This book raises the idea of a new discipline of cultural psychology, the study of the ways that psyche and culture, subject and object, and person and world make up each other. *Cultural Psychology* is a collection of essays from leading scholars in anthropology, psychology, and linguistics who examine these relationships with special reference to core areas of human development: cognition, learning, self, personality dynamics, and gender. The chapters critically examine such questions as: Is there an intrinsic psychic unity to humankind? Can cultural traditions transform the human psyche, resulting less in psychic unity than in ethnic divergences in mind, self, and emotion? Are psychological processes local or specific to the sociocultural environments in which they are embedded?

The volume is an outgrowth of the internationally known Chicago Symposia on Culture and Human Development. It will appeal to an interdisciplinary audience of anthropologists, psychologists, linguists, historians, philosophers, and hermeneutists interested in the prospects for a new discipline of cultural psychology.

Cultural psychology

Cultural psychology

ESSAYS ON COMPARATIVE HUMAN DEVELOPMENT

EDITED BY

James W. Stigler
Committee on Human Development
University of Chicago

Richard A. Shweder
Committee on Human Development
University of Chicago

Gilbert Herdt
Committee on Human Development
University of Chicago

The right of the
University of Cambridge
to print and sell
all manner of books
was granted by
Henry VIII in 1534.
The University has printed
and published continuously
since 1584.

Cambridge University Press

CAMBRIDGE
NEW YORK   PORT CHESTER
MELBOURNE   SYDNEY

Published by the Press Syndicate of the University of Cambridge
The Pitt Building, Trumpington Street, Cambridge CB2 1RP
40 West 20th Street, New York, NY 10011, USA
10 Stamford Road, Oakleigh, Melbourne 3166, Australia

First published 1990

Printed in the United States of America

Library of Congress Cataloging-in-Publication Data
Cultural psychology : essays on comparative human development
edited by James W. Stigler, Richard A. Shweder, Gilbert Herdt.
p. cm.
ISBN 0–521–37154–6. ISBN 0–521–37804–4 (pbk.)
1. Ethnopsychology – Congresses. 2. Cognition and culture –
Congresses. I. Stigler, James W. II. Shweder, Richard A.
III. Herdt, Gilbert. IV. University of Chicago.
Committee on Human Development.
GN502.C85 1989
155.8–dc19 88-37008

British Library Cataloguing in Publication Data
Cultural psychology: essays on comparative
human development
1. Man. Development. Psychological aspects
I. Stigler, James W. II. Shweder,
Richard A. III. Herdt, Gilbert H. *1949–*
155

ISBN 0–521–37154–6 hard covers
ISBN 0–521–37804–4 paperback

Contents

Preface

THE CHICAGO SYMPOSIA ON HUMAN DEVELOPMENT

In 1990 the Committee on Human Development marks its 50th anniversary as a graduate training program and research undertaking at the University of Chicago, which makes it, perhaps, the oldest genuinely interdisciplinary social science program in the United States. The faculty of the committee decided to warm up for the occasion, and to start celebrating early, by having a series of symposia on topics central to its intellectual mission. This volume on "cultural psychology" is a product of two of those symposia, held at the University of Chicago on October 23–25, 1986, and November 5–7, 1987, under the respective titles "Culture and Human Development" and "Children's Lives in Cultural Context."

The symposia were designed with two intellectual aims in mind. The first aim was to provoke debate about conceptions of human nature and development, in the light of our increased sophistication in cultural analysis, in the interpretive study of meaning, and in the symbolic representation of symbolic representations; and to let the voices of context, content, and surface structure vie with the voices of the universal processor, abstract mathematical form, and deep structure. A second (and closely related) aim was to promote the idea of a cultural psychology.

Cultural psychology seems to be very much in the air these days. The basic idea is that our representations of reality (including social and psychological reality) become part of the realities they represent; and many casual processes are constraining precisely because of our representations of them and involvement with them. A central goal of a cultural psychology is to examine the way people make personal use of their customary practices, traditional institutions, symbolic and material resources, and inherited conceptions of things to construct a world that makes sense and to constitute a life-space in which they can feel at home.

There are many signs that this new discipline called cultural psychology is coming of age: the burgeoning interest among anthropologists in ethnopsychological theories (including our own "scientific" psychological theories, now examined as ethnotheories); the interest among cognitive scientists in cultural "artifacts" and collectively organized and socially inherited systems of representation as "tools for thought"; the interest among developmentalists and sociolinguists in discourse, dialogue, social interaction, and the role of intersubjective processes in the construction of the self.

The basic idea of a cultural psychology implies that an "intrinsic psychic unity" of humankind should not be presupposed or assumed. It suggests that the processes decisive for psychological functioning (including those processes promoting within-group or within-family variation and the replication of diversity) may be local to the systems of representation and social organization in which they are embedded and upon which they depend. The philosopher Hilary Putnam has argued that "the mind and the world jointly make up the mind and the world." The dialectical co-construction of a cultural psychology may be more complex, a three-body problem in which self, society, and nature jointly make up self, society, and nature.

Our symposia promoted the idea of a cultural psychology. It did this not by staking out any one position on the relationship of culture and psyche, but by providing a forum for the discussion of empirical and theoretical issues among researchers working on that hazardous yet promising interface of anthropology and psychology, betwixt and between collective systems of representation and individual mental states.

The symposia were public events, held in the sublime setting of the grand lecture hall on the third floor of Swift Hall in the Divinity School at the University of Chicago. Wooden arches support the high vaulted ceiling of the room. Life-sized wooden angels hover overhead, dignifying the proceedings and keeping expectations high. Students and faculty in the Committee on Human Development prepared for the symposia by meeting weekly in a series of "Cross-cultural Workshops" to read and discuss early versions of the symposia papers. The symposia were widely advertised – locally, nationally, and internationally. Hundreds of scholars, students, and social science and medical practitioners from diverse disciplines (anthropology, education, history, linguistics, philosophy, psychiatry, psychology) attended the various sessions. Every presentation was critiqued by two or more members of the University of Chicago faculty and further examined by the community during a question-and-answer period. The first symposium opened with a keynote address by Melford E. Spiro. The second symposium concluded with commentary and a general discussion session led by Clifford Geertz. At those and several other sessions during the days of our meetings there was standing room only.

The excitement surrounding the intellectual and social occasions of the two symposia cannot be fully captured in a book; nor is there a single vision of a cultural psychology to be found diffused throughout the chapters in this edited volume. Yet a general and provocative problematic concerning the cultural context of psychological functioning appears and reappears. The book should thus prove useful for the rapidly increasing number of scholars studying ontogenetic development who are looking beyond the lone child for a more social unit of analysis. It should be useful as well for those scholars who conceive of psychological functioning as being embedded in systems of meaning and social organization and who are disinclined to believe that language is epiphenomenal to psychic life.

The 1986 Chicago Symposium on Culture and Human Development was sponsored by the Committee on Human Development, with welcome local support from the committee's new Center for Culture and Mental Health Research, and from the Council for Advanced Studies in the Humanities and Social Sciences, the Division of the Social Sciences, and the Irving B. Harris Center for Developmental Studies.

The 1987 Chicago Symposium on the Child in Cultural Context was jointly sponsored, by the Committee on Human Development and the Irving B. Harris Center for Developmental Studies. While the Committee on Human Development is about to celebrate its 50th anniversary, the Center for Developmental Studies is a relatively recent addition to the University of Chicago community, supportive of scholarly and training activities in child and adolescent development. The existence of such a center is a tribute to the generosity and kind-spiritedness of its patron saint, Irving Harris, and to years of creative program building by its directors, Bennett Leventhal and Thomas Trabasso. We are very grateful for their support. Donna Wicinski's assistance as a liaison between the committee and the center is much appreciated. David Walton (in 1986) and Sandra Dixon (in 1987) were the intrepid masterminds of the rather considerable organizational effort for the symposia, and Sandra Dixon contributed in innumerable ways to the preparation of this book. Thank you, David. Thank you, Sandy. All but three of the chapters in the book are original publications, revised versions of presentations from the Chicago symposia.

Cultural psychology – what is it?

Richard A. Shweder

A discipline is emerging called "cultural psychology." It is not general psychology. It is not cross-cultural psychology. It is not psychological anthropology. It is not ethnopsychology. It is cultural psychology. And its time may have arrived, once again.

While the authors in this volume were never asked to define or explicitly address the idea of a cultural psychology, several of the chapters turned out to be examples of it. They inspired this essay – which is a preliminary attempt to say, taxonomically and narratively, and briefly – what the discipline of cultural psychology was, is, and ought to be about.[1] Ultimately it is a story of cyclical return.

In the short run, however, the essay is a story of one of the pitfalls of the "cognitive revolution" of the 1960s, the failure of the cognitive revolution to develop an adequate theory of the "person," because of the prevailing Platonism implicit in its scientific agenda. The essay is also a scouting expedition across the boundaries of some very treacherous disciplinary territories in the search to recover an important interdisciplinary identity.

Cultural psychology is the study of the way cultural traditions and social practices regulate, express, transform, and permute the human psyche, resulting less in psychic unity for humankind than in ethnic divergences in mind, self, and emotion. Cultural psychology is the study of the ways subject and object, self and other, psyche and culture, person and context, figure and ground, practitioner and practice live together, require each other, and dynamically, dialectically, and jointly make each other up.

Cultural psychology is premised on human existential uncertainty (the search for meaning) and on a (so-called) intentional conception of "constituted" worlds. The principle of existential uncertainty asserts that human beings, starting at birth (and perhaps earlier), are highly motivated to seize meanings and resources out of a sociocultural environment that has been arranged to provide them with meanings and resources to seize and to use. The principle of intentional (or constituted) worlds asserts that subjects and objects, practitioners and practices, human beings and sociocultural environments interpenetrate each other's identity and cannot be analytically disjoined into independent and dependent variables. Their identities are interdependent; neither side of the supposed contrast can be defined without borrowing from the specifications of the other.

The basic idea of cultural psychology is that no sociocultural environment exists or has identity independent of the way human beings seize meanings and resources from it, while every human being has her or his subjectivity and mental life altered through the process of seizing meanings and resources from some sociocultural environment and using them.

A sociocultural environment is an intentional world. It is an intentional world because its existence is real, factual, and forceful, but only as long as there exists a community of persons whose beliefs, desires, emotions, purposes, and other mental representations are directed at it, and are thereby influenced by it.

Intentional worlds are human artifactual worlds populated with products of our own design. An intentional world might contain such events as "stealing" or "taking communion," such processes as "harm" or "sin," such stations as "in-law" or "exorcist," such practices as "promising" or "divorce," such visible entities as "weeds" and invisible entities as "natural rights," and such crafted objects as a "Jersey cow," an "abacus," a "confessional booth," a "card catalogue," an "oversize tennis racquet," a "psychoanalytic couch," or a "'living' room."

Such intentional (made, bred, fashioned, fabricated, invented, designated, constituted) things exist only in intentional worlds. What makes their existence intentional is that such things would not exist independent of our involvements with them and reactions to them; and they exercise their influence in our lives because of our conceptions of them (D'Andrade, 1981, 1984, 1986; Schneider, 1968, 1984). Intentional things are causally active, but only by virtue of our mental representations of them.

Intentional things have no "natural" reality or identity separate from human understandings and activities. Intentional worlds do not exist independent of the intentional states (beliefs, desires, emotions, etc.) directed at them and by them, by the persons who live in them. Thus, for example, a weed is an intentional thing. It is an intrusive, interfering, or improper plant that you do not want growing in your garden. Consequently, a daisy or a sunflower or a foxglove, or perhaps even a thorny rose that turns up in your vegetable patch might be plucked out as a weed, while one can find intentional worlds where marijuana or dandelions or crabgrass are not constituted as weeds at all. Instead they are cultivated as cash crops.

Because a weed is a weed is a weed, but only in some intentional world, there is no impersonal, neutral, "objective," "scientific," independent-of-human-response, botanical, genetic or (so-called) natural-kind definition of plants that can specify *in the abstract* or *in general* which ones count as weeds. The botanical capacity to self-seed bestows on a plant the power to be a nuisance, if the plant is unwanted. Yet the same plant, if it is wanted, has the power to produce abundant harvests. And there are other routes by which a plant might make itself troublesome or become misplaced in your garden, ultimately to be weeded out.

It would seem to follow that in some fascinating and important sense, the weeds in our gardens achieve their reality because we are implicated in their existence, and we achieve our reality, at least in part, by letting them become implicated in ours. Our identities interpenetrate and take each other into account. Without us, nature knows little of the existence of weeds. Without the existence of weeds and of all the aims, activities, and practices (Wittgenstein's "forms of life") presupposed by their existence and constitutive of it, there would be less to us worth knowing.

And because a weed is a weed is a weed, but only in some intentional world, what is truly true (beautiful, good) within one intentional world (e.g. "that is a 'weed'; therefore it ought to be plucked out of the ground and discarded") is not necessarily universally true (beautiful, good) in every intentional world; and, what is not necessarily true (beautiful, good) in every intentional world may be truly true (beautiful, good) in this one or in that one.

According to the principle of intentional worlds, there is no logical requirement that across intentional worlds the identity of things must remain fixed and universal; while within any particular intentional world (e.g., the 20th-century intentional world of American baseball; or the 16th-century intentional world of English witchcraft) the identity of a thing (e.g., a "foul ball," or a "witch") can be real and the question of its real identity (e.g., was that a "foul ball"? or is she a "witch"?) can be a subject for rational and objective dispute.[2]

Cultural psychology is the study of intentional worlds. It is the study of personal functioning in particular intentional worlds. It is the study of the interpersonal maintenance of any intentional world. It is the investigation of those psychosomatic, sociocultural, and, inevitably, divergent realities in which subject and object cannot possibly be separated and kept apart because they are so interdependent as to need each other to be (see Kleinman, 1986; Shweder, 1986, 1988, 1989).

Finally, cultural psychology is an interdisciplinary human science. It aims to develop several companion disciplines, especially an anthropology (reunited with linguistics) suitable for the analysis of sociocultural environments (meanings and resources – "forms of life") in all their intentionality and particularity, and a psychology (reunited with philosophy) suitable for the analysis of persons in all their intentionality and historicity.

Answering a "what is it?" question

It is a principle of cultural psychology – the principle of intentional worlds – that nothing real "just is," and that realities are the product of the way things get represented, embedded, implemented, and reacted to in various taxonomic and/or narrative contexts. The reality of cultural psychology is no exception to the principle. As a constructed intellectual discipline, cultural psychology has a taxonomic and narrative identity whose reality is not independent of our sharing with each other, debating, and acting upon, our conception of it.

To say what something is, taxonomically, is to say what it is not, to say what it is a kind of, and to point to instances of it. It is to subsume it as a particular example of something more general, and it is to generalize it, so as to turn something more particular than it into its example. In apposition, to say what something is, narratively, is to describe its origination ("once upon a time") and its destiny (its aim, purpose, or function), and to comprehend its current status, in the here and now, as part of a longer story of strivings, achievements, obstacles, growth, adaptations, failures, dormancy, or never-ending cyclical return.

Since cultural psychology can be traced through many ancestral lines, one looks forward to other tellings in other forums as the discipline is rediscovered and reevaluated. Placed in its taxonomic context, an ideal cultural psychology has qualities that distinguish it from general psychology, cross-cultural psychology, psychological anthropology, and ethnopsychology.

It is not general psychology

First, cultural psychology must be distinguished from general psychology. "People are the same wherever you go" is a line from the song "Ebony and Ivory" by Paul McCartney and Stevie Wonder; that line describes pretty well a basic assumption of general psychology. The assumption is sometimes referred to as the principle of "psychic unity" of humankind.

General psychology assumes that its subject matter is a presupposed central (abstract and transcendent = deep or interior or hidden) processing mechanism inherent (fixed and universal) in human beings, which enables them to think (classify, infer, remember, imagine, etc.), experience (emote, feel, desire, need, self-reflect, etc.), act (strive, prefer, choose, evaluate, etc.) and learn.

The aim of general psychology is to describe that central inherent processing mechanism of mental life. Since the central processing mechanism is presumed to be a transcendent, abstract, fixed, and universal property of the human psyche, general psychology has the look, taste, and smell of a Platonic undertaking. For it is that presupposed central and inherent processing mechanism that is the true object of fascination in general psychology and not all the concrete, apparent, variable, and particular stuff, substance, or content that is operated upon by the processor or may interfere with its operation.

It is a necessary step in the general psychology enterprise to distinguish intrinsic (internal) psychological structures and processes from extrinsic (external) environmental conditions, to procedurally abstract and analytically withdraw the knower from what he or she knows, and to insist on a fundamental division between the processing mechanism of the person versus his or her personal or group history, context, stimulus and task environment, institutional setting, resources, beliefs, values, and knowledge.

Of course, people are not the same wherever you go. Not even Paul McCartney and Stevie Wonder are the same. And no general psychology is so unworldly as to overlook that fact. General psychology may be Platonic, but it is certainly not thoughtless. The principle of general psychology – that "people are the same wherever you go" – does not mean that people are the same in *every* respect. It means that transcendentally, "deep down" or "inside," where the central processing mechanism lives, people are the same (or, alternatively, what gives people "psychic unity" is what makes them all the same "deep down" or "inside").

All the other stuff – stimuli, contexts, resources, values, meanings, knowledge, religion, rituals, language, technologies, institutions – is conceived to be external to or outside of the central processing mechanism. Observations on Rajput widows in India, motivated by special beliefs and desires, immolating themselves along with their deceased husband on his funeral pyre; or observations on Chinese abacus experts, assisted by special mental representational techniques, solving arithmetic problems "in their head" at a speed several orders of magnitude faster than the rest of humanity – all that may be rich material for humanistic inquiry, journalistic reporting, and literary representation, yet all of it must, given the Platonist impulse, be viewed, in and of itself, as incidental or secondary to the aim of general psychology.

The aim, as noted, is to get behind superficial appearances, local manifestations, and external resources to isolate the intrinsic central processing mechanism of the mental life and describe the invariant laws of its operation.[3]

It is that Platonic impulse, one suspects, that was behind the memorable remark from an anthropologist who, upon hearing about Mike Cole and John Gay's research in Liberia, argued that the thinking processes of West African tribesmen do not differ from our own; only their values, beliefs, and classifications differ, which is why the Kpelle perform differently on psychological tests (see Cole & Gay, 1972:1066).

It is that same impulse, one suspects, that once led Mel Spiro, with his interest in group differences in personality (1955:257) to express the methodological concern that in demonstrating emotional and behavioral differences across different sociocultural contexts, anthropologists had not demonstrated the existence of *genuine* personality differences at all. They "have merely demonstrated that different stimuli evoke different responses."

The methodological "merely" in Spiro's analysis is revealing. For one might have argued, methodologically and non-Platonically, that the power of a particular stimulus to evoke a particularizing response is not independent of the way a person or people get particularly involved with it psychologically – classify it, reason about it, tell stories about it, appropriate it to their purposes – and that that is what *genuine* personality differences are about. In intentional worlds "stimuli" are not external to, or independent of, our understanding of them, and those understandings are a large part of what we mean by "personality" (see, e.g., Mischel, 1973).

In other words, one might have argued, from the point of view of intentional worlds, that the study of genuine psychological differences between ethnic groups should be conceived as the study of how different sociocultural environments become different *by virtue of* the ways they are differently constituted psychologically by different peoples so as to possess different response evocation potentials.

Platonism is an ancient and formidable school of interpretation. It is crucial to recognize that the long-lived and imaginative idea of an inherent (fixed, universal) and central (transcendent, abstract) processing mechanism, a psychic unity to humankind, will never be seriously threatened by the mere existence of performance differences between individuals or populations. Those performance differences can always be interpreted, and should be interpreted, as the consequence of incomparabilities, incommensurabilities, or just some plain differences in all the other stuff; which leaves permanently unsettled and eternally unsettleable the question of whether there really is, deep down, an inherent and central processing mechanism hidden behind all the other stuff. Platonism and its alternatives will always be with us, offering different interpretations and competing visions of the nature of the human psyche.

It is equally crucial to recognize that general psychology, with its Platonic imagery and premises, is not the only imaginative and interpretive game in town for understanding the mental life. As I try to elaborate in my discussion of cultural psychology later in the chapter, if one subscribes to an alternative, non-Platonic principle of intentional worlds, that nothing in particular exists independent of our involvement with it and interpretation of it, it is possible to conceive of the mental life as variable and plural and substantive and constructively stimulus-bound. And it is possible to characterize a large part of the mental life in terms of the particularizing ways that peoples constitute and get involved with particulars, thereby giving to those constructed stimuli, task environments, and sociocultural contexts the powers they have to evoke the special responses they evoke.

Nevertheless the aim of general psychology is Platonic, and it is its Platonic aim to seek out a presumed central processing mechanism of human beings and to isolate it from all the other stuff. Given that aim, it is not surprising that general psychology has constructed its own special intellectual standards for knowledge representation (its preferred ontology) and knowledge seeking (its preferred epistemology).

Ontologically speaking, knowledge in general psychology is the attempt to imagine and characterize the form or shape of an inherent central processing mechanism for psychological functions (discrimination, categorization, memory, learning, motivation, inference, etc.). Epistemologically speaking, knowledge seeking in general psychology is the attempt to get a look at the central processing mechanism untainted by content and context.

The main intellectually motivating force in general psychology is the idea of that central processing device. The processor, it is imagined, stands over and above, or transcends, all the stuff upon which it operates. It engages all the stuff of culture, context, task, and stimulus material as its content. Given that image, the central processor itself must be context- and content-independent. That means, in effect, that the processor must be describable in terms of either properties that are free of context/content (abstract, formal, structural properties) or properties that are general to all contexts/contents (invariant, universal properties).

Still speaking ontologically, it is that image of an inherent (fixed, universal) and central (abstract, transcendent) processing mechanism – a context/content independent and omnipresent unity to mind – that explains the great esteem conferred in general psychology upon accounts of the mental life in terms of universal mathematical functions and invariant formal limits or constraints, such as exponential decay functions mapped in an abstract psychological space for representing the probability of generalization between pairs of stimulus events in any domain for any sensory modality for any species (Shepard, 1987); or magical numbers, seven plus or minus two, used to represent the maximum capacity of the central processing mechanism for distinguishing values, whatever the values, along any single dimension, whatever the dimension, in any single instant, wherever and whenever the instant (G. Miller, 1956).

Great esteem is also conferred within general psychology upon certain ways of seeking knowledge. Knowledge seeking in general psychology is the attempt to gain direct access to the central processing mechanism without having to become quagmired in all the other stuff. General psychologists qua general psychologists are typically wary of rain forests, swamps, and the complex textures and tones of everyday life, language, and institutional settings. They take comfort in a radically simplifying (some would call it a radically "surreal") article of faith, namely, that the central processor is most likely to reveal its pristine form when lured by meaning-free or unfamiliar or novel stimulus items into a context-free environment.[4]

Nonsense syllables, white coats, and darkened bare rooms may be misguided or monstrous things of the distant past for serious researchers in general psychology, yet the experimental lab is still treated as a privileged space, where, quite fantastically and against much evidence, it is conveniently assumed that one can physically enter a transcendent realm where the effects of context, content, and meaning can be eliminated, standardized, or kept under control, and the central processor observed in the raw.

General psychology presumes that there exists a central processing mechanism that can be isolated from the different particulars it might encounter, and that isolating that processing mechanism is what genuine psychological research is about. That image of a central processing mechanism and the search for a window or a peep hole through which to view it naked and pure may explain why in general psychology there has become entrenched the intuition that real science is the doing of experiments in a lab.

Unfortunately, even if there does exist the presumed inherent central processing mechanism obscured or hidden behind appearances, the psychological laboratory is probably not the mythical enchanted doorway through which one can step straight away into a more fundamental reality. Indeed, one suspects the sociocultural environment of lab life is not even plausibly equivalent to the physicist's vacuum or the physiologist's X ray for directly accessing things that are basic, deep, or hidden from view.

The ideas of a context-free environment, a meaning-free stimulus event, and a fixed meaning are probably best kept where they belong, along with placeless space, eventless time, and squared circles on that famous and fabulous list of impossible notions. For when it comes to the investigation and examination of psychological functioning, there probably is no way to get rid of all the other stuff, even in the lab.

Of course, nothing I have said argues against studying "stuff" in a lab. If the stuff brought into the lab (or simulated there) is interesting enough stuff to study, and if one can bring it into the lab (or reproduce it there) without spoiling it (those are big "ifs"), then one can certainly study it there, and there may even be very good reason to do so (see, e.g., Milgram, 1974). Whether there is a royal road running through the lab to the land of the central processing mechanism of the mental life is, however, quite another issue.

In closing this section on general psychology I would like to comment briefly on Roger Shepard's (1987) discussion (published appropriately enough in *Science* magazine) of "a universal law of generalization for psychological science," for it is a revealing illustration of Platonist presuppositions in general psychology and the way they guide a research enterprise and structure the interpretation of evidence by even the most brilliant of practitioners.

Shepard begins and ends his paper by holding out Newton's mathematical and universal law of gravitation as the standard by which to judge the success or failure of the discipline of psychology. Psychology, Shepard avers, should strive to be the science of the invariant mathematical forms underlying psychological functioning. Three hundred years after the publication of Newton's *Principia* Shepard thinks psychology can finally point to a success, a mathematical law of stimulus generalization "that is invariant across perceptual dimensions, modalities, individuals and species" (p. 1318) and that shows that psychology "may not be inherently limited merely to the descriptive characterization of the behavior of particular terrestrial species" (p. 1323) or the properties of particular stimulus domains (pp. 1317–1318).

Shepard's "universal law" is basically an abstract spatial representation of an exponential decay function for stimulus generalization likelihoods between pairs of stimuli. The exponential decay function is detectable in several data sets from humans and pigeons, which record for selected domains (e.g., consonant phonemes, triangles of different sizes and shapes) the probability that a response learned to any one stimulus within the domain will generalize to any other stimulus within the domain. Shepard believes that this exponential decay function is the central processing mechanism for stimulus generalization in its pristine form – abstract and transcendent (= deeply interior), fixed and universal (p. 1318).

To catch a glimpse of this abstract transcendent processing function, Shepard is quite prepared to, indeed he feels he must, exteriorize, treat as illusory, and withdraw his attention from, several levels of reality that play a major part in human classificatory behavior.

First he must withdraw his attention from measurable similarities and differences in the stimulus materials themselves. For it has been shown – he views the relevant findings as "troublesome" and "discouraging" – that there exists no universal mathematical function for predicting the probability of a generalization response from measurable physical characteristics of pairs of stimuli; those mathematical functions seem to vary by stimulus domain (p. 1317). For example, the mathematical function for the color space may differ from the function for tonal scales, and these may differ by species or individuals; and, within a particular stimulus domain, for example, the color space, a response to a particular color chip may generalize to a distant hue at the opposite end of the spectrum.

So if there is to be a universal law of generalization it is not going to be a law of the stimulus environment. It must be a pure psychological function not a psychophysical function (p. 1318). It cannot tell you which stimulus items in any domain will be generalized to, only that the likelihood of there being generalization behavior across pairs of stimulus items (whichever they should turn out to be) will decay exponentially. To reach the central processing mechanism of stimulus generalization Shepard must get beyond the stimulus environment.

Then he must also get beyond learning processes. For he does not expect his universal law of generalization to describe generalization behavior under multiple learning trials, because "differential reinforcement could shape the generalization function and contours around a particular stimulus into a wide variety of forms" (p. 1322).

Finally, he must get beyond reconstructive memory processes. For it is known that the universal law is *not* descriptive of generalization behavior when learning trials are delayed. This Shepard interprets as a failure of the law due to interfering "'noise' in the internal representation of the stimuli" (p. 1322).

At this point a reader of *Science* interested in similarity and difference judgments might be tempted to ask what he or she has learned about human classificatory behavior. Having withdrawn his attention from the stimulus environment and from processes of learning and memory, why does Shepard think he is looking at something fundamental like a central processing mechanism of mind?

The answer is clear and Platonic. Late in his paper Shepard points out that strictly speaking his universal law is descriptive of stimulus generalization behavior *only* when "generalization is tested immediately after a single learning trial with a novel stimulus" (p. 1322).

Here we come to the great and unbreachable divide between general psychology and cultural psychology. Moved by the Platonic impulse (and perhaps, one speculates, by the prestigious image of Newton's gravitational forces operating in a vacuum), Shepard seems to think that something truly fundamental about the mind – an inherent central processing mechanism – can be divined only if we can transcend the noise and clutter of the environment by bleaching it of familiar things and impoverishing it of feedback, and by isolating the mind from its own mental supports.

The alternative interpretation – the view from cultural psychology – is that the mind left to its own devices is mindless. From that perspective, Shepard's proposed "universal law of generalization for psychological science" is little more than an extremely unqualified description of the special, restrictive (and one might add the rather peculiar) effects on similarity and difference judgments of unfamiliar stuff (novel stimuli) examined in one-trial learning environments.

According to the principles of cultural psychology, the effects of stuff won't go away, even in the lab, for there is no context-free environment. We are intentional beings who live in an intentional world of constituted and represented particulars – domain-specific, concrete, subject-dependent, artifactual things. Absolute transcendence is a great and marvelous thing, but not if you want to keep the psyche in psychology.

The implication, of course, is that genuine success for psychological science will come when we stop trying to get beyond the "noise" and start trying to say interesting things about some of the more interesting, robust and patterned varieties of it.[5] That is the challenge for cultural psychology. But I am getting ahead of my story. First we must consider cross-cultural psychology (not to be confused with cultural psychology), which can be very noisy, perhaps too noisy.

It is not cross-cultural psychology

As we have seen, one of the hazards of general psychology as a Platonic undertaking is the inherent difficulty of distinguishing statements about a presumed inherent central processing mechanism from statements about all the other stuff. It is that difficulty that has kept the discipline of cross-cultural psychology in business.

Cross-cultural psychology is a subdiscipline of general psychology that shares with general psychology the Platonic aim of characterizing the inherent central processing mechanisms of the mental life. Practitioners of the subdiscipline carry the general psychologist's tests and research procedures abroad.

Occasionally cross-cultural psychological research replicates some regularity observed with educated Western subjects (Ekman, in press). The main discovery of cross-cultural psychology, however, is that many descriptions of mental functioning emerging out of laboratory research with educated Western populations do not travel very well to subject populations in other cultures. Thus, for example, almost all adults in Geneva, Paris, London, and New York display so-called concrete operational thinking on Piaget's conservation of mass, number, and liquid quantity tasks. Many adults in many Third World capitals do not (Cole, 1988; Cole & Scribner, 1974; Hallpike, 1979).

The definitive problematic of cross-cultural psychology is the struggle, fought in Platonic terms, over how to interpret population-based differences in performance on psychological tests and tasks. Within the framework of Platonist thinking there are only two possibilities: (1) that the performance differences exist primarily because the central processing mechanism inherent in mind has not yet become fully developed among certain peoples of the world (Hallpike, 1979; see Shweder, 1982, for a critique); and (2) that the performance differences exist primarily because the psychologist's tests and tasks baffle and bewilder certain peoples of the world and deny them a fair opportunity to display the extant central processing mechanisms of their mind (Cole 1988; Cole & Scribner, 1974).

Notice that the principle of psychic unity is presupposed by both interpretations. According to the first interpretation, psychic unity is the anticipated result of central processor development, but the universal and uniform structures inherent in mind will only mature under ideal environmental conditions. This leads some cross-cultural psychologists to become concerned with possible external stimulators of growth of the central processing mechanism – literacy, schooling, toys, Socratic dialogue, and so on.

According to the second interpretation, psychic unity is not just a potential inherent in mind. Psychic unity has already been achieved. It is there, waiting to be revealed. This leads other cross-cultural psychologists to become concerned with "etics" and "emics" and with the incommensurateness or inappropriateness across cultures of test materials and research tasks; and it leads them to search for more "natural" or "realistic" settings, activities, and institutions in everyday life where central processor functioning goes on unimpeded by the artificial or unfamiliar conditions of psychological task environments.

Cross-cultural psychology has lived on the margins of general psychology as a frustrated gadfly, and it is not too hard to understand why. For one thing, cross-cultural psychology offers no substantial challenge to the core Platonic interpretive principle of general psychology (the principle of psychic unity). Moreover, if you are a general psychologist cum Platonist (and a principled one, at that) there is no theoretical benefit in learning more and more about the quagmire of appearances – the retarding effects of environment on the development of the central processing mechanism, the noise introduced by translation or by differences in the understanding of the test situation or by cultural variations in the norms regulating the asking and answering of questions.

Rather, if you are a general psychologist, you will want to transcend those appearances and reach for the imagined abstract forms and processes operating behind the extrinsic crutches and restraints and distortions of this or that performance environment. Perhaps that is why, in the circles of general psychology, cross-cultural psychology has diminutive status, and why its research literature tends to be ignored. Not surprisingly, developmental psychology – the study of age-graded differences in performance on psychological tests and tasks – has suffered a similar fate, and for similar reasons.

It is doubtful that anyone is going to disenchant general psychology of its fascination with the imaginative idea of an inherent central processing mechanism. And certainly not by merely showing that the regularities observed in the Western lab do not travel well to other contexts, or generalize to subjects from other cultures (or age levels) or to stimulus materials from everyday life (see LeVine, n.d., for a discussion of "why cross-cultural evidence is discounted" by psychologists). Platonism is a framework for interpretation that is likely to remain enshrined in general psychology and definitive of its intellectual agenda. Like the scripture of some great religion of the world, it sets the terms for its own assessment, and it has enormous appeal, especially for those devoted to it to whom it appeals.

A far more useful and liberal aim than the demise of Platonism is the revival of other equally powerful and, one might add, equally ancient disciplines for the interpretation of the mental life. Which is one good reason for going beyond cross-cultural psychology and its presupposition of psychic unity to develop a cultural psychology of intentional worlds.

A problem with cross-cultural psychology is that it is not heretical enough, even as it raises its serious concerns. It would not be too great an exaggeration to assert baldly that so-called method effects (major variations in research findings due to slight variations in research procedure, elicitation technique, wording of questions, description and representation of problems, expectations of examiners, subject population, etc.) are the main effects to emerge out of decades of laboratory research in general psychology. That "method effect" phenomenon (see Campbell & Fiske, 1959; Cronbach, 1975; Fiske, 1986) is quite consistent with the discovery that generalizations from psychological research on one population do not travel well across cultural, historical, and institutional boundaries.

Unfortunately, in the face of that evidence most cross-cultural psychologists have been unable to free themselves of the hegemony of Platonistic presuppositions in general psychology. They have continued to assume a psychic unity to humankind and to search for the presumed central processing mechanism, looking for it in growth-stimulating environments (literate, industrialized Western urban centers) or through culture-fair or everyday stimulus materials.

Cultural psychology is far more heterodox vis-à-vis the canon of psychic unity, and thus it differs from cross-cultural psychology. For cultural psychology is built out of a fundamental skepticism concerning all those fateful and presupposed distinctions between intrinsic properties of mind versus extrinsic properties of environments, between form versus content, between the "deep" versus the "superficial," between the inherent central processing mechanism (psychic unity) versus all the other stuff.

Cultural psychology offers an alternative discipline of interpretation of the fundamentals of mind. The mind, according to cultural psychology, is content-driven, domain-specific, and constructively stimulus-bound; and it cannot be extricated from the historically variable and cross-culturally diverse intentional worlds in which it plays a coconstituting part.

Consequently, cultural psychology interprets statements about regularities observed in a lab or observed anywhere else – on the street or in a classroom, in Chicago or in Khartoom – not as propositions about inherent properties of a central processing mechanism for human psychological functioning but rather as descriptions of local response patterns contingent on context, resources, instructional sets, authority relations, framing devices, and modes of construal.[6] It is the aim of cultural psychology to understand the organization and evocative power of all that stuff, to study the major varieties of it, and to seek mind where it is mindful, indissociably embedded in the meanings and resources that are its product, yet also make it up.

It is not psychological anthropology

Whereas cross-cultural psychology has traditionally been a subdiscipline of psychology, psychological anthropology has been a province of anthropology; which means that psychological anthropology is less concerned with behavior in laboratories or on standardized tests or with novel stimulus materials and more concerned with other kinds of stuff. That stuff of anthropology includes rituals and folk tales, games and art forms, family life practices and religious doctrines, kinship categories, and inherited systems of knowledge. Anthropologists in general like to muck around in the stuff of everyday life and language, and psychological anthropologists are no exception.

It should come as no surprise that psychological anthropology is "psychological" anthropology. Its proper and excellent aim is to understand the way ritual, language, belief, and other systems of meaning function or are put together in the lives and experiences and mental representations of persons.

In recent years many psychological anthropologists have turned to the study of cultural psychology and have revised some of the classic assumptions of the discipline. What I write here applies to psychological anthropology prior to its more recent reincarnation as cultural psychology.

Classically, psychological anthropology has tended to conceive of the "psychological" in the general psychology sense, which means that when psychological anthropologists muck around in classic form in their favorite anthropological stuff (e.g., initiation ceremonies, kinship classifications, origin stories, conceptions of the gods, etc.) they do it with the idea of psychic unity in mind. Psychological anthropologists, in classic form, go searching for the transcendental in the world of appearances. They try to explain the stuff of culture by reference to the workings of a central processing mechanism underlying psychological functioning. They try to make use of the stuff of culture to characterize or discover a central processing device.

General psychologists, it has been noted, search for the central processor by trying to eliminate the interfering effects, noise, and distortion produced by any meaningful stimulus environment. Psychological anthropologists, in contrast, look for the central processor in the stimulus environment, on the assumption that there is something about long-surviving sociocultural environments that makes them relatively noiseless and distortion-free.

One of the special marks of classical psychological anthropology is the sanguine premise that there not only exists an inherent central processing mechanism for individual psychological functioning but that its powers and influences extend into the sociocultural environment. It is the assumption of classical psychological anthropology that to remain viable any sociocultural environment must be adapted to, or expressive of the central processing mechanism's abstract form and invariant constraints.

Psychological anthropology can be taxonomized along received fault lines (body versus mind; affect and motivation versus thought) into two subfields: "culture and personality" and "cognitive anthropology." Before the recent reemergence of a cultural psychology, the subfields of classical psychological anthropology were united with each other, as well as with general psychology and cross-cultural psychology, by the now familiar assumption of the "psychic unity" of humankind.

The central problematic for general psychology, as we have seen, is to characterize the central processing mechanism inherent in mental functioning by isolating it from the environment and from all the other extrinsic stuff upon which it operates. The central processor is abstract, transcendent (interior, deep, hidden, beyond, somewhere else, etc.), fixed, and universal.

The central problematic for cross-cultural psychology, as we have seen, is to explain the noteworthy performance differences on psychological tests between human populations without renouncing the idea of an inherent psychic unity to humankind. Performance differences exist, it is argued in cross-cultural psychology, either because the cultural environment has slowed down the full maturation of the central processor in some populations, or because the performance environment of psychological testing has inhibited the central processing mechanism from going on display.

The central problematic of classical psychological anthropology, however, is more imperial – to find expanded into the territory of sociocultural environments the central authority of the psychological processing machine. The imperial premise: that the stuff of sociocultural environments gets shaped or molded by the dictates and constraints of the central processing mechanism into a limited number of possible designs for living; that the central processing mechanism gives structure to a sociocultural environment, either by mediating the relationships between its stuff or by impressing its abstract form upon it.

Thus, for example, within the circle of classical psychological anthropology, sibling terminological systems might be interpreted as revelatory of a universal and inherent disinclination of the central processing mechanism to engage in disjunctive reasoning (Nerlove & Romney, 1967). Cultural origin stories might be interpreted as revelatory of an inherent preference of the human mind for dichotomous categories (Lévi-Strauss, 1963). And almost everything from myths to patterns of kinship avoidance and joking to adolescent circumcision ceremonies might be interpreted as revelatory of that famous presumptive psychic universal known as the Oedipus complex (Stephens, 1962; Spiro, 1983).

Psychological anthropology, classically practiced, is a reductionist enterprise. Unlike Shepard, who searched for the abstract central processing mechanism for stimulus generalization behavior by trying to reach beyond the noisy, autonomous, and resistant physical constraints of any concrete stimulus domain, principled psychological anthropologists assume that the substantive domains of a sociocultural environment are a relatively pliant content operated upon by, or expressive of, deep and invariant psychological laws or processes of motivation, affect and intellect.

Cultural psychology is not psychological anthropology. Psychological anthropology assumes that there is an inherent central processing mechanism. Psychological anthropology assumes that the central processing mechanism not only stands outside the sociocultural environment as an independent, fixed, and universal given of the human psyche; the central processor, it is assumed, also reaches in to the sociocultural environment, leaving its indelible stamp. Psychological anthropology assumes that the structure and functioning of the central processing mechanism is not fundamentally altered by the content, stuff, material, or sociocultural environment on which it operates. Psychological anthropology assumes that whatever the differences between populations in all the other stuff (in religious beliefs, in ceremonial life, in mythology, etc.) those differences can and should be interpreted as just so many products of the deep operations of a psychically unifying central processing device.

Cultural psychology is dubious of all those assumptions; indeed, cultural psychology is psychological anthropology without those assumptions. Many psychological anthropologists today are in fact doing cultural psychology.

It is not ethnopsychology

If cultural psychology is psychological anthropology without the premise of psychic unity, then enthnopsychology is cultural psychology without a psyche at all. Ethnopsychology is the study of ethnic variations in theories of the mental life. It is the investigation of indigenous representations of mind, self, body, and emotion. Such representations might include, for example, biochemical theories linking black bile or tired blood or sluggish neuro-transmitters to depression. They might include interpersonal theories of guilt and possessive states conceiving of the mind as populated with the unplacated spirits or shadows of one's ancestors. They might include lay classifications of subjective states (thinking, feeling, willing). They might even include Platonistic theories positing a psychic unity to humankind.

There are many points of similarity between cultural psychology and ethnopsychology, especially a common concern for the indigenous psychological categories of the folk. The major point of difference is that ethnopsychology is a subdiscipline of ethnosemantics or ethnoscience. It is primarily concerned with the investigation of mind, self, body, and emotion as topics (along with, for example, botany, or kinship) in the ethnographic study of folk beliefs. Ethnopsychology is thus less concerned with the actual psychological functioning and subjective life of persons in the cultures whose doctrines about mind, representations of emotions, formal texts about the self, and gender ceremonies are under examination. Ethnopsychology is cultural psychology without the functioning psyche.

For some general anthropologists, especially those who are psychophobic, the focus in ethnopsychology on folk beliefs and doctrines sanitizes its subject matter (mind, self, emotion) and makes it more acceptable for investigation. The person is allowed in to general ethnography safely contained in the form of an idea or an ideology. Cultural psychology is more person-centered, for it is the ethnopsychology of a functioning psyche, as it actually functions, malfunctions, and functions differently, in different parts of the world. Many ethnopsychologists today are in fact doing cultural psychology.

An origin story for cultural psychology

So far this essay has treated cultural psychology entirely within a taxonomic context of definition. Taxonomically, and by way of summary, cultural psychology is the plural, variable, domain-specific, and constructively "stimulus-bound" psychology of intentional worlds. It is psychological anthropology without the premise of psychic unity. It is the ethnopsychology of the functioning psyche, as it actually functions, malfunctions, and functions differently in the different parts of the world.

Cultural psychology tries to synthesize, or at least combine, some of the virtues of general psychology, cross-cultural psychology, psychological anthropology, and ethnopsychology while seeking to disencumber itself of their vices. It should come as no surprise that a vice in the intentional world of cultural psychology could turn out to be a Platonist's virtue, and vice versa.

Speaking from within the intentional world of cultural psychology, the virtue in general psychology is its concern with the organized nature of the mental life. Its vice is its conception of the mental as a central processing mechanism – abstract, interior (transcendent), universal, fixed, and content-free. The virtue in cross-cultural psychology is its concern with performance differences between ethnic groups. Its vice is its orthodox adherence to the premise of psychic unity. The virtue in psychological anthropology is its focus on psychological functioning in sociocultural context. Its vice is its subordination of the sociocultural environment to the postulated directives of a central processing device. The virtue in ethnopsychology is its attention to indigenous or local conceptions of mind, self, body, and person. Its vice is its psychophobia.

Of course, much more needs to be said and worked out about each of those points. Yet there is also another way to "thicken" (Geertz, 1973) our appreciation of cultural psychology, which is to treat it not only in a taxonomic context of definition but also in a narrative one. Many stories can be told, at varying orders of magnitude of historical time depth, about ups and downs in the life of cultural psychology. The tale I am about to tell is but one story, a short and contemporary one, selected out of the many that could be told. It is the story of a pitfall of the "cognitive revolution" of the 1960s.

It is probably no accident that the present renewal of interest in cultural psychology is occurring after 30 years of intellectual fragmentation in both general anthropology and general psychology. That fragmentation can be interpreted as a salutary reaction against the Platonism hidden in the agenda of the so-called cognitive revolution of the 1960s (see the discussion between D'Andrade and Geertz in Shweder, 1984:7–8).

The cognitive revolution of the 1960s actually got off to a promising start. It was welcomed by many (and I am one of them) as the obvious and necessary corrective to the radical behaviorism that preceded it. The revolution seemed to address a rather serious shortcoming in psychology and anthropology, namely, the lack of a notion of mental representations and intentional states (mind, self, and emotion) in theories of the person and the lack of a notion of mental representations and intentional worlds (subject-dependent objects embedded in constituted "forms of life") in theories of the sociocultural environment.

Unfortunately, the cognitive revolution turned out to be far less than the rediscovery of intentionality and mental representations, and far more than just the displacement of behaviorism. Along with the cognitive revolution came an uninvited "geist" – the spirit of Platonism – which aroused in psychology, and even in some corners of anthropology, that ancient fascination with formal, mathematical, structural models and an inherent central processing mechanism.

As the words of the cognitive revolution spread through the disciplines, so did Platonism. While some cognitivists (e.g., D'Andrade, Lakoff, Lutz) sought to develop the idea of intentionality and mental representations by investigating the specifics of indigenous conceptions of physical, biological, social, and psychological things as those conceptions have a bearing on people's lives (Schank & Abelson, 1977; Holland & Quinn, 1986), for the most part during the cognitive revolution content got set aside in favor of process. The particular got set aside in favor of the general. The substantive got set aside in favor of the abstract and the formal. The person and his or her intentional worlds, meanings, and sociocultural resources, like all other concrete particulars, somehow got lost in the search for the inherent central processing mechanism of the mind.

Today, 30 years into the cognitive revolution, psychology and anthropology are more fragmented than 30 years before. In 1959 it was possible to point to experimental work on animal learning or psychophysics as "real" psychology, or to ethnographic fieldwork on social organization, ritual, and kinship as "real" anthropology, and to have some agreement about it. But no longer. When, in 1987, Shepard reported in *Science* the discovery of a universal law of generalization and compared it favorably to Newton's laws of gravitation, relatively few hearts skipped a beat and many heads shook in dismay.

To everyone's surprise – some scholars are reacting with delight, others with despair – in 1989 it has become increasingly difficult for leading scholars to reach a consensus about the specifications for an excellent psychological research project, or an excellent anthropological one. The criteria for identifying the ideal intellectual core of each discipline have become freely contestable.

With the breakup of general psychology and general anthropology, the usual definitional exercises have become strenuous and fruitless. Now when one asks scholars within the respective disciplines to name the prototypical psychologist or the prototypical anthropologist opinions scatter, with every school of thought fancying a claim to a nonexistent center stage.

Even the recent Platonist nostalgia in some circles of psychology for something abstract and bleached and really real, and the diffuse distraction of attention to the latest intellectual fashion in reductionism and formalism, known as artificial intelligence (AI), has proved to be short-lived. Already other reductive and nonreductive varieties of cognitive science (e.g., neural nets and parallel distributed process models) are screaming like demons for their equal time (see 1988 Winter, special issue of *Daedalus* on artificial intelligence).

For the sake of developing and liberating a "cultural psychology," all the commotion and fragmentation has probably been for the good. Too often in the past the wrong hegemonic general psychology has conspired with the wrong hegemonic general anthropology to divide and conquer the realm. General psychology played its part by reducing and diminishing our conception of the "person" or of "psyche" to a transcendent and abstract and fixed and universal central processing mechanism. General anthropology, fascinated by all the historical and ethnographic variations and diffusional clusterings of concrete sociocultural institutions, practices, and beliefs, played its part by taking no interest in the "person" or "psyche" at all.

The two hegemonic intellectual regimes preserved and deserved each other's disciplinary parochialism. Both research traditions made it difficult to even conceive of a meaningful collaboration between anthropologists and psychologists. Culture and psyche were made to keep their distance by defining what they had in common, the "person" and his or her intentionality, out of both.

Earlier, in my "taxonomic" discussion of general psychology, I analyzed the Platonist prototype for psychological research. At this juncture in the discussion the taxonomic and narrative contexts of definition can be joined: for it was Platonism's taxon that got perpetuated and revivified during the cognitive revolution.

Indeed, under a Platonic influence most high-status research in the psychological sciences during the 1960s came to be guided by five rules of thumb or research heuristics. Modest exposure to those heuristics produced an instant feeling of indifference to the kinds of phenomena (meaning systems, institutional settings, rituals, artifacts, modes of representation, interpersonal power orders, conflicts of motives, goal setting, etc.) of interest to cultural psychology. Those five prescriptions/proscriptions for research went something like this (see Shweder, 1984:3–4):

Heuristic 1. Search for a central processing system and represent it as an abstract structure or as a pure mathematical form; mere content can be ignored.

Heuristic 2. Ignore what people actually say to each other; language use is epiphenomenal to the true causes of behavior. (*Note:* Grammar and phonology remained legitimate topics for investigation, for they were abstract and structural and perhaps even deep – see heuristic 1.)

Heuristic 3. Ignore exterior and extrinsic macrounits such as the sociocultural environment; what is really real (the central processing mechanism) is hidden and interior, and exists solely inside the skin of individuals.

Heuristic 4. Search for universal (timeless and spaceless) laws of nature; the organization of knowledge in Newtonian physics is the ideal form for all true understanding.

Heuristic 5. Do not think about anything that cannot be controlled and measured in a lab, for the lab is the royal road to the central processing mechanism.

Those were, of course, not the only heuristics widely and wildly promoted by Platonism in psychology during the cognitive revolution. I might have mentioned others. And I would not want to deny that there exists at least one, and perhaps even two or three research topics for which those heuristics were, and continue to be, quite useful.

The main point, however, is that during the cognitive revolution those heuristics became reigning heuristics. Their overextension and prevalence lent credence to epithets defining psychology as the "nonsocial social science." Ironically, right in the thick of the cognitive revolution, the psyche and the person were nowhere to be found in psychology, as the discipline designed to study the soul, the subjectivity, the person, the rational strivings of human beings for dignity and self-esteem had turned away from those themes and returned to the mechanistic investigation of automatic processes and deep abstract mathematical forms.

Quite predictably, during the cognitive revolution the person did not succeed in gaining a foothold in anthropology. The local representatives of the revolution, the structural anthropologists (Lévi-Strauss, Leach and family), behaved like Platonists. They searched for the abstract universal principles of organization (e.g., class inclusion, binary opposition) of the central processing mechanism.

The ethnosemanticists and ethnoscientists studied classifications of flora and fauna, later to become ethnopsychologists and study classifications of persons or ideas about emotional states, without studying functioning (or malfunctioning) persons or emotions at all.

The culture and personality theorists – the ones who were really supposed to care about the lived experiences of persons in society – felt disgruntled by the lack of concern for motivation and emotion during the cognitive revolution or played possum, yet they could offer no compelling alternative to the Platonism of the times, since they fully endorsed Platonism's central theme – deep psychic unity.

Most anthropologists, however, simply carried on as usual, just more so, documenting ethnographically and historically the diversity of exotic human institutions, practices, and beliefs and taking no interest in the person at all. Indeed, as if to return (with a vengeance) the compliment of psychology's indifference to the "extrinsic" stuff of culture, society, meaning, and context, the hegemonic prototype for research in general anthropology induced among (too) many a motivated state of psychophobia. The more psychology conceived of the person or the psyche as fixed, interior, abstract, universal, and lawful, the more anthropology chose to interpret sociocultural environments as exterior, historically variable, culture-specific, and arbitrary and to renounce any interest in psyches or persons, or in the general causes of anything.

The person disappeared from ethnography. The question of why people believe the things they believe or practice the practices they practice was either begged, tabooed, or trivialized. The question was reduced to questions of conformity or indoctrination or some other variation on the metaphorical theme of robotics or social pressure. (For a discussion of cultural symbols as personal symbols and an extended critique of conventionalist doctrines in general anthropology, see Obeyesekere, 1981; for a commentary on Obeyesekere, see Shweder, 1987.)

For three decades a person-free psychology of an abstract invariant human nature conspired with a person-free anthropology of local systems of arbitrary, socially sanctioned coercive practices and meanings to keep a cultural psychology of intentional states and intentional worlds off the center stage.

Fortunately for cultural psychology, there were many side shows, and those side shows drew an exciting and excited countercultural crowd. If you knew where to look, or had the right friends, you could find cultural psychology there all along, doing its unorthodox things outside the main pavilions and the center rings.

Some of the side shows were dazzling. There was the tent of Lucien Levy-Bruhl, were exotic ethnic mentalities were put on display in defiance of psychic unity. There was the tent of Ludwig Wittgenstein, where Platonism was turned sour and transmuted into a "form of life." There was the tent of Aaron Cicourel and the ethnomethodologists, where realities were dissolved, contextualized, and infinitely regressed yet still seemed able to reconstruct themselves out of themselves. There was the tent of Roy D'Andrade and other psychesensitive ethnographers of mental representations, where anthropology resisted the Platonism implicit in the cognitivist agenda, on a platform of local or domain-specific territories of meaning.

There was also the tent of Clifford Geertz, where there was magic in his words and reality in his rhetoric, and where they talked manner matters with such sophistication that the same became the different, the formal became contentful, and the fixed began to move. There was the tent of Arthur Kleinman and the "medical anthropologists," where soma revealed psyche and the body exposed its intentionality, and where all could see that there was more to a "splitting head" or a "broken heart" or "frayed nerves" than the matter of disease. There was the tent of Edward Sapir and the "linguistic relativity" hypothesis, where the barker spoke the ultimate mystery (of cultural psychology): "the worlds in which different societies live are distinct worlds, not merely the same world with different labels attached" (Sapir 1924).[7,8]

So what is it?

It still remains to be seen what this new age in anthropology and psychology of seeking to conflate ancient antinomies (form/content, process/content, person/environment, interior/exterior, subjective/objective, psyche/culture) will bring.

In this volume, entitled *Cultural Psychology*, there is some evidence of a new discipline trying to be born. The part titles of the book – Cultural Cognition, Cultural Learning, Cultural Selves, and so on – have been designed as refigurations of the more standard Platonic labels – Culture *and* Cognition, Culture *and* Learning, Culture *and* Selves – and are meant to connote the central theme of cultural psychology, namely, that you can't take the stuff out of the psyche *and* you can't take the psyche out of the stuff.

Cultural psychology, properly understood and practiced, is heretical. It does not presume the premise of psychic unity, that the fundamentals of the mental life are by nature fixed, universal, abstract, and interior.

Cultural psychology presumes instead the principle of intentionality, that the life of psyche is the life of intentional persons, responding to, and directing their action at, their own mental objects or representations, and undergoing transformation through participation in an evolving intentional world that is the product of the mental representations that make it up. According to cultural psychology, intentional persons change and are changed by the concrete particulars of their own mentally constituted "forms of life."

For those who labor for a cultural psychology there are, of course, many difficult analytic, methodological, and substantive issues that must be addressed. There are lots of old habits of thinking to be overcome. Undoubtedly there will be much debate about the true character of the discipline. Even in this volume some of the essays might be read as articulate and challenging expressions from other frameworks (general psychology, cross-cultural psychology, psychological anthropology, and ethnopsychology), or as critiques of cultural psychology or of the principle of intentionality. Perhaps at some future symposium the contrasts between disciplines or frameworks should be addressed more directly.

Nevertheless here I have focused on what I think is trying to be born, a cultural psychology suitable for the study of the role of intentionality in the interdependent functioning and development of coconstituting and coconstituted intentional persons and their coconstituted and coconstituting embodied and materialized intentional worlds.

Betwixt and between anthropology and psychology in the reoccupied zone of cultural psychology the main agenda item these days is how to bridge, fill in, or minimize the gap created by the Platonic separation of an inherent central processing mechanism from all the other extrinsic stuff. There have been many types of attempts. Since a review is not feasible in this context, an illustration or two will have to suffice.

There are many signs of the times. First I would note, without comment, that among those who study formal norms for reasoning (e.g., philosophers of science), the Platonic search has largely been abandoned for a universally binding inductive "logic" or "formal scientific method" that might operate on its own or mechanically to draw sound inferences, free of entrenched local systems for encoding and representing and "abducting" events (Putnam, 1981; see note 4).

Then I would celebrate a bit the emergence among psychologists of an interest in "expertise." For among those who study problem solving, the cognition of virtuosos has become a central topic of investigation, and exemplary cognition is increasingly talked about in non-Platonic ways, as knowledge-based, constructively stimulus-bound, and domain-specific or modular. The current turn toward "content" is significant and widespread.

Indeed what seems to differentiate an expert from a novice (chess player, abacus user, medical diagnostician, etc.) is not some greater amount of content-free pure logical or psychological power. What experts possess that neophytes lack is a greater quantity and quality of domain-specific knowledge of stimulus properties, as well as dedicated mastery of the specialized or parochial "tools" of a trade (see Stigler, 1984; Stigler, Chalip, & Miller, 1986; Stigler & Baranes, 1988).

It is thus no coincidence that those who study expertise do not equate the mental with the abstract. Instead they interpret the mind as it is embodied in concrete representations, in so-called mediating schemata, scripts, and well-practiced tools for thought. The idea of tools for thought is an apposite (and self-referring) metaphor for thinking about thinking. It says that thinking is fundamentally interdependent with the traditional intellectual artifacts, representational schemes, and accumulated knowledge of some cultural or subcultural community. It says that as thinking becomes, as it must, metaphorically displaced away from the operations of any fixed and central processing mechanism, the life of the mind becomes an extension of, or an appendage to, or an analogue of, cultural artifacts and their built-in design features.

Jerome Bruner, speaking in resistance to the Piagetian notion of a deeply interior and abstract central processing mechanism undergoing progressive development, used to talk of cultural "amplifiers" of thought. His idea was that what you think with (and about) can be decisive for how you think; and that it is those amplifiers or collective modes of representation, and the role they play in formal and informal education, that are proper topics for the psychology of thought.

Of course, it is hardly news to point out that one cannot be indifferent to "mere" content and still make sense of everyday cognitive, emotional, and conative functioning. Every Platonist knows that, as we have seen.

From a Platonic point of view, everyday cognitive, emotional, and conative functioning is "noise"-laden and stimulus-bound, which is, of course, precisely why the Platonists believe that the stimulus and task environment must be transcended to discover pure "psychological" laws (see the discussion of Shepard earlier in the chapter). What is new (and renewing) in anthropology and psychology is the return of a this-worldly interest in the study of actual functioning and the reemergence of a genuine respect for all that psychocultural, psychophysical, psychosomatic noise. Indeed, in the land of cultural psychology all of the action is in the noise. And the so-called noise is not really noise at all; it is the message.

Notably, in the language of cultural psychology there are no pure psychological laws, just as there are no unreconstructed or unmediated stimulus events. There are intentional persons reacting to, and directing their behavior with respect to their own descriptions and mental representations of things; and there are intentional worlds, which are the realities we constitute, embody, and materialize out of our descriptions and representations of things. Indeed, according to the premises of cultural psychology, even the transcendent realities portrayed by scientists are part of intentional worlds and cannot really take us beyond our mental representations of "things."[9] In the world of cultural psychology transcendence and self-transformation is possible but only through a dialectical process of moving from one intentional world into the next, or by changing one intentional world into another.

Every person is stimulus-bound while every stimulus is person-bound. That is what I mean when I say culture and psyche make each other up. That is why a cultural psychology signals an end to the purely psychological in psychology, an end to the quest for the inherent central processing mechanism of mental life, and an end to the Platonist legacy of the cognitive revolution. Cultural psychology is a return to the study of mental representations (emotions, desires, and beliefs and their intentional objects) without the presumption of fixity, necessity, universality, and abstract-formalism.

And although the constitutive and meaning-laden act of scientific comparison may require the postulation of a standard or universal Archimedian point of view from which to spot differences and talk sensibly about them (difference does presuppose likeness), it should be remembered that such posits of a universal grid for comparison are constructed and deconstructed by us in order to make our intentional world intelligible. One of the hazards of comparison may be the ease with which the universals that we posit as part of our own intentional activities, in maintaining and enriching our own intentional world, get projected onto some imagined deep and essential structure of the mind.

As interpretive frameworks change, so do perceptions. Thus it is also a sign of the times that the "fundamental" Platonic distinction between "higher"-order and "lower"-order systems (between "deep" structure and "surface" structure) no longer seem quite so easy to sustain. It is not just that there are content-rich mediating schemata bridging the gap between supposed abstract structures and the real life instances to which they apply. (Platonists have no trouble with that. They view the "application" of abstract principles to concrete cases as either beside the point or as rulelike and mechanical.) The most difficult problem for Platonism is that once the gap between abstraction and case has been filled in, a general and rulelike distinction between a central processor and its content is not so readily defined.

A deep suspicion has arisen in cultural psychology that so-called strict or intrinsic dispositions for behavior (Putnam, 1987) and neat linear relationships between things are the exceptions in a world of local nonlinear dynamic processes with circular or dialectical feedback loops between so-called (and once Platonically conceived) levels of analysis, and between subject and object, text and context, manner and matter, content and form, fact and value, belief and directive force. There seems to be far less distinction in those famous old distinctions than there used to be.

At forums in anthropology and psychology these days someone is bound to say "not so fast" if you blithely presuppose a central processing mechanism consisting of abstract universal underlying structures or laws that impose form on any substance that happens to come along; or if you casually presume a self-evident division between an interior psyche and an exterior sociocultural environment. Indeed, with the reemergence of a cultural psychology there has been defined a new aim for anthropologists and psychologists: to find ways to talk about culture and psyche so that neither is by universal nature intrinsic or extrinsic to the other.

That aim for cultural psychology is to imaginatively conceive of subject-dependent objects (intentional worlds) and object-dependent subjects (intentional persons) interpenetrating each other's identities or setting the conditions for each other's existence and development, while jointly undergoing change through social interaction (see the earlier discussion of weeds). That aim is to develop an interpretive framework in which nothing really real is by fundamental nature fixed, universal, transcendent (deep, interior) and abstract; and in which local things can be deeply embedded, but only for a while; and then, having developed the framework, the aim is to see how far it will go. (It may not go everywhere, but that remains to be seen.) That aim is to bridge the gap between psyche and culture by talking about them in new (or is it in very old) ways. Here is one new (and very old way) of talking about psyche and culture.

Psyche refers to the intentional person. Culture refers to the intentional world. Intentional persons and intentional worlds are interdependent things that get dialectically constituted and reconstituted through the intentional activities and practices that are their products, yet make them up (again, see the earlier discussion of weeds).

Psyche animates her vessels and turns them into persons, leaving them mindful, soulful, willful, and full of goals and judgments. The breath of psyche is the stuff of intentional states, of beliefs and desires, of fears and fancies, of values and visions about this or that. Psyche refers to patterns of motivated involvement, subjective states responsive to and directed at our mental representations of things. The breath of psyche is the stuff of intentional processes, goal setting, means–ends calculation, reality testing, embodied emotional reactiveness, self-monitoring, and self-regulation in the pursuit of personal dignity, and so on. Psyche refers to "already-there " intentional states and processes distributed and organized within a person or across a people, and undergoing change, reorganization, and transformation across the life cycle.

In thinking about culture in new (or very old ways) it is crucial to remind oneself again and again that a sociocultural environment is a world constituted, occupied, and used by intentional beings (see Sahlins, 1976, on the symbolic or intentional uses of food and clothing). For psyche imparts to her vessels that charmed and spiritual quality of intentionality (and the teleology and pursuit after mental objects and final causes that accompanies it): Psyche's vessels strive always to keep up appearances, to remain visibly dignified and exemplary of their imagined kind, and to express through their social actions a conception of themselves and of their place in the constituted scheme of things.

Culture is the constituted scheme of things for intending persons, or at least that part of the scheme that is inherited or received from the past. Culture refers to persons, society, and nature as lit up, and made possible by some already-there intentional world, an intentional world composed of conceptions, evaluations, judgments, goals, and other mental representations already embodied in socially inherited institutions, practices, artifacts, technologies, art forms, texts, and modes of discourse. It is those inherited conceptions, evaluations, judgments, and goals embodied in cultural things (institutions, artifacts, discourse), about which the intending think, out of which the intending build their lives, and with respect to which the intending give substance to their minds, souls, wills, and directed actions.

Psyche and culture are thus seamlessly interconnected. A person's psychic organization is largely made possible by, and expressive of, a conception of itself, society, and nature; and one of the best ways to understand cultural conceptions of self, society, and nature is to examine the way those conceptions organize, and function in, the subjective life of intending individuals (see D'Andrade, 1984).[10]

It cannot be repeated enough that a cultural psychology aims to develop a principle of intentionality – action responsive to and directed at mental objects or representations – by which culturally constituted realities (intentional worlds) and reality-constituting psyches (intentional persons) continually and continuously make each other up, perturbing and disturbing each other, interpenetrating each other's identity, reciprocally conditioning each other's existence.

The aim of cultural psychology is to examine the different kinds of things that continually happen in social interaction and in social practice as the intentionality of a person meets the intentionality of a world, and as they jointly facilitate, express, repress, stabilize, transform, and defend each other through and throughout the life of a person or the life of a world. There are histories (narratives) that can be written about each, or both – the history of lives and the history of practices and institutions.

Most of the work of cultural psychology is still ahead of us. To achieve its aims, cultural psychology is going to have to develop an analytic framework for characterizing the relationships between reality-constituting psyches (intentional persons) and culturally constituted realities (intentional worlds) that is at least as rich as the framework developed by behavioral geneticists for characterizing so-called genotype–environment correlations (Scarr & McCartney, 1983; Plomin, 1986: chap. 6).

As ethnographers, economists, and experimental social psychologists have known for a long time, intentional worlds can be strongly disposing and powerfully promoting of certain intentional states and not others. They prompt and dispose in a variety of ways – by the way objects and events are represented and described by local guardians of the intentional world (parents, teachers, leaders, experimenters), by the way resources and opportunities are arranged and managed, by the way rituals and routines are performed, by the way sanctions are allocated (see Whiting & Whiting, 1975; Ochs & Schieffelin, 1984; Shweder & Much, 1987; Miller & Sperry, 1987; Whiting & Edwards, 1988).

Here is a simple yet vivid example of a strongly disposing (micro) intentional world: An alarm clock ringing loudly from where it was deliberately placed the night before, on the other side of the room, tends to stimulate an intense desire to turn it off, which gets you out of bed (see Schelling, 1984, chaps. 2 and 3, on self-regulation and self-deception through the personal management of microenvironments).

For a moment let us borrow from the behavioral geneticists (Scarr & McCartney, 1983; Plomin, 1986) their analytic framework for talking about genotype–environment interactions, and let us transmute it a bit. Since the genotype is irrelevant to the logic of the analytic framework, let us drop it and talk instead about person–environment interactions. Using the Scarr and McCartney framework, one can imagine at least six types of relationships between reality-constituting psyches (intentional persons) and culturally constituted realities (intentional worlds).

The relationship can be either *positive* (when the intentionality of the world amplifies or supports the intentionality of the person) or *negative* (when the intentionality of the world diminishes or contravenes the intentionality of the person). And the relationship can be either *active* (when the target person himself creates or selects his intentional world), *reactive* (when other persons create or select an intentional world for the target person in the light of that person's intentionality or the intentionality that others anticipate in the target person) or *passive* (when a target person ends up living in an intentional world created or selected by others for others or for themselves). That gives us six types: positive (active, reactive, passive) and negative (active, reactive, passive).[11]

The alarm clock arranged to go off just out of reach is a negative active relationship. The reality-constituting person constructs an intentional world using collective resources to contravene his or her own anticipated preference to stay in bed and go back to sleep. Whistling a happy or confident tune in the dark to alleviate one's fear is a second example of a negative active relationship. Hiding one's face from, or not looking at, or avoiding, seductive or attractive things that might tempt you to transgression is a third example. Rituals of transcendence or detachment – for example, Buddhist meditative exercises through which a reality-constituting person strives to make his or her own body ego-alien by conceiving of it as a bag of feces (Obeyesekere, 1985), provide a fourth example.

It is characteristic of the negative *active* relationship that the psyche creates or selects an intentional world to protect itself against itself, often by means of so-called culturally constituted defenses (the alarm clock, the happy tune, etc.). The negative *reactive* relationship, however, is one in which others intervene to protect you against your own intentionality. The institution of purdah for adolescent females is an example of a negative reactive relationship.

In some intentional worlds girls are not permitted to do at age 13 what they were permitted to do at age 5 and whatever desire they may have for autonomy in decision making becomes dangerous with the onset of puberty. Menstruating daughters are kept off the street in that intentional world, for the sake of what is good and true and beautiful, in that intentional world. Purdah, too, is a culturally constituted defense, but a reactive one, choreographed by others for the self rather than written by the self for itself.[12]

In contrast, in the negative *passive* relationship the reality-constituting person experiences the meanings and resources of an intentional world created or selected by others for others or for themselves. For example, during the 10 to 12 days of death pollution in orthodox Hindu communities in India, family members assist the soul of the deceased in detaching from its corpse and in proceeding on its eternal transmigratory journey. The pollution in the corpse is believed to burden the soul of the deceased and keep it bound to its material vessel. To assist the deceased, his or her living relatives absorb the pollution in the corpse into their own bodies.

To facilitate the process of death pollution absorption, family members are careful to avoid other kinds of pollutants (hot foods, hot activities like sex, and hot emotions). They fast. They are abstinent. They stay at home. The mourning period is over when the soul of the deceased has successfully detached itself from its dead body. Family members then cleanse their own bodies of the death pollution they have absorbed. They do that by shaving their hair, cutting their nails, and taking a special bath. They put on new clothes and they return to life in the outside world.

It seems likely that for some members of the family, at some point in the life cycle, the experience of the mourning ritual is a negative passive one. Children or other family members may want to go out, or play or eat hot foods. Adults may want to have sex. Some transgression of the requirements of the intentional world of the funeral practice probably does occur. Yet because children participate passively and vicariously in the practice and experience its meanings, resources, and sanctions, the intentional world of mourning customs (including the end at which it is aimed – salvation of an eternal transmigrating soul through the help of loyal, devout, and self-sacrificing relatives) comes to be upheld and pursued by precisely those reality-constituting persons whose intentions came to be formed through participation in those very practices.

I will not on this occasion illustrate or examine all the positive types of relationships between reality-constituting psyches (intentional persons) and culturally constituted realities (intentional worlds). The main reason for reviewing a logical scheme for types of person–environment interactions in this context is to suggest that it might be fruitful in cultural psychology to conceive of socialization processes in terms of, *at least*, those six forms of relationship between intentional persons and intentional worlds. There is a reciprocal and dynamic relationship between intentional persons and intentional worlds, each setting conditions for the other's existence and development.

All the relationships are self-transforming and dialectical. At stake in these relationships are both the cultivation of a human psyche suited to the historical context of some intentional world and the cultivation of an intentional world, capable of cultivating and supporting the human psyche in one of the various forms of its nobility.

The three "negative" relationships describe "defensive" engagements. Making use of the resources from an already-there intentional world, an already-there personal intention becomes attenuated, modified, or hidden, either through direct self-regulation (active) or through direct or vicarious interpersonal regulation (reactive, passive). The three positive relationships describe "expressive" engagements. Making use of the resources from an already-there intentional world, an already-there personal intention is amplified, reproduced, and displayed, either through direct self-promotion (active) or through direct or vicarious interpersonal subsidization (reactive, passive).

In some orthodox Brahman communities in Orissa, India, for example, there is a positive reactive ritual, which takes place in the context of joint family living arrangements the day after a marriage is consummated. Everyone in the extended household knows that the bride has lost her virginity the night before. (Indeed, some of them may have been listening and giggling at her door.) She knows that everyone knows it. Everyone knows that she knows that everyone knows it. She feels embarrassed to show her face the next morning; she wants to hide. So she is made to hide. They feel embarrassed to face her. So they are not allowed to face her.

The day-after-the-fateful-night-before is explicitly labeled the "day of embarrassment." That day the bride is expected to stay secluded in her room all day or to go away to visit a friend. By means of a positive reactive relationship between a reality-constituting person (yesterday's virgin) and a culturally-constituted world (the "day of embarrassment") the young Hindu bride is protected from humiliation and permitted to safely dramatize her state of mind and realize her intention to hide.

It is tempting but not feasible in the context of this preliminary scouting expedition to view or review the key analytic and empirical contributions of the various intellectual communities that have so much to contribute to a cultural psychology. The territory is too vast. Such a review would include, for example, philosophical work on intentionality and partial translatability (Brentano, Heidegger, Goodman, Rorty, Gadamer, Manicus, Derrida, MacIntyre); linguistic work on discourse processes, performative utterances, and the pragmatics of language use (Austin, Grice, Searle, Labov, Slobin, Silverstein, Dunn, Peggy Miller, Heath, Ochs, Schieffelin, Fred Myers, Much, Haviland); cognitive work on framing effects, construal, and the representation of knowledge (D'Andrade, Tversky, Kahneman, Ross, Nisbett, Quinn, Holland, Schank, Sperber, Trabasso, Siegler, Charles Nuckolls. Ed Hutchins, Kempton); literary work on rhetoric inside and outside of science (Booth, Geertz, Fish, McCloskey, deMan, Herb Simons, Barbara H. Smith, Clifford); sociological work on situated meanings and the construction of realities, including scientific realities (Cicourel, Mehan, Eilberg-Schwartz, Woolgar, Pinch, Latour); critical interpretive work on social and psychological theory (Bernstein, Bloor, Bourdieu, Tambiah, Gergen, Mike Cole, Lave, Haskel Levi, Goodnow); medical work on "placebo," psychosomatic effects and the body as an intentional system (Kleinman, Gendlin, Good, Csordas); developmental work on social referencing and the socialization of emotions (Campos, Dunn, Emde, Camras); clinical work on the role of cultural myths and stories in the self-regulation or emotional states (Kakar, Herdt, Doi, Spiro, Zonis); anthropological work on person-centered ethnography (Robert Levy, Obeyesekere, LeVine, Scheper-Hughes, Luhrmann, Gregor, Whiting and Whiting); ethnographic work on the socialization of motivations, attitudes, and subjective states in institutional settings – families, schools, military units (Lois Peak, Bletso, Alan Fiske, Phil Jackson, Stodolsky, G. W. Skinner, Csikszentmihaly, Edgerton, Weisner, Ogbu); psychological and anthropological work on narrative and dialogue (Bruner, Cohler, Crapanzano, Nancy Stein); and ethnopsychological work on the representation of self and subjective states (Fogelson, Geoffrey White, Lutz, Fitz Porter Poole, Joan Miller, Heelas, Paul Harris, Triandis, Michael Bond, Karl Heider). Some of that work is reviewed and examined in the chapters that follow.

The many insights and refigurations that emerge from those various intellectual communities are stimulating (perhaps even breathtaking) in their own terms. Yet they are also suggestive of a possible unification of intellectual agendas under the banner of a cultural psychology. Even a brief consideration of the several varieties (positive vs. negative; active, reactive, passive) of continual engagement between intentional persons and intentional worlds should make it apparent that neither psyche nor culture can long be denied by anyone genuinely curious about the functioning and development of either.

The challenge is before us, to define more precisely this promising new discipline. How far can one go with an interpretive framework within which, and in whose terms, nothing is by fundamental or intrinsic nature fixed, universal, transcendent, and abstract? What kind of knowledge can we expect from a cultural psychology? Those are questions for other occasions. I won't try to answer them here. They call for deep rethinking and broad discussion across intellectual communities sympathetic to the general framework and aims of a cultural psychology.

It does seem likely, however, that our received images of "real" or honorific science will have to be revised. Although a cultural psychology does not avoid the study of causes, it studies precisely those causal processes that go on because of our understanding of them and involvement with them. It would seem to follow that the truths to be formulated in cultural psychology are typically going to be restricted in scope, because the causal processes they describe are likely to be embedded or localized within particular intentional worlds. What we are likely to discover are patches of institutionalized regularities, stabilized within culture areas during certain historical epochs, perhaps even for centuries, yet subject to change (see Gergen, 1973).

It would also seem to follow that if realities are not independent of our representations of them and involvement with them, then the raising of questions, even "scientific" questions, is no innocent act. Asking people what they want to do is a way of promoting autonomous decision making. Asking about the potential uses of something is a way of constituting it as instrumental. Indeed, to select a not so random illustration, one might argue that the manner of representation of reality known as economics is a normative ideology, which recommends a way of thinking about events ("take care of number one"; "more is better"; "everyone is a whore – the only difference is how much you get paid for it!") that plays a part in making economic principles work; and that economic thinking is a way of thinking about things that turns things into economic "facts." Cultural psychology will undoubtedly have an ideological and critical role to play in society. Platonism certainly has had one.

The world of cultural psychology is a world of dialectical feedback loops and dynamic nonlinear relationships between things undergoing transformation. Given such a world, many of our received expectations for, and models of, successful research are going to make less sense. For example, one may not be able to fix or standardize the definitions of concepts. You can do that in a unitary, homogeneous linear world where things stay put, permitting their presumed essences to be inter-defined, but not in the world of cultural psychology. And one should not expect that the same truths will reappear in every intentional world, or that something more wonderful and fundamental and revelatory has been discovered when and if they do, as sometimes they will (see note 2). Most important, one should not expect reality to be independent of our participation in it. The likelihood that an event will occur in an intentional world is not independent of the confidence we have that it will occur.

Most normative models for decision making have not yet taken into account that simple truth. There are good metaphors and bad metaphors for the actions of intentional persons in intentional worlds. Most normative models for rational choice are metaphorical variations on the properties of roulette wheels, random number tables, dice games, and coin flips. Those rather special, peculiar (and ethically controversial) cultural artifacts and technologies (dice, roulette wheels) have been deliberately designed by us so that their behavior is indepen-dent of our attitudes toward them; and thus they are among the most inappropriate of metaphors for intentional action in general.

The intentional world is not typically the world of a coin flip. It is more often a world in which our confidence in an event influences the likelihood of its occurrence and where we not only monitor but also regulate and control deviations from expectation. It is a world in which, if we did not have the confidence we have in things occurring, then they might not occur, just because of us! Patterns of decision making that are irrational in Las Vegas (e.g., the so-called gambler's fallacy) may well be rational and constructive in most other intentional worlds.

Thinking through others: cultural psychology as an interpretive discipline

Among the most illustrious and chewed-over collections of anthro-pological essays on intentional worlds is Clifford Geertz's *Interpretation of Cultures*. Cultural psychology is an "interpretive" enterprise in Geertz's sense. One of the first questions cultural psychology will need to consider is this: Just what is it one actually does in the interpretation of (intentional) worlds and (intentional) lives? Since I suspect that the answer to that question has something to do with the process of "thinking through others" – thinking through other cultures, thinking through other lives – I would like to conclude this essay with some thoughts about that process of thinking through others.

The expression "thinking through others" (e.g., thinking through

India, thinking through Plato, thinking through feminist criticism, thinking through paranoia) is, of course, polysemous in at least four senses – (1) thinking by means of the other; (2) getting the other straight; (3) deconstructing and going beyond the other; and (4) situated witnessing while there, in the context of your engagement with the other.

First, there is thinking through others in the sense of using the intentionality and self-consciousness of another culture or person – his or her or its articulated conception of things – as a means of heightening awareness of one's less conscious self.

Orthodox Hindus in India, to select a not so random example, have, as intentional beings, for thousands of years reflected on the relationship between moral action and outcome, on hierarchy, on patronage and paternalism, on sanctity and pollution. The more one tries to conceive of an intentional world in their intentional terms, the more their doctrines and rituals and art forms and other modes of representation come to seem like sophisticated expressions of repressed, dormant, and potentially creative and transformative aspects of our own psyche pushed off by our intentional world to some mental fringe.

We do not know how to talk about "karma" or how to comprehend an occasional dread that if we do something bad something bad may happen to us, yet we experience it. We do not know how to justify status obligations and hierarchical relationships, but we live them. We do not quite know how to acknowledge the importance of personal sanctity, yet we feel it.

Thinking through others in the first sense is to recognize the other as a specialist or expert on some aspect of human experience, whose reflective consciousness and system of representations and discourse can be used to reveal hidden dimensions of our self. Some cultures of the world are virtuosos of grief and mourning, others of gender identity, and still others, of intimacy, eroticism, and ego striving. Ruth Benedict, an ancestral spirit of cultural psychology, with her conception of cultures as selections from the arc of human possibilities, understood well the first sense of thinking through others.

Then there is thinking through others in a second sense, of getting the other straight – of providing a systematic account of the internal logic of the intentional world constructed by the other. The aim is a rational reconstruction of indigenous belief, desire, and practice. The assumption is that the organization of the psyche is based on a reality principle, whereby culturally constituted realities and reality-constituting psyches are mutually adjusted to one another until some attractive equilibrium is reached – a graceful or proportionate fit between the world as the other has made it out/made it up and the other's reactions to the world made out and up.

Freud is one of the great champions of the reality principle and the second sense of thinking through others. In his brilliant and inspiring defense of nonbiomedical healing practices, published under the title

"The Question of Lay Analysis," he notes that "if a patient of ours is suffering from a sense of guilt, as though he had committed a serious crime, we do not recommend him to disregard his qualms of conscience and do not emphasize his undoubted innocence; he himself has often tried to do so without success. What we do is to remind him that such a strong and persistent feeling must after all be based on something real, which it may perhaps be possible to discover."

Thinking through others, in its second sense, is a process of re-presenting (and defending) the others' evaluations of, and involvements with the world – for example, a taboo against eating meat or a prohibition against remarriage – by tracing those evaluations and modes of involvement to some plausible alternative intentional world and conception of reality, which, in the ideal case, no rational person, not even Freud, can defeat.

Then there is thinking through others in a third sense, the sense favored by Derrida and other postmodern deconstructionists. It is the sense of thinking one's way out of or beyond the other. It is the sense of passing through the other or intellectually transforming him or her or it into something else – perhaps its negation – by revealing what the intentional world of the other has dogmatically hidden away, namely its own partiality and incompleteness. It is a third sense for it properly comes later, after one has already appreciated what the intentional world of the other powerfully reveals and illuminates, from its special point of view. Thinking through others is thus, in its totality, an act of criticism and liberation, as well as of discovery.

And then there is thinking through others in its fourth sense. It is the sense of a situated perspectival observer, thinking *while there* in an alien land or with an alien other, trying to make sense of context-specific experiences. It is the sense of Geertz's "I-witnessing" author trying to turn a personal field experience into a "they-picturing" account of the other (Geertz, 1988). In that fourth sense of thinking through others, the process of representing the other goes hand in hand with a process of portraying one's self itself as part of the process of representing the other, thereby encouraging an open-ended self-reflexive dialogic turn of mind.

It seems to me that a genuine cultural psychology, the one we can feel proud of, is the cultural psychology that strives to think through others in all four senses, and more.

Finally, we come to the ultimate question: how far can you go with a cultural psychology? Can it take you all the way? It is always a good idea to leave ultimate questions for some other occasion. Still I will express my doubts. I think cultural psychology will take you very far, but not all the way. I do not think it will take you as far as Nirvana, if there is such a place or state of mindlessness. I think there is such a place. And I think that if you get there you won't have the slightest need for a content and context dependent, this-worldly cultural psychology. I certainly hope you won't.

Yet who knows; maybe I am wrong. Perhaps even Nirvana is really a special state of mind in a special intentional world, which it is the proper business of a cultural psychology to understand.

Notes

I am grateful to Roy D'Andrade, Gilbert Herdt, Philip Jackson, Arthur Kleinman, Melford Spiro, James Stigler, and Stanley Tambiah for their helpful comments on an earlier version of this essay; and to all the participants in the 1986 and 1987 Chicago symposia, who unwittingly, and I hope not regretfully, provided the necessary stimulus for the preparation of this manifesto for a cultural psychology.

I am uncertain of the origin of the expression "cultural psychology." It would be fascinating to trace the history of its appearance and reappearance in the writings of 19th- and 20th-century social and psychological theorists. Although conceptions of cultural psychology may differ from scholar to scholar, the expression has certainly been used before, for example, by Michael Cole, by Alan Howard (1985), by James Peacock (1984) and perhaps by several others as well.

The idea of a cultural psychology is very much in the air these days, and my understanding of the possibilities for this reemerging discipline has been significantly deepened through discussions with friends and colleagues at several recent important seminars, workshops, conferences, and planning groups. Those include the seminar and colloquium series "Culture and Personality" at the University of Michigan, organized by Hazel Markus and Richard Nisbett; the conference "The Rhetorics of Science" at the University of Iowa, organized by Donald McCloskey and Allan Megill; the workshop "Accounts of Human Nature: A Workshop in Anthropology and Psychology" at Cumberland Lodge, Windsor Great Park, England, organized by Paul Heelas and Tim Ingold; the faculty seminar "Culture and the Person" at Harvard University, organized by Arthur Kleinman, Jerome Kagan, and Philip Holtzman; the colloquium "Myth, Philosophy, and Practice" at the University of Chicago, organized by Frank Reynolds and David Tracy; the conference "The Person in South Asia" at the University of California, Santa Barbara, organized by Mattison Mines; the workshop "Socialization of Emotions" at the National Institute of Child Health and Human Development, organized by Sarah Friedman and Joseph Campos; and the planning session "Cultural Acquisition" at the Social Science Research Council, organized by Stefan Tanaka.

Well-represented these days within the Gothic quadrangles of the University of Chicago are the three intellectual traditions and frameworks that go under the labels Platonism, positivism (or positive science), and historicism (or cultural relativism). A reconsideration of the possibilities for a cultural psychology is a form of engagement and struggle with the judgments of all three frameworks. My understanding of those traditions has been enriched through ongoing participation in the "Practical Reason Workshop" of the University of Chicago Divinity School, organized by Donald Browning, Philip Jackson, and Jerome Wakefield; the "Rational Choice Workshop," organized by Gary Becker and James Coleman; and the "Cross-Cultural Workshop," of the Committee on Human Development, organized by the three coeditors of this volume.

For well over a decade, Haskel Levi and Marvin Zonis have kept alive at the University of Chicago a remarkable informal faculty seminar known as

"Grounds," where advocates of Platonism, positivism, and historicism have been encouraged to argue with each other in the context of a family affair. We all keep coming back, eagerly.

I owe a great intellectual debt to several scholars, teachers, and friends who over the years have been luminaries in the debates over the possibilities for a cultural psychology. Not all of them may have realized that they were participating in such a debate, and certainly many will want to take issue with my formulation. Nevertheless, my intellectual debt is great to Wayne Booth, Jerome Bruner, Donald Campbell, Ranjit Chatterjee. Bertram Cohler, Mihaly Csikzentmihalyi, William Damon, Roy D'Andrade, Sandra Dixon, Carolyn Edwards, Alan Fiske, Donald Fiske, Daniel G. Freedman, Clifford Geertz, Eugene Gendlin, Kenneth Gergen, Alan Gewirth, Byron Good, J. David Greenstone, Robert Hahn, Sara Harkness, Harry Harootunian, Sophie Haroutunian, John Haviland, Gilbert Herdt, E. Tory Higgins, Martin Hoffman, Janellen Huttenlocher, Philip Jackson, Jerome Kagan, Sudhir Kakar, Julius Kirshner, Arthur Kleinman, Lawrence Kohlberg, Mark Lepper, Haskel Levi, Donald Levine, Robert LeVine, Robert Levy, John Lucy, McKim Marriott, Hugh Mehan, Joan Miller, Peggy Miller, Walter Mischel, John Miyamoto, Nancy Much, Richard Nisbett, Larry Nucci, Charles Nuckolls, Elinor Ochs, Deborah Pool, Michelle Rosaldo, David Rosenhan, Lee Ross, Paul Rozin, Lloyd Rudolph, Bambi Schieffelin, Theodore Schwartz, Herbert W. Simons, Jan Smedslund, Melford Spiro, James Stigler, Charles Super, Stephen Toulmin, Thomas Trabasso, Eliot Turiel, Thomas Weisner, Beatrice Whiting, John Whiting, William Wimsatt, Stanton Wortham, Nur Yalman, and Marvin Zonis. I hope this essay will keep the debate going and that the network of participants in the debate will keep expanding.

1 In defining cultural psychology I shall assume, as did the ancients, that a proper appreciation of a thing integrates its taxonomic and narrative contexts (its being with its becoming). That assumption is characteristic of teleological approaches to definition and understanding, and it is associated with the following conception of reality or nature: What is real or in the nature of things is what a thing of a certain kind strives to become so as to fully realize its identity and become excellent, developed, and exemplary of its kind.

The teleological approach to definition may sound old-fashioned or premodern, which is not surprising since teleology, and all that it implied about nature, society, and persons, was one of the casualties of modern thinking in the West. It was replaced by an "enlightened" positive science conception: the natural order as unanimated, deterministic, and indifferent to human affairs and to all other mental events.

In that modern scientific conception of reality, whatever happened in the world was thought to be an expression of the inexorable deterministic laws inherent in the nature of things. And thus, in modern consciousness, the idea of what was proper or excellent or elevated or cultivated became detached from the idea of what was natural (see Shweder, 1989).

One unfortunate consequence of that separation was that all the traditional and central normative ideals for human functioning and development – ideas of the good, the right, the beautiful, and so on – were deprived of natural or objective force, while the idea of a natural norm was reduced to a nonevaluative statistical notion, the so-called value-neutral positive science idea of regularly occurring or repetitive events. Natural science and normative ethics – is and ought – got in the habit of moving through modern times in entirely divorced ways, and, as I shall suggest later, social science suffered for it.

Yet teleology still has some things to recommend it, not the least of which is the opportunity it affords to move seamlessly back and forth between descriptions of what something is and descriptions of what something ought to be; to see an as yet unrealized regulative ideal immanent and active in the development of instances of its kind; and to promote what is natural in the light of what is.

Hence this essay, which is itself part of a teleological process, lending assistance, quite purposefully, to the discipline of cultural psychology in an attempt to help it discover, and hence realize, its nature.

2 At any historical moment, of course, what has been constituted as true, beautiful, or good within some one, then existing, intentional world might also happen, as a matter of contingency, to have been constituted that way within each of all the then existing intentional worlds. In other words, there may well be some intentional truths that are true universally. However, since an intentional truth becomes true only by virtue of its embeddedness in some particular intentional world, it follows that there is no sense of necessity associated with a universal intentional truth.

A universal intentional truth is universally true because it has been constituted as true within each of the then existing particular intentional worlds, which is no guarantee that it must of necessity be true within every existing intentional world, past or future, or within every imaginable one.

3 For those general psychologists who are, by metaphysical choice or second-nature, materialists, reductionists, and incorrigible utopians, there is also an additional aim, some day to locate Plato's transcendent realm of fixed ideas in some physical realization in the brain or the nervous system, or on chromosome 11.

It may well have been René Descartes, a latter-day Platonist, who turned inward or interiorized the ancient search for the transcendent, and first tried to postulate a physical realization – localized in the pineal gland – for an abstracted central processor of the mind, the "I."

4 Descartes, of course, tried an alternative Platonist route to the central processor, the route of rationalism (deductive reasoning from undeniable premises, for example, "I think, therefore I am") rather than the route of empiricism (inductive reasoning from sense-data or observations). Adhering to his principle of radical doubt, Descartes treated as deceptive or illusory or exterior all sensations and stimulus materials and tried to reconstruct the logically necessary features of the central processing mechanism through deductive reasoning alone.

Both rationalism and empiricism are the offspring of the Platonic imagination, which fancies routes of direct access to a fixed and uniform reality. General psychology is the empiricist child of Platonism, while its rationalist sibling lives on in the philosophy of mind and language, in normative ethics, and in the field of artificial intelligence.

If there is to be a cultural psychology it will have to synthesize rationalism and empiricism into something else or provide an alternative to both, C. S. Peirce's notion of abductive reasoning as the indispensable assistant to the "unaided rationality" of logic and sense-data is a promising starting point.

One version of Peirce's notion, if I understand it, is this: Transcendent realities can be imagined but never seen or deduced, for they are constructions of our own making, which sometimes succeed at binding us to the underlying reality they imagine by giving us an intellectual tool – a metaphor, a premise, an analogy, a category – with which to live, to arrange our experience, and to interpret our experiences so arranged. In other words, the abductive faculty is the the faculty of imagination, which comes to the rescue of sensation and logic by providing them with the intellectual means to see through experience and leap beyond empty syllogisms and tautologies to some creative representation of an underlying reality that might be grasped and reacted to, even if that imagined reality cannot be found, proved, or disproved by inductive or deductive rule following. (On the imaginative conceiving of things, see Levin 1988.)

I hope it goes without saying that just because you cannot get beyond appearances to reality with the methods of science or the rules of logic (or, for that matter, through meditative mysticism) does not mean you should stop trying to imagine the really real, or that the imagination *must* be disrespectful of sense-data or deductive logic, or that "anything goes." Of course there are times and places when it makes good sense to be disrespectful of sense-data and of logical deductions, especially when they lead you places where there is good reason not to go.

5 For a discussion of how the field of geophysics had to get free of the standards of Newtonian mechanics in order to gain some self-respect and make progress, see Richter (1986) on the topic of plate tectonics. For a discussion of the importance in the social sciences of not waiting around for our Newton, see Converse (1986).

6 From within the interpretive framework of cultural psychology researchers in general psychology might be construed as participant observers in the special sociocultural and procedural world of laboratory life, where they talk to and observe the reactions of informants – most often college-age students – from some specific cultural and historical tradition, typically their own.

7 Of course I am being ridiculously selective and contemporary here. I trust that the many ancestral spirits of a cultural psychology – Abelard, Herder, Fichte, Schiller, Hegel, Heidegger, Brentano, Wundt and all the many others – will not take offense.

A short short list of relevant and important contemporary texts critiquing one aspect or more of the Platonic conception of a central processing mechanism (fixed, universal, transcendent = interior or deep, abstract) includes *Primitive Mentality* (Lucien Levy-Bruhl), *Philosophical Investigations* (Ludwig Wittgenstein), *The Structure of Scientific Revolutions* (Thomas Kuhn), *Studies in Ethnomethodology* (Harold Garfinkle), *Human Understanding* (Stephen Toulmin), *Interpretation of Cultures* (Clifford Geertz), *Languages of Art* (Nelson Goodman), *After Virtue* (Alasdair MacIntyre), *Is There a Text in This Class?* (Stanley Fish), *Women. Fire and Dangerous Things* (George Lakoff), and *The Many Faces of Realism* (Hilary Putnam).

8 In the intentional world that is the object of investigation for cultural psychology, people study the past so as to allow it to intrude on the present, and they ignore the past so that it won't. One way to revivify cultural psychology is to pay homage to the many great ancestral spirits of cultural psychology, whose work deserves to be honored and revived. Sapir is one of

those greats, who tried to define an interdisciplinary agenda for anthropology, psychology, and linguistics.

Hardly anyone in the social sciences (historians are an exception) reads things more than 10 years old these days, let alone a poetic, Aristotelian essay from 1924 written by an anthropological linguist and published in a sociology journal. The anthropological linguist in question is Edward Sapir, the less-honored, although more formidable, intellectual figure behind the so-called Sapir–Whorf linguistic relativity hypothesis. Yet in 1924, just before joining the University of Chicago, Edward Sapir published an article in the *American Journal of Sociology* entitled "Culture: Genuine and Spurious," in which he conceived of the way traditions and individuals, cultures and psyches might conspire to make each other up and excellent. There are sections of Sapir's essay "Culture: Genuine and Spurious" that could well have been subtitled "A Manifesto for a Cultural Psychology."

A genuine culture, Sapir argued in that essay, is not an externally imposed set of rules or forms or a "passively accepted heritage from the past" (1963:321) but rather a "way of life" (1963:321), gracefully proportioned to the beliefs, desires, and interests of its bearers, with which it is indissociably linked. A genuine culture consists of institutions, resources, and ideals of excellent performance and expertise that assist individuals in the cultivation of precisely those reactions, skills, and mental states that have "the sanction of a class and of a tradition of long standing" (Sapir, 1963:309).

In a genuine culture, there are processes at work aimed at the achievement of a harmonious interdependent balance between psyche and culture. Traditional ideals for a good and proper life are made salient through diverse forms of representation – art, artifacts, ritual, language, folklore, mundane practice – and individuals willfully and creatively come to terms with and make use of those ideals to refashion their selves, thereby revivifying and confirming the tradition. In a genuine culture, processes of cultural maintenance and personal maintenance serve each other. The tradition gives to the self "the wherewithal to develop its powers" and "a sense of inner satisfaction, a feeling of spiritual mastery" (1963:323).

Sapir's nascent, provocative, and poetic teleological ideas about the processes of genuineness in culture have remained for over 60 years dormant and relatively underdeveloped. Sapir was concerned that the alienation of culture from psyche had, in modern times, become real and pervasive. He held out as a mission for anthropology the examination of the processes by which genuine or unalienated cultures integrate cultural and personal symbol. One promise of today's cultural psychology is that it will carry on where Sapir left off.

9 Relevant here is the work of the so-called Edinburgh School (Woolgar, Pinch, Barnes, and others) in the sociology of science, as well as the work of Donald McCloskey and Allan Megill on the rhetorics of science.

10 It has become increasingly recognized among anthropologists that speculative ontologies and other cultural "texts" can be misleading guides to operative beliefs, which is one reason why the idea of "metaphors we live by" (Lakoff & Johnson, 1980) in our personal and interpersonal functioning has taken hold.

11 My use of the Scarr and McCartney framework to talk about person–environment interactions should carry no implication that those authors are engaged in an exercise in cultural psychology, just as there should be no

implication that my appropriation and extension of their logical scheme is a comment, one way or the other, upon behavioral genetics. The framework of positive (active, reactive, passive) vs. negative (active, reactive, passive) relationships is totally detachable from any concern with the genetic determination of behavior.

I might add that the behavioral geneticists seem all too fascinated with, indeed overjoyed by, the idea of positive person–environment relationships and far too little concerned with the ubiquity of negative ones. At its core, the field of behavioral genetics displays strong Platonist tendencies and is relatively innocent of the idea of intentional persons and intentional worlds. Robert Plomin and Daniel G. Freedman are exceptions.

12 Of course, in some other intentional worlds parents react to displays of timidity or shyness in their teen-agers by encouraging them to date, go to parties, and get out of the house.

If I had to divide all the cultures of the world into two types, putting aside everything else, I think I would partition them into those in which boys and girls are pushed together at puberty and those in which they are kept apart – kissing-game cultures versus purdah cultures. I suspect there are many interesting correlates to that division.

References

Campbell, D. T., & D. W. Fiske, 1959. Convergent and Discriminant Validation by the Multitrait-Multimethod Matrix. *Psychological Bulletin* 56:81–105.

Campos, J. J., & C. R. Stenberg. 1981. Perception, Appraisal and Emotion: The Onset of Social Referencing. In M. E. Lamb & L. R. Sherrod (Eds.), *Infant Social Cognition*. Hillsdale, NJ: Erlbaum.

Cole, M. 1988. Cross-Cultural Research in the Sociohistorical Tradition. *Human Development 31*:137–157.

Cole, M., & J. Gay. 1972. Culture and Memory. *American Anthropologist 74*:1066–1084.

Cole, M., & S. Scribner. 1974. *Culture and Thought*. New York: Wiley.

Converse, P. 1986. Generalization and the Social Psychology of "Other Worlds." In D. W. Fiske & R. A. Shweder (Eds.), *Metatheory in Social Science: Pluralisms and Subjectivities*. Chicago: University of Chicago Press.

Cronbach, L. J. 1975. Beyond the Two Disciplines of Scientific Psychology. *American Psychologist 30*:116–127.

D'Andrade, R. G. 1981. The Cultural Part of Cognition. *Cognitive Science 5*:179–195.

1984. Cultural Meaning Systems. In R. A. Shweder & R. A. LeVine (Eds.), *Culture Theory: Essays on Mind, Self and Emotion*. New York: Cambridge University Press.

1986. Three Scientific World Views and the Covering Law Model. In D. W. Fiske & R. A. Shweder (Eds.), *Metatheory in Social Science: Pluralisms and Subjectivities*. Chicago: University of Chicago Press.

Ekman, P. In press. The Argument and Evidence about Universals in Facial Expressions of Emotion. In H. Wagner & A. Manstead (Eds.), *Handbook of Psychophysiology: Emotion and Social Behavior*. London: John Wiley.

Fiske, D. W. 1986. Specificity of Method and Knowledge in Social Science. In D. W. Fiske & R. A. Shweder (Eds.), *Metatheory in Social Science: Pluralisms and Subjectivities*. Chicago: University of Chicago Press.

Geertz, C. 1973. *Interpretation of Cultures*. New York: Basic Books.

——— 1988. *Works and Lives*. Stanford: Stanford University Press.

Gergen, K. J. 1973. Social Psychology as History. *Journal of Personality and Social Psychology 26*:309–320.

Hallpike, C. R. 1979. *The Foundations of Primitive Thought*. New York: Oxford University Press.

Holland, D., & N. Quinn. 1986. *Cultural Models in Language and Thought*. New York: Cambridge University Press.

Howard, A. 1985. Ethnopsychology and the Prospects for a Cultural Psychology. In G. M. White & J. Kirkpatrick (Eds.), *Person, Self and Experience*. Los Angeles: University of California Press.

Kleinman, A. 1986. *Social Origins of Distress and Disease*. New Haven: Yale University Press.

Lakoff, G., & M. Johnson. 1980. *Metaphors We Live By*. Chicago: University of Chicago Press.

Levin, S. 1988. *Metaphoric Worlds: Conceptions of a Romantic Nature*. New Haven, CT: Yale University Press.

LeVine, R. A. n.d. Environments in Child Development: An Anthropological Perspective. Unpublished manuscript, School of Education, Harvard University.

Lévi-Strauss, C. 1963. *Structural Anthropology*. New York: Basic Books.

Milgram, S. 1974. *Obedience to Authority*. New York: Harper and Row.

Miller, G. 1956. The Magical Number Seven, Plus or Minus Two: Some Limits on Our Capacity for Processing Information. *Psychological Review, 63*:81–97.

Miller, P., & L. L. Sperry. 1987. The Socialization of Anger and Aggression. *Merill-Palmer Quarterly, 33*:1–31.

Mischel, W. 1973. Towards a Cognitive Social Learning Reconceptualization of Personality. *Psychological Review 80*:252–283.

Nerlove, S., & A. K. Romney. 1967. Sibling Terminology and Cross-Sex Behavior. *American Anthropologist 69*:179–187.

Obeyesekere, G. 1981. *Medusa's Hair: An Essay on Personal Symbols and Religious Experience*. Chicago: University of Chicago Press.

——— 1985. Depression, Buddhism, and the Work of Culture in Sri Lanka. In A. Kleinman & B. Good (Eds.), *Culture and Depression*. Berkeley: University of California Press.

Ochs, E., & B. Schieffelin. 1984. Language Acquisition and Socialization: Three Developmental Stories and Their Implications. In R. A. Shweder & R. A. LeVine (Eds.), *Culture Theory: Essays on Mind, Self and Emotion*. New York: Cambridge University Press.

Peacock, J. L. 1984. Religion and Life History: An Exploration in Cultural Psychology. In E. M. Bruner (Ed.), *Text, Play and Story: The Construction and Reconstruction of Self and Society*. Washington, DC: American Ethnological Society.

Plomin, R. 1986. *Development, Genetics, and Psychology*. Hillsdale, NJ: Erlbaum.

Putnam, H. 1981. *Reason, Truth, and History*. Cambridge: Cambridge University Press.

1987. *The Many Faces of Realism*. LaSalle, IL: Open Court Publishing Co.

Richter, F. 1986. Non-Linear Behavior. In D. W. Fiske & R. A. Shweder (Eds.), *Metatheory in Social Science: Pluralisms and Subjectivities*. Chicago: University of Chicago Press.

Sahlins, M. 1976. *Culture and Practical Reason*. Chicago: University of Chicago Press.

Sapir, E. 1924. Culture: Genuine and Spurious. *American Journal of Sociology* 29:401–429. Reprinted in D. Mandelbaum (Ed.), *Selected Writings of Edward Sapir in Language, Culture and Personality*. Berkeley: University of California Press, 1963.

Scarr, S., & K. McCartney. 1983. How People Make Their Own Environments: A Theory of Genotype → Environment Effects. *Child Development* 54:424–435.

Schank, R., & R. Abelson. 1977. *Scripts, Plans, Goals and Understanding*. Hillsdale, NJ: Erlbaum.

Schelling, T. 1984. *Choice and Consequence*. Cambridge, MA: Harvard University Press.

Schneider, D. M. 1968. *American Kinship: A Cultural Account*. Englewood Cliffs, NJ: Prentice-Hall.

1984. *A Critique of the Study of Kinship*. Ann Arbor: University of Michigan Press.

Shepard, R. N. 1987. Toward a Universal Law of Generalization for Psychological Science. *Science* 237:1317–1323.

Shweder, R. A. 1982. On Savages and Other Children. *American Anthropologist* 84:354–366.

1984. Preview: A Colloquy of Culture Theorists. In R. A. Shweder & R. A. LeVine (Eds.), *Culture Theory: Essays on Mind, Self and Emotion*. New York: Cambridge University Press.

1986. Divergent Rationalities. In D. W. Fiske & R. A. Shweder (Eds.), *Metatheory in Social Science: Pluralisms and Subjectivities*. Chicago: University of Chicago Press.

1987. How to Look at Medusa without Turning to Stone. *Contributions to Indian Sociology* 21:37–55.

1988. Suffering in Style. *Culture, Medicine and Psychiatry* 12:479–497.

1989. Post-Nietzschian Anthropology: The Idea of Multiple Objective Worlds. In Michael Krausz (Ed.), *Relativism: Interpretation and Confrontation*. Notre Dame: University of Notre Dame Press.

Shweder, R. A., & N. C. Much. 1987. Determinations of Meaning: Discourse and Moral Socialization. In W. M. Kurtines & J. L. Gewirtz (Eds.), *Moral Development through Social Interaction*. New York: Wiley.

Spiro, M. 1955. Symposium: Projective Testing in Ethnography. *American Anthropologist* 57:245–270.

1983. *Oedipus in the Trobriands*. Chicago: University of Chicago Press.

Stephens, W. N. 1962. *The Oedipus Complex: Cross-Cultural Evidence*. New York: Free Press.

Stigler, J. W. 1984. "Mental Abacus": The Effect of Abacus Training on Chinese Children's Mental Calculation. *Cognitive Psychology* 16:145–176.

Stigler, J. W., & R. Baranes. 1988. Culture and Mathematics Learning. In E. Rothkopf (Ed.), *Review of Research in Education* 15:253–306.

Stigler, J. W., L. Chalip, & K. F. Miller. 1986. Consequences of Skill: The Case of Abacus Training in Taiwan. *American Journal of Education* 94:447–479.

Whiting, B. B., & C. P. Edwards. 1988. *Children of Different Worlds: The Formation of Social Behavior.* Cambridge, MA: Harvard University Press.

Whiting, B. B., & J. W. M. Whiting. 1975. *Children of Six Cultures.* Cambridge, MA: Harvard University Press.

PART I
The keynote address

1
On the strange and the familiar in recent anthropological thought

Melford E. Spiro

It is a pleasure to join with you in commemorating the anniversary of the Committee on Human Development. While the other important ventures in interdisciplinary teaching and research – most notably Yale's Insititute of Human Relations and Harvard's Department of Social Relations – have long passed from the academic scene, the committee has not only survived, but it has grown. For that, Chicago should be proud, and the rest of us (those of us, at least, who deplore parochial specialization) should be grateful.

In commemorating this occasion, I had originally intended to discuss cultural internalization, an especially appropriate topic for a conference like this because it is both developmental in content and interdisciplinary in focus. Upon further reflection, however, it occurred to me that such a topic is too complex to address in this brief space. Therefore I have chosen instead to speak on the dialectical relationship between the strange and the familiar in the history of anthropological thought. Although the latter topic does not have a developmental focus, it is interdisciplinary inasmuch as the changing anthropological views on this matter have been informed by, and have in turn informed, recent developments in the other human sciences.

Because a scholarly essay does not, like Athena, spring full-grown from the brow of its genitor – even though its birth, like Athena's, may have been precipitated by a prolonged headache of the genitor – it is perhaps desirable to indicate the genesis of this essay. The germ was implanted in my brow many years ago by T. S. Eliot, but it was born only recently following a short, but concentrated, immersion in some current anthropological and philosophical writings preparatory to writing a paper on contemporary cultural relativism (Spiro, 1986), and then capped by a passage in a recent essay by Renato Rosaldo. But first to T. S. Eliot.

In his essay on Andrew Marvell, Eliot (1950:259) writes that in Marvell's verse there is "the making the familiar strange, and the strange familiar," a characteristic that, Eliot adds (attributing this notion to Coleridge), is the hallmark of all "good" poetry.[1] When I first read that essay, it struck me – in that "shock of recognition" that Edmund Wilson describes so well – that Eliot's characterization of "good" poetry aptly characterizes "good" anthropology, as well. The *ability* of the anthropologist to make the familiar strange, and the strange familiar, may not equal that of the poet, but that *that* is what he does seemed to me at that time to be self-evident.

Convinced of the aptness of that comparison, and more than a little pleased that it was inspired by my favorite contemporary poet, that idea nevertheless remained dormant until my exposure, many years later, to the anthropological writings I mentioned above. For after encountering for the *n*th time (*n*, in this case, being a *very* large number) one of the critical terms of that work, namely, "the Other," that line of Eliot's suddenly obtruded into my consciousness. And this time, just like the first time, I had one of those "Aha!" experiences that we all know so well.

What struck me this time, however, was the very opposite of what had struck me the first time. For while Eliot's characterization of the poet is applicable to contemporary poets, no less than to their predecessors, my extrapolation of that characterization to the anthropologist, although applicable to the anthropologists of that earlier period, does not, however, apply to a significant percentage of their successors. Many of them, together with many other social scientists, reject explicitly and on principle the making of the familiar strange, and the strange familiar. In them, it struck me, anthropology had undergone a sea change, one that occurred, roughly, some two decades ago.

Before describing this sea change, it is perhaps useful to explain why it was that I originally believed that Eliot's characterization of the good poet also characterized the good anthropologist – in his three roles of teacher, scholar, and cultural critic. Let us begin with the role of teacher.

Consider, in that regard, the typical introductory course in anthropology. By observing, for example, that most human societies are unilineal, such a course encourages the undergraduate students to view the familiar – the bilateral descent system of their own society – as strange, "strange" in the sense of being deviant from a comparative, or statistical, human norm. Conversely, by locating the veneration of saints in a cross-cultural, rather than merely a Catholic perspective, that same course encourages those same students to view polytheism as familiar, "familiar" in that it enables them to comprehend a strange religious system by reference to an analogous one that is found in their own culture.

Notice, moreover, that by this device of making the familiar strange, and the strange familiar, teacher and student, alike, come to view the familiar with a greater degree of objectivity than would otherwise be the case. For if, in respect to one or another cultural system or social institution, the first operation makes their own group different from other groups, while the second makes it similar to them, then the familiar can be seen as both *more* and as *less* strange than it had previously been assumed to be.

But the dual operation of making the familiar strange, and the strange familiar, has been employed by anthropologists not only as a pedagogical device, but also as a scientific method. In the first place, because it makes cross-cultural comparison and classification possible, that dual operation has been used as an indispensable first step in the attempt to discover social and cultural generalizations. It does that through translation.

By "translation" I do not mean the rendering of the cultural systems and social institutions of strange groups by the concepts of one's own group: That might make the strange familiar, but it does not make the familiar strange. Rather, I mean rendering of both, the strange and the familiar alike, by a third set of concepts – that is, anthropological concepts – which, being familiar to neither, and strange to both, permits the anthropologist to compare the strange and the familiar in accordance with one and the same classificatory system.

For the anthropologist, that procedure makes the strange familiar because the scientific concepts by which he classifies strange cultures are familiar to him, qua scholar; and it makes the familiar strange because the latter concepts, in principle at least, exclude the connotative meanings and affective resonances of the anthropologist's own culture, which for him, qua native, are its important distinguishing features.

The operation of making the familiar strange and the strange familiar has been employed as a method not only for cross-cultural generalizations, but also for single-culture explanations. For it compels the anthropologist to include in his explanatory net a variety of variables which, because that culture – depending on whether the anthropologist is a native or a foreigner – is either too familiar or too strange, would otherwise remain opaque to his perceptions. In sum, because the strange and the familiar, alike, foster intellectual distortion, if not blindness, those dual operations are a necessary first step – or so it was formerly believed – for social and cultural explanation.

To put it differently, if philosophers, as Thomas Nagel (1986) has recently put it, are driven to adopt "the view from nowhere" without, however, being able to relinquish "the view from here," then anthropologists have believed that they could overcome that quandary by adopting (what might be called) "the view from everywhere" – a view that encompasses the entire human experience on this planet, from the earliest hominids to our own time, and from Zuni to Zaire.

Anthropologists, it may now be observed, have been concerned not only with teaching and scholarship, but also (and as a consequence of the latter role) with cultural criticism – the third in their trinity of roles. One has only to mention Boas and Benedict, or Herskovits and Mead to recognize that from its very inception the combating of Western racism and ethnocentrism, to take only two examples, has been an important objective of American (but not only American) anthropology. And in the service of that objective, its most important strategy has consisted of making the strange familiar – a strategy that has been deployed to combat the alleged *moral* inferiority of other peoples and cultures, on the one hand, and their alleged *cognitive* inferiority, on the other.

In respect to the former allegation, that strategy has been deployed to demonstrate that those characteristics of primitive societies that, by the criteria of Western culture, are morally objectionable, have their analogue in Western society, as well. Thus, although *they* might practice headhunting, *we* – so the argument goes – kill many more people in war, or else permit them to starve to death in the midst of economic plenty.

This, of course, is the tu quoque argument, for by arguments of that kind, primitive societies are not so "primitive" after all; or if they are, then our own, familiar society can be considered just as, if not more "primitive." Moreover, if these strange cultures are the moral equals of our own, then correlatively their creators (generally, peoples of races other than our own) are not biologically inferior to ourselves (people, mainly, of the white race), not at any rate in respect to their moral values.

In respect, now, to the alleged cognitive inferiority of primitive cultures, the strategy of making the strange familiar has been deployed in a somewhat different way. Rather than arguing that primitive and Western cultures have uniformly attained a similar level of intellectual achievement, it has been argued that although in certain domains – technology, for example – Western culture may be more complex than primitive cultures, in other domains – kinship, for example – it is often the other way around. That being the case, neither the cultures of primitive peoples, nor the people themselves, are cognitively inferior to our own.

This argument, too, is a species of the tu quoque argument because the criterion used to assess mental achievement – intellectual complexity – is again Western. Thus, a much-favored argument in support of the thesis that peoples with technologically simple cultures are nevertheless capable of complex cognitive functioning is that the eight-class kinship system of the Australian aborigines is so complex that it took some three generations of anthropologists to understand its underlying principles.

Thus far I have attempted to explain why it is that when I first read Eliot I believed that the "good" anthropologist, like the "good" poet, makes the familiar strange, and the strange familiar. Lest, however, I be misunderstood, I should stress that in describing *how* anthropologists have performed those operations, I do not mean to suggest that I believe (either now or in retrospect) that the *means* they have employed for their achievement were, or are, always valid or successful. Indeed, it is my belief that in many cases, they were, and are, neither the one nor the other. Nevertheless, it is because the *attempt* to achieve those ends was one of the distinctive characteristics of anthropology that, as a graduate student, I myself chose to study anthropology rather than any of the other social sciences.

I now wish to turn to my second thesis – that for a decade or so many anthropologists (together with many other social scientists) have undergone a sea change in respect to those two operations. In addressing that thesis I must begin, however, by immediately qualifying it: The sea change has occurred primarily in the anthropologist's role as scholar. As teachers, both operations, as far as I can tell, remain our standard stock-in-trade, and as cultural critics it is my impression that one of these operations – the making of the familiar strange – is, if anything, practiced even more rigorously than previously.

In short, although in their roles as teacher and cultural critic, both operations are alive and well for most anthropologists, in their role as scholar one of these operations – the making of the strange familiar – is virtually dead for more than a few; dead, however, not from benign neglect, but from a principled rejection. And in that regard, as I mentioned previously, anthropologists stand shoulder to shoulder with many other social scientists. (Since it is cumbersome to reiterate the refrain "and other soical scientists," henceforth "anthropologists" is to be taken as a synecdoche for social scientists in general.)

One group of anthropologists rejects the making of the strange familiar on the ground that the range of cultural diversity makes this operation *impossible* to achieve; a second group rejects it on the ground that, even if it were possible, Western "domination" of non-Western societies makes it *undesirable* to achieve. Although somewhat different, these grounds nevertheless overlap (which is why, I may now add, there is still a third group – there is *always* a third group – who reject that operation on both grounds).

The overlap between these groups can be expressed in the proposition that the non-Western peoples that comprise the "object" for the Western "subject" (to employ the currently fashionable terms) are "strange" – that is, they are different from ourselves – not in some simple sense, but in a fundamental and irreducible sense. In brief, the non-Western object is the *Other*. (I have thus finally returned to my second "Aha!" experience.)

For the first group, the irreducible strangeness of the Other is a function, as I said, of the extraordinary degree of diversity among the cultures of the world, as well as the social and psychological diversity of the peoples and societies that, purportedly, are molded and shaped by those cultures.

"But," it might now be objected, "what else is new?" That cultures are different, one from another – although the stimulus for anthropological inquiry – was hardly the discovery of anthropologists. That discovery, surely, was made some few millennia ago by the Hellenes, the Hebrews, and the Han. Moreover, having discovered that cultures are different one from another, all three – the "three H's," as we shall call them – agreed that insofar as other cultures differed from their own, they were strange, so strange that each of the three H's viewed itself as civilized, and other peoples as barbarians. I shall shortly return to that *comparative* judgment, for it is crucial for my unfolding story.

Although the three H's, admittedly, recognized cultural diversity long before it was ever commented upon by anthropologists, nevertheless there *is* something new (to return to my rhetorical question) in the view of those anthropologists with whom we are concerned here. What is "new" is their conception of the magnitude of that diversity. For in their view, cultures not only differ from each other, but each is unique – "unique" not in the trivial sense that every snowflake, for example, is unique, but in the radical sense that each is *incommensurable*.

That claim – the claim that cultures share few, if any, nontrivial similarities – is related of course to the translation problem mentioned previously. For if every human group inhabits its own culturally constituted conceptual world, and if the concepts of any one are incommensurate with those of any other, then there is no way by which the members of one group can translate the cultural concepts of any other group – none, at any rate, that is at once both meaningful and intelligible.

But if the members of any group G cannot meaningfully and intelligibly translate the cultural concepts of any other group into their own concepts, then for G, other groups are not only strange; they are fundamentally and irreducibly strange. In short, for G, any other group is, like the *deus absconditus* of Calvinism, wholly Other – unknown, because unknowable.

Now, such a radical conception of cultural diversity (as its proponents correctly observe) poses an equally radical challenge to the traditional conception of anthropological scholarship described earlier. For if cultures are comprehensible only in their own terms, then it is clearly not possible for a comparative anthropology to achieve its twin desiderata of translating the different cultural worlds comprising human cultural diversity in a manner that at one and the same time makes each of them both meaningful and intelligible, on the one hand, and yet com*para*ble with all the others, on the other hand.

The first desideratum, clearly, cannot be achieved by any natural language; even traditional anthropologists agree with that proposition. More important, it cannot be achieved, as was formerly believed, by the technical language of anthropology because, as the creature of Western culture, anthropology is not the transcultural science that it was formerly conceived to be; rather, it is more accurately conceived as an ethnoscience of Western culture, reflecting and being informed by the Western conceptual world. In sum, contrary to the conception of traditional anthropological scholarship, according to this conception there is no way, even in principle, to break the culture barrier.

But if now the first desideratum of traditional anthropological scholarship is in principle impossible to achieve, then so also (according to the new anthropological conception) is the second, that is, cultural comparison. For in the absence of a language that might in principle render the variety of human cultures in a manner that is at once both meaningful and intelligible, there is then no way by which cultures might possibly be classified and compared – none, at any rate, that is at once both accurate and sensible.

Those twin claims bring me back to my point of departure. For if cultures are as radically dissimilar as has just been described, then (as the proponents of this view properly argue) the dissimilarity between the culture of the Western scholar, on the one hand, and any non-Western culture that he might choose to study, on the other, is just as radical. Hence, inasmuch as the former and the latter – the familiar culture and the strange – share few, if any, nontrivial characteristics, it is impossible in principle for Western scholarship to make the strange familiar. In short, for the Western scholar, the strange cannot possibly be anything other than Other.

Let us now turn to the group of anthropologists who reject the making of the strange familiar on the second ground – the ground that such an operation is *undesirable* to achieve. For this group, the non-Western "object" is Other, in the first instance, not so much because cultures are incommensurable (which they are), but because the West – in the service of colonialism, imperialism, and, more recently, the modern world system – has *defined* non-Western peoples as Other. That construction, inasmuch as it makes non-Western peoples fundamentally inferior, was motivated, so it is claimed, by the need of the West to justify its political and economic domination over non-Western peoples.

According to this view, traditional anthropological scholarship has contributed to that construction by its procedure of making the strange familiar. In brief, when anthropologists attempt to make Third World cultures familiar – by translating them into anthropological concepts, and then explaining them by means of anthropological theory – they only succeed (however good their intentions) in making those cultures even more strange. That is because, relative to the Western values that inform the concepts and theories of anthropology – anthropology being a Western ethnoscience – Third World cultures are willy-nilly inferior.

That, now, Third World peoples have been subjected to the procrustean conceptual bed of anthropological theory is, according to this view, as much an instance of their *cultural* domination by the West, as their economic subjugation by Western imperialists is an instance of Western *political* domination. In short, the cultural subjugation of Third World peoples, just like their political subjugation, reflects the asymmetrical power relationship between these two peoples.

The only solution to the cultural subjugation of Third World peoples by Western anthropology, so it is claimed, is to create a non-Western anthropology – one that is informed not by Western values, but by the radically different values of Third World cultures. When these cultures are conceptualized by that alternative – their own – ethnoscience, they still, of course, remain Other vis-à-vis Western culture, but they achieve a status (at the very least) of equality with it. In sum, the strange can only become the equal of the familiar not, paradoxically enough, by being made familiar, but by remaining strange.

I have now completed a sketch of a sea change that has occurred over the past decade, or so, in the thought of an influential group of contemporary anthropologists, together with other social scientists, and some few philosophers and literary scholars. The magnitude of that change is best captured, I believe, by Renato Rosaldo, who characterized their view (in a passage I alluded to at the beginning of this paper) as follows: "My own group aside, everything human is alien to me" (Rosaldo, 1984:188).

I would now suggest that this view constitutes a change in the history not only of anthropological thought, but also of human thought – at least of recorded human thought. For consider. When those three great ethnocentrists – the Hellenes, the Hebrews, and the Han – proclaimed the familiar civilized, and the strange barbaric, such a *comparative* judgment rested on the belief that in principle the strange and the familiar *could* be compared. Without such a belief, that invidious judgment (or, for that matter, any other) could not have been made.

In sum, although for the three H's other people and cultures were strange, they were not all *that* strange – that is, not incommensurably strange. That is why a Hellene could proclaim (in a *mot* that, I presume, is the one that inspired Rosaldo's) that he was part of all that he met. And it is also why a Roman could say (Rome, after all, is not that far from Greece) that being human himself, nothing human was alien to him. For both statements entail the claim – that, at any rate, is how I read them – that although the familiar and the strange are different, they are yet also similar in some nontrivial respects.

These two Mediterranean worthies do not, of course, go nearly as far as the great Vedic sage, who, in one of the ringing exclamations of classical Indian religion – *tat tvam asi*, Thou art That – proclaimed that man is similar to the godhead, itself. In short, for the Vedic sage, even divinity is not all that strange. But then in such matters, as in so many others, India of course is always the extreme, while the Greeks (and to a lesser extent the Romans) preached, if they did not always practice, moderation.

Thus far my discussion of the sea change that has occurred in recent anthropological thought in respect to the relationship between the familiar and the strange has been confined to the anthropologist as scholar. In order to grasp the full magnitude of that change, however, we must turn now to the anthropologist as cultural critic. In doing so – in turning, that is, from the scholarly treatment of the strange to the critical treatment of the familiar – we shall find (to prefigure my conclusion) that the quotation from Rosaldo is only half right.

Earlier, I described one type of cultural criticism whose aim is to combat Western ethnocentrism and racism. It attempts to achieve this aim, it will be recalled, by showing that although in respect to certain domains primitive and other Third World cultures may be judged inferior to Western culture, both morally and cognitively, in respect to other domains they are its superior, and that on balance the two are more or less equal.

In addition, however, to this type of cultural criticism, there is a second type, which is best characterized as inverted ethnocentrism. Practiced not only by anthropologists, but also by other social scientists as well as by literary scholars, this type of criticism argues that Western culture is inferior to Third World cultures not only in respect to certain domains, but globally. This type, it might be observed, is almost as old as the first – indeed, frequently, both types have been practiced by one and the same critic – and it has had some distinguished practitioners.

Consider, for example, the following passage from an anthropologist whose intellectual and emotional roots antedate both the countercultural and neo-Marxist ideologies of the 1960s (the inspiration for many contemporary critics of this type), one moreover who is arguably the most distinguished anthropologist of our time. Writing in 1955, Claude Lévi-Strauss (1964:388) observed that anthropology is a Western creation because the West

> was so tormented by remorse that it had to compare its own image with that of other societies, in the hope that they would either display the same shortcomings or help the West to explain how these defects could have come into being. . . . The general average of which I spoke earlier throws into relief the existence of a few sociological ogres, among whom we ourselves must be numbered. Nor is this an accident: if it were not that we deserved, and for that matter still deserve, first prize in this grim competition, anthropology would not have come into being; we should have felt no need of it. . . . [To be sure] other societies have shared in the same original sin, though they are doubtless few in number, and fewer still as we descend the ladder of progress.

Although, as this quotation indicates, the inverted ethnocentrism that characterizes the second type of cultural criticism predates the period of the sea change, still, it is my impression (as I suggested earlier) that with the coming of neo-Marxist criticism, feminist criticism, and some few others (mostly of Parisian origin), its scope has become more sweeping, and its voice less modulated than formerly. Indeed, I sometimes have the impression that some of these critics may perhaps be commiting the error of which Socrates was (falsely) accused by the Athenians – that of making the better seem the worse, and the worse the better.

Be that as it may, since my concern with this type of criticism is not with how well, or how responsibly, it is conducted, but with its relationship to my central topic – the making of the familiar strange, and the strange familiar – in that regard, it differs from the first type not only in its global judgment of the inferiority of the familiar, but also in the manner by which it reaches that judgment.

While the first type of criticism attempts to achieve its aim by arguing that the familiar is similar (both morally and cognitively) to the strange, this type attempts to achieve *its* aim by arguing that the familiar, itself, is strange (both morally and emotionally) for its own actors. In that regard, modern Western culture, it is argued, is different from Third World cultures – if not the actual cultures of contemporary primitive (and other Third World) societies, then the hypothetical cultures of societies of a putatively earlier stage of social evolution.

The latter proviso is important, for insofar as contemporary primitive (and other Third World) societies have been corrupted as a consequence (so it is argued) of Western influence, their actors are no different from Western actors. As Stephen Tyler (1986:128) has recently put it, "The savage of the twentieth century is sick too; neutered, like the rest of us, by the dark forces of the 'world system.'"

Cultural criticism of this (the second) type derives its inspiration, as is well known, from one or the other – sometimes both – of two Western intellectual traditions: from Primitivism and Utopianism, on the one hand, and, on the other hand, from any number of theories that (beginning with Marx) view Western capitalist society as the seedbed of alienation. Hence, although all cultural critics of this type are similar in most respects, they yet differ to some degree, depending on whether their inspiration is derived from the one or the other of these two intellectual traditions. Let us then, briefly and schematically, delineate their differences.

Those critics who derive their inspiration from Primitivism proceed from a list of characteristics that putatively distinguish primitive (in either of the two meanings of "primitive" mentioned above) and other Third World societies from modern Western society. Thus, the former are authentic, the latter is inauthentic; the former are genuine, the latter, spurious; the former are cooperative, the latter, competitive; the former are egalitarian, the latter, hierarchical; the former are integrated, the latter, conflictual; the former are solidarious, the latter, anomic. And so on. There is no need to detail all of the other familiar contrast sets that make up that list.

According, now, to this group of critics, any or all of these contrasts signify one and the same thing: The cultural characteristics of Western society are morally *estranging*, hence ego-dystonic, for Western actors. In brief, globally speaking, the familiar culture is strange, not familiar, for the actors themselves.

For those critics who derive their inspiration from the second intellectual tradition, the cultural characteristics of modern Western society – economic, scientific, political, religious, medical, whatever – when compared to those of primitive and other Third World societies, are uniformily *alienating*. Hence, Western actors, it is held, are alienated from their psyches (which, I suppose, is what the Marxist notion of "false consciousness" refers to), from their bodies, from their families, from their work, from their social groups, from their ecosystems – indeed, from the cosmos itself.

In sum, since modern Western culture is (to use one of the favorite terms of this group of anthropologists) "totalizing" in its alienating effects, for Western actors their own culture is ego-alien. Once again, then, the familiar culture is strange, not familiar, for the actors themselves.

Taking into account both the cultural criticism and the scholarship of contemporary anthropology, I would now submit that what we have witnessed over the past decade or so among a large group of anthropologists is nothing less than an unremitting perception of the entire human world as "strange." For if as scholars these anthropologists have *minimized* the familiar characteristics – the comprehensible and intelligible characteristics – of the strange, then as cultural critics they have *maximized* the strange characteristics – the ego-dystonic and ego-alien characteristics – of the familiar. In sum, for many anthropologists, and (to reiterate my cautionary note at the beginning of this chapter) for many other social scientists and literary scholars, as well, the familiar, no less than the strange, has become Other.

We may now perhaps understand why, previously, I claimed that Rosaldo's characterization of this group of anthropologists – "my own group aside, everything human is alien to me" – is only half right. In order for that characterization to be entirely right, the qualifier ("my own group aside") would have to be deleted.

How, now, it might be useful to ask, have we arrived at such a state of affairs? To begin with the conception of the familiar, is the judgment that Western society is ego-dystonic and ego-alien, while Third World societies (those not yet corrupted by the West) are ego-syntonic and ego-integrative – is that judgment grounded in the *evidence* of anthropological scholarship, or is it rather, at least to some degree, a *construction* – as Lévi-Strauss, for one, has suggested – of anthropological criticism?

Although the cultural critic would claim that the first alternative is the case, such a claim, surely, is paradoxical. For consider: in order for the anthropologist, qua critic, to make that invidious judgment regarding Western society, he must be able to determine, qua scholar, that one or another non-Western society is ego-syntonic and ego-integrative for its actors. In short, he must possess the ability to enter into and mentally inhabit *their* cultural world, to perceive it through *their* (not his) eyes, to grasp it by *their* (not his) concepts, and then to experience it through *their* (not his) emotions.

But if Third World cultures are Other, then the anthropologist, qua scholar, cannot possibly possess the ability to comprehend the thoughts and emotions that make up the minds of Third World actors since their cultures, ex hypothesi, are incommensurate with his own. And if that is the case, then when that same anthropologist claims, qua cultural critic, that compared to Third World cultures, Western culture is ego-alien and ego-dystonic, that judgment cannot possibly be empirically grounded.

Until or unless that paradox is resolved, we might perhaps want to consider the explanation offered by Lévi-Strauss for that judgment. "It is not by chance," Lévi-Strauss (1964:381) writes,

> that the anthropologist is rarely on terms of neutrality with his own social group. . . . Objective factors in his past can probably be adduced to prove that he is ill- or unsuited to the society into which he was born. . . . If he tries to think straight, he will have to ask himself whether he is really justified in setting such great store by exotic societies (and the more exotic they are, the more he will prize them). Is this not rather a function of the disdain, not to say the hostility, which he feels for the customs of his own milieux? At home, the anthropologist may be a natural subversive, a convinced opponent of traditional usage; but no sooner has he in focus a society different from his own than he becomes respectful of even the most conservative practices.

Because Lévi-Strauss's observations are consistent with my own, I am highly tempted, as a clinician manqué, to offer a psychodynamic gloss on that quotation. Since in this essay, however, I am wearing the hat of cultural critic (a critic, that is, of one subculture of contemporary social science), I must resist that temptation. Let us instead turn from the Otherness-of-the-familiar of anthropological criticism to the Otherness-of-the-strange of anthropological scholarship.[2]

Since the Otherness-of-the-strange is based on the claim of cultural incommensurability, it too is paradoxical. For if that claim is valid, then Hilary Putnam's comment on the analogous claim made by some few historians of Western science applies to anthropologists, as well: Namely, if cultures were incommensurable, then for the investigator who studies a cultural group other than his own, the communications of its actors would mostly consist of uninterpretable "noise." And, to quote Putnam (1981:114–115), if

> we cannot interpret organisms' noises at all, then we have no grounds for regarding them as *thinkers, speakers,* or even *persons.* In short, if Feyerabend (and Kuhn at his most incommensurable) were right, then members of other cultures, including seventeenth-century scientists, would be conceptualizable by us only as animals producing responses to stimuli (including noises that curiously resemble English or Italian). To tell us that Galileo had "incommensurable" notions *and then go on to describe them at length* is totally incoherent. [Italics in original]

Substitute, now, "Navaho" for "Galileo," and the application of that passage to anthropology is clear. If strange cultures are not only different from, but are also incommensurate with, Western culture, then anthropologists would be incapable of describing, let alone interpreting, the cultures of the strange groups in which they conduct research. But since the proponents of this view (together with other anthropologists) do precisely that – they themselves describe and interpret strange cultures – those strange cultures cannot be so strange, after all. In short, they cannot really be Other.

Why it is, then, that the proponents of this thesis theoretically insist upon it, when their own work empirically confutes it, is – to say the least – yet another paradox. Although I can offer no simple resolution for that paradox, Lévi-Strauss – that great master of paradox – once again has. "Never," Lévi-Strauss (1964:58) writes, "can [the anthropologist] feel himself 'at home' anywhere: he will always be, psychologically speaking, an amputated man."

Now I don't know whether that is a valid resolution of that paradox, or not. But having been previously informed by Tyler that all of us are "neutered," and now being told by Lévi-Strauss that anthropologists are "amputated" – that combination of metaphors has (at least for a psychoanalytically oriented theorist like myself) some rather specific symbolic meanings, which are more than a little anxiety producing. Hence, having refrained from offering a gloss on the previous quotation from Lévi-Strauss, it is best to let this quotation speak for itself, especially since I would prefer to close on an upbeat note – to close it, that is (with apologies to the poet who stimulated the writing of this paper) not with a whimper, but a bang.

For consider: If anthropologists *can* describe and interpret other cultures, then the strange cultures cannot be as strange as many contemporary anthropologists claim; and if anthropologists *cannot* describe and interpret other cultures, then there are no valid grounds for believing that our *own* – familiar – culture is as strange as they claim. Since, whichever is the case, only one of us – either we or they – can be Other, I was clearly wrong in claiming that contemporary anthropologists (or at least many of them) have made the *entire* human world strange; they have made only *half* of it strange.

That still leaves us with one unresolved question. Which half?

Notes

1 In preparing this essay, I did not recall in which of Eliot's essays I had originally read this line, nor did I remember that Eliot had credited the line (with a little license) to Coleridge. I am grateful to Helen Singer for refreshing my memory on both accounts.
2 It might be observed that in viewing their own culture as inferior to primitive and Third World cultures, these anthropologists represent only the first point on a scale of (what might be called) "the depreciation of the familiar," by some few Western academics and intellectuals. This scale can be delineated as follows: (a) As human beings, Westerners are culturally inferior to non-Western (primitive and Third World) peoples. (b) As a species, humans (b1) are little different from non-human species, if not (b2) inferior to them. (c) As psychological beings, humans (c1) are little different from machines, and (c2)

inferior to inert matter. Having already dealt with *a*, the first point on this scale, let us proceed to (b1), its second point.

Here is psychologist Edward Tolman (who himself, it will be recalled, opposed the simple S-R theories of his time):

> I believe that everything important in psychology (except perhaps such matters as the building up of the superego, that is, everything save such matters as involve society and words) can be investigated in essence through the continued experimental and theoretical analysis of the determiners of rat behavior at a choice point in a maze. (Tolman 1938:34)

Again, listen to psychologist Kenneth Lashley who, having described how the microstoma (a tiny marine worm) acquires the nettles it needs for its protection by ingesting hydras, writes: "Here in the length of half a millimeter are encompassed all of the major problems of dynamic psychology" (Lashley 1938:446).

For the third point on the scale, (b2), listen to biologist Stephen Jay Gould:

> I do not see how we, the titular spokesmen for a few thousand mammalian species, can claim superiority over three quarters of a million species of insects who will surely outlive us all, not to mention the bacteria, who have shown remarkable staying power for more than three billion years. (quoted in Shaw 1986:31)

Let us proceed, now, to (c1), the fourth point on the scale. In a delightful passage, psychologist Edward Boring (1946:192) says:

> I believe that robotic thinking helps precision of psychological thought, and will continue to help it until psychophysiology is so far advanced that an image is nothing other than a neural event, and object constancy is obviously something that happens in the brain. That time is still a long way off, and in the interval I choose to sit cosily with my robot, squeezing his hand and feeling a thrill – a scientist's thrill – when he squeezes mine back again.

With the coming of cognitive science, and its emphasis on mental representations, one might have thought that the machine model would have been discarded. If anything, the reverse is the case, especially among some few specialists in artificial intelligence (AI), for whom the equivalence of the computer and the human mind is virtually axiomatic. Thus, for the proponents of the "claim of strong AI," "the appropriately programmed computer really is a mind and can be said literally to understand and to experience other cognitive states" (Gardner 1985:171).

As a measure of the strong conviction (and affect) with which its proponents hold this claim, consider the response of computer scientist Douglas Hofstadter to the measured critique of philosopher John Searle (1980). "This religious diatribe against AI, masquerading as a serious scientific argument, is one of the wrongest, most infuriating articles I have ever read in my life" (quoted in Gardner 1985:176).

The fifth (and final) point on the scale, (c2), is represented, startlingly enough, by some few contemporary poets. Thus, after observing that the most popular key word in new poetry is "stone," critic Paul Breslin cites the following passage, taken from an interview from Galway Kinnell (the Pulitzer Prize-winning poet). "If you could go even deeper," Kinnell is quoted as saying, "you'd not be a person, you'd be an animal; and if you went deeper still, you'd be a blade of grass, eventually a stone. If a stone could speak, your poem would be its words" (quoted in Shaw 1986:31).

Viewed from the perspective of these commentators, the *cultural* alienation of the anthropologists considered in this paper seems rather moderate. In either event, an intellectual historian might profitably address his energies to the question of how it is that a civilization (Western civilization) in which the Psalmists viewed humans as "little lower than the angels" could have undergone a transformation of such a magnitude that contemporary biologists could come to view humans as inferior to insects, psychologists as little better than machines, and poets as inferior to stones.

References

Boring, Edwin G. 1946. Mind and Mechanism. *American Journal of Psychology* 54:173–192.

Eliot, T. S. 1950. *Selected Essays* (new ed.). New York: Harcourt, Brace and Company.

Gardner, Howard. 1985. *The Mind's New Science.* New York: Basic Books.

Lashley, Karl S. 1938. Experimental Analysis of Instinctive Behavior. *Psychological Review 45*:445–471.

Lévi-Strauss, Claude, 1964. *Tristes Tropiques.* New York: Atheneum.

Nagel, Thomas. 1986. *The View from Nowhere.* Oxford: Oxford University Press.

Putnam, Hilary. 1981. *Reason, Truth and History.* Cambridge: Cambridge University Press.

Rosaldo, Renato. 1984. Grief and a Headhunter's Rage: On the Cultural Force of Emotions. In Edward Brunner (Ed.), *Text, Play and Story.* Washington, DC: Proceedings of the American Ethnological Society.

Searle, John. 1980. Minds, Brains and Programs. *The Behavioral and Brain Sciences 3*:417–457.

Shaw, Peter. 1986. The Demotion of Man. *Commentary 10*:30–36.

Spiro, Melford E. 1986. Cultural Relativism and the Future of Anthropology. *Cultural Anthropology 1*:259–286.

Tolman, Edward C. 1938. The Determiners of Behavior at a Choice Point. *Psychological Review 45*:1–41.

Tyler, Stephen A. 1986. Post-Modern Ethnography: From Document of the Occult to Occult Document. In James Clifford & George E. Marcus (Eds.), *Writing Culture.* Berkeley and Los Angeles: University of California Press.

PART II
Cultural cognition

2
Some propositions about the relations between culture and human cognition

Roy D'Andrade

Cognitive anthropology has been an ongoing enterprise for more than 25 years. In this period much has been learned about the relationship between culture and cognition. This chapter summarizes some of that work. I have tried to organize what has been learned as a series of interrelated propositions with supporting material. These propositions represent not proven facts but rather my assessment of what is most probably the case.

Before the propositions are presented, something should be said about the terms *culture* and *cognition*. With respect to human cognition, this essay assumes an information-processing approach based on the model developed at UCSD by Mandler, Norman, Rumelhart, and associates. This model treats the mind as a complex of structures composed of parallel-distributed processing networks. Through these structures events are interpreted, remembered, and acted upon (Mandler, 1984; Rumelhart & McClelland, 1986).

It is assumed here that culture consists of learned and shared systems of meaning and understanding, communicated primarily by means of natural language. These meanings and understandings are not just representations about what is in the world; they are also directive, evocative, and reality constructing in character. Through these systems of meanings and understandings individuals adapt to their physical environment, structure interpersonal relationships, and adjust psychologically to problems and conflicts (D'Andrade, 1985). These systems of meanings and understandings are only one set of variables that influence human behavior; social and evironmental conditions, the distribution of power, economic opportunity, personality characteristics, genetic constitution, and other classes of variables also influence what people do and think.

The abstract definition of culture first given fails to indicate the pervasiveness and importance of culture in normal human life. If we try to enumerate the actions that a normal person carries out in an average day, we quickly discover that a great deal of what people do is culturally shaped – culturally shaped in the sense that both the goal and the means

This paper has benefited from critiques by James Boster, Paul Kay, Willet Kempton, and Naomi Quinn.

to the goal are part of a learned and shared system of understandings about the appropriate thing to do (Swartz & Jordan, 1976). For example, an average American adult, on waking, does things like shaving, showering, dressing, eating breakfast, and reading the morning newspaper. These conventional actions, evaluated by conventional standards, are replicated daily by millions of other Americans, but not performed at all by millions of non-Americans.

It is sometimes said that social scientists are unsuccessful at predicting behavior. Whether this statement is true for other fields, it is clearly untrue with reference to the study of culture. Since culture tends to be stable over time, a description of yesterday's conventions will serve as predictions of tomorrow's actions. A simple English dictionary, for example, can be viewed as a huge compilation of predictions about tomorrow's discourse. Similariy, a standard ethnography can also be considered a predictive account of what people will do. For example, Le Vine (1984) writes:

> From 1955 to 1957, I conducted fieldwork in a Gusii community. I had read the publications of Philip Mayer, who carried out fieldwork among the Gusii from 1946 to 1949 in an area about ten miles away. Guided by his descriptions of Gusii culture, I was nevertheless constantly searching for points in which my community might deviate from what he had written. I found that his account of Gusii beliefs concerning witches (Mayer, 1954) forecast my informants' descriptions down to the smallest details, not only as beliefs attributed to the community in general but also in narratives concerning personal experience. In other words, the Gusii I worked with for eighteen months told me stories of their own current encounters with witches for which Mayer's account provided the basic script, though his statements were based on interviews with other informants in a community some distance away. I discovered that Gusii accounts of personal experience with witches were in fact highly predictable in the social situations of their occurrence, the images of witches and victims, the narrative sequences of action, the emotional reactions attributed to self and other, and the outcomes of attempts to combat witchcraft. These were the most intense emotional experiences reported by my friends and neighbors about themselves and members of their immediate families, yet the form and contents of their reports were standardized, apparently following a conventional script with a single set of symbols and meanings. (p. 71)

If anthropologists are so good at predicting behavior, is there anything left for psychologists and other social scientists to do? First, it should be noted that although large chunks of behavior come culturally "packaged," there is always selection at the individual level among alternative packages. In greeting a friend, one can say "hello," or "how's it going," or "good morning," and it is reasonable to expect that extracultural variables – psychological and social – will account for who selects which alternatives. Second, culture changes, and a theory is needed that can account for the way the chunks get repackaged. Third, there is much behavior that is not already conventionalized – some idiosyncratic, some aberrant, some produced in laboratories – which cannot be accounted for by referring to culture and convention. Finally, there is more to doing science than making successful predictions. Success at prediction is not a good measure of how well a science is progressing. If the only theory in anthropology were that people continue to do the conventional actions they did before, anthropology would make many successful predictions but would not be a very good science (see D'Andrade, 1986, for further discussion of this point).

One issue taken up in this chapter has to do with the ways in which culture "structures" or "packages" or "conventionalizes" human cognition. Given that so much of human behavior is culturally shaped, it would be surprising indeed if culture did not also shape human cognition. Can culture affect the way people perceive, reason, and feel? If so, to what degree? And, conversely, is culture shaped by the way human cognitive processes work? If so, to what degree? Any attempt to understand the human condition must pay close attention to these issues.

Symbolic representation

What then, have anthropologists, psychologists, and others discovered about relationships between culture and cognition? To start off, a basic area of continuing interest is the general process of *categorization*, especially the type of categorization found in natural language. The emphasis on natural language leads immediately to questions about the nature of symbolic representation. What does it mean to say that something is a *symbol*? A considerable amount of work has been done on defining a symbol, but most of it seems to involve synonym mongering. It does not help to say that "a symbol is a physical sign that stands for something else," without saying what "stands for" means. One can, however, get at what representation by symbols really is by discovering something about what an animal has to learn before one can say that the animal is really using symbols.

To my knowledge, the most effective experimental paradigm for the investigation of symbolic representation by animals is that developed by Savage-Rumbaugh and her associates (1980), who taught chimpanzees to label objects and classes of objects using plastic tokens (lexigrams). First, the animals were taught to sort real objects (bread, orange, key, stick) into two different bins – one for the "foods," and one for the "tools." Next, the animals were taught to sort these objects into the proper bin and then select the proper lexigram representing either food or tool. The bins were then removed, and subjects taught to label each object as a food or tool. Once the animals reached a high level of expertise in performing this task, a test was made by introducing new tools and foods, testing whether or not the animals could make the appropriate generalization and label correctly the new items. It turned out that two of the three chimpanzees could do this, and one – Lana – could not. Lana had been trained just to label specific objects, and had not used lexigrams to communicate with other animals. It is interesting that Lana could, when shown new tools, correctly place them in the original bins. Thus she understood the distinction between food and tool, but had not learned that the lexigrams stood for this distinction.

In further work, the two successful animals were also taught to label photographs of the original training items with the food and tool lexigrams, and then were tested to see if they could label correctly photographs of new items. Again, both animals were successful. Finally, the animals were taught to select the appropriate food or tool lexigram when presented with previously learned lexigrams for the specific training items. The test for this phase was to present the animals with lexigrams for new items that they had not learned to label with the food or tool lexigram, and to see if they could correctly label these new lexigrams. In fact, both animals were quite successful at this final test of labeling labels.

It seems clear that symbolic representation is involved in these animals' ability to generalize a sign from a small class of specific objects to a larger abstract class of tools or foods, and further to generalize a sign from a small class of signs to a larger class of signs. What appears to have been learned is not just a link between a specific object and a physical sign (something any mammal can learn), but rather a complex linkage between physical signs, physical objects, *and abstract concepts*.

However, the success of some chimpanzees in learning symbolic representations should not obscure the great difference between humans and other animals with respect to the degree to which humans are genetically ready and eager to learn a language (Lenneberg, 1967). For example, research by Goldin-Meadow and Feldman (1977) with deaf children who have never been exposed to a sign language indicates that even without tuition of any direct kind children will spontaneously invent a structured sign system that not only uses symbolic representation, but also combines signs into semantically meaningful phrases. In sum,

1. *Humans and some other animals are capable of using true symbolic representations, but humans differ from other animals in being much more interested in and successful at acquiring and using language.*

Cognitive effects of categorization

Given the capacity and importance of language for humans, the question of the relationship between culture and cognition has been investigated primarily in terms of the relationship between language and cognition. One historically important formulation of this relationship is the *Sapir–Whorf hypothesis*. This hypothesis has been stated in a number of ways, but one reasonable form, derived from Kay and Kempton (1984), is

2. *Language differences in the way objects are categorized and distinguished are paralleled by cognitive differences in the perception of similarity between such objects, and in the degree to which these objects are accurately remembered.*

As Kay and Kempton point out, for the Sapir–Whorf hypothesis to be of any interest there must be at least moderate differences between languages, or between domains in categorization within languages. They quote Whorf: "In our language...plurality and cardinal numbers are applied in two ways: to real plurals and imaginary plurals. Or more exactly if less tersely: perceptible spatial aggregates and metaphorical aggregates: We say 'ten men' and 'ten days' " (Whorf, 1956:139). Kay and Kempton (1984) go on to say:

The claim here is that some things really are plural (or really are experienced directly as plural) while other things have the conceptual structure of plurality imposed on them by a metaphor that in another language could be and often is avoided. Everybody, Whorf seems to be saying, has to experience ten men as an aggregate, but we English speakers extend this aggregate schema to days, while the Hopi do not. A few lines later Whorf again suggests that he conceives of experience having two tiers: one, a kind of rock bottom, inescapable seeing-things-as-they-are (or at least as human beings cannot help but see them), and a second, in which the metaphors implicit in the grammatical and lexical structures of language cause us to classify things in ways that could be otherwise. (p. 76)

Thus there is a factor that potentially limits any effects of the Sapir–Whorf hypothesis, namely, the amount of human experience that rests on the bottom tier of inescapable seeing-things-as-they-are in contrast to the amount of human experience that could be seen differently.

Much of the research on the Sapir–Whorf hypothesis has been carried out in the domain of color. Color is a practical domain for this type of research because there are between-language and within-language differences in the way in which various parts of the color space are categorized, and because it is difficult to discriminate among the many fine gradations of color. Consequently, at least some color perception must rest on Whorf's second rather than first tier of human experience. Munsell color chips have been used to elicit ethnographic color terms in response to standardized stimuli, and to make a controlled comparison between the ranges of color terms in languages as different as English and Zuni (Lenneberg & Roberts, 1956). In their landmark study, Brown and Lenneberg (1954), using an array varying by hue and brightness at the highest level of saturation, found that Munsell color chips with short agreed-upon names were more accurately remembered than chips without short agreed-upon names. However, using a different array, in which chips vary by hue but are at the same level of saturation and brightness, Lenneberg (1961) found that chips *without* short agreed-upon names were more accurately remembered than chips with short names. It should be noted that the chips in this second array, the Farnsworth Munsell array, do not include the focal colors, since focal colors are defined at high levels of saturation, and the Farnsworth Munsell array chips are all at *relatively low* levels of saturation. One hypothesis about why Lenneberg got these results is simply that basic color terms are poor descriptors of the chips in the Farnsworth Munsell array.

Research by Lantz and Stefflre (1964) reestablished the potential of the Sapir–Whorf hypothesis by using a different linguistic measure. Rather than using the short agreed-upon names as a measure of how language categorizes a domain, Stefflre developed a measure of communication accuracy, which measures the degree to which a speaker of a language can describe a chip within an array so that other speakers of the same language can correctly select that chip from the array. Using the Farnsworth Munsell array, Lantz and Stefflre found this measure of communication accuracy correlated strongly with accuracy of recognition. Stefflre, Castillo Vales, and Moreley (1966) extended the study of communication accuracy to Spanish and Yucatec Mayan speakers, and found the same strong correlation between communication accuracy and recognition accuracy for each language, although, in general, the speakers of these languages differed with respect to which chips were most easily remembered and described. These researchers also found that mistakes in memory are *systematically distorted*, for when subjects misremembered which chip they had seen, they tended to select a chip in the direction of the median chip selected as typical of that chip's description. For example, a chip that is called *rose* may not be as good an example of the color rose as some other chip. When trying to select from memory this "rose-but-not-the-best-rose" chip, subjects will tend to err in the direction of the "best-rose" chip.

In the late 1960s the emphasis in research shifted from how language influences perception and memory to how the bedrock of human experience of color is so inescapably what it is that languages naturally conform to this experience. In *Basic Color Terms*, Berlin and Kay (1969), using Munsell's 320-chip array of varying hue and brightness at maximal saturation, found that speakers of different languages agreed closely on the best exemplars for basic color terms, and that although languages had varying numbers of basic color terms, these terms form a Guttman scale-like order. Rosch (Heider 1972), using a 160 Munsell array, found that the chips universally selected as best exemplars of basic color terms (focals) were more accurately remembered, regardless of naming. However, Lucy and Shweder (1979) observed that the focal color chips were easier to find (they gave a subject a chip and timed how long it took the subject to find the same chip in a randomized array), and that in an array in which the discriminability of chips was controlled, that focality did not correlate with accuracy of recognition, but that communication accuracy did. Later work by Garro (1986) and Lucy and Shweder (1988) revealed that under certain conditions both focality and communication accuracy correlate with recognition.

Up to this point, the discussion of the Sapir–Whorf hypothesis has been solely concerned with memory effects. Recently Kay and Kempton (1984) tested the Sapir–Whorf hypothesis by comparing American-English speakers to Tarahumara speakers using specific color chips in the blue-green area. Tarahumara differs from English in having only one basic-level term for the blue and green region. Kempton and Kay used three chips differing only in hue, where the middle and one end chip fall on the same side of the English blue-green boundary, but the middle and the other end chip are actually closer together with respect to hue. They found that American English speakers, compared with Tarahumara speakers, tended to select as the most different the chip that has a different English color name, whereas Tarahumara speakers more often selected on the basis of actual similarity in hue.

In a second, ingenious experiment, Kay and Kempton devised an apparatus in which three chips were arranged in a container with a sliding top so that the subject could see either of two pairs of the three chips, but not all three at once. The chips selected for this experiment were the same as those selected for the first experiment in which two chips fell on one side of the boundary and one fell on the other. The subject was then asked "tell me which is bigger: the difference in greenness between the two chips on the left or the difference in blueness between the two chips on the right." The central chip, which is in-termediate in hue between the other two, is in view at all times.

Although formally the same judgment was being asked in this experiment as in the first experiment, where subjects could see all three chips at once, the use of the apparatus apparently blocked the ap-plication of different names as a factor in the perception of difference. What happened here was that American subjects reversed the judgment about which two chips were furthest apart, and more accurately saw a greater difference between the two chips on the same side of the blue-green boundary. The effect is like a perceptual illusion – as soon as the sliding cover is taken off and all three chips are seen, the difference between the two chips of the same color suddenly appears to be the smaller difference. Kay and Kempton (1984) concluded:

> There do appear to be incursions of linguistic categorization into apparently nonlinguistic processes of thinking, even incursions that result in judgments that differ from those made on a purely perceptual basis. Thus... the English speaker judges chip B to be more similar to A than to C because the *blue-green* boundary passes between B and C, even though B is perceptually closer to C than to A. The name strategy seems to demand two facilitating conditions:

> (1) it must not be blocked by context, as in experiment 2; (2) the original judgment must be in some sense hard to make. (p. 77)

It would be interesting to determine the age at which American children begin to show this linguistic effect on color perception. One might guess the effect would not show up until some period after the age at which the child can use color terms correctly, since rehearsal time should be needed to establish what Whorf called *habitual* thought.

Another example of the effect of categorization on memory can be found in the various studies of the *systematic distortion effect* in memory-based personality assessment procedures (D'Andrade, 1965, 1974b, 1985; Shweder, 1972, 1977a, 1977b, 1977c; Shweder and D'Andrade, 1979, 1980). These studies show that the correlational structure of memory-based assessment ratings, such as the Norman five factors or the MMPI Alpha factor, can be replicated using only informants' judgments about the similarity of the rating items, and that in many cases the correlational structure of directly observed behavior does not correspond to the correlational structure of memory-based ratings. These findings are just part of a wide range of studies that show that recall data are influenced by preexisting ideas about the world – that memory is constructive and schema-driven (Mandler, 1984).

The cross-cultural study of emotion is like the cross-cultural study of color in that it also involves problems concerning potential universals of experience and the cognitive effects of different lexically coded systems of categorization (see Lutz & White's 1986 review of studies of emotion in anthropology). Although there is evidence that the facial patterns that are postulated to express the basic emotions are universally lexically differentiated (Ekman, 1971), exactly what is meant when a speaker of a non-Western language uses a particular term to refer to a particular facial expression remains controversial. Anthropologists (e.g., Gerber 1975, 1985; Levy, 1973, 1985; Lutz, 1982, 1985; Poole, 1985) who have studied discourse about emotion ethnographically have found that emotion terms often are defined with reference to complex culturally stereotyped scenarios. Since these complex scenarios are often culturally idiosyncratic, emotion terms are difficult to translate exactly from one language to another, although partial synonyms can usually be found. Wierzbicka (1986), for example, discusses the Polish term *tesknota*, a frequently used emotion term that has no exact English translation. Wierzbicka defines this feeling as follows:

X feels "tesknota" to Y *means*
X is far away from Y
X thinks of Y
X feels good feelings towards Y
X wants to be together with Y
X knows he (she) can't be together with Y
X feels something bad because of that.

Wierzbicka discusses the ways in which *tesknota* differs from such partial English synonyms as *pine* (for which the object can be places and things as well as people, and which carries the connotation that the person becomes sickly as well), *miss* (which is not necessarily a strong feeling, and also can take as its object places and things as well as people), and *homesick* (which is for a place where certain people are, not an individual person). The problem is not just with Polish, however, although the evidence is not as systematic as one would like. Wierzbicka suggests that the distinctions between the English terms *disgust*, *revulsion*, and *dislike*, and the distinctions between *shame*, *embarrassment*, and *fear* are quite different from the distinctions found in many other languages around the world. The issue here is not whether there are universal basic affects, but whether the distinctions found in English make the best prototype for basic affects.

Gerber, in her investigation of Samoan emotion terms (1985), sums up the problem of the relation between *basic affects* and cultural influence as follows:

> The subjective experience of all but a few emotions is shaped both by basic affect patterns and by complex cultural influences. Some emotions, however, have relatively specific cultural scenarios to which they are considered relevant. . . . Because of this specificity, terms that express such feelings cover relatively narrow ranges of meaning. Other terms are more global, and therefore available to be used to express something closer to a basic affect pattern. "Nostalgia-for-the-lilacs-of-yesteryear" is an example of the former sort of emotion, while "sadness," . . . is an example of the latter. . . . Both of these concepts are given force by the same basic affect; to the extent that nostalgia is capable of moving us, it is because we are innately programmed to respond to loss. Equally, every experience of loss, whether described by a specific or more global term, is culturally defined and conditioned. We are taught which experiences appropriately trigger the loss program, what behavioral reactions to it are expectable, and what the appropriate subjective tone of the experience ought to be. (pp. 129–130)

An important question here is to what extent do the different cultural organizations of emotion terms affect perception and memory? In languages that do not distinguish between "fear" and "shame," what do people feel when something "frightening" happens to them? And do they have the same feeling when something "shameful" happens to them? Feelings appear to be difficult to tell apart, which makes them good material for "incursions of linguistic categorization into apparently nonlinguistic processes of thinking."

Cultural understandings about emotions do more than segment the domain of basic affects. Because culturally defined eliciting situations and behavior responses are included as part of the definition of emotions, emotion terms can convey covert cultural ideologies. Gerber

(1985) has analyzed some of the cultural ideology carried by Samoan emotion terms. For example, the term *alofa*, best translated by the English term *love*, has the following basic culturally conventional scenario: An old person, hot, tired, and perhaps ill, is seen walking down the road carrying a heavy load. This makes one feel *alofa*, which prompts one to provide help, perhaps by taking the burden or by offering a cool drink and a place to rest. The emphasis in *alofa* is on caring, giving, and obligation, not intimacy, physical affection, and the appreciation of individual uniqueness, as expressed by the English term *love*. *Alofa* is the normal feeling toward kin, and the behaviors that are thought to express and are prompted by this feeling are generally morally correct and socially obligatory. Thus a good child works for his or her parents and thereby expresses *alofa*. The emotions thought to be similar to *alofa* are feelings of peacefulness, absence of angry thoughts, forgiveness, humility, generosity, and agreeableness. *Alofa* is thought to be the way good people feel. The cultural ideology here, an ideology that strengthens obligations to elders and kin and mutes resentment and rebellion, is readily apparent to most Americans, since they have not been raised within this particular reality-defining system. The ideology invoked by English emotion terms is probably less apparent to most Americans (see Lutz, 1986, for an analysis of this ideology).

3. *Category systems that bring together definitional attributes from a number of domains, such as emotion terms, have the capacity to reinforce certain values. Typically, these systems bring together representations of situations, actions, and the self along with a strong evaluational component.*

There is an interesting relation between emotion terms and colors. A series of studies of the association between emotion terms and Munsell color chips in four cultures (D'Andrade & Egan, 1974; Kieffer, 1974; Johnson, Johnson, & Baksh, 1986) demonstrates that informants tend to select similar chips out of various arrays as the best examples of translations of the English emotion terms *happy*, *sad*, *angry*, and *frightened* in all four cultures. There is also considerable agreement among all four cultures on which color chips are *good*, *bad*, *strong*, and *weak*. This is not to say there are no cultural differences. However, the cultural differences seem to be small compared to the general similarity in emotional response to colors.

The problem of definition

There is a great deal of controversy about how the meaning of words is formulated. Linguists, psychologists, and anthropologists have proposed a number of models to explain this process. Miller and Johnson-Laird (1976) carried out an early pioneering effort to relate word meaning to explicit cognitive processes. Recent empirical work by researchers such as Chafe, Fillmore, Kay, Kempton, Labov, Lakoff,

Langacker, Rosch, Sweetser, and Talmy has brought to light a wide range of phenomena that are badly in need of critical examination. Unfortunately, only a brief summary of some of this work can be presented here.

At present there is some agreement that the so-called classical view of meaning as an if-and-only-if relation between the item to be defined and a conjunctively connected class of features or attributes is insufficient to describe the semantics of natural language. Perhaps the most detailed metalanguage for semantics is that developed by Langacker (1986, 1987). For Langacker, the unit to be defined, whether a grammatical particle, word, phrase, or sentence, has two basic parts, a *base* and a *profile*. The base is the background object, relation, or event that is differentiated by the profile. For example, the term *hypotenuse* has as its base a right angle triangle and as its profile the line segment opposite to the right angle; the term *finger* has as its base some kind of hand and as its profile an elongated terminal segment of the hand; and the term *mother* has as its base a woman and as its profile the fact that this woman has given birth to a child. Langacker does not give a set theoretical formulation for the terms *base* and *profile*; rather he conceives of these terms as having a psychological relationship of a gestaltlike *figure/ground* type. (Interestingly, Langacker's base/profile relationship is closer to the true classical analysis of meaning – that is, Aristotle's notion that definition is constituted by the specification or differentiation of a "genus," the type example being *man* is a *rational animal*, where *animal* is the base and *rational* is what is profiled – than it is to the classical checklist model.)

The assumption of a psychological foundation for meaning is quite explicit in Langacker's work. For Langacker, the base that is profiled by a term is really a knowledge base, composed of cognitive schemas. The right-triangle base of the term *hypotenuse*, for example, involves the coordination of the cognitive schemas of *line segment* and *angle*, which in turn are complex conceptualizations built of even simpler schemas involving conceptually basic representations of space, markings, straightness, and so on. An exhaustive definition of the meaning of a term would require a complete description of all the hierarchical levels of schemas presupposed by the term, but such an endeavor generally is not feasible.

Langacker has developed a set of concepts and a method of using diagrams to describe the way predications are built up. This approach permits one to identify relatively subtle aspects of meaning. Consider the meanings of *go*, *away*, and *gone*, as in

a. You have been here long enough – please *go* now.
b. California is very far *away*.
c. By the time I arrived, she was already *gone*.

The time process designated by *go* is diagrammed in Figure 2.1(a). This example is taken directly from Langacker (1986). Time, which is one

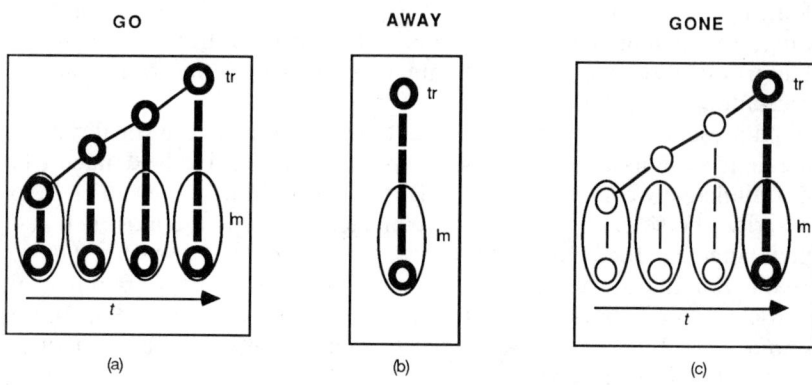

Figure 2.1.

salient domain for this verb, is indicated by an arrow. The diagram for *go* displays only four states out of a continuous series. There are two main participants, represented by circles. Langacker calls one of these the *trajector* and the other the *landmark*. The dotted lines signify "correspondence"; they connect the trajector from state to state, and the landmark from state to state. The heavy dashed lines connecting the trajector and the landmark within each state represent the profiled interconnection marking the distance of the trajector relative to the region to the landmark. In the initial state the trajector is in the neighborhood of the landmark, as given by the ellipse. The trajector's position changes from state to state over time, and in the final state it lies outside the neighborhood of the landmark. For *away*, time is not an active domain. Figure 2.1(b) shows a single configuration that is identical to the final state of *go*. Thus the process designated by *go* results in the locative state of being *away*.

The analysis for *gone* is more complex. As diagrammed in Figure 2.1(c) *gone* matches *away* in profiling (the dark lines) a single locative arrangement in which the trajector is outside the neighborhood of the landmark. However, these two terms differ in their base; for *away*, the base is just a spatial region, whereas for *gone* the base is the entire process diagrammed for *go*. That is, something is *gone* because it is the result of the process of *going*.

This brief excursus gives some indication of the complex relations to be found in the construction of meaning. *Profile* and *base*, *trajector* and *landmark* are complex relational terms needed to analyze the information carried by a term like *gone*. These relationships are basically psychological; they involve cognitive processes that have not been well studied in the laboratory. However, if Langacker is right about the necessity of postulating such relationships in semantic analysis, then these must be frequently used and highly practiced cognitive processes, and one would expect to find them in other areas of intellective functioning outside natural language.

4. *Semantic analysis of natural language terms requires an understanding of complex cognitive processes such as the profiling of a base and the establishment of the relationship of a trajector to a landmark. Meaning is not reducible to a conjunctive association of features, or some similar logically based formulation.*

The way in which the word *gone* builds on the structure of *go*, which is built on the structure of increasing "awayness" across time, illustrates a major characteristic of human semantics: the "chunking" of structures into cognitive "units" that serve as the parts of more complex structures. An early finding in the field of cognitive psychology was that humans are limited in their capacity to process information (Miller, 1956). Anthony Wallace extended Miller's finding to cultural terminological systems (Wallace, 1961). In a survey of kin-term systems and other lexical sets in which every item is in direct contrast with every other item – such as an alphabet, a phonemic system, pieces of a game, and verb systems – he found that the number of items in such systems range from 14 to 50 and seem to be constrained to a number smaller than the number of items that can be discriminated by 2^6 binary bits of information.

The limitations of short-term memory also appear to affect both the depth and width of folk taxonomic systems. Rarely do folk taxonomies exceed more than five hierarchical levels (since each level down adds an independent predication to the level above, and so the most specific level involves at least five different chunks). Also, rarely do the terms that fall directly under any one node (and so form a direct contrast set) exceed the 50-item limit, as would be expected from the size constraints just discussed (Berlin, Breedlove, & Raven, 1966, 1973).

Since human short-term memory is limited with regard to the number of items it can independently discriminate, natural language symbol systems have developed elaborate uses of chunking to get around this constraint. That is, by treating a complex structure such as the structure of awayness, as a single item, a number of such structures can be cognitively processed simultaneously, as in the term *go*. This more complex structure can then be packaged into a single chunk and made part of even more complex structures, such as *gone* (or *deserted*).

5. *Limits on short-term memory restrict the number of items that can be independently discriminated, and thereby constrain the size of directly contrasting lexical sets to 64 or so items and constrain the size of folk taxonomic systems to five or so levels. However, the complexity of structure found within a single term may exceed what might be expected from short-term memory constraints alone because of the cognitive operation of chunking, which makes it possible to package together previously formed structures and treat them as if they were single objects.*

ring

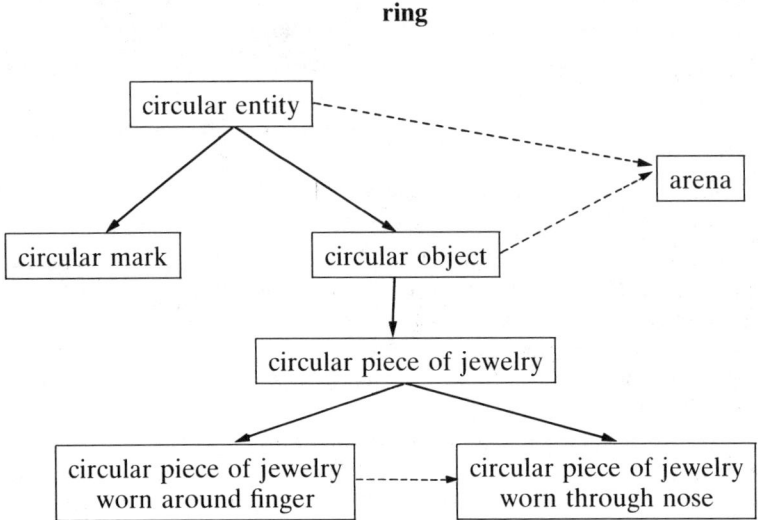

Figure 2.2.

The way in which meanings are constructed cannot be fully explained without taking into account *polysemy*, or the multiple senses of a single term. Take the term *ring*. It has a number of senses. These senses are diagrammed in Figure 2.2 (taken from Langacker, 1986). The solid arrows in the diagram indicate that the sense under the arrow is a more elaborated or more highly specified conceptualization of the sense above the arrow. The dotted arrows indicate an *extension* of the sense; that is, some features of the original sense have been retained, but contrasing features have also been added. Thus a *boxing ring* is an enclosed area, but, unlike the other senses of *ring*, does not refer to a circular form.

Anthropological studies provide numerous discussions of polysemy in connection with kinship terms. In many cultures the basic kin terms (*mother, father, son, daughter*) have at least two senses. One sense is genealogical – genealogically, a *father* is related to someone else by being that person's genitor. Another sense is *role designating* – behaviorally, a *father* is someone who provides basic support and guidance for ego (Schneider & Roberts, 1953). The two senses contrast in the following sentences:

Sam never even met his father.
Jim wasn't the father he wanted to be.

According to one view of polysemy, the meaning of any term can be reduced to a single sense and its other senses derive from the basic sense from context, or are metaphorical extensions that need not be treated as lexical meanings. This may be done by taking the most *abstract* sense as the basic or primary meaning. For the term *father*, one might posit an upper-level sense defined as "the male generally responsible for the reproduction of offspring," and then treat the genealogical and role-designating senses as contextually defined specifications of being "generally responsible for reproduction." A different tactic is to arrange the terms in some kind of logical, temporal, or physical order of *priority* and take the most prior sense as the basic or primary sense. For the term *father*, one might argue that the genealogical sense is prior because the role-designating sense is based on an understanding of what it is that genealogical fathers *do*, and hence the genealogical sense is the basic or primary sense, whereas the role-designating sense is given by context.

Each of these tactics depends on being able to trace out kinds of relations among the senses of terms, and then arguing that analysis of these relations allows the analyst to fix one meaning as primary or basic. Their major drawback is that there is no principled reason to accept any one of these ways of deciding which sense is primary as the right method (D'Andrade, 1976, 1986; Fillmore, 1977; Lakoff, 1987; Langacker, 1987). However, the analyses of the relations between senses point to an important empirical generalization:

6. *The different senses of a term tend to be related to each other in complex ways; by abstraction, or by logical, spatial, or temporal priority, or by empirical or culturally based associations, and so are motivated rather than arbitrary.*

This argument is made with an extensive range of cultural materials by Lakoff (1987).

An aspect of meaning that is often overlooked in linguistic and anthropological treatments of semantics is its *intersubjective* character. To communicate what one means to someone requires not just that the speaker have a set of meanings for the sounds produced, but also that the hearer have the *same* set of meanings. Further, the speaker must assume that the hearer has the same set of meanings for the words produced, for otherwise there would be no communication and no point in speaking. Still further, the speaker must assume that the hearer assumes that the speaker has the same set of meanings for what is said; otherwise the hearer could not assume that the speaker had intended to communicate whatever was said. Interestingly, the assumption of inter-subjectivity has the secondary effect of producing a psychological sense of intersubjectivity, in that talking to someone who talks back appropriately appears to establish that it must be true that both parties are in contact with the same realities. However, the often-cited example of people who do not know they are *not* talking to a therapist when using the Eliza program shows that people can be fooled about this relatively easily.

7. *Symbolic communication requires the establishment of intersubjectivity, although it may be the case that much actual language use in which intersubjectivity is assumed in fact rests only on a limited commonality.*

	direct		collateral	
	male	*female*	*male*	*female*
ascending	father	mother	uncle	aunt
descending	son	daughter	nephew	niece

Figure 2.3.

Semantic networks

The simplest kinds of networks among terms are those created by the very attributes of the terms. One of these is the *contrast set*. A contrast set is composed of terms that all possess at least one salient attribute in common but that differ from each other with respect to other attributes. In some special domains the attributes on which terms differ are orthogonal or cross-cutting, which result in *paradigmatic sets* such as the often-used example of kinship terms. Thus, within the domain of genealogical relationships the paradigmatic relations of *mother*, *father*, *aunt*, *uncle*, *daughter*, *son*, *niece*, and *nephew* can be displayed as shown in Figure 2.3. These terms all share the attribute of being nonaffinal kin, but differ on the attributes of gender (*male* vs. *female*), descent (*direct* vs. *collateral*), and generational polarity (*ascending* vs. *descending*). (For a detailed analysis of American kin terms, see Romney & D'Andrade, 1964.)

There are few fully paradigmatically organized sets of terms in the lexicon. They occur mainly in domains containing dyadic relationships between a small class of objects, such as kin terms, pronouns, and verb inflections. In some cases alternative analyses can be made using different selections of attributes. In these cases it is possible to use information judgments of various kinds to determine which analysis corresponds best to the psychological distinctions made by native speakers (Romney & D'Andrade, 1964; Wexler & Romney, 1972).

An interesting empirical finding about paradigmatic sets based on the space defined by the attributes is that the great majority of terms are conjunctively or relationally composed, and are *not* disjunctively composed. To illustrate, consider the attributes by which sibling terms can be distinguished (Nerlove & Romney, 1967). One such attribute is gender; in English, for example, *brother* refers to a male sibling and *sister* refers to a female sibling. Another attribute is the *relative age* of the sibling; some languages contain just two sibling terms, one for *older* sibling, one for *younger* sibling. A third attribute is the *cross/parallel* relation between the sex of the speaker and the sex of the sibling; some languages have just two sibling terms, one for sibling of the *same sex* as the speaker, one for sibling of the *opposite sex* of the speaker. These three binary attributes define a space of eight kin types. Working from ethnographic and linguistic sources, Nerlove and Romney collected the sibling kin-term systems for 245 distinct cultural groups and found that only 4 of these systems contained any disjunctive categories.

8. *Although natural language categories are often polysemous, containing motivated extensions that make definition by a simple conjunctive or relational composition of attributes impossible, it is nonetheless rare for natural language categories to be arbitrarily disjunctive.*

Psychological processes and contrastive features

Several examples from my own and related work spanning several decades can serve to give an idea of the way in which cultural models affect basic psychological processes such as judgment and inference. The research is illustrative rather than definitive, however, and some of the conclusions given here are controversial.

The first example consists of a simple attempt to assess the degree to which certain kinds of judgments might be affected by or be under the control of contrastive attributes. To return to the paradigmatic analysis of American kin terms, consider the three attributes used to partition the terms – *direct* versus *collateral*, *ascending* versus *descending*, and *male* versus *female*. Suppose that respondents are presented with pairs of kin terms and asked to select the term that refers to the relative with whom one expects to have the greater *solidarity*. To the extent that respondents are reacting to the prototypic kin as if they were made up of these attributes, it should be possible to predict the degree of solidarity ascribed to each kind of kin solely from knowledge of the degree of solidarity contained in the attributes.

This hypothesis was tested by means of a simple experiment. Nineteen college students were given a questionnaire that consisted of a randomized list of all possible pairs of the fifteen American consanguineal kin terms: *father, mother, son, daughter, brother, sister, grandfather, grandmother, grandson, grandmother, uncle, aunt, nephew, niece* and *cousin*. Respondents were asked to circle in each pair the relative "you would expect to be the warmer, friendlier, and more trustworthy person." Respondents were told that their rating should be based on "how people generally expect kin to be." The solidarity score for each kin term for each respondent was calculated by counting the number of times the term was circled. Mean scores for all respondents are presented in Figure 2.4.

To derive the solidarity weight for each of the attributes, the mean for all terms containing that attribute was computed. The difference between the attribute mean and the grand mean of all the kin terms constitutes the solidarity weight for that feature. To compute the predicted value for each kin from its attributes, the attributes scores are added together with a constant for the grand mean of all the solidarity scores. The predicted score for *nephew*, for example, consists of the sum

		Direct		Collateral	
		male	*female*	*male*	*female*
	ascending	grandfather	grandmother		
		5.6	8.3		
2nd Generation		<u>6.1</u>	<u>8.1</u>		
	descending	grandson	granddaughter		
		4.5	5.9		
		<u>4.1</u>	<u>6.1</u>		
	ascending	father	mother	uncle	aunt
		9.9	12.7	3.6	6.3
1st Generation		<u>10.1</u>	<u>12.1</u>	<u>3.9</u>	<u>5.7</u>
	descending	son	daughter	nephew	niece
		8.4	9.7	2.0	3.6
		<u>8.1</u>	<u>10.1</u>	<u>1.9</u>	<u>3.9</u>
		brother	sister	cousin	
Own Generation		9.5	10.8	4.1	
		<u>9.2</u>	<u>10.1</u>	<u>4.0</u>	

r between observed and predicted scores = .92

Figure 2.4. Observed and predicted solidarity scores for American kin terms (predicted scores underlined)

of the weight for a *male* (-1.0), *descending* (-1.0), *first generation* $(+1.3)$, *collateral* (-3.1), plus the grand mean constant (5.7), yielding a predicted score of 1.9.

The predicted scores for the 15 kin terms are presented under the actual scores in Figure 2.4. The fit between the two sets of scores is relatively good. The Pearson r between the two sets of scores is .91. Even the discrepancies between the observed and predicted-scores appear to be neatly patterned. In every case the ascending female terms and the descending male terms have slightly higher solidarity scores than predicted by the attribute weights, while the ascending male terms and the descending female terms have lower solidarity scores than predicted. Respondents seemingly agree that one can expect a little more from senior female kin and junior male kin than either sex or generation alone would predict.

The data above are aggregated, so the degree to which individuals show consistent attribute weightings cannot be determined. To check on the way individuals perform, six respondents were selected randomly and presented the same questionnaire given to the group. The correlation between predicted and observed solidarity scores was still impressive, although slightly lower (r's were .87, .89, .72, .86, .65, and .93). In every case the attribute *female* had a higher solidarity score than the attribute *male*; *ascending* had a higher weight than *descending*; and *direct* had a higher weight than *collateral*. Only the attribute of *generation* showed large shifts, with considerable variation between *first-* and *second-generation* weights.

The contrastive attributes of a paradigmatic analysis can also be used to predict the ease with which children learn proper definitions of kin terms. Haviland and Clark (1974) studied the degree to which children can appropriately define the 15 American consanguineal kin terms, in a group of 30 children ranging in age from 3 to 10 years. The children were interviewed individually and asked "What is a mother?" "What is an uncle?" and so on. The children's definitions were recorded and then classified by category level: Category 1 consisted of responses in which the child said he or she didn't know, or gave an irrelevant answer; category 2 consisted of responses in which the child used only absolute or nonrelational criteria, such as sex or age, to define the term; category 3 consisted of responses that gave relational criteria; and category 4 consisted of definitions that were relational and also recognized the potential reciprocal nature of the relationship involved in the term.

Figure 2.5 gives the percentages of children whose definitions had reached category 3 or better for each of the 15 kin terms. Using the same procedures to estimate attribute weights, as in the analysis of solidarity scores, the predicted percentages are also presented below the observed scores. The largest difference is between collateral and direct terms; there is a tendency for ascending terms to be learned before descending terms, and for second-generation terms to be more difficult than first or own-generation terms. Overall, the Pearson correlation between observed and predicted frequency is .89.

The results of these two experiments support the hypothesis that the contrastive attributes used to partition kin terms have an effect on how much solidarity one expects from that class of relative, and also on how hard the term is to define, and indicate that there is little interaction between attributes in producing these effects. Although there are undoubtedly cases in which contrastive attributes are not related to various characteristics of a category, or in which there are strong interaction effects between attributes (consider the kin term *mother-in-law*, for example, which would have a much worse observed solidarity score than predicted from the contrastive attributes because the close relation of the mother-in-law to her child is expected to create conflict with the child's spouse), the evidence here is that each attribute acts as an independent force. More generally,

9. *Given any category, people can give judgments about it – how much they like it, what it costs, and so on. In many cases these judgments are made by simply summing or averaging the judgments to the various attributes that are distinctive of that category. This makes for cognitive*

		Direct		Collateral	
		male	female	male	female
2nd Generation	ascending	grandfather 30.0% <u>38.5%</u>	grandmother 30.0% <u>39.5%</u>		
	descending	grandson 30.0% <u>27.5%</u>	granddaughter 30.0% <u>28.5%</u>		
1st Generation	ascending	father 43.3% <u>42.7%</u>	mother 53.3% <u>43.7%</u>	uncle 30.0% <u>22.7%</u>	aunt 23.3% <u>23.7%</u>
	descending	son 30.0% <u>31.7%</u>	daughter 33.3% <u>32.7%</u>	nephew 13.3% <u>11.7%</u>	niece 6.7% <u>12.7%</u>
Own Generation		brother 36.7% <u>39.7%</u>	sister 43.3% <u>40.7%</u>	cousin 23.3% <u>20.2%</u>	

r between observed and predicted scores = .89

Figure 2.5. Observed and predicted percentage level three or better definitions for American kin terms (predicted scores underlined)

efficiency, in that the judgments about a great many categories can be generated from the combinations of the judgments about a much smaller number of attributes.

Taxonomy

Another kind of network between terms created by the attributes of the terms themselves is a *taxonomic* network. A taxonomic relation, in which A is a kind of B, is created whenever A has all the attributes of B, but B also has additional attributes that distinguish it from A (Werner & Schoepfle, 1987). For example, a *cottage* is a kind of *house* (a *cottage* has the attributes of a *house*, plus other attributes involving small size), a *ponderosa* is a kind of *pine* (a *ponderosa* has all the attributes of a *pine*, plus specific attributes involving needle form, size, trunk, etc.), and a *cousin* is a kind of *relative* (a *cousin* has all the attributes of a *relative*, plus specific attributes involving collaterality and generation). In some domains, such as the domain of plant taxa, relatively extensive taxonomic hierarchies can be elicited (Conklin, 1962; Berlin et al., 1966).

Note that the taxonomic relationship, as defined here, is not the same as the subset/superset relationship (D'Andrade, 1976; Werner, 1985). Every taxonomic relationship is a subset/superset relationship, but some subset/superset relationships are not taxonomic relationships. For example, *comic books* are a subset of *stuff I haven't read for years*, but the attributes of the complex term *stuff I haven't read for years* are not included in the term *comic books*; the subset/superset relationship is empiricially or contingently true, but not definitionally true. In some cases it is hard to decide if a true taxonomic relationship holds; for example, is it true by definition that *lamps* are a subset of things that are *furniture*? This question is discussed further in the following paragraphs.

Taxonomies in the plant domain have been investigated extensively, and a series of generalizations about the structure of this kind of hierarchical system have been proposed (Berlin et al. 1973), along with various modifications (Hunn, 1976, 1985; Randall 1976; Brown, 1977; Wierzbicka, 1984; Dougherty & Keller, 1985). The basic generalizations are as follows:

10. *Folk biological taxonomies are based on the identification of generic taxa. Generic taxa correspond approximately to biological genera, which form natural groupings with many more attributes in common. Generics often consist of strongly related species that exhibit a family resemblance, but that cannot be defined by some necessary and sufficient set of attributes. These generics are also called basic-level categories.*

In a recent study of Jivaro folk ornithology, Boster, Berlin, and O'Neill (1986) found that not only do Jivaroan bird generics generally correspond to scientific generics, but also that there is a strong degree of correspondence between folk and scientific systems of classification with respect to the pattern of resemblance between organisms, where resemblance is measured for the scientific systems by taxonomic depth and for the folk system by an information theoretic measure of the degree to which there is specimen overlap in naming.

11. *Folk taxonomies rarely exceed five levels. These levels are definable in terms of linguistic and taxonomic criteria. The five levels are labeled unique beginner, life form, generic, specific, and varietal. Unique beginner refers to the largest inclusive grouping of taxa, and is often unlabeled linguistically by a single term. Life form taxa are invariably few in number (5 to 10). The generic taxa are more numerous (approximately 500). Sometimes unusual generics (cacti, cassowary, platypus) are not included in any lexically distinct life form. Specific and varietal taxa are generally less numerous than generics, typically forming small sets of a few members within a single generic. Specific and variental taxa are commonly labeled in binomial (e.g., white pine) or trinomial (e.g., American golden plover) terms.*

These generalizations hold not only for folk taxonomies of plants and animals, but also for other domains. Brown et al. (1976) found the same structure for cultural artifacts (American automobiles and Finnish winter vehicles), religious figures (Thai spirits), and partonomies (Huastic body parts).

Using the notion of generics, Rosch (1975) extended Berlin's generalizations to include a wide range of interesting psychological phenomena. Rosch used the term *basic-level category* to refer to genericlike classes, that is, classes composed of "intrinsically separate things" that have many attributes in common, many motor movements in common, and strong similarity in shape. She showed that given three-level taxonomies consisting of a life-form, generics, and specifics (e.g., life-form: *tool*; generics: *hammer, saw, screwdriver*; specifics: *ball-peen hammer, hack hand saw, Phillips screwdriver*) that subjects could list many more attributes and more motor movements for generics than for life-forms, but could not list significantly more attributes and motor movements for specifics than for generics. However, Rosch found that for the categories of *trees, fish,* and *birds,* her subjects could *not* list more attributes for generics than for life-forms. Apparently, for normal urban Americans *tree, fish,* and *bird* are psychologically basic-level objects. With respect to shapes, Rosch found that figure outlines of specifics of the same generic were much more similar in form than generics of the same life-form, and that the basic level is also the most inclusive level at which an average shape of an object can be recognized.

Within the categories of objects, Rosch proposed that where there are different exemplars (different *generics* of some *life-form*, or different *specifics* of some *generic*), that people form a *prototype* (clearest case, best example), which serves to "define" the object, and that nonprototype members can be ordered from better to poorer examples. Rosch (1975) showed that subjects are able to make reliable ratings of "goodness of example" (and that such ratings predict reaction time in categorization tasks), and are also able to predict the order in which subjects list examples of a category. Uyeda and Mandler (1980) replicated Rosch's ratings for 28 categories on a different sample of subjects, and found their ratings correlated with a Spearman's r of .867 with Rosch's ratings, a mean Spearman's r of .546 with Battig and Montague (1969) norms for production frequency, and a mean Spearman r of .199 with the Kucera and Francis (1967) norms of word frequency.

12. *People grade examples of some types of categories as good or bad examples of those categories, and are quicker at identifying good examples than bad examples, and generally more likely to think of good examples than bad examples in free recall, and generally more likely to use the good examples when they reason about categories than the bad examples.*

Although prototype-related phenomena appear to be robust, there are some limitations to these findings. Rosch (1973) was unable to obtain similar results for certain other types of categories, such as categories of action (*walking*, *eating*, etc.). The hypothesis, derived from Rosch's work, that people categorize by computing similarity distances between the object to be categorized and various prototypes, and then place the object in the category belonging to the closest prototype, has met with considerable criticism, since there is ample evidence that in some cases a prototype will be most similar to a particular exemplar that is not categorized under the same term as the prototype. For example, most informants judge a *paper cup* to be more generally similar to a *glass* than to a *cup* (Kronenfeld, Armstrong, and Wilmoth, 1985; Ripps, in press; Werner, 1985). However, a number of hypotheses about the *general* process of categorization do use the notion of prototype (Kempton, 1981; Kronenfeld et al., 1985; Lakoff, 1987; Fillmore, 1975).

While Berlin's formulation of folk taxonomy has proven to be valuable to ethnobiological study, and his generalizations about the differences between generics, life-forms, and specifics have been validated in a number of studies, various problems have arisen concerning this formulation. First, it has often been pointed out that folk taxonomies are unlike true scientific taxonomies in that the folk taxonomic relation is not always transitive or mutually exclusive. For example, American informants will say that *strawberries* are a kind of *berry*, and *berries* are kinds of *bushes*, but that *strawberries* are not *bushes* (Randall, 1976), or that although some *oaks* are *bushes*, *oaks* are really *trees* (D'Andrade, 1976). One response to this criticism is that the folk taxonomic relation is defined on the prototypic forms of the term, not every exemplar. Furthermore, the taxonomic relation does not really hold between *life-forms* and generics, but does hold between generics and specifics (Hunn, 1985). That is, generics like *oak* and specifics like *live oak* are really *natural kinds*, defined by a Kripke-like causal contingency between the name and the objects referred to by the name. We use a variety of attributes to identify the objects, but definition is not accomplished by means of a small number of "arbitrary" necessary and sufficient criteria, as it is in the case of life-forms. According to this view, the terms *tree*, *grass*, and *bush* are not *taxonomically* related to anything, although some natural kinds do happen to have these attributes, and therefore it is not surprising that various kinds of exception to the taxonomic relation are found between the life-form terms and the generics.

It might also be argued that the problem lies in the application of the concept of taxonomic relation, which should be restricted more than it is at present (Wierzbicka, 1984). According to this view, the taxonomic relation should be limited to cases in which the superordinate category is part of the definition of the subordinate category. Thus an *oak* is really a kind of *tree*, because, in Langacker's terminology, the *tree* domain serves as the *base* for term *oak*. The term *bush*, on the other hand, does not typically serve as a *base* domain for plant terms. A *blackberry* or *lilac* may grow in a bushlike form, but being a *bush* does not happen to be part of their definition. Some supporting evidence for this is that if one asks informants to list kinds of *trees*, informants produce a reasonable set of terms. However, if one asks informants for kinds of *bushes*, one gets primarily confused reactions from informants.

Wierzbicka also extends her analysis to a number of other kinds of superset/subset relations. She distinguishes true taxonomic *kinds of* relations from the relationship found between terms like *bike* and *toy* or *gun* and *weapon*, which she points out are not relations between two kinds of *things*, but relations between a kind of thing and a function. She argues that the superset/subset connection between *functionals* and *things* is not as tight as the taxonomic relation between *things* and *things*, in that *things* like *knives* can be either *weapons* or *toys* or *silverware*, depending on context.

In addition to these two relationships, Wierzbicka distinguishes other types of superset relation. Terms such as *furniture*, *cutlery*, *clothing*, and *fruit* are *collections* of objects defined partly by function and partly by unity of place. *Furniture*, for example, is made up of objects used to furnish a house or place of residence, and contrasts with the *fittings* of a house. Other collective terms like *leftovers*, *groceries*, and *refreshments* are even more ad hoc collections, defined partly by function, place, or common fate. Terms like *vegetable*, *drugs*, *medicines*, and *dyes* can be distinguished from the collective terms by the fact that they are not used or treated as a group, but still do not form true taxonomic superclasses, since they refer to *uses* of a certain kind of stuff, not to a *kind of thing*.

13. *Basic-level categories are typically kinds of things, but many super-ordinates (life-forms) are not kinds of things, but rather types of functions, or special collections, or uses of things. This explains Rosch's finding that basic-level terms typically have many more attributes than superordinate terms, since many superordinates are not things.*

This also explains why Rosch found that in the case of the biological taxonomies (birds, trees, and fish) there was little difference in number of ascribed attributes between the basic-level terms and the superordinates, since here the superordinates were the same kinds of thing as the basic-level objects. In sum, what Rosch found was not that there are intrinsic conceptual differences between different levels of a taxonomy, but rather that there are conceptual differences between terms that refer to kinds of things in the world versus terms that refer to functions of things, or to collections of things. This is not to deny the point made by Dougherty (1978), that the salience of different taxonomic levels varies by culture and subcultural interests.

Other objections to the use of taxonomic models have been made on ethnographic grounds. Randall (1976) points out that just because an ethnographer can, by careful questioning, elicit a large, extensive, taxonomic tree, this does not mean that informants actually use any such cognitive schema. Instead, Randall argues, the available evidence indicates that informants use "dwarf trees" – essentially small networks consisting of a basic object and its attributes. Hunn (1985) points out that biological taxonomies only lexicalize a small portion of the total number of available plant and animal taxa, and that what is lexicalized are the plants and animals that have some special importance to people. For Hunn, terms like *bush* are *residual categories*, constructed to refer to a large number of taxa that are not worth distinguishing further. Hunn, like Wierzbicka, considers the terms at the life-form level to have a different status than the true generics, which he treats as a difference between the multiattribute, general-purpose definitions of generics and the single-attribute, special-purpose definitions of the life-forms. Hunn argues that the taxonomic system developed by Berlin is a compromise between the Linnean hierarchical model and what Hunn calls the *natural core model*, which treats folk biological domains as "composed of a general purpose, polythetic core of taxa surrounded by special purpose, monothetic concepts in peripheral position" (1985:124). Hunn's position seems right, and suggests a general formulation:

14. *Human beings are opportunistic information processors, and in constructing systems of symbols will make use of any kind of structure that will help to communicate information of interest. There are always trade-offs between consistency and generality in categorization. Phenomena such as polysemy and the mixture of terms for kinds of things, functions, and collections within a single hierarchical system represent compromises between the need to have symbols that are defined by simple consistent formulations and the need to organize great varieties of experience by means of a limited number of symbols.*

Another kind of semantic network can be isolated by selecting some class of terms and then analyzing the kinds of distinctions utilized by these terms. Talmy (1978), for example, has carried out an extensive analysis of the distinctions conveyed by grammatical particles like *a*, *the*, *in*, *across*, *-ed* (past tense), *-s* (plural), and so on, in contrast to the distinctions conveyed by lexical items, such as *tree*, *write*, and *angry*. Talmy finds that grammatical particles are preponderantly *relativistic* or *topological*, and exclude fixed or metrically Euclidean distinctions. For example, many languages inflect nouns to specify the *uniplex* or *multiplex* character of the object, but no language has inflections that specify the particular color or size of a noun. Deitics like *this* or *that* specify the location of an object by setting up a *partition* that divides a space into region, and then *locate* some *entity* at a *point* or *region* that is on the *same* or *different* side as the speaker. The specifications of *this* or *that* appear to be truly topological, in that the partitions and regions set up by using such terms are "rubber-sheet geometry" – they have no metric constraints and may apply to the most concrete or the most abstract "spaces." Prepositions, like verb inflections and various deitics, also have topological rather than metric or absolute specifications:

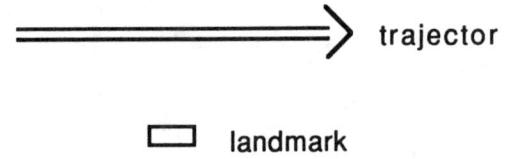

Figure 2.6.

An illustrative case here are the twenty-odd motion related prepositions in English, such as *through* or *into*, which together subdivide the domain of "paths considered with respect to reference-objects." This domain covers a great and varied range, but any particular "path" falls within the purview of one or another preposition, associated there with other "paths." The associations are often language specific and sometimes seem arbitrary or idiosyncratic. Thus, . . . classed together by *through* are such dissimilar cases as a straightforward liquid parting course (walking through water) and a zig-zag obstacle-avoiding course (walking through timber). The question arises why such distinctions should be effaced by the grammatical system, while they are observed by the lexical and other cognitive systems. Why are grammatical elements – say, such prepositions – not a large and open class marking indefinitely many distinctions? One may speculate that the cognitive function of such classification lies in rendering contentful material manipulable – i.e., amenable to transmission, storage, and processing – and that its lack would render content an ineffective agglomeration. (Talmy, 1978:9)

Considerable work has been done on the semantics of English prepositions. Linder (1981), using Langacker's concepts of *landmark* and *trajector*, has analyzed in detail the prepositions *up* and *out*. A similar analysis of *over* has been carried out by Brugman (1981). These analyses support Talmy's hypothesis that grammatical elements are defined by relatively few criteria, and that these criteria are relational and topological in character.

The extensive polysemy of these prepositions is most dramatic. Each of the senses has a specific *image schema*, that is, a schematic pictorial representation, or a metaphoric extension of such an image schema. Lakoff, for example, discusses how one spatial sense of *over*, as in

The plane flew over the hill,

is transformed into the metaphorical sense found in

He was passed over for promotion.

The spatial sense of the first sentence can be represented by the relation between a landmark and a trajector, as in Figure 2.6.

The arrow in the figure represents the path that the trajector is moving along. The trajector has a horizontal path, and is *up* from the landmark, with no contact between them. The metaphorical sense of being "passed over for promotion" is based on the metaphorical equivalences *control is up* and *choosing is touching*. Using these equivalences, the hearer infers that the person was not contacted by whatever is up there, and therefore not chosen for promotion (Lakoff, 1987).

15. *Grammatical elements are predominantly relativistic and topological, and can often be represented by simple image schemas. Specific grammatical elements may have a large number of senses, including complex extensions based on metaphoric equivalences.*

In another kind of semantic organization, discussed by Fillmore (1977), sets of terms are all based on the same schema (Fillmore sometimes uses the terms *scene* and *scenario* to refer to what are here called *schemas*). Fillmore uses as an example terms that refer to the schema of a commercial event. Elements of the schema are the *buyer*, the *seller*, the *price*, and the transfer of *money* and *goods*. There is a large class of terms that all use this event as part of what Langacker would call the *base* of the term. Thus, *sell, buy, loan, borrow, rent, lease, purchase, charge, embezzle, defraud, haggle, bid, tip, ransom, refund, pension, allowance, tuition, salary, alimony, reward*, and so on, each profile a different aspect of the same underlying commercial transaction.

Fillmore also points out that *base schemas* (defined here as schemas that serve as the *definitional base* of some term) are highly simplified representations of the world, and the application of a particular term to a specific situation that does not reasonably fit the base schema results in odd or inappropriate usage (Fillmore, 1975, 1977). For example, the base schema for the term *widow* does not fit cases in which the woman is a triple bigamist who has lost one of her three husbands. To ask of such a woman whether or not she is a *widow* is inappropriate not because the *profile* of the term does not apply (the profile of *widow* involves the death of a husband), but because the *base* does not have a reasonable fit to the actual situation. As Fillmore (1975) puts it,

> How old does an unmarried man have to be before you can call him a bachelor? Is someone who is professionally committed to the single life properly considered a bachelor? (Is it correct to say of Pope John XXIII that he died a bachelor?) If so, is bachelorhood a state one can enter? That is, if a man leaves the priesthood in middle life, can we say that he became a bachelor at age 47? When we say of a divorced man or a widower that he is a bachelor, are we speaking literally or metaphorically? How can we tell? Would you call a woman a widow who murdered her husband? Would you call a woman a widow whose divorce became final on the day of her husband's death? Would you call a woman a widow if one of her three husbands died but she had two living ones left?
>
> ...According to the prototype theory of meaning, these concepts are defined in the context of a simple world in which men typically marry around a certain age, they marry once, they marry exclusively, they

stay married until one partner dies. Men who are unmarried at the time they could be married are called bachelors. Women whose husbands have died are called widows. (pp. 128–9)

A nice example of the way in which the base schema of a term creates unconscious presuppositions about its meaning has been described by Sweetser (1987), who presents evidence that the way people define the term *lie* is based on simplified schema or folk theory of discourse. The basic assumptions of this folk theory are the maxims

1. Try to help, not harm.
2. Knowledge is a beneficial thing.

These two maxims entail

3. Try to inform others; don't misinform.

Further assumptions are

4. Normally people obey the rules.
5. People's beliefs normally have adequate justification.
6. Adequately justified beliefs are normally true.

The result of this set of assumptions – this folk theory of discourse interaction – is that if somebody tells you something, normally that something is true. What then, is a *lie*? Coleman and Kay (1981) found that of the three prototypic conditions of lying,

a. Speaker believes statement is false
b. Speaker intends to deceive hearer by making the statement
c. The statement is false in fact,

when respondents were given various combinations of these statements, condition (a) was strongest in producing a judgment that the speaker was lying, and (c) was weakest. This makes sense given the folk theory Sweetser outlines, for if the speaker believes the statement is false, and if most belief is justified, then the statement would be false in fact. Furthermore, since to be beneficial one should not misinform, one would not give a false statement unless one wanted to deceive. Therefore, (b) and (c) follow from (a) and the folk model. Sweetser also points out that, when the prototypic assumptions do not hold, a special sense of *lie* is created, as in a *white lie*, in which the speaker wants to be beneficial, but believes the truth would not be beneficial, and so says what is intended to be beneficial but not true.

Kay (1987) has carried out a similar type of analysis on linguistic *hedges*. Kay finds that certain hedges are defined relative to schemas or models of language itself. The terms *loosely speaking* and *strictly speaking* are defined with reference to a folk theory of language that portrays words as referring to a world that is independent of our talk, and that can be more or less faithful to the nonlinguistic facts they represent (an intentional theory of reference). In the sentence

Loosely speaking, the first human beings lived in Kenya,

"loosely speaking" serves as a pragmatic hedge, indicating that what is being referred to as the "first human beings" and "Kenya" are only approximate fits to the actual objects. "Loosely speaking" takes a Fregean view of language. In contrast, the hedge *technically speaking*, as in the expression

The movers have come for your furniture, which technically includes TV sets,

assumes a very different theory of language; one in which there is a body of experts who have the power to fix particular words to particular objects and events (a causal theory of reference). This theory is like the baptismal-causal theories of Kripke and Putnam in which a word refers to the things it does because someone stipulated that henceforth this word would designate this particular kind of thing. The point here is that the semantics of English are not frozen, but are manipulable by ordinary speakers using appropriate hedges.

16. *Cultural schemas serve as the definitional bases for whole sets of terms. Typically such cultural schemas portray simplified worlds, making the appropriateness of the terms that are based on them dependent on the degree to which these schemas fit the actual worlds of the objects being categorized. Such schemas portray not only the world of physical objects and events, but also more abstract worlds of social interaction, discourse, and even word meaning.*

Nondefinitionally based semantic networks

All the types of semantic networks discussed so far are based on relations among definitional attributes of some type. A quite different type of network can be constructed by linking objects with non-definitional, extrinsic relationships. Frake (1964), in advance of the work on semantic networks in artificial intelligence, presented a simple network of relations among the elements for yeast making involving relations of *use, part, source,* and *kind.* Metzger and Williams, in a series of pioneering papers (1963a, 1963b, 1966) demonstrated how ethnographic descriptions could be generated by constructing queries that elicited relationships of various types. The goal of this type of research was to find a method to effectively elicit and display cultural knowledge. The following excerpt is taken from Black and Metzger (1965:151–152) and concerns the administration of justice in the Tzeltal-speaking municipio of Tenejapa in highland Chiapas, Mexico:

Q. *banti ya smuk te ?anima e*	Where do they bury the dead person?
A. *ya smuk ta yutna*	He is buried inside the house.
A. *ya smuk ta kapasanto*	He is buried in the cemetery.
Q. *mas lek bal ya smuk ta yutna mak ya smuk ta kapasanto*	Is it better to bury a person in the house or in a cemetery?
A. *mas lek ta yutna*	It is better in the house.
Q. *bi yu?un mak lek ta yutna*	Why is it better in the house?

A. *melel k'usobel sba yu?un ha?al*	Because otherwise he will feel the rain.
Q. *bi ya spas te hmilawai e te me lom p'ih*	What does the killer do if he is smart?
A. *ya s?an*	He flees.
A. *ya spakan hilel te ?anima e*	He turns the dead man face down.
Q. *bi yu?un ya spakan hilil te ?anima e*	Why does he turn the dead man face down?
A. *ma sk'an ta scuhk*	He does not wish to be captured.
A. *ma ba ya stak yil sc'ulel ?animal*	The soul of the dead man will not be able to see him.

This kind of nonimpressionistic, rigorous ethnography has proved extremely demanding and is rarely used. However, frame-elicitation techniques have been more generally adapted for the systematic study of specific domains as a means of investigating cultural knowledge. For example, D'Andrade, Quinn, Nerlove, and Romney (1972) used a simplified frame-elicitation technique in a study of American and Mexican beliefs about illness. To construct frames, they collected a series of ordinary statements about specific illness from informants. These statements were then put in frame form by replacing the particular illness term with a blank – for example, "It is safer to have _____ as a child and get it over with." From a large collection of such statements, the 30 most general, unambiguous, and semantically independent sentence frames were selected. A list of diseases was also elicited, and the 30 best-known and most common diseases were selected. From this collection of sentence frames and disease terms a systematic elicitation task was constructed in which each informant was asked for every sentence frame whether or not the insertion of each disease term into the frame would make the sentence true or false (for the American sample of 10 Stanford undergraduates a five-point scale from "definitely true" to "definitely not true" was used). Thus an informant doing the American-English task would be asked for sentence frame 1. *You catch _____ from other people*, whether that was true for (a) *appendicitis*, (b) *arthritis*, (c) *asthma*, and so on. The modal response was then taken as culturally representative. A small piece of the final matrix is presented in Figure 2.7.

A matrix of this type is an efficient way to store a large network of information. It is unlikely, however, that people actually store information in such a manner. The question is, once one has obtained a large matrix of cultural information how is it cognitively organized? One heuristic method of investigating this question is to use multidimensional scaling (MDSCAL) to uncover clusters or dimensions. A median-based cluster analysis technique (D'Andrade et al., 1972) revealed three major clusters of frames and disease terms for the American data. One cluster consisted of contagious diseases (*colds, mumps, mononucleosis*, etc.) and associated frames; another cluster consisted of serious, life-

	cancer	acold	polio	stroke	ulcers
__ is caused by germs	no	yes	yes	no	no
__ comes from emotional upset	no	no	no	yes	yes
__ is serious	yes	no	yes	yes	no
__ is a sign of old age	yes	no	no	yes	no
__ runs in the family	no	no	no	yes	yes

Figure 2.7.

threatening noncontagious diseases (*stroke, leukemia, heart attack,* etc.) and associated frames; and the third cluster consisted of less severe, old age, inherited, or emotion-caused diseases (*rheumatism, epilepsy, ulcers,* etc.) and associated frames. A MDSCAL dimensional analysis and a principal components factor analysis both produced similar results. The major conclusion of this research was

17. *The defining properties of a set of terms are not always the properties that determine how people categorize or react to the objects referred to by these terms.*

Thus, the categories discovered by the analysis of how disease terms distribute across beliefs do not seem to be related to the features that define these disease terms. Our informants agree that *cancer is serious, noncontagious,* and not a *childhood* illness. These properties are major foci for how Americans conceive of diseases. But these are neither necessary nor sufficient conditions for making the decision that someone has cancer.

A major drawback of this research is that multidimensional scaling, although an effective means of detecting structure and summarizing data, does not yield results that fit a cognitive processing model. That is, one cannot, from scaling results, construct a computer program that reproduces the original judgments in a manner that even roughly simulates human thinking processes. But, then, how *are* ordinary people able to fill out large matrices of the type used in this research? Perhaps attention to how people actually process cultural information can yield more effective and general models than multidimensional scaling.

Cultural schemas and cultural models

To construct a model that has the capacity to reproduce the original judgments in a reasonably human manner, a propositionally based model was developed with some simple rules of inference for the American disease terms and frame data (D'Andrade, 1976). To

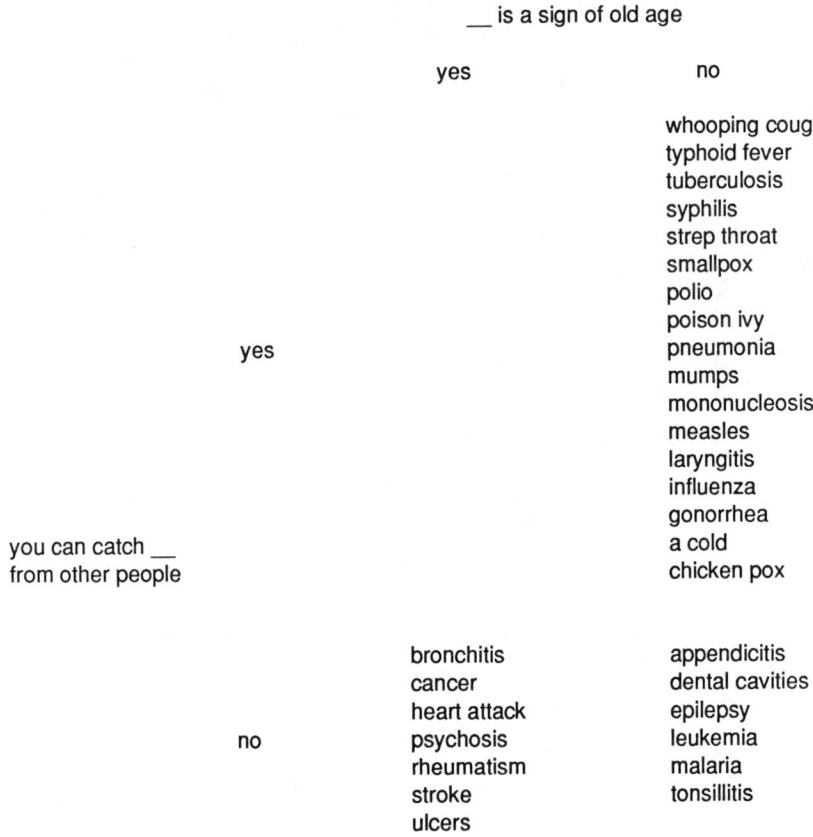

Figure 2.8.

determine the inferential relations between all pairs of attributes, contingency tables for all pairs of attributes were computed, and those with zero cells or near-zero cells were selected, as indicated in Figure 2.8.

The contingency table shows that there is no disease that is both *catching* and *a sign of old age*. Thus one can infer the absence of the old age property from the presence of the contagion. More generally, whenever there is a zero in any of the four cells of a two-by-two contingency table, one can use the fact that a certain combination of variables does *not* occur to make inferences about what *can* occur. In the example in Figure 2.8,

               1. not (*catching* and *a sign of old age*)

therefore   2. if *catching* then not (*a sign of old age*)

and therefore 3. if *a sign of old age* then not (*catching*).

The next step was to use the fact that inference relations of this sort are transitive to eliminate redundant relationships. For example, if any disease is a *children's* disease then it is a *contagious* disease, and if any disease is a *contagious* disease then it is a *germ-caused* disease. Because implicational relations are transitive, the fact that if any disease is a *children's* disease then it is a *germ* disease does not need to be "remembered" by the system, but can be generated from the separate relationships.

The final result was a model that contained 31 primary relationships, from which 81 further relationships could be generated. Interestingly, three major chains of if–then relationships were found to correspond to the same three clusters just described. Despite some success however, as a more process-oriented generative model, overall, the effort was a failure. Perhaps because the format of the model was closer to a "natural" representation than the scaling analyses were, one could see immediately that some aspects of it were wrong. The model lacked any description of the nature of germs, routes of infection, the development of antibodies, the structure of the human body, the functions of various organs, and the like. It is knowledge of these things that lie behind the inferences that can be made from the zero cells. Without a representation of this knowledge, the inferences appear arbitrary. *Children's* diseases are a subset of *contagious* diseases. This is not some arbitrary cultural formulation, but rather something that makes good sense given the nature of germs, getting older, resistance, and antibodies. The problem was that the model had propositions and inferences, but it did not represent the basic objects and causal events on which the propositions and inferences are based.

Thus, much of the work on cultural models leads to the same kind of result that work on representation of meaning did, and also that work on taxonomies and related semantic networks did. That is to say,

18. *Evaluation of attempts to represent the use of symbols, ranging from the word level to the level of large knowledge systems, indicates that construction of adequate cultural representations requires explication of the basic cognitive schemas that underlie the use of these symbols.*

What, precisely, is meant by a *cognitive schema*? A good summary is presented in Casson's (1983) review paper "Schemata in Cognitive Anthropology":

> Schemata are conceptual abstractions that mediate between stimuli received by the sense organs and behavior responses. They are abstractions that serve as the basis for all human information processing, e.g. perception and comprehension, categorization and planning, recognition and recall, and problem solving and decision making. . . . Bartlett, who is generally credited with being the first to use the term schema in its contemporary sense (although Kant used the term in much the same manner in his *Critique of Pure Reason*), argued that "the past operates as an organized mass rather than a

group of elements each of which retains its specific character" (1932, 197). Remembering, Bartlett maintained, is constructive. Not all stimuli are stored in memory; rather, schemata are employed to provide a "general impression of the whole" and to construct (or reconstruct) "probable details" (1932, 206)....[S]chemata occur at differing levels of abstraction. At relatively low levels of abstraction there are schemata for perceiving geometrical figures, colors, faces, etc., while at higher levels there are schemata for comprehending complex activities and events. There are no important differences in kind between schemata for perception and comprehension.... schemata, unlike associations, are organic wholes comprised of parts that are oriented both to the whole and to other parts....Schemata are autonomous and automatic – once set in motion they proceed to their conclusion. (pp. 430–431)

Consider, for example, the normal schema for a cat that most of us share. It is really a most remarkable device; it can come up with the interpretation *cat!* with a great range of minimal information – the sound of a certain kind of growl, or the sight of a waving tail, or the physical sensation of something rubbing against one's leg, or a crude line picture on a sheet of paper, or a particular combination of letters. The cat schema contains imagistic, acoustic, sensory, and propositional materials at varying levels of abstraction, from highly schematic line figures to detailed images of the mangled ears of an elderly male. The schema is flexible, and can accommodate new forms, such as a blue point Burmese, or even a *dasyure,* the marsupial cat. The schema has a great number of default values – things that get filled in even if they are not observed or stated. This schema is not a picture in the mind, because no picture can be both pure black and pure white, yet the standard schema contains both these possibilities and more. The schema is well organized, both with respect to how a cat is put together physically and what it does, and contains parts and subparts, each of which is a separate schema in its own right. Yet, despite its detail and organization, the cat schema leaves out an enormous amount and is a great simplification of the potential visual, acoustic, sensory, and propositional information that could be experienced about cats. The values that get filled in by default create prototypic cats – the cats we expect when nothing is known except that it is a cat. Thus the cat schema, which is already a simplification, through the operation of default values, creates further simplifications, or senses of what could be a cat. Finally, the cat schema is sensitive to context, so that in certain places and at certain times we are ready to see a cat, and need only minimal cues to make the identification.

To create such a mechanical device would be a remarkable achievement. Recent work on parallel-distributed processing models indicates that such a device may be constructed by a relatively simple network of interconnected neuronlike elements (Rumelhart & McClelland, 1986).

The ability of such parallel processing networks to mimic the behavior postulated for schemas is quite impressive. The possibility of constructing flexible, contextually sensitive, default value-filling, accommodating, and assimilating interpretative devices from simple parallel processing networks can be expected to have a large impact on the various subfields of cognitive science.

Schema theory has served as the underlying psychological mechanism for the development of the concept of a *cultural model*. A cultural model is a cognitive schema that is *intersubjectively shared* by a social group. Because cultural models are intersubjectively shared, interpretations made about the world on the basis of a cultural model are experienced as obvious facts of the world. A wild pitch is obviously a *ball*, except to those who do not know baseball. A further consequence of the intersubjectivity of cultural models is that much of the information relevant to a cultural model need not be made explicit, since what is obvious need not be stated. If the announcer says that the pitch was wild, he need not say that it was a ball.

To get around the limits of short-term memory, cognitive schemas tend to be organized *hierarchically*, so that the parts of any one schema can often be unpacked into further complex subparts. One consequence of the hierarchical structure of schemas is that certain cultural models have a wide range of application because they serve as parts of many other cultural models. Thus the cultural model of *money* is found as a part of a great many other cultural models, such as the models of *buying, interest, banking, inflation,* and *salary*. Knowing a culture requires at least knowing the cultural models that are widely used as parts of other cultural models.

An important characteristic of many cultural models is the fact that informants usually cannot produce an organized description of the entire model. They can *use* the model, but they cannot produce a complete *description* of it. The model is like a well-learned set of procedures one knows how to carry out rather than a body of fact one can recount. However, most cultural models do not seem to be purely procedural, since most informants can describe in part how the model operates when asked questions about specific matters.

In psychology one of the best-known examples of a cultural model is the *restaurant script* (Schank & Abelson, 1977). Of course, the restaurant script is dependent on a sociocultural *institution* – that is, the existence of a particular kind of business that sells cooked food, called a "restaurant." The script concept is intended to refer to stereotyped sequences of events. However, event sequences are just one type of organization of elements. As Casson (1983) has pointed out, some schemas are cultural *object* models (plants, animals, manufactured objects, persons, kinsmen, occupations, ethnic identities, personality descriptors, illnesses, and emotions have all been studied, for example), *orientation* models (e.g., cognitive maps for cities, or even spatial mnemonic devices such as the "method of loci"), as well as *event* models, such as scripts (see, e.g., Randall's 1986 study of Samal fishing, and Frake's 1975 study of how to enter a Yakan house). A special kind of cultural model, the *expressive* model, has been studied in detail over the past two decades (Roberts, 1987). These are models "of and for" behavior, ranging from *riddling* to *trap shooting*, which permit people to express strong affective generalized orientations and which can be both conflict reducing and conflict enhancing.

Quinn and Holland (1987) recently reviewed the cultural model approach, placing it within the general framework of cognitive anthropology. They stress the shift in semantic analysis from earlier work toward greater diversity in methodological techniques, more reliance on native intuitions in formulating the model, with subsequent testing of the adequacy of the model using different kinds of data, and greater reliance on the analysis of natural discourse. They also point to the convergence between anthropologists and linguists in the study of cultural models:

> Understandably, linguists are most concerned with the important implications of underlying cultural models for their theories of word definition, metaphor, polysemy, hedging, and other linguistic phenomena. Anthropologists tend to orient their analyses in the opposite direction, treating linguistic usages as clues to the underlying cultural model, and working towards a more satisfactory theory of culture and its role in non-linguistic tasks such as reasoning, problem solving, and evaluating the behavior of others. But the different questions which draw linguists and anthropologists should not obscure the common insight which brought together this particular group of linguists and anthropologists in the first place: that culturally shared knowledge is organized into prototypical event sequences enacted in simplified worlds. That much of such cultural knowledge is presumed by language use is as significant a realization to anthropologists as to linguists. For the latter, these cultural models promise the key to linguistic use, while for the former, linguistic usage provides the best available data for reconstruction of cultural models. (p. 48)

Quinn and Holland discuss the relation between what they term, following Lakoff (1983), *image-schemas* and *proposition schemas*. Basically, image-schemas are highly abstract visual representations, whereas proposition schemas are abstract language-based representations. They conclude that, although cultural models may be based solely on one or the other kind of representation, most cultural models contain both kinds of representation.

An important process in the construction of schemas of all types, including cultural models, is the use of analogy and metaphor. Lakoff and Johnson (1983), in pointing out the pervasiveness of metaphor in ordinary talk, ask why it is that certain things are used as metaphors and other things are metaphorized. They suggest that metaphors generally carry structure from physical-world models into nonphysical domains, perhaps because physical-world structures are well formed and experientially universal, although this is not always the case (Holland, 1982). Quinn and Holland (1987) point out that physical-world models, since they are things that can be seen and have spatial properties, allow the construction of image-schemas that can be transferred to nonphysical domains. Thus, for example, *marriage* can be conceptualized as a *manufactured object*, and hence more or less likely to *fall apart*. Even more specifically, there is the question of why one kind of physical object rather than another is used as the source of metaphor. Quinn and Holland say that

> the classes from which speakers select metaphors they consider to be appropriate are those which capture aspects of the simplified world, and the prototypical events unfolding in this world, constituted by the cultural model. Chosen metaphors not only highlight particular features of the cultural model; as we have discussed, they also point to entailments among these elements. Thus, one husband's metaphor of marriage as a "do-it yourself project" at once suggests for him the durable quality of something made in this manner – "it was very strong because it was made as we went along" – and implies, additionally, the craft and care and effort which must go into such a thing to make it well. Speakers often favor just such metaphors, which allow two or more related elements of the source domain to be mapped onto a corresponding set of related elements in the cultural model (Quinn 1985), and a comment upon that relation to be made. At the same time, other metaphors which fail to reflect, or even contradict, aspects of the cultural model in the target domain to which they are mapped, are likely to be rejected. Quinn (ibid.) gives an anecdotal example in which marriage was likened to an ice-cream cone which could be eaten up fast or licked slowly to make it last longer – a metaphor in such clear violation of our understanding of marriage as an enduring relationship that it bothered and offended members of the wedding at which it was voiced. (p. 61)

Several detailed analyses of cultural models are presented in Quinn and Holland's *Cultural Models in Language and Thought* (1987). Quinn, for example, summarizes her work on American marriage. Marriage, as a cultural model, is related to the social institution of marriage, which consists of a complex set of formal and informal behavioral norms concerning licenses, co-residence, sexual partnerships, etc. There are numerous studies of marriage as a social institution, but much less work on what marriage *is* to the people who are involved in this institution.

Quinn's data consist of over 350 hours of taped and transcribed interview material from 11 husband-and-wife couples in which each spouse was seen separately. Analysis involved culling hundreds of linguistic usages from the transcripts and sorting and interpreting these usages. These usages include metaphors for marriage (some of the common metaphors are MARRIAGE IS A MANUFACTURED PRODUCT, MARRIAGE IS AN ONGOING JOURNEY, MARRIAGE IS A DURABLE BOND BETWEEN TWO PEOPLE, A SPOUSE IS A FITTING PART, and MARRIAGE IS AN INVESTMENT), sequences of reasoning about marriage, and key words, such as *commitment, fulfillment,* and *love,* used to talk about marriage. Quinn finds four propositional schemas around which metaphors, key words, and reasoning appear to be organized; these are MARRIAGE IS ENDURING, MARRIAGE IS MUTUALLY BENEFICIAL, MARRIAGE IS DIFFICULT, and MARRIAGE IS EFFORTFUL.

Using these propositions and their specific metaphorical formulations, Quinn (1987) is able to show how particular sections of discourse can be analyzed to present in explicit form the reasoning of her informants about marriage. Her analysis uses the general method developed by Hutchins in his study of inference among Trobriand Islanders (1980). First, a transcribed section of discourse is presented in which an informant is making some point about something. At first glance, the informant's argument may appear rather scattered and even illogical. Next, the cultural model of the object about which the informant was talking is described, typically formulated in terms of a series of interrelated propositions. Then the informant's sentences are reformulated using the cultural model, and the missing material that the informant ignored because it was too obvious to state is filled in. Finally, the logical form of the argument, using some form of sentential or predicate calculus, is displayed. Often, this type of analysis can show that what seemed to be a rather scattered argument on the part of an informant was in fact a neatly and intricately reasoned piece of work.

One of the models Quinn finds embedded within the model of marriage is that of *need satisfaction.* In simple form, this cultural model is based on the notion that each person has certain needs (needs are wants that, in some sense, *must* to be satisfied if the person is to function properly), and that human relationships, which are seen as essentially dyadic, maintain themselves because each partner in the dyad satisfies enough of the needs of the other to keep the relationship going. Marriage relationships are expected to provide a large part of any human's social needs – that is, companionship, sex, affection, communication, intimacy, caring, nurturance, and so on. It is the problem of mutual need fulfillment that makes for the difficulty and needed effort of marriage, and for its failure. This model of need fulfillment is general in American culture; it is found in other cultural models such as models for friendship and family life, and in models of achievement and accomplishment. This model of need satisfaction is thought to be common sense, a truth beyond ordinary questioning. Of course, like most cultural models, it is not always true, but, like most cultural models, it seems so true that exceptions fail to invalidate the model.

Another cultural model that has been described in some detail is the American folk model of the mind (D'Andrade, 1987). Unlike marriage,

a. Perceptions
    i. simple state - *see, hear, smell, taste, feel*
    ii. achieved state - *spot, sight, notice*
    iii. simple process - *look, observe, watch, listen, touch*

b. Belief/Thought
    i. simple state - *believe, know, remember, expect, assume, doubt, imagine, recall*
    ii. achieved state - *understand, realize, infer, learn, discover, guess, conclude, forget*
    iii. simple process - *reason, think*
    iv. accomplished process - *figure out, plan*

c. Feelings/Emotion
    i. simple state - *love, like, fear, hate, blame, approve, pity, feel sad, feel happy*
    ii. achieved state - *forgive, surprise, scare*
    ii. simple process - *enjoy, be frightened, be angered, be bored, mourn, emote*

d. Desires/Wishes
    i. simple state - *want to, desire, like to, feel like, need*
    ii. achieved state - *choose, select*
    iii. simple process - *wish, hope for*

e. Intention
    i. simple state - *intend to, aim to, mean to, plan to*
    ii. achieved state - *decide to*

f. Resolution, Will
    i. simple state - *determined to*
    ii. achieved state - *resolved to*
    iii. simple process - *strive, make oneself, force oneself*

Figure 2.9.

or the restaurant script, this model is unrelated to any specific social institution, although it is widely used in ordinary talk. It is a *folk* model in that it contrasts with a *scientific* model, which is something experts know about, and which ordinary people don't. This model has six major elements (see Figure 2.9).

The distinction between states and processes is a basic image-schema difference. A state is the condition of some entity, a uniform condition that exists through time. In general, when talking about the mind as an entity, the specific metaphor used is the *container* metaphor – a person is said to be "full of" *knowledge, fear, desire, resolve*. The mind as an entity does not change whether the person is sleeping or awake – Einstein would still know the theory of relativity whether or not he was thinking about it. But only if Einstein's mind was doing something could we say that he was *figuring out* a unified theory, or *worrying about* nuclear war, and so on. That is, the mind is alternately conceived of as a set of processes that occur repetitively, like the action of walking. Thus all the process verbs can be put in an -ing form; one can say "I am *looking/thinking/enjoying/hoping for/striving*," but outside of idiomatic use we do not say "I am *hearing/believing/loving*."

Both the state and process occur in time, but a process is marked by the repetition of some action and thus has continuous tenses. In the model of the mind, states are linked to process. Typically, someone is in a particular state because of the occurrence of some process. Thus, for example, John *hears* Bill because he is *listening* to Bill; Sally *believes* Lisa is her friend because she went through the process of *assessing* her relationship with Lisa and *concluded* she was a real friend; and Roger has been *frightening* his cousin, which is why his cousin *fears* him.

There is another relevant time distinction in English verbs based on the notion that certain processes and states are defined by a climax or terminal point that marks the end of the state or processes. When such a terminal point defines a state, it is called an *achievement,* and when it defines a process it is called an *accomplishment.* For both achievements and accomplishments, we can ask "How long did it take to....?" but not for simple states or processes. We do not ask "How long did it take you to *think* that?" but we do ask "How long did it take you to *realize* that?" For simple states and processes, events are treated as if they were homogeneous across the entire period through which it occurs, but for achievements and accomplishment, the event is defined by its terminal point. Thus, even if one *thinks* for only an instant, one has *been thinking,* but, no matter how long one has been at it, one does not *realize* something until the exact instant the light dawns (Vendler, 1967).

In the model of the mind, these six major states/processes are linked together in a complex causal chain: Because of what one *perceives,* one *believes* certain things to be true; because of what one *believes* to have happened, one has certain *feelings* or *emotions*; because of what one *feels,* one has certain *wishes*; because of what one *wishes,* one has certain *intentions*; and certain second-order *intentions* to keep to one's *intentions* constitute *resolve.* This is the major causative order, but a reverse order for some of the elements is also thought to happen, although it is considered to be inappropriate. Thus, strong *feelings* can influence what one *thinks* (but it shouldn't), and if one *thinks* certain things are true, it can influence what one *perceives* (but it shouldn't).

Another important type of relation within the model of the mind is the way in which the things that one *intends* to do, or that one *wants,* are created by one's own *thoughts.* One can only *intend to* do something or *want to* do something that one can *think* of doing, and perhaps one is most likely to *want to* do and *intend to* do what one *thinks of* most often – *evil he who evil thinks.* The situation with respect to emotions is complex, since in the folk model sometimes the object that arouses the feeling is purely an object of thought – for example, "John is afraid of nuclear winter" – while sometimes it is an actual object – for example,

"Tom thinks he is afraid of flying, but actually he is afraid of traveling away from home."

There are a number of other complex relationships among these elements (see D'Andrade, 1986). One of these concerns the experiential *self* and the things that can affect it. Clearly, things outside the body can affect the self – we say "The rock hit me." However, things inside the body, and even inside the mind can affect the experiential self – we say "The idea struck me," placing the idea outside the self that experienced the idea. We can even say "The feeling struck me" or "The desire to have a cigarette struck me." That is, almost all the elements of mind can be placed metaphorically outside the self. There is one exception here; *intentions* cannot be placed outside the self. We do not say "The intention struck me." Thus the very core of the self is its *intentions*, from which it cannot be separated.

The model of the mind sketched out here and more elaborately described in D'Andrade (1986) was developed from intuition and from the work of various linguistic philosophers such as Anscombe, Vendler, and Searle. In an attempt to validate this model, interviews were carried out with five college and high school students who had never had courses in psychology. In these interviews the informants were systematically queried about each of the major propositions of the model. None of the interview material contradicted the model, although some of the responses made by informants could not be derived from the model.

When this Western cultural model was compared with the model of the mind described by Lutz (1985) for the people of Ifaluk, a small Micronesian atoll, it was found that both models have the same overall framework. *Thoughts, feelings,* and *desires* are distinguished. Feelings are considered a natural response to experience, not under self-control, and are thought to have the power to move the person to action. The emotions are distinguished from physical sensations. Understanding is considered necessary for appropriate behavior; without the ability to understand, the person is thought to go out of control. The major difference seems to be that on Ifaluk there is no clear distinction between desire and intention, and there is a greater fusion of the categories of thought and feeling. The emotion terms are defined slightly differently on Ifaluk, and the interpersonal role of emotion is more distinctly conceptualized than in the West, as is the role of emotion in causing illness and the therapeutic role of catharsis.

Another interesting question has to do with the way in which children learn a model of the mind. Since mental events are private, the teacher cannot point directly to the learner's mental machinery and say "What you just experienced is a *thought*, not a *feeling*," or "That is *anger*, not *fear*, which you just experienced." The question is, how, even if everyone's private experience is highly similar, are the words of others matched to the learner's private experience? It appears that the model can be learned because it is not *just* a model of private experience. The model contains systematic links of public events. Thus thinking is like speech, and speech is public. Feelings are defined in part by the public events that are likely to elicit them, and by the actions we are likely to take because of them. Furthermore, human beings have an innate communication system for the emotions, signaled by patterns of facial expression (Ekman, 1971). To understand what wishes and desires are, we have the speech act, which gives them public expression; requests and commands. Wanting is feeling that makes one say "Gimme, gimme." Intentions are related to the speech acts that are based on making commitments; a promise is the public statement of an intention with the assertion that one has the ability to bring about the intention. The tight connection pointed out by Vendler (1972) between verbs for speech acts and verbs for internal states is not fortuitous; speech acts are one of the major classes of public events used as identifying marks of internal states and processes.

The cultural models presented so far have been purely conceptual in nature, but cultural models may also be *physically realized*. Frake (1985) has described the nature and operation of the medieval *compass rose*, the 32-point compass found printed on many maps. Historical research shows that this compass was used in calculating tides, not just in naming directional points.

The operation of the compass rose depends on the knowledge that high and low tides are related to the position of the moon in the sky. Tide times may vary considerably from place to place along any particular sea coast, but the relation between the position of the moon and the high tide for any particular place along the coast will remain constant. Thus, at La Jolla Shores, along the southern coast of California, high tide occurs at a little less than two hours before the moon crosses the meridian (lunar noon) or two hours before the moon crosses the opposite meridian on the other side of the earth (lunar midnight), and low tide occurs approximately four hours after lunar noon or lunar midnight. A sailor or surfer finds it helpful to know when the moon will be at the meridian. However, during the day, and often much of the night, one cannot see the moon.

The compass rose is used to calculate the time of high and low tides from knowledge of the time of the last full moon and the time of high tide relative to the moon's position for specific places along some coast. This is done by treating the compass rose like a clock, with due south as noon, west as 6 p.m., north as midnight, and east as 6 a.m. Each of the 32 points divides the day into 45-minute intervals. Just like sun time, lunar time can also be represented as a compass bearing, with lunar noon as south, moonset as west, lunar midnight as north, and moonrise as east. Medieval sailing directions gave the tide for any given coastal place by giving the lunar time at which there would be high tide – for La Jolla Shores this would be approximately southeast by south – that is, about 9:45 a.m. moon time.

The solar time of the high tide can be calculated from the date of the last full moon by using the compass rose as a counting device. Each day the tides rise and fall approximately 48 minutes later than they did the day before – close to the 45-minute intervals of the compass rose. This means that 5 days after the full moon the high tide at La Jolla Shores would be 5 points past southeast by south, which is south/southwest, corresponding to approximately 1:30 p.m. Of course, to use the compass rose, one must learn the times of day for each of the 32 points. The compass rose is a cultural model that organizes both time and direction and has the capacity to coordinate solar time with lunar time so that tide times can be estimated.

The problem of isolating the basic cognitive operations that are involved in the use of physically realized models has been addressed in a recent paper by Hutchins (n.d.). Even an extremely simple physical device such as the *checklist* can be seen to be an example of a *mediating structure*. In using a checklist, the user does not coordinate his or her behavior directly with the task environment, but rather coordinates with a mediating object that has a structure that is like the task environment in some important way. Suppose one has to perform a complete ordered sequence of actions to do something (say, start an airplane), and one has a printed checklist of these actions.

For the checklist to work, the printed list of actions must correspond to the user's descriptions of the actions that must be taken to actually start the plane. The user must invoke a sequential execution strategy to determine which step is the next step, and possibly determine an index to the next step so that it can be remembered. One simple way to do this is to start reading at the top of the list, and to place a mark next to the item being performed. The user must then read and understand the printed instructions at some level and then construct a representation of the world from what was read that maps onto the relevant task world. To read "engage the clutch" is not helpful if one does not know what in the environment corresponds to the "clutch." Then the user must coordinate his or her actions with this representation and mapping into the task environment. Thus what might at first look like a simple device in fact turns out to be a complex of mediations – that is, of coordinations between structures.

Hutchins points out that the internalization and automatization of a checklist involves the gradual transfer of control from different coordinating structures. First one learns the list, and in doing the task, one remembers an instruction, then creates a representation of the instruction, then coordinates this representation with the task environment, then coordinates an action with this representation and the task environment. After the task has been even more thoroughly learned, one recalls one task representation after another rather than remembering verbal instructions. Finally, when the checklist is fully automated, one directly recalls the actions to be taken and their associated environmental changes. At that point the mediating structure has become unconscious and all that one is aware of is the task environment and the need to do one thing after another. A good example of this kind of learning has been described by Stigler, Chalip, and Miller (1986) for abacus training. They found that children who had learned the abacus had a different representation of numerical calculations based on a "mental abacus" that enabled them to manipulate numbers with remarkable speed.

For Hutchins (n.d.), all cultural models, whether embodied in artifacts or as image and propositional schemas, are mediating structures:

> In this view, what we learn and what we know, and what our culture knows for us in the form of artifacts and social organizations are these hunks of mediating structure. Thinking consists of bringing these structures into coordination with each other such that they can shape (and be shaped by) each other. The thinker in this world is a special medium that provides coordination among many structured media, some internal, some external, some embodied in artifacts, some in ideas, and some in social relationships. (pp. 13–14).

19. *Cultural models, constructed out of complex cognitive schemas, are found in a great range of domains, including events, institutions, and physical and mental objects. Some of these cultural models have special computational properties, serving as inferential and orientational devices of considerable complexity.*

Cultural idea systems

Cultural models are not the only form in which cultural knowledge is packaged. There is a long tradition of investigation of cultural world views, or *cultural idea systems* in anthropology. These idea systems appear to be made up of interrelated and intersubjectively shared propositional schemas that form a coherent (if not always perfectly consistent) perspective or ideology about how the world is. There are a large number of excellent ethnographic studies of cultural idea systems, such as Fortes's *Oedipus and Job in West African Religion* (1983), which use standard ethnographic techniques of investigation. The drawback of such studies is that they fail to make clear exactly what individual natives really believe, since these studies focus primarily on collective representations of various kinds, such as myth and ritual.

One of the contributions of cognitive anthropology has been to develop methods of research – sometimes derived from methods already used in psychology – for investigating the beliefs of individual natives. Shweder and Bourne (1984), for example, in their study of the cultural conceptions of the self in India (Orissa) and the United States, constructed a task in which informants were asked to describe a close acquaintance ("How would you describe so-and-so's personality"). The resulting descriptions were then broken into constituent subject-predicate-object phrases (a total of 3,451 phrases were coded). A coding system was developed to determine if the phrase referred primarily to an *abstract trait* ("she is stubborn"), an *action* ("she uses dirty language"), or an *emotive-evaluative term* ("he is a good man"). Contextual qualifications were also coded: *personal reference* ("he gets angry with his father"), *qualification* ("he gets irritated if provoked"), and *no qualification* ("he is irritable").

The results show strong patterned differences in which Oriyas are more likely to use contextual qualifications whereas Americans are more likely to use no qualifications at all. When Americans do use qualifications, they are most likely to use self-referential qualifiers ("she is beginning to accept herself") and inferential qualifiers ("judging from what others say, he is very reserved"). Oriyas are more likely to describe someone by telling you what the person does ("he shouts curses at his neighbors"), whereas Americans are more likely to use traits ("he is friendly").

Since these results could be caused by differences in level of schooling, Shweder and Bourne checked them against individual years of education, but found that the differences could not be accounted for by this variable. Educated Oriyas were as context dependent in their descriptions of the person as illiterate Oriyas. Shweder and Bourne suggest that these results are due not to differences in the development of cognitive skills, but to differences in the metaphorlike idea systems of these two cultures. Indian culture contains a highly developed holistic idea system that makes extensive use of the metaphor of the body for society, whereas American culture contains a highly developed individualistic idea system that treats the person as distinct from his or her social roles and group affiliations. Thus the use of context and action on the part of Indians to describe others is not due to some failure on their part to attain abstract constructs of the person, but to a different system of ideas about how the person is embedded in a social matrix.

In a study of American and Oriya moral conceptions, Shweder, Mahapatra, and Miller (1987) examined 39 cultural practices involving kinship avoidances, forms of address between inferiors and superiors, sleeping arrangements, incest avoidance, dietary practices, forms of dress, marriage and remarriage, personal possessions and private property, begging, nepotism, monogamy, wife beating, physical punishment for children, family division of labor, inheritance of property, and so on. One aim of the study was to determine the degree to which each of these practices is conceived of as a *moral* versus *conventional* versus *personal* matter. A second aim was to investigate the general character of American and Indian moral codes. A third goal was to investigate the course of development over the life cycle of moral ideas in each culture.

The American sample consisted of 180 children and 60 adults from Hyde Park; the children were divided into three age ranges (5–7, 8–10, 11–13). The Indian sample consisted of two subsamples, Brahmans and Untouchables from Bhubaneswar, Orissa. The Brahman subsample had the same size, age, and gender distribution as the American sample. The Untouchable sample included 30 male and 30 female informants in the 8–10 age range and 30 male and 30 female adults. The informants were examined individually using a short standard set of interview questions and probes designed to assess the moral/conventional/personal status of the obligations pertinent to the case. Questions were asked about each of the 39 practices, and informants were instructed to rank the "seriousness" of the perceived breach or transgression in each case. Standard back-translation procedures were used to ensure translation equivalences for all cases.

The results are somewhat surprising. First, there is no correlation between the Indian and the American rankings of the "seriousness" of the transgression involved in each case. One cannot predict from knowing that a particular practice is regarded as a serious moral matter in one culture anything about how seriously the same issue will be considered in the other. Second, both Americans and Indians consider *most* issues to be matters of objective moral law rather than matters of convention. Third, *only* Americans use the notion that some practices are conventional. Fourth, the children in each culture are most like the adults from that culture, and *not* like the children in the other culture. Fifth, American children are less likely to use the notion of convention than American adults. Sixth, there is more consensus on the moral character of the various practices among the adults in each culture than among the children. Seventh, as Americans get older they are more likely to engage in relativistic moral reasoning and less likely to engage in universal moral reasoning, whereas the reverse in true for Indians.

These findings provide no indication of universal age trends – contrary to the predictions from Kohlberg's theory of moral development (Kohlberg, 1981) or Turiel's theory that certain issues are inherently moral in all cultures (Turiel, 1979). Although the particular practices are understood differently with respect to moral issues by the different cultures, the *justifications* for the moral judgments are much the same in both cultures. According to Shweder et al. (1985),

> Under some description, at some abstract level, justice, harm and protection of the vulnerable might qualify as "deep" universals of all moral codes. The rub, and the irony, is that if one merely focuses upon the abstract principles underlying a judgment about a particular case, then the principles so abstracted do not make it possible to predict informants' judgments about particular cases. . . . If we are to understand our informants' moral judgements about particular cases we are going to have to understand the culture specific aspects of their moral codes, and we are going to have to understand the way those culture-specific aspects interact with the more universal aspects to produce a moral judgment. (p. 97)

One can extrapolate from the work of Shweder and his associates on morality and conceptions of the person to idea systems in general:

20. *Cultural idea systems – about morality, aesthetics, science, human nature, and so on – typically have both universal and culturally specific*

components. There is little evidence that cultures can be characterized as more or less advanced according to stages of cognitive development, or even that children understand the universal components of these systems more easily than the culturally specific components.

Inference and cultural models

Another important area of research in the relation between culture and cognition is the study of inference. A classic problem in this area is the so-called Wason problem (Wason, 1969). One presentation of the problem is as follows:

> All labels made at Pica's Custom Label Factory have either the letter A or the letter E printed on the front of the label, and have either the number 2 or the number 3 printed on the back side. The machine never makes a mistake about this – it always puts the letter A or E on the front, and the number 2 or 3 on the back.
>
> As part of your job as a label checker at Pica's, you have the task of making sure that *if a label has an E printed on the front, it has a 2 printed on the back side.* You have to check this, because sometimes the machine makes a mistake and breaks this rule.
>
> Which of the labels would you have to turn over to make sure that the label had been printed following the rule? Mark an X under the labels you would have to turn over.

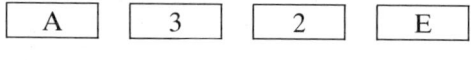

The results for this problem are universally poor; typically, 85% or more of the subjects in the experiment fail to get the correct answer. The correct answer is that one should turn over the label with an E on it and the label with a 3 on it. The modal incorrect answer is that one should turn over the label with an E on it and the label with a 2 on it.

There have been a great number of studies about why people get this problem wrong. Subjects do not get the problem wrong if told "No label should have both an E and a 3 on it," which is logically equivalent to the first rule. Interestingly, it is also hard to convince subjects that they have made a mistake – they often try to argue that they are following the rule, whatever combination they have chosen. However, these arguments are never coherent (except for the very few who interpret the rule as an "if and only if" relation between E and 2). One can demonstrate that one should turn over the label with the 3 on it by making up some real labels, and showing subjects that a misprinted label will have a 3 on its back side, therefore if the 3 is showing, it should be turned over to check its correctness.

Johnson-Laird, Legrenzi, and Legrenzi (1972) discovered an interesting thing about this problem; that is, if the problem is translated into a "realistic" example, subjects will get it right. Here is realistic form that I have found easy for American college students:

As part of your job as an assistant at Sears, you have the task of checking sales receipts to make sure that any sale of $30.00 or more has been approved by the section manager. The amount of the sale is written on the front of the form, while the section manager's approval is initialed on the back of the form.

Which of the forms would you have to turn over to make sure that the sales clerk had been following the rule? Mark an X under the forms you would have to turn over.

1 chair $77	approved __	1 lamp $12	approved __

About 70% of American college subjects get the correct answer on the realistic form of the test. A number of realistic forms have been developed, such as the form that uses rules about the drinking age (Cox & Griggs, 1982). It is interesting that subjects who have just gotten the right answer on the realistic form of the test still get the wrong answer on the letter-number form of the test.

One explanation for these results is that the subjects are unfamiliar with the problem and therefore have some difficulty in understanding it, most probably because their misunderstand the logical connective *if-then*. However, subjects understand the rule well enough, since 86% could correctly translate it for the label problem into "No label should have an E on the front and a 3 on the back." However, only 36% could translate the *if-then* for the label problem into the contrapositive: "Every label that has a 3 on the back should have an A on the front." (D'Andrade, in press-b). Note that this is much like the situation in the Wason problem in which the subject has to decide whether or not to turn over the label with the 3 on the back. In fact, those who got the label problem right were significantly more likely to get the contrapositive right; a phi correlation of .41 was found between a correct answer for the contrapositive label rule question and giving the correct answer for the label version of the Wason problem.

It is generally recognized that one's ability to solve the Wason problem is strongly affected by the kind of content that is used to instantiate the problem. There is much less general agreement on what it is about arbitrary content that makes the Wason problem hard. The hypothesis here is that the difficulty with the Wason problem is an example of a more general problem, the difficulty of the contrapositive. The simplest example of a logical problem with the contrapositive is modus tollens which has the form (1) *if p then q*, (2) *not q*, (3) *therefore not p*. To test the hypothesis that subjects would have difficulty with the contrapositive, a simple questionnaire containing a variety of modus tollens problems was administered to college students. Following is an example of a typical modus tollens with arbitrary content:

GIVEN: If Roger is a musician, then Roger is a Bavarian.

SUPPOSE: Roger is not a Bavarian.
THEN: a. It must be the case that Roger is a musician.
     b. Maybe Roger is a musician, maybe he isn't.
     c. It must be the case that Roger is not a musician.

No widely shared cultural schema links someone's being a musician with someone's being a Bavarian, which leaves the subject who tries to solve this problem more dependent on logical form alone. Only 53% of a sample of undergraduates gave the correct answer to this problem (D'Andrade, in press-b).

Subjects do much better when the problem contains a well-formed cultural schema linking p and q, as in the following problem:

GIVEN: If this rock is a garnet, then it is a semiprecious stone.
SUPPOSE: This rock is not a semiprecious stone.
THEN: a. It must be the case that this rock is a garnet.
     b. Maybe this rock is a garnet and maybe it isn't.
     c. It must be the case that this rock is not a garnet.

In this instance, 96% of the undergraduate sample gave the correct answer. For this problem there is a well-shared cultural schema linking something being a garnet and something being semiprecious – that is, garnets are semiprecious stones. Here are some other examples of modus tollens problems with well-formed schematic links between p and q that have been tested on UCSD undergraduates:

If Tom was born is San Diego, then Tom is a native Californian. (86% correct)
If Janet lives in San Cristobal, then Janet lives in Mexico. (80% correct)
If Bill cut himself, then Bill would be bleeding. (77% correct)
If it is raining, then the roof is wet. (68% correct)
If John bought a present, then John spent some money. (65% correct)

The following examples illustrate problems that lack well-formed schematic linkages between p and q and that subjects had more difficulty solving:

If Janet went to town, then Janet brought home some bread. (57% correct)
If Roger drank Pepsi, then Tom sat down. (53% correct)
If James is a watchman, then James likes candy. (51% correct)
If D is true, then E is true. (E is false). (45% correct)
If Harold is a politician, then Harold is from New York. (40% correct)
If J is true, then K is true (not K is true). (33% correct)

Samples sizes for these results range from 30 to 50.

It is not the case that people always have difficulty reasoning with arbitrary content. People do seem to be able to reason correctly with certain *simple* logical forms irrespective of content. Perhaps the simplest of all logical forms is modus ponens: (1) *if p then q*, (2) *p*, (3) *therefore q*, as in the following modus ponens problem:

GIVEN: If James is a watchman, then James likes candy.

SUPPOSE: James is a watchman.

THEN: a. It must be the case that James likes candy.
      b. Maybe James likes candy, maybe he doesn't.
      c. It must be the case that James does not like candy.

Ninety-six percent of an undergraduate sample gave the correct answer. In general, people seem to be able to solve modus ponens problems no matter how bizarre the content. In solving modus ponens problems, people act like true logicians for whom only form counts. Other logical forms besides modus ponens that people seem to be able to use effectively no matter what the content are

Not not *p*. Therefore *p*.
P or *q*. Not *p*. Therefore *q*.

These findings raise the question, "How do people reason when not using logical forms?" Although a long way from a full answer, work on reasoning carried out in natural settings has given some clues. An examination of legal disputes among the Trobriand Islanders (Hutchins, 1980) indicates that connectives such as *and, if-then, not, or*, and so on, are apparently culturally universal and of central importance in reasoning. The conceptual materials that these universal connectives organize into larger structures are typically made up of parts of cultural models. Furthermore, these connectives are not understood in terms of truth table relations, but rather in terms of various kinds of temporal and causal contingencies (D'Andrade, in press-b; Johnson-Laird, 1983).

21. *In reasoning, people use logical form only for the simplest inferences. Most commonly, people use well-learned cognitive models in reasoning, mentally manipulating these models to compute what could or could not happen, or what is likely or unlikely to happen. When these models are well learned, as is usually the case with cultural models, people can do quite complex manipulations, such as the kind of manipulation that is abstractly described as modus tollens. When the models are not so well learned or well structured, as is usually the case for the arbitrary situations given in logic problems, people can do only the simplest manipulations without error.*

The representations that are mentally manipulated in reasoning are often surprisingly concrete and particular. For example, in a study of the missionaries and cannibals puzzle, Hutchins and Levin (1979) found that subjects were less likely to detect that they had attempted illegal moves when they imagined events taking place on the river bank away from them compared with imagined events on their side of the river (the subject's point of view with respect to the river was determined by the subject's use of deixis in verbal protocols – for example, "they go to the other side, then I bring them back here"). It is as if events that are imagined to occur on the subject's side of the river are closer and hence easier to see than events that are imagined to occur on the other side of the river. Similarly, it is said that chess players prefer to play with familiar-shaped chess sets, and that they complain if they have to use pieces of unusual shapes because they say such pieces are harder to manipulate mentally. Preferred mental models appear to be those that are most familiar, immediate, and best understood.

One major effect of this limitation in formal reasoning is to make complex reasoning appear context bound. That is, somebody may be able do a certain problem in one domain, but not be able to do a problem with the same logical or mathematical form in a different domain. However, if the analysis given here is correct, the reason for the differential performance has nothing to do with context per se. One can do some mental manipulation of a well-formed schema in one domain that one cannot do in another domain simply because one lacks a well-formed schema of the relations within that domain.

This means that one cannot know from any test of reasoning ability how well someone is likely to be able to reason about some particular topic, because from a test one does not know how well formed that person's schemas are about that topic. This also means that the ability to reason will be strongly influenced by culture, since many of any person's schemas come from their culture – they are cultural models. To the extent that a culture has good cultural models (*good* in the sense that the representation captures the real world contingencies of interest), one will be able to reason well about the objects and events represented within these models.

Schemas and motivation

Cognition, if sealed off from everything else in the world, would not be very interesting. It is in its relation to action that cognition is of interest to most social scientists. The main relation between cognition and behavior that has been assumed in cognitive anthropology is a competence relation – if you don't have a well-formed cognitive representation of something, you can't identify it, remember it, or make inferences about it. But, if you do have a well-formed representation of that something, then identification, memory, inference, and actions dependent on such processes are possible. According to this view, cognitive schemas and other forms of knowledge representation give one the competence to do certain things – to use kin terms, solve a hard puzzle, be appropriately deferent to a chief, choose the right market, label manioc, go ocean fishing, or predict the time of high tide.

This competence model is useful and powerful. But there is the possibility that cognition is also related to behavior in another even more immediate and direct way. The idea is that some cognitive schemas – and hence some culturally formed schemas or cultural models – have motivational properties.

During the 1940s and 1950s motivation was a central concept in psychology and the social sciences. To understand someone's behavior, one had to understand what moved that person – that is, what motives that person had. Although theorists differed on the details, the common notion was that motives acted like a strong stimulus that pushed toward action and was rewarding if relieved, painful if not.

A major problem in the research on motivation, however, has been that it is difficult to determine which motives are "driving" which behaviors at any one time. Second, no consensus has developed on how many kinds of drives there are. Every motivation theorist has presented a different list of drives. Third, drives are difficult to measure. Fantasy measures, such as the TAT, are generally not too reliable and have only moderate correlations to most outcome measures. Finally, the great situational variance that exists among humans has made predictions to any given situation on the basis of motivation uncertain. A very "dependent" child, for example, as measured by whatever motivational measure, might prove to be quite independent in certain situations (say, in school settings) but very dependent in others (say, at home). Mischel's book, *Personality and Assessment*, published in 1968, summarized these problems and thus marked the end of an era of a certain type of motivational research.

However, the question of how people categorize things, make decisions, and infer things is not the question that the early motivational theorists were trying to answer. For example, some students work hard and some don't. Some colleagues like to get involved in collaborative research and some don't, some publish up a storm and others don't. In some places people put much time and effort into religious endeavors, and in some places religion is a minimal concern. These differences cannot be explained by standard cognitive analyses. The problems that motivational theorists have tried to solve have not gone away.

Recent work in cognitive anthropology and cognitive psychology indicates that there is a relatively direct relation between cognitive schemas and action and that it may account for a significant part of the phenomena that the motivational theorists have been studying (Mandler, 1984). The basic idea is that some cognitive schemas are connected to behavior through the activation of goals.

There appear to be large differences among schemas in the degree to which they activate goals *autonomously*. Some schemas have only weak connections to goals, so that goals are triggered only if other schemas also activate these same goals. The schema for dirt, for example, is typically linked to goals concerning cleaning, but the cleaning goal will normally be activated only if the thing that is dirty is one's own responsibility, it is an appropriate time for cleaning, one has a way to dispose of the dirt, and so on. However, some schemas are more autonomous and less dependent on contextually related schemas for the activation of their goals. Physical danger would be a simple example of such a schema – given the interpretation that one is in real physical danger, the goal of removing oneself from the danger tends to be strongly activated regardless of other concurrent interpretations.

The hierarchical organization of schemas plays an important part in human motivation. Schemas are hierarchical in the sense that interpretations created by one schema are passed on to higher-level schemas in order to make more general interpretations. It seems reasonable to assume that it is the topmost level of interpretation that is typically linked to the actions by which the organism operates in its environment. This is, of course, not a hard and fast expectation – sometimes one makes a general interpretation just to understand what is going on, as in watching a play and trying to understand why one character is hiding something, or pursuing some issue. However, it seems reasonable to expect that a person's most general interpretation of what is going on will be strongly attached to important goals, since top-level schemas are typically used to guide action at the most general effective level that the organism has learned.

In summary, the argument here goes as follows:

22. *To understand people, one needs to understand what leads them to act as they do; to understand what leads them to act as they do, one needs to know their goals; to understand their goals, one must understand the overall interpretive system they have that triggers these goals; and to understand their interpretive system – their schemas – one must understand something about the hierarchical relations among these schemas. When a schema is frequently activated (by whatever drives), functions at a high level of interpretation, and triggers in a relatively context-free way particular goals, we can say such a schema has motivational force.*

This account does not replace the drive model. Physiological or psychological drives, in this account, are special sources of activation that energize particular schemas. A complete analysis of motivation would determine not only particular schemas and goals, but also the specific drives that activate these schemas. The network of connections between goals and drives, however, is without doubt extremely complex and can rarely be empirically determined. Perhaps it is this complexity and indeterminacy in the linkage of drive to goal that led Freud to group all the drives together into one motivational source, the libido. The complexity of human drive–goal linkages would seem to be the product of a general evolutionary process in which, as intelligence increases, the connections between instinct and action become more complex, indirect, and modifiable.

Treating motives as activated schemas with embedded goals results is quite different from treating motives as vectors. Basically, a vector is something that has a direction (to get food, to help others, to make money) and an amount – a scale to measure the strength of a drive as indicated by frequency, persistence, emotionality, or fantasy. One might characterize someone with the vector model of motivation by saying that he is very hostile. This is quite different from saying that someone has a top-level schema in which this individual sees himself surrounded by enemies who wish to humiliate him, and whom he must attack to keep himself from being destroyed. And to say something about the nature of the situations that most strongly activate this interpretation, the characteristic feelings that go along with this interpretation, and the more specific goals that are activated whenever this interpretation is regnant presents a picture of a kind of organized complexity that outlines the way in which various goals are organized and activated. One of the important advantages of treating motivation as drive-activated schemas with embedded goals is that such an account not only connects cognition to behavior – it also shows how behavior may be organized through schemas.

A question that has received relatively little attention is how it is that some people learn – come to possess (or be possessed by) – *particular* goal-embedded schemas that organize their behavior. Many of the *general* schemas learned by individuals are culturally learned, shared, and transmitted. Achievement, love, security, recognition, freedom – all these terms refer to intersubjectively shared schemas, or collections of schemas – cultural models – through which events are interpreted and responded to. We assume that these cultural schemas, when internalized, are used extensively to interpret the world and organize sets of goals that deal with the world.

This formulation also rests on the assumption that many general human motives are culturally shaped. Things like achievement, acquisition, affiliation, power, and so on are, from an anthropological point of view, basically cultural models. Not only is what counts as achievement, acquisition, affiliation, and power dependent on the culture, but the very recognition that such things exist is dependent on the culture. With the increasing sophistication in the methods and techniques used to identify and analyze schemas, anthropologists and other social scientists may soon be able to determine the motivational force of cultural models, and thereby link cultural analyses to predictions about action.

Individual variability

One of the persistent problems in cognitive anthropology is individual variability. Cognitive anthropology has emphasized the role of the psychological functioning of the individual as a carrier of culture. The problem is that when human groups are systematically surveyed, there is considerable disagreement about most items (Roberts, 1964).

One way to avoid this problem is to treat the most frequently held items – the *modal* items – as if they were *the* culture of the group. The disadvantage of this approach is that it takes a purely statistical characteristic and treats it as if it had some kind of "reality." A descriptive procedure should do more than just make it easy to say what is in the culture and what is not. It has been argued that characterizing a culture by its modal items is not a bad thing to do because the degree of sharing across items shows an almost bimodal pattern, in which most items are either highly shared or are unique (D'Andrade, in press-a).

But the assurance that the modal items are held by large percentages of the population still does not give any special status to the description – it simply says that this strategy catches a lot of what is there. It would be much more satisfying theoretically if there were something about the more highly shared items that indicates that they have some special kinds of psychological or social *reality* – something that marked off these items from the less highly shared items besides frequency. Therefore some attention should be given to the recent work by Boster, Romney, Weller, and others on intracultural variation, which demonstrates that selection of modal items is associated with a special set of social and psychological characteristics (Boster, 1985). These characteristics are, first,

23a. *Reliability: Persons who are more likely to give modal responses on a task are more likely to be reliable, that is, to give the same responses if the task is presented at a later time.*

For example, Boster (1985) found that Aguaruna Jivaro informants who tended to use the modal names for a set of manioc plants were much more likely to be consistent when asked to name these same plants on a second occasion. The agreement measure was computed by counting the number of plants (out of a total of 90) on which each informant agreed with the majority name for the plant. The reliability measure was computed for each informant by counting the number of plants given the same name on both occasions. Boster found that the correlation between reliability and agreement across six informants was .92.

23b. *Consistency: Persons who are more likely to give modal responses on some task are more likely to give responses that are consistent with each other.*

For example, Weller (1984) found that rural Mexican women who gave the majority response (when there are only two alternatives, the modal response will also be the majority response) about which of a pair of diseases was the hotter, or more severe, or more contagious, were more likely to be consistent in their choices as measured by the likelihood that they would not fall into the "error" of saying that disease A is hotter than B, and that B is hotter than C, but that A is not hotter than C. Agreement with the majority was measured by computing the number of pairs of diseases for which the informant agreed with the majority choice. Consistency was measured by the number of triples of disease terms for each informant that did not show the "intransitivity error" described earlier. The correlations between consistency and agreement was .57 for contagion, .21 for severity, but only .07 for the hot–cold dimension.

23c. *Normality: Persons who are more likely to give modal responses on a task are more likely to have had "normal" experiences with respect to the material symbolized by the task.*

For example, Weller, Romney, and Orr (in press) found Orange County high school students who agreed most with the majority response about the truth or falsity of 135 statements about parental sanctions for rule breaking were less likely to have been physically abused by their parents as measured by their response to a question about parental use of physical punishment. It is interesting that the abused children did not have a special pattern of their own – they merely appear to be less knowledgeable about these cultural norms.

23d. *Education, intelligence, and experience: Persons who are more likely to give modal responses on a task are more likely to be better educated with respect to that task and judged more intelligent with respect to their ability in that task domain, and tend to have more experience in that task domain.*

Weller (1984), in her Mexican study of disease characterisitics, found that literate and educated women were most likely to give modal responses on the contagion and hot–cold dimensions, whereas older women were more likely to give modal responses on the severity and age dimensions. Further evidence for the association of education and intelligence with modal responses can be found in data from word association tests (D'Andrade, 1987). In a study by Moran, Mefferd and Kimble (1964) a standard word list of 125 words was given to subjects on four successive days. After being tested on each set of 25 words, subjects were retested on the same sets of words but were instructed to give the same responses that they had given the first time. From the word association data, Moran et al. constructed a measure of modality they called *commonality*. Commonality was computed by giving a value for each response corresponding to the percentage of times that response was given by the total sample of subjects. Responses were also coded for *reliability* (the number of times the subject gave exactly the same associations to the same stimulus word), *speed* (reaction time), being *blank* (failing to give any response within 20 seconds), and being *distant* (giving a response that has no apparent semantic connection to the stimulus word). The number of years of *education* of each subject, and the subjects' scores on the vocabulary part of the Wexler–Bellvue IQ test were also obtained. Pearson correlations of all variables across subjects were computed. It was found that those who most frequently chose the modal response (measured here by "commonality") had higher IQs ($r = .42$), were somewhat better educated ($r = .29$), were more reliable ($r = .58$), gave their responses faster ($r = .45$), were less likely to give semantically unrelated responses ($r = -.66$), and were less likely to fail to give any response at all ($r = -.33$).

The kind of intelligence postulated here as being associated with modal or majority responses on some task is not *general* intelligence (whatever that may be), but rather a specific ability to do well with the kinds of materials that are involved in the task. The ability to choose good definitions is clearly related to word association tasks, in that both involve the cognitive manipulation of semantic relations. It may seem strange that the "smart" people were more likely to give the "common" response in word association tests. The average respondent gave only 10% common responses across all stimulus words (with the "smart" people tending to give a few percentage points more than this), which still leaves plenty of opportunity for "creative" responses. If Moran et al. had measured the number of different words used by each subject they would likely have found that the subjects with higher IQs used both more common associations *and* a greater number of different word types.

The greater degree of reliability, consistency, normality, education, intelligence, and experience of those who are more likely to give modal or majority responses can only be expected when the conditions that Romney, Weller, and Batchelder (1986) stipulate for a *consensus model* are in effect. For the consensus model to apply, there must first be only one major factor in the person-to-person correlation matrix; that is, the sample must be homogeneous and must not contain major subcultural groupings. Second, the sample must show a reasonable level of agreement on what constitutes "correct" responses – otherwise, it will be impossible to distinguish the data from random "noise."

Assuming that there is evidence to support the propositions presented in the preceding paragraphs, the question is *why* – why should those who give modal or majority responses in doing various tasks tend to be more reliable, consistent, normal, educated, intelligent, and experienced? There are probably a number of related causes at work here, but one possibility is that most cultural domains are characterized by a kind of coherence and substance. Consider a set of questions about algebra. Those people who know algebra well are more likely to give the more highly shared answers – since in most cases the "right" answer will be the most frequent answer because the many possible "wrong" answers will each have only a small number of adherents. Those who know algebra well are also more likely to be more reliable since they are more likely to "compute" the same answer to the same problem every time because they have a more highly practiced set of skills. They are also more likely to be experienced because learning and domain usually requires practice. And they are more likely to show up as "smart" in domain-related tests because the same kinds of cognitive computations are likely to be involved in both tasks, and, to the extent that they have "natural" ability, they will learn the "correct" procedures better than others with less ability. Thus the pattern that emerges is that *those who give more modal responses display the behavioral characteristics of an expert.*

All of this seems reasonable for algebra. But in what sense is labeling types of manioc (or determining which of two diseases is more contagious, or deciding what are appropriate parental sanctions, or giving word associations) like doing algebra problems? Certainly these domains are less organized and less clearly matters of provable truth than algebra. However, all these domains do involve complex relations and discriminations in which the criteria used to answer one series of questions are likely to recur in answering other series of questions. Once a domain has enough structure so that it is possible to generalize from one thing to another, then expertise becomes possible. To label plants one must use combinations of complex discriminations, and the discriminations needed to label one series of plants are likely to be needed to label another series. Similarly, common word associations are derived from a relatively small set of semantic relationships, such as opposition on a dimension of contrast (dark/light), coordinate members of a contrast set (red/blue), superordinate relations (cabbage/vegetable), subordinate relations (jewel/diamond), and so on, which form a structured field. If one can use these relations effectively with one series of stimulus words, it is more likely that one will be able to use these same relations effectively with another series of stimulus words.

Thus, there is a reasonable sense in which one can speak of being an *expert* in each of these domains, where being an expert means that one not only knows a lot about some domain, but also that one can operate cognitively in an especially effective way, using the internal consistencies within the domain to reason, extrapolate, remember, and discriminate more accurately than ordinary folk. These findings substantiate the intuitive judgment of many ethnographers that some informants are experts on some topics, and that their single judgments can sometimes represent the group consensus more accurately than the judgments of a number of less expert informants.

The fact that one can be an expert in a cultural system implies that such cultural systems are indeed real. There would be no way for people to become experts in some cultural system if the system were just something in the mind of the ethnographer, totally dependent on the ethnographer's classificatory strategies. Further, if becoming adept at understanding a system were just an individual matter (rather than a social matter), there would be no reason to expect an association between being an expert and giving modal responses. Knowledge in most if not all cultural systems is socially distributed – that is, some people know things that others do not (Roberts, 1964). Even with respect to the simplest cultural systems, it is rare for any individual to control all the relevant knowledge. To become an expert, one must gather and integrate knowledge from a number of other people, and this type of communication requires *common* meanings and understandings with respect to the system being learned or used. Since the most general and widely accessible common meanings are those that are modal in the group, the expert gains a large advantage by knowing and using them. Although a developing expert could negotiate separate agreements about the relevant meanings and procedures with each person he or she worked with, this would be extremely costly and inefficient. The expert is more likely to maximize "communicative accuracy" across persons by using modal meanings and understandings.

To return to the issue of individual variability, one can consider the observed disagreement about cultural items to be the cost of the social distribution of knowledge and belief. Given that large numbers of people must each learn at least some part of a system, there are bound to be errors in transmission because of the difficulties inherent in learning and recall. These errors would snowball over time and eventually make the system totally idiosyncratic, were there not other processes continuously pushing people to adopt the more highly shared items. There are probably many processes by which to increase commonality, such as imitating people with high social standing and not sanctioning those who act differently. I suggest that one such force that has not been widely recognized is the communicative advantage of using the most common meanings and understandings in developing expertise in a cultural system. This suggestion is supported by the data discussed earlier, which show that those who perform most consistently and reliably are also most likely to use modal meanings and understandings.

End remarks

The discussion in this chapter points to one general trend, which I call the move from *extension* to *intension*. Early work in cognitive anthropology often assumed that it is possible to work primarily from extensional definitions – that is, from the natives' statements about what things got what labels, or what sentences were true rather than false, or what terms could be filled into what sentence frames. With an extensional approach, the investigator could avoid trying to understand what was in the native's mind, and instead concentrate on finding out how what the native said correlated with what was in the world. Indeed, this kind of approach made it possible to find out a great deal about native systems of knowledge and understanding. At the same time, however, it became difficult to formulate definitions, to account for the properties of classificational and taxonomic systems, to represent the productive capacities of informants, and to formulate the descriptions of complex objects. Consequently, there was greater reliance on models based on the *sense* that the native had of things. The schema notion is an example of this; a schema is an internal mechanism through which interpretations are made – it is a general sense-maker. There probably has been a certain loss of rigor in this trend, since work with extensional meaning is more explicit and directly verifiable than work with sense and intensional meaning, which requires the investigator to develop a cognitive model of how the native represents things that can only be indirectly verified. However, the gain has been worth the loss, in that many of the generalizations about the relationship between culture and cognition described here could not have been discovered without such models of native representation.

References

Battig, W. F., & Montague, W. E. 1969. Category norms for verbal behavior in 56 categories: A replication and extension of the Connecticut category norms. *Journal of Experimental Psychology Monographs 80* (3, part 2).

Berlin, B., Breedlove, D., & Raven, P. H. 1966. Folk taxonomies and biological classification. *Science 154*:273–275.

1973. General principle of classification and nomenclature in folk biology. *American Anthropologist 75*:214–242.

Berlin, B., & Kay, P. 1969. *Basic Color Terms*. Berkeley: University of California Press.

Black, M., & Metzger, D. 1965. Ethnographic description and the study of law. *American Anthropologist 67* (6, part 2):141–165.

Boster, J. S. 1985. Requiem for the omniscient informant: There's life in the old girl yet. In *Directions in Cognitive Anthropology*, J. Dougherty (Ed.), pp. 177–197. Urbana: University of Illinois Press.

Boster, J., Berlin, B., & O'Neill, J. 1986. The correspondence of Jivaroan to scientific ornithology. *American Anthropologist 88*:569–583.

Brown, C. 1977. Folk botanical life-forms: Their universality and growth. *American Anthropologist 79*:317–342.

Brown, C., Kolar, J., Torrey, B., Truon-Quan, T., & Volkman, P. 1976. Some general principles of biological and non-biological folk classification. *American Ethnologist 3*:73–85.

Brown, R., & Lenneberg, E. 1954. A study in language and cognition. *Journal of Abnormal and Social Psychology 49*:73–85.

Brugman, C. 1981. The Story of Over. Master's thesis, University of California, Berkeley.

Casson, R. 1983. Schemata in cognitive anthropology. *Annual Review of Anthropology 12*:429–462.

Coleman, L., & Kay, P. 1981. Prototype semantics: The English verb "lie." *Language 57*, 26–44.

Conklin, H. C. 1962. Lexicographic treatment of folk taxonomies. In *Indiana University Research Center in Anthropology, Folklore, and Linguistics, Publication 21. Problems in Lexicography*, F. Householder & S. Saporta (Eds.), pp. 119–141. Bloomington: University of Indiana Press.

Cox, J. R., & Griggs, R. A. 1982. The effects of experience on performance in Wason's selection task. *Memory and Cognition 10*:496–502.

D'Andrade, R. G. 1965. Trait psychology and componential analysis. *American Anthropologist 67*:215–228.

1974a. The colors of emotion. *American Ethnologist 1*:49–63.

1974b. Memory and the assessment of behavior. In *Social Measurement*, T. Blalock (Ed.), pp. 139–186. Chicago: Aldine-Atherton.

1976. A propositional analysis of U.S. American beliefs about illness. In *Meaning in Anthropology*, K. Basso & H. Selby (Eds.), pp. 155–180. Albuquerque: University of New Mexico Press.

1985. Character terms and cultural models. In *Directions in Cognitive Anthropology*, J. Dougherty (Ed.), pp. 88–119. New York: Cambridge University Press.

1986. Three scientific world views and the covering law model. In *Metatheory in Social Science*, D. Fiske & R. Shweder (Eds.), pp. 19–41. Chicago: University of Chicago Press.

1987. A folk model of the mind. In *Cultural Models in Language and*

Thought, D. Holland & N. Quinn (Eds.), pp. 112–148. New York: Cambridge University Press.

In press-a. Cultural sharing and diversity. In *Models of Culture: Essays in Honor of John Roberts*, R. Bolton (Ed.). New Haven: HRAF Press.

In press-b. Culturally based reasoning. In *Cognition and Social Worlds*, A. Gellatly & D. Rogers (Eds.), Oxford: Clarendon Press.

D'Andrade, R. G., & M. Egan 1974. The colors of emotion. *American Ethnologist 1*:49–63.

D'Andrade, R. G., Quinn, N., Nerlove, S. B., & Romney, A. K. 1972. Categories of disease in American-English and Mexican-Spanish. In *Multidimensional Scaling, Volume II*, A. K. Romney, R. N. Shepard, & S. B. Nerlove (Eds.), pp. 11–54. New York: Seminar Press.

Dougherty, J. 1978. Salience and relativity in classification. *American Ethnologist 5*:66–80.

Dougherty, J., & Keller, C. 1985. Taskonomy: A practical approach to knowledge structures. In *Directions in Cognitive Anthropology*, J. Dougherty, (Ed.), pp. 161–174. Urbana: University of Illinois Press.

Ekman, P. 1971. Universals and cultural differences in facial expressions of emotion. In *Nebraska Symposium on Motivation*, J. Cole (Ed.), pp. 207–283. Lincoln: University of Nebraska Press.

Fillmore, C. 1975. An alternative to checklist theories of meaning. In *Proceedings of the First Annual Meeting of the Berkeley Linguistics Society*, C. Cogen, H. Thomson, G. Thurgood, K. Whilstler, & J. Wright (Eds.), pp. 123–131. Berkeley: Berkeley Linguistic Society.

1977. Topic in lexical semantics. In *Current Issues in Linguistic Theory*, R. Cole (Ed.), pp. 76–138. Bloomington: Indiana University Press.

Fortes, M. 1983. *Oedipus and Job in West African Religion*. Cambridge: Cambridge University Press.

Frake, C. 1964. Notes on queries in ethnography. *American Anthropologist 66*:(3, part 2):132–145.

1975. How to enter a Yakan house. In *Sociocultural Dimensions of Language Use*, M. Sanches & B. Blount (Eds.), pp. 25–40. New York: Academic Press.

1985. Cognitive maps of time and tide among medieval seafarers. *Man 20*:254–270.

Garro, L. 1986. Language, memory, and focality: A reexamination. *American Anthropologist 88*:128–136.

Gerber, E. 1975. The Cultural Patterning of Emotion in Samoa. Ph.D. dissertation, University of California, San Diego.

1985. Rage and obligation: Samoan emotion in conflict. In *Person, Self, and Experience*, G. White & J. Kirkpatrick (Eds.), pp. 121–167. Berkeley: University of California Press.

Goldin-Meadow, S., & Feldman, H. 1977. The development of language-like communication without a language model. *Science 197*:401–403.

Haviland, S., & Clark, E. 1974. "This man's father is my father's son": A study of acquisition of English kin terms. *Journal of Child Language 1*:23–47.

Heider, E. 1972. Universals in color naming and memory. *Journal of Experimental Psychology 93*:10–20.

Holland, D. 1982. Conventional metaphors in human thought and language. *Reviews in Anthropology 9*:287–297.

Hunn, E. 1976. Toward a perceptual model of folk biological classification. *American Ethnologist 3*:508–524.

1985. The utilitarian factor in folk biological classification. In *Directions in Cognitive Anthropology*, J. Dougherty (Ed.), pp. 117–140. Urbana: University of Illinois Press.

Hutchins, E. 1980. *Culture and Inference: A Trobriand Case Study.* Cambridge, MA: Harvard University Press.

n.d. Mediation and automatization. Manuscript, University of California, San Diego.

Hutchins, E., & Levin, J. A. 1979. *Point of View in Problem Solving.* CHIP Technical Report, University of California, San Diego.

Johnson, A., Johnson, O., & Baksh, M. 1986. Cognitive and emotional aspects of Machiguenga color terms. *American Anthropologist* 88:674–681.

Johnson-Laird, P. N. 1983. *Mental Models.* Cambridge, MA: Harvard University Press.

Johnson-Laird, P. N., Legrenzi, P., & Legrenzi, M. 1972. Reasoning and a sense of reality. *British Journal of Psychology* 63:392–400.

Kay, P. 1987. Linguistic competence and folk theories of language: Two English hedges. In *Cultural Models in Language and Thought*, D. Holland & N. Quinn (Eds.), pp. 67–77. New York: Cambridge University Press.

Kay, P., & Kempton, W. 1984. What is the Sapir–Whorf hypothesis? *American Anthropologist 86*, 65–79.

Kempton, W. 1981. *The Folk Classification of Ceramics.* New York: Academic Press.

Kieffer, M. 1974. Color and Emotion: Synesthesia in Tzutujil Mayan and Spanish. Ph.D. dissertation, University of California, Irvine.

Kohlberg, L. 1981. *The Philosophy of Moral Development: Moral Stages and the Idea of Justice, Volume 1: Essays on Moral Development.* San Francisco: Harper and Row.

Kronenfeld, D., Armstrong, J., & Wilmoth, S. 1985. Exploring the internal structure of linguistic categories: An extensionist semantic view. In *Directions in Cognitive Anthropology.* J. Dougherty (Ed.), p. 110. Urbana: University of Illinois Press.

Kucera, H., & Francis, W. N. 1967. *Computational Analysis of Present-day American English.* Providence: Brown University Press.

Lakoff, G. 1987. *Women, Fire, and Dangerous Things: What Categories Reveal about the Mind.* Chicago: University of Chicago Press.

Lakoff, G., & Johnson, M. 1983. *Metaphors We Live By.* Chicago: University of Chicago Press.

Langacker, R. 1986. An introduction to cognitive grammar. *Cognitive Science 10*:1–40.

1987. *Foundations of Cognitive Grammar.* Stanford, CA: Stanford University Press.

Lantz, D., & Stefflre, V. 1964. Language and cognition revisited. *Journal of Abnormal and Social Psychology* 69:472–481.

Lenneberg, E. 1961. Color naming, color recognition, color discrimination: A reappraisal. *Perceptual and Motor Skills 12*:375–382.

1967. *The Biological Foundations of Language.* New York: Wiley.

Lenneberg, E., & Roberts, J. 1956. The language of experience; A study in methodology. *International Journal of Linguistics*, Memoir no. 13.

LeVine, R. 1984. Properties of culture: An ethnographic view. In *Culture Theory: Essays on Mind, Self, and Emotion*, R. Shweder & R. LeVine (Eds.), pp. 67–87. New York: Cambridge University Press.

Levy, R. L. 1973. *Tahitians: Mind and Experience in Society Islands.* Chicago: University of Chicago Press.

1985. Emotion, knowing, and culture. In *Culture Theory: Essays on Mind, Self, and Emotion*, R. Shweder & R. LeVine (Eds.), 214–237. Cambridge: Cambridge University Press.

Linder, S. 1981. A Lexico-Semantic Analysis of Verb–Particle Constructions with UP and OUT. Ph.D. dissertation. University of California, San Diego.

Lucy, J., & Shweder, R. 1979. Whorf and his critics: Linguistic and non-linguistic influences on color memory. *American Anthropologist 81*:581–615.

1988. The effect of incidental conversation on memory for focal colors. *American Anthropologist 90*(4):923–931.

Lutz, C. 1982. The domain of emotion words on Ifaluk. *American Ethnologist 9*:113–128.

1985. Ethnopsychology compared to what: Explaining behavior and consciousness among the Ifaluk. In *Person, Self, and Experience*, G. White & J. Kirkpatrick (Eds.), pp. 35–79. Berkeley: University of California Press.

1986. Emotion, thought, and estrangement: Emotion as a cultural category. *Cultural Anthropology 1*:287–309.

Lutz, C., & White, G. 1986. The anthropology of emotions. *Annual Reivew of Anthropology 15*:405–436.

Mandler, G. 1984. *Mind and Body.* New York: W. W. Norton.

Metzger, D. & Williams, G. 1963a. A formal ethnographic analysis of Tenejapa Ladino weddings. *American Anthropologist 65*:1076–1101.

1963b. Tenejapa medicine I: The curer. *Southwestern Journal of Anthropology 19*:216–234.

1966. Some procedures and results in the study of native categories: Tenejapa "firewood." *American Anthropologist 68*:389–407.

Miller, G. A. 1956. The magical number seven plus or minus two: Some limits on your capacity for processing information. *Psychological Review 63*:81–96.

Miller, G. A., & Johnson-Laird, P. N. 1976. *Language and Perception.* Cambridge, MA: Harvard Univeristy Press.

Mischel, W. 1968. *Personality and Assessment.* New York: Wiley.

Moran, L. J., Mefferd, R. B., & Kimble, J. P. 1964. Idiodynamic sets in word association. *Psychological Monographs: General and Applied 78*(2):1–22.

Nerlove, S., & Romney, A. K. 1967. Sibling terminology and cross-sex behavior. *American Anthropologist 74*:1249–1253.

Poole, F. J. P. 1985. Coming into social being: Cultural images of infants in Bimin-Kuskusmin folk psychology. In *Person, Self, and Experience*, G. White & J. Kirkpatrick (Eds.), pp. 183–242. Berkeley: University of California Press.

Quinn, N. 1985. American marriage through metaphors: A cultural analysis. *North Carolina Working Papers in Culture and Cognition No. 1.* Durham, NC.: Duke University Department of Anthropology.

1987. What discourse can tell about culture: Convergent evidence for a cultural model of American marriage. In *Cultural Models in Language and Thought*, D. Holland & N. Quinn (Eds.), pp. 173–192. New York: Cambridge University Press.

Quinn, N., & Holland, D. 1987. Introduction. In *Cultural Models in Language and Thought*, D. Holland & N. Quinn (Eds.), pp. 3–40. New York: Cambridge University Press.

Randall, R. 1976. How tall is a taxonomic tree? Some evidence for dwarfism. *American Ethnologist 3*:543–553.

——— 1986. Steps toward an ethnosemantics of verbs. In *Directions in Cognitive Anthropology*, J. Dougherty (Ed.), pp. 249–268. Urbana: University of Illinois Press.

Rips, L. In press. Similarity, typicality, and categorization. In *Similarity and Analogical Reasoning*, S. Vosniadou & A. Ortony (Eds.). Cambridge: Cambridge University Press.

Roberts, John M. 1987. Within culture variation. *American Behavioral Scientist 31*(2):266–279.

Romney, A. K., & D'Andrade, R. G. 1964. Cognitive aspects of English kin terms. *American Anthropologist 66*:146–170.

Romney, A. K., Weller, S. C., & Batchelder, W. H. 1986. Culture as consensus: A theory of culture and informant accuracy. *American Anthropologist 88*:313–338.

Rosch, E. 1973. On the internal structure of perceptual and semantic categories. In *Cognitive Development and the Acquisition of Language*, T. Moore (Ed.), pp. 123–142. New York: Academic Press.

——— 1975. Cognitive representations of semantic categories. *Journal of Experimental Psychology 104*:192–233.

Rumelhart, D., & McClelland, J., 1986. *Parallel Distributed Processing: Explorations in the Microstructure of Cognition. Volume 1: Foundations.* Cambridge, MA: MIT Press.

Savage-Rumbaugh, S., Rumbaugh, D., Smith, S., & Lawson, J. 1980. Reference: The linguistic essential. *Science 210*:922–925.

Schank, R., & Abelson, R. 1977. *Scripts, Plans, Goals, and Understanding: An Inquiry into Human Knowledge Structures.* Hillsdale, NJ: Erlbaum.

Schneider, D., & Roberts, J. 1953. Role designating and role classifying aspects of kin terms. *Papers of the Peabody Museum 32*:121–133.

Shweder, R. A. 1972. Semantic Structures and Personality Assessment. Doctoral dissertation. Department of Social Relations, Harvard University.

——— 1977a. Illusory correlation and the M.M.P.I. controversy. *Journal of Consulting and Clinical Psychology 45*:917–924.

——— 1977b. Illusory correlation and the M.M.P.I. controversy: Author's reply to some allusions and elusions in Block's and Edward's commentaries. *Journal of Consulting and Clinical Psychology 45*:936–940.

——— 1977c. Likeness and likelihood in everyday thought: Magical thinking in judgments about personality. *Current Anthropology 18*:637–648.

Shweder, R. A., & D'Andrade, R. G. 1979. Accurate reflection or systematic distortion? A reply to Block, Weiss, and Thorne. *Journal of Personality and Social Psychology 37*:1075–1084.

——— 1980. The systematic distortion hypothesis. In *New Directions for Methodology of Social and Behavioral Science 4*:37–58. San Francisco: Jossey Bass.

Shweder, R. A., & Bourne, E. J. 1984. Does the concept of the person vary cross-culturally? In *Culture Theory: Essays on Mind, Self, and Emotion*, R. Shweder & R. LeVine (Eds.), pp. 158–199. New York: Cambridge University Press.

Shweder, R. A., Mahapatra, M., Miller, S. G. 1987. Culture and moral development. In *The Emergence of Morality in Young Children*, J. Kagan & S. Lamb (Eds.), pp. 1–83. Chicago: University of Chicago Press.

Stefflre, V., Castillo, V., & Moreley, L. 1966. Language and cognition in Yucatan: A crosscultural replication. *Journal of Personality and Social Psychology* 4:112–115.

Stigler, J. W., Chalip, L., & Miller, K. F. 1986. Consequences of skill: The case of abacus training in Taiwan. *American Journal of Education* 94:447–479.

Swartz, M. J., & Jordan, D. K. 1976. *Anthropology: Perspective on Humanity*. New York: Wiley.

Sweetser, E. 1987. The definition of *lie*: an examination of the folk models underlying a semantic prototype. In *Cultural Models in Language and Thought*, D. Holland & N. Quinn (Eds.), pp. 43–66. New York: Cambridge University Press.

Talmy, L. 1978. The relation of grammar to cognition – a synopsis. In *Proceedings of TINLAP-2 Theoretical Issues in Natural Language Processing*, D. Waltz (Ed.), pp., 3–23. Champaign: Coordinated Science Laboratory, University of Illinois.

Turiel, E. 1979. Distinct conceptual and developmental domains: Social-convention and morality. In *Nebraska Symposium on Motivation, Volume 25*, C. Keasy (Ed.). Lincoln: University of Nebraska Press.

Uyeda, K., & Mandler, G. 1980. Prototypicality norms for 28 semantic categories. *Behavioral Research Methods and Instrumentation* 12:587–595.

Vendler, Z. 1967. *Linguistics in Philosophy*. Ithaca, NY: Cornell University Press.

——— 1972. *Res Cognitans: An Essay in Rational Philosophy*. Ithaca, NY: Cornell University Press.

Wallace, A. F. C. 1961. On being just complicated enough. *Proceedings of the National Academy of Sciences* 47:458–464.

Wason, P. 1969. Regression in reasoning. *British Journal of Psychology* 60:471–480.

Weller, S. C. 1984. Consistency and consensus among informants: Disease concepts in a rural Mexican town. *American Anthropologist* 86:966–975.

Weller, S. C., Romney, A. K., & Orr, D. P. 1986. The myth of a sub-culture of corporal punishment. *Human Organization* 46:39–47.

Werner. O. 1985. Folk knowledge without fuzz. In *Directions in Cognitive Anthropology*, J. Dougherty (Ed.), pp. 73–90. Urbana: University of Illinois Press.

Wexler, K., & Romney, A. K. 1972. Individual variations in cognitive structures. In *Multidimensional Scaling Vol. II*, R. Shepard & S. Nerlove (Eds.), pp. 73–92. New York: Seminar Press.

Whorf, B. L. 1956. Science and linguistics. In *Language, Thought, and Reality*, J. B. Carrol (Ed.). Cambridge, MA: MIT Press.

Wierzbicka, A. 1984. Apples are not a "kind of fruit": The semantics of human categorization. *American Ethnologist* 11:313–328.

——— 1986. Human emotions: Universal or culture specific? *American Anthropologist* 88:584–594.

3
Culture and moral development

Richard A. Shweder, Manamohan Mahapatra, and Joan G. Miller

This essay reports the results of a cross-cultural development study of ideas about the moral (its form) and ideas about what is moral (its content). The informants for the study are children, five to thirteen years of age, and adults, male and female, from Brahman and "Untouchable" families in the orthodox Hindu temple town of Bhubaneswar, Orissa, India; and from Judeo-Christian families in the secular university neighborhood of Hyde Park in Chicago, Illinois.

One aim of the essay is to assess the strengths and limitations of two prominent and important theories about the origins and development of moral understandings: Kohlberg's "cognitive developmental" theory (Kohlberg 1969, 1981; Kohlberg, Levine, and Hewer 1983) and Turiel's "social interactional" theory (Turiel 1979, 1983; Nucci and Turiel 1978; Turiel and Smetana 1984). A second aim is to highlight

Reprinted by permission from *The Emergence of Morality in Young Children*, Jerome Kagan and Sharon Lamb, eds. Chicago and London: University of Chicago Press, 1987.

The research reported was supported by a grant from the Human Learning and Behavior program of the National Institute of Child Health and Human Development (R01 HD17067). The research in India would not have been possible without the support, encouragement and advice of S. K. Misra, S. K. Mahapatra and M. K. Rout. Our deep gratitude to those scholars and to those who, over the years, have eased our way: P. K. Badu, Ashoy Biswal, Rita Biswal, N. K. Das (Nabi Babaji), R. N. Das, Babaji Patnaik, K. S. Ramachandran, M. T. Rath, Babla Senapati, and Nilamani Senapati. An earlier version of the chapter was read by several colleagues, whose comments, both critical and supportive, were appreciated. Our thanks to Augusto Blasi, Roy G. D'Andrade, Donald W. Fiske, J. David Greenstone, Jerome Kagan, Larry Nucci, James Stigler, Elliot Turiel, and Alan Young. Manamohan Mahapatra's mailing address is Punama Gate Area, Bhubaneswar 751002, Orissa, India.

A special thanks to those who directly assisted in the development, translation, collection, coding and interpretation of research materials, especially Barbara Byhouwer, Kathleen Chattin, Sandy Dixon, Alan Fiske, Chita Mohanty, Swapna Pani, Deborah Pool, Mary Ruth Quinn, and Candy Shweder.

the role of social communication processes in the ontogeny of moral understandings by outlining a "social communication" theory of moral development and using it to interpret the similarities and differences in the moral understandings of children and adults in the two cultures.

Three theories of moral development

The three theories to be discussed present different portraits and accounts of the ontogenetic origins of the idea of a moral obligation. Kohlberg's "cognitive developmental" theory hypothesizes that a genuine understanding of the idea of a moral obligation (stages five and six) has its origins in the idea of a conventional, or consensus-based, obligation (stages three and four). The theory proposes, as a developmental universal, that the idea that obligations are rooted in convention precedes the idea that obligations are rooted in natural law.

According to the "cognitive developmental" theory, the development of the idea of a moral obligation is related to the development of general skills of rational reasoning. Those skills include deductive logic and the ability to distance oneself from what is personal, ego-centered or consensus-based. Movement through the stages is related to the cognitive ability to construct, and to transcend to, a detached, impartial vantage point from which one evaluates right and wrong objectively.

By contrast, Turiel's "social interactional" theory proposes that the idea of morality and the idea of convention are not connected in development. Furthermore, it is proposed that the idea of a moral obligation and the idea of a conventional obligation are both present universally and differentiated from each other in early childhood.

According to Turiel's theory, the development of the idea of a moral obligation is related to social experiences with a restricted class of events that have objective or intrinsic implications for justice, rights, harm, and the welfare of others. A paradigmatic moral experience is the child's personal observation of the consequences of hitting and hurting a helpless victim. On the other hand, the idea of a conventional obligation arises from social experiences with a class of socially regulated events that lack any objective or intrinsic implications for justice, rights, harm, or the welfare of others. For Turiel, a paradigmatic conventional experience is the extrinsic or externally imposed social demand to use clothing styles (for example, skirts) as a mark of gender differences.

The "social communication" theory, to be outlined in this essay, presents a third account of moral development, diverging in different ways from both Kohlberg and Turiel. In contrast to Kohlberg, the "social communication" theory proposes that the idea of a moral obligation is a universal of childhood and is not preceded by the idea that obligations derive their authority from consensus or convention.

In that respect the "social communication" theory converges with Turiel's "social interactional" account.

In contrast to Turiel, however, the "social communication" theory questions the hypothesis that there are universal developmental processes leading the child to differentiate and contrast moral versus conventional obligations. The research suggests that it is not a universal idea that social practices are conventional formations, deriving their authority from a culture-bound consensus. According to the theory a culture's ideology and worldview have a significant bearing on the ontogenesis of moral understandings in the child, and not all cultures have a place in their view of the world for the idea that social practices are conventions.

A basic claim of the "social communication" theory is that children develop an idea of a conventional obligation in those cultures, like our own, where the social order has been separated ideologically from the natural moral order. One way that separation can occur is by reducing, as far as possible, what's moral to free contracts, promises, or consent among autonomous individuals. In the purest version of our free contract worldview, "markets" are absolutely neutral as to the particular social arrangements into which individuals choose to enter. The terms of a contract are decided by those who enter it; between "consenting adults" anything goes. The "social communication" theory proposes that the idea that social practices are conventional or consensus-based takes on significance only in those cultures where social arrangements are thought to be secondary formations, derived from a more fundamental, natural moral authority – the will of the individual, voluntarily expressed through consent, promise, or contract.

As we shall see, not all cultural worldviews are like our own. The Latin word "mores," from which the term "morals" is derived, meant "custom" (Gewirth 1984), and in many parts of the world, including orthodox Hindu India, customary practices (for example, menstrual seclusion, arranged marriage, food taboos, kin avoidance, naming practices) are viewed as part of the natural moral order. Society is not separated conceptually from nature. What is natural or moral has not been narrowed down to the idea of an individual, empowered and free to create relationships at will through contract. Forms of human association are thought to be found (natural law), not founded (conventionism). In those parts of the world, the idea that social practices are conventions plays a minimal role in the child's developing understanding of the source of obligations.

Social practices are the primary focus of our study. The Hindu temple town of Bhubaneswar is a place where marriages are arranged, not matters of "love" or free choice; where, at least among Brahman families, widows may not remarry or wear colored clothing or ornaments or jewelry; where Untouchables are not allowed in the temple; where menstruating women may not sleep in the same bed as their husbands or enter the kitchen or touch their children; where ancestral spirits are fed on a daily basis; where husbands and wives do not eat together and the communal family meals we find so important rarely occur; where women avoid their husbands' elder brothers and men avoid their wives' elder sisters; where, with the exception of holy men, corpses are cremated, never buried; and where the cow, the first "mother," is never carved up into sirloin, porterhouse or tenderloin cut.

The study focuses upon thirty-nine practices including kinship avoidance, forms of address between inferiors and superiors, sleeping arrangements, incest avoidance, dietary practices, forms of dress, marriage and remarriage, personal possessions and private property, begging, nepotism, monogamy, wife beating, physical punishment for children, the division of labor in the family, the inheritance of property, the protection of persons from physical and psychological harm, funeral rites, and various practices surrounding the birth of a child.

One aim of the study is to determine how the obligations associated with those practices are understood by Indian and American children and adults, with special reference to the distinction between morality and convention. A second aim of the study is to make explicit the premises and principles that are implicitly conveyed by social practices. What do Indian and American practices tell us about each culture's conception of persons, society, morality, and nature and about the relationships among those orders of things? Similarities and differences are identified in the form and content of moral codes across different cultural or subcultural traditions. A third aim of the study is to use our cross-cultural evidence on moral thought to appraise Kohlberg's and Turiel's contrastive theories of moral development. Thus, before turning to our study it is necessary to review and critique in detail those two theories.

Kohlberg's cognitive developmental theory: overview and evaluation

OVERVIEW

Kohlberg (1969, 1971, 1981) has proposed a comprehensive scheme for developmental and comparative research on moral understandings. The scheme builds upon the work of Piaget ([1932] 1965) by identifying three major levels in the attainment of moral understandings and dividing each level into two stages.

In the lowest, "preconventional" level of understanding (stages one and two) young children define the meaning of "rightness" and "wrongness" in terms of the subjective feelings of the self. What is right is what avoids punishment or brings one rewards. If the self likes it, it is right, if the self doesn't like it, it is wrong. There are no "higher" obligations. Egoism reigns.

In the intermediate, "conventional" level of understanding (stages three and four), older children and adults continue to define the meaning of "rightness" and "wrongness" by reference to subjective feelings, but now it is the collective feelings of others that matter. What is correct and virtuous is whatever agrees with the will and dictates of authority figures (the commands of parents; the role expectations of society; the laws of legislatures). If one's reference group likes it, it is right. If one's reference group does not like it, it is wrong. The idea of obligation is equated with the rules and regulations of society or the state. Conformity and consensus reign.

In the third and highest "postconventional" level of understanding (stages five and six in Kohlberg's earlier formulations; stage five in more recent formulations; Kohlberg, Levine, and Hewer, 1983) "rightness" and "wrongness" are defined by reference to objective principles detached from the subjective feelings and perspective of either the self or the group. What is correct and virtuous is defined in terms of universalizable standards, reflectively constructed by the individual, of justice, natural rights, and humanistic respect for all persons, regardless of sex, age, ethnicity, race, or religion. For the post-conventional thinker, there are objective obligations that any rational person can come to discover and is bound to respect, that stand above the feelings of the self or the demands of others. In Kohlberg's theory, the source of the idea of being obliged to do something is related to the hypothetical act of entering into a contract to form a society. Postconventional thinkers recognize that among the terms of any voluntary and rationally based contract to form a society, justice, fairness, and natural rights must reign.

There are several noteworthy features of Kohlberg's three-level scheme. First, the scheme is organized around the contrast between subjectivity and objectivity. By "objectivity," Kohlberg means relative distance from the perspective of the self, or seeing things from a detached or "decentered" vantage point. In principle, perfect objectivity, a transcendental state, is seeing things from "nowhere in particular" (Nagel 1979). Thus, for Kohlberg, the first major move in moral development is away from solipsistic subjectivism, away from exclusive involvement with personal pleasure and pain and one's own individual needs (preconventional understanding) toward a recognition of external group consensus, a concern with the approval of significant others and conformity to social conventions and laws (conventional understanding). The second major move is toward transcendental objectivity, away from exclusive concern with conformity to custom, law, or group consensus (conventional understanding) and toward respect for rationally defensible objective standards for right conduct (postconventional understanding).

A second noteworthy feature of Kohlberg's three-level scheme is that the three levels correspond to three different conceptions in moral philosophy about the meaning of the expression "It's right to do that." According to one view, associated with so-called emotivist conceptions of moral discourse (Stevenson 1944; see MacIntyre 1981), obligations, like tastes, are merely expressions of personal preferences. The underlying meaning of the expression "It's right to do that" can be translated as an exhortation: "I like it; you like it as well." According to a second view, associated with so-called positive-law or legal positivist conceptions of moral discourse (see Hart 1961) obligations are nothing more than the promulgations of other human beings. The underlying meaning of the expression "It's right to do that" can be translated as an empirical report that "It is permitted by existing rules, laws, and other commands promulgated by your group, and there are no existing penalties for doing it." According to a third view, associated with so-called natural-law conceptions of moral discourse, there are such things as "objective" obligations which rational persons can discover. The expression "It's right to do that" can be translated as an implicit argument that "There are certain impersonal, objective standards to which social practices and institutions, man-made rules and laws, and personal desires must conform if those practices, institutions, rules, laws, and desires are to be valid." Whether or not Kohlberg is fully aware of it (although see Kohlberg 1981, chap. 9), he has arranged these three conceptions of moral discourse in a single developmental sequence with emotivism at the bottom, positive-law conceptions in the middle, and natural-law conceptions at the top. Thus, there appear to be several alternative ways to label Kohlberg's three levels: preconventional, conventional, postconventional; egoistic, consensual, moral; emotivist, positive-law, natural-law (see figure 3.1).

A third noteworthy feature of Kohlberg's three-level scheme is that adequate moral understandings are portrayed as emerging out of prior conventional understandings. Kohlberg's image of the development of moral understandings is a sequential process of differentiation and replacement in which postconventional or natural-law conceptions of right versus wrong come to be distinguished from conventional or positive-law conceptions and supersede them (Kohlberg, Levine, and Hewer 1983, 17, 32). Likewise, conventional or positive-law conceptions emerge out of prior preconventional egoistic, or emotivist conceptions.

A fourth noteworthy feature of Kohlberg's three-level scheme is that adequate moral understanding is equated with the postconventional level of thinking. It is Kohlberg's view that the postconventional level of understanding is rationally preferable to the conventional level, which in its turn is rationally preferable to the preconventional level. He argues that with the development of processes of rational reasoning (for example, formal operational reasoning as described by Piaget) and exposure to proper education (for example, engagement in Socratic dialogue), the individual will recognize the conceptual inadequacies of the lower level of understanding and adopt a higher, more rationally defensible conceptual level. The underlying assumption is that in a creature endowed with the capacity for rational thought, as that capacity is cultivated, the development of moral understanding will tend in the direction of what is most rational.

Level 3	Postconventional	Morality	Natural law	Principle	It's right	Transcendent objectivity	Formal operations
Level 2	Conventional	Convention	Positive law	Consensus	The group approves	Collective subjectivity	Concrete operations
Level 1	Preconventional	Personal preference	Emotivism	Self-ego	I like it	Solipsistic subjectivity	Preoperational

Figure 3.1. Schematic representation of the parallel distinctions running through Kohlberg's three-level cognitive developmental theory of moral development.

A fifth noteworthy feature of Kohlberg's three-level scheme is that the various criteria for characterizing postconventional understanding are not all equally secure in the moral philosophy literature. Consistent with Kohlberg's claims, most recent analyses in moral philosophy suggest that adequate moral understandings have something to do with the idea of objective obligations that rational people can come to know, and that moral understanding cannot be reduced to the idea of positive law, social convention, or personal desire. It is a matter of dispute, however, whether a formal decision criterion involving the ideas of justice and harm can account for all cases where we judge a moral transgression to have occurred (for example, incest, using contraceptives, between consenting adult brother and sister) (Feinberg 1980; Perelman 1963). Furthermore, there is disagreement in the moral philosophy literature about whether there are such things as natural or objective rights as described in the Bill of Rights (MacIntyre 1981) and about whether reference in moral justification to the commandments of a superior or divine being set forth in "sacred text" is to be classified as an instance of positive law, level two, as Kohlberg classifies it (1981, chap. 9), or natural law, level three (Dworkin 1977). There is disagreement about whether the theory of free contract or the idea of consent can provide a comprehensive or even compelling account of the sources of obligation to those shared expectations that constitute a society. In other words, it is not a settled fact that all Kohlberg's proposed criteria are mandatory features of any rationally based moral understanding. Some of the proposed criteria may be discretionary or permit rational alternatives or substitutes. There may be other rationally based moral codes besides the one proposed. Kohlberg may not have sufficiently distinguished between mandatory versus discretionary features in his conception of postconventional understanding. There may be alternative postconventional moralities for which no place has been provided in his scheme.

An evaluation of Kohlberg's cognitive developmental theory

THE STRENGTH OF THE THEORY

It is widely acknowledged in moral and legal philosophy that moral understandings are not the same as conventional understandings. The difference is exemplified, for Americans, by the difference in the way they understand their obligation, construed to be moral, to feed their children, versus their obligation, construed to be conventional, to send their son to school in pants instead of a skirt. One of the more defensible ways to distinguish the two types of understanding is by reference to the abstract idea of natural moral law basic to Kohlberg's scheme.

One way to think about the abstract idea of natural moral law is to imagine that there are certain standards to which social practices, man-made rules, and personal desires must conform if those practices, rules, and desires are to be valid. These standards are natural, in at least two senses. First, adherence to those standards is thought to lead factually to certain ultimate, important, or categorical ends of life like liberty, equality, safety, salvation, or the elimination of suffering. Secondly, the standards themselves are thought to be objective or external, hence natural. Just as the shape of an object is said to inhere in that object regardless of a human perceiver, so too, certain actions (starving a child to death) are thought to be wrong independent of any human acknowledgment of it. The wrongness is there regardless of whether anyone recognizes it as such. Declaring that a round object is square does not make it so. So too, an action that is wrong by virtue of natural law cannot be made right by any declaration, vote, or legislation.

To select a parochial example, in those places in the world where the idea of natural law is associated with the idea of natural "rights," there are certain freedoms (speech, travel) that are placed beyond the realm of the subject and out of the reach of majority vote, above convention and consensus. Of course, a government, a state, or a court may fail to realize its objective obligations and may fail to grant its citizens any rights at all. But, according to those who believe that civil liberty is part of the natural order of things, the obligation is present nonetheless. Being objective it does not go away for having been misperceived.

Kohlberg is probably on the side of the angels in his use of the abstract idea of objective obligations to describe the nature of genuine (or postconventional) moral understandings. It is the appeal to an objective ought, a natural law, that genuine moral understanding is about, both in Kohlberg's scheme and in the schemes of most moral philosophers. Nonetheless, Kohlberg's account of moral development and his conceptual scheme have been the target of much legitimate criticism. Before summarizing those legitimate criticisms, however, it is necessary to digress for a moment to discuss Kohlberg's most recent reformulation of his theory.

THE REFORMULATION

Kohlberg's recent reformulation of his theory (Kohlberg, Levine, and Hewer 1983) is a lucid but complex statement, packed with revisions, qualifications, concessions, and several new distinctions. It is complex enough to dazzle even the most sympathetic critic. An unsympathetic critic might view the reformulation as the beginning of the epicycle stage of the theory. "Soft" stages are now distinguished from "hard" stages. Two substages (A and B) are introduced within each of Kohlberg's stages to accommodate the Piagetian distinction between autonomy and heteronomy. And while a "soft" seventh stage is added to the scheme, the previously proposed "hard" stage six is dropped because it is not an empirically identifiable form of moral reasoning (1983, 60).

The domain of the theory is narrowed. What was once to be a

theory of moral development is now described as a theory of justice reasoning. Kohlberg, Levine, and Hewer (1983, 19) write: "We admit, however, that this emphasis on the virtue of justice in Kohlberg's work does not fully reflect all that is recognized as being part of the moral domain."

The claims of the theory are weakened. Kohlberg, Levine, and Hewer (1983, 63) state that they agree with their critics that genuine postconventional moral understandings need not be tied to any particular normative ethical position. They accept the criticism by Carter (1980) that "'what Kohlberg really achieves with clarity is nothing more than a sequential typology of development in moral thinking from egoism to universalism, and from situation-specific rules to universalizable and reversible judgments of principle.'" Carter probably overstates the case. For Kohlberg has not discovered that adults are typically principled or universalistic postconventional thinkers, and stage one egoism is not a frequent empirical occurrence, even among children (Snarey 1985). What Kohlberg has firmly established empirically is that, with his interview methodology and scheme of concepts, children are more likely than adults to justify action verbally by reference to the subjective feelings of the self, and that adults make more reference to social and political institutions – majority vote, the state, the law – in discussing their obligations. The only empirically established sequential typology emerging from the Kohlberg framework is the shift in verbal justifications from reference to self to reference to social institutions. Research concerned with how society and social institutions are represented by mature adults does not support the idea of a sequential end point on the side of abstract universal principles. Most adults in most societies stabilize at stage three with a conception of society built up out of the mutual reliances and interdependencies, and the specific agreements and obligations, associated with particular status or role relationships – husband to wife, parent to child, friend to friend, stranger to stranger (Edwards 1980, in press; Gilligan 1982).

It is ironic that with the publication of his "current formulation" there is somewhat less clarity about what it is that Kohlberg believes. Some of his most fundamental reformulations are difficult to reconcile with each other, and his thinking seems to be in the midst of a, perhaps productive, process of change. For example, Kohlberg, Levine, and Hewer state that "at this point, our stage findings do not allow us to claim evidence for certain normative ethical conclusions which nevertheless remain Kohlberg's own philosophical preference for defining the ontogenetic end point of a rationally reconstructed theory of justice reasoning. In particular we cannot claim either that there is a single principle which we have found used as the current empirically highest stage, nor that that principle is the principle of justice or respect for persons. There may be other principles" (1983, 63). They allude to alternative principles such as "responsible love," and they acknowledge the existence of a rationally appealing "morality of particularistic relationships" (see Gilligan 1982). This particularistic morality need not be based on such principles as "contract" or universal respect for persons but is founded instead on such ideas as loyalty, caring, and responsibility (1983, 20). Yet later in the text Kohlberg, Levine, and Hewer (1983, 75) assert: "We claim that there is *a* universally valid form of rational moral thought process which all persons could articulate, assuming social and cultural conditions suitable to cognitive-moral stage development" (our emphasis).

One way to reconcile the two apparently contradictory assertions would be to postulate that Kohlberg's idea of a single, universally valid form of moral reasoning does not include, as a mandatory feature, the principle of justice or respect for persons but only some very general features like the abstract idea of an objective obligation. The problem with that attempted reconciliation is that Kohlberg quite clearly wants to deny that *any* moral principles are culturally variable "in a fundamental way" (1981, 73–74). He wants to assert that *all* divergences of moral belief can be reconciled by rational principles and methods (1982, 73–74). To eliminate the apparent contradictions in the text, one is tempted to ask: Are the principles of justice and respect for persons, then, not "fundamental" principles? Are discrepancies between normative ethics founded on justice versus those founded on particularistic relationships, loyalty, caring, and benevolent love, not to count as "divergences in moral beliefs"?

Kohlberg's theory has become a perplexing and shifting target, which, given its current complexities and flexible epicycles, is more difficult to represent in 1985 than it was in 1982. At present, the theory that is influential in the field is the one that preceded the current reformulation, and it is that theory that we have tried to represent. Nevertheless, the only criticisms of Kohlberg worth considering are those that still seem relevant after reflection on his latest reformulations. It is to those enduring criticisms that we now turn.

THE LIMITATIONS OF THE THEORY

Is cognitive development stagelike? One criticism of Kohlberg's theory addresses his claim that the development of rational reasoning, specifically the attainment of the cognitive stage of formal operational thinking as described by Piaget, is a precondition for genuine moral understanding. Unfortunately, the moral development literature has not clarified what is purely logical, as distinct from what is purely moral, about moral concepts like commitment, harm, duty, trust, or rights. Empirical studies have been inconclusive on the relations between performance on Piagetian logical tasks and performance on Kohlberg's moral dilemma interview (Haan, Weiss, and Johnson 1982).

Moreover, the Piagetian account of cognitive development has taken a beating in recent years (Shweder 1982c). It has come to be acknowledged that human cognitive growth is not very stagelike, and no single cognitive stage (preoperational, concrete operational, formal operational) is a characteristic property of an individual's cognitive functioning. The most recent comprehensive review of Piagetian concepts concludes that "the experimental evidence available today no longer supports the hypothesis of a major qualitative shift from preoperational to concrete operational thought" (Gelman and Baillargeon 1983, 167).

One implication of that evidence is that how an individual functions in Kohlberg's scheme may depend on what he or she is thinking about. Varying the manner of presentation of a problem limits the generality of a conclusion about conservation of number or liquid quantity. Similarly, by changing the content of a moral dilemma it may be possible to alter the modal stage response of a subject. For example, a subject may be stage four when thinking about stealing, but stage three when thinking about extramarital sex (see Gilligan et al. 1971).

Doubts about whether moral growth is very stagelike are reinforced by two facts. Approximately one-third of the responses of a typical subject come from stages other than the modal stage, and for any particular subject almost all responses come from only two stages, typically in a two to one ratio. As a theoretical structure Kohlberg's scheme has three levels, each divided into two stages. Hence, *in theory*, there are six stages. As an empirical phenomenon, however, stages one, two, five, and six occur rarely in pure form among adults, and stages one, four, five, and six occur rarely in pure form among children. The typical child mixes concepts and principles from stages two and three. The typical adult mixes concepts and principles from stages three and four. The main thing that distinguishes children from adults is that adults stop talking about personal likes and dislikes and start talking about social institutions and social systems. Both children and adults talk about social roles and status obligations (which, as we shall discuss later, may be a promising starting point for an alternative conception of a rationally based postconventional morality). In the study of moral development, it may be time to set aside the theoretical machinery of Piaget's stage theory of cognitive growth. The evidence suggests there are diverse concepts and forms of reasoning available to children and adults. What we do not yet understand is how the particular case one thinks about and the way it is represented make it more or less difficult to engage in one form of reasoning or another.

Is the test biased in favor of Westernized elites? A second criticism builds on Kohlberg's observation that certain populations receive higher stage scores than others. While it is not true, as is sometimes claimed, that men score higher than women on Kohlberg's moral development interviews (Walker 1984; Snarey 1985), social class is a major correlate of stage level. On a worldwide scale, the highest scores are achieved by Israelis of European origin, upper middle-class Americans and Western-oriented members of the urban elite in countries like Taiwan and India. Some critics see this as an indication of bias in

Kohlberg's scheme (Simpson 1974). An alternative interpretation, compatible with Kohlberg's theory, is that processes of rational reasoning and opportunities to engage in Socratic dialogue are unequally distributed across human populations. In other words, upper middle-class Americans are more rational than lower class Americans; Israelis of European origin are more rational than Israelis of African or Middle Eastern origin; and urban elite populations in Taiwan and India are more rational than traditional rural populations in those countries.

The thesis that there is an unequal distribution of rationality across populations has both supporters (Hallpike 1979) and critics (Cole and Scribner 1974; Shweder 1982a, 1982b, 1982c). It is important, however, to distinguish this thesis from a less controversial one with which it is sometimes confused, namely the thesis about the distribution of self-consciousness or deliberate meta-analysis. It is widely acknowledged among cognitive anthropologists and cross-cultural psychologists that individuals and populations do differ in the extent to which they reflect on what they know and explicitly formulate it. Few researchers would deny that those who are schooled are better at self-reflection and more likely to think about or even write down the rules for moral or logical thinking (see Scribner and Cole 1981). Self-consciousness about thinking probably is a useful cross-cultural and developmental variable. Not everyone has good verbal access to their own processes of rational reasoning.

Notice, however, that the thesis about meta-analysis has nothing to say about the types of rational processes available to a person or people. There is an important difference between implicit versus explicit understanding of principles. The fact that some cultures are more rational*ized* (self-reflective or "meta") than others does not mean that they are more rational. What is controversial is the question of the distribution of rational reasoning processes, as distinct from the mental skills of self-reflection, verbal access, and meta-analysis.

Why is postconventional thinking so rare? A third criticism comes closer to the concerns of this chapter. Perhaps the most striking research finding using Kohlberg's scheme is that very few people are postconventional thinkers. On a worldwide scale, only 1 or 2 percent of all responses are pure postconventional, and mixed conventional/postconventional responses (so-called stage four/five) account for only about 6 percent of responses (Snarey 1985). Even pure preconventional responses are infrequent. The vast majority of responses fall within the loose boundaries of the conventional level of understanding (stages three and four). If one accepts Kohlberg's moral dilemma interview methodology and the underlying interpretive logic of his scheme, then one must conclude that almost all adults in all cultures conceive of virtue as conformity with the subjective preferences of the group, and most never attain the idea that there are objective obligations that take precedence over the preferences and will of the group. That conclusion is not consistent with several more ethnographically based research findings on moral codes (Read 1955; Ladd 1957; Malinowski [1926] 1976; Firth 1951; Fortes, 1959). Firth's remarks on the Tikopia are typical of ethnographers' accounts of moral codes: "The spirits, just as men, respond to a norm of conduct of an external character. The moral law exists in the absolute, independent of the Gods" (quoted in Nadel 1957, 270–71). Moreover, if the idea of objective obligation does not occur to most people in most societies, it would suggest that most members of our species adhere to a rationally inadequate conception of morality. Not surprisingly, that conclusion has led some moral development researchers to raise doubts about Kohlberg's interview methodology, the logic of his conceptual scheme, or both.

THE METHODOLOGICAL CRITIQUE: WHY IS POSTCONVENTIONAL THINKING RARE?

Kohlberg's theory of moral development is about the development of moral understandings, yet his moral dilemma interview methodology is a verbal production task that places á high premium on the ability to generate arguments, verbally represent complex concepts, and talk like a moral philosopher. It is hazardous to rely on such a procedure when studying moral understandings because one of the most important findings of recent developmental research is that knowledge of concepts often precedes their self-reflective representation in speech. Young children know a great deal more about the concept of number, causation, or grammaticality than they can state. As Nisbett and Wilson (1977) have put it, people "know more than they can tell." A distinction is needed between implicit, tacit, or intuitive knowledge of a concept and the ability to state explicitly the knowledge one has.

To clarify the distinction between implicit and explicit knowledge of principles, consider research on adult understandings of natural language grammar. Most people do not have good verbal access to their own available concepts or intellectual processes. The ability to describe grammatical principles is a rather poor index of an individual's knowledge of the grammar of his language or of his ability to discriminate between grammatical and ungrammatical utterances. Most competent speakers of a language can make use of grammatical decision rules without being able to state what those rules are. Researchers would not confuse a theory about the development of grammatical competence with a theory about the development of the skills of a grammarian.

That, curiously, seems to be what has happened in the study of moral understandings. Those who study moral understandings with Kohlberg's moral dilemma interview have reduced the study of moral concepts to the study of verbal justification of moral ideas. The study of moral understanding has been narrowed, by methodological fiat, to the study of what people can propositionalize. That is dangerous because what people can state is but a small part of what they know.

Kohlberg's interview methodology requires subjects to access verbally their moral concepts, produce moral arguments, and talk like a moral philosopher. Several researchers (Turiel 1979, 1980; Nucci and Turiel 1978; Nucci 1981, 1982; Nucci and Nucci 1982; Smetana 1981a, 1981b, 1982, 1983; also see Shweder, Turiel, and Much 1981; Shweder 1982a) have relaxed the demand characteristics of the moral dilemma interview situation, requiring only that subjects be consistent in their responses to direct probes about the objective versus consensual status of moral versus conventional obligations. For example, children are asked whether an obligation is merely relative to the child's group or universally binding. "Suppose there is another country where parents and schools allow children to [pull each other's hair; wear no clothes at school]. Is that all right?" Others (e.g., Much and Shweder 1978) use a somewhat different technique and look at distinctions drawn between moral and nonmoral obligations, as revealed in the way children use language in "situations of accountability" to justify or excuse apparent violations of normative standards.

The findings from that research, where subjects are permitted to display their understandings by means of responses to simple, direct probes (or through naturally occurring language use), suggest a different portrait of the emergence of moral understandings, at least among children who are exposed to the family and school practices of Western liberal democracies. Probing their subjects about the impersonality, alterability, and relativity of obligations, Turiel, Nucci, and Smetana discover that even young children (ages three to five years) have an implicit understanding of the idea of an objective obligation. Young children distinguish moral rules (the prohibition on destroying the property of others without their permission) from conventional rules (it is wrong to eat horses but not wrong to eat cows; it is wrong for a boy to wear a dress to school every day). They recognize that, unlike conventional obligations, moral obligations cannot be altered by majority vote or the preferences of this or that group.

The Turiel, Nucci, and Smetana research suggests that young children understand the idea of an objective obligation. It also suggests that what children know is not necessarily revealed during a Kohlbergian interview. More directed probes may be needed to get at their implicit understandings. For example, children sometimes say such things as "it is wrong to steal because you'll be caught and sent to prison" (an apparent egoistic, preconventional response). However, when probed directly – "what if you would not be caught, you would get away with it?" – many of those same children maintain that stealing would still be wrong, and it would be wrong even if your father told you to do it, and even if most people voted to make it right. When children say "it is wrong to steal because you will be punished" they often mean "wrong things get punished, and stealing is punished because it is wrong." They do not usually mean "it's the punishment that makes something wrong." What children know and intend to communicate is not equivalent to the literal and surface interpretation of their often feeble attempts to identify and state in words the abstract principles underlying their judgments.

THE CONCEPTUAL CRITIQUE: WHY IS POSTCONVENTIONAL THINKING RARE?

A second reaction to Kohlberg's finding that so few people around the world exhibit genuine moral understandings is to question the underlying interpretive logic of his scheme (Shweder 1982a, 1982b; Shweder and Miller 1985). One reason so few people are postconventional may be that most people reject the particular conceptual reference points from which Kohlberg constructs his notion of a rationally appealing objective morality. It is important to recognize that for a person to reject Kohlberg's postconventional level of moral understanding is not the same as defining morality as positive law or subjective preference; there may be alternative conceptual starting points from which rationally to construct an objective morality. That type of critique of Kohlberg's interpretive logic is associated with the position that there are "divergent rationalities" in the moral domain (Shweder 1986).

The idea of "divergent rationalities" in the moral domain can be analyzed into the following claims. (1) There exists more than one rationally defensible moral code. (2) In any moral code with rational appeal, some concepts are "mandatory"; without those mandatory concepts the code loses its rational appeal. Other concepts are "discretionary"; they permit replacement by alternative concepts whose substitution into the code would not diminish its rational appeal. (3) Every moral code that is rationally defensible is built up out of *both* mandatory and discretionary concepts. The rational appeal of a moral code would be diminished, it would become empty, if it were divested of all discretionary concepts. (4) Kohlberg's particular conception of postconventional morality is not advocated by most rational thinkers around the world because they reject one or more of the particular discretionary concepts incorporated into his scheme.

What are the mandatory and discretionary features built into Kohlberg's conception of postconventional morality? As far as we can judge, there are at least three mandatory features. Those features have broad appeal among moral philosophers and are candidates for moral universals. There are also at least six discretionary features. Not all rational thinkers will find those particular features rationally appealing; they may elect to construct a moral code with substitute concepts or principles.

The three mandatory features are the idea of natural law, the principle of harm, and the principle of justice. The six discretionary features are a conception of natural law premised on natural "rights"; a conception of natural law premised on "voluntarism," "individualism," and a "prior to society" perspective; a particular idea of what or who is a "person"; a particular conception of where to draw the boundaries around the "territories of the self"; a conception of justice in which likenesses are emphasized and differences overlooked; and, finally, a rejection of the idea of divine authority. We consider briefly each of these features.

The Mandatory feature 1: the abstract idea of natural law. The idea of natural law has already been described at some length. The idea is implicated whenever we speak of a discrepancy between what is and what ought to be. The idea of natural law implies that there are certain practices and actions that are inherently wrong regardless of how much personal pleasure they might give us and despite the existence of rules or positive laws that might permit their occurrence. It is the idea of an objective obligation.

Mandatory feature 2: the abstract principle of harm. The principle of harm states that a legitimate ground for limiting someone's liberty to do as they want is a determination that harm is being done to someone. Life in society is made up of the direct and indirect effects of people's actions and inactions. Every rationally appealing moral code defines what consequences are permissible and justifies the regulation of certain actions by reference to their harmful effects, however those are conceived.

Mandatory feature 3: the abstract principle of justice. The principle of justice states that like cases must be treated alike and different cases differently (Hart 1961). Alternatively, what is wrong for one person is wrong for any similar person in similar circumstances (Singer 1963). The principle of justice is the normative or prescriptive side of the abstract idea of categorization. In effect, the principle of justice forces us to group people into those we treat one way (in like fashion) and those we treat another way (in like fashion). Any social categorization (kin versus nonkin, teacher versus student) implements the principle of justice by defining the kinds of people there are to have similar or different kinds of relationships with.

Discretionary feature 1: a rights-based conception of natural law. One discretionary feature of Kohlberg's moral code is a rights-based conception of natural law. The feature is discretionary because not every rationally defensible moral code must be founded on a conception of natural "rights." A moral code may be founded on a conception of natural "duties" or natural "goals" and remain rationally defensible. Dworkin (1977) has important things to say about the difference between rights-, goal-, and duty-based moral codes. He points out that while all moral codes may have some place for social goals, individual rights, and individual duties, rational moral codes differ significantly in the scales over which goals, rights, and duties range, and in the priority given to goals over rights, duties over goals. In a goal-based code, a good like "improving the general welfare" or "national security" is taken as fundamental and given priority. In a rights-based code, a right like "the right of all men to the greatest possible overall liberty" is taken as fundamental and given priority. In a rights-based code, a duty like "the duty to obey God's will as set forth in the Ten Commandments" is taken as fundamental and given priority.

It is crucial for Dworkin's conceptualization that rights, duties, and goals are not merely three idioms for saying the same things. If they were merely idioms, then every right could, in principle, be translated without loss of meaning into a parallel duty or goal, every duty into a goal or right, every goal into a duty or right. There are two reasons why perfect intertranslation cannot be achieved.

For one thing, there are duties and goals without correlative rights. In India, for example, it appears that the duty of a householder to feed a guest is owed to some third party or force like God or Hindu dharma, without any implication that the guest has a right to be fed, and in our own historical tradition parents had duties towards their children long before children could make rights claims against their parents.

Secondly, as Dworkin notes, rights and duties are not perfectly intertranslatable because even in those cases where duties and rights correlate "one is derivative from the other and it makes a difference which is derivative from which." He points out that the idea that "you have a duty not to lie to me because I have a right not to be lied to" is quite different in meaning from the idea that "I have a right that you not lie to me because you have a duty not to tell lies." They are different in meaning because "in the first place I justify a duty by calling attention to a right; if I intend further justification it is the right I must justify, and I cannot do it by calling attention to the duty. In the second case it is the other way around."

Duty-based codes have several distinctive features. In a duty-based code attention is focused on the moral quality of individual acts per se, on the degree of conformity of each act to a code for proper conduct. It is the code that takes precedence and it is the code that is the object of interpretation and elaboration, while the individual per se and his various "interior" states, preferences, appetites, intentions, or motives are of little interest or concern. The purity of the motive is less important than the quality of the act.

When moral codes are duty-based, the individual is supposed to match his or her actions to the code "or be punished or corrupted if he does not." The individual is not at liberty to deviate from the rule, or to call on others to do so. Within a duty-based code there is no such thing as a natural right (e.g., free speech) to encourage others to engage in wrong actions. In a duty-based code it would be incoherent to proclaim: "Do not impose your private morality on other people." Indeed, in duty-based moral codes, individual rights and the domain of what is private are typically subordinated to duties, and it is the duties associated with particular role relationships, of a wife to her husband, a host to his guest, that receive the most elaborate treatment in the code. It is the performance of duty, not the defense of liberty or personal conscience, that stimulates feelings of righteousness. To the extent that Kohlberg's scheme presupposes the existence of natural "rights" and gives them priority, the scheme will seem alien to any rational thinker who constructs a moral code on the basis of natural duties or natural goals.

Discretionary feature 2: natural individualism in the abstract. A second discretionary feature of Kohlberg's moral code is the priority given to individualism. Societies are built out of roles and statuses (mother-child, doctor-patient, teacher-student, etc.), for which there are performance obligations, and out of individuals, who have differential talents, abilities, powers, intelligences, resources, and beauty. Both are necessary for social action. A discretionary feature in any moral code concerns what is taken as more fundamental, real, natural, or of value: "roles and statuses" (the parts to be played) or "individuals" (the people who play the parts).

The most fundamental entity in Kohlberg's moral code is the "abstract individual." Kohlberg's individual is "abstract" in two senses. First, the individual is abstracted from society. Conceived to exist as an autonomous entity prior to or outside of the social arrangements in which he or she is found, hypothetically stripped of any distinguishing social identity, each individual is assumed to have an intrinsic, and equal, moral value quite apart from that which attaches to him or her as an occupant of a particular status. Second, the individual is abstracted out of his or her personality and divested of all distinguishing marks of character, such as differential power, intelligence, beauty, charisma; the abstract individual, by definition, has no individuality.

The abstract individual is the fundamental entity in Kohlberg's scheme because society is viewed as a logically derivative product, formed when abstract individuals enter into a social contract. Kohlberg's commitment to an abstract individual is most apparent in his attempt, following Rawls (1971), to derive a just society from the idea of a social contract forged under an aptly labeled "veil of ignorance." Rawls and Kohlberg argue that a just society is the one to which any individual (free of duress and concerned only with self-interest) would voluntarily bind himself if he had to form a society ignorant of who the comembers of the society were going to be, that is, ignorant of his relative intelligence, talent, power. The most basic unit in Kohlberg's moral code is a theoretically idealized individual abstracted from society and abstracted from his own psychological qualities.

An alternative approach to the rationalization of a moral code is to start with the assumption that social arrangements are primary or fundamental and to attribute moral significance to the universal fact of role differentiation (for example, within the family) and the unequal distribution of health, wealth, status, beauty, and intelligence across individuals. That view argues that a differentiated social morphology is part of the natural order of things, that the moral value of a person is dependent on the position occupied within a system of particularistic interpersonal relationships (see Read 1955) and that the moral value of a person can be measured by reference to the skills, talents, and psychological qualities that are his or her just desert. It judges as fair whatever actions ensure that the proportions between differentiated social functions and social roles are adapted to the society as a whole (see Dumont 1970). This idea that social arrangements are part of nature, and that social forms are more permanent and fundamental than the individuals who happen to pass through them, has had its appeal to many rational thinkers.

Discretionary feature 3: who is a person? A third discretionary feature in Kohlberg's moral code is his substantive conception of what or who is a "person" or "moral agent." Every moral code has some kind of more or less inclusive definition of who must abide by the standards of natural law and is entitled to just treatment and protection from harm. What is discretionary, however, are the category boundaries of the "person" or "moral agent." The rational defensibility of a moral code is probably unaffected by such decisions as, for example, whether illegal aliens have the same rights as citizens of the state or whether such entities as corporations, fetuses, cows, or dogs should receive protection from harm.

Kohlberg adopts a relatively inclusive definition of moral agent and treats as moral equivalents prisoners and free men, men and women, citizens and aliens, children and adults, heathens and nonheathens. His definition of a moral agent does not include fetuses, cows, fish, insects, plants, or other nonhuman living things. His definition is probably too inclusive for some rational thinkers who might argue that, just as the claims of one's children ought to take precedence over the claim of a stranger, so too the claims of a fellow "tribesman" ought to take precedence over the claims of an outsider. His definition of a person may not be inclusive enough for other moral thinkers who might argue that life is continuous and that even animals have a soul and should not be bred and raised in order to be killed and eaten.

Discretionary feature 4: which territories of the self? A fourth discretionary feature in Kohlberg's moral code is his substantive conception of where to draw the boundaries around the "territories of the self." Within any moral code "moral agents" or "persons" are entitled to protection from harm; yet, even after it is decided who is a "moral agent," another discretionary decision must be made: how expansively to define the realm worthy of protection that surrounds the "person."

In other words which invasions of which territories of the self are to be considered harmful attacks? Are the protected territories to include only our bodies and physical possessions, or are they to include also our feelings, reputation, and honor? Not all rational thinkers would care to defend the proposition that "sticks and stones can break your bones, but words can never harm you," or that honor is always less important than life, so suffer the insult.

Discretionary feature 5: justice as equality. A fifth discretionary feature is a substantive conception of justice in which likenesses are emphasized and differences overlooked. Kohlberg argues that justice requires every person's claims to be treated as equal, regardless of the person (1981, 144). What is moral vis-à-vis an American is moral vis-à-vis a Vietnamese; what is moral vis-à-vis a father is moral vis-à-vis a son (1981, 135). Kohlberg believes that in employing the utilitarian rule for maximizing general welfare the only just thing to do is count each individual as equal to one unit; no weighting is allowed. Thus, saving more lives is better than saving fewer lives, regardless of who it is that is saved, the old or the young, the good or the wicked. That conception of justice is not implied by the abstract idea of justice, which merely states "treat like cases alike and different cases differently." The abstract idea of justice does not state which likenesses or differences should count, whether or how they should be weighted, or how, in particular, like cases should be treated, other than being treated in the same way. When relevant differences can be cited it is not unjust to treat different cases differently. That is the reason why some rational thinkers argue that it can be a moral act to prohibit the son but not the father from casting a vote, and by analogy that no one should be allowed to vote who is uninformed about the issues or candidates or unable to exercise mature rational judgment. Within a population, rationality is not equally distributed, and some individuals may have greater vulnerabilities than others and require greater protection from themselves.

Discretionary feature 6: secularism. A final discretionary feature of Kohlberg's code is a secularism that rejects divine authority (1981, 312–18). That rejection is revealed when Kohlberg (1981, 315) argues that the statement "X ought to be done because it is a command of God (or is in the Bible, or is one of the Ten Commandments)" is equivalent to the statement "X is right because it is approved of by a majority of the Gallup Poll." In other words, the knowledge possessed by a superior or divine being set forth in sacred text has no greater epistemological status than majority votes or other expressions of the subjective preferences of a group of human beings. That idea commits Kohlberg to a particular, and in our view peculiar, definition of natural law, in which the only things that count as natural laws are things that human beings can discover *for themselves* (1981, 313), without the assistance of revealed or handed-down truths about right and wrong.

It is reasonable to presume that Kohlberg does not believe in superior beings who have privileged access to truths about natural laws. He seems to reject the idea that there might exist natural laws that human beings are unable to discover on their own, or that there might exist natural laws whose underlying rationale is difficult for mere human beings to understand, even after the natural law is revealed. Yet the idea of a superior or divine being (whose privileged access to truth is revealed in sacred texts) is neither incoherent nor irrational. Unless Kohlberg is prepared to argue that all rational thinkers must be atheists or that it is irrational to accept an account of the truth from beings thought to have superior powers of understanding, his attempt to equate divine commands with convention or group consensus must be seen as a discretionary act of a secular humanist that need not have universal appeal to all rational thinkers.

We have examined in some detail several discretionary features in Kohlberg's conception of postconventional moral understanding. Most of those features are variations on the idea that society has a rational foundation in a hypothetical social contract, and the related claim that the idea of an abstract, rational individual standing outside of, or prior to, society can be used as the fundamental and common measure of moral conduct. The underlying logic of Kohlberg's scheme is premised on voluntarism, secularism, and individualism, premises that not every rational thinker must adopt. There is the possibility that there is more than one form of postconventional thinking and that individualism is not the only premise out of which to construct a rationally appealing objective ethics.

We suspect that so few people around the world meet Kohlberg's criteria for postconventional thinking because they reject his particular rationalization of morality. Subjects classified as conventional thinkers (stages three and four) may be expressing an alternative form of postconventional thinking that cannot be easily classified within the terms of Kohlberg's scheme. We believe that is the case with our Hindu informants, as we shall see later. It may be true of Kohlberg's American informants as well.

Turiel's social interactional theory: overview and evaluation

OVERVIEW

Turiel, Nucci, and Smetana examine the young child's implicit understanding of abstract moral principles like natural law or universalizability. The research, however, does more than just provide a methodological critique of Kohlberg's verbal production interview task; it suggests an alternative theory of moral development. One way to conceptualize their theory is to imagine that Turiel, Nucci, and Smetana have turned Kohlberg's three-level scheme on its side. Instead of three levels of understanding (egoistic, conventional, and moral) they posit three domains of understanding (personal, conventional, and moral) which are distinguished from each other by young children, and which

	Domain A	Domain B	Domain C
	Moral	Conventional	Personal
Material conditions	Justice, harm, rights, welfare, allocation of resources	Social uniformities and regularities, food, clothes, forms of address, sex-roles	Psychological states, personal tastes and preferences
Formal conditions	Rational Universal Unalterable Objective Self-constructed More serious	Arbitrary Relative Alterable Consensus-based Socialized Less serious	

Figure 3.2. Turiel's social interactional domain theory of moral development turns Kohlberg's scheme (Figure 3.1) on its side.

undergo separate courses of elaboration, and increased sophistication (see figure 3.2). Moral understandings do not emerge out of conventional understandings but rather coexist with them during early childhood. The differentiation of what is moral from what is conventional is explained not by reference to the development of rational reasoning and exposure to Socratic dialogue but by reference to the distinguishing qualities of social interactional events. "Qualitatively distinct types of social interactions with different classes of events or actions lead to the construction of different types of social knowledge" (Smetana 1983, 134).

Turiel, Nucci, and Smetana accept Kohlberg's proposed criteria for distinguishing moral understandings from conventional ones, although they believe the distinction exists in early childhood. Morality refers to objective obligations concerning justice, harm, rights, and human welfare, and it is instantiated by actions (e.g., hitting and hurting; stealing personal property) that have an objective effect upon the well-being and rights of others. The idea of convention, in contrast, refers to certain actions that are right (or wrong) by virtue only of social consensus (e.g., men wearing pants instead of dresses; the idea that all work should stop on Saturdays for a day of rest).

A convention is the idea of an obligation for which there is no natural law. It is the idea that the rightness or wrongness of an action (shaking hands when greeting another) is arbitrarily designated and historically limited to a social consensus that happens to have formed. It is arbitrarily designated in that, from an objective or rational point of view, what happens to be right or wrong (eating beef but not pork) could have been designated otherwise. Turiel, Nucci, and Smetana hypothesize that socially demanded behavioral uniformities (traffic regulations, dress codes) are functionally advantageous for coordinating social interaction among members of a social system. That functional advantage, they argue, is the major reason that any social consensus develops at all around such issues as what to wear, what to eat, how to eat, how to address others (first name or title) (see Lewis 1969).

Turiel, Nucci, and Smetana believe there are intrinsically moral events. They argue that, through social interaction, children quickly come to distinguish those events that inherently possess a moral quality (connecting them to issues of harm, justice, and welfare) from those events whose rightness or wrongness is merely an extrinsic matter of social consensus. Young children are said to develop the idea of a moral event and the idea of a conventional event and to distinguish them from each other because they have had direct experience with both types of events and have learned that they are not the same.

The Turiel, Nucci, and Smetana theory does not postulate that every event must be purely moral or purely conventional. The theory acknowledges fuzzy boundaries and various blendings of types (Smetana 1983; Turiel and Smetana 1984; Turiel and Davidson, 1985). The theory does postulate the existence of enough pure moral events and pure conventional events to stimulate in the mind of the child a distinction between morality and convention.

For Turiel, Nucci, and Smetana, morality refers to objective obligations concerning harm, justice, rights, and the welfare of others. They argue that actions or events possess that moral quality if those actions or events involve physical or psychological harm, personal or private property, promises or commitments, or the allocation of scarce resources. Conventional events do not possess a moral quality, since their rightness or wrongness is acquired solely by virtue of social consensus, should such a social consensus develop. Those conventional events include food "customs," clothing "styles," sex-role definitions, forms of address, and sexual practices. According to the theory, ridiculing a cripple will be universally viewed by children as a moral event, while the norms prohibiting male business executives from wearing a dress to work will be viewed as conventional.

Turiel, Nucci, and Smetana credit young children with inferential ability to recognize the moral quality inhering in some events. These skills include means-ends analysis, the recognition of cause and effect connections, and simple forms of hypothetical and counterfactual reasoning (for example, "if everyone were to do that, then...."). Those cognitive skills make it possible to recognize the objective connection between pulling someone's hair and inflicting harm and the desirability of the presumption that such behavior is wrong, unless overridden by other moral considerations.

Young children are also credited with the ability to detect regularities in their social environment. They recognize that some actions are, for no apparent objective or rational reason, consistently considered wrong by members of the group. Turiel, Nucci, and Smetana argue this leads children to infer that conventionally based wrongness is arbitrary, relative to one's group, alterable by consensus, and less serious in the breach. According to the theory, conventional wrongs, but not moral wrongs, can only be learned through exposure to group consensus via social transmission processes – commands, sanctions, instructions. Moral wrongs are learned primarily through direct observation of the harm or injustice caused by a transgression. Finally, Turiel, Nucci, and Smetana argue that children take an interest in regulating, sanctioning, and intervening in other children's actions when those actions violate moral standards but remain relatively indifferent when children violate conventional norms for right conduct. Social conventions, they imply, are the concern of adults, not children.

In sum, Turiel, Nucci, and Smetana introduce an alternative methodology into the study of moral understandings, broad enough to include both implicit and explicit knowledge of moral concepts. They propose a theory of moral development in which moral understandings do not develop out of conventional understandings, but rather coexist with them from an early age. The central claims of the theory concern (a) the determinate content of moral versus conventional events (e.g., pulling hair vs. wearing brightly colored clothes to a funeral); and (b) the parallel series of oppositions (universal vs. relative; unalterable vs. alterable; serious vs. not serious; objective vs. subjective; inherent vs. extrinsic; rational vs arbitrary; directly observed vs. socialized) that distinguish both moral events and the idea of morality from conventional events and the idea of convention.

An evaluation of Turiel's social interactional theory

THE STRENGTH OF THE THEORY

The Turiel, Nucci, and Smetana research suggests that the mandatory principles of a rationally appealing moral code – the abstract or formal ideas of natural law, harm, and justice – are available between the ages of three and five years and can be elicited utilizing direct probes about the relativity, alterability, and importance of obligations. From the point of view of the young child, obligations are not overwhelmingly viewed as conventional, and, for at least a subclass of material events, the young child grasps the difference between objective, natural-law, reason-driven obligations and consensus-based, collective-preference, conformity-driven obligations. Happily, the research directs our attention to "social interaction" and to the child's intellectual and emotional appraisal of the consequences of his or her own actions (e.g., pulling someone's hair and making him or her cry), although the research gives relatively little weight to the way interactional events and their consequences are socially construed, or to the way children are assisted by others in appraising an event.

THE LIMITATIONS OF THE THEORY

Are events free of social meaning? One potential difficulty with the Turiel, Nucci, and Smetana theory is that it underplays the way ritual observances and customary practices involving food, sex, dress, the exchange of greetings, and terms of address may be linked through social meanings to mandatory moral principles like harm, justice, and natural law. The theory underestimates the potential importance and moral significance of events classified by the theory as conventional.

That tendency to overlook the role of social meaning in the development of moral understanding may be a by-product of Turiel, Nucci, and Smetana's definition of morality. Morality is defined not only by reference to the idea of natural law and objective obligation (a mandatory feature of any rationally appealing moral code), but by reference to natural "rights" (a discretionary feature). And morality is defined not only by reference to the abstract idea of harm (a mandatory feature) but by reference to only certain kinds of harms (direct and intended physical and psychological attacks) on certain types of "persons," namely sentient beings (a discretionary feature). Given that definition of morality, Turiel, Nucci, and Smetana have no difficulty identifying arbitrary assault (hitting and hurting), biased arbitration, and theft as prototypical examples of moral infractions. Yet with that definition of morality, how are we to classify the failure to perform funeral rites for deceased parents, or kissing and sexual foreplay between consenting adult brother and sister?

The theory is faced with a difficulty. On the one hand, the principle of harm could be broadened to include the distress or emotional upset that is caused when someone witnesses in others what they believe to be a violation of obligations. The concept of a "person" could be broadened to include such entities as the souls of deceased ancestors, God, nature, or anything else that is believed to be vulnerable to harm, insult, or abuse. Yet if the discretionary features that define a moral code are broadened in that way, it is no longer obvious why a domain of conventional events must be separated out from a domain of moral events; nudity or the violation of a dress code might be emotionally upsetting to someone, hence a moral event. On the other hand, if morality is equated with such discretionary features as natural "rights" and direct physical or psychological assaults on a sentient being, then we must classify as conventional events the obligation to perform funeral rites for your parents, and the taboo on incest between cautious, consenting adult siblings. That would be a misclassification from the point of view of most peoples of the world.

Such examples cannot be readily explained away as domain mixtures or second-order phenomena. It is not the case that our obligations concerning incest avoidance and a proper burial for the dead are understood as primarily conventional with secondary moral implications. On the contrary, at least for some peoples, the expectations associated with the incest taboo and funeral rites are the prototypes of a moral obligation.

An indirect, but fascinating, source of evidence on the issue of whether Turiel, Nucci, and Smetana's hypothesized domain of conventional events *must* be separated in development from the moral domain comes from Murdock's (1980) cross-cultural survey of theories about the causes of illness in 139 societies. Among the theories of illness surveyed by Murdock is the theory of "mystical retribution," in which acts in violation of some taboo or moral injunction cause illness directly (rather than through the mediation of some offended or punitive supernatural being) (1980, 18). Murdock lists six major types of rules, injunctions, and taboos in order of the frequency with which their violation is associated with subsequent illness.

It seems reasonable to assume that a rule whose violation is thought to make you sick is perceived as important. Thus, it is noteworthy that many of the actions that are thought, on a worldwide scale, to cause illness are from the class of actions Turiel, Nucci, and Smetana classify as "conventional." Violations of food taboos (e.g., a Muslim eating pork) are at the top of Murdock's list. Violations of sex taboos (e.g., adultery and incest) come next. Next come violations of "etiquette" taboos, especially "breaches of appropriate behavior towards kinsmen, strangers or social superiors," and violations of "ritual" taboos, defined as "breaches of appropriate behavior toward the supernatural." Fifth on the list are violations of "property taboos" (theft, trespass), a class of actions that Turiel, Nucci, and Smetana classify as "moral." The final class of transgressions frequently associated with illness are violations of "verbal taboos" (e.g., "blasphemy or the use of forbidden words"). In Murdock's data on theories of illness through mystical retribution, actions classified by Turiel, Nucci, and Smetana as conventional (e.g., forms of address to social superiors) are not necessarily treated as different from actions classified as moral (e.g., theft).

Turiel, Killen, and Helwig (1987, 155–244) have noted that children and adolescents sometimes make distinctions between moral and conventional (nonmoral) events by weighing the seriousness of the transgression; the more serious breaches are considered moral. If seriousness of breach is an indication of the moral (versus nonmoral) quality of an event, and if the belief that a breach will cause illness is an indication of perceived seriousness, then the cross-cultural evidence surveyed by Murdock does not support the proposition that food customs, sexual practices, modes of dress and address, and ritual practices will be excluded from the moral domain. One possible conclusion consistent with Murdock's result is that if food customs, ritual observances, sexual practices, and modes of dress are inherently nonmoral, then perceived seriousness of breach is not a measure of what is moral (versus nonmoral). A second, more appealing conclusion is that there are no inherently nonmoral events. Nothing in the first-order interactional experience of events per se demands a distinction between morality and convention.

In a discussion of "domain mixtures," Smetana (1983, 134–41) stops just short of drawing that latter conclusion. Noting that events classified in her theory as conventional are not always viewed as conventional by her child informants, Smetana describes ways in which what she views as conventional events can be reinterpreted as moral. For example, a child addressing a teacher in front of the whole class by her first name or a child answering a question without raising his hand can be viewed as morally wrong by interpreting those events as psychological insults, unfair to the rights of others, causing injury, or hurting someone's feelings. While it is our view that there are other ways to moralize an event, for example, by reference to violations of natural duties, or by direct reference to a scriptural code of natural law, Smetana's observations on "domain mixtures" are sufficient to raise an important doubt for us about the *inevitablity* of the development of domain distinctions between morality and convention in moral development. We are skeptical about the proposition that a class of nonmoral events must universally be distinguished from, and set in contrast to, a class of moral events in the minds of children and adults. We are skeptical because we do not believe there exists a universal class of inherently nonmoral events. Nor do we believe that every culture draws a distinction between what is moral and what is conventional, although some cultures do.

Is thinking free of social communication? A second potential difficulty with the Turiel, Nucci, and Smetana theory is that it underplays the importance of tacit and explicit social communication in the interpretation of an event as moral. It is conceivable that there are certain actions (e.g., poking someone in the eye with a stick) whose wrongness young children might, in principle, be able to figure out for themselves by observing the consequence and empathizing with the victim, or by working out the counterfactual, "what if that had happened to me?" That is the type of self-construction process, through direct interaction, that Turiel, Nucci, and Smetana associate with the acquisition of primary moral understandings; processes of social communication, they argue, are decisive only in the acquisition of conventional obligations.

While it is possible to conceive of self-construction processes in the development of certain primary moral obligations, it seems to us an open empirical question whether the wrongness of moral actions is learned that way in practice. It is also an open empirical question whether wrongs that are learned through social communication will be viewed as conventional and consensus-based, deriving their authority exclusively from the commands of the parent or group. Whether an event is interpreted as moral or conventional – indeed, whether a distinction is drawn between morality and convention – may be related to how events are talked about and represented.

The relevance of social communication to moral development is highlighted by Edwards' work (1985) on naturally occurring transgressions among Luo children in the South Nyanza district of Kenya. Edwards analyzed a corpus of 105 transgression events, observed in connection with a study by Carol R. Ember. The recorded events, which include verbatim transcripts of verbal accusations, commands, threats, excuses, and accounts between child caretakers (ages seven-and-a-half to sixteen) and their young charges, consist of violations that Turiel, Nucci, and Smetana classify as moral (e.g., aggression toward peers, aggression toward animals) and violations they classify as conventional (e.g., terms of address, displays of deference, appropriate greetings, etc.). Edwards draws several pertinent and pro-vocative conclusions from the analysis of her corpus.

First, with regard to events that Turiel, Nucci, and Smetana classify as moral (e.g., aggression toward small children or animals), "the victim's response is not the main, and certainly not the only, source of information for Oyugis children. Luo culture contains strong prohibi-tions against the striking of infants and toddlers by older children. Adults clearly communicate to children, first, that infants and toddlers are too little to be beaten no matter what, and second, that hurting and striking small children is a punishable offense." Furthermore, observations suggest that children are not left to construct moral rules concerning cruelty to animals on their own, by simply observing the victim's response. Rather, aggressive children are assisted in inhibiting action by intervening adults and children, "who rely a great deal on the use of commands, threats and sanction statements to stop aggressive behavior." Edwards points out that prohibitions against hitting and hurting and other forms of aggression require "enforcing by sanction-ing agents to convince children that these matters are serious and not to be forgotten."

Second, with regard to events that Turiel, Nucci, and Smetana classify as conventional, Edwards points out that the Luo "put a great deal of stress on proper social forms" – the correct use of titles, kinship, age and status terms, appropriate greetings, avoidance, and joking to communicate interpersonal difference in rank, status, and power. On the basis of the recorded episodes it appears that the Luo consider those events to be just as important as those events that we would view as harmful or unjust. Younger children are called by older children to account for violations of so-called conventional events, just as they are for violations of moral events. Indeed, Edwards argues that "justice, harm and welfare rules, on the one hand, and conventional rules, on the other, are not necessarily learned in different kinds of social encounters."

Third, with regard to the command, threat, and sanction statements that frequently accompany transgressions in both the moral and "con-ventional" domain, Edwards suggests that they do not lead the Luo child to conclude that rules are arbitrary or consensus-based, or that rules derive their force simply from punishment. She argues that in the Luo cultural context, commands and sanction statements convey in-formation about the basic importance and unconditionality of rules. Luo children interpret a command or threat to mean, "These rules are not to be taken lightly. Obey them whether I am there or not."

Fourth, with regard to the finding that American children view conventional rules (dress styles, forms of address, food customs, manners, and etiquette) as less important and more negotiable than moral rules, Edwards suggests that such a differentiation of convention versus morality may not be a developmental universal. At least for the Luo, relationships of status, power, age and kinship, and the proper forms of address, greeting, avoidance, and deferential display are understood as part of the moral-natural order of things and do not stand in contrast to morality. One is tempted to suggest that for the Luo, and for many other people as well, forms of address are as important as the status relationships they are meant to signal or express.

Turiel, Nucci, and Smetana may be able to accommodate the Luo evidence within their theory. They might argue, for example, that, for the Luo, certain conventional events have moral implications that are lacking in our society. Two decisive questions would still remain. First, at what point do conventional events with moral implications become moral events with moral implications? Second, why is it not possible for all conventional events to become moral events with moral implications? If it is possible, then a domain distinction between morality and convention may not be a cross-cultural or developmental universal.

From review to preview

Kohlberg and Turiel have made important contributions to our understanding of moral development. But as indicated in our review, the cognitive-developmental and social interactional theories of moral development have raised as many conceptual and empirical issues as they have resolved. Several of those problematic issues are addressed in the cross-cultural developmental research from India and the United States reported below.

The research assesses Kohlberg's central claim that conventional understandings precede moral understandings, and the Kohlbergian finding that children and most adults do not possess an idea of natural law or objective obligations. The research assesses Turiel, Nucci, and Smetana's central claim that the distinction between conventional obligations and moral obligations is a universal of childhood and adulthood, and that some events are inherently moral and other events inherently nonmoral.

We have discovered through our research that moral events cannot be distinguished from conventional events on substantive grounds. For example, among orthodox Brahmans and Untouchables in India, eating, clothing and naming practices, and various ritual events are viewed in moral, rather than conventional, terms, and several practices (wife beating, sleeping in the same bed with a menstruating woman) that one culture views as harmful are not seen as harmful by the other culture.

Second, while we have discovered that some principles and practices (e.g., keeping promises, protecting the vulnerable, avoiding incest, justice, unprejudiced judgment, reciprocity, respect for personal property) are strong candidates for universal features in any moral code, we are far less confident that there exists a universal class of inherently nonmoral events. Those "deep" moral principles that are shared across cultures do not characteristically lead to similar judgments about what is right or wrong in particular cases. Any event can be made moral by appropriately linking it to a deep moral principle.

Third, we have discovered (pace Kohlberg and Turiel) that, on a worldwide scale, the idea of convention plays a relatively minor role in everyday understandings of obligations. Postconventional moral conceptions of obligation represent the dominant mode of rule understanding held by all informants, Indian and American, child and adult, male and female. The postconventional emphasis in America is on the natural "right" to free contract, personal choice, and individual liberty. The postconventional emphasis in India is on the natural "duty" to respect the "truths" of Hindu dharma, which concern the justice of received differences and inequalities, the moral implications of asymmetrical interdependencies in nature (for example, parent-child), and the vulnerabilities and differential rationality of social actors.

The idea of convention, the idea that obligations are consensus-based, relative, and alterable, is not absent from the interviews, but it occurs almost exclusively in the thinking of American adults and older American children. American children and adults express the democratic ideology that any collection of like-minded individuals is free to construct for themselves their own design for living, as long as other differently minded individuals are free to "exit" and form their own society. When a practice (serving horse meat but not dog meat for dinner) is viewed as conventional, typically it is by an American adult or eleven- to thirteen-year-old. Orthodox Hindu informants make little use of the idea of convention. They view their practices as direct expressions of natural law. Among American children under age ten, there is not a single practice in our study that is viewed predominantly in conventional terms, although as American children get older certain practices and events do evoke the idea of convention.

Fourth, we have discovered that the communication and the socialization of a moral code proceed rapidly over ontogeny and seem to influence the direction of developmental change in social cognition. The culture-specific aspects of a moral code seem to be acquired as early in childhood as the more universal aspects, although socialization pressures and communication channels seem to be far more intense and/or effective in Hyde Park than in Bhubaneswar. There is relatively little evidence for a spontaneous universal childhood morality unrelated to adult attitudes and doctrines. For the most part, the moral thinking of Indian and American children is much like the thinking of adults in their respective cultures and distinct from the thinking of the children in the other culture.

Moreover, the directionality of change in moral thinking seems to be culture-specific. As Americans grow older they rely more on the idea of convention and become more pluralistic or relativistic in their judgments. As Indians grow older they show a greater and greater tendency to view their practices as universally binding and unalterable.

While it is possible to argue from the data for a culture-specific domain distinction between morality and convention among American adults and older American children, the research suggests that the idea of a conventional practice does not necessarily stand in contrast to the idea of morality. Rather the idea of a convention may be a second-order moral concept, distinctive of a democratic world view with an ideology of free contract. In democratic societies with a preponderant free-market mentality, one ideally grants to people the natural right to freely choose the way they want to live, and the natural right to enter voluntarily into a covenant to "convene" a society with other free, like-minded individuals. The emerging consensus about how to organize a society becomes a natural source of obligations, and respect for the conventions set forth in the covenant becomes a moral obligation.

Finally, the research suggests that the abstract idea of natural law or objective obligation may be universal to childhood and adulthood while several discretionary features of moral codes, which help constitute the rationality of any particular code, need not be universal. There may be more than one type of postconventional moral understanding. Having previewed the major findings of the study we turn to the study itself.

The development of moral understanding in Bhubaneswar and Hyde Park

METHOD

Informants. The American sample includes thirty male and thirty female children from each of the age ranges five to seven, eight to ten, and eleven to thirteen, as well as thirty male and thirty female adults, a total of 180 children and sixty adults. The informants, predominately white, and of middle-class or upper milddle-class background, are descendants of the reformed to secularized branches of the Christian or Jewish traditions. Most of the informants would describe themselves as Protestant, Catholic, or Jewish. Some of the adults would describe themselves as secular humanists or atheists. Few would describe themselves as orthodox. Children were recruited from schools in Hyde Park, the residential community surrounding the University of Chicago. The adults in the sample were, for the most part, parents of children attending these schools, although only children and adults from different families were recruited in the sample. While the majority of the adults sampled are Hyde Park parents, there are some informants who are not parents of school-age children.

The Indian sample consists of two subsamples, Brahmans and "Untouchables." The Brahman subsample includes thirty male and thirty female informants from each of the age ranges five to seven, eight to ten, and eleven to thirteen, as well as thirty male and thirty female adults, a total of 180 children and sixty adults. The informants are orthodox Hindus residing in the old temple town of Bhubaneswar, Orissa, a residential community surrounding the eleventh–twelfth century Hindu temple of Lingaraj.

The Lingaraj temple is a pilgrimage site for Hindus from all over India. Most of the informants in the Brahman sample come from families in which at least one male member performs hereditary duties in the cycle of ritual activities in this functioning Hindu temple. The deity residing in the temple is Lingaraj, a form of the Hindu god Siva, represented through a stone lingam. Each day in the temple the deity is awakened, bathed, and dressed. Food is cooked for him and he is fed. He takes a nap. He holds audience. Functionaries from the resident Brahman castes assist him in these activities. They also serve as guides for pilgrims, possessing as they do hereditary privileges to escort pilgrims from designated districts throughout India. In addition to the scores of functions performed every day in the temple, there are astrologically determined dates during the annual cycle of the temple when the deity is brought out of the temple to, for example, visit his married sister, beg forgiveness for his sins at the nearby temple of the god of death (Yama), take a vacation to the temple of a maternal aunt, or go on an outing with his wife, the goddess Parvati.

Temple duty is not a full-time occupation for most of the adult male informants in the sample. Most are employed or engaged in other activities or occupations, as shopkeepers, tailors, civil servants, teachers, or property owners and landlords. Nevertheless, the status of the Brahman families in the sample is defined by their role in the ritual activities of the temple. The orthodoxy of the social and family practices of the Brahman community in the old town is not unrelated to their desire to maintain the sanctity of the temple and preserve the pilgrimage trade. All of the adult Brahman women in the sample have maintained traditional female roles in a Brahman household or joint family, as wife, mother-in-law, or widowed matriarch. Brahman children in the sample were recruited from schools in the old town community and from families familiar to the authors. The adults in the sample were recruited by word of mouth through friendship networks from Brahman families resident in neighborhoods surrounding the Lingaraj temple.

The "Untouchable" sample includes thirty male and thirty female informants in the age range eight to ten years, as well as thirty male and thirty female adults. The informants are members of those castes referred to as "scheduled" castes by the government of India (scheduled for affirmative action programs), as Harijans or "children of God" by Gandhi, and as "unclean" castes by the local Brahmans. They come primarily from the local Bauri, Hadi, and Pana communities.

The traditional occupations of these informants include agricultural labor, latrine cleaning, and basket making. The men and women in the sample regularly seek employment as physical laborers in road and house construction, stone quarrying, and harvesting. Informants from these "scheduled" castes reside either in the old temple town of Bhubaneswar or in neighboring villages. A few of the children were recruited through local schools. Many were recruited with the assistance of local members of the respective communities. Adult informants were recruited through friendship networks. According to local doctrine, members of "Untouchable" castes do not maintain their own sanctity and thus are not permitted to enter or come in contact with any holy ground. And in India there are many holy grounds, including the physical body of a Brahman, the house of a high-caste family, the purificatory waters of sacred rivers, ponds and wells, and all temples. Untouchables are not permitted entry to the Lingaraj temple.

The thirty-nine cases. The core of the study is an examination of American and Indian childhood and adult interpretations and understandings of thirty-nine behavioral cases. The thirty-nine cases, representing a range of family life and social practices, were developed over a period of several months on the basis of ethnographic knowledge of community life in Bhubaneswar and Hyde Park. Mahapatra is an anthropologist and a native resident of the old temple town. At the time the study began (October 1982) Shweder had previously conducted eighteen months of field research in Bhubaneswar.

The examination of informant interpretations was undertaken by means of a standard set of interview questions designed to assess an informant's understanding of obligations as subjective versus objective or conventional versus moral. The interview questions are described below. Informants were also presented with a ranking task to assess the perceived seriousness of the potential transgression event in each of the thirty-nine cases. The thirty-nine cases were developed with several objectives in mind.

One aim was to determine the extent to which the social order is perceived as moral or conventional by children and adults in India and America. Thus, cases were selected to sample a set of existential issues that must be addressed by any social system. The existential issues of concern in this study are personal boundaries (what's me/what's not me?), sexual identity (what's male/what's female?), maturity (what's grown-up or responsible/what's childish or irresponsible?), autonomy (am I autonomous and self-reliant/am I interdependent and mutually reliant?), ethnicity (what's our way/what's not our way?), hierarchy and status (who's up/who's down; how should life's burdens and benefits be distributed?), identification-empathy-solidarity (whose interests do I take into account/whose interests do I not take into account?), personal protection (avoiding a power order or "the war of all against all") and the "state" (what I want to do versus what the group wants me to do) (see Shweder 1982a). Cases were developed that related to one or more of those issues.

A second aim was to test Turiel, Nucci, and Smetana's hypothesis that a distinction between moral and conventional obligations can be drawn on substantive grounds. Thus, certain cases were selected to exemplify practices that Turiel, Nucci, and Smetana would classify as primarily conventional (e.g., regulations and restrictions concerning dress, food, terms of address, ritual practices, sex role definitions). Other events were selected to exemplify practices that their theory would classify as primarily moral (e.g., regulations concerning property, promises, and physical and psychological attacks on another person).

A third aim was to identify principles and concepts that might be candidates for moral universals. The moral philosophy literature from Hobbes to Kohlberg suggests several candidate concepts: justice, harm, reciprocity, protection of the vulnerable, altruism, honesty, loyalty, the honoring of commitments, and various prohibitions related to theft, ingratitude, biased arbitration, arbitrary assault, and the use of irrelevant classifications. Cases were selected to represent those candidate principles.

The fourth and final aim in selecting a corpus of behavioral cases was to further the development of an ethnography of family life. Thus, culture-specific practices were included in the study, in addition to practices that might have a more universal distribution. Cases were developed having to do with sanctity (pollution), chastity and respect for status (central themes for Indians), personal liberty, privacy, and equality (central themes for Americans). The thirty-nine behavioral cases are listed in table 3.1. They are listed in order of the perceived seriousness of the transgression involved, as judged by eight- to ten-year-old Brahman children in the old town of Bhubaneswar.

The descriptions of the thirty-nine cases and the interview questions (to be described below) were developed first in English, then translated into Oriya (the state language of Orissa) for use with Indian informants, and then back-translated into English for use with American informants.

The interview. Questions were developed to assess features of an informant's understanding of the nature of obligations. Some questions probed the extent and seriousness of the obligation. Other questions indexed the perceived impersonality or objectivity of the obligation, with special reference to the features of relativity and alterability. Responses to the questions made it possible to classify informant understanding along several axes and into several categories, including the distinction between conventional and moral obligations.

The thirty-nine cases were divided into three thirteen-case subsets for use with the standard series of questions. Each subset of cases was administered to one-third of the males and one-third of the females in

Table 3.1. *Thirty-nine cases in order of perceived "seriousness of breach" as judged by Hindu Brahman eight- to ten-year-olds*

1. The day after his father's death, the eldest son had a haircut and ate chicken.
2. One of your family members eats beef regularly.
3. One of your family members eats a dog regularly for dinner.
4. A widow in your community eats fish two or three times a week.
5. Six months after the death of her husband the widow wore jewelry and bright-colored clothes. (the widow)
6. A woman cooked rice and wanted to eat with her husband and his elder brother. Then she ate with them. (the woman)
7. A woman cooks food for her family members and sleeps in the same bed with her husband during her menstrual period. (the woman)
8. After defecation (making a bowel movement) a woman did not change her clothes before cooking.
9. A man had a wife who was sterile. He wanted to have two wives. He asked his first wife and she said she did not mind. So he married a second woman and the three of them lived happily in the same house. (the man)
10. Once a doctor's daughter met a garbage man, fell in love with him and decided to marry him. The father of the girl opposed the marriage and tried to stop it because the boy was a garbage man. In spite of the opposition from the father, the girl married the garbage man. (the daughter)
11. A widow and an unmarried man loved each other. The widow asked him to marry her. (the widow)
12. A beggar was begging from house to house with his wife and sick child. A homeowner drove him away without giving him anything. (the homeowner)
13. In a family, a twenty-five-year-old son addresses his father by his first name. (the son)
14. It was the king's order, if the villagers do not torture an innocent boy to death, twelve hundred people will be killed. The people killed the innocent boy. So the king spared the life of the twelve hundred people. (the people)
15. A poor man went to the hospital after being seriously hurt in an accident. At the hospital they refused to treat him because he could not afford to pay. (the hospital)
16. A brother and sister decide to get married and have children.
17. The day after the birth of his first child, a man entered his temple (church) and prayed to God.
18. A woman is playing cards at home with her friends. Her husband is cooking rice for them. (the husband)
19. A father told his son to steal flowers from his neighbor's garden. The boy did it. (the boy)
20. While walking a man saw a dog sleeping on the road. He walked up to it and kicked it. (the man)
21. Two people applied for a job. One of them was a relative of the interviewer. Because they were relatives, he was given the job although the other man did better on the exam.

Table 3.1. *(continued)*

22. Immediately after marriage, a son was asked by his parents to live in the same house with them. The son said he wanted to live alone with his wife and that he and his wife had decided to live in another town and search for work there. (the son)
23. A man says to his brother, "Your daughter's skin is dark. No one will say she is beautiful. No one will wish to marry her." (the man)
24. A father said to his son, "If you do well on the exam, I will buy you a pen." The son did well on the exam, but his father did not give him anything, spending the money on a carton of cigarettes. (the father)
25. Two brothers ate at home together. After they ate, the wife of the younger brother washed the dishes. (the wife)
26. A man had a married son and a married daughter. After his death his son claimed most of the property. His daughter got a little. (the son)
27. At night a wife asked her husband to massage her legs. (the wife)
28. A wife is waiting for her husband at the railway station. The train arrives. When the husband gets off, the wife goes and kisses him. (the wife)
29. There was a rule in a hotel: Invalids and disfigured persons are not allowed in the dining hall.
30. You went to a movie. There was a long line in front of the ticket window. You broke into line and stood at the front.
31. You meet a foreigner. He is wearing a watch. You ask him how much it cost and whether he will give it to you.
32. In school a girl drew a picture. One of her classmates came, took it, and tore it up.
33. A father, his eldest son and youngest daughter traveled in a boat. They had one life jacket. It could carry one person. The boat sank in the river. The father had to decide who should be saved. He decided to save his youngest daughter. The father and the eldest son drowned. (the father)
34. A letter arrived addressed to a fourteen-year-old son. Before the boy returned home, his father opened the letter and read it.
35. A young married woman went alone to see a movie without informing her husband. When she returned home her husband said, "If you do it again, I will beat you black and blue." She did it again; he beat her black and blue. (the husband)[a]
36. In a family, the first-born son slept with his mother or grandmother till he was ten years old. During these ten years he never slept in a separate bed. (the practice)[a]
37. A boy played hookey from school. The teacher told the boy's father and the father warned the boy not to do it again. But the boy did it again and the father beat him with a cane. (the father)[a]
38. A man does not like to use a fork. Instead he always eats rice with his bare hand. He washes it before and after eating. He does this when he eats alone or with others.[a]
39. Two men hold hands with each other while they wait for a bus.[a]

[a] Not considered a breach.

Table 3.2. *The standard questions*

1. Is (*the behavior under consideration*) wrong?
2. How serious is the violation?
   (*a*) not a violation
   (*b*) a minor offense
   (*c*) a somewhat serious offense
   (*d*) a very serious violation
3. Is it a sin?
4. What if no one knew this had been done. It was done in private or secretly. Would it be wrong then?
5. Would it be best if everyone in the world followed (*the rule endorsed by the informant*)?
6. In (*name of a relevant society*) people do (*the opposite of the practice endorsed by the informant*) all the time. Would (*name of relevant society*) be a better place if they stopped doing that?
7. What if most people in (*name of informant's society*) wanted to (*change the practice*). Would it be okay to change it?
8. Do you think a person who does (*the practice under consideration*) should be stopped from doing that or punished in some way?

each age-community subgroup. Having informants answer the questions concerning thirteen rather than thirty-nine cases was a strategy designed to avoid possible fatigue or boredom effects that might have resulted from a more lengthy interview. A list of the question probes appears in table 3.2.

The questions can be viewed as criteria for distinguishing moral or objective obligations from conventional or consensus-based obligations while identifying those areas of conduct where it is perceived that one has the moral right to do whatever one wants. The first three questions assess the existence or nonexistence of an obligation and the perceived importance of the obligation, should one exist. Question 4, concerning self-regulation in the absence of external observers, indexes one aspect of the difference between moral and conventional obligations. Questions 5 through 7 tap the perceived universality (versus relativity) and unalterability (versus alterability) of obligations.

Obligations that are thought to be relative to particular groups and alterable by consensus or majority will are readily classified as conventional obligations. Obligations that are perceived as universally binding and unalterable are readily classified as moral obligations.

The perceived relativity of an obligation is a necessary but not sufficient criterion of conventional understandings, because obligations need not be perceived as universally binding to be perceived as objective or moral. It is not incoherent or self-contradictory for an informant to believe that a moral or objective obligation may be tailored to the special requirements of a population, its temperament, its climate, its local context. We return in a moment to the issue of how to classify obligations that are thought to be unalterable, but only binding on some particular groups and not other groups. Finally, question 8, concerning sanctions, and the perceived legitimacy or illegitimacy of outside regulation, makes it possible to identify cases where informants believe there is a moral right to freedom of choice to do what one wants.

Our use of the questions in assessing an informant's understanding of obligations is illustrated in the following responses given by a hypothetical Brahman adult and American adult to case 4 (table 3.1), concerning a widow in your community who eats fish two or three times a week. First, the Brahman interview:

1. Is the widow's behavior wrong? (Yes. Widows should not eat fish, meat, onions or garlic, or any "hot" foods. They must restrict their diet to "cool" foods, rice, dhal, ghee, vegetables.)
2. How serious is the violation? (A very serious violation. She will suffer greatly if she eats fish.)
3. Is it a sin? (Yes. It's a "great" sin.)
4. What if no one knew this had been done? It was done in private or secretly. Would it be wrong then? (What difference does it make if it is done while alone? It is wrong. A widow should spend her time seeking salvation – seeking to be reunited with the soul of her husband. Hot foods will distract her. They will stimulate her sexual appetite. She will lose her sanctity. She will want sex and behave like a whore.)
5. Would it be best if everyone in the world followed the rule that widows should not eat fish? (That would be best. A widow's devotion is to her deceased husband – who should be treated like a god. She will offend his spirit if she eats fish.)
6. In the United States, widows eat fish all the time. Would the United States be a better place if widows stopped eating fish? (Definitely, it would be a better place. Perhaps American widows would stop having sex and marrying other men.)
7. What if most people in India wanted to change the rule so that it would be considered all right for widows to eat fish. Would it be okay to change the rule? (No. It is wrong for a widow to eat fish. Hindu dharma – truth – forbids it.)
8. Do you think a widow who eats fish should be stopped from doing that or punished in some way? (She should be stopped. But the sin will live with her and she will suffer for it.)

Next consider the American interview.

1. Is the widow's behavior wrong? (No. She can eat fish if she wants to.)
2. How serious is the violation? (It's not a violation.)
3. Is it a sin? (No.)
4. What if no one knew this had been done. It was done in private or secretly. Would it be wrong then? (It is not wrong, in private or public.)

5. Would it be best if everyone in the world followed the rule that it is all right for a widow to eat fish if she wants to? (Yes. People should be free to eat fish if they want to. Everyone has that right.)
6. In India, it is considered wrong for a widow to eat fish. Would India be a better place if it was considered all right for a widow to eat fish if she wants to? (Yes. That may be their custom but she should be free to decide if she wants to follow it. Why shouldn't she eat fish if she wants to?)
7. What if most people in the United States wanted to change the rule so that it would be considered wrong for a widow to eat fish? Would it be okay to change it? (No. You can't order people not to eat fish. They have a right to eat it if they want.)
8. Do you think a widow who eats fish should be stopped from doing that or punished in some way? (No!)

It should be noted that questions 5 through 7 are asked regarding the rule or obligation that is endorsed by the informant and perceived by the informant as relevant to the case. In some cases, as in the Brahman example, this rule or obligation may concern the regulation or proscription of a particular practice. In some cases, as in the American example, the rule or obligation may concern the protection of an agent's freedom of choice or autonomous decision making, in which case the interview assesses whether personal freedom in such matters is moral or conventional.

In the two sample interviews presented above neither informant viewed the dietary practices of widows in conventional terms. Although they disagreed about the morally right thing to do, both the Indian Brahman and the American viewed the issue as a moral issue. Both viewed the obligations involved as universally binding (questions 5 and 6) and unalterable (question 7). For the Brahman the relevant obligation was a status obligation associated with widowhood and the continued mutual reliance of husband and wife. For the American the relevant obligation was the obligation to protect the personal liberties and zones of discretionary choice of autonomous individuals. For the American whether you eat fish or not is your own personal business. The right to personal liberty and discretionary choice concerning what you eat is a moral issue. The obligation to protect that liberty is an objective obligation. Neither informant argued that the obligations involved were relative to this or that group or alterable by consensus or majority vote.

Crossing the relativity versus universality criteria (questions 5 and 6) with the alterability versus unalterability criteria (question 7) produces four categories for classifying informants' understandings of obligations. See table 3.3.

Classifying responses as conventional versus moral. Much of our discussion of conventional and moral obligations will focus on informant responses to questions 5 and 6, concerning the relativity of obligations,

Table 3.3. *Categorizing obligations into types*

	Questions 5 and 6	
	Universal Obligation	Relative Obligation
Unalterable obligation	Universal moral obligation	Context-dependent moral obligation
Question 7		
Alterable obligation	Incoherent	Conventional obligation

and question 7, concerning the alterability of obligations. For the sake of that discussion it is useful to distinguish the idea of a universal moral obligation from the idea of a context-dependent or culture-specific moral obligation. It is also useful to distinguish further both those types of moral obligations from conventional ones that are perceived not only as context-dependent or culture-specific but also as alterable. Treating relativity (versus universality) and alterability (versus unalterability) as independent dichotomous variables in a 2×2 factorial design, we generate four possible types of understandings of obligations: universal moral obligations (universal and unalterable), context-dependent moral obligations (relative and unalterable), conventional obligations (relative and alterable), and a logically incoherent fourth category in which it is held that obligations are universally binding but can be altered by consensus in a particular society.

The understanding of obligations as universal moral obligations is exemplified by a Brahman informant who argues that it is wrong to let young children sleep alone in a separate room and bed because children awaken during the night and are afraid, and that all parents have an obligation to protect their children from fear and distress. The understanding of an obligation as a context-dependent moral obligation is exemplified by a Brahman informant who argues that an Indian parent has an objective moral obligation to physically punish his errant child, but that the obligation does not universalize to American parents because the temperamental qualities of American children make them less responsive to physical punishment and more responsive to warnings or reasoning. The understanding of an obligation as a conventional obligation is exemplified by an American informant who argues that it is all right for people in other cultures to eat dogs, just as it is all right for us to eat sheep, cows, or rabbits, and that the prohibition on Kentucky Fried Canine for dinner would cease to have force if most Americans wanted it to. After all, we raise turkeys for slaughter. Why not raise dogs for slaughter?

Ranking task: seriousness of violation. A ranking task was administered to a subset of informants from the main sample. This subset included ten male and ten female children in each age-community subsample, ten male and ten female American adults, ten male and ten female "Untouchable" adults and twelve male and twelve female Brahman adults.

The thirty-nine cases, written on separate index cards, and also read aloud to most Indian children and some adults, were presented to informants for ranking. Informants were asked first to identify the cases in which they felt the practice under consideration was wrong. They were then asked to rank order those cases in response to the question, "How serious is each violation? Which is the most serious, the next most serious, and so forth?" To ease the cognitive demands of the ranking task, the ranking was undertaken in steps. Informants first divided the wrong behaviors into three or four gradations (e.g., minor offense, somewhat serious offense, very serious offense) and then rank-ordered the behavioral incidents within each subcategory. Ties were not permitted, except for the cases considered nonviolations.

Subsequent analysis of the data focused on the ranks accorded each of the thirty-nine cases, with the most serious breach numbered 1, and the least serious, 39. In that correlational analysis, cases considered nonviolations were considered ties and assigned the mean value of the nonoccupied rank positions. For example, in a case in which an informant judged four cases to be nonviolations, each of those incidents would be assigned the rank value of 37.5 (that is, the mean of the nonoccupied rank positions of 36, 37, 38, 39).

RESULTS

The results section is organized around a series of questions posed below.

Question 1: Are there, in fact, cultural differences in judgments about what is right and what is wrong? Anthropologists have long noted the existence of major culturally based variations in judgments about what is right and wrong. Some anthropologists have even set as their task the understanding and explication of the unstated premises, metaphors, and lines of reasoning that lend ethical force and justification to those startling judgments of right and wrong ("It's a sin to comb your hair during a thunderstorm") that to an outsider seem opaque or bizarre.

Murdock (1980) describes the category of sin among the Semang people of Malaysia. For the Semang, the category of sin includes combing one's hair during a thunderstorm or during the mourning period, teasing or mocking a helpless or tame animal, watching dogs mate, killing a sacred black wasp, sexual intercourse in the daytime, drawing water in a vessel blackened by fire, and casual informal behavior with one's mother-in-law.

As far as we know, there is little reason to doubt anthropological accounts of cross-cultural differences in judgments of right and wrong.

Some scholars, however, have raised doubts about whether those native judgments are moral judgments, while still others are skeptical that there is any moral justification for such errant judgments of right and wrong. Even Murdock (1980, 89) expresses the view that for the Semang the category of sin is "arbitrary and devoid of ethical justification," and that to the extent the Semang conform at all to their prohibitions, it is merely out of fear of external sanctions by a superhuman, omniscient god.

Question 1 of the results section addresses the noncontroversial proposition that there are major cross-cultural differences in judgments of right and wrong. Question 2 addresses the more challenging issue whether those judgments of right and wrong are, from the point of view of the native, moral judgments, or merely judgments about obligations perceived to be conventional or conformity-based. Later, in a discussion of the conceptual foundations of the Hindu code in everyday reasoning in Orissa, we will explicate some of the premises, principles, goals, metaphors, and lines of reasoning that give ethical justification, and thus "internal" force, to apparently alien judgments about what's right and what's wrong.

With regard to the thirty-nine practices and cases examined in this study (see table 3.1) the judgments about what is right and wrong elicited from Americans and Oriyas are virtually independent. In contrast, there are high levels of agreement between Oriya Brahmans and Oriya Untouchables, with the notable exception of normative judgments about practices concerning widows (widows' diet and widow remarriage), practices over which there is considerable dissensus within the Untouchable community. Henceforth in this essay "dissensus" of judgment refers to judgments of right (or wrong) shared by less than 75 percent of informants within an age-community subsample. Conversely "consensus" of judgments refers to agreement about what's right (or wrong) among at least 75 percent of informants within an age-community subsample. Since sex differences are not an important factor in the findings, the responses of males and females have been pooled within each age-community subsample.

Table 3.4 presents the intercorrelations (r) among the mean ranks of the thirty-nine practices in terms of perceived seriousness of breach, as judged by each age-community subgroup. Within the American community there are very high levels of mean agreement between each age group on the ranking task. On the average, American five-year-olds and American adults make very similar judgments about what is right and what is wrong ($r = .86$). Levels of agreement are also high within and across the Brahman and Untouchable samples (the average within India, between age group correlation $= .59$). In contrast there are weak negative intercorrelations between the mean rankings of American children and adults versus the mean rankings of Brahman and Untouchable children and adults (mean cross-cultural correlation $= -.21$). At an unaggregated level of analysis, individual rankings of

Table 3.4. *Intercorrelations (r) of mean rankings of thirty-nine cases in terms of seriousness of breach*

		Americans				Brahmans				Untouchables	
		Ad	11	8	5	Ad	11	8	5	Ad	8
Americans	Adults		.94	.92	.85	−.16	−.21	−.34	−.19	−.29	−.03
	11–13			.93	.90	−.26	−.27	−.39	−.25	−.33	−.13
	8–10				.92	−.17	−.25	−.27	−.11	−.29	−.03
	5–7					−.22	−.27	−.32	−.12	−.24	.01
Brahmans	Adults						.67	.74	.62	.70	.61
	11–13							.54	.38	.60	.44
	8–10								.68	.56	.52
	5–7									.49	.63
Untouchables	Adults										.72
	8–10										

American adults intercorrelate with each other in the .60 range, Brahman, adult rankings intercorrelate with each other in the .50 range, while American-Brahman rankings intercorrelate with each other in a range that varies around .00, in a slightly negative direction.

Table 3.1 lists the full ranking of the thirty-nine cases in terms of seriousness of breach as perceived, on average, by Brahman eight- to ten-year-olds. To appreciate fully the magnitude of the cross-cultural differences in judgments about right and wrong, the reader should compare his own judgments of seriousness of breach with those shown in table 3.1. With regard to the practices that are the focus of the study we seem to have found a relatively high consensus code, at least within each of the communities that are the focus of the study. There may, of course, be other issues over which there is more dispute within each community, and there may be other communities within each nation (e.g., the urban elite in India) who would display different patterns of judgments.

Over the entire set of cases, the judgments of our Oriya and American informants about right and wrong are virtually unrelated. The judgments are not uniformly opposed, nor are they typically in agreement. A display of the points of agreement and disagreement in normative judgments can be found in table 3.5. Inspection of table 3.5 reveals that, of the thirty-nine practices or cases, Brahman and American adults display similar judgments of right versus wrong concerning ten practices and opposed judgments concerning sixteen practices. For eleven other practices there is disagreement about what's right or wrong within one community or the other, although never in both.

What is not shown in table 3.5, and is important to note, is that several of the culture-specific wrongs are viewed by Brahman infor-

Table 3.5. *Patterns of disagreement and agreement among American and Brahman adults*

Case no.	Type of practice
	Disagreement: Brahmans think it is right/Americans think it is wrong
26	Unequal inheritance, male vs. females
35	Beating disobedient wife
37	Caning an errant child
	Disagreement: Brahmans think it is wrong/Americans think it is right
6	Eating with husband's elder brother
2	Eating beef
27	Wife requests massage
13	Addressing father by first name
1	Cutting hair and eating chicken after father's death
8	Cooking in clothes worn to defecate
5	Widow wears bright clothes
17	Entering temple after birth
18	Husband cooks
10	Love marriage out of status
11	Widow remarriage
4	Widow eats fish
7	Menstruating woman cooks, etc.
25	Washing plates of husband's elder brother
	Agreement: Brahmans and Americans think it is wrong
15	Ignoring accident victim
24	Breaking promise
30	Cutting in line
32	Destroying another's picture
20	Kicking a harmless animal
16	Incest – brother/sister
21	Nepotism
19	Stealing flowers
29	Discrimination against invalids
31	Asking foreigner for his watch

Practices with dissensus in one or the other culture, with indication of consensual views of the other culture (B = Brahmans; A = Americans)

Brahman Dissensus	American Dissensus
34 Father opens son's letter (A = wrong)	36 Ten-year-old sleeps with mother (B = not wrong)
33 Father saves daughter over son (A = not wrong)	9 Polygyny (B = not wrong)
28 Kissing in public (A = not wrong)	12 Helping beggar (B = not wrong)
22 Neo-local residence (A = not wrong)	38 Eating with hands (B = not wrong)
14 Sacrificing innocent child (A = wrong)	23 "No one will marry your daughter" (B = wrong)

mants as more serious transgressions than many of the events viewed as wrong in both cultures (see table 3.1). In the Oriya Brahman community it is considered a serious wrong for a doctor at a hospital to refuse to treat an accident victim because he is too poor to pay (table 3.1, no. 15), but that transgression is not quite as serious as a widow eating fish (table 3.1, no. 4), a relative eating beef (table 3.1, no. 2), or the firstborn son cutting his hair the day after his father's death (table 3.1, no. 1).

Tables 3.1, 3.4, and 3.5 illustrate what anthropologists have long known: different cultures display many differences in social and family practices and in ideas about what is right and what is wrong, and it is not always apparent at first blush, or to an outsider, why a particular event (like a widow eating fish or a man entering the temple the day after the birth of his child) is considered wrong at all.

It is, of course, important to recognize that the level of cross-cultural normative agreement and disagreement discovered in our study, or any study, is relative to the particular cases selected for investigation. With sufficient cunning it might have been possible to preselect cases to demonstrate higher levels of agreement or disagreement. What we would claim for our own findings is that the thirty-nine cases sample a broad range of practices of importance in India or America and represent key issues in the moral philosophy literature. With reference to those practices and issues one discovers what anthropologists experience when doing fieldwork: many things viewed as wrong on one side of the Atlantic are not viewed as wrong on the other side.

A far more controversial question is whether a culture's distinctive, and in many cases opaque, practices are invested with moral force. As noted above, Murdock described Semang sins as arbitrary cultural taboos without ethical justification. To what extent does the native agree with the anthropologist that culture-specific practices are conformity- or consensus-based matters of convention or "culture" rather than expressions of natural moral law or objective obligations? Later in the essay we will address the further question: Why is it that certain "innocent" events (e.g., cooking while menstruating) are viewed with disgust, outrage, or horror? What does the native know about such "innocent" events that we do not know? What does the native "see" in the event that we do not see? What premises, analogies, and lines of reasoning does the native use to comprehend the significance of the event and to render a judgment that it is morally wrong? Is there a rational ethical justification for such judgments?

Question 2: "Culture" from the native point of view: a moral or a conventional order? Our evidence suggests a strong tendency for informants to invest their practices with moral force and to view even their distinctive "cultural" practices from a naturalistic moral perspective. The dominant view among all informants, adult and child, male and female, American, Brahman, and Untouchable, is that society is a moral order, although the idea of a conventional obligation does play some part in the thinking of older American children and especially in the thinking of American adults. It is almost a nonexistent form of thought in our India data.

Table 3.6 examines sixteen culture-specific practices (see table 3.5), practices about which there is clear-cut disagreement between Brahman and American adults about what is right and what is wrong. Table 3.6 indicates whether informants perceive the obligation associated with each practice as a universal moral obligation (unalterable and universally binding), a context-dependent moral obligation (unalterable but relative) or a conventional obligation (alterable and relative). (See table 3.3 for a clarification of those distinctions.)

As indicated in table 3.6, the primary form of understanding among all informants is that the obligations associated with social practices are universal moral obligations. Understanding by reference to conventions occurs much less frequently than moral understanding. Notably, and in contrast to Kohlberg's theoretical formulations, American adults engage in reasoning by reference to convention more frequently than American five- to seven-year-olds. Conversely, American five- to seven-year-olds are more likely than American adults to engage in moral (versus conventional) judgment and to view their own obligations and rights (e.g., individual freedom of choice in matters of food, clothing, marriage) as universally binding, unalterable obligations. That developmental increase in the use of the idea of convention and "relativism" seems to be a culture-specific conceptual change, about which more will be said later.

The basic finding with reference to question 2 is that social practices and institutions are not typically, and certainly not universally, understood as conventional forms, and are usually perceived as part of the natural-moral order of things by most natives. One secondary finding with reference to question 2 is that the idea of objective moral obligation may be more, not less, widely distributed than the idea of convention, and the idea of morality may be ontogenetically prior to the idea of convention.

Question 3: Can the distinction between moral and conventional events be predicted on substantive ground? Is there something about certain events, for example, food, clothing, forms of greeting, that makes them resistant to moralization? In our review of theories of moral development we asked whether the abstract idea of the moral and the abstract idea of the conventional have an objectively determinate content. That is to say, is there something about an event per se that determines whether the obligation associated with the event will be understood as moral or conventional? According to Turiel, Nucci, and Smetana's "social interactional" theory, certain types of events (food, clothing, terms of greeting and forms of address, the sexual division of labor)

Table 3.6. *Sixteen culture-specific practices (see table 3.5) and percentage of responses of each type (see table 3.3)*

Practice (case no. per table 3.1)	Brahmans									Americans								
	Children (5–7)			Adults						Children (5–7)			Adults					
	UM	CDM	Conv	UM	CDM	Conv				UM	CDM	Con	UM	CDM	Conv			
Love marriage out of status (10)	56	31	00	100	00	00				85	05	10	85	15	00			
Menstruating woman cooks, etc. (7)	66	11	16	94	00	00				85	00	15	60	30	05			
Cooking in same clothes used to defecate (8)	62	18	12	94	05	00				70	00	25	55	15	30			
Addressing father by first name (13)	75	12	06	87	06	00				85	05	10	20	50	30			
Husband cooks (18)	83	16	00	75	20	05				75	15	10	70	20	10			
Widow eats fish (4)	75	15	00	79	21	00				85	15	00	75	25	00			
Beating disobedient wife (35)	75	12	00	100	00	00				100	00	00	95	05	00			
Caning errant child (37)	100	00	00	60	33	07				90	00	10	85	10	05			
Widow wears bright clothes (5)	60	33	06	71	14	00				95	05	05	35	45	20			
Eating beef (2)	77	22	00	82	17	00				90	00	05	44	40	20			
Entering temple after birth (17)	66	33	00	93	06	00				95	00	05	55	40	05			
Eating with husband's elder brother (6)	75	00	00	56	18	18				85	00	10	55	35	10			
Wife requests massage (27)	40	09	20	79	15	00				90	10	00	60	25	15			
Widow remarries (11)	53	38	07	77	11	05				85	00	15	90	05	05			
Cutting hair and eating chicken after father's death (1)	50	21	21	84	10	05				80	05	15	20	45	35			
Washing plates of husband's elder brother (25)	62	25	00	94	00	05				100	00	00	60	20	20			
Average	67	18	05	83	14	03				87	04	08	60	27	13			

Note: UM = Universal Moral (unalterable and universal); CDM = Context-Dependent Moral (unalterable but relative); Conv = Conventional (alterable and relative).

have no inherent consequences vis-à-vis justice, harm, and the welfare of others. Those events are, according to theory, inherently nonmoral, or at least resistant to moralization, and the obligations associated with such events are more likely to be understood as conventional or consensus-based. Other types of events (physical and psychological attacks, allocation of resources, etc.) do have inherent consequences concerning justice, harm and the welfare of others, and it is highly likely that the obligations associated with those events will be understood as moral.

Table 3.7 presents data on informants' understanding of the moral versus conventional status of twenty-two practices. Eleven of those practices involve the type of material events (food, clothes, forms of address) theoretically defined as conventional by Turiel, Nucci, and Smetana. Those practices include the prohibition on eating beef, the restrictions on the color of clothes worn by widows, and the taboo against an adult son addressing his father by personal name. The other eleven practices involve the type of material events that would be theoretically defined as moral by Turiel, Nucci, and Smetana. Those practices include, for example, a husband physically beating a wife, a father breaking a promise to his son, and a child destroying a picture drawn by a schoolmate. For a full list of the twenty-two practices, see table 3.7.

In discussing the results presented in table 3.7 the first eleven events will be referred to as "morality-resistant" events. The second eleven events will be referred to as "morality-prone" events. The major claim we make for that division is that, within the framework of Turiel, Nucci, and Smetana's theory, the eleven "morality-resistant" events ought to elicit relatively higher levels of reference to conventions than the "morality-prone" events, all of which are relatively pure moral events.

A noteworthy feature of table 3.7 is that both types of events are viewed predominantly in moral terms. The obligations associated with such events as food (the prohibition on eating beef), clothing (the prescription that widows must wear white clothes for the rest of their lives), or forms of address (the prohibition against addressing your father by first name) are not typically viewed as alterable and relative. The hypothesized "morality-resistant" events are readily moralized. Over all age groups and cultural communities the "morality-resistant" events evoke the idea of conventionality only 7 percent of the time. Even among American adults, who are most likely to view obligations as conventional, the "morality-resistant" events are viewed as conventional only 20 percent of the time.

A second noteworthy feature of table 3.7 is that for three subpopulations, all American, the "morality-resistant" events elicit higher levels of reference to convention than the "morality-prone" events. Differences in levels of reference to convention between the types of events are statistically significant (t-test, $p = <.05$) for the American

Table 3.7. *Mean percentage of universal moral, context-dependent moral, and conventional reasoning for each age-community subgroup for eleven "morality-resistant" events and eleven "morality-prone" events*

	Reasoning vis-à-vis					
	Eleven Turiel-like "morality-resistant" events			Eleven Turiel-like "morality-prone" events		
	UM	CDM	CONV	UM	CDM	CONV
	Americans					
Adult	46	28	20	79	13	05
child:						
11–13	61	21	17	89	06	03
8–10	69	11	12	89	05	03
5–7	86	05	06	95	01	02
	Brahmans					
Adult	76	15	04	88	04	00
child:						
11–13	68	21	01	79	11	06
8–10	69	29	02	81	14	00
5–7	66	18	05	78	09	06
	Untouchables					
Adult	62	27	03	80	09	03
child:						
8–10	65	27	04	71	20	04
Average	66	20	07	82	09	03
Total average of UM and CDM	86			91		

Note: "Morality-resistant" events = table 3.1, cases 1, 2, 3, 4, 5, 6, 13, 18, 25, 27, 38. "Morality-prone" events = table 3.1, cases 15, 19, 20, 21, 24, 26, 29, 30, 32, 35, 37.

children ages eight to ten and eleven to thirteen, and for American adults. The differences in levels of reference to conventions between the two types of events are not statistically significant for any of the Brahman or Untouchable subsamples, or for the American five- to seven-year-olds.

The idea that obligations are conventional seems to be most prevalent among American adults. Over all samples and all thirty-nine cases there are six instances where an event is more likely to be classified as conventional rather than moral. All those instances come from the response of American adults or American eleven- to thirteen-year-olds. Importantly, those six events are much like the type of events Turiel, Nucci, and Smetana have often used to exemplify their theoretical domain of inherently nonmoral or conventional events. The six events are those referring to food and eating practices (nos. 3, 38, 1), forms of address (no. 13), and social organization (nos. 9, 36). For the Brahman and Untouchable samples, and for the American five- to seven-year-olds, there is no difference in frequency of reasoning by reference to convention between the two types of events and little support for the idea of a universal domain distinction in the mind of children or adults between conventional and moral practices.

The evidence in table 3.7 is not inconsistent with Turiel, Nucci, and Smetana's claim of a domain distinction between morality and convention in the reasoning of American subjects. For American subjects there are events that elicit relatively high levels of reasoning by reference to conventions, and those events are like the ones described by Turiel, Nucci, and Smetana. It is noteworthy, however, that even in our American sample, the idea of conventional obligations seems less pervasive, and begins to be evoked at a later age, than we had anticipated from the findings of earlier studies.

Methodological factors may explain the divergence between our findings and those of Turiel, Nucci, and Smetana. We find that reasoning by appeal to conventional obligations occurs relatively late among Americans and is a high-frequency mode of reasoning for only a restricted set of events. They find that such modes of reasoning by reference to convention occur early in childhood and are fairly common among Americans. A methodological factor that may explain that discrepancy concerns the specific questions used to assess the perceived relativity of obligations. Our interview questions concerning the "relativity" of obligations (table 3.2, questions 5 and 6) required that informants judge whether another society would be a "better place" if it stopped engaging in practices (for example, eating dogs) that the informant disapproved of in his or her own society. It is possible that the probes used in previous research were not as stringent tests of the perceived relativity of obligations.

In previous research on the perceived relativity of obligations, subjects have typically been asked whether it is "all right" for another society to permit practices that are prohibited in one's own society. Unfortunately, the question is ambiguous and potentially misleading, especially for subjects who are hesitant to meddle in the internal affairs of other nations. It has been our experience that when a subject says it is "all right" for another society to do things differently, all they may mean is "what right do I have to tell another society how to live." Such subjects may say "it's all right" even when they believe the practices of the other society are morally wrong. Thus, in our research an informant who stated (perhaps moved by a liberal impulse to respect cultural differences) that it is all right for people in Nagaland to eat dogs would not be scored relativistic unless he or she also agreed, under cross-examination, that Nagaland would not be a better place if they stopped eating dogs (table 3.2, question 6).

The appeal to the idea of a convention is a rare occurrence among the Oriya Brahmans and Untouchables and the American five- to seven-year-olds. The young American children, like their American elders, believe that it is not wrong for a twenty-five-year-old son to address his father by his first name. But, unlike the American adults, the American five-year-olds do not think it is acceptable for Indians to prohibit first name use. Nor do these children believe, as do the American adults, that it would be legitimate to prohibit the practice if a majority of Americans decided it was wrong to be so informal with one's elders. Indeed, the idea of a natural right to personal liberty is highly developed in the American five- to seven-year-olds, and they are less willing than American adults to delimit that right or to relativize it. For the young American children (who believe one may address the father by his first name) and for the Oriya children and adults (who believe it is wrong to address the father by his first name), the issue is a moral issue, not a conventional one.

There is, however, one noteworthy difference between the "morality-resistant" events and the "morality-prone" events. Depending on the type of event, there seems to be a difference in the likelihood that informants will contextualize their moral obligations. Thus, while none of the events can be said to be truly "morality-resistant," and while the predominant view among all informants is that the obligations associated with social practices are universally binding and unalterable, there is a statistically significant tendency (t-tests) for the "morality-resistant" events to elicit higher levels of context-dependent moral reasoning (unalterable but relative, see table 3.3) from the adults in all three communities (Untouchable, Brahman, and American) and from eleven- to thirteen-year-old Americans. The differences in levels of context-dependent moral reasoning between the two types of events are not statistically significant for any of the five- to seven- or eight- to ten-year-old samples or for the eleven- to thirteen-year-old Brahman sample.

That finding is supportive of Turiel, Nucci, and Smetana's notion that not all obligations are of the same kind. On a worldwide scale, however, the crucial distinction is not between objective moral obligations and consensus-based, conventional obligations. Rather the distinction seems to be between context-dependent moral obligations and universally binding moral obligations. The obligations associated with food, clothes, terms of address, and sex roles are not typically perceived as conventional. However, in comparison with the obligations concerning physical assault, theft, and promises, the obligations associated with food and clothes are less likely to be universalized.

It is imporatant to emphasize that when context-dependent moral thinking does occur, which is not often (20 percent with the so-called morality-resistant events; 9 percent with the so-called morality-prone events, see table 3.7), it is not because the practices in question are understood as arbitrary. On the contrary, a moral obligation is contextualized because the practice in question is viewed as distinctively expressive of, or adaptive to, the special conditions, temperament, or moral qualities of a population. One variant of that view is verbalized in the minority position among Brahmans that it is immoral for Brahmans to eat beef because (a) the human body is a temple in which a holy spirit dwells (what we call the "self" or the "witness" or the "observing ego" they view as a spirit or soul or deity); (b) beef is a "hot" food; (c) "hot" foods stimulate the body as a biological organism; (d) to stimulate the body as a biological organism is to violate the sanctity of the body as a temple in which a holy spirit dwells. But it is permissible for Americans to eat beef because the colder American climate will counteract the effects of the "hot" food.

As noted, that is a minority argument. Most Oriyas accept all the premises of that argument. But, additionally, most Oriya Brahmans also believe that the cow is an incarnation of the "first mother," about whom there is much lore. They argue that we nurture our children using one of her holy gifts, her milk, and that even Americans should not eat their mother! For most Oriya Brahmans the taboo on eating beef is universally binding and its violation is a "great sin."

A second variant of context-dependent moral thinking is contained in the minority position among Brahmans that it is immoral for a Brahman widow to wear brightly colored clothes and jewelry because (a) she will appear attractive; (b) if she appears attractive she will invite sexual advances; (c) if she gets involved with sex she will disregard her meditative obligations to the soul of her deceased husband and behave disloyally. But it is acceptable for American widows to wear bright clothes and jewelry because (a) it is the destiny of America, *at this stage in its development as a civilization*, to be a world conqueror and the ingenious inventor of technology; (b) the offspring of illicit sexual unions are more likely to be clever, dominating, and adventurous; (c) widow remarriage and other American practices, adolescent dating, and "love marriage," encourage illicit sexual unions, thereby producing those qualities of character appropriate to the stage level of American civilization.

A more abstract formulation of that context-dependent moral argument goes something as follows. America is a young civilization. India is an ancient civilization. It takes a long time for a civilization to figure out and evolve good or proper practices and institutions, those that are in equilibrium with the requirements of nature. You should not expect the young to possess the wisdom of the old. America is doing what is fitting or normal for its early stage of development. Its practices are not arbitrary.

In sum, there is little support for the hypothesis that a distinction between moral and conventional obligations is a universal of early childhood, encoding in thought the substantive differences between "morality-resistant" events and "morality-prone" events. For all samples, the obligations associated with practices in the proposed "morality-resistant" domain are understood primarily in moral terms.

The evidence is not inconsistent with the hypothesis of a culture-specific distinction between morality and convention in the American sample. American adults and older children do seem to show significantly higher levels (although not high levels) of reasoning by reference to conventions for the proposed "morality-resistant" events (food, clothes, forms of address, etc.) over the proposed "morality-prone" events (physical and psychological harms, etc.). For a small subset of events (tabooed foods, polygyny, titles versus personal names, eating with your hands) the idea of conventional obligations predominates in the reasoning of American adults or older children.

In both cultures the proposed "morality-resistant" events seem to elicit higher levels (although, again, not high levels) of context-dependent moral thinking, whereby informants appeal to an unalterable objective obligation that is tailored or specifically adapted to the distinctive nature or environment of a particular group. Nevertheless, for all groups, the predominant understanding of the proposed "morality-resistant" practices is not that they are arbitrary, alterable, and relative, but rather they involve universally binding objective obligations that cannot be altered by consensus or majority vote.

Question 4: Is there universal agreement among young children about what is morally right and wrong? Do young children "spontaneously" develop their own moral code? By age five, the young children in our study are well on their way to expressing distinctive culturally appropriate judgments about what is morally right and wrong; the Oriya children sound very Oriya, and the American children sound very American. That, of course, is not to say that the capacity to feel "lowered" or "elevated," "cleansed" or "stained," "pure" or "sinful," or to experience empathy, outrage, dread, shame, disgust, terror, guilt, pride, virtue, or any other moral sentiment is culturally acquired. It is to suggest, however, that what one feels "lowered" *by*, empathy *towards*, disgust *at*, pride *in*, or outrage *about* (that is to say, how moral sentiments are directed) is related to a judgment, not necessarily conscious or even verbally accessible, that bears many of the markings of received understandings by five years of age. The implication is that if children do subscribe to a universal moral code spontaneously generated independently of participation in social practices and socialization experiences, then researchers must search for it within the first four years of life. By age five, children around the world do not typically agree with each other about what is morally right or wrong.

As indicated in table 3.4, the rankings of the thirty-nine practices in terms of seriousness of breach by five- to seven-year-old Brahman and American children are virtually independent of one another ($r = -.12$), while the rankings display marked similarities to the rankings of adults in the respective cultures ($r = .62$ between Brahman five-year-olds and adults; $r = .85$ between American five-year-olds and adults).

Whatever divergence in moral beliefs exists at age five becomes greater with age. The process of reproducing, in the next generation, the premises, principles, metaphors, and intuitions that make it possible to participate in social practices and generate culturally appropriate moral judgments seems to be a continuous one that goes on well into adolescence and probably adulthood. That can be seen by comparing table 3.8 with table 3.5. Table 3.8 shows the areas of agreement and disagreement about what is right (or wrong) between Brahman and American five- to seven-year-olds.

One noteworthy feature of table 3.8 is that there are fourteen practices about which the young children in both the cultures have strong convictions (75 percent agreement within a subsample) about what is right (or wrong). Across the two cultures, those convictions are virtually independent of one another. Brahman and American five- to seven-year-olds agree about the moral status of seven practices and disagree about the moral status of seven other practices.

A second noteworthy feature of table 3.8 is that, at ages five to seven, there are still many practices about which children in one or the other culture have not yet formed a consensus. In adulthood the moral judgments of the two populations will still remain virtually orthogonal, but there will be many more practices (twenty-eight practices instead of fourteen) around which a consensus of moral understanding has emerged within each culture (see table 3.5).

A final noteworthy feature of table 3.8 is that, with the exception of driving away a beggar (no. 12), the wrongs about which Brahman and American five- to seven-year-olds universally agree are a subset of the set of wrongs about which there is universal agreement between Brahman and American adults. In other words, in areas of convergence in the moral judgments of young children, the children's views do not run contrary to adult views and may well have a common source in direct or indirect experience with routine social practices.

Table 3.9 compares the judgments of Brahman five- to seven-year-olds with those of Brahman adults. One feature to be noted in table 3.9 is that, of the sixteen practices for which there is a clear consensus within the child and adult samples, there is no case in which the children's and adult's view of right and wrong deviate from each other. In no case do the children think "X" is wrong while the adults think "X" is right, or vice versa. Either the adults have acquired their judgments from the children or the children have acquired their judgments from the adults, or both the children and the adults have acquired their judgments through participation in the same social practices, or some combination of those possibilities.

A second finding illustrated in table 3.9 is that there are twenty-three practices for which there is dissensus within either the adult sample or the child sample. That dissensus is typically among the

Table 3.8. *Patterns of disagreement and agreement among Brahman and American five- to seven-year-olds*

Case no.	Type of practice
	Disagreement:
	Brahman children think it is right/American children think it is wrong
37	Caning an errant child
38	Eating with hands
34	Father opens son's letter
	Disagreement:
	Brahman children think it is wrong/American children think it is right
13	Addressing father by first name
2	Eating beef
8	Cooking in clothes worn to defecate
1	Cutting hair and eating chicken after father's death
	Agreement: Brahman children and American children think it is wrong
12	Ignoring beggar
24	Broken promise
32	Destroying another's picture
20	Kicking harmless animal
19	Stealing flowers
7	Menstruating woman cooks[a]
	Agreement: Brahman children and American children think it is right
39	Men holding hands

For the remaining twenty-five practices there was dissensus within one or the other community.

[a] The Oriya term for menstrual pollution is *mara*. The general term for pollution, which can also be specified and applied to menstrual pollution is *chuuan*. Oriya children know those terms and associate with them certain menstrual practices (seclusion, no cooking by mother, etc.). They are not, however, aware of the fact of bleeding. There is no adequate translation in English of *mara* or *chuuan* for use in interviews with American children. The term "unclean," which was used, it obviously inadequate. With regard to case 7 the translation problem is theoretically fascinating yet may be practically insurmountable. Thus, the results on case 7 for American children, and the apparent agreement between American and Brahman youth, must be discounted.

children and not the adults. The one major exception is the practice of fathers opening and reading the mail addressed to their adolescent sons. The five- to seven-year-old Brahman children overwhelmingly think that practice is permissible while the Brahman adults are divided on the issue. In general, however, while the young children have many consensually shared views, the adults have convictions about many more issues. Not all practices are directly known or available to children, and it takes time to induce or comprehend the messages implicit in those practices that are directly experienced.

A third feature of table 3.9 is that the culture-specific and universal aspects of the adult code seem to be acquired or constructed in the same way, or by the same process. Stated more cautiously, culture-specific moral beliefs and universal moral beliefs are constructed at the same rate. There are nine practices that seem to be strong candidates for universal moral prohibitions across adults in all three populations, American, Oriya Brahman, and Oriya Untouchable. Those nine moral universals are listed in table 3.10. There are fourteen moral prohibitions that are specific to Brahman adults (nos. 1, 2, 4, 5, 6, 7, 8, 10, 11, 13, 17, 18, 25, 27) and five prohibitions that are specific to American adults (nos. 14, 26, 34, 35, 37). By age five to seven years, Brahman children have developed consensual moral convictions concerning four (44 percent) of those nine universal adult moral prohibitions (breaking promises, arbitrary assault, destruction of private property and incest).

Table 3.9. *Patterns of disagreement and agreement among Brahman five- to seven-year-olds and Brahman adults*

	Disagreement: Brahman children think it is right/ Brahman adults think it is wrong NO CASES
	Disagreement: Brahman children think it is wrong/ Brahman adults think it is right NO CASES
	Agreement: Brahman children think it is wrong/ Brahman adults think it is wrong
Case no.	Type of practice
1	Cutting hair and eating chicken after father's death
8	Cooking in clothes worn to defecate
2	Eating beef
12	Ignoring beggar
24	Breaking promise
32	Destroying another's picture
20	Kicking innocent animal
16	Incest – brother/sister
19	Stealing flowers
7	Menstruating woman cooks, etc.
10	Love marriage out of status

Agreement: Brahman children think it is right/Brahman adults think it is right

Case no.	Type of practice
36	Ten-year-old sleeps with mother
38	Eating with hands
37	Caning an errant child
39	Men holding hands

Table 3.9. *(continued)*

Practice with less than 75% consensus within Brahman adults or
Brahman children between five and seven years of age

Practice	Is there consensus among children?	adults?
Eating with husband's older brother (6)	No	Yes
"No one will marry your daughter" (23)	No	Yes
Unequal inheritance, males vs. females (26)	No	Yes
Cutting in line (30)	No	Yes
Wife requests massage (27)	No	Yes
Ignoring accident victim (15)	No	Yes
Polygyny (9)	No	Yes
Eating a dog (3)	No	Yes
Beating disobedient wife (35)	No	Yes
Widow wears bright clothes (5)	No	Yes
Entering temple after birth (17)	No	Yes
Husband cooks (18)	No	Yes
Discriminating against invalids (29)	No	Yes
Widow remarriage (11)	No	Yes
Nepotism (21)	No	Yes
Washing plates of husband's elder brother (25)	No	Yes
Widow eats fish (4)	No	Yes
Asking foreigner for watch (31)	No	Yes
Father opens son's letter (34)	Yes	No
Father saves daughter over son (33)	No	No
Neo-local residence (22)	No	No
Kissing in public (28)	No	No
Sacrificing innocent child (14)	No	No

American five- to seven-year-olds have developed consensual convictions concerning seven (77 percent) of the nine prohibitions (all except incest and reciprocity-gratitude, asking for the watch; see table 3.10).

The same rate of acquisition seems to hold for the culture-specific moral practices and beliefs. Brahman five- to seven-year-olds hold consensual convictions concerning five (35 percent) of the fourteen culture-specific Brahman adult moral prohibitions (see table 3.9), while American children of the same age hold consensual convictions about all five (100 percent) of the culture-specific American adult moral prohibitions. Thus, while it remains to be explained why the moral judgments of their respective cultures are being acquired more rapidly by American than by Brahman children, in both cultures young children seem to be constructing the universal aspects of their moral code at about the same rate as they are constructing the culture-specific aspects of the code (44 percent versus 35 percent for Brahman children; 77 percent versus 100 percent for American children).

It seems reasonable to hypothesize that the same process, whatever

Table 3.10. *Nine candidates for moral universals across adult popula-tions – high consensus virtues and vices for Brahman, Untouchable, and American adults*

Case no.	Type of practice
24	Keeping promises (a virtue)
32	Respect for property (a virtue)
30	Fair allocation (a virtue)
15	Protecting the vulnerable (a virtue)
31	Reciprocity – gratitude (a virtue)
16	Taboo on incest (a virtue)
20	Arbitrary assault (a vice)
21	Nepotism (a vice)
29	Arbitrary ("biased") classification (a vice)

that might be, is responsible for the construction of the universal and culture-specific aspects of the code. Little support is to be found in this evidence for the hypothesis that the universal aspects of the code are constructed one way (e.g., self-constructed through the personal observation of objective consequences) while the culture-specific aspects are constructed in a different way (e.g., through acceptance of adult doctrines).

Whatever process explains the early similarity in the moral judg-ments of children (five years and older) and adults within a culture, it influences not only the content of judgments about right and wrong but also the more formal or structural aspects of those judgments. In the present context, what we mean by the formal or structural aspect of thinking is the idea of an obligation as a universal moral obligation (unalterable and universally binding) versus the idea of an obligation as a context-dependent moral obligation (unalterable and relative) versus the idea of an obligation as a consensus-based conventional obligation (alterable and relative).

There is a culture-specific directionality of change for some of the more formal or structural features of moral thinking. Thus, as Amer-icans get older they are more likely to engage in reasoning by refer-ence to convention and by reference to context-dependent moral reasoning, and less likely to engage in universal moral reasoning. Conversely, as Brahmans and Untouchables get older they are more likely to engage in universal moral reasoning, and less likely to engage in context-dependent moral reasoning or reasoning by reference to convention. Those culture-specific developmental trends are dia-grammed in figures 3.3–3.5, where the average percentage of each type of response (universal moral, context-dependent moral, conventional) over all thirty-nine cases is indicated for all subjects interviewed in each age-community subgroup.

Examining the three types of thinking for each of the thirty-nine

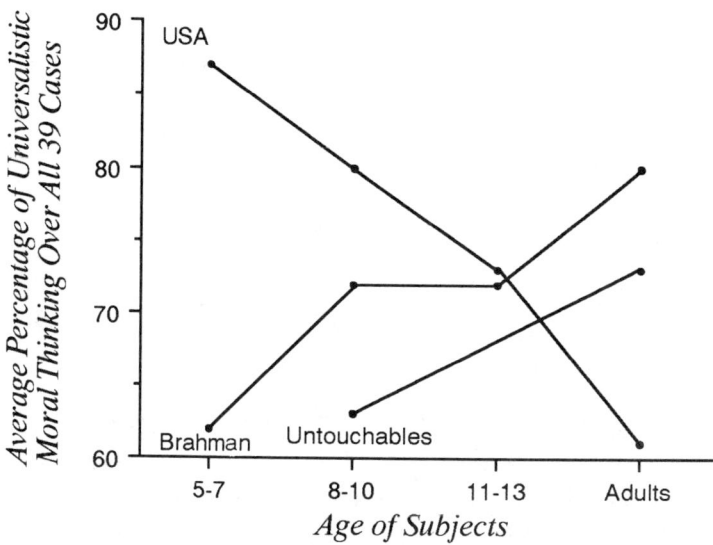

Figure 3.3. Universalistic moral thinking in children and adults in India and America. Universal moral – unalterable and not relative (see Table 3.4).

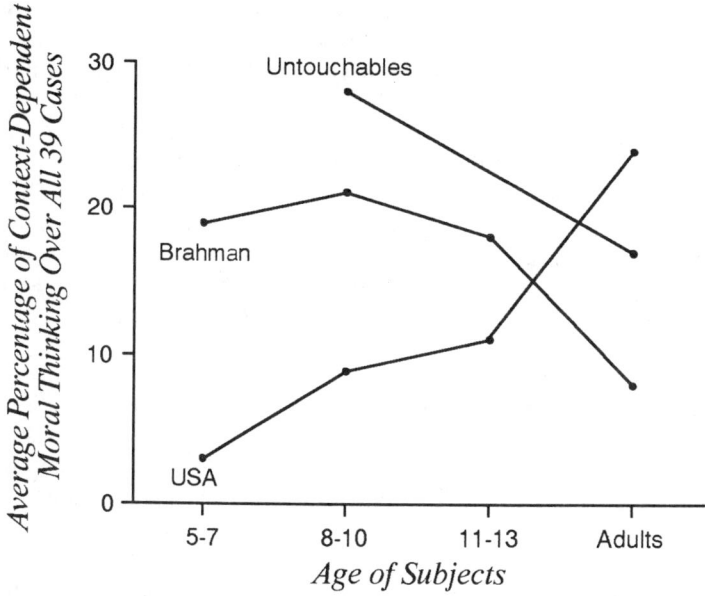

Figure 3.4. Context-dependent moral thinking in children and adults in India and America. Context-dependent moral – unalterable but relative (see Table 3.4).

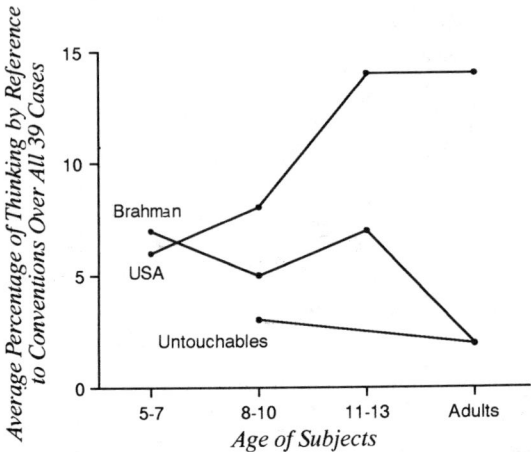

Figure 3.5. Conventional thinking in children and adults in India and America. Conventional – alterable and relative (see Table 3.4).

cases, the most general of all trends across the thirty-nine cases is the developmental waning of universalistic moral thinking in the American sample. While we cannot give a definitive interpretation to the trends displayed in figures 3.3–3.5, the five- to seven-year-old American children seem to believe there exists a universal natural right to eat beef if you want to, to choose your wife for yourself if you want to, to kiss your wife in public if you want to, to wear brightly colored clothes and jewelry even if you are a widow, if you want to. The young American children are less willing than older American children and American adults to grant that rights to liberty in such matters are conventional or to accept that other societies can legitimately choose to do things differently. The developmental increase of universal moral thinking in the Indian sample is also relatively general across cases, while the higher average level of reference to conventions among American adults over young American children seems to be carried by a subset of cases, especially cases 1, 2, 3, 5, 13, 23, 25, 26, 27, 28, 34, 38 (see table 3.1).

There are several implications to the pattern of findings in figures 3.3–3.5. First, figure 3.5 raises the possibility that a distinction between moral and conventional practices may not be a universal of childhood or adulthood. The level of reference to conventional obligations in the Indian sample seems too insignificant to support the hypothesis of a universal domain distinction. Second, figure 3.3 suggests that obligations are not typically viewed as conventional or consensus-based by either children or adults. The idea of universal moral or objective obligations seems to be more widely distributed across ages and cultures than the idea of conventional obligations, and developmentally the idea of morality seems to take precedence over the idea of convention, even at an early age. Finally, taken together, figures 3.3–3.5 raise the possibility that the emergence of reasoning by reference to conventional or consensus-based obligations is a culture-specific development; however, the reason for the emergence of the idea of convention, in some cultures, like our own, but not in other cultures, like orthodox Hindu society, remains to be explained.

Far more research on these issues is needed, utilizing alternative methodologies. Directly probing about the relativity and alterability of family life and social practices, as we did in our study, is but one way to search for a domain distinction between conventional and moral obligations. Murdock's (1980) work on illness as a perceived conse-quence of transgression and Edwards' (1985) work on caretaker re-sponse to transgression suggest two other ways to study the degree of differentiation of domains. If a culture does distinguish conventional from moral obligations, that separation of domain might reveal itself in anything from differential patterns of emotional response to transgres-sion to different types of sanctions or punishments. Reviewing our own research in light of Murdock's cross-cultural survey on illness and Edwards' study of caretaker response in Kenya raises for us the strong possibility that the distinction between conventional and moral obliga-tions is not a developmental universal.

Question 5: What are the universal and culture-specific aspects of a moral code? This essay is concerned with identifying the universal and culture-specific, mandatory and discretionary, features of rationally based moral codes. Given that aim, it is perhaps worth noting that to identify genuine differences in moral codes is to presuppose some common criteria for identifying moral issues. Meaningful differences presuppose a general likeness. However, contrary to Kohlberg's view that there are no fundamental differences from culture to culture in the ideal form of a rationally based moral code (1981, 71–74), it is our view that all rationally based moral codes are alike in some ways (the mandatory features) and in some ways different (the discretionary features). And, because the ways that moral codes differ are rationally discretionary, those differences (for example, in the assertion or denial of divine authority) are likely to persist even in the face of cognitive development and Socratic dialogue.

For the moment we shall put aside the issue of universal moral emotions (see Kagan 1984, especially chap. 4, on that issue). We believe there are such universal emotions – empathy, shame, guilt, outrage, pride, repugnance, disgust – and we believe the emotional reactions of others, their anger, disappointment, or hurt feelings, can play an important cuing function in the acquisition of a moral code. Recent experimental research on "social referencing" in infants and young children (Feinman 1982; Feinman and Lewis 1983; Campos and Stenberg 1981; Bretherton 1984) suggests that internalization of the evaluations of significant or powerful others is a prepotent ontogenetic process that does not wait patiently for an Oedipus complex to develop. By ten months of age, infants make use of the mother's or experimenter's verbally or nonverbally conveyed affective interpretations of events (for example, distress or pleasure at the entrance of a stranger) and modulate their own emotional and behavioral reactions accordingly.

We even believe that some emotional responses are retained in the presence of conscious reflection and deliberate judgment, and that feelings (for example, righteous indignation) can form part of a rational response to a perceived transgression. Within the terms of a rationally based moral code, actions that are wrong, sinful or polluting may make you feel guilty, angry, afraid, or disgusted, and they may, in some cases, even carry with them an obligation to feel that way.

To acknowledge the universality and functional importance of moral emotions is not, however, the same as saying that actions become wrong, sinful, or polluting *because* they make you feel guilty, angry, afraid, or disgusted; or that you believe that actions are wrong, sinful, or polluting because they were learned in association with feelings of guilt, anger, fear, or disgust. We would reject, as do our informants, a pure emotivist view of the meaning of moral discourse. You may feel guilty because you have transgressed, but the transgression is not defined by the guilt, and, in many cases, a transgression is a transgression whether you feel guilty or not. To understand why a transgression has become defined as a transgression is to look outward, away from the emotions, in the direction of the moral code as a rational organization of concepts and principles. That is what our research is about. Thus, in considering moral universals, we put moral emotions to the side, for the moment, and focus on the form and content of the code itself.

Table 3.10 lists those nine moral prohibitions that are shared by American adults, Brahman adults, and Untouchable adults. One noteworthy feature of table 3.10 is that the nine universal prohibitions listed are *moral* prohibitions. They are viewed by all informants as objective, unalterable, and universally binding prohibitions. That suggests that the idea of an objective obligation, the idea of morality as natural law, is a universal. As we have seen (see table 3.6), the abstract idea of natural law is displayed relatively early in life, certainly by age five.

A second noteworthy feature of table 3.10 is that it is difficult to decide on a proper level of abstraction for describing moral universals. Some would argue that universality arguments are merely arguments about the generality of coding categories: the less specific the content written into the coding category the more universal the category. While there is much merit in that argument (see Shweder and Bourne 1982 on the "higher-order generality rule") it overlooks the fact that the peoples of the world sometimes do agree about relatively particularistic issues (e.g., that such-and-such a color chip is the reddest red, or that the offspring of an incestuous union are more likely to be deformed or in some way grotesque; see Berlin and Kay 1969; Burton 1973), and they frequently disagree about more general issues (e.g., whether people have transmigratory souls or whether or not justice means "to each according to his needs"). It is possible to discover pancultural universals without having to bleach one's coding categories of all interesting substance.

The research reported examines informants' judgments about particular cases (kicking a sleeping dog, cutting into a line at a cinema). As it turns out, it is possible to discover moral universals at the "case" level of description; Brahmans, Untouchables, and Americans all agree, for example, that "it is wrong when meeting a foreigner for the first time to ask him how much his watch costs and whether he will give it to you" (no. 31, table 3.1), and that "it is wrong for a hotel to make a rule that invalids and disfigured persons are not allowed in the dining hall" (case no. 29, table 3.1). It is possible for a concrete case to elicit a universal reaction of moral repugnance.

There is, however, an understandable temptation to identify the more general or abstract principle underlying a judgment about a particular case. In table 3.10 we have given in to that temptation. Thus, case 31 (asking the foreigner for his watch) is described as "reciprocity" and case 29 (no invalids in the dining hall) is described as arbitrary (biased) classification. There is also a temptation to reduce the list of principles in table 3.10 to a smaller set of highly abstract ideas. Thus, for example, the taboo on incest could perhaps be reduced to the idea of protection of the vulnerable (protecting children from sexual exploitation), and perhaps the idea of justice and the presumption that harm is wrong could "cover" most of the "middle-level" principles listed in table 3.10. Under some description, at some level of abstraction, justice, harm, and protection of the vulnerable might qualify as "deep" universals of all moral codes.

The rub is that if one focuses only upon the abstract principles underlying a judgment about a particular case, the abstracted principles do not make it possible to predict informants' judgments about particular cases. Thus, for example, while Oriya Brahman adults disapprove of kicking a dog that is sleeping on a street (no. 20), they do not disapprove of beating "black and blue" a wife who goes to the movies without the husband's permission (no. 35). And, while they disapprove of unfair treatment (nepotism, no. 21, cutting in line, no. 30, the hotel rule excluding invalids, no. 29), they believe it is permissible for a married son to inherit far more than a married daughter (no. 26). Indeed 60% of the female adult members of the Brahman community believe there is a positive moral obligation to save the life of the firstborn son over the life of the lastborn daughter if only one life can be saved (no. 33).

Needless to say, Oriya Brahmans do not view beating an errant wife as an instance of arbitrary assault, and they do not believe it is unfair to choose the son over the daughter in matters of life or inheritance. What Americans view as similar cases (kicking the dog, beating the wife) Oriyas view as quite different cases, and what Americans view as quite different cases (for example, addressing the father by first name, no. 13, and the wife requesting a massage, no. 27) Oriyas view as similar. The appeal to some small set of common abstract principles (justice, harm, protecting the vulnerable) does not help us understand or predict which cases will be seen as alike or different.

If we are to understand our informants' moral judgments about particular cases we are going to have to understand the culture-specific aspects of their moral codes and the way those culture-specific aspects interact with the more universal aspects to produce a moral judgment. Oriya Brahmans, for example, believe that beating a wife who goes to the movies without permission is roughly equivalent to corporal punishment for a private in the army who leaves the military base without permission. For Oriyas there are rationally appealing analogical mappings between the family as a unit and military units (differentiated roles and status obligations in the service of the whole, hierarchical control, drafting and induction, etc.). One thing the family is not, for Oriyas, is a voluntary association among coequal individuals.

Discussion

IMPLICATIONS FOR KOHLBERG'S COGNITIVE DEVELOPMENTAL THEORY

Our research in India and America suggests a portrait of the development of the understanding of obligations that differs from Kohlberg's. If one relaxes the demand characteristics of the interview task, utilizing direct probes about universality and alterability of obligations, it appears that major structural features of postconventional moral understanding are universals of early childhood and adulthood. Those features include the idea of objective obligations and natural moral law. And, if one relaxes the demand characteristics of the interview task, it appears that the idea of obligations as conventional or consensus-based is not the predominant form of understanding among either children or adults. Our research suggests that the idea of moral obligation does not develop out of the idea of conventional obligation. On the contrary, the idea of a conventional obligation is a special development related to certain discretionary features of a moral code, such as the ideas of individualism, individual rights, and "freedom of contract."

IMPLICATIONS FOR TURIEL'S SOCIAL INTERACTIONAL THEORY

Turiel's theory hypothesizes an early, universal differentiation of a domain of moral obligations from a domain of conventional obligations. The theory hypothesizes that certain obligations are "morality-prone" while other obligations are "morality-resistant" because the events they regulate do not involve issues of justice, harm, or the welfare or rights of others. Our research suggests that the differentiation of moral events from conventional events is not necessarily a developmental universal and that the distinction between morality and convention, useful as it is within certain cultural worldviews, may well be culture-specific.

While it is not possible to prove definitely that *any* event can be moralized (i.e., treated as an objective obligation related to harm and justice), within the framework of our research, a moral and a conventional domain could not be distinguished on substantive grounds. For orthodox Hindus in the old town of Bhubaneswar, food, clothing, terms of address, sex roles, and ritual observances are conceived of as part of the moral order. The received orthodox Hindu conception of objective obligations or natural moral law leaves little room for the idea that culture or society is conventional, consensus-based, and arbitrary rather than an expression of natural law. Within a culture like our own where the morality versus convention distinction does play a part, there are undoubtedly events that fall on the boundaries or partake of both domains, and it is relevant and important to ask the question proposed by Turiel, Nucci, and Smetana, "Which are the pure moral or conventional events and which are the mixed events?" Within orthodox Hindu culture, however, the relevant question may well be, "Are any events purely conventional?"

IMPLICATIONS FOR FUTURE RESEARCH
Social communication. What has not been emphasized sufficiently in past research on moral development is that children discern the moral order as it is dramatized and made salient in everyday practices. Children are assisted in constructing their notions of right and wrong. The inferences they draw about the moral (its form) and what's moral (its content), are, in substantial measure, personal reconstructions created within a framework of tradition-based modes of apperception and evaluation. The moral concepts of a people and their ideas about self, society, and nature are powerful ways of seeing the world that have been worked on, and applied to experience, over many generations. Every child is the beneficiary of a conceptual inheritance, received through communication with others.

Our "social communication" theory of moral development emphasizes the ways a culture's ideology and worldview have a bearing on the ontogenesis of moral understandings in the child. That highlighting is done by relating the ontogenesis of ideas about obligations to the representation of received premises and ideological tenets through routine social practices.

In our conception of "social communication," morally relevant interpretations of events by local guardians of the moral order (e.g., parents) are typically presented and conveyed to young children in the context of routine family life and social practices. Those moral premises are carried by the messages and meanings implicit in the emotional reactions of others (anger or disappointment or "hurt feelings" over a transgression). They are carried by the verbal exchanges – commands, threats, sanction statements, accusations, explanations, justifications, excuses – necessary to maintain routine social practices. Indeed, moral premises may be expressed through, and hence are discernible in, institutionalized behaviors; and those premises may be validated by the child, and hence reinforced for the child, because they help make sense of the experience of routine practices. Finally, it is an assumption of our theory that the emerging moral intuitions or unconscious moral inferences of the child are not only the product of social practices but are also the grounding for the child's later attempts to reflectively reconstruct is own moral code.

As an illustration of the social communication process we have in mind, consider the following case concerning one aspect of the socialization of moral understandings in the domain of pollution-purity-sanctity, with obvious implications for matters of interpersonal affiliation (see Shweder 1985, from which the following illustration is drawn and partly excerpted; see also Shweder and Much, 1986).

"*Mara heici. Chhu na! Chhu na!*" is what a menstruating Oriya mother exclaims when her young child approaches her lap. It means, "I am polluted. Don't touch me! Don't touch me!" If the child continues to approach, the woman will stand up and walk away from her child. Of course, young Oriya children have no concept of menstruation or menstrual blood; the first menstruation arrives as a total surprise to adolescent girls. Mothers typically "explain" their own monthly "pollution" to their children by telling them that they stepped in dog excrement or touched garbage, or they evade the issue. Nevertheless, Oriya children quickly learn that there is something called "*Mara*" (the term "*chhuan*" is also used) and when "*Mara*" is there, as it regularly is, their mother avoids them, sleeps alone on a mat on the floor, is prohibited from entering the kitchen ("*Handibahari heici*" – "I'm out of the kitchen" – is a local euphemism for talking about menses), eats alone, does not groom herself and is, for several days, kept at a distance from anything of value. Children notice that everything their mother touches is washed. In interviews, most six-year-olds think it is wrong for a "polluted" ("*mara*") woman to cook food or sleep in the same bed with her husband; most nine-year-olds think that "*mara*" is an objective force of nature and that all women in the world have a moral obligation not to touch other people or cook food while they are "*mara*."

Oriya children learn that "touching" can be dangerous. They learn that "purity," "cleanliness," and status go together. Just as the pure must be protected from the impure, the higher status and the lower status must be kept apart or at a distance. These ideas are effectively conveyed in several ways. "Don't touch me" is heard on many occasions in many contexts. There's not only the menstruating mother (whose status in the family is roughly that of an Untouchable for three days, and who is sometimes discussed as possessed by an evil spirit while bleeding). There's the father who tells his children not to touch him in the interim between bathing (a purification rite) and worshipping the family deity. There's the grandmother who does not want her grandchildren to touch her or climb into bed with her until the child has removed all his "outside" clothes, which have become polluted ("*chhuan*") as the child mixed with lower castes at school. Those attitudes and sentiments towards "*mara*" or "*chhuan*" also get coded and expressed in a children's game on the theme, "pollution tag." Several children stand apart from a lone isolated child and all together chant and tease: "You ate in the house of a Hadi (the lowest Untouchable caste). Don't touch me! Don't touch me!" The children scurry off, pursued by the hand of the "polluted" child.

The culture is providing the child with a practical moral commentary in which one of the many messages is ultimately that menstrual blood, feces, and lower status go together. For the sake of physical and spiritual well-being, they must be kept at a distance from what is clean, pure, and of higher status. Daily bathing and acts of purification and cleanliness become associated with status elevation and feelings of personal well-being. Ultimately, one's body becomes conceptualized as a "temple" with a spirit, the self, dwelling in it. Keeping the temple pure becomes a major goal of daily life, in eating, in bathing, in avoiding contact with pollutants and anyone of lower status.

The socialization process just described is affect-laden. The child wants to get in bed with his or her grandmother and is rejected. The child wants to approach the mother and is put off. The distress aroused in grandmother or mother can be palpable. Furthermore, the socialization process is carried by discourse that indexes a great deal of implicit knowledge. Since a great deal of what we call moral socialization is done through talking with others, the study of moral development calls for the identification of propositions about the way the world is and ought to be that are carried by discourse and other forms of symbolic action (see Much and Shweder 1978; Much 1983; Ochs and Schieffelin 1984; Shweder and Much, 1986).

Finally, it is also interesting to note that the concepts that are inherited – pollution, impurity, separation, loss of status, purification, cleanliness – succeed at making sense of experience, from "the native point of view." Children reason, but not all the concepts they reason with are of their own making. Children observe the consequences of action, but those consequences include the enculturated emotional reactions of others, and even those enculturated emotional reactions are interpreted for the child by others, using concepts from tradition-based doctrines about psychological and social functioning. The child of moral development, it turns out, is not a lonely subject and is rarely left alone.

Alternative postconventional moralities. Our analysis of the mandatory and discretionary features in Kohlberg's conception of postconventional morality raised the theoretical possibility of alternative rationally based moral codes, based on a conception of natural law, justice, and harm (mandatory features), yet not founded on individualism, voluntarism, natural "rights," secularism, or the idea of a social contract (discretionary features). In the light of our experience in India and knowledge of the anthropological literature on moral codes, we think that it is more than just a theoretical possibility. We hypothesize that most adults around the world do not talk on Kohlberg's tasks like postconventional thinkers because they reject the discretionary features built into Kohlberg's definition of genuine moral understandings, not because they confuse objective obligations with consensus, convention, or positive law. There may be alternative rationally based moral codes that Kohlberg's scheme, founded on abstract individualism, voluntarism, and secularism, does not illuminate.

Our hypothesis implies that there is more than one way to rationalize a moral code and that the cluster of ideas associated with individualism, consent, voluntarism, promise, and free contract are discretionary rather than mandatory features of a rationally based moral code. The hypothesis raises the possibility that the ubiquitous stage three–four reasoning discovered by Kohlbergian researchers could be defended as a rationally based form of postconventional thinking, especially if interpreted in the light of a different set of discretionary moral concepts (see Gilligan 1982; Shweder and Much, 1986).

One of the attractions of India for moral development reserchers is the possibility that the orthodox Hindu moral code is an example of an alternative postconventional moral understanding. This is not the occasion to attempt a rational reconstruction of the moral judgments of our Hindu informants (see Shweder and Much, 1986). Such a rational reconstruction would distill the numerous arguments, analogies, and premises used by our informants in defense of their practices (e.g., arranged marriage, the prohibition against widow remarriage, etc.) and form them into an "ideal" argument structure. By an "ideal" argument structure we mean a reasoned defense of family life and social practice that is not vulnerable to the criticism that its empirical claims are false or that its reasoning is viciously contradictory.

Our interviews with Hindu adult informants are rich in arguments. A distilled argument, for example, might go as follows: "A marriage is something that affects so many people, relatives, ancestors, neighbors, and friends, in serious ways. How can you possibly leave it up to one young person, driven by lust and passion, to make a sound decision?" Informants often reason by reference to similes and analogies. One argument asserts, "The husband is a moving god and should be treated with comparable respect." Another argument holds, "The body is a temple with a spirit dwelling in it. Therefore the sanctity of the temple must be preserved. Therefore impure things must be kept out of and away from the body." Factual claims are asserted, such as "Life on earth is organized around the division of things into male and female, and there is a natural asymmetrical interdependency between them"; or, "The family is a natural institution." Fundamental assumptions and premises are implicitly or explicitly announced: "Nature is just. Virtue is rewarded and vice punished"; "Souls reincarnate"; "Received inequalities (male over female, elder over younger, Brahman over Untouchable) are a form of just desert"; "The family is the ideal prototype for all social relationships."

What one finds in the reasoning of our Hindu informants is a preference for paternalism and asymmetrical interdependency, the idea that most people need to be protected against their own vulnerabilities, and a rejection of the idea of autonomous functioning and self-sufficient voluntarism. There is an inclination to view the family, not the marketplace. as the prototype of moral relationships. There is a corollary tendency to represent the moral order as a natural order built up out of status or role obligations (wife to husband, stranger to stranger) rather than out of promises or commitments between abstract individuals living in the marketplace of a free-contract regime.

It is our hunch that the arguments of our Hindu informants are informed by an alternative postconventional morality (Shweder and Much, 1986). A recent series of essays by the economist Schelling (1984), on the need to protect oneself against oneself, hints at one way for us rationally to reconstruct the Hindu code. States Schelling (1984, 100): "Actually, there is no a priori basis for confidence that enforceable contract is a generally good thing. People might just get themselves tied up with all kinds of regrettable contracts, and the custodians of legal wisdom might have decided that enforceable contract is a mischief. Suppose promises to second parties tended usually to get people into trouble, so that a wise legal tradition would readily excuse people from promises incurred in haste, or in passion or in disgust. Duress is recognized; if impetuosity were a problem, legally binding contracts might require something like a second or third reading before acquiring status. It is an empirical question whether the freedom to enter into contract, the freedom to make enforceable promises, or the freedom to emancipate oneself from a nicotine habit would prove generally to be a good thing."

What Schelling's remarks suggest is that, as a matter of fact, the human beings of a society may be highly vulnerable to exploitation or self-destruction and may not assume the idealized, and somewhat utopian, state of "voluntariness" presupposed by a free-contract regime. When people in the real world agree to the terms of a contract, they may do so impetuously, or under duress, while angry or depressed, or without foresight, willpower, or knowledge of relevant information, or lacking the skill to calculate consequences properly. An unwed mother in postpartum depression signs a contract permitting a childless married couple to adopt her infant in exchange for a sum of money. Later, no longer depressed, and willing to return the money, she wants her child back. Does she have an obligation to honor her contract? The legal system of a free-contract regime tries to adjust for the discrepancy between the idealized presumption of a "voluntary" agent and the fact of "involuntary" choice by specifying conditions (fraud, duress) for disqualifying contracts, by mandating certain terms that must be included in any contract, and by withholding freedom to contract from certain classes of agents (minors, the insane). (See Kennedy 1982, for a discussion of those issues and the role of paternalistic motives in a free-contract regime.)

It is instructive to construct hypothetically an alternative postconventional moral code, starting with the assumption that agents are naturally vulnerable. Since agents frequently display features of "involuntariness" – weakness of will, impetuosity, emotionality, ignorance, addiction, etc. – freedom to contract would not be deemed a general good. It either promotes exploitation, if the freedom is genuine and general, or promotes costly monitoring, regulations and correction by external authorities (judges and bureaucrats), if exploitation of the vulnerable is to be controlled.

Such an alternative postconventional conception of moral obligations might be self-consciously paternalistic, modeled after the family as a moral institution. It is noteworthy that in the Western legal-moral tradition, family obligations and law stand as a major exception to the general theory of free contract among autonomous, rational, voluntary agents (see Kennedy 1982). In contrast, it appears that in orthodox Hindu thought the family is not the exception to the basic principles of the moral order but rather the prototype of the moral order. It is credible to argue that the family exists as an institution because of the natural vulnerabilities and interdependencies of its members. Through a complex of relationships based on mutual reliance (e.g., husband and wife), asymmetrical interdependency (e.g., parent to child) and the obligations and agreements associated with kinship status (father, son, mother, daughter) the family seems to be able to function without the necessity of either a contract or outside regulation. In nonabusive families, of which there are many, a combination of loyalty, deference, empathy, altruism, love, and hierarchy protects the vulnerable from exploitation, while rewarding the powerful for caring for the weak. And all that is done without bureaucracies, legislatures, or the costly devices of centralized control.

Any rational reconstruction of a postconventional Hindu moral code is likely to be a rational defense of paternalism, sympathetic to the sentiment expressed in Tolkien's famous trilogy about the Middle Earth in its latter days: "'Few now remember them,' Tom murmured, 'yet still some go wandering, sons of forgotten kings walking in loneliness, guarding from evil things folk that are heedless.'" In family relationships, we may come as close as we dare to restoring that lost sense of noble, or at least paternal-maternal, obligation.

References

Berlin, B., and P. Kay, 1969. *Basic Color Terms: Their Universality and Evolution*. Berkeley: University of California Press.

Bretherton, I. 1984. Social Referencing and the Interfacing of Minds: A Commentary on the Views of Feinman and Campos. *Merrill-Palmer Quarterly 30*:419–27.

Burton, R. V. 1973. Folk Theory and the Incest Taboo. *Ethos 1*:504–16.

Campos, J. J., and C. R. Stenberg, 1981. Perception, Appraisal and Emotion: The Onset of Social Referencing. In M. E. Lamb and L. R. Sherrod, eds., *Infant Social Cognition*. Hillsdale, N.J.: Erlbaum.

Carter, R. E. 1980. What Is Lawrence Kohlberg Doing? *Journal of Moral Education 2*:9.

Cole, M., and S. Scribner, 1974. *Culture and Thought: A Psychological Introduction*. New York: John Wiley.

Dumont, L. 1970. *Homo Hierarchicus*. Chicago: University of Chicago Press.

Dworkin, R. 1977. *Taking Rights Seriously*. Cambridge, Mass.: Harvard University Press.

Edwards, C. P. 1980. The Development of Moral Reasoning in Cross-cultural Perspective. In R. H. Monroe, R. Munroe, and B. B. Whiting, eds., *Handbook of Cross-Cultural Human Development*. New York: Garland Press.

1985. Another Style of Competence: The Caregiving Child. In A. D. Fogel and G. F. Melson, eds., *Origins of Nurturance*. New York: Erlbaum.

In press. Cross-cultural Research on Kohlberg's Stages: The Basis for Consensus. In S. Modgil and C. Modgil, eds., *Lawrence Kohlberg: Consensus and Controversy*. London: Falmer Press Limited.

Feinberg, J. 1980. *Rights, Justice and the Bounds of Liberty*. Princeton: Princeton University Press.

Feinman, S. 1982. Social Referencing in Infancy. *Merrill-Palmer Quarterly 28*:445–70.

Feinman, S., and M. Lewis, 1983. Social Referencing at Ten Months: A Second-order Effect on Infants' Responses to Strangers. *Child Development 54*:878–87.

Firth, R. 1951. Moral Standards and Social Organization. In *Elements of Social Organization*. London: Watts and Co.

Fortes, M. 1959. *Oedipus and Job in West African Religion*. Cambridge: Cambridge University Press.

Gelman, R., and R. Baillargeon, 1983. A Review of some Piagetian Concepts. In J. H. Flavell and E. M. Markman, eds., *Manual of Child Psychology*. Vol. 3, *Cognitive Development*. New York: John Wiley.

Gewirth, A. 1984. Ethics. *Encyclopedia Britannica*. 15th ed. Vol. 6.

Gilligan, C. 1982. *In a Different Voice: Psychological Theory and Women's Development*. Cambridge, Mass.: Harvard University Press.

Gilligan, C., L. Kohlberg, J. Lerner, and M. Belenky, 1971. Moral Reasoning about Sexual Dilemmas: The Development of an Interview and Scoring System. In *Technical Report of the U.S. Committee on Pornogrpahy and Obscenity*. Vol. 1.

Haan, N., R. Weiss, and V. Johnson, 1981. The Role of Logic in Moral Reasoning and Development. *Developmental Psychology 18*: 245–56.

Hallpike, C. R. 1979. *The Foundations of Primitive Thought.* Oxford: Clarendon Press.

Hart, H. L. A. 1961. *The Concept of Law.* London: Oxford University Press.

Kagan, J. 1984. *The Nature of the Child.* New York: Basic Books.

Kennedy, D. 1982. Distributive and Paternalist Motives in Contract and Tort Law, with Special Reference to Compulsory Terms and Unequal Bargaining Power. *Maryland Law Review 41*:563–658.

Kohlberg, L. 1969. Stage and Sequence: The Cognitive-Developmental Approach to Socialization. In D. A. Goslin, ed., *Handbook of Socialization Theory and Research.* New York: Rand McNally.

——— 1971. From Is to Ought: How to Commit the Naturalistic Fallacy and Get Away with It in the Study of Moral Development. In T. Mischel, ed., *Cognitive Development and Epistemology.* New York: Academic Press.

——— 1981. *The Philosophy of Moral Development: Moral Stages and the Idea of Justice.* Vol. 1 of *Essays on Moral Development.* San Francisco: Harper and Row.

Kohlberg, L., C. Levine, and A. Hewer, 1983. *Moral Stages: A Current Formulation and a Response to Critics.* In J. A. Meacham, ed., *Contributions to Human Development.* Vol. 10, New York: Karger.

Ladd, J. 1957. *The Structure of a Moral Code: A Philosophical Analysis of Ethical Discourse Applied to the Ethics of the Navaho Indians.* Cambridge, Mass.: Harvard University Press.

Lewis, D. K. 1966. *Convention: A Philosophical Study.* Cambridge, Mass.: Harvard University Press.

MacIntyre, A. 1981. *After Virtue.* South Bend, Ind.: University of Notre Dame Press.

Malinowski, B. [1926] 1976. *Crime and Custom in Savage Society.* Totowa, NJ: Littlefield, Adams and Co.

Much, N. 1983. The Microanalysis of Cognitive Socialization. Ph.D. diss., University of Chicago.

Much, N., and R. A. Shweder, 1978. Speaking of Rules: The Analysis of Culture in Breach. In W. Damon, ed., *New Direcctions in Child Development.* Vol. 2, *Moral Development.* San Francisco: Jossey-Bass.

Murdock, G. P. 1980. *Theories of Illness: A World Survey.* Pittsburgh: University of Pittsburgh Press.

Nadel, S. F. 1957. *The Theory of Social Structure.* Glencoe, Ill.: The Free Press.

Nagel, T. 1979. *Mortal Questions.* Cambridge: Cambridge University Press.

Nisbett, R. E., and T. D. Wilson, 1977. Telling More than We can Know: Verbal Reports on Mental Processes. *Psychological Review 84*:231–59.

Nucci, L. P. 1981. The Development of Personal Concepts: A Domain Distinct from Moral or Societal Concepts. *Child Development 52*:114–21.

——— 1982. Conceptual Development in the Moral and Conventional Domains: Implications for Values Education. *Review of Educational Research 52*:93–122.

Nucci, L., and M. Nucci, 1981. Children's Social Interactions in the Context of Moral and Conventional Transgressions. *Child Development 53*:403–2.

Nucci, L. P., and E. Turiel, 1978. Social Interactions and the Development of Social Concepts in Preschool Children. *Child Development 49*:400–407.

Ochs, E., and B. B. Schieffelin, 1984. Language Acquisition and Socialization: Three Developmental Stories and their Implications. In R. A. Shweder and R. A. LeVine, eds., *Culture Theory: Essays on Mind, Self and Emotion.* New York: Cambridge University Press.

Perelman, C. 1963. *The Idea of Justice and the Problem of Argument.* New York: Humanities Press.

Piaget, J. [1932] 1965. *The Moral Judgment of the Child.* New York: Free Press.

Rawls, J. 1971. *A Theory of Justice.* Cambridge, Mass.: Harvard University Press.

Read, K. E. 1955. Morality and the Concept of the Person among the Gahuku-Gama. *Oceania* 25:233–82.

Schelling, T. C. 1984. *Choice and Consequence.* Cambridge, Mass.: Harvard University Press.

Scribner, S., and M. Cole, 1981. *The Psychology of Literacy.* Cambridge, Mass.: Harvard University Press.

Shweder, R. A. 1982a. Beyond Self-constructed Knowledge: The Study of Culture and Morality. *Merrill-Palmer Quarterly* 28:41–69.

1982b. Liberalism as Destiny. Review of *The Philosophy of Moral Development: Moral Stages and the Idea of Justice.* Vol. 1 of *Essays on Moral Development,* by Lawrence Kohlberg. *Contemporary Psychology* 27:421–24.

1982c. On Savages and Other Children. *American Anthropologist* 84:354–66.

1985. Menstrual Pollution, Soul Loss, and the Comparative Study of Emotions. In A. Kleinman and B. Good, eds., *Culture and Depression.* Berkeley: University of California Press.

1986. Divergent Rationalities. In D. W. Fiske and R. A. Shweder, eds., *Metatheory in Social Science.* Chicago: University of Chicago Press.

Shweder, R. A., and E. Bourne, 1982. Does the Concept of the Person Vary Cross-culturally? In A. J. Marsella and C. White, eds., *Cultural Conceptions of Mental Health and Therapy.* Boston: Reidel. Reprinted in R. A. Shweder and R. A. LeVine, eds., *Culture Theory: Essays on Mind, Self and Emotion.* New York: Cambridge University Press.

Shweder, R. A., and J. G. Miller, 1985. The Social Construction of the Person: How Is It Possible? In K. Gergen and K. Davis, eds., *The Social Construction of the Person.* New York: Springer Verlag.

Shweder, R. A., and N. C. Much. 1986. Determinations of Meaning: Discourse and Moral Socialization. In W. Kuritines and J. Gewirtz, eds., *Moral Development through Social Interaction.* New York: John Wiley.

Shweder, R. A. E. Turiel, and N. C. Much, 1981. The Moral Intuitions of the Child. In J. H. Flavell and L. Ross, eds., *Social Cognitive Development: Frontiers and Possible Futures.* New York: Cambridge University Press.

Simpson, E. L. 1974. Moral Development Research: A Case Study of Scientific Cultural Bias. *Human Development* 17:81–106.

Singer, M. 1963. *Generalization in Ethics.* London: Eyre and Spottiswoode.

Smetana, J. G. 1981a. Reasoning in the Personal and Moral Domains: Adolescent and Young Adult Women's Decision-making Regarding Abortion. *Journal of Applied Developmental Psychology* 2:211–26.

1981b. Social-Cognitive Development: Domain Distinctions and Coordinations. Paper presented at meeting of The Society for Research on Child Development, Boston.

1982. Children's Reasoning about Mixed Domains (Moral and Social).

Paper presented at the annual meeting of the American Educational Research Association, New York.

1983. Social Cognitive Development: Domain Distinctions and Coordinations. *Developmental Review* 3, no. 2, 131–47.

Snarey, J. R. 1985. Cross-cultural Universality of Social-Moral Development: A Critical Review of Kohlbergian Research. *Psychological Bulletin 97*, no. 2, 202–32.

Stevenson, C. L. 1944. *Ethics and Language.* New Haven, Conn.: Yale University Press.

Turiel, E. 1979. Distinct Conceptual and Developmental Domains: Social-convention and Morality. In C. B. Keasy, ed., *Nebraska Symposium on Motivation*, 1977. Vol. 25. Lincoln: University of Nebraska Press.

1980. Domains and Categories in Social Cognition. In W. Overton, ed., *The Relationship Between Social and Cognitive Development.* Hillsdale, N.J.: Lawrence Erlbaum.

1983. *The Development of Social Knowledge: Morality and Convention.* New York: Cambridge University Press.

Turiel, E., and P. Davidson, 1985. Heterogeneity, Inconsistency and Asynchrony in the Development of Cognitive Structures. In I. Levin, ed., *Stage and Structure.* Norwood, NJ: Ablex.

Turiel, E., C. Helwig, and M. Killen, 1987. Morality. In J. Kagan and S. Lamb, eds., *The Emergence of Morality in Young Children.* Chicago: University of Chicago Press.

Turiel, E., and J. G. Smetana, 1984. Social Knowledge and Action: The Coordination of Domains. In W. M. Kurtines and J. L. Gewirtz, ed., *Morality and Moral Development.* New York: John Wiley.

Walker, L. J. 1984. Sex Differences in the Development of Moral Reasoning: A Critical Review. *Child Development 55*:677–91.

4

The laws of sympathetic magic
A PSYCHOLOGICAL ANALYSIS OF SIMILARITY AND CONTAGION

Paul Rozin and Carol Nemeroff

For some years, the first author and our colleague April Fallon have been investigating the emotion of disgust (Rozin & Fallon, 1987). We consider this emotion to be food-related at its core, and define it, in accordance with Angyal (1941) as "revulsion at the prospect of oral incorporation of an offensive substance." In our investigations with subjects in the University of Pennsylvania community we noted that offensive objects that elicit disgust, such as cockroaches, worms, or human body excretions, have potent contaminating properties. When they contact an otherwise edible food, they tend to render it inedible, even though there is no sensory trace of this contact. Furthermore, replicas of disgusting substances, even when known to be made of edible materials (e.g., a realistic fly made of candy), are often rejected as food. Our puzzlement about these expressions of the potency of disgust objects was resolved, in a sense, with the discovery that they were prototypical instances of the laws of sympathetic magic, as described in Frazer's *The Golden Bough* ([1890] 1959). Engaged by the fact that these widespread disgust responses in American culture fit with "beliefs" supposedly common only in traditional cultures, we began an investigation of the operation of the laws of sympathetic magic in everyday life, in disgust and other domains (Rozin, Millman, & Nemeroff, 1986). This research prompted us to think through the meaning and significance of the laws of sympathetic magic. This chapter presents some of the first fruits of this work.

The laws of sympathetic magic

The laws of sympathetic magic are descriptions of a consistent pattern of beliefs, thoughts, and practices observed across a wide range of

Preparation of this paper, and some of the research reported in it, was supported by funds from the John D. and Catherine T. MacArthur Foundation, Mental Health Research Network on Determinants and Consequences of Health-Promoting and Health-Damaging Behaviors. Thanks to Alan Fiske for critical comments on the manuscript, and to Fiske and Richard Shweder for invaluable discussions in which many of the ideas presented in this paper were clarified.

traditional cultures. Their widespread occurrence suggests that they may constitute laws of human thought. Three laws of sympathetic magic, contagion, similarity, and opposites, were originally described by E. B. Tylor ([1974] 1871) in *Primitive Culture*, and were substantially elaborated by Sir James Frazer ([1890] 1959) in *The Golden Bough*, and Marcel Mauss ([1902] 1972) in *A General Theory of Magic*. The explication of the laws that follows is based on the writings of all three of these authors, with our own interpretations and extensions. We discuss only the laws of contagion and similarity.

The law of contagion holds that things that have once been in contact with each other may influence or change each other for a period that extends well past the termination of contact, perhaps permanently. This effect can be summarized as "once in contact, always in contact." It is illustrated in the domain of disgust in U.S. culture by the enduring offensiveness acquired by foods that have been in contact with a cockroach, and in the interpersonal domain by the enhanced value of objects that have been in contact with celebrities. The transfer of properties – which can be psychological or physical attributes, or intentions – seems to be accomplished through transfer of an "essence." Animate objects seem particularly potent sources or recipients of essence but inanimate objects may also be sources or recipients. The essence, now in the recipient, remains in some sort of nonphysical relation to the source. This allows for the possibility that action taken on the recipient can affect the source (what we call backward causation [Rozin, Millman, & Nemeroff, 1986]). Thus, it is common practice in sorcery to obtain a personal residue (e.g., fingernail paring) from the victim, scorch the residue, and hence harm the victim.

The law of similarity holds that things that resemble one another share fundamental properties ("the image equals the object"), or that superficial resemblance indicates deep resemblance or identity. It is illustrated in the domain of disgust by the reluctance of many people to consume what they know is a tasty food if it is fashioned to look like a disgusting object (e.g., a large insect, or body excretions). As with contagion, the image has some sort of contact with the source, such that action on the image can affect the source ("like produces like") – another example of backward causation. An example of the latter is sticking pins into a replica of a person as a means of causing harm to that person.

Tylor, Frazer, and Mauss thought of the laws of sympathetic magic as laws of thought. They recognized the parallel between these laws and the laws of association of the British empiricist philosophers (Hume, [1748] 1959; J. S. Mill, [1843] 1963; see Warren, 1921, for a review). These philosophers and their contemporaries put forth a set of laws of association of ideas; most prominent among these were the laws of contiguity, similarity, and opposites. According to Mill, the law of contiguity holds that "when two impressions have been frequently experienced (or even thought of) either simultaneously or in immediate succession, then whenever either of these impressions or the idea of it recurs, it tends to excite the idea of the other" (p. 852). The focus in the law of contiguity is on temporal coincidence, as opposed to spatial coincidence for the law of contagion. Mill explained the associative law of similarity as "similar ideas tend to excite one another."

It is not surprising that two sets of candidates for universal laws of thought should be similar. However, they are far from identical. Tylor, Frazer, and Mauss recognized one fundamental difference between the two sets of laws: The laws of association are limited to the domain of thought; they operate only within the head. The laws of magic project these laws into the real world; that is, the physical world is held to be organized along principles similar to the laws of thought. The idea that one can harm an enemy by burning his hair does not follow from the laws of association (although gaining emotional satisfaction from it might). Another fundamental difference pertains only to the laws of contagion and contiguity. Whereas contiguity speaks to any type of proximity, with temporal proximity in the forefront, contagion refers explicitly to spatial contact. As a result of these and other differences, the laws of association and the laws of sympathetic magic often suggest different topics of investigation.

The scope of the laws of sympathetic magic and association is very large. The ideas of similarity and contagion/contiguity arise repeatedly in ethnographies and in studies of human thinking, and seem to hold a position among the more important aspects of human thought.

The motivation to explore this topic comes from two sources. First, the pattern of thought suggested by the laws of sympathetic magic is not known to psychologists, and hence not integrated into theories of thinking. Although the laws are widely known within anthropology, there has been little analysis of them from the psychological point of view (but see Freud, [1913] 1950, and Piaget, 1967, for some discussion). Second, the laws give rise to an intriguing contradiction. They are generally thought to be "primitive," and yet we find many examples of their operation in educated adults in Western-developed cultures. Furthermore, one of the laws, contagion, does not seem to be operative in young children (at least in the domain of disgust; Fallon, Rozin, & Pliner, 1984), which is an unlikely state of affairs for a supposedly "primitive" notion.

This essay explores the psychological underpinnings of two of the laws of sympathetic magic, the range of situations in which they operate, and their development within the individual.

Contagion

For convenience in exposition, we designate the contagious entity an *essence*. We use the verb, *to contaminate*, to refer to contact between an entity capable of transmitting essence and some other object. Unfortunately, contaminate has a negative connotation, but we use it in a neutral way, with the designation "positive contamination" when the effects are explicitly positive. In any situation to which the law of contagion applies, there is a *source* of contagious effects, and a *recipient* of these effects. Often there is a *medium* that serves to transfer the effects from source to recipient.

DIMENSIONS OF CONTAGION

In examining the structure and foundation of contagious beliefs, we have found it useful to isolate two dimensons of contagion (Rozin, Nemeroff, Wane, & Sherrod, in press). One dimension deals with forward versus backward action, and the other with positive versus negative effects.

Forward versus backward contagion. In forward contagion, or forward causation, an essence from the source reaches the recipient, either directly or via a medium, and exerts some effect on the recipient. This sequence resembles, but is not identical with, microbial contamination, in which the source might be a diseased person, the medium might be water or an implement that contained germs from the source, and the recipient might be a person who contacted the medium. The effect of this might be that the microorganism induced a disease state in the recipient. In a contagion situation, the source is usually, and the recipient is almost always, a person. An essence from the source reaches the recipient by direct contact, or through a medium (such as a piece of hair, or a food cooked by the source). In backward contagion, the generally accepted causal arrow is reversed, leading to a result that is not compatible with microbial infection. The essence is again transferred to the recipient, although in the backward cases, the recipient often actively seeks the contagious item. The item is usually possessed rather than incorporated by the recipient. The recipient now operates upon the essence (usually causing some "damage" to it) with the intent that the source itself will be similarly damaged. Backward contagion, in a negative context, is the basis for a common form of sorcery. In a positive context, it is often the basis for love spells that cause the source to feel desire for the recipient who has acted on his or her personal residue.

Positive versus negative contagion. In the anthropological literature, contagion is more often associated with negative effects, and is closely tied to the concept of pollution. However, as pointed out forcefully by Meigs (1978, 1984), there are abundant examples of positive contagion, that is, situations in which the transferred essence has a desirable effect on the recipient. Meigs's ethnography of the Hua of Papua New Guinea is replete with examples of transfer of positive effects among people in positive relations to one another. Meigs appropriately points out that substances (e.g., body residues) are not inherently negative or positive; rather, it is the context, the relation between source and recipient, that determines their value. Thus, among the Hua, it is beneficial to consume food cooked by someone in a positive relationship to the recipient, and a food is enhanced if it is spat upon by such a person. Similarly, food offerings in a Hindu temple are enhanced in value because the gods are presumed to partake of the offerings before they are returned to the donor (Breckenridge, 1986). More generally, amulets, talismans, and the laying on of hands are examples of positive contagion. Examples of positive contagion occur in U.S. culture, as in the valuation of possessions of one's ancestors, or the enhancement in value of clothing previously worn by a loved one (see later discussion in the chapter on the extent of contagion beliefs in U.S. culture).

Although positive contagion is a reality, negative contagion seems to be both more common and more salient, even among the Hua, perhaps the reigning champions of positive contagion. There is no salient opposite to the concept of pollution (although in ancient Greece, there was a term, *katharmos*, that stood for the opposite of pollution [*miasma*] [Parker, 1983]). The strength of this bias is well illustrated by a Nebraska car mechanic who pointed out that "a teaspoon of sewage spoils a barrel of wine, but a teaspoon of wine does nothing for a barrel of sewage." Stevenson (1954) captures this same relation, with respect to Hindu India, in his claim that "pollution always overcomes purity." Our survey of contagion beliefs in U.S. culture, while uncovering many examples of positive contagion, generally reveals a higher incidence, and greater potency for, negative contagion.

The negative bias may be related to the potency of harmful microorganisms that surely are the most salient form of physically based contagion in the natural world. Only some antibiotics and psychoactive drugs in the natural world have the powerful positive potency, in trace amounts, to match the negative potency of harmful microorganisms. In general, it may be the case that negative biological (and perhaps, social) forces have an urgency that requires high vigilance and urgency in response. There appears to be a negative bias in learning and in emotion, as well as in contagion, perhaps for this same reason; one cannot afford to learn slowly about imminent dangers, like predators or poisons (Rozin, 1986; Rozin & Fallon, 1987). Interpersonal bonding and attitudes to kin, both common arenas for positive contagion, do not have the same urgency.

CONTAGION AND THE TRANSMISSION OF ESSENCE

At the core of the idea of contagion is the existence of a contagious entity. Some authors (e.g., Mauss, [1902] 1972) refer to this entity as *mana*, but this term has many connotations, some of which extend well beyond "contagious entity." Meigs (1984) uses the term *vital essence* to describe the entity. In this discussion, the term of choice is *essence*.

The question we ask is, in the light of the actual practice of contagious magic and beliefs about contagion, what are the presumed properties of this essence and how is it transmitted? In particular, to what extent can the essence be considered to be (or to function as) a trace of a physical substance? And to what extent is essence analogous to a microbe? We are currently exploring this possibility through in-depth interviews with adults in U.S. culture. What follows results from our discussions and review of the literature.

In most practices and belief systems, essence seems to pervade the source. We describe this as the holographic principle. Thus, one lock of hair seems to contain the essential nature of the person from which it comes, just as each part of an animal contains the essential nature of the animal (a point commented upon by a number of authors; see, e.g., Werner, 1948). Crawley (1902) points out that any part of a person, or anything that has been in contact with him, is believed to retain this connection, and when acted on, to affect its owner. This illustrates the metonymic principle that the part can stand for the whole. Although the essence presumably contains all of the characteristics of its source, including the physical and mental properties of the source and the source's intentions, only a limited set of these properties may be operative in any contagious interaction. Thus, among the Hua (Meigs, 1984), and in many other cultures, it is often the intention of the source that is transmitted by the essence; foods contacted by people in a positive relation to the recipient cause improvement in the recipient, whereas foods contacted by people in a negative relation to the recipient cause harm to the recipient. In such cases, the particular personal attributes of the source are irrelevant; the outcome is general benificence or harm.

Essence has a number of characteristics that suggest that it is a physical substance. Most critically, it is passed on by physical contact. Furthermore, in many cases the effects of an essence in a recipient, or its transmissability in a medium, can be ameliorated by the same operations that would be effective against a physical substance: For example, washing is partly effective in rendering contaminated clothing more neutral. Washing with water was the principal means of purification (ridding a person of pollution) in ancient Greece (Parker, 1983). We do not yet know the extent to which other operations, such as maceration or burning, have similar effects on physical substances and essence. We also do not know the extent to which the effectiveness of a medium as a transmitter of essence is related to its ability to transmit physical substances. So, for example, are moist or rough media more susceptible to transfer than dry and smooth ones? In Hindu India, earthenware vessels are considered more likely to convey pollution, on account of their porosity, than cooking vessels of smoother and harder composition (Stevenson, 1954). Furthermore, among Oriya Brahmins and other groups in India, cotton is more pollutable than silk (Shweder, 1987). Similar distinctions are made in the kosher dietary rules, for example, between earthenware and glass vessels (Grunfeld, [1972]

1982). Many traditional means of removing a person's pollution (e.g., washing, purging, wiping, fumigating in ancient Greece) would operate upon physical entities (e.g., would reduce microbial contamination). One can imagine a physical transmission of essence that is nonmaterial, as in the transmission of energy. Thus, when a hot rock is placed in water, the temperature of the water changes without there being any transfer of rock-substance to the water. On this model, transformations that might not affect substance would be predicted to affect essences.

There are also a number of senses in which essences seem to be nonphysical. On the whole, contagion does not necessarily seem to be dose dependent (unlike microbial illness or other physical models). That is, very small amounts of essence seem capable of passing the full effect to the recipient. A number of operations, such as washing, which should rid an object of all traces of a foreign essence, are only partly effective in eliminating the effects of the essence. Furthermore, the permanence of some contagious effects, though consistent with what is known about physical substance, strain the physical limits a bit. As one subject in an interview spontaneously commented, with respect to a much-laundered shirt that once was worn by a despised person, X: "Once on X, always on X." To the extent that ritual is effective in removing pollution, there is a strong suggestion of a nonphysical entity. Although the Hindu practice of purification by ingestion of the products of the sacred cow (milk, ghee, curd, urine, dung) (Simoons, 1974) could be conceived as acting on physical entities, it is more compatible with a nonphysical model. The most nonphysical feature of contagion is backward causation. Unlike the tight physical link between source and recipient represented by the critical role for contact in forward contagion, backward causation is a prime example of action at a distance (a state abhorred by natural scientists, but one that they conveniently put aside in considering gravity, a perfect example of such action).

The reader is invited to explore the physical status of essences, for him or herself (it varies across people, within U.S. culture), by conducting a simple experiment. Consider a sweater that was owned and worn by Adolf Hitler. We presume most readers would be uncomfortable about wearing such a sweater, even after it was laundered. Now ask what manipulations on that sweater could make it neutral: heating, unraveling and reknitting, burning, being worn for a period of time by a greatly loved or admired person? Note that the latter manipulation, which some may find effective (notwithstanding that it might contaminate an admired figure), can be accounted for by both physical and spiritual interactions.

ESSENCE, ODOR, AND CONTAGION

There is a relation between essence, viewed as a physical substance, and odor. Both can constitute individual, unique, and invisible carriers of identity. An individual's odor can be left behind, as a residue to be incorporated by others, as can his or her essence. If one simply adduces to odors the possibility of carrying personal characteristics and intentions, then odor becomes a special case of essence. Crawley (1902) in reviewing a large number of instances of contagion, concludes that there is a belief that one's body odor may contain one's properties. The Ilahita Arapesh of New Guinea believe that odor is the distillation of physical, and more importantly, moral essences (Tuzin, 1986). For them, smell is the medium of moral recognition, and knowing a person's smell is to experience shared substance with them. Odor became an important, and highly threatening, carrier of personal properties and disease in the beliefs of 18th-century western Europeans, leading to a great interest in masking with pleasant odors, disinfection, and ventilation by the end of the 18th century and a tendency to rid oneself of odor-retaining things (Corbin, 1986).

The point is that odor shares many properties with essence, and may be, at some level in development or cultural evolution, the origin of ideas of contagion.

THE SOURCES OF CONTAGION

Any object, and any part of that object, is a potential source of contagion, but most sources of contagion are living things; plants, nonhuman animals, or humans. For the case of humans, it is often the personal relation between source and recipient that critically determines the degree and sign of contagion. In interpersonal cases, intent is often transferred, as well as or instead of characteristics. For the case of plants and animals, specific properties are transferred. Although there are examples of plants that pass on their properties (e.g., fast growth, femaleness with respect to the shape, color, and texture of the fruit) to humans by ingestion, there are sharp limits to the contagious potency of plants, in almost all cases. That is, they have to be ingested in modest amounts, and slight contact rarely causes significant pollution. Animals are much more potent sources of contagion; animal products are particularly potent sources of pollution (negative contagion). Thus, disgusting substances, which are always contaminating to some extent, are almost entirely of animal origin, cross-culturally (Angyal, 1941; Rozin & Fallon, 1987). The special potency of animals as sources of contagion may relate to their salient properties, and to their similarity to humans. Leach (1964) and Tambiah (1969) have pointed out that, for humans, animals are emotionally highly charged entities.

As Meigs (1984) has pointed out, body substances have a particular potency in terms of contagion. The potency is primarily on their negative side, leading to suggestions that decay (Meigs, 1984), anomaly (Douglas, 1966), or animalness (since these substances are also produced by animals) may be an important determinant of contagious potency.

The sign and potency of a source of contagion are not simply properties of the object. Meigs (1984) has provided many examples of how the context (e.g., the relation of a source person to a recipient) can modulate the sign of contagion (for some people for example, in U.S. culture, some body substances that normally induce strong negative contagious effects can become positive in the context of romantic love). Furthermore, the contagious link between the same source-recipient pair may shift over time. Meigs (1984) discusses these conditional polluting relations in some detail. For example, among Oriya Brahmins in India, during the first three days of menstruation a woman is not permitted to touch her children and is not allowed to cook (Shweder, 1987).

CONTACT AND CONTAGION

At its base, contagion seems to be about the incorporation into the self of foreign, friendly, or unfriendly essences. One can conceptualize both the essence and the self in physical terms, but the self has many forms (James, [1890] 1950). In particular, there is the virtually universal view of a soul, a moral, perhaps nonphysical entity, that resides within the body (Shweder, 1987). Essences would seem to be able to make contact with (and perhaps be comprised of) the soul/self.

The bodily self is clearly in intimate relation with the environment, and constantly engaged in exchange of materials. This fluidity involves exchange of inanimate, animate, and interpersonal essences; it is a particularly salient part of life in Hindu India (Kakar, 1982; Stevenson, 1954). Individual persons are constantly, via contact, leaving residues of themselves in the environment, while other individuals incorporate these essences. There is a vast, complex interpersonal exchange set up in this way, which can be described as the shedding of self and the permeability of the person.

Although the ultimate event may be contact of essence with the soul, individuals behave as if the physical body is the critical structure, and contact with it constitutes some form of entry. Thus, in the domain of disgust, Allport (1955) noted the striking phenomenon that while people are not disgusted by their own saliva as part of their body, most are offended by the prospect of drinking a glass of water after they have spit into it (confirmed by questionnaire for U.S. culture by Rozin et al., 1986).

There is something compelling about contact. Simply consider the difference between the presence of a piece of dog feces 1/2 inch from one's hand as opposed to touching one's hand. The skin is a clearcut boundary of the self. Objectively, one can imagine three routes of "contact," that is, entry of substance, into the body. One is surface contact. A second, perhaps a special case of the first, is entry through an orifice, most commonly in the act of ingestion, but also in sexual behavior. A third route of contact is inhalation of odorants, gases, vapors, or dusts. Although most contagious belief focuses on contact and ingestion, odor often assumes an important role (see e.g., Tuzin,

1986, for an example from New Guinea). Odor as a source of pollution assumed a major role in Western Europe from the 18th century onward (Corbin, 1986), and airborne entities, in some sort of vague way, played an important role in 19th-century conceptions of disease transmission (Rosenberg, 1962, 1986). Without intending to slight the airborne route, we focus on the more salient and universal direct-contact route.

There is no question that actual contact greatly enhances contagious effects; this holds for contact with corpses in ancient Greece (Parker, 1983) and the day-to-day phenomena of pollution in India. Both in terms of psychological reactions and the actual invasion of the body by foreign matter, the oral contact/ingestion route seems most highly charged and potent (leaving aside the one competitor for this dubious honor, the vagina). The mouth accounts for almost all of the overt material transaction between the rest of the world and the self. It is, approximately, THE incorporative organ. At the most basic biological level, this incorporation involves the essential acquisition of nutrients, made more emotionally salient by the real risk of ingestion of natural (and later in human history, culturally produced) toxins.

The process of ingestion carries a finality and intimacy that is not equaled by skin contact. Thus, in India, ingestion of a polluting substance is considered more dangerous than contact. Water can be used as purification for skin contact, but internal contact requires ingestion of ghee or the sacred panchgavya (a combination of different products of the sacred cow) (Stevenson, 1954). Daniel's (1984) observation and analyses of interpersonal exchanges in India led him to comment in *Fluid Signs*: "In the human body, the mouth is certainly the most vulnerable orifice, through which not only food substances enter but also evil spirits and the spirit of dead persons. Conversely, when an evil spirit is exorcised, it is believed to leave the body through the mouth" (p. 130).

You are what you eat. Contagion via the oral route is exemplified in the folk saying, "Man ist was Man isst" (you are what you eat). This maxim generally refers to the passage of physical or personality characteristics, as opposed to intentions, and captures a belief that is widespread in traditional culture. It illustrates the potency of the mouth (there is no equivalent saying, "you are what you touch"). The contagious principle is invoked since there is a presumed passage of essence; however, for the case of you are what you eat, there is usually a substantial amount of matter that is transferred, as opposed to a trace. In at least some such cases, there may be marked dose dependence and, in some cases, repeated ingestion is required to produce an appropriate transfer of characteristics.

According to Frazer (1959:573): "The savage commonly believes that by eating the flesh of an animal or man he acquires not only the physical but even the moral and intellectual qualities which were characteristic of that animal or man." Frazer illustrates with many examples, including the fact that bushmen avoid the flesh of slow animals, the belief in northern India that if one eats the eyeball of an owl one will be able to see in the dark, or the Australian belief that ingestion of kangaroo will lead to an improvement in jumping ability. Crawley (1902) also offers abundant examples, including the Hottentot belief that consumption of hare will induce faintheartedness, while consumption of lion will produce courage and strength.

On reflection, "you are what you eat" seems like an eminently reasonable idea (Nemeroff & Rozin, 1989). In the real world, mixture of entities (one version of what happens in ingestion) often gives rise to a product that shows properties of the constituents. Why shouldn't one turn orange after eating a lot of oranges, or become a good swimmer after eating fish? It is only the knowledge of the process of digestion in modern developed cultures that makes this idea implausible. Indeed, transmission of digestible entities can lead to some documented instances of you are what you eat. Virtually all yellow/orange pigmentation in animals traces ultimately to ingested carotenoids of plant origin. In particular, the pink-orange color of flamingoes comes in large part from carotenoids contained in the algae they consume (Gray, 1961; Thomson, 1964). Extensive ingestion by humans of foods containing carotenoids, such as carrots or tomatoes, can result in carotenemia, a marked symptom of which is orange pigmentation of the skin (reviewed in "The Orange Man," Roueché, [1947] 1982).

It is possible that you are what you eat is a universal belief, present in all children, and stamped out of adults through a scientific education. Indeed, according to Keith Thomas (1983), in his survey of the development of attitudes to the natural world in 17th- to 19th-century England: "It was generally accepted that food affected the character" (p. 292).

We pursued this idea by testing whether there is an implicit, unacknowledged belief in you are what you eat among educated American adults (Nemeroff & Rozin, 1989). We used the impressions technique originated by Solomon Asch (1946) to measure this belief. Subjects (a few hundred undergraduate students) read a half-page vignette describing a hypothetical culture. There were two versions of the vignette (unknown to the subjects), which were identical except that in one case, the people were described as eating marine turtle, and hunting wild boar, but only for its tusk, whereas, in the opposite case, wild boar was eaten and marine turtle was hunted, but only for its shell. So the two vignettes differed with respect to what was eaten (and fabricated), and not in terms of other contact with the two animals in question. After reading the vignette, subjects were asked to rate male members of the culture on a number of personality scales, including good swimmer versus good runner, irritable versus good-natured, phlegmatic versus excitable, long-lived versus short-lived. Many of these traits had been selected to discriminate boar from turtle. We found that subjects reading the boar-eating vignette rated the people in this culture as more boar-like than those rating the turtle-eating culture. We obtained similar findings, with other subjects, using a contrast between an elephant-eating culture and a vegetarian culture that hunted elephants for their tusks. We are in the process of extending these findings, and exploring other interpretations of them.

THE THREAT OF CONTAGION

Given the negative bias that we have already referred to, it is difficult to avoid a negative frame in discussing the consequences of contagion. In this section, we surrender to this impulse, and lay out the threats (as opposed to benefits) of contagion. Negative contagious interactions can lead to any of four types of bad consequences: (1) acquisition of negative physical or personality characteristics; (2) moral degradation; (3) "bad luck"; or (4) illness or death. A dominant theme in the first two consequences is the distinction between humans and animals. We discuss this first, and then another theme that distinguishes these consequences: the moral/physical distinction.

Acquiring animal properties and defending the animal/human distinction. Humans in traditional and modern cultures seem deeply concerned with defining themselves as distinct from all other animals. "We are not animals" is a theme that appears in an important way in many ethnographies (e.g., Ortner, 1973). Animal names as terms of abuse illustrate, as well, the low regard in which animals are held, with respect to humans (Leach, 1964). The human animal distinction plays an important motivating role in the development of sensibilities in Western European culture, as illustrated in Keith Thomas's (1983) *Man and the Natural World*. In previewing his analysis of the development of manners in medieval Europe, Elias (1978, p. 120) comments, "It will be shown how people, in the course of the civilizing process, seek to suppress in themselves every characteristic that they feel to be 'animal.'"

The manifestations of you are what you eat often focus on the acquisition of animalness, which appears both in terms of acquiring specific animal properties and a general moral degradation. Grunfeld ([1972] 1982), in his elaboration of the Talmudic interpretations of the Hebrew dietary laws, says that a major aim of many of these laws is to prevent the transfer of animal instincts into man, by consumption of certain foods. In particular, flesh eating and cruel habits are believed to be transmitted by consumption of carnivorous animals. Grunfeld states: "This is the general principle: The nearer the animal is to the vegetable world in its habits and composition, the less likely it is to arouse the animal nature in man, and its meat becomes the more suitable for human consumption" (p. 8).

In a more modern context, in 19th-century England, one of the great arguments against vaccination was that the use of cow fluids would animalize humans (Thomas, 1983). Similarly, Gandhi (1949) argued for a vegetarian diet on the grounds that it allayed animal passion, and DesPres (1976) argued that a powerful aspect of the concentration camp horror was to get both the guards and the inmates to think of the inmates as animals.

In their analysis of disgust, Rozin and Fallon (1987) conclude that the widespread disgust expressed at the prospect of consuming animal foods relates directly to the issue of animalness. There is concern both with eating what was once a living animal, and for the possibility of acquisition of animalness. All of these examples simply serve to emphasize the importance of the animal/human distinction, and the power of contagion to blur this boundary.

While humans clearly seek to distinguish themselves from animals, humans also admire animals. This is illustrated by a desire to identify with animals, illustrated by the existence of totems and, in U.S. culture, the naming of sports teams after admired animals. Overall, the human response to animals, and their consumption, is ambivalent, but with respect to contagion, negative features often predominate.

The moral/physical distinction. Our typical college student subject goes through the following sequence when offered a cockroach to eat. It is, of course, rejected. When asked why, the response is usually: "Roaches are filthy creatures that carry all sorts of germs. I could get sick." We respond with: "OK, then, let's consider a sterilized, dead roach. That would have no germs." The subject's response is (often with a certain amount of embarrassment): "Oh, well, I still wouldn't eat it." Experimenter: "Why not, it's perfectly safe." Subject: "Because, because, it's a cockroach!" This exchange represents a shift from a health-threatening ("physical") to a symbolic/moral reason. It illustrates a fundamental conflict in accounting for rejection of contaminating or contaminated entities that occurs both historically and in development. There is a confusion between physical/health and moral/symbolic accounts, and a tendency to frame or rationalize the threat in terms of bodily harm. Thus, Elias (1978), in his analysis of the rise of modern table and other manners in medieval Europe, concludes that the original motivation for suppression of belching, eating from a common pot at the table, or spitting at the table, and the like was social/moral – that is, it established a distinction between upper, more civilized, and lower classes. These manners were later justified in terms of sanitation. Similarly, the Hebrew dietary prohibitions such as the pork taboo arguably have a moral basis (Grunfeld, [1972] 1982), but have been justified, incorrectly in most cases, in terms of health (e.g., prevention of trichinosis).

Especially since many contaminating entities can be disease vectors, there is a strong tendency, as with the cockroach example, to explain rejection in terms of health risk. But a major case for which such a shift to physical risk does not hold is modern Hindu India. Traditional Hindus reject foods that have had a certain degree of contact with members of lower castes. The more the lower caste member has been engaged with the food (the more of him that is "in" the food), the more unacceptable it is (Douglas, 1966). As a result, of foods that have been in contact with a lower caste member, cooked foods, which are in fact safer to eat from the point of view of microbial contamination, are less acceptable than raw foods.

FRAMING AND THE LIMITS OF CONTAGION

From a contagion perspective, the world is suffused with essences; footsteps, money, clothing, all foods, and many other items bear the residues of insects and other people, savory or unsavory. The most neutral object may become highly charged (usually negatively) if we contemplate its history. And yet, neither we, nor the much more contagion-sensitive Hua, are crippled by this prospect. How is this managed? (Note that we again revert to negative contagion in this discussion.) We put all but the most salient instances of contagion out of our minds; we frame situations so as to reduce the salience of past history. We do not think that the air we breathe during a ride on public transportation or at a lecture was just exhaled by some of our neighbors (unless it is called to our attention by an unsavory odor). We do not think of the history of the money we handle, or where our dog's face has been as he licks us. We also arrange, sanitize our environment to make personal and offensive linkages less salient. Food is purchased at supermarkets in sanitized packages, as if processed by machine. In this context, it is inappropriate to think about WHO prepared the food. In U.S. culture it is primarily the obsessives who worry excessively about cleanliness and past history, and who become crippled on this account. There have been situations at other times, and in other cultures, where contagion has become crippling. In 18th- and 19th-century France, there was excessive concern over corruption via inhaled air. Disinfection, deodorization, and ventilation came to be of major importance (Corbin, 1986). Fear of sorcery via contagion may become extreme. Frazer ([1890] 1959) reports that among the Betsileo of Madagascar, "blue blood" or ramanga have the job of eating all nail parings and licking up all spilled blood of nobles to prevent sorcery. They follow their masters around in order to dispose of residues.

We have already identified two mechanisms for reducing the effects of contagion. One is disregarding it (framing out) and the other is reducing the salience of contagion in the environment (e.g., by packaging foods in the supermarket). A third mechanism invokes explicit rules, and is probably most common in cultures in which contagion is a more serious threat. Thus, among Hindus in India, the left hand is reserved for toilet functions, and not used in the serving of food or in greetings. (Of course, there are limits to this, since it is hard to believe all cooking is done with the right hand, and then there is, of course, the problem of left-handers). This left-hand specialization is common in many parts of the Middle East and Africa.

It is within the Hebrew tradition of dietary laws that we see some of the most elaborate treatments of minimal contagion. According to the interpretations of the prohibitions developed in the Talmud and later works (Grunfeld, [1972] 1982), explicit limits on the provenance of contagion are set to prevent cessation of all activity by the possibility of microcontamination. The basic principle, known sometimes as the 1/60th rule, holds that if a nonkosher contaminant (e.g., pork, or a dairy product in meat) falls *accidentally* into a kosher food, the food remains kosher as long as the contaminant constitutes no more than 1/60th of the total volume. This neat rule does not solve all problems, however. Suppose that there are two contaminants, one that constitutes 1/70th and the other 1/90th of the total volume. Together they would activate the 1/60th rule, but, if that is so, then any contaminant, when summed with tiny amounts of other unknown contaminants might also trigger the 1/60th level. This problem was appreciated by the Hebrew sages so the 1/60th rule applies only to the principal contaminant. All others may be ignored. There are other fascinating elaborations of this problem (Grunfeld, [1972] 1982); the point of the example is to illustrate the problem and the most cerebral approach to its solution.

Of course, a rule delimiting significant contamination effects does not directly solve the problem of emotional responses to contamination. Indeed, we (Nemeroff & Rozin, 1988) have shown that kosher Jews commonly reject as undesirable foods that have been contaminated with nonkosher items at sufficiently low levels that they remain technically kosher by the 1/60th rule.

THE REAL-WORLD BASIS FOR CONTAGION

As represented in the interpersonal domain (e.g., the food cooked by X contains X's essence), and especially in terms of backward contagion, the law of contagion seems maladaptive and irrational. However, there are physical bases, or at least physical analogues, to the law (in the forward version). Microbial contamination, as we have mentioned, is a direct parallel to negative, forward contagion, and could arguably be the adaptive basis and origin of contagion beliefs. For an intensely social species like Homo sapiens, passage of disease by invisible entities is a major risk.

In an important sense, contagion has to do with the history of entities, in particular, their past contacts. It emphasizes history over appearance in the evaluation of objects. In this regard, contagion is closely related to kinship, where history (genealogy) is the central concern, and a major determinant of the nature of social relations.

As we have shown, analysis of contagion leads to the presumption that a holographic principle is operating, akin to the metonymic principle that the part equals the whole. As contagion usually operates, any part of a source contains the essence of that source, as if the essence is distributed throughout the source. Although this is clearly untrue for matters such as personality, it is actually the case for the genetic blueprint, since an identical and unique set of DNA molecules is present in all cells of a given person.

THE EXTENT OF BELIEF IN CONTAGION IN THE UNITED STATES

In recent research, we have sought to determine the degree of belief in the law of contagion among educated Americans (primarily, students at the University of Pennsylvania). Our basic technique has been to compare (usually in a questionnaire) an uncontaminated object with this same object after contact with a potent source. In most cases, subjects rate their readiness to consume, wear, or otherwise interact with the object on a 200-point scale, with +100 as "the most pleasant thing you can imagine," -100 as the "most unpleasant thing you can imagine," and zero as neutral.

Not surprisingly, 46 of 49 subjects reported a drop in desirability of their favorite juice after it was actually contacted by a sterilized, dead cockroach (mean drop in rating on the 200-point scale was 99 points; Rozin et al., 1986). In a more wide-ranging questionnaire study of 140 subjects, interpersonal contagion was explored with four personal sources: a lover, a best friend, a disliked person, and an unsavory person (e.g., a street person) (Rozin et al., in press). Subjects selected persons to meet each description from their own experience before answering the questions about these people. Subjects then answered questions about a number of media before and after they had appropriate contact with each of the sources. The sources and interactions we shall discuss are wearing a laundered sweater previously owned by each of the sources (one sweater per source, all sweaters identical except with respect to their history), taking a bite from a hamburger previously bitten by each of the sources, and using a hairbrush previously used by each of the sources and then thoroughly cleaned.

In general, positive contagion reactions were somewhat (but not strikingly) stronger to lovers than best friends, and negative contagion reactions were somewhat (but not strikingly) stronger to unsavory than disliked persons. Using as a criterion a change of at least 20 points in the rating scale as a result of contact, about 90% of the subjects showed a drop in the sweater rating as a result of contact with the negative persons (unsavory or disliked), whereas only about 20% of the subjects showed an increase of 20 points as a result of contact with a positive person. The corresponding figures for hamburger were 85% negative and 10% positive, while the figures for hairbrush were 79% negative and 5% positive. Thus, across these three common media, negative contagion effects appear in the great majority of the subjects while positive contagion appears in a small minority. We also explored a case of backward contagion, in which one's own hairbrush (which one will never see again) comes into the possession of each of the four sources. Surprisingly, although the magnitude of the effect was not enormous, there was clear evidence for backward contagion in both the negative and positive directions. Using the criterion of a shift of at least 20 points, from neutrality, abot 30% of the subjects showed discomfort at the thought of having their hairbrush possessed by an unsavory or disliked person, and about 37% showed pleasure at the thought of having their hairbrush possessed by a best friend or lover.

The principal findings of this survey were (1) negative forward contagion was ubiquitous; (2) positive forward contagion was clearly present in a subset of subjects; and (3) evidence pointed to both positive and negative backward contagion. Over the range of questions asked in this survey (including more media than indicated above), none of the 140 subjects showed clear signs of contagion beliefs for *all* media, directions (forward and backward), and signs (positive and negative). On the other hand, *all* subjects showed *some* signs of contagion beliefs on one or another of the questions. There was a weak tendency for a person who held one contagion belief to hold another one.

This contemporary survey evidence is supported by a wide variety of findings and observations from Western-developed cultures. Positive contagion is illustrated, in general, by the existence of objects to which people have sentimental attachments. More specifically, Crawley (1902) refers to the European folk custom in which a lover applies a piece of his hair, drops of his blood or sweat, or water in which he has washed his hands, to the garments of the girl whose affection he desires. A recent survey documents the importance of objects with personal histories in the lives of adult Americans; indeed, the authors of the study comment that objects (in particular, photographs) "can acquire an almost mystical identification with the deceased person" (Csikszentmihalyi & Rochberg-Halton, 1981, p. 69).

A recent television commercial in which the well-known football player, Mean Joe Green, gives a thrilled young admirer his towel illustrates positive contagion with respect to heroes. A striking instance of contagion is the great value placed on the ashes of a cremated loved one. In a recent court case in California, a company that disposed of such ashes was sued for 200 million dollars, because, instead of being scattered over the Sierras, the ashes were unceremoniously dumped in a lot (*Sacramento Bee*, 1984). As we commented earlier, kinship loyalty and affection is construable as an instance of contagion; that is, the definition of kinship centers around a continuity of substance, whether or not this continuity is perceptible.

Examples of the operation of negative forward contagion are even more common. Even prior to germ theory, contagion was a popular view of disease transmission. Indeed, during the 18th-century cholera epidemics in the United States, common folk treated the disease as contagious even though the medical profession preferred a moral interpretation of contraction of the disease (Rosenberg, 1962). Many people are reluctant to buy used clothing because of their fear of contagion; in a recent survey, 76% of the sample refused to buy underclothing, and 20% refused to buy used overcoats (O'Reilly, Rucker, Hughes, Gorang, & Hand, 1984).

The most striking illustration of negative contagion beliefs in recent times relates to the current AIDS epidemic. There is a strong response among many people to *any* contact with AIDS victims, in spite of medical evidence indicating minimal risk. This appears to be a powerful belief, which, like other contagion beliefs, is almost dose independent. The current abhorrence of any sugar in foods among some Americans is another possible example of a belief in contagion. The idea seems to be that if sugar is toxic, then even tiny amounts of sugar carry this toxicity (again, the dose-independence principle).

We conclude from these selected examples that even in American culture, where the personal history of objects is often suppressed, contagion plays a substantial role. In modern Hindu India and some other places, that role is much more powerful.

THE DEVELOPMENT OF CONTAGION

Because of its association with traditional cultures, there is a strong inclination to think of belief in the law of contagion as a sign of a "primitive" mentality. However, we will argue on both empirical and theoretical grounds that contagion is a complex and sophisticated concept.

Although contagion beliefs about illness are present in a great many cultures, the salience of these beliefs is often not high. Thus, in his cross-cultural survey of beliefs about disease, Murdock (1980) reports that only 49 of 139 cultures attribute disease to a contagious entity (contact with a polluting substance, such as menstrual blood), and only 31 of these 49 cultures have anything like a germ theory.

The view that contagion is "primitive" predicts that it would be present in young children and would decrease with age and education. The view that it is sophisticated would hold that contagion would be absent in young children. The latter seems to hold. Until the age of about seven or eight, American middle-class children do not show contagion in response to disgusting or dangerous items (Fallon et al., 1984). Although young children reject consumption of "poison" or insects when presented with stories in which contamination occurs, they do not show signs of rejecting a beverage that has been in contact with dangerous or disgusting items for a brief time. Further experimentation, using actual contamination of a beverage with a fly, or an apparently used comb, also indicate that below the age of seven, there is little evidence for disgust-based contagion (Rozin, Fallon, & Augustoni-Ziskind, 1985).

It is conceivable that our failure to observe disgust contamination results from a weakness in the child's disgust response, rather than an absence of contagion. Contagion may appear earliest in a domain other than disgust. Anecdotal reports of strong attachments of children to particular toys or dolls, or blankets, have a contagion aspect (that is, *their* blanket has *them* in it, and is different from any other similar-looking item). Anecdotal reports of children who refuse to eat a food if it has touched a disliked food on their plate are suggestive of contagion, as are some "contagion" transfer games such as Cooties (Opie & Opie, 1969), or a form of "pollution tag" played by children in the Orissa region of India (Shweder, 1987). We know of no firm evidence concerning the ages at which such games are regularly played.

As indicated in the discussion of essence above, the cognitive basis for contagion is, in fact, quite sophisticated. Most centrally, essence is invisible, and perhaps, insensible. Thus, the principle of contagion is built on the premise that things are seldom what they seem, or that appearance is not equal to reality. As we will indicate in the discussion of the development of similarity, the equation of appearance and reality, which we take to be the basis of similarity, is indeed a simple and "primitive" aspect of mentation. (The appearance–reality confusion is present in American children until the early school years [Flavell, 1986; Keil, 1986].) This being the case, contagion, as its opposite, cannot be simple and primitive.

The notion of essence, or its equivalent, may presume a notion of the particulate nature of matter and the idea that these particles are not visible. Before the age of seven, children have very limited conceptions of the particulateness of matter (Smith, Carey, & Wiser, 1985), and the nature of the process of dissolving (disappearance of matter through particulation; Piaget & Inhelder, [1941] 1974). Furthermore, germ theory does not appear in an articulated manner before seven years of age (e.g., Bibace & Walsh, 1979; Nagy, 1953).

It is particularly surprising that contact, which seems a most elemental notion, does not seem to have a specially important role. Thus, it is not until about seven years of age that children focus on contact as a major source of disease transmission (Bibace & Walsh, 1979), even though younger children have a definite sense of disease transmission by proximity without contact.

Contagion, by its nature, depends on the conception of a continuing history of persons and objects, since otherwise the past contacts of an object would not be relevant to one's current commerce with that object. It is critical that one realize that this food or item of clothing is the *same* one that had a particular contact in the past. Although some conception of the continuity of objects over time is surely present in even the youngest humans, there are limitations to the range and domain of such continuity ideas in early childhood. Before the age of six, children do not usually recognize the continuity of a child with the adult that it will later become (Guardo & Bohan, 1971).

If contagion is an acquired belief, how is it acquired? It is unlikely that children are explicitly instructed in this domain. However, there are many opportunities to observe adult behavior that would reveal adults' belief in contagion, so that contagion might be acquired implicitly, as is the case for many aspects of culture. We suggest that one route to acquisition is learning that odor is an enduring characteristic that can represent a presence in the absence of appearance cues. A person's possessions may carry his odor, which in this sense, serves as a sign of the contagion history of these possessions. It is conceivable that children first learn about contagion by attending to odor, as opposed to just appearance. Indeed, among the Ilahita Arapesh of New Guinea, odor is the major vehicle and sign of contagion (Tuzin, 1986). Alternatively, contagion may be a natural and inevitable outgrowth of cognitive advances in the understanding of matter.

The law of similarity

According to the descriptions and analyses of Tylor, Frazer, and Mauss, the law of similarity holds that the image equals the object. That is, things that show a superficial resemblance, which in most cases amounts to looking alike, also have a deep resemblance. Furthermore, because like produces like, or like acts on like, action against an image can influence the object that it corresponds to. That is a form of backward causation. Indeed, a particularly common manifestation of similarity occurs in the sorcery practice of attempting to harm someone by damaging his image. Perhaps as a result of the dominance of the visual sense in humans, similarity is almost always evaluated in terms of visual resemblance. In this respect, it is appropriate to summarize the law of similarity as "appearance equals reality" (where appearance is a distinctly visual word).

It does not seem necessary to invoke the concept of essence to explicate the law of similarity. Of course, one could say that the image, by some mysterious process, contains the essence of the source (object). Under such circumstances, the backward causation belief that occurs in sorcery could share a mechanism with backward causation by contagion.

As with contagion, similarity can invoke positive or negative response, depending on the nature of the object (source). Forward and backward "causation" both occur. Forward causation describes the satisfaction or discomfort, potential benefit or harm, resulting from intimacy with a replica of a valued or offensive entity, and backward causation describes feelings that sources will be influenced if action is taken on their images.

Belief in the law of similarity is widespread in traditional cultures, and is documented at length by Tylor, Frazer, and Mauss. A particularly interesting recent example is the reluctance of members of some traditional cultures to have their picture taken, on the grounds that something of them will be taken away when the developed replica leaves their community in the hands of a tourist or researcher.

It is possible to infer from the appearance-equals-reality claim the more inclusive claim that if two entities resemble one another on certain attributes, they also have a deep resemblance (resemblance in visible traits is one special case of this). In a sense, the attributes of an entity may instantiate the entity (something akin to the holographic principle mentioned in the discussion of contagion). One particularly salient attribute of an object is its name. There is widespread reverence for names of respected entities, along with a feeling that to defile the name is like defiling the entity it refers to. The name is perceived as an integral part of its referent, perhaps something that partakes of its essence. Piaget (1967) refers to this view as nominal realism (referred to as word realism by Werner & Kaplan, 1963). Nominal realism is normal in children in the Western cultures Piaget studied, up until the age of six. The name of an object is perceived as an integral part of the object, and the carrier of all the object's properties. Hesse (1962) points out that name and object are equated commonly in Western culture, as can be seen in the prohibition on mentioning the name of "God" in Judaism. There are widespread examples of nominal realism in traditional cultures, often manifested as a prohibition on speaking the name of someone who has recently died.

THE REAL WORLD BASIS FOR SIMILARITY

Similarity can be viewed as an overextension of a useful principle. Surely, sometimes appearances are deceiving. But, as a general rule or heuristic, the principle that if X looks like a Y, it is a Y, is a good one. Indeed, it is wise to operate on the principle that what looks like a tiger is a tiger. The problem arises when this heuristic has major influences on behavior in situations where appearances are deceiving. There is mimicry in the natural world.

The extent of belief in similarity among Americans. Although similarity may be the more "simple-minded" of the two laws of sympathetic magic, we find its operation to be commonplace among educated, adult Americans (Rozin et al., 1986). Thus, 49 of 50 University of Pennsylvania community subjects showed more reluctance to hold between their lips what was obviously a clean rubber replica of vomit (from a prank store) than a clean rubber drain mat of the same size. Similarly, 45 of 50 of these same subjects rated themselves less desirous of consuming a well-crafted mound of chocolate fudge, shaped to appear like a "doggie-doo," than an equivalent mound of the same fudge shaped in the form of a disc (Rozin et al., 1986). Furthermore, these same subjects were significantly poorer in accuracy in throwing darts at the point midway between the eyes of a picture of a revered figure (John F. Kennedy) or an imagined head of a loved person, than at a blank paper or picture of a disliked person (Rozin et al., 1986).

We believe that nominal realism is also common among adults. We suspect that many adults would be uncomfortable tearing up a piece of paper on which the name of a loved one is written. How many of those who use computers a lot have had second thoughts about erasing a file named for a liked person, especially when the erase command is "KILL," e.g. "KILL MILDRED," followed by the computer display "KILLING MILDRED." We demonstrated such tendencies in the laboratory by offering people a choice of two glasses of sugar water. One glass was made with sugar taken from a bottle labeled "sucrose, table sugar," and the other with sugar from a bottle labeled "sodium cyanide, poison" (Rozin et al., 1986). People rate the "cyanide" water significantly less desirable. There can be no question that the subjects thought there might really be cyanide in the cyanide-labeled bottle. Subjects watched sugar poured into both of the bottles. They were then given the two sticky labels (sugar and cyanide), and asked to put one label on whichever bottle they wanted to.

There are many other manifestations of similarity in our culture. A striking set of examples that can be construed as similarity is the reliance on resemblance as opposed to contingency in the formation of impressions (Shweder, 1977). Indeed, Shweder argues for the prevalence of related magical beliefs in Western-developed cultures.

THE DEVELOPMENT OF SIMILARITY

The developmental picture for the "primitive" belief in similarity is what might be expected (in contrast to contagion). Similarity does seem to be a childish way of thinking, which becomes less salient (but does not disappear) with age.

In an impressive and extensive series of recent studies, John Flavell and his colleagues have demonstrated that young U.S. American children (below the age of 5 or 6) fail to make the appearance–reality distinction in many situations (reviewed in Flavell, 1986). For example, they believe that a yellow object actually becomes red when it is seen behind a red filter, even if a part of the yellow color sticks out from the side of the filter. This finding is in keeping with Keil's (1986) work on natural kind, where preschoolers hold that a skunk shaved and otherwise superficially altered to look like a raccoon, *is* a raccoon.

Nominal realism was described by Piaget (1967) and Werner and Kaplan (1963) as a normal feature of childhood in Western cultures. Through the age of six years, children believe that the name is inseparable from the referent. Up to the age of nine or ten, children continue to believe that things must have a name.

Similarity and contagion: contrasts and similarities

JOINT OPERATION OF SIMILARITY AND CONTAGION

Since beliefs in both similarity and contagion are widespread, and since both focus on significant entities, we would expect both to operate with respect to some of the same entities. And they do. Both are operative with respect to attitudes to pork and other nonkosher foods or combinations of foods by kosher Jews (Nemeroff & Rozin, 1989). Responses to offensive animals or decay in many cultures follow both laws. Within American culture, the correlations between degree of belief in contagion and similarity, as gauged by a number of questionnaire and laboratory tests, is positive, but very small (Rozin et al., 1986). There is no question that the laws can act independently. In the case of sorcery, creating a replica of a person and then damaging it is a pure example of similarity. Obtaining a personal residue (e.g., hair, fingernail paring) and damaging it is a pure example of contagion. Among kosher practices, rejection of soy imitation bacon bits is a pure example of similarity, and rejection of an eggroll that contains tiny amounts of pork is a pure example of contagion.

In many situations, both laws operate simultaneously, to reinforce one another. Thus, Frazer ([1959] 1890) cites the Malay custom in which a clay figure of an enemy is constructed (similarity) incorporating residues from that person (contagion). The figure is then scorched, causing harm to the enemy by both laws.

The laws can operate in sequence, in a situation we call contagion by similarity. That is, the contagious entity is not the original source of contagion, but a replica of it. Thus, among the Moose of Burkina Faso, a medicine that will aid an individual in his ambition to be head of a village includes a rock from the highest mountain, an epiphyte from the top of a tall tree, the bark of a tree that fell opposite to the wind, and a piece of lion. These similarity-based entities are compounded into a powder or burnt to charcoal and then mixed with food and ingested (contagion) (Fiske, personal communication). Among the Hopi, the navel cord of a newborn boy is attached to an arrow shaft (contagion) so he will become a good hunter (similarity). For the female child, a stirring stick is used, so that she will become a good cook. In a questionnaire used with college students to measure disgust sensitivity, subjects were asked about the extent to which they would be discouraged from consuming their favorite soup if it was stirred by a brand new comb. The new comb is a negative entity by similarity to a used comb. By stirring the soup, the principle of contagion is engaged, by an item similar to a disgusting item. Sixty-four percent of subjects rated the stirred, previously favorite soup as neutral or disliked as a result of this hypothetical maneuver, a clear example of contagion by similarity. Similarly, stirring of a favorite soup with a brand new flyswatter resulted in equivalent effects in 71% of subjects (data from Rozin, Fallon, & Mandell, 1984).

In the same manner, we (Nemeroff & Rozin, 1989) have found that many kosher Jews will reject a kosher food that has been contaminated by contact with a kosher item that is similar to a nonkosher item. Thus, 42% of our 56 kosher subjects were reluctant to eat vegetarian lasagna into which a trace of vegetarian bacon bits had fallen, while

Table 4.1. *Comparison of similarity and contagion*

Similarity	Contagion
Similarities	
Image $\equiv$ object	Parallel to: Part $\equiv$ whole
Forward-backward dimension	Forward-backward dimension
Positive-negative dimension	Positive-negative dimension
Differences	
Appearance $\equiv$ reality	Appearance $\neq$ reality
Decreases with age	Increases with age

57% were reluctant to eat kosher chicken soup into which a drop of nondairy creamer had fallen.

In general, it seems that when a source is sufficiently negative, and a person sufficiently swayed by the magical principles in this context, contagion by similarity can occur.

COMPARISON OF SIMILARITY AND CONTAGION

Both laws of sympathetic magic (and the law of opposites, as well) are empirical generalizations that supposedly describe universal laws of thought. The laws have notable similarities and differences (summarized in Table 4.1).

Similarities. Both laws are manifested in terms of forward and backward causation, and both have both positive and negative forms. Although both have a basis in predicting events in the world, both fail under some conditions, particularly in the backward causation form. In this sense, there is something irrational about some of the applications of both laws.

There is a close parallel between similarity and contagion. The image equals the object, a shorthand for similarity, can be glossed as a part of the object (its name or image), can stand for the whole object, and behaves in significant ways (e.g., with respect to backward causation) as the real object. The part equals the whole, a gloss of the holographic aspect of contagion, represents basically the same relation. Although these two relations have been distinguished as metaphoric and metonymic (e.g., Leach, 1976), they share the part/whole feature. In other words, both can be thought of as generalizations, or overgeneralizations.

Differences. The fundamental contrast between the laws is in degree of sophistication. The law of similarity can be glossed as "appearance equals reality." The law of contagion, in its emphasis on insensible traces of past interactions, emphasizes that appearance does not always represent reality. The latter is clearly the more sophisticated, less sense-based notion. Perhaps it is because of this greater sophistication of the law of contagion that contagion seems to increase with age, whereas similarity decreases with age.

Conclusions

This discussion has different functions for psychologists and anthropologists. For psychologists, it calls attention to unfamiliar cousins to the familiar laws of association. These cousins, the laws of sympathetic magic, call attention to phenomena ignored by psychologists, which, especially in the form of contagion, may have major implications for social interaction. We hope to harness the considerable experimental skills of psychologists in an effort to explain these so far untouched-by-psychology aspects of human thought. For anthropologists, the essay should serve as a reminder of something familiar, and a reminder that although the laws of sympathetic magic are familiar, we know very little about how they operate, what they entail, their development, and their psychological basis.

The laws of sympathetic magic may well be universal beliefs or laws of thought. The overtness of belief, and the domains in which the laws operate, vary both across cultures and across individuals within cultures. We believe that the laws are factors in decision making in U.S. culture. We have argued that the two laws are very different, if not opposite, in the degree of sophistication that they presume. We hope that this contrast, the ubiquity of the laws, and their almost pristine state as subjects of investigation will encourage interest in further explorations.

References

Allport, G. W. (1955). *Becoming. Basic considerations for a psychology of personality*. New Haven, CT: Yale University Press.

Angyal, A. (1941). Disgust and related aversions. *Journal of Abnormal and Social Psychology, 36*:393–412.

Asch, S. E. (1946). Forming impressions of personality. *Journal of Abnormal and Social Psychology, 41*:258–290.

Bibace, R., & Walsh, M. E. (1979). Developmental stages in children's conceptions of illness. In N. E. Adler et al. (Eds.), *Health psychology. A Handbook* (pp. 285–301). San Francisco: Jossey-Bass.

Breckenridge, C. A. (1986). Food, politics and pilgrimage in South India, 1350–1650 A.D. In R. S. Khare & M. S. A. Rao (Eds.), *Food, society and culture: Aspects in South Asian food systems* (pp. 21–53). Durham, NC: Carolina Academic Press.

Corbin, A. (1986). *The foul and the fragrant: Odor and the French social imagination*. Cambridge, MA: Harvard University Press.

Crawley, E. (1902). *The mystic rose. A study of primitive marriage*. London: Macmillan.

Csikszentmihalyi, M., & Rochberg-Halton, E. (1981). *The meaning of things*.

Cambridge: Cambridge University Press.

Daniel, E. V. (1984). *Fluid signs: Being a person the Tamil way*. Berkeley, CA: University of California Press.

DesPres, T. (1976). *The survivor*. Oxford: Oxford University Press.

Douglas, M. (1966). *Purity and danger*. London: Routledge & Kegan Paul.

Elias, N. (1978). *The history of manners. The civilizing process: Vol. I* (E. Jephcott, Trans.), New York: Pantheon Books. (original work published 1939)

Fallon, A. E., Rozin, P., & Pliner, P. (1984). The child's conception of food: The development of food rejections with special reference to disgust and contamination sensitivity. *Child Development*, 55:566–575.

Flavell, J. (1986). The development of children's knowledge about the appearance–reality distinction. *American Psychologist*, 41:418–425.

Frazer, J. G. (1959). *The golden bough: A study in magic and religion*. New York: Macmillan. (Reprint of 1922 abridged edition, edited by T. H. Gaster; original work published 1890)

Freud, S. (1950). *Totem and taboo* (J. Strachey, Trans.). New York: W. W. Norton. (Original work published 1913)

Gandhi, M. K. (1949). *Diet and diet reform*. Ahmedabad, India: Navijivan.

Gray, P. (1961). *The encyclopedia of the biological sciences*. New York: Van Nostrand/Reinhold.

Grunfeld, D. I. (1982). *The Jewish dietary laws. Volume One. Dietary laws regarding forbidden and permitted foods, with particular reference to meat and meat products* (3rd ed.). London: Soncino Press. (original work published 1972)

Guardo, C. J., & Bohan, J. B. (1971). Development of self-identity in children. *Child Development*, 42:1909–1921.

Hesse, M. B. (1962). *Forces and fields: The concept of action at a distance in the history of physics*. Westport, CT: Greenwood Press.

Hume, D. (1959). *Enquiry concerning human understanding and concerning the principles of morals*. New York: Dover. (Original work published 1748)

James, W. (1950). *Principles of psychology*. New York: Dover. (Originally published 1890)

Kakar, S. (1982). *Shamans, mystics and doctors: A psychological inquiry into India and its healing traditions*. Boston: Beacon Press.

Keil, F. C. (1986). The acquisition of natural kind and artifact terms. In W. Demopoulos & A. Marras (Eds.), *Language learning and concept acquisition: Foundational issues* (pp. 133–153). Norwood, NJ: Ablex.

Leach, E. (1964). Anthropological aspects of language: Animal categories and verbal abuse. In E. Lenneberg (Ed.), *New directions in the study of language* (pp. 23–64). Cambridge, MA: MIT Press.

——— (1976). *Culture and communication*. Cambridge: Cambridge University Press.

Mauss, M. (1972). *A general theory of magic* (R. Brain, Trans.). New York: W. W. Norton. (Original work published 1902; Esquisse d'une theorie generale de la magie. *L'Annee Sociologique*, 1902–1903)

Meigs, A. S. (1978). A Papuan perspective on pollution. *Man*, 13:304–318.

——— (1984). *Food, sex, and pollution: A New Guinea religion*. New Brunswick, NJ: Rutgers University Press.

Mill, J. S. (1963). System of logic: Ratiocinative and inductive. In *Collected works of John Stuart Mill. Volume VIII*. Toronto: University of Toronto Press. (Original work published 1843)

Murdock, G. P. (1980). *Theories of illness: A world survey*. Pittsburgh, PA: University of Pittsburgh Press.

Nagy, M. H. (1953). The representation of "germs" by children. *Journal of Genetic Psychology, 83*:227–240.

Nemeroff, C., & Rozin, P. (1989). "You are what you eat" Applying the demand-free "impressions" technique to an unacknowledged belief. *Ethos: The Journal of Psychological Anthropology, 17*:50–69.

——— (1988). Sympathetic magic in kosher practice and belief at the limits of the law of Kashrut. *Jewish Folklore & Ethnology Review, 9*(1):31–32.

Opie, I., & Opie, P. (1969). *Children's games in street and playground*. Oxford: Oxford University Press.

O'Reilly, L., Rucker, M., Hughes, R., Gorang, M., & Hand, S. (1984). The relationship of psychological and situational variables to usage of a second-order marketing system. *Journal of the Academy of Marketing Science, 12*:53–76.

Ortner, S. B. (1973). Sherpa purity. *American Anthropologist, 75*:49–63.

Parker, R. (1983). *Miasma. Pollution and purification in early Greek religion*. Oxford: Clarendon Press.

Piaget, J. (1967). *The child's conception of the world*. Totowa, New York: Littlefield & Adams. (Original work published 1929)

Piaget, J., & Inhelder, B. (1974). The child's construction of quantities. (A. J. Pomerans, Trans.). London: Routledge & Kegan Paul. (Original work published 1941)

Rosenberg, C. E. (1962). *The cholera years*. Chicago: University of Chicago Press.

——— (1986). Disease and social order in America: Perceptions and expectations. *Millbank Quarterly, 64* (Suppl. 1), 1–22.

Roueché, B. (1982). The orange man. In *The medical detectives*. New York: Washington Square Press (pp. 147–160). (Originally published 1947)

Rozin, P. (1986). A survey of one-trial acquired likes and dislikes in humans: Disgust as a US, food predominance and negative learning predominance. *Learning & Motivation, 17*:180–189.

Rozin, P., & Fallon, A. E. (1987). A perspective on disgust. *Psychological Review, 94*:23–41.

Rozin, P., Fallon, A. E., & Augustoni-Ziskind, M. (1985). The child's conception of food: The development of contamination sensitivity to "disgusting" substances. *Developmental Psychology, 21*:1075–1079.

Rozin, P., Fallon, A. E., & Mandell, R. (1984). Family resemblance in attitudes to food. *Developmental Psychology, 20*:309–314.

Rozin, P., Millman, L., & Nemeroff, C. (1986). Operation of the laws of sympathetic magic in disgust and other domains. *Journal of Personality and Social Psychology, 50*:703–712.

Rozin, P., Nemeroff, C., Wane, M., & Sherrod, A. (In press). Operation of the sympathetic magical law of contagion in interpersonal attitudes among Americans. *Bulletin of the Psychonomic Sciences*.

Sacramento Bee (1984). Ashes dispute in court. *Sacramento Bee*, June 15, 1984, B4.

Shweder, R. A. (1977). Likeness and likelihood in everyday thought: Magical thinking in judgments about personality. *Current Anthropology*, *18*:637–658.

(1987). Menstrual pollution, soul loss and the comparative study of emotions. In A. Kleinman & B. J. Good (Eds.), *Culture and depression: Towards an anthropology of affects and affective disorders*. Berkeley: University of California Press.

Simoons, F. J. (1974). The purificatory role of the five products of the cow in Hinduism. *Ecology of Food and Nutrition*, *3*:185–201.

Smith, C., Carey, S., & Wiser, M. (1985). On differentiation: A case study of the development of the concepts of size, weight, and density. *Cognition*, *21*:177–237.

Stevenson, H. N. C. (1954). Status evaluation in the Hindu caste system. *Journal of the Royal Anthropological Institute of Great Britain and Ireland*, *84*:45–65.

Tambiah, S. J. (1969). Animals are good to think and good to prohibit. *Ethnology*, *8*:423–459.

Thomas, K. (1983). *Man and the natural world*. New York: Pantheon Books.

Thomson, Sir A. L. (1964). *A new dictionary of birds*. New York: McGraw-Hill, pp. 143, 297–299.

Tuzin, D. (1986). Sensory contact and moral contagion in Ilahita. Paper delivered at 85th annual meeting of the American Anthropological Association, Philadelphia, PA, December.

Tylor, E. B. (1974). *Primitive culture: Researches into the development of mythology, philosophy, religion, art and custom*. New York: Gordon Press. (Original work published 1871)

Warren, H. C. (1921). *A history of the association psychology*. New York: Scirbner.

Werner, H. (1948). *Comparative psychology of mental development* (rev. ed.). New York: International Universities Press.

Warner, H., & Kaplan, B. (1963). *Symbol formation. An organismic-developmental approach to language and the expression of thought*. New York: John Wiley.

5

The development from child speaker to native speaker

Dan I. Slobin

[The forms of each language] establish a definite relational feeling or attitude towards all possible contents of expression and, through them, towards all possible contents of experience, in so far, of course, as experience is capable of expression in linguistic terms.

Edward Sapir ([1924] 1958:152)

The child encounters culture, to a great extent, through speech. The *content* of speech conveys the norms, the values, the accumulated knowledge and folkways of the society. However, the *form* of speech – that is, structured *language* – bears an uncertain relation to culture. Linguists, anthropologists, psychologists, and philosophers have taken every possible position on the role played by linguistic form in the thought and behavior of individuals and social groups. In my own comparative research on child language development I have sought to avoid these uncertain issues by attending to the acquisition of linguistic form itself, characterizing my approach as cross-*linguistic*, but not as cross-*cultural*. This approach is based on the empirical finding – from our early cross-cultural research (Slobin, 1970, 1973) – that patterns of grammatical development are strikingly similar in widely differing cultural settings; and on the psychological conviction that the course of language development is determined by biological and cognitive factors that are common to our species. Thus I have made use of linguistic diversity as a kind of "natural experiment" in which the world presents children with different tasks to solve. In this laboratory, by carefully selecting contrasting linguistic systems for study, one can tease out the strategies that human children use in constructing grammar.

My interests have focused on linguistic structure – on patterns of

Presented to the First Annual Chicago Symposium on Culture and Human Development, October 23–25, 1986. Work reported in this paper was supported by a fellowship from the John Simon Guggenheim Memorial Foundation, by grants from the Linguistics Program of the National Science Foundation and from the Israel–U.S. Binational Science Foundation (with Ruth A. Berman), by the Sloan Foundation Program in Cognitive Science (Berkeley), and by the Max Planck Institute for Psycholinguistics (Nijmegen). I am grateful to Ruth Berman for her major role in helping to develop the research program and the ideas presented here.

word order and grammatical morphemes – and on the relations of these patterns to developing systems of cognition and communication. Linguistic structures seem to vary independently of cultural factors, such as political-economic organization, social structure, religion, and so forth. Many examples of the independence of language and culture could be cited. For example, consider Hungary – clearly part of European culture, yet differing radically in its linguistic structure from the languages of its neighbors. The Austro-Hungarian monarchy would have worked no better, or no worse, if Hungarian had case-marked articles, like German, rather than its Uralic pattern of agglutinative noun suffixes. Nor has the structure of Hungarian accommodated to the historical changes from a society of nomadic warriors, through feudalism, Central European monarchy, and present-day communism. Indeed, if one seeks languages similar in grammatical structure to Hungarian, one finds, for example, Turkish and Japanese. Yet an anthropologist or sociologist would be hard-pressed to find common features in the cultures or social systems of Hungary, Turkey, and Japan that could be attributed to their agglutinative morphology and verb-final syntax.

As a psycholinguist, however, one does find common features in the ways in which languages of this type are acquired by children and used by adults. For example, these three languages place their grammatical morphemes at the ends of words and sentences, thereby facilitating children's discovery of formal marking of notions such as agency and spatial and temporal relations (Slobin, 1973). Thus, in reaching for an object, a Hungarian or Turkish or Japanese child of 18 months might add a noun-final or utterance-final particle, grammatically indicating an object of desire, whereas an American or German child of the same age may lack clear grammatical means to mark the same intent. To this extent, then, linguistic *typology* can influence patterns of acquisition.

At the same time, however, utterances expressing such basic notions as requests for objects are found universally in 18-month-old speech. Indeed, regardless of the particular grammatical means of expression, there is a striking commonality in the content and functions of children's early speech across languages and cultures. In a sense – abstracting away from surface characteristics of word order and morphology – there are universal starting points for language in terms of children's concepts and communicative intentions. The "child speaker," cross-linguistically, makes claims on objects and services, reports sudden changes of state, notes locations and absences of objects, announces intentions, and so forth. At first, the child's eye view of the world seems to transcend specific peculiarities of language and culture, presenting us with a broadly cross-cultural view of the beginnings of language. Consider, briefly, two examples: references to object manipulation and to resultant states (for details, see Slobin, 1985).

In widely differing languages, children younger than 2 use some grammatical marker in utterances expressing control or direct physical manipulation of objects. For example, in Russian child speech the accusative inflection appears on nouns that are the direct objects of verbs like "give", "put", and "throw", but not on nouns that are the direct objects of non-manipulative verbs like "see" and "read" – although in adult Russian this inflection is required in all instances (Gvozdev, 1949). What we have here is a restriction of the application of a grammatical marker on a childish basis. Similar distinctions are found in widely differing languages. For example, the Kaluli of New Guinea speak an ergative language – that is, a language in which a special grammatical marker is required on the *subject* of a transitive verb, rather than the object, as in Russian. Kaluli children begin their grammatical speech with the same semantic restriction as Russian children, although in this instance restricting the marker on *subject* nouns to utterances in which the verbs express control or direct physical manipulation of objects (Schieffelin, 1985). Because the semantic definition of grammatical marking appears to be so similar across language types and cultures, it seems appropriate to describe the behavior of a generalized "child speaker," rather than a native speaker of Russian or of Kaluli. In order to become a *native* speaker of Russian, for example, the child will have to learn how that particular language deals with direct objects – for example, that verbs of non-manipulative semantics, like "see" and "read" also mark their objects with the accusative inflection; but that this inflection is not used when the proposition is negated; that a different inflection is used if the direct object is masculine and animate; and so forth. That is to say, the distinctions that are grammatically marked by the native speaker are not childlike, but are distinctly Russian. Similarly, the Kaluli native-speaker will use the ergative inflection on the subjects of various semantic types of verbs, but will not use it in every word order.

Let me give another example of the transition from child speaker to native speaker – one that plays a role in the study I report on in this chapter. It seems that some kinds of *results* are more salient to little children than are the *processes* that lead up to those results. This is reflected in the finding, in many different kinds of languages, that the first uses of verb markings for past tense tend to mark immediate changes of state, like "feel", "broke", and "dropped". For example, Bloom, Lifter, and Hafitz (1981:398) noted that in the speech of American 2-year-olds, verbs that occurred in the past tense "named nondurative, momentary events that tended to be completive, with a relatively clear result." Again, we have a cross-linguistic pattern of child speech that must evolve into the verb tense/aspect categories of particular native languages. In English, for example, the past tense in adult speech also refers to events that are durative, extended in time, and noncompletive: not only *fell* and *broke*, but also *played* and *thought*. That is, the past tense is semantically *general* in adult English. At the same time, however, it is *differentiated*, in that it is possible to mark a range of distinctions of aspect and modality for any particular verb, depending on larger discourse considerations – consider, for example, some possible differences in reporting that someone dropped something: *he dropped it, he was dropping it, he kept on dropping it, he was going to drop it, he used to drop it, he has dropped it, he had dropped it, he has been dropping it, he might have dropped it.*... Thus the native speaker has gone beyond the child speaker in at least two ways: (1) the use of formal grammatical marking is generally not closely tied to particular events or situational meanings, and (2) a wide range of semantic/pragmatic *perspectives* on events can be marked grammatically. Both of these developments should have important consequences for the restructuring of child thought. To revive an ancient controversy, consider the epigraph to this chapter, a quotation from the linguist Edward Sapir in one of his milder versions of the doctrine of linguistic relativity and determinism – one that I will try to support in presenting some new cross-linguistic research on the transition from child speaker to native speaker. In 1924 Sapir wrote: "[The forms of each language] establish a definite relational feeling or attitude towards all possible contents of expression and, through them, towards all possible contents of experience, in so far, of course, as experience is capable of expression in linguistic terms" (1958:152).

The categories that determine grammatical choice in child speech seem to be well-motivated and fairly easily definable semantic/ pragmatic "core" notions, whereas those of adult speech are much less obvious – as indicated by the vigorous and ever-expanding field of linguistics. Each language requires the speaker to make use – automatically and systematically – of a collection of semantic distinctions that are not immediately tied to everyday perception and action or to the demands of practical life. The core notions expressed in early child grammar do not have to be taught through language; rather they seem to stem from primordial and universal patterns of thought and action. However, the distinctions that are grammaticized in developed human languages cannot be easily pointed out by ostensive reference or mapped directly from general experience; rather, they must be learned through the linguistic devices themselves, which are the only means for "pointing" to the relevant event categories. This learning moves the child from child speaker to native speaker of a particular language. Rather than continue on this general level, let me now turn to one specific investigation in progress, trying to fill out these general observations with examples.

Five ways of learning how to talk about events: a cross-linguistic study of children's narratives[1]

The investigation that I draw from is currently in progress. It began, several years ago, as a joint endeavor with an Israeli linguist, Dr. Ruth Berman of Tel-Aviv University, directed at the development of temporal systems in child language. We picked Hebrew and English because they lie at two ends of a continuum with regard to grammatical marking of temporal relations: Hebrew, with its simple system of past-present-future and no grammatical marking of aspect, and English, with its complex and interacting systems of past and present tense, progressive and perfect aspect, and modality. We began with preschoolers, but as we moved into work with schoolage children it became evident that we were involved with more than just marking of temporal reference on individual verbs and clauses. Having picked a *narrative* task, we quickly became involved with issues of *plot* and *perspective* in their relations to developing language. Soon other languages were added to the study, and it became evident that children were learning verb forms to express particular types of discourse functions, as guided and limited by the perspectives provided by particular languages. For the purposes of the present discussion, I will pull out only a few main trends that are emerging from this research. First, an orientation to the task and the languages.

In order to standardize narrative content, we used a picture storybook, *Frog, Where Are You?* (Mayer, 1969), that tells a story without words. (For a synopsis of the book and sample pictures, see the appendix on p. 250.) The strength of this technique, of course, is that whatever variation we find by age or by language cannot be attributed to the stimulus materials, but to the ways in which these materials are interpreted by the children. It is these varying and developing interpretations that are the focus of our study. Here I discuss stories that were gathered from children aged 3, 5, 9, and adults, speaking English, German, Hebrew, Spanish, and Turkish as native languages.[2]

These languages can be placed on a rough continuum in terms of the number of aspectual distinctions that are marked in the grammar – that is, distinctions like the English *ran/was running*, which do not differ in deictic tense (both of these are "past"), but differ in the "temporal contour" or "temporal perspective" from which an event is described. Verbal aspects can be classified in various ways, but the following presents a rough summary of our continuum, ignoring various interactions of aspect with tense for simplicity of presentation:

Language	*Aspects*
Spanish	PROGRESSIVE (*corriendo*)
	PERFECT (*ha corrído*)
	IMPERFECTIVE (*corría*)
	PERFECTIVE (*corrió*)
English	PROGRESSIVE (*running*)
	PERFECT (*has run*)
	HABITUAL (*runs*)
Turkish	PROGRESSIVE (*koşuyor*)
	HABITUAL (*koşar*)
German	PERFECT (*ist gelaufen*)
Hebrew	(none)

What might one expect, developmentally, from such an array of languages? Our expectation was that our 3-year-olds would resemble each other cross-linguistically, beginning with similar, simple event descriptions, and adding the aspectual coloring of their native languages starting around age 5. And we expected that 9-year-olds learning languages with sparse aspectual systems, like German and Hebrew, would try to find other means – adverbial and periphrastic – to make distinctions that are not grammatically marked in their language. What we found, however, was quite different: Children seem to be closely guided by the options provided by the native language. Our 3-year-olds are already distinguishable by language: The more tense/aspect options available, the more they are used. Thus Spanish children of this age use six different forms, English and Turkish use four, and German and Hebrew use two:

Language	3-year-old tense/aspect forms
Spanish	PAST PERFECTIVE, PAST IMPERFECTIVE, PAST PROGRESSIVE, PRESENT, PRESENT PROGRESSIVE, PRESENT PERFECT
English	PAST, PAST PROGRESSIVE, PRESENT, PRESENT PROGRESSIVE
Turkish	PAST, PAST PROGRESSIVE, PRESENT, PRESENT PROGRESSIVE
German	PRESENT, PRESENT PERFECT
Hebrew	PAST, PRESENT

The forms are used appropriately, and, as we will see, are mastered before the larger discourse frames of coherent narrative have been established. Thus these children have apparently already passed beyond the universal developmental period that I have characterized as "child speaker," and already have begun to sound like native speakers of their particular languages – even if they do not yet sound like mature speakers.

Let me follow this last distinction a bit further, since there are two developmental paths that deserve our attention. The child is learning how to talk like a speaker of Spanish or English, and is also learning how to tell a story, conduct an argument, make a request, and so forth. These two paths seem to be fairly separate. We can read English versions of our story texts from the five languages and can readily identify the age of the child on the grounds of features of plot structure and character development, as I will show. At the same time, a fine-grained clause-by-clause analysis can reveal the native language of the child, at all ages. In essence, with a bit of simplification, we can identify a common cross-linguistic course of development at the level of *macrostructure* – a development that results in *mature speakers*; and a language-specific course of development at the level of *microstructure*, that results in *native speakers* of one language or another. The macrolevel deals with the story as a whole and with relations between segments of the story in terms of features such as foreground–background relations, causality, and motivation. The microlevel deals with the structure of individual clauses or adjacent clauses, and especially with their verbs and predicates. Of course, there are relations between these two levels, but here I want to focus particularly on the microlevel. First, however, a few observations about macrolevel development will set the stage.

DEVELOPMENT OF STORY ORGANIZATION

Few of our 3-year-olds tell coherent stories, while almost all of the 9-year-olds do. Yet even 9-year-old narrators are not as flexible and competent as adults. Here I must point out that our cross-*linguistic* research design undoubtedly misses interesting cross-*cultural* differences at the macrolevel. Although we gathered data in five countries (United States, Spain, West Germany, Turkey, and Israel), we were careful to minimize cultural differences in the interest of using only language and age as the major independent variables. Thus we chose only urban and suburban children of educated families, representing a fairly common Western life-style across societies. These children have been read to, have gone to preschools and kindergartens, and become literate at about the same age. Within this common background, there are no striking cultural differences in their interpretations of the frog story. Indeed the 9-year-old stories are so stereotyped that one sometimes has to read twice to convince oneself that one hasn't read the same story over again by mistake!

The 3-year-olds tend to talk about the book picture-by-picture, even though all children first looked through the whole picture book silently, being encouraged to follow the story. The following segment of an American 3-year-old narration is typical:[3]

> This dog is looking into the bowl. And then the frog is still in there. And now, look what happened. And now, he got away. The frog got away, and then, look what happened. He tried to go in, but, see, he didn't, couldn't go in! And then, he licked the boy, and he was mad! And then, some bees came out of the tree, and then he tried to get the bees, but he couldn't. [E-3f]

Compare this with an American 5-year-old:

> When the boy and the dog were asleep the frog jumped out of the jar. And then the boy and the dog woke up. The frog was gone. Then the boy got dressed, and the dog stuck his head in the jar. And then the boy opened up his window and called out for his frog, and the dog still had the jar on his head. Then the dog fell [out of the window],[4] and the boy was scared. And then the boy was mad at the dog, and picked him up. And then he called for his frog again. He called in a hole, and the dog called in the beehive. And the dog got some bees out of the hive. And then the dog made the beehive

fall, and all the bees came out of the beehive. And the boy looked in the tree. And then the boy fell out, and the owl was flying, and the bees were flying after the dog. And the boy got up on some rocks, and the owl flew away. And the boy was calling for his frog on the rocks. And a deer...the boy got caught on the deer's antlers. And then the deer carried him over a cliff and threw him [over the cliff into a pond]. And the boy and the dog fell, and they splashed in some water. And they looked, and they saw a log. And the boy said "shh" to the dog. And they looked over the log. And they saw the frog, and some baby frogs too. And the boy said goodbye to the frogs, and brought a baby frog home. [E-51]

Here we find such narrative features as stage setting ("*When* the boy and the dog were asleep"), internal states ("...and the boy was *scared*. And then the boy was *mad* at the dog..."), continuing goal orientation ("And the boy was calling *for his frog* on the rocks"), and relation of the end to the initial situation ("And they saw *the* frog"). Still, however, the story is "jumpy" and not as well integrated as the following typical 9-year-old version, which is clearly more mature:

Once there was a boy who had a pet frog and a dog. And that night he was watching it. And when he went to sleep, the frog got out of his jar and got away. The next morning, when he woke up, he saw that the frog was gone. So he put on his clothes, and the dog accidentally got his head stuck in the jar which the frog was kept in. They called out the window, and the dog fell down, and the glass jar broke, and the boy was mad at him. So they went off to find his pet frog. And he looked in a hole, and the dog was chasing the beehive. It was a home to a ground squirrel. And he got his nose scratched. And the dog was still over playing with the bees. The bees started to chase him, 'cause the beehive fell. The boy was calling the frog in this tree. And then the dog was running away, because the bees were all chasing him, and he had fallen down because an owl poked him out of the tree. And the bees chased the dog, and the dog chased the boy to a rock, and he stood on the rock and called the frog. But a deer was on top, and it got him by his horns, and carried him to the edge of a cliff, with his dog chasing after, and threw them both into the lake, that was down below, and they both fell in. And then they heard some frogs chirping on the other side of the log. So they went to the log, and they went over and saw his pet frog with a mate. And when they climbed over they saw that he had babies too, and so the frog let them have one of his babies to keep, instead of him. [E-9a]

Here we have much more elaborate stage-setting and indication of temporal transitions ("And that night he was watching it.... The next morning, when he woke up..."). The story does not relentlessly move forward in time, but allows for flashbacks or retrospection ("...the dog...got his head stuck in the jar which the frog was kept in"; "...he

Table 5.1. *Percentage of stories with sustained search*

	Age		
	Three	Five	Nine
English	8	42	100
German	42	67	100
Spanish	33	42	100
Turkish	10	50	90
Hebrew	8	75	100
Average	21	57	98

had fallen down because an owl poked him out of the tree"). Motives and causes of events are repeatedly and explicitly stated ("The bees started to chase him *'cause* the beehive fell." "And then they heard some frogs chirping on the other side of the log. *So* they went to the log..."). And the conclusion is more clearly related to the overall theme of loss and search (which is mentioned several times in the narrative) ("...and saw his pet frog...and so the frog let them have one of his babies to keep, instead of him").

Such differences between 5- and 9-year-old stories are found in all five languages. (Compare the Spanish and Turkish stories in the appendix.) Numerically, one can indicate such macrolevel developments in several ways. Consider, for example, Tables 5.1 and 5.2.

In Table 5.1 we ask whether the narrator made some mention of the fact that the boy and dog were looking for the frog after having left the house. Note that overall, only about one-fifth of the 3-year-olds have any sort of sustained search in their stories; more than half of the 5-year-olds do; and, with one exception, all of the 9-year-olds do. Table 5.2 looks at one particular key transition in the plot – namely, the cause of the boy and dog falling from the cliff. Note a steady increase with age in the percentage of children who make some mention of the causal role of the deer in bringing about this important

Table 5.2. *Percentage of stories mentioning causal role of deer*

	Age		
	Three	Five	Nine
English	30	56	92
German	50	67	95
Spanish	58	82	90
Turkish	44	70	100
Hebrew	33	50	83
Average	43	65	92

change of location. The 9-year-olds also make more frequent mention of participants' inner states, often attributing causal import to them. For example, they say that the boy was "amazed", "upset", "sorry" not to find the frog in the morning; that he was "happy", "pleased" to have a frog he could take home with him again. Compare, for example, the Spanish 5- and 9-year-old stories (in the appendix) in regard to the role of the owl. The younger child says: "An owl came out that threw the boy"; while the older child adds a causal link in terms of an internal change of state: "Then an owl came out and the boy got scared and he fell." Or note the developing attribution of intentions as motivating actions: The Turkish 5-year-old (in the appendix) simply reports: "Then the dog put the jar on his head. Then the boy came and got mad at the dog. Then the dog fell from the window." The Turkish 9-year-old attempts to motivate this event by saying, "The dog put his head inside the jar. He couldn't get it out at all. In order to get it out, he jumped from the window. And when the jar broke he managed to save himself."

On the linguistic level, the 9-year-old stories are identifiable by their greater use of subordination and embedding. Broadly, from age 3 to adulthood, there is a steady development from simple *pointing* at separate events, to *chaining* of events, and finally to *nesting* (Berman, 1986). Only 9-year-olds give us such marvelous interweavings of change of perspective between events as the English: "And then the dog was running away, because the bees were all chasing him, and he had fallen down because an owl poked him out of the tree." Compare this with an English 5-year-old's chaining of events: "And then the boy fell out and the owl was flying, and the bees were flying after the dog."

MICROLEVEL DEVELOPMENTS

Macrolevel trends in story organization, such as those I have just briefly alluded to, cut across our five language samples. More striking psycholinguistically, however, are the subtle differences between languages on the microlevel. Here each language predisposes a particular "narrative slant" or "perspective" with regard to the local encoding of such issues as temporal overlap and sequence of events, location and change of location, and causality and agency. Mature language use requires the ability to *choose* between forms of a verb, depending on the function of the predicate in connected discourse – particularly on the *perspective* taken by the speaker with regard to the represented event. These perspectives reflect a set of options in the flow of discourse – options to present an event, for example, as ongoing or completed, or to present a protagonist as agent or patient or something in between. Each of the five languages has its own ways of encoding temporal, spatial, and causal relations, and children seem remarkably sensitive to the available means of expression from early on. None of these language-specific categories are in any sense "present in" or "required by" the picture. The picture story has its own logic, whoever looks as it. Yet, even the 3-year-olds recount events in accord with the particular slant of their language, as opposed to presenting simple, unelaborated versions that would be roughly identical across languages. (And, as I will suggest later, the set of available perspectives offered by a given native language may well constrain the range of conceptualizations of events developed by the child.) With a practiced eye, one can even read English translations of the foreign stories, together with original versions in American English, and identify the real language of the narrator. To simplify the presentation, I will consider four broad issues: *temporality*, *change of location*, *agency*, and *definiteness* – primarily with regard to English, Spanish, and Turkish.

TEMPORALITY

As I pointed out earlier, 3-year-olds have already acquired the basic range of obligatory tense/aspect distinctions offered by the native language: the richer the language, the more distinctions acquired. Furthermore, these distinctions are generally used appropriately in the youngest stories.

Progressive. In languages with progressive aspect, children find it easy to differentiate between ongoing and completed events in the past, as shown by our American 5-year-old: "And then the boy *fell out*, and the owl *was flying*, and the bees *were flying* after the dog." Compare this with a Hebrew 5-year-old: *ve hu [yanshuf] hipil et hayeled, ve az kol hadvorim racu axarey hakelev, ve hu barax* "and he [the owl] threw the boy, and then all the bees ran after the dog, and he ran away" [H-5k]. It apparently does not occur to a Hebrew-speaker to indicate differences in duration between events, whereas such distinctions are made naturally and with ease by speakers of languages with progressive or imperfectives.

Perfective/imperfective. Languages like Spanish, with a perfective/imperfective aspectual distinction, allow one to consider an event from an external perspective, as a closed or completed event (perfective), or from an internal perspective, as having extent in time (imperfective). This distinction is somewhat different from that marked by the progressive – and it is one that is rather hard for English-speakers to fully grasp. The distinction is mastered clearly in our Spanish 5-year-old story (in the appendix), where the same verb, *ver* "see", occurs in three different – and appropriate – combinations with a complement verb. (*I* = imperfective, *P* = perfective, in the following examples.)

> When the boy sees the dog fall, both events are interpreted as having extent, and overlapping in time; therefore both verbs are given in the imperfective: *el niño vería que se caía el perro* "the boy saw-*I* that the dog fell-*P*".

> When the dog looks in the jar and realizes that the frog is gone, his seeing is momentary, and therefore perfective, while the absence of

the frog is durative, and therefore imperfective: *y vió que no estaba la rana* "and he saw-*P* that the frog wasn't-*I* there".

When the boy and dog find the frog, they see – at a moment in time, and therefore perfective – the frog that ran away – a single completed event, and therefore also perfective: *vieron a la rana que se escapó* "they saw-*P* the frog that escaped-*P*".

These aspectual juxtapositions between verbs are not easily conceived of in the other languages, yet they are quite accessible to very young Spanish children (Slobin & Bocaz, 1988). Again, let me remind you that they do not directly come from the events in the picture, or from the ways in which human beings perceive events; rather, they come from the ways in which a language like Spanish chooses to categorize temporal qualities of events.

Temporal subordination. Turkish has a system of forming nonfinite clauses – that is, verbs that are not marked for person or number – that allows for easy mention of contingent circumstances. Our 9-year-old story is full of such forms, reflecting a subtlety of narrative syntax not found in the other languages. These forms allow for a series of antecedent conditions, with only the verb of the final clause establishing tense/aspect and person/number. For example: *sessizce patırdı yapmadan, kurbağa kavanozundan çıkarak kaçtı* "quietly, not making a sound, the frog, slipping out of its jar, ran away". Such forms are both "native" and "mature," in that we find them only in Turkish, and, by and large, not before age 9 (Slobin, 1988).

CHANGE OF LOCATION

Our five languages differ with regard to the compactness or elaboration with which they encode changes of location. For example, consider the scene in which the boy and dog fall from the cliff into the water. My English description has already revealed particular features of English (and also German), in which we have a rich set of locative particles and prepositions: *fall from...into*. Even 3-year-olds say things like "he fell off in the pool" [E-3e], and 5-year-olds have elaborations like "threw him over the cliff into a pond" [E-5j]. Spanish, Turkish, and Hebrew, by contrast, tend to use verbs of inherent directionality – the equivalents of our Latinate verbs like *enter, exit, ascend, descend*, but as everyday vocabulary items – with much more restricted use of locative particles. Thus our Spanish 5-year-old simply says *la cabra tiró al niño al agua* "the deer threw the boy to the water"; and our Turkish 5-year-old, similarly, says *keçi onu bir itmiş, suya düşmüşler* "the goat [=deer] gave him a push, he fell to the water". Narrators in these languages are often content to say no more than "he fell" or "he threw him", while English and German children always add more locative specification ("he fell off," "he fell down," "he threw him down," etc.). Since it is possible in English and German to use bare verbs of motion, without further locative specification, we must conclude that children (beginning with our youngest subjects) have already assimilated the pattern of pervasive use of locative particles characteristic of their languages. They *could* simplify, but they do not.

By age 9 there is an interesting difference between the two Germanic languages (English and German) in comparison with the other three languages in our sample. (By the way, it is important to note that the languages divide in different ways, typologically, depending on the semantic domain under consideration. English and German are at opposite ends of a continuum in regard to aspect, but fall together in regard to directionality. Facts like this should make one suspicious of general claims relating language typology *as a whole* to cognition or language use.) The English- and German-speaking 9-year-olds tend to put together directionality, source, and/or goal in one complex clause with locative phrases, as, for example, "he tips him off over a cliff into the water" [E-9k], or the equivalent German *schmiß ihn den Abhang hinunter genau ins Wasser* "hurled him down from the cliff right into the water" [G-9d]. By contrast – as if they sense that their language does not provide the means for such compact expression – a widespread narrative strategy in the other three languages consists in setting the scene in separate locative phrases, especially relative clauses with existential or stative verbs, and then referring back to this scene with a general verb of motion. The Spanish and Turkish versions in our 9-year-old stories (in the appendix) are typical, and similar examples are also found in Hebrew stories:

> *El ciervo le llevó hasta un sitio, donde debajo había un río. Entonces el ciervo tiró al perro y al niño al río. Y después, cayeron.* "The deer took him to a place, where below there was a river. Then the deer threw the dog and the boy to the river. And then, they fell". [S-9b]
>
> *Ancak önlerinde bir uçurum vardı. Altıda göldü. Çocuk hız yaptığı için, geyiğin başından köpeğiyle birlikte düştü.* "Just in front of them was a cliff. Below was a lake. Because of the boy's making speed, he fell from the deer's head together with his dog". [T-9j]
>
> *Ve ha'ayil nivhal, ve hu hitxil laruts. Ve hakelev rats axarav, ve hu higia lemacok she mitaxat haya bitsa, ve hu atsar, ve hayeled ve hakelev naflu labitsa beyaxad.* "And the deer was startled, and he began to run. And the dog ran after him, and he reached a cliff that had a swamp underneath, and he stopped, and the boy and the dog fell to the swamp together". [H-9i]

What is of special interest here is that the unavailability of a particular grammatical device – in this instance, a system of locative particles related to verbs – has rather large consequences for narrative organization (Slobin & Bocaz, 1988). These children are driven to a procedure of scene setting, in which a vaguely specified change of location becomes interpretable. Whether or not grammar has consequences on a broad cognitive plane, it certainly seems to have consequences on the level of verbal art.

AGENCY

Reading through the English stories presented here, a particular sort of phrase stands out – a sort of "middle voice" between the description of an event as an agentive act or a completely passive description of a resultant state. We find such expressions as: "the boy got caught on the deer's antlers" [E-51] and "the dog accidentally got his head stuck in the jar" [E-9a]. This form is most common in English (with some similar passive forms, though used less frequently, in Turkish and Hebrew), suggesting that English gives children a particular *perspective* that can be taken on agency and responsibility. German-speakers do not have an available colloquial passive like the English *get*-constructions, and, as a consequence, many narrators apparently find it necessary to set up an extended scenario to indicate, for example, that the dog cannot extricate himself from his situation: *Dann kuckt der Hund ins Glas. Dann kommt er nicht mehr raus.* "Then the dog looks into the glass. Then he doesn't come out anymore" [G-5i]. Again, narrative structure on the microlevel seems to be sensitive to the availability of grammatical structures on the level of morphology, lexicon, or clause.

DEFINITENESS

Finally, a short remark about definiteness. It seems obvious to us, in English, to indicate each noun as definite or indefinite: to introduce it as indefinite and then refer back to it as definite. The same is true in German, Hebrew, and Spanish – for example, in our 9-year-old Spanish story: *...un niño cogió UNA rana...LA rana se escapó* "...a boy caught A frog...THE frog escaped" [S-9b]. But Turkish is quite different. Our 5-year-old says, quite appropriately: *Kurbağa bulmuşlar. Kurbağayla oyun oynuyorlar.* "They found frog. They are playing with frog" [T-5i]. There is no definite article in Turkish. Rather, specificity of reference is indicated only for *direct objects*, by use of an accusative inflection: *Kurbağa YI bulamamış.* "He couldn't find THE-frog" [T-5i]. And, if we had gathered Russian or Polish stories, we would have found that children never have to pay grammatical attention to definiteness. Here, surely, the language itself guides the speaker to attend to definiteness, since it cannot be shown in the picture, yet each speaker must know, on some level, when a participant is new on the scene and when he is not.

Linguistic relativity and determinism

In this concluding section let me face head-on the "neo-Whorfian" asides I have been making all along. I want to suggest that, in the course of becoming what I have termed a native speaker, the child is not only learning a collection of language-particular features on the microlevel of grammatical morphology and clause structure, but that the child is also being led to take a particular perspective on the description of the microstructure of events. This is a strong claim, and it is difficult to substantiate beyond the kind of cross-linguistic differences I have summarized. But the "Sapir–Whorf Hypothesis," or the doctrine of "linguistic relativity and determinism," has always foundered on the rocks of *non*linguistic thought and action. Here I have carefully picked, as my guiding epigraph, an early and cautious statement by Sapir. Let me restate it, emphasizing the final clause: "[The forms of each language] establish a definite relational feeling or attitude towards all possible contents of expression and, through them, towards all possible contents of experience, *insofar, of course, as experience is capable of expression in linguistic terms.*" Using this formulation, we can remain within the bounds of linguistic expression and ask whether languages differ in how they direct our attention to the structure of experience *for the purposes of talking about experience.* Even my brief presentation of different kinds of frog stories in five languages clearly leads to an affirmative answer. There is nothing in the pictures themselves that leads English speakers to note whether an event is in progress or Spanish speakers to note whether it has been completed; to encourage Germanic speakers to formulate elaborate descriptions of trajectories; to make Turkish speakers indifferent to definiteness or Hebrew speakers indifferent to conceiving of events as durative or bounded in time.

Among developmental psycholinguists, Melissa Bowerman has most recently advanced such a position on linguistic determinism, using cross-linguistic child language data to study *differences* in the semantic organization of developing grammatical systems. She concludes:

> One important factor that can influence the meanings children adopt is the *semantic structure of the input language* – i.e. the specific meaning categories associated with the grammatical forms of the language in the speech of fluent speakers. I argue that children are prepared from the beginning to accept linguistic guidance as to which distinctions – from among the set of distinctions that are salient to them – they should rely on in organizing particular domains of meaning. (1985;1284–1285)

There is, however, something dissatisfying in limiting ourselves to evidence so bound up with the acquisition and use of native languages. In conclusion, I would like to point to two different types of *dynamic* evidence that seem to support these general conclusions. What I have in mind are two types of situations in which language use changes over time: an individual's learning of a second language, and the changes that languages undergo in historical time. Both of these dynamic situations seem to me to provide evidence for the ways in which learning a language as a child constrains one's sensitivity to "the possible contents of experience as expressed in linguistic terms."

THE FIRST LANGUAGE PATTERNS THE SECOND

Consider the list of linguistically encoded perspectives that we have been examining: temporal contours of events marked by aspectual forms, movement and trajectories in space, perspectives on agency, indication in definiteness of participants mentioned in connected discourse. These are precisely the sorts of things that make it so hard to master a second language like a native (ignoring control of pronunciation and vocabulary, which are not at issue here). In discussing Spanish aspect, I noted how hard it is for English speakers to grasp the perfective/imperfective distinction that is lacking in their native language. In fact, native English speakers who learn Spanish seem never to fully master this system. By contrast, however, we have little difficulty in figuring out how to use the Spanish progressive and perfect, or the Spanish definite and indefinite articles – since we have already learned how to make decisions about the linguistic expression of these notions in our native language. But there is nothing inherently easy or hard about *any* of these Spanish distinctions. For example, French speakers have no trouble with the Spanish imperfective, since they have a similar category in French; but the progressive and perfect pose problems to them, since these are not French ways of looking at events. Turkish speakers have difficulty with definite and indefinite articles in learning to speak Spanish, English, and German. German speakers of English use the progressive where they should use simple present, although Turks do not make this error in English. Spanish learners of English object that we make too many obscure distinctions with our large collection of locative prepositions and particles. And so on. In brief, each native language has trained its speakers to pay different kinds of attention to events and experiences when talking about them. This training is carried out in childhood and is exceptionally resistant to restructuring in adult second-language acquisition, even – as we hear about us in academia – in the English of fluent, immigrant intellectuals who use the second language daily in personal and professional life.

Much of value could be learned from a systematic study of those systems in particular second languages that speakers of particular first languages find especially difficult to master. I think that these systems, including the ones we have considered here, have something important in common: *they cannot be experienced directly in our perceptual, sensorimotor, and practical dealings with the world.* I would guess, for example, that if your language lacked a plural marker, you would not have unsurmountable difficulty in learning to mark the category of plurality in a second language, since it is evident to the nonlinguistic mind and eye.[5] Or if your language lacked an instrumental marker, it should not be difficult to learn to add a grammatical tag to nouns that name objects manipulated as instruments. But there is nothing in everyday interactions with the world that changes when you describe an event as "I've been to London" or "I went to London," or when you refer to the same object in successive utterances as "a car" and "the car." Distinctions of aspect, definiteness, voice, and the like, are par excellence, distinctions that can only be learned through language, and have no other use except to be expressed in language. And, further, once our minds have been trained in taking particular points of view for the purposes of speaking, it is exceptionally difficult to be retrained.

PERSISTENT ORIENTATIONS OVER TIME

If one follows a particular language or group of languages over historical time, it is often striking that these kinds of linguistic perspectives remain stable across centuries or millennia, and across large-scale organizational changes in the grammar. For example, many things indeed have changed between Latin and the modern collection of Romance languages, but one thing that has remained is a sense of the imperfective aspect (see, e.g., Harris, 1978). The imperfective is used sometimes more, sometimes less; sometimes it contrasts with one other past tense, sometimes with a collection. But what remains constant is the sense that it is important to think of past events as possibly imperfective.

This distinction is not marked in present-day Turkic languages, nor does it appear in their histories. Rather, what we find across almost two thousand years is a constant reinvention of some sort of progressive aspect (see, e.g., Serebrennikov & Gadžieva, 1979). A small collection of verbs of location and motion – "stand", "sit", "lie", "walk" – provides the source of auxiliaries that first have progressive meaning, and then become gradually reduced and suffixed to become a more general present tense. At the same time, speakers reach for another one of these verbs, as if from old habit, to once again encode an ongoing, continuous event as viewed from inside or in progress. Again, I suggest that this "old habit" is taught to each generation of speakers through the particular linguistic of the language.

On a broader level than the imperfective or the progressive alone, it seems that language families "specialize" in the sort of temporal cognition that they attend to grammatically. The Turkic languages not only renew and grammaticize progressives, but also iteratives, inchoatives, and cessives. All of these aspectual categories treat events as having temporal *extension* – that is, Turkic languages focus on segments or stretches of events, but do not grammaticize the distinction between line and point. The latter distinction seems to be the specialty of Romance and Slavic languages, which have been tenacious in maintaining perfective/imperfective categories that attend to events as durative/nondurative or completive/noncompletive (depending on one's linguistic analysis). What we have here are deeply ingrained *patterns* – sets of filters that are used for the verbal reflection of experience.

Let me conclude, then, by once again quoting Sapir, who spoke of the persistence of *patterns* of culture: "It may be pointed out...that the value to social science of...comparative study of languages...is that it emphasizes the extraordinary persistence in certain cases of complex *patterns* of cultural behavior regardless of the extreme variability of the content of such patterns" ([1931] 1958:82). I would suggest that patterns of culture are extraordinarily persistent because they are laid down in childhood through structured interaction with the bearers of culture – in our case, through communication that is, of necessity, framed in terms of the grammatical categories of the native language.

Appendix

PICTURE STORY (MAYER, 1969)

Sample pictures from *Frog, Where Are You?* appear on p. 251. The following is a page-by-page description of the complete pictures. (The book is usually easy to obtain in the children's section in many bookstores.) Some scenes are contained in a single page, while others are spread across two pages. Except for page 1, which is a single page, the numbering of pages indicates single page scenes with a small letter after the number, and double page scenes with a number only.

Page 1: A boy and a dog are sitting in a bedroom, looking at a frog that is sitting inside a lidless jar.

Page 2a: The boy and dog are in bed, asleep. The frog is halfway out of the jar. A crescent moon in the window indicates it is nighttime.

Page 2b: Sunshine streams through the window. The boy is staring at the frog's jar, which is empty.

Page 3a: The boy looks inside his boot as he holds it upside down over his head. The dog's head is inside the frog's jar.

Page 3b: The boy is leaning out of the window, calling. The dog is precariously balanced on the window sill, with his head still inside the jar.

Page 4a: The boy is still at the window, watching the dog, who is in the middle of falling from the window to the ground outside the boy's room.

Page 4b: The boy is holding the dog, and has an angry expression. The dog is licking the boy's cheek. Pieces of the broken jar lie scattered on the ground.

Page 5: The boy and dog are standing in a clearing, with trees and a house in the distance. Ahead of them are a beehive, hanging from the nearest tree, and many bees. The boy is calling toward the trees and beehive. The dog is sniffing toward the bees.

Page 6a: The boy and dog are nearer to the tree with the beehive. The boy calls into a small hole in the ground. The dog jumps toward the beehive.

Page 6b: A small animal is halfway out of the hole. The boy is leaning away from the animal and touching his nose with both hands, as if having been bitten. The dog has his two front paws on the trunk of the tree in which the beehive is hanging.

Page 7: The beehive is on the ground. The dog still has his two front paws on the tree trunk. The boy is sitting high up in a large tree, looking into a large hole in the trunk.

Page 8: An owl stands on the trunk of the large tree, as if he just emerged from the large hole. The boy is lying on the ground below the owl. A stream

Picture 10B

Picture 11

Picture 8

Picture 4a

Picture 3a

Picture 14a

of bees is nearly in contact with the dog, who is running away from them.

Page 9a: The boy has one foot up on a small rock, while he leans against a larger rock and shields his head with his arm. The owl is directly above him. Behind the rock are shrubs and branches.

Page 9b: The boy is standing on top of the larger rock, holding onto some of the branches, and calling. The dog is skulking or cowering at the base of the rock.

Page 10a: (The branches the boy was holding in Page 9b are shown to be the antlers of a deer.) The boy is lying between the antlers of a deer that is standing immediately behind the larger rock. The implication is that the boy unwittingly held onto the antlers, the deer stood up, and the boy became ensnared in the antlers.

Page 10b: The boy is still on the deer's head. The deer and dog are both running toward a cliff that drops off at a 90° angle.

Page 11: The deer stands at the edge of the cliff. The boy and dog are in mid-fall from the cliff to a pond below.

Page 12a: The boy's and dog's feet are sticking up out of the water in the pond.

Page 12b: The boy is sitting (right-side-up) in the pond, with the dog on his head. The boy has his hand to his ear, and is listening in the direction of a nearby large, fallen log.

Page 13a: The boy leans against the fallen log and puts his hand to his mouth in a "shhh" gesture as he looks at the dog swimming toward him.

Page 13b: The boy leans forward against the log and looks on the far side of it. The dog stands on top of the log and also looks on the far side.

Page 14a: The boy is lying along the log, and the dog is leaning down toward two frogs, who are sitting on the ground beside the log. Both the boy and dog are looking at the frogs.

Page 14b: The boy and dog are still on the fallen log. The two frogs are still sitting on the ground. Eight smaller frogs are sitting near the two larger ones.

Page 15: The two larger frogs and seven smaller ones are sitting on the fallen log. One smaller one is still on the ground beside it. The boy and dog are walking through the pond, away from the frogs, and the boy is waving to them. He has a frog in his hand. The frogs are looking at him.

END OF STORY

SAMPLE STORIES[6]

Spanish 5-year-old.[7] The boy, the dog, and the frog were-*I* at home. The boy went-to-sleep-*P* with the dog. The boy was-*I* covered and the dog outside of the bed. The frog went-*I* [= was going] to-escape...he escaped-*P*. And the dog looked-*P* down and saw-*P* that the frog wasn't-*I* there. (He) picked-up-*P* a boot and got-up-*P* from the bed. The boy was-*I* calling the frog, and the dog had-*I* the jar on his face. The boy learned-*P*...and the boy saw-*I* that the dog fell-*I*. The dog, when (he) fell-*P*, broke-*P* the jar. The boy went-down-*P* and picked-up-*P* the dog. The dog licked-*P* the boy. (He) went-out-*P* of his house and called-*P* the frog. The dog was-*I* seated there. (He) saw-*P* lots of bees. The dog wanted-*I* to-take the beehive that was-*I* hung in a tree. The boy saw-*I* a hole and was-*I* calling in the hole. A rat came-out-*P*, and the boy put-*P* his hand on his nose, said-*P* "ooh!" The dog still wanted-*I* to-take the beehive. Here the dog went-*I* [= was going] to-go-up, but the hive was-*I* already down from the tree. The rat kept-on-*P* looking. The boy looked-*P* in a hole of a tree.

An owl came-out-*P* that threw-*P* the boy. The dog came-*P* running and the bees behind. (He) wanted-*I* to-go-up on a rock. (He) went-up-*P* and (he) hung from a deer. The deer started-*P* to-run and the dog too. The dog made-*P* a jump to get the boy, but (he) couldn't-*P*. The deer threw-*P* the boy to the water, and the dog. The boy ended-up-*P* sitting in the water. The dog was-*I* on top of the boy and the boy looked-*P*. Later the boy sat-down-*P* and the dog was-*I* on his head. The boy said-*P* "shh" and (they) went-up-*P* on a tree trunk. There (they) saw-*P* the frog that escaped-*P*, and the father and the mother, and there were-*I* little froggies. The boy took-away-*P* a little froggie and the others went-away-*P*, behind...the little ones went-away-*P* behind the mother and the father, and (they) were-*I* on the trunk. One remained-*P*. And that's the end of the story. [S-5d]

Turkish 5-year-old.[8] (They) found (a) frog. (They) are-playing with (the) frog. (It) got to be evening. (The) frog went outside (and) ran-away. When (the) boy got-up (he) couldn't find the-frog. (He) called everywhere. (He) couldn't find the-frog. Then (the) dog put the-jar on his head. Then (the) boy came (and) got-mad at-(the)-dog. Then (the) dog fell from-(the)-window. (He) came (and) got-mad at-(the)-dog. (The) glass broke too. (They) went-out-to-look-for the-frog. (They) called all over, but (they) couldn't see the-frog. (They) went to a tree. There was (a) beehive at that tree. (They) touched the-beehive. All (the) bees in the-beehive came-out and bit their-noses and everywhere. Then (they) went to a hole in a tree. Then (they) looked-at the-tree, (they) looked in a hole, there wasn't any frog. Then an owl came-out from-inside (and) (the) dog ran-away so fast that (the) boy fell to-(the)-ground. Then the boy's head hurt a lot. Then (he) called all over but (he) couldn't find any frog. (A) deer caught him and then (the) deer gave him a push. (They) fell to-(the)-water. When-they-fell to-(the)-water (they) saw a tree. (They) climbed over the-tree. (The) boy said "shh" to-(the)-dog. "Let's climb behind the-tree," (he) said. When-they-climbed behind the-tree (they) saw seven babies and (they) saw a mother and a father too. Then they took one of the-frogs. Saying bye-bye to-them (they) went-away. [T-5i]

Spanish 9-year-old. It was-*I* at night-time that a boy caught-*P* a frog and put-*P* it in a jar. Then (he) went-*P* to sleep and the frog escaped-*P*. The next day (she) wasn't-*I* in the jar, and (they) started-*P* to look-for her everywhere. Then (they) started-*P* to look and look in the boots. And (they) went-out-*P* to the window. And the dog, in searching for it, put-*P* himself in the bottle and (he) couldn't-*I* get-out. And (they) started-*P* to search for her and the dog fell-*P* from the window and the jar broke-*P*. And then the boy went-down-*P* and picked-*P* him up. And (they) searched-*P* in the forest. And the bees came-out-*P* of a hive. Then (they) went-on-*P* looking in a place where rats live in the field. And the dog searched-*I* where there was-*I* a hive. But the rat smelled-*I* very bad. Then the boy left-*P* the rat and climbed-*P* a tree, and the hive fell-*P*. Then an owl came-out-*P* and the boy got-scared-*P* and (he) fell-*P*. And the bees started-*P* to chase the dog. Then the owl left-*P* the boy and (he) climbed a rock, the boy. Then (he) held-onto-*P* some horns of a deer. And the boy, since (he) didn't know-*I*...well...the deer took-*P* him to a place, where below there was-*I* a river. Then the deer threw-*P* the dog and the boy to the river. And then (they) fell-*P*. The dog climbed-*P* on the boy's head. And (they) saw-*P* a trunk, thinking that it was-*I* the place where the frog was-*I*.

Then the boy told-*P* the dog to-be-quiet. And (they) looked-*P* at the other side of the tree and saw-*P* the frog and its sweetheart. Then (they) found-*P* its children, and then when (they) went-away-*P* (they) took-*P* a little frog that the frog gave-*P* them, and (they) went-*P* home. [S-9b]

Turkish 9-year-old.[9] A boy had a frog, that (he) kept inside of that jar, and a dog. Because (it) got-to-be night-time (the) boy together with his-dog got into bed, (and) immediately on-shutting their-eyes, fell-asleep. Quietly, not making (a) sound, (the) frog, slipping-out of-its-jar, ran-away. (The) next morning (the) boy, not being able to find his-frog in the-jar, got very sad Getting-dressed right away, (he) set-off to-look-for him right away. (The) dog, (he) put his-head inside the jar. (He) couldn't get-(it)-out at all. In order to get-(it)-out, (he) jumped from-(the)-window. And when (the) jar broke (he) managed-to-save himself. The-dog's master got very mad. After that, calling the bees in order to find his-frog, (he) wanted help from-them. (The) dog wanted to-eat the-honey that the-bees made. (The) boy asked (the) mole if (he) had seen the-frog. (The) mole didn't know where the-frog was. (The) boy, climbing (a) tree, thought the-frog was-hidden in a hole, but just then an owl came-out of-that-hole. (The) boy fell to-(the)-ground. (The) owl, chasing the-boy, scared him. (The) boy, calling the-deer, wanted help from-him. (He) sat on his head right away and (the) deer started to-run. Just in-front-of-them was a cliff. Below was (a) lake. Because of (the) boy's making speed, (he) fell from the-deer's head together with his-dog. (He) swam to (the) other side. (The) boy told (the) dog to-be-quiet because (he) was-barking continuously. There was a tree trunk. When (they) looked behind (they) saw their frog and the-wife (he) had-married. There were little ones with-them. (The) boy got very happy. Taking one in his hand, he loved it. They lived in (a) happy family together. [T-9j]

Notes

1 This heading is the title of a 1987 working paper reporting part of a study by Ruth A. Berman and Dan I. Slobin, distributed by the Cognitive Science Program, Center for Cognitive Studies, University of California at Berkeley. Further details can be found there, in Berman, 1986, 1987; Renner, 1988; Slobin, 1988; Slobin & Bocaz, 1988; and in forthcoming publications. The study was supported by the U.S.-Israel Binational Science Foundation, the Linguistics Program of the National Science Foundation, the Sloan Foundation Program in Cognitive Science at the University of California at Berkeley, and the Max-Planck-Institute for Psycholinguistics in Nijmegen. The data were gathered, analyzed, and discussed in collaboration with: Ayhan Aksu-Koç (Boğaziçi University, Istanbul), Michael Bamberg (Clark University), Esther Dromi (Tel-Aviv University), Virginia Marchman (University of California, Berkeley), Yoni Ne'eman (Tel-Aviv University), Tanya Renner (University of California, Berkeley), Eugenia Sebastián (Universidad Autónoma, Madrid), and Christiane von Stutterheim (Universität Heidelberg).

2 The "frog book" method was developed by Michael Bamberg, and the first full-scale analysis of German stories appears in his 1985 Berkeley dissertation (Bamberg, 1985, 1987). Additional data, not analyzed here, were gathered from 4-year-olds in English, Spanish, and Hebrew; and from 7- and 11-year-olds in Hebrew. (Currently, additional data are being gathered in

Icelandic, Russian, Chinese, American Sign Language, and from Broca's aphasics in Turkey.) There were 12 Ss in each child group in English, German, Spanish, and Hebrew; there were 6 Spanish adults and 14 Hebrew adults; all Turkish groups consisted of 10 Ss. Quoted Ss are referred to by language, age, and ordinal identifying letter (e.g., "T-5c" = Turkish 5-year-old, third oldest child in the sample of fives).

3 English stories were gathered in Berkeley by Tanya Renner (1988).

4 The two bracketed locative phrases in this passage are drawn from the story of another American 5-year-old, so that a single prototypical story can be used to illustrate a general tendency toward locative elaboration in English-speaking children (discussed under "Change of Location").

5 Having learned to mark plurality, of course, you may not remember to mark it in every instance, but this is a different issue – one of habitual use of a distinction, rather than ability to grasp the underlying semantic category.

6 For purposes of comparison, typical 5- and 9-year-old stories are given here in rough translation from Spanish and Turkish. (Spanish stories were gathered in Madrid by Eugenia Sebastián; Turkish stories were gathered in Istanbul by Ayhan Aksu-Koç.) To simplify the discussion in this brief chapter, German and Hebrew stories have been omitted. Full texts in all five languages are available from the author, and will be analyzed in detail in forthcoming publications from the research project.

7 Words joined by hyphens are single words; words in parentheses are not required in the language, and were not spoken by the child. Spanish verbs are suffixed with *-I* for Imperfective and *-P* for Perfective. Progressives in the English translation correspond to Spanish Progressives.

8 All of the verbs (except for "are-playing") are in the narrative past tense (*-mlş*), with no aspectual distinctions. Inflections for definiteness are indicated by "the-", although there is no definite article in Turkish; "a" represents the indefinite article (the numeral "one"). Words joined by hyphens are single words; words in parentheses are not required in the language, and were not spoken by the child.

9 Tenses are past (*-dl*) and past progressive (*-yordu*), corresponding to English translations, along with a variety of nonfinite (tenseless) forms, translated as gerunds.

References

Bamberg, M. G. W. (1985). Form and function in the construction of narratives: Developmental perspectives. Unpublished doctoral dissertation, University of California, Berkeley.

(1987). *The acquisition of narratives: Learning to use language*. Berlin: Mouton de Gruyter.

Berman, R. A. (1986. The development of temporality in narrative: A cross-linguistic perspective. Paper presented to Workshop/symposium "Acquisition of Temporal Structures in Discourse," University of Chicago, April 16.

(1987). Changing predicates, changing perspectives. Paper presented to Fifth Annual Workshop in Human Development and Education, Tel-Aviv University, December 16–21.

Berman, R. A., & Slobin, D. I. (1987). *Five ways of learning how to talk about events: A crosslinguistic study of children's narratives*. Berkeley Cognitive

Science Report No. 46, Institute of Cognitive Studies, University of California, Berkeley.

Bloom, L., Lifter, K., & Hafitz, J. (1980). Semantics of verbs and the development of verb inflection in child language. *Language*, *54*:386–412.

Bowerman, M. (1985). What shapes children's grammars? In *The crosslinguistic study of language acquisition*, Vol. 2: *Theoretical issues*, ed. D.I. Slobin. Hillsdale, NJ: Lawrence Erlbaum.

Gvozdev, A.N. (1949). *Formirovanie u rebenka grammatičeskogo stroja russkogo jazyka*. Moscow: Izd-vo Akademii Pedagogičeskix Nauk RSFSR.

Harris, M. (1978). *The evolution of French syntax: A comparative approach*. London: Longman.

Mayer, M. (1969). *Frog, where are you?* New York: Dial Press.

Renner, J. A. T. (1988). *Development of temporality in children's narratives*. Unpublished doctoral dissertation, University of California, Berkeley.

Sapir, E. (1924). The grammarian and his language. *American Mercury*, *1*:149–155. [Reprinted in *Selected writings of Edward Sapir in language, culture and personality*, ed. D. G. Mandelbaum. Berkeley/Los Angeles: University of California Press, 1958]

——— (1931). The concept of phonetic law as tested in primitive languages by Leonard Bloomfield. In *Methods in social science: A case book*, ed. S.A. Rice. Chicago: University of Chicago Press. [Reprinted in (1958) ibid.]

Schieffelin, B. B. (1985). Acquisition of Kaluli. In *The crosslinguistic study of language acquisition*, Vol. 1: *The data*, ed. D. I. Slobin. Hillsdale, NJ: Lawrence Erlbaum.

Serebrennikov, V. A., & Gadžieva, N. Z. (1979) *Sravnitel'no-istoričeskaja grammatika tjurkskix jazykov*. Baku: Izd-vo Maarif.

Slobin, D. I. (1970). Universals of grammatical development in children. In *Advances in psycholinguistics*, ed. G. B. Flores d'Arcais & W. J. M. Levelt. Amsterdam: North-Holland.

——— (1973). Cognitive prerequisites for the development of grammar. In *Studies of child language development*, ed. C. A. Ferguson & D. I. Slobin. New York: Holt, Rinehart & Winston.

——— (1985). Crosslinguistic evidence for the Language-Making Capacity. In *The crosslinguistic study of language acquisition*, Vol. 2: *Theoretical issues*, ed. D. I. Slobin. Hillsdale, NJ: Lawrence Erlbaum.

——— (1988). The development of clause chaining in Turkish child language. Paper presented to Fourth Conference on Turkish Linguistics, Middle East Technical University Ankara, August 17–19.

Slobin, D. I., & Bocaz, A. (1988). Learning to talk about movement through time and space: The development of narrative abilities in Spanish and English. *Lenguas Modernas* (Universidad de Chile), *15*:5–24.

PART III
Cultural learning

6
The socialization of cognition
WHAT'S INVOLVED?

Jacqueline J. Goodnow

The title of this chapter sets out a topic (the socialization of cognition) and asks a question (what is involved?). To introduce my answer, and to explain what I mean by the socialization of cognition, I start by differentiating between psychologists' approaches to the study of social development and to the study of cognitive development. From the beginning the study of social development reflected a strong interest in the acquisition of values or value-laden qualities: honesty, reponsibility, empathy, friendliness, healthy adjustment, prosocial behavior. It also pointed to the social environment as the main factor in the acquisition of these qualities. What came later was an interest in skills and strategies – the skills needed, for instance, to enter a social group, make friends, ask for help, or refuse a request without disastrous consequences. Often as an accompaniment to the interest in skills and strategies (although not dictated by it), there appeared as well an interest in the effect of internal factors, with a particular emphasis on the unfolding of cognitive capacity – the capacity, for instance, to take the perspective of another, to judge interactions, or to estimate the consequences of an action.

In contrast, the study of cognitive development reflected from the start an interest in skills and strategies, and in capacities that unfolded with age. Interest in the impact of the social environment was slow to develop, as was the recognition that cognitive development is marked by the acquisition of values. We do not simply learn to solve problems. We learn also what problems are considered worth solving, and what counts as an elegant rather than simply an acceptable solution. We do not simply acquire knowledge. We learn also that some particular pieces of knowledge are expected of us, that some can be happily ignored, and that some are inappropriate for all but a few to own. This is the knowledge that is private, restricted, confidential, or even taboo.

This essay was presented at the conference, Culture and Human Development, Chicago, November 5–17, 1987. I am happy to acknowledge the benefit of discussions with Jeannette Lawrence and Millicent Poole on the acquisition of "evaluation frameworks," the advice of May-Jane Chen on ways to analyze the consistency of value judgments, and the contribution of financial support from the Australian Research Grants Council.

Finally, we learn that some ways of acquiring knowledge are more acceptable than others, and that particular ways of seeking are expected for particular areas of knowledge. As a child, for instance, it may seem that the easiest way to gain knowledge is to ask one's parents. Children in Western-style cultures soon learn, however, that direct questions in some areas – family income or sex, for instance – are not encouraged. The approved way is to wait until information is volunteered or to gather information as best you can from peers, books, or other indirect sources.

It may sound as if I am talking mainly about the acquisition of knowledge within some privatized areas in our society: areas such as money or sex. That is not the case. I use these areas to tap into ideas that are already familiar. In these areas, it is easy to recognize the presence of cultural values about what should be learned and when, what knowledge may be acquired but not openly displayed, and what should not be asked about in any direct fashion. In these areas also, it is easy to recognize that the social environment does not take a neutral view toward the acquisition of knowledge and skill, but is instead highly interested, and often directive, controlling or even denying access to information. I now want to extend the awareness of values to areas of cognitive development that seem more mundane, that appear at first blush to be "value-free." I also want to extend into the analysis of how cognitive development takes place the concept of a social environment that takes an active, nonneutral interest in determining which values are acquired. Finally, I want to ask about the consequences of an alertness to cognitive values and controlling environments. What difference would such notions make to the research we do and to our prevailing theories about cognitive development?

The material covered in this chapter is organized around three central questions:

1. Why focus on the acquisition of values about ways of thinking and learning?
2. What specific research does an emphasis on values – on good performances, appropriate knowledge, proper ways of learning – give rise to? (I describe a few studies already completed and suggest some further possibilities.)
3. How does attention to the acquisition of values and to nonneutral environments alter the way one regards some prevailing views of cognitive development? (I refer briefly to theories with a Piagetian and with a Vygotskian base, and to the type of approach represented by sociologists such as Bourdieu and Foucault.)

The discussion throughout the chapter refers both to product and to process – that is, to what is acquired and how this occurs – although the emphasis on "what" and "how" varies from one section to another. My original concern was with what developed: that is, with forms of cognitive development that seemed to be poorly understood. Questions about the adequacy of accounts of process came a little later. Both aspects, however, call for some rethinking.

Why consider values?

One of the interesting changes in analyses of cognitive development is the move away from the notion that cognitive skills or structures simply unfold with age, or are entirely "self-constructed" (Shweder, 1982) from each individual's encounters with objects and events. It is now almost commonplace to refer to the social bases of cognitive development. The debate has shifted to ways of specifying how a social basis has its effects. On that issue, there is so far no consensus. There is also no shortage of proposals. Some scholars see cognitive growth as emerging out of social dialogue and conflict (see, e.g., Doise & Mugny, 1984; Doise & Palmonari, 1984). Others see cognitive skills as emerging out of cultural practices (see Cole & Scribner, 1974; Lave, in press; Scribner, 1984), or out of the carefully phased support provided by an expert transferring skills to a novice learner, a view exemplified by emphasis on "scaffolding" (see Wood, Bruner, & Ross, 1976) and by much of the material on Vygotsky's zone of proximal development (see Rogoff & Wertsch, 1984).

Why not be satisfied with such widespread recognition of the social aspects of cognitive development?

Basically, all these social accounts expand our concepts of how development takes place, but do little to broaden our ideas about what is developing. On that score, the current accounts seemed to me narrow, especially compared with the descriptions offered by anthropologists and sociologists. Psychologists tend to discuss specific "logical structures," or "knowledge structures." Anthropologists and sociologists talk in larger and more metacognitive terms. They note the presence of worldviews, modes of thinking, or "aspects of consciousness": pervasive notions such as the belief that time is valuable, that numbers always provide the best evidence, or that learning is best achieved by a carefully controlled sequence of segmented pieces (Berger, 1977; Berger, Berger, & Kellner, 1974).

In addition, the psychological accounts seemed to me to be oriented primarily toward explaining what people could or could not do, toward describing their skills and strategies or their capacity to solve particular problems. I felt, uneasily, that I was being presented with a world where only ability counted or where ability, once present, was readily translated into performance. Where gaps between ability and performance were recognized, they were often moved out of cognition and labeled problems of "style" or "motivation": a form of tidying up that seemed to me rather arbitrary.

More specifically, I found a number of observations were difficult to fit into the standard schemes. Let me review some of these. They all involve values about cognition that one is likely to acquire in the course of socialization. They are also all cases in which I had to take note of a phenomenon, begin trying to find a conceptual place for it, and begin asking: How does this come about? What are its implications?

Some behaviors are more "smart" or "intelligent" than others. I am not advocating a totally relativistic view of intelligent action. Some actions are undoubtedly more adaptive than others. Across cultures there are also undoubtedly some basic similarities in what is regarded as intelligent action. There are also cultural differences – differences that emerge especially in what is regarded as good style, good taste, good form, an "elegant" argument, or as "interesting". You may gain some sense of those differences when you read the journals in another country. North Americans, for instance, typically find European journals very philosophical and historical. Many Europeans find U.S. journals empty of background, individuality, and depth. From two Englishmen with a European orientation, for instance, comes a judgment that may surprise North Americans. It characterizes articles in *Child Development* and *Developmental Psychology* – regarded by many in the United States as especially prestigious journals – as representing "the lowest common denominator" in developmental research (Richards & Light, 1986, p. 3).

My own strongest sense of the presence of differences in definition came from using several Piagetian tasks with unschooled Chinese children in Hong Kong and with black children in Washington, D.C. I emerged from those experiences with the feeling that the interesting difference lay not in the acquisition of particular logical skills but in the definition of what was the intelligent action to take in a particular situation (Goodnow, 1976).

That concern with the definition of intelligent behavior led to one decision. I would use Piagetian tasks only with children who felt the task made sense and who made much the same sense of it that I did. It also led to an alertness to the extent to which people – myself included – attach evaluative tags to intellectual endeavors, labeling some elegant or original, whereas others are solid, pedestrian, facile, boring, "clever," or even "too clever by half." I began to wonder how labels come into being and how it happens that labels are not always agreed upon (Goodnow, 1984). The work that elicits "brilliant" or "original" from one person, for instance, may elicit "odd" from another. What features of a piece of work or of a judge could give rise to such differences?

At this point, however, I took no research steps and began to work on a different research problem – but the problem of evaluative judgments about cognitive performances did not go away.

Some approaches to problem solving are better than others, on some occasions. This observation is similar to the first, but has a sharper form to it. The basic question is not why some ways of problem solving are regarded as better than others but, *when* is one particular style regarded as best? For what kinds of problems? My thinking on this issue was influenced by a couple of situations, one of which arose when I was taken to task by some of my colleagues for being a "cool," "pragmatic" administrator, seldom taking an overtly ideological stand. I was at first surprised: I thought my style was a virtue! I then began to think about the extent to which, in Anglo-Saxon circles, it is taken for granted that the best or only way to approach and to discuss any problem is in a cool, rational style. Emotions are to be kept in check or kept hidden while one considers the costs and benefits of various alternatives.

Habermas (1970), I discovered, had a great deal to say about rationality as an idealized hallmark of Western thought. On a much smaller scale, I came to see that the issue is not one of a pragmatic style versus a style more closely governed by one's heart. Even in Anglo-Saxon circles, the pragmatic style is regarded as appropriate only for some kinds of problems (Goodnow, 1987). Social occasions, for instance, have to wear an air of spontaneity, with the organization and planning carefully hidden. In affairs of the heart, one is expected to be "swept off one's feet." In short, the value of planning and of rationality applies only to some problems and to some contexts, and part of one's socialization into a culture must consist of learning when the cool planning style is appropriate and when it signals to others that a problem is not taken seriously or that one "has no heart," "no abiding ideology." The differences between cultural groups – or between individuals – lie, then, in the way problems are sorted into those that should be dealt with coolly and those where the accepted way of signaling that one cares is to display strong emotion (at least at the start of negotiations or problem solving). My own socialization into a full appreciation of such categories for problems is still occurring.

Some problems are significant, others are trivial. The Kpelle find it astonishing that grown European men are interested in problems that the Kpelle find trivial (Cole, Gay, Glick, & Sharp, 1971). Luria (1976) reports a similar response to many of the problems he presented to Russian peasants. In each case, a cultural group has acquired its own definition of "worthwhile" versus "trivial" problems.

One could multiply the examples. My own sharpest awareness came when I was helping to organize a symposium on women, social science, and public policy (Goodnow & Pateman, 1985). For my share, I undertook a review (Goodnow, 1985) related to the question: What impact has the rise of feminism had on the way research is conducted in the social sciences? I rapidly became aware, far more explicitly than before, that an interest in topics tagged as "women's issues" is interpreted in some circles as a sign of not being truly interested in one's science. I came especially to admire the sociologist Anne Oakley for insisting on studying, for her Ph.D. thesis, the nature of housework as an occupation (Oakley, 1974). At that time, the notion of housework as an occupation or as a form of work was a definite break from tradition and she had, as she reports, some difficulty in finding a supervisor who would take the project seriously. Her work has become a classic, but even in 1986, as I discovered when I began some work on the perceived ownership of housework (a superb example of constraints on everyday problem solving), I found the topic can be interpreted by some as a descent into utter frivolity.

I do not wish to suggest that the issue of trivial versus significant applies only to topics related to women's lives. It has always been an issue in any science. The debate over "women's issues" has simply made more visible one form of such evaluative judgments, just as social historians – with their emphasis on the daily lives of "small people" – have made recognizable the extent to which we have regarded as worthwhile in history only the stories of kings, popes, and parliaments (see Lerner, 1979).

Some skills and some areas of knowledge belong to some people more than to others. For this last observation, let me stay with gender marking for a moment and then give it a broader conceptual place. I have already introduced one phrase that implies ownership, namely, "women's issues." Now let me add the comment that women are often advised to avoid some forms of knowledge. "Be good, sweet maid, and let who will be clever" is one form of such advice. Present in our culture also is the view that skill in mathematics is more relevant for males than for females and that success in mathematics requires more effort from females than it does from males. That view is apparently part of socialization into the culture of the United States. It is held at least by adolescent males, adolescent females, and their parents (Parsons, Adler, & Kaczala, 1982).

Here is clearly an area where specific research is possible. One might ask: What areas of knowledge or skill are most strongly gender marked? And how do people acquire ideas about such gender marking? First, however, I needed to ask whether gender marking might not be one form of a wider phenomenon, namely, the "ownership of knowledge." The term comes from anthropology (see Sharrock, 1974). It covers the way we use terms such as "Western science," "Eastern philosophy," or "Chinese medicine," often with the implication that these are most strongly developed and best studied in particular places. It covers also the way in which, within some cultures, particular songs, rituals, or designs belong to some particular people. They are their "copyright" and can be performed only by them or, if by others, only for a fee and/or with the owner's consent. To say that a skill is "natural" to some people and not others, I suggest, is a further way of establishing ownership. It may not be culturally possible to copyright that area of knowledge. It may be illegal to place overt restrictions on its being taught. A great deal of ownership can still be exercised, however, if one can make would-be performers feel that they will find the material hard to learn and that the display of knowledge or interest may mark them as "unnatural."

Next steps. I have sketched out some observations that kept bringing me back to the acquisition of values about cognitive performances and cognitive areas. In the course of socialization, I reasoned, we acquire not only interpretive frameworks – allowing us to assign meaning – but also evaluative frameworks, allowing us to categorize performances and areas of knowledge as "better" or "poorer" in a variety of ways.

The same observations kept pushing me toward a different view of how development comes about. I became less and less happy with the emphasis on spontaneous curiosity or spontaneous interest in pursuing particular areas of knowledge or skill. With evaluative judgments, it seemed far more likely that an individual's concepts were being shaped by an environment that was often active and controlling rather than neutral, and often restrictive rather than giving a benign blessing to all intellectual endeavors.

I began to move in two directions. On the one hand, I began developing some ways of exploring the nature and the development of cognitive values. On the other, I began a theoretical exploration, which consisted of taking a second look at some classic psychological accounts of cognitive development.

Locating some researchable questions

Of the four observations sketched out in the previous section, two dealt with judgments about specific performances (some are more intelligent than others; some are better styles of problem solving on some occasions). The other two dealt with areas of knowledge and skill (some are more significant than others; some belong to particular people). I decided to begin with judgments about particular performances, and with two general questions:

1. *What kinds of value judgments are children likely to acquire?* Ideally, I wanted to locate some forms of judgment that could apply to a variety of performances. Two judgments appeared to fit that criterion, both dealing with aspects of "good" performances. One has to do with the *age-grading of performances* – that is, the sense that a performance is appropriate, or "the norm" for a particular age. The other has to do with *a sense of audience* – that is, the sense that particular audiences will value or regard as "good" some kinds of performance more than they do others.
2. *What particular aspects of a judge give rise to particular judgments?* The qualities of the judge could take many forms. I decided to vary the age of the child. That quality is a familiar one in developmental

studies. Varying it was also a step toward acknowledging that the processes involved in the socialization of cognition were unlikely to be all top-down in type. The qualities of the person being socialized must play some part in the process.

I had in mind two other questions: What particular aspects of a performance give rise to a particular judgment? And how does any change in judgment come about? I decided, however, not to attack these directly but to let them emerge as I proceeded with the others.

The final strategic decision was to use *children's drawings as an area of performance*. At various times, I have been tempted to use verbal productions (written or spoken) as a content area for asking questions about value judgments, and I have been pleased to learn that Nancy Stein and Tom Trabasso have already done so (see Stein, 1982; Stein & Policastro, 1984). Drawings, however, have several advantages. Young children produce them and find them interesting. They can readily be compared with one another, with few memory demands involved. I knew something about how they are produced (Goodnow, 1977) and knew that children often make spontaneous comments about what is good or not. Above all, there is available an explicit age grading based on U.S. groups, which is used also in Australia. The Goodenough–Harris measures of developmental status (Harris, 1963) provide one with a ready-made statement of age norms, quantified to a degree that makes it possible to pin down the size of the difference that expert adults see as occurring between any two performances.

In the following paragraphs I describe three studies, outlining both their rationale and their results. The results are abstracted from a longer report (Goodnow, Wilkins, & Dawes, 1986). Basically, I am presenting them here as demonstrations of feasibility – evidence that one can specify evaluative judgments, pinpoint changes in their acquisition, and find ways to begin asking about underlying processes. I also point to the ways in which the results are linked to some general paths that socialization into cognitive values may take.

STUDY 1: JUDGMENTS ABOUT AGE NORMS

Why select the acquisition of age norms as a form of socialization into cognitive values? To start with, ours is a culture in which age grading is pervasive. Birthdays, school years, permission to drive, marry, or drink alcohol, parental reminders that "you're too big for that kind of thing any more" – it is hard to find an area where age norming does not intrude. (It is, of course, not only age that is taken into account. We say, for instance, "not bad for a beginner," but I shall stick with age for the moment.) It seems reasonable to assume that children will acquire a sense of what is appropriate for a given age and will do so fairly early. In my experience, even preschoolers make such statements as "Well, I'm only four" or "I'm not very big yet."

How to proceed? One could ask children to assign marks to various productions, varying the information given about the age of the producer, telling one group, for instance, that "this is by a 7-year-old" and another that "this is by a 4- or a 10-year-old." I was reluctant to use that procedure with drawings. One of the reasons that art is an attractive activity for primary school children is that a variety of productions can be regarded as acceptable (Goodnow & Burns, 1985). I was personally unwilling to add to the notion that everything one does should attract a specific, single mark. I opted instead for a more basic and less objectionable question: Can young children discriminate between the productions of "younger" and "older" children?

Figure 6.1 shows the drawings we used.

In the Goodenough–Harris Scale, these range in age from the norm for 4 years (drawing 1) to the norm for 10 years (drawing 8). The intervals between drawings are either 3 or 4 points. The procedure was one of paired comparisons. On each comparison a child was asked which was by an older child (we had first checked for the understanding of this term by asking about other school grades and siblings). The

Figure 6.1. Stimulus figures used for paired comparisons, varying in Goodenough–Harris scores (DDS) by progressive intervals of 3 points (drawings 1, 2, 3, 4, 5) or 4 points (drawings 6, 7, 8). Drawing 1 (DDS = 9 points) is slightly below the mean (standard score 96) for children aged 4 years (Harris, 1963:294). Drawing 8 (DDS = 33) is slightly below the mean (standard score 98) for children aged 10 years.

children were in five age groups. The mean ages of these groups were 4:4, 5:4, 7:5, 9:3, and 11:7 years. The first two groups were in preschool (mean age 4:4) or in kindergarten (mean age 5:4). In effect, all children had had some exposure to the work of other children and, probably, to comments by adults other than their own parents.

Briefly, the results are as follows:

1. Across age groups, children display *an increase in similarity to expert judgments*. The youngest group generally performs at chance level. The 5-year-olds, however, are above chance; the second-graders are well beyond it; the 9- and 11-year-olds are at ceiling. The percentage of children in each group who were accurate on 75% or more of their choices was 25, 44, 88, 100, and 100.

2. Across age-groups, children display *an increase in the consistency of judgment*. That is an important result, and I wish to acknowledge the help of May-Jane Chen in finding a way to pin it down. In theory, socialization into adult judgments could take two paths: (a) the child moves from no particular position to adopting an adult-type position; (b) the child gives up an established position of its own, leaving behind or setting aside an articulated child-view. For age judgments about drawings, the former path applies. Accuracy and consistency were highly correlated ($r = .72$) and the age paths for the two aspects of judgment were similar. I think there are still areas where the second path of socialization occurs, but this form of value judgment is not one of them.

3. *The bases of change*. I had started with an awareness that a change in age could mean a change in experience with the production of drawings, in exposure to the work and the judgments of others, and in general intellectual capacity, with the last of these altering the capacity to use the information available. I had started also with an interest in checking on each of these possible sources and, if possible, in eliminating some. I did not expect to gather definitive data but I hoped to gain some insights.

At this point, we can eliminate the notion that the critical aspect of age is increased experience in production. There were occasional signs of judgment being influenced by experience in production. For example, one child who was firm about the last drawing in the series being by an older child based her judgment on the fact that she herself had tried to draw people sitting down and she knew how difficult it was. In general, however, experience in production was not needed for accuracy in judgment. Children could make judgments about drawings that were well beyond the level of their own production. Their major hesitations had to do with drawings for which the interval of difference was small rather than large. There may still be areas of socialization where judgment has to be closely informed by the experience of production, but age judgments about drawings do not fit that model. Most judgments about performances in art, music, or sport probably do not fit it either – that is, few skilled critics are skilled performers.

STUDY 2: A SENSE OF AUDIENCE

One of the basic aspects of socialization has to do with producing the right behavior for the right occasion. One must be consistent enough to avoid the labels of being "two-faced," "inconsistent," or "having opinions that depend on the last person spoken to." At the same time, performances and displays should be flexible enough to avoid the labels of being "rigid" or "having only one song to sing."

Accounts of cognitive change already contain some information to show that cognitive performances vary not only with ability but also with audience. That information comes from research on modes of speech. We all acquire several ways of speaking, and we learn to vary our speech to fit what we think the audience expects, will accept, or will respond to. Even children at the age of 4 can shift from one mode to another. They use shorter sentences and more imperatives, for instance, with 2-year-olds than they do for adults (Shatz & Gelman, 1973). Why they do so, however, is not clear. It may be because they regard younger children as less able to understand more complex speech. But children also use more imperatives with peers regarded as lower in status (Becker, in press), and they use less polite forms of request with friends than they do with acquaintances (Lefebvre-Pinard, Bouffard-Bouchard, & Fielder, 1982). In effect, the variation by audience may reflect assessments of audience ability, audience tolerance, audience approval, or the probable effectiveness of an action even if it is not rated highly on other grounds.

I wanted to reduce these alternatives, and decided to eliminate – or make unlikely – the influence of estimates of ability to understand. I also thought it reasonable to move away from ratings as an index of value judgments and to work instead from performances, inferring the sense of audience from variations in what was displayed.

The material again consisted of drawings. This time, they were the children's own drawings. The children were either in kindergarten (mean age 6:0) or in Grade 1 (mean age 7:1). They produced drawings under two conditions. In one, they produced drawings of people mainly for themselves during free time. The teacher collected these unobtrusively and marked them for us with the date and the child's name. In the other, the children were asked by a visiting adult to draw a person: "Make the very best picture that you can; see what a good picture you can make." The adult was not completely unfamiliar. She had visited each classroom on an earlier occasion helping the teacher. In both conditions, children used the same-sized paper and the same drawing tools.

In all, we gathered from these children four drawings of a person. Two we have labeled "spontaneous" (that is, there was no overt request for a "good" drawing). Two we have labeled "request." The order of drawings, collected over a one-month interval, was R1, S1, S2, R2. We collected two drawings of each type because we expected children's productions to vary somewhat, especially in their spontaneous drawings, and felt on surer ground working with two instances in each case. The critical quantitative measure is the number of points that adults would assign using the Goodenough–Harris scoring system. This is our index of the degree of maturity or the age grade that adults would read into a drawing.

1. On average, *request drawings attract higher scores* than do spontaneous drawings, more so in Grade 1 than in kindergarten. The difference in Grade 1 is close to a year's difference in the assigned developmental age.
2. *Variation by audience increases from one grade to the other.* In kindergarten (mean age 6:0) children tend to produce much the same formula on all four occasions. In Grade 1 (mean age 7:1), they vary productions for the audience. Figure 6.2 illustrates the difference. It could be that children in kindergarten are less well socialized into a sense of audience than are children in Grade 1. I think it more likely that kindergarteners are like novices with a second language. In all situations, they produce what they can.
3. The *variations occur predominantly in two features: the amount of detail included and the presence of attempts at drawing action.* The second row in Figure 6.2 illustrates the way that the request drawings add detail to a basic formula (elaborated feet and arms, for instance, plus pupils to the eyes). Figure 6.3 illustrates both the attention to detail in the request drawings and their "still life" quality. They lack the vigor and vitality of the spontaneous attempts to represent movement and to find alternatives to a rigidly upright position. Action was not represented in any request drawing. In contrast, it was present in 69% of the spontaneous drawings from Grade 1 (0% from kindergarten). I might add also that it was a rare child who attempted any new structure in the course of a request drawing. One who did so is shown in the second row of Figure 6.3. She used the first request drawing as an attempt at something new for her, namely, a figure drawn with an all-embracing line.

A number of questions about acquiring a sense of audience still remain to be answered. I cannot tell, for instance, why children varied their productions. In any situation that asks for a "good" performance, children may fall back on tried-and-true procedures, avoiding novel but risky performances. Alternately, they may feel that adults will prefer pictures in which all parts are "present and correct" to pictures in which an attempt at an advanced structure means that some details go by the board. With a few children, I asked which pictures they thought teachers would prefer. These were children whom I knew to have a strong attachment to their own standards, so that the question did not suggest to them any need to give special attention to teachers'

Figure 6.2. Examples of differences in kindergarten between drawings requested by an adult ("the very best picture you can make") and spontaneous drawings. Each set of 4 drawings is by one child. The same basic formula is maintained throughout but request drawings contain more detail and more control over proportion. For Child 1, the difference score between R1 and S1 is 5 DDS points; between R2 and S2 it is 2 points. For Child 2, the differences are 4 and 2.5 points, respectively.

preferences. These children held the view that most teachers would like the detailed still lifes, even though the drawings with attempts at movement were "more fun." Since the spontaneous drawings, from the point of view of structure, are actually more advanced than the request drawings, such comments are somewhat depressing. Even at the age of 7 years, public and private displays are diverging, and the public display is the safe one.

STUDY 3

A third study was concerned with adult preferences. We wanted to know whether children come to like the same performances that adults do. We also wanted to know how children would deal with a situation in which adults may express two bases to their preferences – that is, adults may send two messages as to what constitutes a preferred performance but the messages are not always compatible. Mixed messages or contradicting messages are not unusual in the real world, but in experimental paradigms they are rare.

REQUEST   SPONTANEOUS

Figure 6.3. Examples from two children in Grade 1 of the effect of including action in spontaneous drawings. For Child 1, action accounts for the difference between R1 and S1 (4 points) and between R2 and S2 (5.5 points). For Child 2, action accounts for the difference between R2 and S2 (11 points). The reversed difference between R1 and S1 (S1 higher by 10.5 points) results from a similar attempt at something new, namely an attempt at a novel body structure based on an all-embracing line.

We pitted two possible cues against one another, both possible bases of adults' judgments. One cue is a higher versus a lower score on the Goodenough–Harris criteria. The other is a higher versus a lower score on ratings by preschool teachers for the extent to which they liked a child's drawings. We constructed sets containing four drawings each:

One with a high Goodenough–Harris score, and a high rating by preschool teachers for the extent to which they liked it – in effect, a *High-High* drawing.

One with a *High-Low* combination. It rated highly on the Goodenough–Harris system, but teachers did not especially like it.

One with a *Low-Low* combination.

One with a *Low-High* combination of features. An example of a set is shown in Figure 6.4.

A further group of preschool teachers and two groups of children (kindergarten and Grade 1) were asked to sort each set of four into

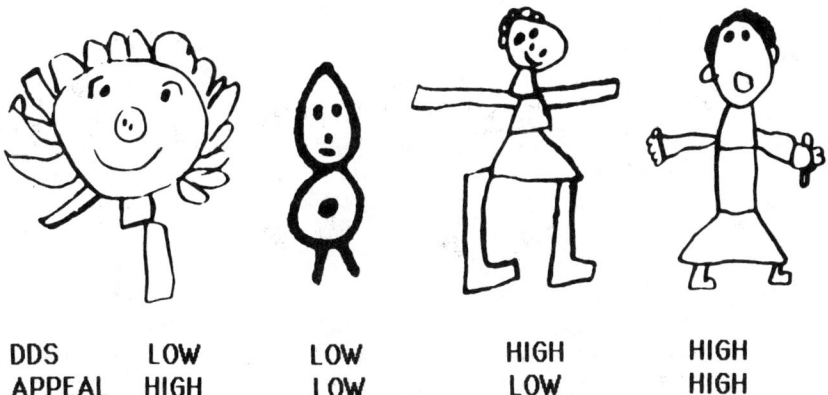

| DDS | LOW | LOW | HIGH | HIGH |
| APPEAL | HIGH | LOW | LOW | HIGH |

Figure 6.4. Example of stimulus figures for expressions of preference. In each set of 4, Ss selected 2 they "liked more" and 2 they "liked less." Each set contained drawings that were high vs. low in appeal to adults and high vs. low in DDS.

two groups: those they "liked more" and those they "liked less". (The preschool teachers would not admit the possibility of disliking a child's work.) The basic results are as follows:

1. The correlations between teachers' preferences and children's preferences were not significant (they were about .20). In contrast, correlations were high (about .80) between the two groups of children.
2. The children differed from teachers mainly in the way they gave their preferences to drawings with high Goodenough–Harris scores.

The second result is the interesting one because it suggests two possible sources of difference among people at various stages of socialization. First, one's own stage of learning may highlight particular qualities of performance. The children are more oriented toward technical skill because that is what they are trying to acquire. They have not yet acquired an interest in the expressive qualities of drawings. Second, a combination of stage and social position may prompt the use of some judgment categories and the avoidance of others. Teachers, for instance, used the category "cute" to describe some drawings. The children in these samples did not do so. One begins to wonder what factors prompt the use of categories such as "cute," "charmingly naive," or "skilled but cold." Some factors probably have to do with the area of performance. The area has to be one in which expressive qualities can be a legitimate part of evaluation. Few people, for instance, would describe a street map as "charmingly naive." The factors probably also have to do with who is making the judgment. "Cute," for instance, is a judgment that seems more likely to be made about people judged to be younger or inferior in status than about peers, elders, or oneself.

SOME FURTHER POSSIBILITIES

I have described some ways in which it is possible to study the nature and acquisition of evaluative judgments about specific performances. There is no shortage of further possibilities. I am still attracted, for instance, to the notion of testing judgments about the *significance of various kinds of error*. This interest is prompted in part by the observation that people often differ with respect to what they regard as a "serious" or a "trivial" error, and what they make an effort to correct. It is prompted also by d'Andrade's (1981) suggestion that judgments about errors mark some essential differences between novices and experts, and by Schieffelin's (1979) comment that asking parents in New Guinea about the significance of errors in children's speech was an excellent window into underlying ideas about both the competence and the social place of children.

I am also attracted by the possibility of exploring further the issue of a sense of audience, but this time with a stronger emphasis on *the rules of display*. Children and adults both learn – often with some pain – when and where to assume a "becoming modesty" about one's knowledge or skill, walking a line between the charge of concealment and the charge of boasting. I single out that aspect of socialization in part because there seem to be large cultural differences in the rules of display. There may also be gender differences, with girls being more strongly socialized into modesty and silence. I single out rules of display also because there is one challenging account of how socialization proceeds – this time, by peers. This is an account by Davies (1982) of some occasions when a group of Australian children used the phrase "sucked in." In these situations, peers encouraged an individual to try for an achievement that might not come off (for instance, to try to kick a football, beyond what the person had done before or beyond what others had done). The cry "sucked in" came when the "sucker" rose to the bait and failed. That form of socialization may be specifically Australian. Its virtue lies not in its being universal, however, but in its drawing attention to the need to analyze specific ways in which people socialize each other into the cultural rules of display.

So far I have not followed any of those possibilities. The reason is that I was very much aware of three large gaps in the picture being developed of cognitive values. One had to do with the bases of judgment. Another had to do with judgments about areas of knowledge and skill. The third had to do with the processes of socialization, more specifically, with what was happening in the social environment.

The bases of specific judgments. A judge or assessor presumably pays attention to particular features of a piece of work. What are the features they respond to? Why these features? What inferences do they draw from them? Up to this point, I had given only minimal attention to such questions. If I were to choose a study illustrating what is possible, I would choose one in which all the judges are adult and the variation is in experience. The judges in this case are literally that. They are magistrates hearing cases, deciding on guilt and, if the judgment is guilty, then deciding on a penalty. The study is by Lawrence (in press) who has laid out in detail the features of the case that magistrates attend to, the inferences they draw, and the overarching orientation to their own role (e.g., administer the law, protect society, deter repetition, promote rehabilitation and reform). Brought out also is a difference between experienced magistrates and a novice in all three respects: features noted, inferences drawn, and the overall definition of role. This type of analysis, based on thinking-out-loud protocols, is labor-intensive but Lawrence (in press) has nicely demonstrated that it is feasible.

Areas of knowledge and skill. Note that the studies mentioned all have to do with judgments about performances. They do not get into the issue highlighted by the latter pair of the observations I started with, namely, judgments about areas of knowledge and skill. That gap bothered me because I was increasingly moving toward the view that in the course of socialization we encounter information that is already tagged in a variety of ways – tagged, for example, as important, difficult, ignorable, not for you, reserved for group X, best approached by method Y, and so on (Goodnow, in press). If that is what socialization involves, then the next questions must ask whether children come to recognize these tags, how they do so, and how they cope with them.

Once again, research of that kind is certainly feasible. There is, for example, a very interesting study by Buescher and Olzewski (1987) on the ways in which girls with high ability in mathematics find ways of maneuvering around stereotypes. They recognize the tag – "boys' subject" – but move into the area anyhow. To underline their own "normalcy," however, they give their achievements as low a profile as possible and choose, as friends, girls of lower ability. Boys, in contrast, mix with peers of equal ability, and do not try to keep their achievements invisible. Instead, they try to gather other forms of visibility (e.g., prominence in sport or class activities) that make the skill in maths less unique.

In addition, it would be perfectly feasible to explore children's categorizations of areas of knowledge and skill. Of particular appeal to me are categorizations into areas that allow "*one right way*" as against those that allow more. It appeals first of all because it suggests an alternative view of socialization. In most areas socialization is directed toward increasing approximation to the prevailing parental or expert view. In some areas, however, one is allowed to depart from the establishment view. The world of art is one example. It contains some tolerance for asserting "I know what I like" even if experts would class one's choice as "kitsch" or "simply awful." In some circumstances, a person may even assert comfortably that "I like kitsch"; that is, I know how it's viewed, I know what it's called, but I claim it as my preference in an acceptable defiance of the orthodox expert view. It would be interesting to know more about the way we come to recognize when, where, and how one may disagree with an establishment view or an establishment agenda.

A second reason for singling out categorization in terms of "right ways" is that there is one challenging account of how such categories develop. This is a study by Susan Stodolsky (1988). She has observed teachers – the same teachers – in their math and social studies classes. In the former, they teach "by the book." They seldom provide projects or encourage students to try to discover principles by themselves. In the latter, projects abound. Small wonder, Stodolsky (1988) proposes, that we emerge with the notion that mathematics and statistics can only be learned by sitting at the feet of experts, writing down prescriptive suggestions, assuming that there is only one right way, and probably never understanding why that should be the case.

The processes of socialization. This is the most obvious gap in the account so far. Empirically, I had concentrated on exploring some forms of value judgment and their changes from one age to another. I was also aware that these changes could be accounted for by several processes: changes, for instance, in exposure to the work or the standards of others, changes in one's own experience in production, changes in the intellectual capacity to absorb the views presented and in the willingness to do so. These specific processes aside, the basic question had to be faced: *For the acquisition of cognitive values, can one get by with the same processes proposed for the acquisition of other forms of knowledge?* Do questions about values simply extend the domains of development one considers, leaving unchanged any account of process? Or do they highlight the need to add further processes? For such basic questions, I did not feel ready to start any empirical work. I needed first to return to some standard theories and look again at what they offered.

Examining some accounts of cognitive development

I should start by placing some of my own values on the table. I regard theories as essentially heuristic devices for thought or research. I am a poor believer in any theory. For me, the interesting aspect of theory is that it provides a starting point, which will prompt me to ask: What will this position illuminate? Where are the limits to what it will cover?

Let me apply these questions to three theoretical accounts of cognitive development, paying particular attention to concepts of how development comes about, but noting also any ideas about differences among areas of knowledge and skill.

CLASSIC PIAGETIAN THEORY

I have in the past found Piagetian theory a useful starting point. I have also found appealing the kind of image presented of human life. People emerge as active, alert, curious, always eager to make sense of the world. And the world by and large lets them happily pursue their search for meaning.

An interest in cognitive values and active socialization brought me first of all to the recognition that Piagetian theory presents a very particular view of the world. The world is essentially free-market and benign. All the information is available. You may help yourself and act for yourself. The only limitations are imposed by the nature of your own abilities – the extent to which your schemas or logical structures allow you to take in the information. The only area where I have found an alternate picture is in the area of moral judgment (Piaget, 1965). Here Piaget makes it clear that adults may in fact take an active role and have a negative effect on development, in the sense that their emphasis on obedience rather than independent thought may retard a child's progression to advanced levels of moral reasoning. This is still some distance, however, from the notion that information might be restricted or denied.

Classical Piagetian accounts also contain a particular view of the content of cognitive development. With the exception of moral reasoning, areas of knowledge are presented as varying only in difficulty. In contrast, as I noted earlier, I was beginning to develop a picture of encounters with information that was already tagged in various ways: tagged with labels such as important, relevant, O.K. to ignore, reserved for group X, best approached by method Y, no room for error, O.K. to be original and so on. I found myself less in sympathy with the classic Piagetian account than with D'Andrade's (1981) observation that cognitive scientists seemed to ignore the fact that, at each point in our lives, we are *expected* to acquire certain kinds of information, in fact, we are sanctioned if we do not.

Overall, the world in Piagetian theory appeared to be a long way from Glick's (1985) description. In real life, Glick argued, the pendulum you are trying to understand is seldom readily available or reliable. On the contrary, it may be owned by someone else, available but rigged so that the results you get are what someone else wants you to know, or available but accompanied by the warning that experimentation might make you blind (Glick, 1985). This does not mean that classical Piagetian theory needs to be set aside. It does, however, narrow down the domains to which it best applies. I see it, for example, as applying quite well to areas such as the conservation of amount, weight or volume, or the understanding of spatial coordinates. More broadly, it fits well only those areas of knowledge where adults have little investment in the ideas children acquire (Goodnow, Knight, & Cashmore, 1985). If one's goal is to go beyond those domains – to construct an account of cognitive development that cuts across many domains or that takes place in everyday life – then classical Piagetian theory will certainly need some additions.

SOCIAL GENEVAN THEORY

Perhaps, I began to think, better answers are to be found in the work of the Social Genevans (see Doise & Mugny, 1984; Doise & Palmonari, 1984). This work certainly has a far more social cast to it. A basic tenet is the argument that the discrepancy or conflict that best sparks cognitive development takes a social form. That is, the discrepancy one responds to most strongly is a difference in opinion or perspective between one's own view and that of another. The critical process is not any discrepancy but "social conflict." In addition, Social Genevan theory proposes that social conflict leads to cognitive advance only if there is a dialogue between the two parties. If one person simply insists on his or her view, and the other accepts without challenge, the exchange does not lead to any advance. Finally, Social Genevan theory contains – especially in the work of Perret-Clermont (1980) on the effects of class – the proposal that social background can predispose an individual to particular views about how dialogue should proceed, particular interpretations of the attempts of others to enter into dialogue, and differences in the ability to make use of contrasting viewpoints or dialogue.

This later Genevan material is a major step toward building in social bases to cognitive development. I still felt, however, that the world being presented was relatively benign. People might be high-handed and refuse to enter into constructive dialogue. There was little place as yet, however, for less amiable forms of control over areas of knowledge and skill, for people denying knowledge, for instance, or actively resisting it. The Social Genevans are not uninterested in these other forms of social interaction (Doise, personal communication), and Doise (1986) certainly has been very much aware of French sociologists who define knowledge as a commodity and a source of power. To date, however, the empirical work and the discussion of social conflict have not been extended to cover these interests.

Does Social Genevan theory provide any expansion or change in the *description of areas of knowledge or skill*? There is an interesting beginning to a differentiation of domains in terms other than the type of logical reasoning required. Domains are noted as varying in what is termed "social marking" – essentially in the extent to which the relationships among parts of a problem have a representation in social life that will frame the way one sees the problem or is able to think about it (see De Paolis, Doise, & Mugny, 1984). Let me provide an example. The spatial position of teachers in relation to pupils is typically one of teachers at the "front" of the room, facing pupils. A problem that calls for changing spatial relationships will be more difficult to solve if the materials of the problem consist of teacher and pupils rather than if the materials contain no such social constraints on what might be done. Duncker (1945) would have said that some parts of the problem are perceived as functionally fixed. The Social Genevans describe the problem as "socially marked."

VYGOTSKIAN-BASED ACCOUNTS

What if one turns away from the Genevans – classic or social – and asks about Vygotskian-based accounts of cognitive development? These accounts contain a strong emphasis on social interactions, especially those where the more and the less expert combine to work out a shared definition of a situation and to move the novice from a state in which performance can proceed only with help to a state in which performance can be carried through unaided.

This type of account has inspired a sizable number of studies and many a second look at what experts and novices do (see Rogoff & Wertsch, 1984). My disappointment with the picture usually presented is that once again the world is benign and relatively neutral. To be more specific, the standard picture is one of willing teachers on the one hand and eager learners on the other. Where are the parents who do not see their role as one of imparting information and encouraging understanding? Where are the children who do not wish to learn or perform in the first place, or who regard as useless what the teaching adult is presenting? Those questions were prompted especially by trying to fit Vygotskian analyses to the interactions involved in teaching children to be skilled at some household tasks and to take responsibility for them (Goodnow, 1988). On the surface, this type of teaching/learning situation should allow a Vygotskian analysis. It is very much an interpersonal situation. And it contains an expert who is usually eager to pass on both skills and a particular definition of the situation. Success, however, is often elusive; resistance is often open and prolonged.

If one looks more closely, one will find that Vygotskian-based work departs in some ways from the picture of willing teachers and eager learners. Wertsch, Ninick, and Arns (1984) describe a group of Brazilian mothers as being interested only in their child turning in a correct performance, even if there was little understanding and the mother had simply told the child how to solve the puzzle. Griffin and Cole (1984) describe two boys whose original definition of a situation was that, if they waited, the more knowledgeable adult would step in and do the job assigned to them. "Doing it by yourself" did not appear to be at the core of their value system. Valsiner (1984) notes precisely that mothers, when it comes to a young child's learning to crawl or to feed itself with a spoon, are at times slow to move into an encouraging role. They may in fact actively restrict the child's attempts to learn, sometimes for the child's good and sometimes for their own convenience. Finally, Azmitia (1987) has begun to take a closer look at the negotiations that occur – especially between peers – over who may play teacher and who will play student, and Verdonik (1987) has pointed to the presence of "power relations" between expert and novice, affecting not only the nature of the negotiation but also the likelihood that the information imparted will be listened to, heard accurately, and absorbed. In short, there are some signs of additions to the usually serene scene, and more may be expected.

SOME SOCIOLOGICAL ACCOUNTS

The most explicit interest in unwillingness and resistance, especially on the part of teachers, is to be found in some sociological accounts of knowledge acquisition. I have already given some notice of the view that knowledge is a source of power, a commodity controlled by one group, dispensed to others only on certain conditions, and denied to others (see Bourdieu & Passeron, 1977; Foucault, 1980). In these accounts, the well-socialized individual not only encounters a world of control but also comes to accept this state of affairs as natural – comes to believe, for instance, that the only place to learn anything worthwhile is in school, that failure to learn is attributable to one's own lack of ability or effort, or that one should know one's place in life and aim only at the knowledge appropriate for that place.

Such pictures of how knowledge is acquired could cover a number of the observations for which I was seeking a conceptual home, observations about areas of knowledge tagged as "not for children," or "not for girls," means to knowledge tagged as "proper" or "wrong," and the promotion of such an air of naturalness to the whole system that one neither questions it nor even becomes aware that it calls for thought.

I must, however, be difficult to please. This view of the world, I must admit, is at times too heavily conspiratorial for my taste. It is also too exclusively concerned with what is being done by the dispensers of knowledge. Above all, I found too little place for the individuals who resist the information, the skill, or the worldview held out to them. Ideally, I seek an account of socialization that goes beyond saying that the individual must be regarded as agent or actor, or that influences are bidirectional. I want to include such statements, but also to go beyond them. Like Berger and Luckman (1966), I like to believe that – even if much of one's life is spent in puppet fashion – there remain at least the occasional times when one notices the strings and decides to cut them. To the notion of the individual as agent or actor, then, I would like to add more information about what one resists, the source of resistance, and the occasions that prompt one to look up and cut.

NEXT STEPS

What comes after this submersion into theories? I suggest two conclusions. One has to do with evidence. For a start, we need more evidence to indicate that the acquisition of knowledge or skill proceeds differently in areas where there are strong cultural values about the way one should think than it does in more neutral areas. We may thank Piaget (1965) for one line of evidence. Moral dilemmas that bring attention to parental edicts and sanctions appear to be reasoned about at a less sophisticated level than are dilemmas that refer to differences among peers. That type of result, however, says only that the *pace* of cognitive development may be different for areas where adults discourage independent thought, encourage it, or are not involved. It does not cover the possibility that the process might be different.

The second conclusion has to do with the processes we consider in the course of accounting for cognitive development. I would argue for closer attention to two processes that seem to be shortchanged in current accounts of cognitive development. One has to do with what I call "modeled messages," the other with the linking of knowledge or skill to social identity.

Modeled messages. I have taken the term "messages" from Shweder (1982). He and Nancy Much argue that moral socialization proceeds through messages that are implicit in the routine arrangements of living and are conveyed with particular force and richness through discourse – through comments on a child's actions, expressions of concern or satisfaction, and, on occasion, the explicit statement of a rule (see Shweder, 1982; Shweder & Much, in press).

A "message" view of socialization can readily be extended to the acquisition of cognitive values. In fact, one can take the proposal a little further and say that the next questions must then deal with effects from qualities of the message (e.g., its clarity, redundancy, embeddedness in practice, or lack of competition) and qualities of the sender and the receiver (including their vested interests in sending clearly, receiving accurately, or – to borrow a phrase from Shweder and Much – "monitoring the uptake of a message"). One may also move toward distinguishing forms of agreement (actual and perceived) and toward asking about effects on both the perception and the acceptance of a message (see Cashmore & Goodnow, 1985).

In the main, I would depart from Shweder and Much (in press) by giving less attention to discourse and more attention to the impact of routine arrangements, to the way that people teach (Stodolsky, in press), or the way space, time, and activities are arranged. When clocks abound in public space, for instance, and most adults wear watches, the message is clear that keeping track of time is important. When the A and B streams in English schools take Latin whereas the C and D streams take art, a message is clearly being given about the relative importance of each school subject (Jackson & Marsden, 1966). In some ways, the process is a broad form of "social marking" (dePaolis et al., 1984). It is also similar to Jean Lave's emphasis on learning that is embedded in practice rather than in text (Lave, this volume; Lave, in press). Regardless of the name given, I would like to see us pay particular attention to these less verbal ways of conveying messages. I would also like to raise the possibility that messages conveyed in this tacit, uncommented-upon form may have a particular impact. For instance, they may appear to have a particular objective validity and be the least likely to be reflected upon and recognized as being matters of custom and value rather than of nature.

Social identity. For this second neglected process, I shall – for the last time – start with a personalized observation. I have wanted for some time to find a way of accounting for why I am a poor typist, despite four periods of training or attempts at self-instruction. At base, I feel it has something to do with the fact that, in the schools of my socialization, typing was only for the girls who were expected not to do well academically. The discovery of U.S. schools where everyone was taught to type was a revelation, and in theory I believe this is the way the world should be. In practice, I still sense some reluctance on my own part.

Once again I needed a conceptual home for an observation. For the moment, I am placing it within the larger notions that areas of knowledge and skill are differentially linked to one's social identity, and that the linkings can help account for both acceptance and resistance to learning, especially the latter. Aboriginal children, for instance, appear to resist literacy in English because they and their parents regard literacy in English as being in conflict with aboriginal identity (Seagrim & Lendon, 1981). Immigrants and members of minority groups may resist acquiring the accent of the dominant group, or even fail to move beyond a certain level of control over the syntax of the second language (Schumann, 1978; Shapira, 1978). It is not a matter of exposure. Neither is it simply that these immigrants or minorities are unable to conquer the structure or accent of the dominant language. Nor is it that they simply do not bother to do so. Under certain social conditions, they actively resist. They may, in time, even persuade the dominant group to acquire their language and speech. English settlers in Wales, for instance, are reported to be learning Welsh; English speakers in New Zealand are reported to be learning Maori. The work of Giles and several other social psychologists is a particularly rich source for a variety of such examples, all detailing the ways in which a sense of social identity or self-categorization can affect what one will or will not notice, learn, and remember (see Giles, 1977; Turner, 1987; Turner & Oakes, 1986).

If I had to choose one process that is essential to consider for the acquisition of cognitive values and that should be considered for any domain, it would probably be the linking of areas of knowledge and skill to social identity. That linking seems essential in any Genevan account of social conflict. The differences in opinion or definition that stand out in cases of social conflict are most likely to be differences with people one sees as similar to oneself or as members of a group one would like to belong to. A link to social identity seems essential also in any Vygotskian account of negotiations toward a transfer of skill or a shared definition of a task. The negotiations one is willing to work on are likely to be those with people one perceives as similar, wishes to be like, or wishes to impress.

I am reluctant, however, to end with a narrowing-down to any specific possibility when my goal has been to expand horizons. Basically, I have wanted to present some different views about what is acquired in the course of cognitive development, about the quality of environments and about the ways in which the social environment has its impact on development. If I have raised some new questions or suggested some new ways of looking at old theories, I shall have achieved my current purpose.

References

Azmitia, M. (1987). Expertise as a moderator of social influence on children's cognition. Paper presented at biennial conference of the Society for Research in Child Development, Baltimore, MD, April.

Becker, J. A. (in press). Bossy and nice requests: Children's production and interpretation. *Merrill-Palmer Quarterly*.

Berger, P. L. (1977). *Facing up to modernity*. Harmondsworth: Penguin.

Berger, P. L., Berger, C., & Kellner, H. (1974). *The homeless mind*. Harmondsworth: Penguin.

Berger, P. L., & Luckman, T. (1966). *The social construction of reality*. New York: Doubleday.

Bourdieu, R., & Passeron, J. (1977). *Reproduction in education, society and culture*. Beverly Hills, CA: Sage.

Buescher, T. M., & Olzewski, P. (1987). Influences on strategies adolescents use to cope with their own recognized talents. Paper presented at biennial meeting of the Society for Research in Child Development, Baltimore, MD, April.

Cashmore, J. A., & Goodnow, J. J. (1985). Agreement between generations: A two-process approach. *Child Development, 56*: 493–501.

Cole, M., Gay, J., Glick, J. A., & Sharp, D. W. (1971). *The cultural context of learning and thinking*. New York: Basic Books.

Cole, M., & Scribner, S. (1974). *Culture and thought*. New York: Wiley.

d'Andrade, R. C. (1981). The cultural part of cognition. *Cognitive Science, 5*: 179–195.

Davies, B. (1982). *Life in the classroom and playground: The accounts of primary school children*. London: Routledge & Kegan Paul.

De Paolis, P., Doise, W., & Mugny, G. (1984). Social marking in cognitive operations. In W. Doise & S. Moscovici (eds.), *Current issues in social psychology*. Vol. 2. Cambridge: Cambridge University Press.

Doise, W. (1986). Les représentations sociales: définition d'un concept. In W. Doise & A. Palmonari (Eds.), *L'étude des représentations sociales* (pp. 81–94). Neuchâtel: Delachaux & Niestlé.

Doise, W., & Mugny, G. (1984). *The social development of the intellect*. Oxford: Pergamon Press.

Doise, W., & Palmonari, A. (Eds.). (1984). *Social interaction in individual development*. Cambridge: Cambridge University Press.

Duncker, K. (1945). On problem-solving. *Psychological Monographs*, *58* (No. 5, Serial No. 270).

Foucault, M. (1980). *Power-knowledge: Selected interviews and other writings.* London: Brighton & Harvester Press.

Giles, H. (Ed.) (1977). *Language, ethnicity and intergroup relations.* London: Academic Press.

Glick, J. (1985). Culture and cognition revisited. In E. Neimark, R. deLisi, & J. L. Newman (Eds.), *Moderators of competence* (pp. 99–115). Hillsdale, NJ: Erlbaum.

Goodnow, J. J. (1976). The nature of intelligent behavior: Questions raised by cross-cultural studies. In L. B. Resnick (Ed.), *The nature of intelligence* (pp. 169–188). New York: Erlbaum.

(1977). *Children drawing.* Cambridge, MA: Harvard University Press.

(1984). On being judged intelligent. *International Journal of Psychology*, *19*: pp. 391–406.

(1985). Topics, methods and models: Feminist challenges in social science. In J. J. Goodnow & C. Pateman (Eds.), *Woman, social science and public policy* (pp. 1–31). Sydney: Allen & Unwin.

(1986). Organizing and re-organizing: Some lifelong everyday forms of intelligent behavior. In R. J. Sternberg & R. Wagner (Eds.), *Practical intelligence: Nature and origins of competence in everyday life* (pp. 143–162). Cambridge: Cambridge University Press.

(1987). Social aspects of planning. In S. I. Friedman, E. K. Skolnick, & R. R. Cocking (Eds.), *Blueprints for thinking: The role of planning in cognitive development* (pp. 179–204). Cambridge: Cambridge University Press.

(1988). Children's household labor: Its nature and functions. *Psychological Bulletin 103*:5–26.

(In press). Using sociology to expand psychological accounts of cognitive development. *Human Development.*

Goodnow, J. J., & Burns, A. (1985). *Home and school: Child's-eye views.* Sydney: Allen & Unwin.

Goodnow, J. J., Knight, R., & Cashmore, J. (1985). Adult social cognition: Implications of parents' ideas for approaches to social development. In M. Perlmutter (Ed.), *Social cognition: Minnesota symposia on child development* (Vol. 18, pp. 287–324). Hillsdale, NJ: Erlbaum.

Goodnow, J. J., & Pateman, C. (Eds.). (1985). *Women, social science and public policy.* Sydney: Allen & Unwin.

Goodnow, J. J., Wilkins, P., & Dawes, L. (1986). Acquiring cultural forms: Cognitive aspects of socialization illustrated by children's drawings and judgments of drawings. *International Journal of Behavioral Development*, *9*: 485–505.

Griffin, P., & Cole, M. (1984). Current activity for the future: The Zo-ped. In B. Rogoff & J. V. Wertsch (Eds.), *Children's learning in the zone of proximal development* (pp. 45–64). San Francisco: Jossey Bass.

Habermas, J. (1970). *Towards a rational society: Student protest, science, and politics.* Boston: Beacon Press.

Harris, D. B. (1963). *Children's drawings as measures of intellectual maturity.* New York: Harcourt, Brace & World.

Jackson, B., & Marsden, D. (1966). *Education and the working class.* Harmondsworth: Penguin.

Lave, J. (In press). *Cognition in practice*. Cambridge: Cambridge University Press.

Lawrence, J. A. (In press). Expertise on the bench: Modelling magistrates' judicial decision-making. In M.T.H. Chi, R. Glaser, & M. Farr (Eds.), *The nature of expertise*. Hillsdale, NJ: Erlbaum.

Lefebvre-Pinard, M., Bouffard-Bouchard, T., & Fielder, H. (1982). Social cognition and verbal requests among preschool children. *Journal of Psychology, 110*: 133–148.

Lerner, G. (1979). *The majority finds its past: Placing women in history*. New York: Oxford University Press.

Luria, A. R. (1976). *Cognitive development: Its cultural and social foundations*. Cambridge, MA: Harvard University Press.

Oakley, A. (1974). *The sociology of housework*. London: Robertson.

Parsons, J. F., Adler, T. F., & Kaczala, C. M. (1982). Socialization of achievement attitudes and beliefs. *Child Development, 53*: 310–321.

Perrer-Clermont, A. N. (1980). *Social interaction and cognitive development in children*. London: Academic Press.

Piaget, J. (1965). *The moral judgment of the child*. New York: Free Press.

Richards, M., & Light, P. (1976). *Children of social worlds*. Cambridge, MA: Harvard University Press.

(1986). *The possible futures of developmental psychology*. Cambridge, MA: Harvard University Press.

Rogoff, B., & Wertsch, J. (Eds.). (1984). *Children's learning in the zone of proximal development*. San Francisco: Jossey Bass.

Schieffelin, B. (1979). Getting it together: An ethnographic approach to the study of the development of communicative competence. In E. Ochs & B. Schieffelin (Eds.), *Developmental pragmatics* (pp. 73–107). New York: Academic Press.

Schumann, J. H. (1978). *The pidginization process: A model for second language acquisition*. Rowley, MA: Newbury House.

Scribner, S. (1984). Studying working intelligence. In B. Rogoff & J. Lave (Eds.), *Everyday cognition: Its development in social context*. Cambridge, MA: Harvard University Press.

Seagrim, G., & London, R. (1981). *Furnishing the mind: Aboriginal and white*. New York: Academic Press.

Shapira, E. C. (1978). The non-learning of English: Case study of an adult. In E. M. Hatch (Ed.), *Second language acquisition: A book of readings*. Rowley, MA: Newbury House.

Sharrock, W. W. (1974). On owning knowledge. In R. Turner (Ed.), *Ethnomethodology* (pp. 45–53). Harmondsworth: Penguin.

Shatz, M., & Gelman, R. (1973). The development of communication skills: Modifications in the speech of young children as a function of listener. *Monographs of the Society for Research in Child Development* (Serial No. 152).

Shweder, R. A. (1982). Beyond self-constructed knowledge: The study of culture and morality. *Merrill-Palmer Quarterly, 28*: 41–69.

Shweder, R. A., & Much, N. C. (In press). Determinations of meaning: Discourse and moral socialization. In W. Kurtines & J. Gewirtz (Eds.), *Moral development through social interaction*. New York: Wiley.

Stein, N. L. (1982). The definition of a story. *Journal of Pragmatics, 6*: 487–507.

Stein, N. L., & Policastro, M. (1984). The concept of a story: A comparison between children's and teachers' perspectives. In H. Mandl, N. L. Stein, & T. Trabasso (Eds.), *Learning and comprehension of text* (pp. 113–155). Hillsdale, NJ: Erlbaum.

Stodolsky, S. (1988). *The subject matters: Classroom activity in mathematics and social studies.* Chicago: University of Chicago Press.

Turner, J. C. (1987). *Rediscovering the social group.* Oxford: Blackwell.

Turner, J. C., & Oakes, P. J. (1986). The significance of the social identity concept for social psychology with reference to individualism, interactionism, and social influence. *British Journal of Social Psychology, 25*: 237–252.

Valsiner, J. (1984). Construction of the zone of proximal development in adult–child joint action. In B. Rogoff & J. Wertsch (Eds.), *Children's learning in the zone of proximal development* (pp. 65–76). San Francisco: Jossey Bass.

Verdonik, F. (1987). *The role of power relationships in children's cognition: Its significance for research on cognitive development.* Paper presented at biennial conference of the Society for Research in Child Development, Baltimore, MD, April.

Wertsch, J. V., Minick, N., & Arns, F. J. (1984). The creation of context in joint problem-solving. In B. Rogoff & J. Lave (Eds.), *Everyday cognition: Its development in social context* (pp. 151–167). Cambridge, MA: Harvard University Press.

Wood, D., Bruner, J. S., & Ross, G. (1976). The role of tutoring in problem-solving. *Journal of Child Psychology and Psychiatry, 17*: 89–100.

7
Indexicality and socialization

Elinor Ochs

Introduction

As long as society has been an object of interest and inquiry, scholars have been struggling to understand the process of socialization, roughly defined as a process in which a novice transitions toward becoming a member of a social group (Cicourel, 1973; Wentworth, 1980). In addition, societies the world over have promoted their own folk views about how novices become competent participants in the social group. Both scholarly and folk views of socialization strongly reflect and encode notions of human nature. These notions cover a wide range. For example, in 19th-century Europe, in consonance with the philosophy of Hobbes, human nature was thought to be aggressive and self-centered and socialization to be the process by which this asocial nature was transformed into a pro-social disposition. In contrast, functionalist theories of this century (Parsons, 1937, 1951; Merton, 1949) saw individuals as social by nature and the process of socialization not as a battle between the individual and society, but rather as a smooth and gradual conformity to and internalization of social values and expectations.

Currently the process of socialization is receiving considerable attention as a result of a renewed interchange between social and cognitive psychology and a renewed interest, in philosophy and the social sciences, in how individuals construct a sense of reality through ordinary day-to-day social practices (see Bakhtin, 1981; Bourdieu, 1977; Cole, 1985; Giddens, 1979, 1984; Griffin & Cole, 1984; Heath, 1983; Miller, 1982; Much & Shweder, 1978; Ochs & Schieffelin, 1984; Schieffelin & Ochs, 1986a, 1986b; Vygotsky, 1978; Wentworth, 1980; Wertsch, 1985).

Together with my colleague Bambi Schieffelin, I have been considering for several years the process of *language socialization* (Ochs & Schieffelin, 1984; Schieffelin & Ochs, 1986a, 1986b). Language socialization entails both socialization *through* language and socialization to *use* language.

Social scientists concerned with the relations between language and society have tended to see language as being expressive of local ideologies and social orders. That is, they have looked at language as a repository of local meanings. A basic tenet of language socialization is that language must be studied not only as a symbolic system that encodes local social and cultural structures, but also as a *tool* for establishing (i.e., maintaining, creating) social and psychological realities. Both the symbolic and the tool-like properties of language are exploited in the process of language socialization. Language socializes, and in this sense it is a social tool. To a large extent, however, this socializing function relies upon the symbolic aspect of language. That is, among the many means through which language socialization is accomplished, symbolic expression looms large. In this sense, the symbolic function of language serves the social tool-like function of language. The importance of language to socialization has been recognized by a number of scholars, including Edward Sapir, who noted that "language is a great force of socialization, probably the greatest that exists" (Sapir, 1974:53).

As already mentioned, the socializing function of language may be achieved through the *symbolic* or *propositional content* of utterances. However, language socialization relies also on the *manner* in which utterances are delivered. By manner, I refer to a range of verbal phenomena such as grammatical forms, voice quality, codes, and written, spoken, or signed modes. Of particular interest here are structures that vary across contexts and hence index (point to) contexts when used (Silverstein, 1976). These features may index something about the social identities of the participants, for example, or about the activities taking place, or about the feelings or knowledge of the speaker. Such context-bearing features of language and language behavior serve a number of functions, including that of *modulating* the meanings of linguistic constructions. That is, they regulate the breadth and range of situational or social meanings that a construction may convey, in much the same way as tones or chords function to circumscribe the key of a composition. For example, the use of neutral and sympathy-marked first-person pronouns in Samoan modulates the range of possible meanings of particular constructions. The imperative "Give it to me" using the neutral form of "me" (*Mai ia te a'u*) sets the meaning of the construction as a demand. If the speaker uses the sympathy-marked pronoun (*Mai taita*), this pronoun establishes a different meaning for the construction. Specifically, the sympathy-marked pronoun indexes that the speaker is begging. An important goal of this chapter is to outline ways in which, among other routes, children and other novices gain sociocultural knowledge as they gain knowledge of such indexes and as they come to understand the impact of such indexes on the construction of meaning in social interactions and social life.

Working definitions of culture and discourse

LINGUISTIC AND SOCIOCULTURAL KNOWLEDGE

The approach to language socialization advocated here is tied to a particular perspective on sociocultural and linguistic knowledge. In this perspective, knowledge of language and sociocultural knowledge are not universally shared by all members of a social group and hence not contained within any one individual's competence. To draw on an earlier analysis by Ochs and Schieffelin (1984), language and culture constitute

> bodies of knowledge, structures of understanding, conceptions of the world, and collective representations [which] are extrinsic to any individual and contain more information than any individual could know or learn. [Language and] culture encompass variations in knowledge between individuals but such variation, although crucial to what an individual may know and to the social dynamic between individuals, does not have its locus within the individual. (1984:284)

In this view, language and culture are open systems, and individuals have the potential to modify linguistic and sociocultural knowledge *throughout the course of their life spans*.

GRAMMAR AND DISCOURSE

The notion of language used in this account encompasses not only grammar but also discourse. The approach to discourse here is somewhat different from that taken in other research models. Discourse has often been considered coterminous with structures beyond the sentence or beyond the clause. In the present discussion, however, discourse plays a role comparable to grammar. Whereas *grammar* can be defined as a set of rules and constraints generating all allowable sentences in a language, *discourse* can be defined (and is defined here) as *a set of norms, preferences, and expectations relating language to context, which speaker-hearers draw on and modify in producing and making sense out of language in context.*

Discourse relates language to both social and psychological contexts, including affect, knowledge, beliefs, social acts, activities, and identities. Although domains of discourse knowledge are shared among members of a speech community, members may vary in their understanding of discourse. Such variation underlies the dynamics of constructing meaning in interactions and underlies the claim that socialization is a life span process.

Grammar and discourse are two closely related domains of linguistic knowledge, and most linguistic structures are organized by both. For example, all contextually variable structures have a grammatical and discourse organization, including variable word orders, tense-aspect marking, case marking, verb voice, lexical selection, speech acts, conversational turns, sequences, rounds, speech events, and registers, among other structures. As an anthropological linguist, I can, for example, describe the grammar of ergative case marking in Samoan. I can also describe the discourse of ergative case marking, that is, the norms, preferences, and expectations surrounding its use (see Ochs, 1982b, 1988). Every native speaker-hearer has a tacit understanding of grammatical and discourse principles underlying the use of such constructions and it behooves linguistic scholarly research to explore both of these domains.

For language socialization research, discourse lies at the heart of the process we are pursuing. Discourse knowledge is not only an endpoint of language socialization; it is also a path to sociocultural knowledge. As children and other novices come to understand discourse, they also come to understand social order and cultural meanings.

Explicit and implicit language socialization

As noted earlier, two major dimensions of language behavior – propositional content and manner, including linguistic forms, modes, and communicative strategies – facilitate language socialization. Using these resources of utterance content and manner, the members of a social group can convey sociocultural information explicitly or implicitly.

There is no doubt that the most salient and most widely described examples of language socialization pertain to relatively explicit language practices as a mechanism of socialization. The best example of this kind of socialization activity is the *elicited imitation routine*. In this routine a member of the group models a verbal behavior for a novice and directs the novice to repeat the behavior. Such routines have been reported for a number of societies and are probably universal; however, the length and frequency of these routines as well as the scope of functions and situations they serve vary greatly across societies. In societies such as Kwara'ae (Watson-Gegeo & Gegeo, 1986), Kaluli (Schieffelin, 1979, 1986, in press), Mexican-American (Briggs, 1986; Eisenberg, 1986), white working-class South Baltimorean (Miller, 1982, 1986), Basotho (DeMuth, 1986), and Samoan (Ochs 1982, in press), these routines can be pursued for long periods of time and can be used in teasing, insulting, challenging, and reprimanding a third party in multiparty interactions. For this reason, such relatively explicit practices have been of great interest. The novice is provided with explicit prompting in how to participate in a verbal activity – including content and manner of participation. The novice may then use this knowledge to gain an understanding of social relations and situations.

In another type of relatively explicit socialization practice, caregivers simply make an assertion concerning social norms, values, beliefs, and the like. Such practices, which rely on propositional content, are described in Bernstein's accounts of language socialization across social classes in Great Britain (Bernstein, 1972). Bernstein discusses, for example, how mothers provide explicit information concerning the expected demeanor of their sons and daughters. A working-class mother may tell her son "Boys don't cry," for example, as a means of social control. In the literature on middle-class simplified caregiver speech, we can also find examples of relatively explicit rendering of sociocultural information through propositional content. Middle-class caregivers often announce to young children what is going to take place, is taking place just now, or has just taken place – in all cases defining an activity in sociocultural terms (Keenan [Ochs] & Schieffelin, 1976). This information is characteristically conveyed through rhetorical questions and responses, such as "Do you know what we are doing? We're having a tea party." or "Do you know what that was? That was a nurse."

Although these relatively explicit practices and routines can be complex linguistically and socioculturally and have provided us with an initial entry point into the process of language socialization, they represent only a fraction of language socialization activity. The greatest part of sociocultural information is keyed *implicitly*, through language use. Indeed it was difficult to discuss the earlier examples strictly in terms of explicit socialization, for covert messages about the sociocultural context are always conveyed along with explicit goals of direct instruction (Bateson, 1972). The more explicit practices such as prompting and announcing provide a high degree of scaffolding for the novice, but the vast majority of language socialization practices do not. Rather, most sociocultural information on acts and activities, identities and relationships, feelings and beliefs, and other domains must be inferred by children and other novices. Texts and conversational activity of the most ordinary sort are related to other situational phenomena, and these relations allow novices to interpret and otherwise participate in verbal interactions.

Indexicality

CONTEXT OF SITUATION AND CONTEXT OF CULTURE
As one delves into the process of language socialization, one is ultimately faced with specifying more precisely the relation of language to sociocultural context. Initially, one is faced with explicating more precisely how language form and content signal sociocultural dimensions of specific communicative events (e.g., social identities of participants and speech acts). But the task of relating language to sociocultural context is not complete at this point. We have as well to account for how the sociolinguistic organization of these specific communicative events in turn interfaces with more general systems of social order and cultural knowledge. We know that particular communicative events relate to each other in systematic and complex ways within a defined speech community. Although cultures are not perfectly tidy systems, as noted by Geertz (1973), there are nonetheless dispositions, preferences, and dispreferences that cut across numerous communicative events and organize those events.

For example, in traditional Samoan communities, members view activities and tasks as social and not individual accomplishments. This perspective underlies several verbal activities, including verbal acknowledgments of physical labor, verbal responses to oratory in chiefly councils, and judicial responses to acts of wrongdoing in court proceedings. In all these speech activities, no one individual is praised or blamed for his or her actions. It is not the individual but the social group that is responsible for accomplishments and transgressions (Duranti and Ochs, 1986).

Three important questions to consider in research on language socialization are (1) What are the overarching sociocultural dispositions for particular social groups? (2) How do these sociocultural dispositions organize communicative practices? and (3) How do communicative practices generate sociocultural knowledge among novices in the course of becoming a member of a social group?

These issues can only be tackled in a multidisciplinary effort. Psychological models of mental representation and information processing, linguistic models of meaning and use, and sociological and anthropological models of social practices, social order, and cultural knowledge are all needed to shed light on the interface of language and sociocultural knowledge. Several scholars have commented on the importance and the enormity of this undertaking. Lyons, for one, observes:

> If linguistic semantics is taken to be that branch of semiotics which deals with the way in which meaning (of all kinds) is conveyed by language, it must be accepted that a comprehensive theory of linguistic semantics will need to be based upon, or include, a theory of contextual appropriateness. It is arguable, however, that, at the present time at least, the construction of such a comprehensive theory of contextual appropriateness is too ambitious a task. (1977:590)

PROPERTIES OF THE INDEX

To go beyond shaking in our boots or throwing up our hands at the complexity of sociocultural knowledge and its impact on language practice and interpretation, let us consider how language signals or *indexes* sociocultural information at the level of particular communicative events. After all, children and other novices build up tacit knowledge of language use and other sociocultural phenomena through their participation in particular but recurrent communicative events. To go back to our earlier example, Samoan children may be socialized into an ideology of collective task accomplishment through receiving, producing, and overhearing verbal acknowledgments of completed actions. Through linguistic form and message content, these acknowledgments index sociocultural dispositions concerning responsibility for actions taken.

To this end, we have several theories of indexicality available, including that of Peirce (1931–1958), Morris (1946), Jakobson (1960), Lyons (1977), and Silverstein (1976). All of these approaches provide global frameworks for relating linguistic signs to some dimension of temporally and spatially located events. Lyons's definition of indexicality as "some known or assumed connexion between a sign A and its significatum C such that the occurrence of A can be held to imply the presence or existence of C" (1977:106) is clear and useful as a starting point for unraveling sociocultural deixis. Silverstein (1976, 1985) has expanded this notion of index to include not only referential indexicals but also nonreferential indexicals. Whereas a referential index contributes to the denotational or strict referential meaning of a sentence uttered in a context, a nonreferential index does not. The pronouns "I" and "you" are referential indexicals. They both index the communicative context (i.e., the presence of speaker and addressee) and they contribute to the referential meaning of propositions in which they appear. Choices of one dialect or one language rather than another, on the other hand, can be nonreferential indexes, in that code choices may index the communicative context (e.g., the social status of the speaker or the social relationship between speaker and addressee), but do not contribute to the referential or literal meaning of propositions.

The pragmatic and sociolinguistic literature indicates that the following *kinds of sociocultural information* may be so indexed through linguistic signs: social status, roles, relationships, settings, actions, activities, genres, topics, affective and epistemological stances of participants, among others. This literature also informs us that a wide range of *grammatical and discourse structures* index sociocultural information in different speech communities. We know, for example, that phonological and morphological structures are widely used to key speakers' social status, role, affect, and epistemological perspective. Text structures such as repetition, reformulation, code switching, and various sequential units are also linguistic resources for indexing such local contextual dimensions.

Unfortunately, to get a grip on the process of language socialization, it is not enough to list contextual dimensions and the linguistic structures that index those dimensions. Indexical relations are more complex than one-to-one mappings between linguistic forms and contextual features. They cannot be fully understood without additional mappings – between a particular contextual dimension and sets of linguistic forms, and between a particular linguistic form and several contextual dimensions. Further, it must be recognized that an index or set of indexicals may recontextualize the past and precontextualize the future as well as contextualize the communicative context of the moment. Each of these indexical properties must be specified before we can propose a model of language socialization.

Indexing through single features and the collocation of features. Two means of indexing sociocultural context stand out in the pragmatic and sociolinguistic literature: (1) a single linguistic form may index some contextual dimension, or (2) a set of linguistic forms may index some contextual dimension. Honorific morphology provides good examples of how single linguistic forms can index sociocultural context, in this case, affective and social relationships between speaker and addressee or speaker and referent. Personal pronouns that index sex of speaker or hearer in many languages also illustrate how single linguistic items signal sociocultural context of the utterance.

In other cases, contextual information is indexed through a set of cooccurring structures. Let us call this process "collocational indexing." The work of Ferguson (1977), Andersen (1977), Biber (1986), Biber & Finegan (in press), and others on registers, communicative styles, and text types illustrates this process. Here social identity of speaker or addressee, genre, communicative activity taking place, and the like are indexed through a set of linguistic features that systematically cooccur rather than through a single feature.

The important point here is that *isolated linguistic features often have broad indexical scope*. For example, in communities where Standard American English is spoken deletion of the copula (as in "That bad") indexes a wide range of possible social contexts. For example, it may index the social status of one's addressee as child, foreigner, patient, or elderly person (Ferguson, 1977). To narrow the scope of possible contexts to one of these social statuses, speaker-hearers must consider other linguistic forms that cooccur in the text. High pitch along with deletion of the copula, for example, might index that the addressee is a child, whereas loudness might index foreigner status of the addressee. It is the combination of indexes that narrows the indexical scope.

Another example of indexical narrowing through collocation can be found in the domain of affect. Most linguistic constructions that index affect across the world's languages indicate a broad domain of speakers' or others' affective dispositions (Ochs & Schieffelin, in press). For example, in many languages, particular features index only positive affect or negative affect. Further specification of affective dispositions of participants lies in the relation of that feature to others expressed in the text (as well as to nonverbal features of the situation). Morphosyntactic indexes of affect, for example, must be related to phonological and lexical indexes.

That context is indexed through collocation of indexes as well as through single indexes is a sociolinguistic generalization that must be incorporated into a developmental model of how sociocultural and linguistic knowledge interface in the course of language socialization. We must represent the fact that children come to understand constraints on cooccurrence and ordering of indexes and, further, that they come to understand how indexes interact to signal contextual information.

Direct and indirect indexical relations. In addition, our model of language socialization needs to attend to another form of indexical complexity. In many examples of indexicality cited in the literature, there appears to be a *direct* – that is, unmediated – relation between one or more linguistic forms and some contextual dimension. A particular particle in one language may be described as a direct index of the speaker's feelings, or a set of linguistic forms may be described as collectively directly indexing the activity of gossiping or lecturing or oratory.

In looking over numerous examples of indexical relations, I, together with a group of graduate students, have begun to discern a second, more complex type of indexical relation, in which indexicality is achieved *indirectly*. A feature of the communicative event is evoked indirectly through the indexing of some *other* feature of the communicative event. In these cases, the feature of the communicative event directly indexed is conventionally linked to and helps to constitute some second feature of the communicative context, such that the indexing of one evokes or indexes the other.

Good examples of indirect indexes come from the work on Japanese sentence-final particles (see, e.g., Clancy, 1986; Cook, 1987; Seki, 1987; Uyeno, 1971). Certain particles, such as *zo*, *ze*, and *wa*, index both an affective disposition and gender. By gender, I do not mean biological distinctions between men and women but rather cultural constructs of men and women (Ortner & Whitehead, 1981), that is, local assumptions about being male and being female. When speakers use the particles *zo*, *ze*, and *wa*, they index their gender identity along with their affective disposition. Using Bakhtin's (1981) framework, we can say that through these particles Japanese speakers index male or female "voice," along with affect. *Zo* and *ze*, for example, index both a disposition of affective intensity and male voice of speaker. *Wa* indexes almost the reverse: a more hesitant disposition in that it softens the force of an assertion and female voice of speaker.

Within the proposed framework, affect and gender stand in different indexical relations to the particles *zo*, *ze*, and *wa*. Specifically, the particles *directly* index affective dispositions and *indirectly* index gender of speaker. Speakers' gender is indirectly indexed through the indexing of speakers' affect in the sense that gender identity in Japanese society is partly defined in terms of these affective dispositions. Softness and hesitancy are expected constituents of female comportment, and forcefulness is part of local conceptions of being male. Because of the strong conventional and constitutive relations between affect and gender, the direct indexing of affect evokes gender identities or gender voices of participants as well. This relationship between the indexing of affect and gender identity is represented in Figure 7.1.

In the perspective suggested here, features of a communicative event may be related to one another in *constitutive* ways, such that certain features help to define or constitute others. Participants' affect helps to constitute participants' gender identity, for example, and speech acts help to constitute speech activities and so on. The indexical

Particle	Direct meaning	Indirect meaning
Zo, ze	Coarse intensity	Male "voice"
Wa	Affect of softness or delicate intensity	Female "voice"

Figure 7.1. Indexical meanings of *zo*, *ze*, and *wa*.

potential of linguistic forms can thus extend to the contexts so constituted.

I would like to suggest here that sociocultural dimensions of communicative events do not display themselves randomly with respect to
being in a direct or indirect indexical relation to linguistic forms. Major
sociocultural dimensions include social identities of participants, social
relationships among participants, affective dispositions of participants,
beliefs and knowledge (epistemological dispositions) of participants,
social (including speech) acts, social (including speech) activities, and
genre. Within this set, two contextual dimensions are recurrently used
to constitute other contextual dimensions, namely, *affective* and *epistemological dispositions*. Affective dispositions include feelings, moods,
and attitudes of participants toward some proposition. Epistemological
dispositions refer to some property of participants' beliefs or knowledge vis-à-vis some proposition – for example, the source of their
knowledge or the degree of certainty of their knowledge. These two
dispositions are directly indexed in all languages, are central dimensions of all communicative events, and are central constituents of other
dimensions of communicative events. Furthermore, recent linguistic
literature on affect and epistemological dispositions suggests that these
two are probably the most highly grammaticized of the features that
define sociocultural context (Ochs & Schieffelin, in press; Besnier, in
press-a, in press-b; Haviland, in press; Biber & Finegan, in press;
Labov, 1984).

Although other features can help define more complex contextual
features, I propose that affect and epistemology are the most widely
employed to this end. Participants' affect and participants' beliefs and
knowledge help to establish their social identity, the social relationship
obtaining between them, and the speech act or speech activity they are
endeavoring to perform. In this sense, an understanding of indexes of
affect and epistemological stance are basic to interpreting the
sociocultural organization of a communicative event. And, following
this line of thought, such indexes are building blocks of children's
linguistic and sociocultural competence. The constitutive role of affect,
on the one hand, and beliefs and knowledge, on the other, in defining
sociocultural context is schematized in Figure 7.2.

To provide an exhaustive account of the ways in which affective and

		SOCIAL IDENTITY
		SOCIAL RELATIONSHIP
AFFECT	→	SPEECH ACT
BELIEFS/KNOWLEDGE	→	SPEECH ACTIVITIES
		GENRE

KEY:
(→ = Constitutive relation)

Figure 7.2. Constituting sociocultural context.

epistemological stances enter into the constitution of other contexts is beyond the scope of this discussion. We briefly note, however, that affect is a strong component not only of gender identity but of social identity more generally. Many of the linguistic features previously analyzed solely as indexes of social status and role – for example, honorific marking and respect vocabulary systems – can be reanalyzed as direct indexes of affective dispositions of the speaker (e.g., humility, admiration, love), which in turn help to constitute or establish the social positions of participants in a communicative situation. Indexes of affect also help to define numerous speech acts such as praising, protesting, begging, disagreeing, teasing, accusing, complimenting, and assessing.

Epistemological dispositions play an equally important role in constituting context. Indexes of sources and certainty of speakers' beliefs and knowledge, for example, help to constitute communicative activities such as telling stories, gossiping, prophesying, confessing, interrogating, delivering messages, and writing academic papers. Similarly, the indexing of beliefs and knowledge is fundamental to defining speech acts such as speculating, asking questions, accusing, and asserting. Evidential forms in many languages serve the dual function of directly indexing some property of speakers' knowledge and in so doing indirectly indexing for interlocutors the nature of the speech act or activity taking place. In Samoan, for example, there are several linguistic forms that indicate degrees of certainty of speakers' knowledge. Those forms that directly index lack of certainty indirectly index the speech act of speculation (Ochs, in press). Epistemological dispositions also help to constitute social identities and social relationships. In many societies, for example, lower-status persons talking to higher-status persons are expected to evidence confused speech or to otherwise index that they do not know as much as their addressees (see Albert, 1972).

Children come to an understanding of speech acts and speech activities taking place, genres in use, social identities and social relationships in play to a great extent through an understanding of linguistic forms that index affect and beliefs and knowledge. In becoming linguistically and socioculturally competent, children and other novices must learn the social work that these indexes perform, particularly their potential for establishing social personae and social goals.

Vectors of indexicality. A third powerful socializing property of linguistic indexes is their capacity to index not only the ongoing or current context but past and future contexts as well. Thus far we have been considering cases in which one or more linguistic forms index some immediate contextual feature, such as the Japanese particles indexing affective stances and gender identities. And I have emphasized how children's understandings of the meanings of such indexes interfaces with their understanding of social order and cultural orientations. The power of indexicality, however, extends beyond the immediate situational context. Indexes also have the potential to redefine prior contexts, that is, to *recontextualize*, and anticipate future contexts, that is, to *precontextualize*. And these additional vectors of indexicality augment the world-creating potential of language in the process of communication and socialization.

A good example of retrospective indexing comes from the use of linguistic forms that directly index epistemological stance, such as evidential markers in many languages. I mentioned that in Samoan, linguistic forms that directly index speakers' lack of certainty may indirectly index the speech act of speculation. So far, we have been speaking only of indexing the immediate or current context. But speculation, in turn, involves other contexts, particularly past events, and in so doing speculation functions to recontextualize those past events in a different light.

For several years I have been concerned with just one of the many interesting aspects of recontextualization through speculation: the type of topic that is subjected to speculation across different societies. What does or does not become a topic of speculation? What are the conditions under which speculation is appropriate? This concern has led me to consider perhaps the most basic recontextualizing function of speculation, namely, the function of recontextualizing some object as an object of speculation. Comparative studies suggest that societies constrain what can or cannot be subjected to speculation. In this sense, certain evidentials across languages and communities indirectly index for children and other novices the *limits of speculation* for the social group they are entering.

One of the most striking results of cross-cultural research is the finding that societies differ in their willingness to verbally speculate about *what is in the mind of another person* (see Ochs & Schieffelin, 1984; Ochs, 1982a; Schieffelin & Ochs, 1986a). Members of Western European societies generally show no dispreference with respect to explicitly guessing at what another person might be thinking or feeling. Indeed, members of these societies devote considerable attention to speculating about what is or was in someone's mind. Our legal system, for example, assesses the gravity of an action in terms of mental states and allows speculation concerning the premeditation of actions and the mental fitness of the actor at the time of the action. Further, a major pedagogical procedure in these societies is to get novices to explicitly guess what the instructor is thinking about. This procedure is codified in the test question, where the questioner knows the information and is eliciting from others the information the questioner already has in mind. The interest in this sort of mind probing is also evident in riddles and in games such as "Twenty Questions" and "I Spy," which require others to verbally hypothesize about what is in the speaker's mind. That unclear mental states are an acceptable object of verbal specula-tion is made linguistically evident to children early in their lives. Dozens of times a day caregivers in middle-class mainstream communi-ties explicitly guess at unclearly formulated thoughts of young children. The caregivers make a wild or educated guess at what these children may have in mind and ask them to confirm or disconfirm their hypoth-eses. Through speech acts of this sort, caregivers contextualize some mental state of the child as an object of verbal speculation and in so doing, socialize children through language into a component of the local epistemology.

Other societies – including Samoan (Ochs, 1984, 1988), Kaluli of Papua New Guinea (Schieffelin, in press), and Athapaskan (Scollon, 1982) communities – strongly disprefer verbal speculation on what someone else might be thinking or feeling. In traditional Samoan households, interlocutors do not typically pose test questions nor do they engage in mind-reading games or riddles. Legal assessments of wrongdoing do not rely on properties of mental states, and verbal conjectures on this topic are not part of legal proceedings. When Samoan caregivers hear an unclearly expressed thought of a young child, they do not engage the child in hypothesis testing vis-à-vis that thought. Rather, as in other societies, Samoan caregivers prefer to elicit a more intelligible reformulation of the thought – asking "What did you say?" for example – or to terminate the topic.

Through speech-act responses of this sort, Samoan caregivers index mental states as uncertain objects but they do not index mental states as objects of explicit speculation. In this way, Samoan caregivers, like mainstream middle-class caregivers and caregivers the world over, socialize young children into their own particular epistemological per-spective.

Evidential particles marking uncertainty in Samoan are not dedi-cated to speculating about mental states of others; rather they are dedicated to speculating about reported events, actions, and condi-tions. Speculation in these cases addresses the accuracy of the report and poses possible alternative accounts. The use of these particles by caregivers and others, then, indexes for Samoan children (1) a disposi-tion of uncertainty (direct indexing of current context), (2) the speech act of speculation (indirect indexing of current context), and (3) the set of objects that speculation addresses (indirect indexing and recontextualization). Each of these contextual components is related to the other in the sense that the indexing of uncertainty evokes the speech act of speculation and the speech act of speculation evokes an object subjected to speculation.

INDEXICALITY, DISCOURSE, AND SOCIOCULTURAL KNOWLEDGE

The example of verbal speculation just discussed displays the relation between indexicality, discourse, and sociocultural knowledge advocated in this paper. As children in different communities gain competence in the discourse of speculation, they gain sociocultural knowledge as well. In each society, the norms, preferences, and expectations surrounding the activity of speculation are tied to local theories of knowledge. Children acquiring the discourse of speculation are at the same time acquiring these folk epistemologies. Through participation in the activity of speculation, children in different communities come to understand what constitutes knowledge, what a person can know and what a person cannot know, what are the legitimate linguistic paths to knowledge, who can travel these paths and who cannot.

This example is one of dozens that have been investigated in language socialization research. We could see the same relation between indexicality, discourse, and socialization if we turned to the discourse of evidentials in Japanese (Clancy, 1986; Cook, 1987; Seki, 1987), Kaluli (Schieffelin, 1986, in press), Athapaskan (Scollon, 1982) or Samoan (Ochs, 1988); or to the discourse of Kaluli turned-over talk (Feld & Schieffelin, 1982); or deictic verbs in Samoan (Platt, 1980, 1982, 1986); or narratives among white working class Americans (Heath, 1982, 1983); or problem-solving talk among the Kawara'ae (Watson-Gegeo & Gegeo, 1986). As all these examples illustrate, language and culture interface in the domain of discourse, particularly in the area of indexicality, and as such, linguistic knowledge and sociocultural knowledge organize each other.

Language socialization, linguistic relativity, chaos, and reorganization

THE SAPIR—WHORF HYPOTHESIS

The view of language socialization advocated here is in harmony with several other perspectives, particularly Sapir's well-known suggestion, at the heart of the Sapir—Whorf hypothesis, that "we see and hear and otherwise experience very largely as we do because the language habits of our community predispose certain choices of interpretation" (Mandelbaum, 1949:162). The Sapir—Whorf hypothesis has had rather a bad beating in the annals of social science. One of the problems has been a deterministic reading of this hypothesis, a reading grounded in other remarks by Sapir, which suggest that language does not just predispose but "pre-determines for us certain modes of observation and inter-

BIOLOGICAL/PSYCHOLOGICAL → MEMBERS' COMPETENCE
CONSTRAINTS ↓
MEMBERS' PERFORMANCE
↓
NOVICE'S COMPETENCE ↘

KEY:
→ DIRECTION OF IMPACT

Figure 7.3. Unidirectional models

pretation" (Mandelbaum, 1949:74). A second weak point has been the focus on grammar as the locus and source of culture.

I believe that the Sapir–Whorf hypothesis can be taken in other directions, that it can be applied to discourse and culture rather than grammar and culture. Knowledge of discourse – that is, knowledge of norms, preferences, and expectations relating language to context – is a part of our linguistic competence but at the same time such knowledge is part of our sociocultural competence. This means that children developing a knowledge of discourse are developing a knowledge of both language and culture.

The deterministic reading of the Sapir–Whorf hypothesis has been roundly criticized for over two decades in numerous psycholinguistic studies suggesting that indeed at least some features of worldview cut across languages and cultures and are the outcome of psychological and biological processes common to our species. The language socialization perspective taken here is opposed to linguistic determinism, but for reasons other than the arguments just mentioned. Such a strong interpretation of Sapir's statement gives the novice – here the child – little control in the creation of linguistic and cultural understandings. The child is locked into a grammatical system and a cultural system that that grammar encodes. Moreover, according to this interpretation, *members* are little changed by their communication with children. It is the child and not the member who is psychologically altered by their social and linguistic experience with one another.

THE "ACQUISITION" PROBLEM

The notion that novices have little impact on members is not unique to the so-called strong version of the Sapir–Whorf hypothesis. Indeed, many current theories of development, including theories of language development, consider the child as an individual apart from others; or, if social environment is considered, its relation to children is viewed either as input or as a constraint on development. Figure 7.3 illustrates this perspective.

In this perspective, the focus tends to be on how someone or something external to the child may affect the child rather than the converse. In most current views, the child *is* highly active, busily

MEMBERS' KNOWLEDGE

↕

JOINT ACTIVITY

↕

NOVICES KNOWLEDGE

KEY:

↔ DIRECTION OF IMPACT

Figure 7.4. Dialogical models.

constructing systems of knowledge (Piaget, 1926, 1952). *The child, however, is not viewed as actively modifying the systems of competent speaker/members.*

The use of the term "acquisition," as in "language acquisition," codifies this perspective. The terms "acquirer" and "acquisition" imply that little or no bidirectional transformation of knowledge and meaning takes place between members and novices. The notion of acquirer implies that there is a cognitive system out there, or perhaps I should say "up there," and the role and goal of the child/novice is to reach a level of competence in this system. The course of development is seen as a movement toward the adult model. *The adult model is not seen as being moved through interactions with the child,* as part of the process of negotiating reality. It must be that for certain areas of language and culture that the term "acquisition" is entirely appropriate. There are linguistic and sociocultural structures that are nonnegotiable and must be acquired. The term does not seem appropriate to *all* areas of knowledge, however, particularly not to all areas of discourse and sociocultural knowledge. Although I am in no position to say which areas of knowledge are relevant to this claim, I nonetheless suggest that *both* novices and more competent speaker/members transform their structures of knowledge and understanding vis-à-vis discourse and culture. Such a position is dialogical and allows for bidirectional change, as represented in Figure 7.4.

Figure 7.4 indicates that members' and novices' knowledge impacts joint or social activity, but at the same time that joint activity between novice and member impacts both members' and novices' tacit knowledge. In many cases, for example, members' understandings of family roles are modified through joint activities with infants and children. Despite the asymmetry of their relationship and their competence, children and caregivers may jointly construct these domains of knowledge. In this sense, caregivers may be socialized by the children they are socializing. Teachers, too, may be socialized by the students they are inducting into some area of expertise. Their understanding of the subject matter may be transformed by the responses and questions of students. Similarly, novices and members may impact each other's discourse knowledge. For example, in certain cases children and caregivers may impact how they are to speak to one another in the course

BIOLOGICAL/PSYCHOLOGICAL $\rightarrow$ MEMBERS' KNOWLEDGE

$\updownarrow$

JOINT ACTIVITY

$\updownarrow$

NOVICES' KNOWLEDGE

KEY:

$\rightarrow$/ $\updownarrow$ = DIRECTION OF IMPACT

Figure 7.5. Integrated socialization model.

of their communications with each other. And teachers and students may in certain cases impact each other's knowledge of classroom communication. Language socialization has the potential then to be bidirectional, even though asymmetry exists between novice and member.

One of the goals of language socialization research should be to assess the areas of members' language and culture that are more and less resistant to change from "below" (from novices' influence) and to determine the communicative procedures that either discourage or stimulate such bidirectional socialization. A socialization procedure that allows question asking by novices may change members' behavior and worldviews more than a socialization procedure that relies on members modeling and novices repeating some form of knowledge or behavior. Do certain societies more than others rely on particular forms of communication between member and novice? Do we find that certain forms of member–novice communication are linked to certain domains of knowledge within and across societies?

An integrated theory of language socialization, as represented in Figure 7.5, excludes neither unidirectional (i.e., acquisitional) nor bidirectional (i.e., dialogic) processes. This integrated perspective recognizes the social and psychological dominance of the member vis à vis the novice, and the immense impact of this fact on novices' understanding of the world. This perspective also recognizes psychological and biological constraints on the thought and behavior. At the same time, our model allows for members' knowledge to be impacted by novices through the medium of social activity and for social activity to alter biological and psychological parameters over evolutionary time. In this model, both members and novices are active, interactive, and vulnerable.

LANGUAGE SOCIALIZATION AND CHAOS THEORY

This view of language socialization is compatible with current scientific theories – such as chaos theory proposed by the physicist Prigogine – that envision systems as open-ended, active, and probabilistic. Prigogine and Stenzers (1984) suggest, first, that matter is active and inherently unstable. This idea parallels our idea that both novice and knowing member are agents of change – no participant in a socializing interaction is passive. Prigogine further states that the active nature of matter may lead to irregular behavior, that is, to disorder. Although previous scientific paradigms looked on such disorder as detrimental (codified in the term "entropy"), Prigogine suggests that such disorder may lead to new dynamic states. A normal pattern is for matter to assume a new order and stability following this state of instability or chaos. Although I am not suggesting that social relationships are inherently chaotic, I propose that both the member and novice are vulnerable to change and that communication between them may lead to what Prigogine and others call "far from equilibrium" conditions for both, which in turn lead to new organizations of knowledge for both. Questions by novices to members may reorder the thinking of both, despite their differences in knowledge and power. In other words, the relation between novice and member is not static and the direction of change is not always unilateral.

LANGUAGE SOCIALIZATION AND ACTIVITY-CENTERED SOCIAL SCIENCE

Within the social sciences, this view of language socialization is compatible with the set of theories that are performance or activity based and critical of structuralist views that treat activity exclusively as a product of structure. These activity-based approaches include the sociological theories of Bourdieu (1977) and Giddens (1979, 1984) and the psychological theories of Vygotsky (1962, 1978; cf. Wertsch, 1985), Leontyev (1981) and others within a sociohistorical perspective (Griffin & Cole, 1984; Laboratory of Comparative Human Cognition, 1983). Within their own paradigms, each theory emphasizes the creative and generative dimensions of social activity or "practice," to use the term preferred by Bourdieu. Each takes into account the role of unintended consequences of social activity in restructuring mind and society. At the same time, each recognizes that psychological and social structures organize social activity. Structures are thus the source and the outcome of social behavior. These ideas parallel the notion that both linguistic and sociocultural knowledge organizes social activity and that such knowledge is the outcome of social activity. In this approach, linguistic and sociocultural knowledge of both novice and member is vulnerable and can be transformed through social activity.

Concluding remarks

Socialization is a process whereby children or other novices, together with members, come to understand and participate meaningfully in society. Language behavior socializes and it carries out this function largely (although not exclusively) through its indexical structures. The scope of indexicality is vast but not unanalyzable. Contexts are systematically constituted through single indexes or through the collocation of indexes, either directly or indirectly, and either retrospectively, prospectively, or immediately. Members and novices use language in these ways to create contexts of understanding for one another. The dialogic potential of language socialization suggests that linguistic and sociocultural change over historical time may be motivated from below, from the influence of the novice, as well as from other sources. Future research on the impact of immigrant speakers, novice computer users, women in the workplace, male caregivers, and other socialization situations is needed to bear out the reasonableness and scope of this claim. I urge readers to support if not pursue interdisciplinary scholarship so that this and other complex and far-reaching questions regarding language, mind, and society can be responsibly explored.

References

Albert, E. 1972. Cultural patterning of speech behavior in Burundi. In J. Gumperz & D. Hymes (Eds.), *Directions in sociolinguistics* (pp. 72–105). New York: Holt, Rinehart & Winston.

Andersen, E. 1977. Learning how to speak with style. Unpublished Ph.D. dissertation, Stanford University.

Bakhtin, M. 1981. *The dialogic imagination* (M. Holquist, Ed.). Austin: University of Texas Press.

Bateson, G. 1972. *Steps to an ecology of mind.* New York: Ballantine Books.

Bernstein, B. 1972. A sociolinguistic approach to socialization, with some reference to educability. In J. Gumperz & D. Hymes (Eds.), *Directions in sociolinguistics* (pp. 465–497). New York: Holt, Rinehart & Winston.

Besnier, N. In press-a. Reported speech and affect on Nukulaelae. In J. H. Hill & J. Irvine (Eds.), *Responsibility and evidence in oral discourse.* Cambridge: Cambridge University Press.

In press-b. Conflict management, gossip and affective meaning on Nukulaelae. In K. Watson-Gegeo & G. White (Eds.), *Disentangling: The discourse of conflict and therapy in Pacific cultures.* New Brunswick, NJ: Rutgers University Press.

Biber, D. 1986. Spoken and written textual dimensions in English. *Language* 62:2:384–414.

Biber, D., & Finegan, E. In press. Adverbials as markers of stance: A multivariate approach. *Discourse Processes.*

Bourdieu, P. 1977. *Outline of a theory of practice.* Cambridge: Cambridge University Press.

Briggs, C. 1986. *Learning how to ask.* Cambridge: Cambridge University Press.

Cicourel, A. 1973. *Cognitive sociology.* Harmondsworth, England: Penguin Books.

Clancy, P. 1986. The acquisition of Japanese. In D. Slobin (Ed.), *The cross-linguistic study of language acquisition.* Hillsdale, NJ: Lawrence Erlbaum.

Cole, M. 1985. The zone of proximal development: Where culture and cognition create each other. In J. Wertsch (Ed.), *Culture, communication and cognition: Vygotskian perspectives* (pp. 146–161). Cambridge: Cambridge University Press.

Cook, H. 1987. Social voice and individual voice in Japanese: The particle NO and bare verbs. Ms., University of Southern California.

Demuth, C. 1986. Prompting routines in the language socialization of Bosotho children. In B. Schieffelin & E. Ochs (Eds.), *Language socialization across cultures* (pp. 51–78). Cambridge: Cambridge University Press.

Duranti, A., & Ochs, E. 1986. Literacy instruction in a Samoan village. In B. Schieffelin & P. Gilmore (Eds.), *The acquisition of literacy: Ethnographic perspectives. Advances in discourse processes*, vol. 21. Norwood, NJ: Ablex.

Eisenberg, A. 1986. Teasing: verbal play in two Mexican homes. In B. Schieffelin & E. Ochs (Eds.), *Language socialization across cultures* (pp. 182–198). Cambridge: Cambridge University Press.

Feld, S., & Schieffelin, B. 1982. Hard talk: A functional basis for Kaluli discourse. In D. Tannen (Ed.), *Analyzing discourse: Text and talk. Georgetown University round table on languages and linguistics 1981* (pp. 350–370). Washington, DC: Georgetown University Press.

Ferguson, C. 1977. Baby talk as a simplified register. In C. Snow & C. Ferguson (Eds.), *Talking to children* (pp. 219–237). Cambridge: Cambridge University Press.

Geertz, C. 1973. *The interpretation of cultures*. New York: Basic Books.

Giddens, A. 1979. *Central problems in social theory: Action, structure and contradiction in social analysis*. Berkeley and Los Angeles: University of California press.

1984. *The constitution of society*. Berkeley and Los Angeles: University of California press.

Griffin, P., and Cole, M. 1984. Current activity for the future: The zo-ped. in B. Rogoff & J. Wertsch (Eds.), *Children's learning in the "zone of proximal development." In New Directions for Child Development*. San Francisco: Jossey-Bass.

Haviland, J. (In press). "Sure, sure": Evidence and affect. In E. Ochs (Ed.), *The pragmatics of affect*. Special Issue. *Text*.

Heath, S. 1982. What no bedtime story means: Narrative skills at home and school. *Language in Society 11*:49–77.

1983. *Ways with words: Language, life and work in communities and classrooms*. Cambridge: Cambridge University Press.

Jakobson, R. 1960. Concluding statement: linguistics and poetics. In T. Sebeok (Ed.), *Style in language* (pp. 350–373). Cambridge, MA: MIT Press.

Keenan (Ochs), E., & Schieffelin, B. 1976. Topic as a discourse notion: A study of topic in the conversations of children and adults. In C. Li (Ed.), *Subject and topic* (pp. 335–385). New York: Acedemic Press.

Laboratory of Comparative Human Cognition. 1983. Culture and cognitive development. In W. Kessen (Ed.), *Mussen's handbook of child psychology*, 4th ed., vol. 1. New York: Wiley.

Labov, W. 1984. Intensity. In D. Schiffrin (Ed.), *Meaning, form, and use in context: Linguistic applications. Georgetown round table on languages and linguistics: Meaning, form, and use in context: Linguistic applications* (pp. 43–70). Washington, DC: Georgetown University Press.

Leontyev, A. N. 1981. *Problems of the development of the mind*. Moscow: Progress.

Lyons, J. 1977. *Semantics*, vols. 1 & 2. Cambridge: Cambridge University Press.

Mandelbaum, D. G. (Ed.). 1949. *Selected writings of Edward Sapir.* Berkeley/ Los Angeles: University of California Press.

Merton, R. 1949. *Social theory and social structure.* New York: Free Press.

Miller, P. 1982. *Amy, Wendy and Beth: Learning language in south Baltimore.* Austin: University of Texas Press.

1986. Teasing as language socialization and verbal play in a white working-class community. In B. Schieffelin & E. Ochs (Eds.), *Language socialization across cultures* (pp. 199–211). Cambridge: Cambridge University Press.

Morris, C. W. 1946. *Signification and significance.* Cambridge, MA: MIT Press.

Much, N., & Shweder, R. A. 1978. Speaking of rules: The analysis of culture in breach. In W. Damon (Ed.), *Moral development.* San Francisco, CA: Jossey-Bass.

Ochs, E. 1982a. Talking to children in Western Samoa. *Language in Society* *11*:77–104.

1982b. Ergativity and word order in Samoan child language: A sociolinguistic study. *Language 58*:646–671.

1988. *Culture and language development: Language acquisition and language socialization in a Samoan village.* Cambridge: Cambridge University Press.

Ochs, E., & Schieffelin, B. 1984. Language acquisition and socialization: Three developmental stories. In R. Shweder & R. LeVine (Eds.), *Culture theory: Essays in mind, self, and emotion* (pp. 276–320). Cambridge: Cambridge University Press.

In press. Language has a heart. In *Text.*

Ortner, S., & Whitehead, H. 1981. *Sexual meanings: The cultural construction of gender and sexuality.* Cambridge: Cambridge University Press.

Parsons, T. 1937. *The structure of social action.* New York: Free Press.

1951. *The social system.* Glencoe, IL: Free Press.

Peirce, C. 1931–1958. *Collected papers,* vols. 1–8 (C. Hartshorne & P. Weiss, eds.). Cambridge, MA: Harvard University Press.

Piaget, J. 1926. *The language and thought of the child.* London: Routledge & Kegan Paul.

1952. *The origins of intelligence in children.* New York: Norton.

Platt, M. 1980. The acquisition of "come," "give," and "bring" by Samoan children. *Papers and Reports in Child Language Development,* No. 19. Stanford, CA: Stanford University.

1982. Social and semantic dimensions of deictic verbs and particles in Samoan child language. Unpublished Ph.D. dissertation, University of Southern California.

1986. Social norms and lexical acquisition: A study of deictic verbs in Samoan child language. In B. Schieffelin & E. Ochs (Eds.), *Language socialization across cultures* (pp. 127–151). Cambridge: Cambridge University Press.

Prigogine, I., & Stengers, I. 1984. *Order out of chaos.* New York: Bantam.

Sapir, Edward. 1924. Culture, genuine and spurious. *American Journal of Sociology 29*:401–492.

Schieffelin, B. 1979. How Kaluli children learn what to say, what to do, and how to feel: An ethnographic study of the development of communicative competence. Unpublished Ph.D. dissertation, Columbia University.

1986. Teasing and shaming in Kaluli children's interactions. In B. Schieffelin & E. Ochs (Eds.), *Language socialization across cultures*. Cambridge: Cambridge University Press.

In press. How Kaluli children learn what to say, what to do, and how to feel. Cambridge: Cambridge University Press.

Schieffelin, B., & Ochs, E. 1986a. Language socialization. In B. Siegel (Ed.), *Annual Review of Anthropology*. Palo Alto, CA: Annual Reviews.

1986b. *Language socialization across cultures*. Cambridge: Cambridge University Press.

Scollon, S. 1982. Reality set, socialization and linguistic convergence. Unpublished Ph.D. dissertation, University of Hawaii, Honolulu.

Seki, M. 1987. Final particles in the speech of 2-year-old Japanese children and their mothers. Ms., University of Southern California.

Silverstein, M. 1976. Shifters, linguistic categories, and cultural description. In K. Basso & H. Selby (Eds.), *Meaning in anthropology* (pp. 11–55). Albuquerque: University of New Mexico Press.

Uyeno, T. 1971. A study of Japanese modality: A performative analysis of sentence particles. Unpublished doctoral dissertation, University of Michigan, Ann Arbor.

Vygotsky, L. S. 1962. *Thought and language*. Cambridge, MA: MIT Press.

1978. *Mind in society: The development of higher psychological processes*, M. Cole, V. John-Steiner, S. Scribner, & E. Souberman (Eds.). Cambridge, MA: Harvard University Press.

Watson-Gegeo, K., and Gegeo, D. 1986. Calling out and repeating routines in Kwara'ae children's language socialization. In B. Schieffelin & E. Ochs (Eds.), *Language socialization across cultures* (pp. 17–50). Cambridge: Cambridge University Press.

Wentworth, W. M. 1980. *Context and understanding*. New York: Elsevier.

Wertsch, J. 1985. *Vygotsky and the social formation of mind*. Cambridge, MA: Harvard University Press.

8
The culture of acquisition and the practice of understanding

Jean Lave

When I began research on craft apprenticeship among Vai and Gola tailors in Liberia 15 years ago, the community of scholars who worked on cross-cultural comparative studies of education and cognitive development had definite opinions about "informal education." Learning through apprenticeship was assumed to be concrete, context-embedded, intuitive, limited in the scope of its application, mechanical, rote, imitative, not creative or innovative – and out of date. Views have changed. There is considerable interest, currently, in situated learning, embodied knowledge, and the mutual constitution of the person and the lived-in world. The math-learning research community, which certainly claims a stake in debates about crucial forms of thinking and knowing, has begun to explore apprenticeship learning, or "the new cognitive apprenticeship." By this they mean that it might be possible to learn math by doing what mathematicians *do*, by engaging in the structure-finding activities and mathematical argumentation typical of good mathematical practice (e.g., Brown, Collins, and Newman, in press; Schoenfeld, 1985). They emphasize the situated character of problem-solving activity while focusing on learning in doing. There is agreement, then, about the situated character of learning and knowing in apprenticeship, while the significance of this fact has become subject to quite different valuation over time. Indeed, those same math-learning researchers are likely to describe conventional school math learning as the all too mechanical transmission of a collection of facts to be learned by rote, a process devoid of creative contributions by the learner. Current critical concerns about math learning in school sound very much like descriptions of informal learning some years ago.

There are several puzzles to be addressed here: How are we to account for the change over time in the significance attributed to apprenticeship, while no one disputes its situated character? Why talk

I want to thank Rick Shweder and Jim Stigler, the organizers of the Symposium on Children's Lives in Cultural Context (November 1987), for the opportunity to participate in the symposium and to write this essay. The essay was prepared during my stay as a visiting scholar at the Institute for Research on Learning, Palo Alto, CA.

about apprenticeship at all – after all, this is not the feudal era, and the typical contemporary child is not engaged in learning a craft. How can studies of apprenticeship and adult math practice help us understand what's wrong with the way children learn math in school?

The answers may be sought through discussion of two theories of learning, characterized as "the culture of acquisition" and "understanding in practice." The first theory proposes that learning is a naturally occurring, specific kind of cognitive functioning, quite separate from engagement in doing something. Educational institutions such as schools are assumed to function by specializing in learning. Teachers and curricula concentrated on teaching make it possible to intensify learning processes and to make explicit and specific the content to be learned. School students are considered to differ only by being better or worse at "getting it."

"The culture of acquisition" also refers to the practice of social scientists who think that culture *is* "something to be acquired." This view is based on contemporary assumptions about culture as an accumulation of factual knowledge (e.g., D'Andrade, 1981; Romney, Weller, and Batchelder, 1986). There is a further assumption that cognitive benefits follow only when the process of learning is removed from the fields in which what is learned is to be applied. This belief underlies standard distinctions between formal and informal learning, so-called context-free and context-embedded learning, or logical and intuitive understanding. Schooling is viewed as the institutional site for decontextualizing knowledge so that, abstracted, it may become general and hence generalizable, and therefore transferable to situations of use in the "real" world. Bartlett (1958) talks about freeing learners from the shackles of immediate time and place. This view is reflected in the removal of children's activities into the school, the transmission of information verbally and "from the top down," and tests as the measure of knowledge. Another major theme in this approach is the conception of the teaching/learning process as one of cultural *transmission*. This implies that culture *is* a body of knowledge to be transmitted, that there is no learning without teaching, and that what is taught is what will be learned (if it gets learned).

Recent research on learning has turned to apprenticeship for theoretical inspiration because it offers a shorthand way of "saying no" to the theoretical position of "the culture of acquisition." Those interested in an apprenticeship approach, or more generally in theories of learning-in-practice, assume that processes of learning and understanding are socially and culturally constituted, and that what is to be learned is integrally implicated in the forms in which it is appropriated, so that, for example, *how* math is learned depends on its being *math* that is learned, and how math is learned in school depends on its being learned *there*. Apprenticeship forms of learning are likely to be based on assumptions that knowing, thinking, and understanding are generated in practice, in situations whose specific characteristics are part of practice as it unfolds. The gulf in time, setting, and activity assumed to separate school learning from the life for which it is "preparation" is neither reflected nor generated in the process by which apprentices gradually come to be master practitioners. Apprentices learn to think, argue, act, and interact in increasingly knowledgeable ways, with people who do something well, by doing it with them as legitimate, peripheral participants.

None of the researchers who have explored this approach is suggesting that it would be a good idea, or even possible, to borrow some form of craft apprenticeship from China or medieval Europe, or for that matter from Liberia in the 1970s, and transplant it into contemporary school classrooms. Researchers who have recently taken up the idea of "apprenticeship learning" have either drawn on their common sense notions about what "apprenticeship" might mean (e.g., Brown, Collins, & Newman, in press), or on some particular, historically/ culturally situated instance of craft apprenticeship that appears to have theoretically relevant characteristics (e.g., Lave, n.d.). They are interested in apprenticeship not because it offers a prize to capture, bring home, and install in schools, but because scenarios of apprenticeship learning are useful to "think with."

In sum, there is a theoretical tradition, part of Western history, institutionalized in Western schooling, in which teaching/transmission is considered to be primary and prior to learning/internalizing culture. What is transmitted is assumed to be received in an unproblematic fashion, while processes of instruction and learning are assumed to be general and independent of what is to be learned. Let's call this a functionalist theory and note that it offers explanations of how school works and of what is the matter when it doesn't work, and that it is embedded in a theory about relations between society and the individuals who pass through and are socialized into it. This theory also treats socialization or cultural transmission as the central mechanism for the reproduction of social systems.

There are comparable things to be said about learning, schooling, and sociocultural order subsumed in a theory of situated practice (Lave, 1988). But this is not a familiar theoretical position, and an extended example may provide opportunities to work out some of its concepts in immediate terms. A more general theoretical description appears later in the chapter. Suffice it for the moment to mention some of the theorists who have considered issues concerning the nature of practice – Marx ([1887] 1957), Bourdieu (1977), Giddens (1979, 1984), and Sahlins (1976), among others, and the new activity theorists (e.g., Engestrom, 1987; Davydov & Radzikhovskii, 1985). Their theories take as crucial the integral nature of relations between persons acting (including thinking and learning) and the social world, and between the form and content of learning-in-practice. The discussion that follows is focused on what learning-in-practice might mean. Analytic resources developed in the studies of craft apprenticeship and dieting cooks may then be brought to bear on the analysis of learning in school as an everyday practice.[1]

The curriculum of tailors' apprenticeship

My field research with the tailors took place during five field trips to Monrovia between 1973 and 1978 (Lave, n.d.). At that time, a number of Vai and Gola tailors clustered their wood, dirt-floored, tin-roofed tailor shops along a narrow path at the edge of the river bordering the city's commercial district. Tailors' Alley sheltered 120 master tailors and as many treadle sewing machines in 20 shops. With apprentices, the shops had a working population of about 250 men. No women worked as tailors there. (However, women do tailor clothes for sale, learning and working in their homes.) There were several masters present in each shop, visibly doing what masters do – each ran a business, tailored clothes, and supervised apprentices. Apprenticeship, averaging five years, involved a sustained, rich structure of opportunities to observe masters, journeymen, and other apprentices at work; to observe frequently the full process of producing garments; and, of course, to observe the finished products.

The tailors made clothes for the poorest segment of the population, and their specialty was inexpensive, ready-to-wear men's trousers. But they made other kinds of garments as well. Indeed, in the course of research in Tailors' Alley I asked many times what an apprentice needed to learn in order to become a master tailor. Repeatedly the response was an inventory of garments: hats, children's underwear, short trousers, long trousers, Vai shirts, sport shirts, Muslim prayer gowns, women's dresses, and Higher Heights suits (the latter are two-piece men's suits with elaborately tailored, short-sleeved jackets). When I first discovered that this was to be the most common response to my inquiries, it appeared to be a ritualistic litany, a list without internal form. Gradually it became clear that the list of garment types in fact encoded complex, intertwined forms of order integral to the process of becoming a master tailor. The tailors engaged in dressing the major social identities of Liberian society. Apprentices first learn to make hats and drawers, informal and intimate garments for children. They move on to more external, formal garments, ending with the Higher Heights suit. Along the way they learn to create the material markers of gender, religion, age, and politics.

The organization of the process of apprenticeship is not confined to the level of whole garments. The earliest steps in the process involve learning to sew by hand, to sew with the treadle sewing machine, and to press clothes. Subtract these from the corpus of tailoring knowledge and the apprentice must learn how to cut out and sew each garment. Learning processes do not merely reproduce the sequence of production processes. In fact, production steps are reversed, as apprentices begin by learning the finishing stages of producing a garment, go on to learn to sew it, and only later learn to cut it out. This pattern regularly subdivides the learning process for each new type of garment. Reversing production steps has the effect of focusing the apprentices' attention first on the broad outlines of garment construction as they handle garments while attaching buttons and hemming cuffs. Next, sewing turns their attention to the logic (order, orientation) by which different pieces are sewn together, which in turn explains why they are cut out as they are. Each step offers the unstated opportunity to consider how the previous step contributes to the present one. In addition, this ordering minimizes experiences of failure and especially of serious failure (errors in sewing may be reversed; those made while cutting out are more often irrevocable).

There is one further level of organization to the curriculum of tailoring. The learning of each operation is subdivided into phases that I have dubbed "way in" and "practice." "Way in" refers to the period of observation and attempts to construct a first approximation of the garment. An apprentice watches masters and advanced apprentices until he thinks he understands how to sew (or cut out) a garment, then waits until the shop is closed and the masters have gone home before trying to make it. Once an apprentice produces a first garment that has all the parts correctly oriented in relation to each other, with all the necessary construction steps, he moves on to the phase of practice in which he makes many of the same item until he can do so at high speed, and well. The practice phase is carried out in a particular way: Apprentices reproduce a production segment from beginning to end (doing what masters do), although they might be more skilled at carrying out some steps in the process than others. Whole-activity practice is viewed as more important in long-term mastery than is the consistent, correct execution of decomposed parts of the process.

There are no formal tests in tailors' apprenticeship to screen out learners at any stage, and this reflects an assumption that equal accomplishment is possible and expected for all learners. Apprentices are rarely praised or blamed, yet they know when they have made mistakes, and they have rich means of gauging their own skill. They can decide for themselves whether the clothes they make are good enough to sell and what price to set, and they discover how much customers are willing to pay for their efforts compared with garments made by other tailors.

A high percentage of apprentices become masters (85% of those I observed over a period of years). Those who quit do so, with rare exceptions, for reasons extraneous to the process of learning. And, it might be added, masters do not distinguish greater or lesser mastery among themselves. To be a master tailor implies mastery of the curriculum of tailoring. This is no mechanical reproduction of a traditional repertoire – the tailors generate new styles and procedures for making clothes and expect innovation to be part of their "craft."

This form of craft apprenticeship has a greater rate of successful completion than does contemporary schooling, which is a good reason to give it closer study. But there are crucial differences between apprenticeship and schooling that argue against direct adoption of apprenticeship forms of learning in classrooms. One important feature of the tailors' apprenticeship is that the increasing skill of the apprentice is of direct value to masters as well as to their apprentices. Even hemming cuffs helps the master to produce trousers for sale more efficiently; by the time the apprentice can construct trousers skillfully he can contribute to the master's output in a much more substantial way. Apprentices have the privilege of learning from *masters*, in two senses – masters have truly mastered their craft, for one thing, and they are also highly respected, which gives value to the project of learning to be "like them." Apprentices know from the beginning that when they complete apprenticeship there will be a legitimate field for the practice of tailoring in which they are already peripheral participants.

In sum, the tailors' form of education seems remarkably successful – apprentices learn a substantial trade without being taught, in practice. This educational form does not involve separation of learning from practice. "Motivation" is not a problem. Rewards appear to be intrinsic. People spend a lot of time doing what they are learning and vice versa. The process has order to it – there is a multilevel curriculum. The order does not depend much on intentional pedagogical activities by teachers/masters. Learners know clearly what the curriculum is, and it organizes the basic outlines of their everyday practice but does not specify what they should do or precisely how to do it.

Two points may be made about this analysis in anticipation of the exploration of math-learning practice in a school setting. The curriculum of tailoring differs sharply in intentions and organization from school curricula. The curriculum of tailoring is more a set of landmarks *for* learners than specific procedures to be taught *to* learners. It shapes opportunities for tailoring activity and hence the processes of learning to tailor. We might consider the possibility that in school, the prescriptive curriculum embodied in teachers' teaching plans, specific lesson plans, and textbook assignments creates unintended opportunities to learn math in practice. Teaching may have powerful indirect effects on math learning through the ways it shapes possibilities for developing a math practice.

If there are systematic differences between the organization of what children are intended to learn and what in fact they learn, then the question of what motivates activity – what gives it meaning and impels people to act – looks increasingly important. The question rarely surfaces in discussions of learning in school where demands for compliance mask other means by which learners fashion meaning in action. It is difficult, indeed, to see *why* people do what they do in any situation (including craft apprenticeship) that is organized in multiple, pervasive ways to enable them to do it. In the supermarket and in the kitchen people have to generate math problems if they are going to "have a problem," and if they "have" problems it can be said that they "own" those problems themselves. It may be easier, then, to work out what is meant by problems and problem-solving activity, and what motivates problem solving in situations of everyday practice. The study of math learning in the kitchen, while new Weight Watchers learn how to manage a new diet, offers such an opportunity.

Dilemmas and problems: learning math as a Weight Watcher

The Weight Watchers study (de la Rocha, 1986) explored the activities of nine new members of the dieting program as they incorporated new measurement practices into meal preparation over a period of weeks. Because of its emphasis on meticulous control of portions of food consumed, this particular diet program promised to generate many opportunities for calculation in the kitchen, and we hoped to see new math skills coming into existence in a setting far removed from school (Lave, 1988). The Weight Watchers study involved intensive interviewing, including an exploration of the participants' biographies as dieters. The participants were observed repeatedly as they prepared meals in their kitchens, and at the end of the six-week observation period they took part in a variety of arithmetic-testing activities. The participants also kept diaries of all food items they consumed each day. We conducted interviews with the food diaries in hand about the process of dieting, how each person learned the Weight Watchers' system of food portion control, and the specific procedures used in weighing and measuring each item.

There was lots of measuring and calculating activity to be observed. All dieters calculated portion sizes for half the food items they prepared, on average, across the six weeks. But this pattern requires qualification in two respects. Some dieters calculated considerably more often than others. And there was much more measurement and calculation going on as the dieters began the new program than was to be observed after six weeks. I shall try to account for both of these points. Second, comparisons of individuals' in situ success in solving math problems with their success on mathematically isomorphic problems in a test situation produced the result that the same problems were solved consistently more successfully in other settings than scholastic ones. All of the participants demonstrated the level of success (65–70%) on formal arithmetic tests characteristic of market vendors, dairy workers, and grocery shoppers in closely related research studies (cited later in this chapter). Third, in general, the problematic quantitative relations that troubled the cooks were not as difficult arithmetically as the math at which they were successful on the math tests. Formal test results suggested that scholastic math "expertise" did not constrain the dieters' math activities in their kitchens. Fourth, having carefully coded the measuring and calculating activities involved in the preparation of the hundreds of food items by the dieting cooks, de la Rocha showed that none of the following factors that might plausibly account for differences between the cooks' measuring patterns was useful in doing so. Things that *didn't* explain their uses of arithmetic included their age, the number of children living at home, the dieters' years of education, the amount of weight they hoped to lose, the amount of weight they had already lost, and their scores on the arithmetic tests.

All of these factors that might have led to lower or higher incentives to employ school math in the kitchen had to be discarded. Further, the Weight Watchers organization did not treat the preparation of meals as a series of lessons, homework assignments, or occasions for formal arithmetic problem solving. We could not easily invoke school math knowledge, incentives to use it, nor formal demands for math problem solving in order to account for the observed patterns of variation. There was reason to wonder why the dieting cooks bothered to calculate at all, what led them to calculate on some occasions but not others, and what led them to view some events as involving math *problems*. These may be reduced to one central question: Wherein lies the motivation for generating and solving problems in settings where there are not set tasks imposed on the problem solver?

De la Rocha's analysis of the dieters' accounts of their lives and diets offers considerable insight into the dilemmas that impel dieters to engage in math problem solving. She found it possible to work out, in a series of steps, an answer to the question about why dieters engage in math in the kitchen. The analysis begins with Western culture writ large. The abundance of food products in the United States and Americans' fascination with the self-mastery reflected in a slim physique have provoked an obsession with body weight and its control. For most plagued by it, excessive weight is a blight on the image of the body and the self. Although it can be remediated by dieting, this is accomplished with great difficulty and often for only brief intervals. In translating the determination to lose weight into practical action, the dieter faces the dilemma of, on the one hand, a strong desire to alter the distortions of the body that come with being overweight, and on the other, cravings for the solace and pleasure of food. Dieting is a long process that requires not just one decision, but a continual struggle in which the question of self-denial arises many times each day over many months and even years. Inconsistent commitment leads to backsliding or the end of a diet cycle and resulting feelings of failure and depression. From interviews about their history as dieters, it appeared that participants in the project had relatively long-term, consistent resolutions to these dieting dilemmas. Some espoused the view that meticulous control of food portions was the way to control weight. Others expressed their approach as "so long as you feel hungry you must be losing weight." Each of them put their resolution to these dilemmas into practice: Long-term dieting styles clearly shaped measurement activity differently. Earlier I pointed out that as a group the dieters measured half of the food items they prepared. But methodical dieters used arithmetic measurement and calculation techniques on 61% of the food items they recorded in their food diaries, whereas the "go hungry" dieters measured only 26%.

Gaining control over food intake or over decisions not to eat, is the central dilemma of dieting. But attempts to control food portions come into conflict with other concerns of the dieters: The more elaborate the steps to gain control of quantity, the greater the conflict with getting food efficiently on the table. While the dieter calculates, the family and the evening meal wait. The conflict between dieting rules and efficient food handling appeared most directly to generate the dieters' arithmetic "problems" and clearly shaped the long-term shift from more to less calculation over time.[2] All the dieters responded to this conflict in two ways, by generating reusable solutions to recurring math problems, and by finding ways to *enact* solutions as part of ongoing activity. One simple example may illustrate both. Initially, to find the correct serving size for a glass of milk, the dieter had to look up the correct amount in the Weight Watchers' manual; get out a measuring cup, a drinking glass, and the carton of milk; pour the milk into the measuring cup; pour the milk from the measuring cup into the glass; wash the measuring cup and later the glass. This procedure was shortly transformed into get out glass and milk and pour milk into the glass up to just below the circle of blue flowers. This is one among a myriad of examples, for the cooks invented literally hundreds of units of measurement and procedures for generating accurate portions (de la Rocha, 1986). In the process they made it possible to do less and less measurement and calculation over time.

There are two other points to be made briefly about the generation of problems in conflict and their resolution in ongoing activity. First, it is the specific character of action-impelling conflicts that generally determines which of several problems lurking in a situation needs to be solved. Indeed, the history and structure of particular activity-motivating conflicts gives shape and meaning to what comes to constitute "the problem." Second, in school-like settings, where closed-puzzle problem solving is common, the solution to a problem is assumed to mark the endpoint of activity. But in other activities (re)solutions to math problems generate conflict in ongoing activity as often as they resolve it. There is a good example in which the dieters were asked to make peanut butter sandwiches according to Weight Watchers' guidelines. Having made the necessary calculation correctly (in nine unique ways), the cooks discovered a new problem. As a result of their calculations they now had a grossly overburdened slice of bread. Each responded with a protest that it was too much peanut butter and promptly scraped some off, in spite of knowing that the amount was (arithmetically) correct.

For the cooks, math problem solving is not an end in itself; procedures involving quantitative relations in the kitchen are given shape and meaning by the dilemmas that motivate activity; school math knowledge does not constrain the structure of their quantitative activity, and it does not specify what shall constitute math problems. It may serve as an initial resource but not in its form as remembered-school-procedure so much as in an embodied form in tables in kitchen manuals and in kitchen tools. (School algorithmic math is more likely to circulate through the printed page and utensils than through the heads of people cooking meals.) Algorithmic math gets in the way when the person engaged in activity does not need a formal proxy for quantities and their relations, because those quantities and relations are directly at hand.

One reflection of the belief that it is crucial to separate learning from practice and therefore schooling from the everyday world, is a widespread assumption that it is the responsibility of schooling to *replace* the (presumably) faulty and inefficient mathematical knowledge acquired by people in the real world. But research on everyday math, by Scribner (Scribner & Fahrmeier, 1982; Scribner, 1984), de la Rocha (1986), Carraher, Carraher, and Schliemann (1982, 1983), Carraher and Schliemann (1982), Acioly and Schliemann (1985), Murtaugh (1985a, 1985b), Lave, Murtaugh, and de la Rocha (1984) and Lave (1988) challenges the view that school is the central source of everyday math practice. In the situations explored here math is dilemma driven, as the study of Weight Watchers shows vividly. A prerequisite for working on a math problem is "owning" the problem – a felt dilemma and a ballpark sense of its solution. Otherwise it is not a problem but only a constraint. When people own problems about quantities and their relations, they act to relate them in ways that make sense within ongoing activity. They do not "pop out" to represent them in mathematical formulas, which furnish only an impoverished representation when the world is available as a "model" of itself. This research suggests that quantitative relations are assembled inventively and effectively in everyday situations, independently of problem solvers' past school biographies.

It is now possible to distinguish two conceptual developments from the particularities of apprenticeship and dieting. In both cases learners encounter opportunities to develop a practice derived from the multiple and varied (but not infinitely varied) circumstances of their activity day by day. These self-and-other, and activity-organized opportunities for activity might be called a learning curriculum (as opposed to a teaching curriculum). And second, activity is dilemma-motivated: Practice will be so shaped. It is important, therefore, to inquire into the activity-motivating aspects of situations as these are experienced by learners if we are to discover what they are coming to understand in practice.

In making these claims I am leading up to the assertion that what children engage in day by day in school *is* an everyday practice, like dieting for adults, and learning to tailor for apprentices in Tailors' Alley. Several questions follow. How is learning-in-practice given order in school? What is the learning curriculum for this practice? How does the teaching curriculum affect the learning curriculum? What motivates children, in both senses, to solve math problems in schools? Children's typical classroom math understanding has been described by math-learning researchers over the last 10 years in searching and penetrating ways. If we begin with these descriptions of what appears to be the effects of a common learning curriculum of primary school mathematics, perhaps we can account for faulty math learning in school *as* a matter of learning-in-practice.

As soon as we examine this body of math-learning research closely, the negative side of the "culture of acquisition" becomes apparent, for this work implicates the functional theory of learning-at-a-distance in children's learning difficulties. Thus, in spite of generally held beliefs that powerful learning must occur "out of context" for use in other situations, and that "out-of-context" learning should lead to abstraction, generalization, mental exercise, transferable knowledge, and cognitive efficacy in the rest of life, it is also the case that schooling is a compartmentalized and at the same time pervasive institutional setting of children's everyday lives. What is learned "out of context" is in danger of being suspended in vacuo. This danger is reflected in the concerns of learning researchers that everyday life provides too little relevant experience, or erroneous experience, or children actively construct erroneous concepts out of it, or the connection between what is taught and intuitive everyday experience is too weak (e.g., Schoenfeld, 1987, in press; Resnick, 1986; Brown et al., in press). School alumni also maintain a version of this diagnosis of their encounters with math in school. Whether discussing their uses of math in the supermarket (Lave et al., 1984), or discussing home heating use or electric bills (Kempton, personal communication) they inevitably deny that they engage in "real math" and disclaim the value of their everyday math practice in "real life." In sum, it appears that the academic and educational establishments are caught in a serious dilemma concerning the role of distance from experience in strengthening and at the same time weakening learning. And this in turn strongly shapes the sociocultural form of teaching and learning in school.

Resnick (1986) sums up the extensive body of research on what children do and don't learn about math in school in the following way. First, there is good evidence that learners learn actively, and through construction and invention of mathematical procedures. But there is no guarantee that in so doing learners will understand mathematical principles. In fact, by Resnick's assessment, school learners (a) have reasonably correct calculational rules; (b) they learn, in the classroom, rules for manipulating the syntax of symbolic notation systems; but (c) they fail to learn the meaning of symbols and the principles by which they represent quantity and its permissible constrained transformations. In other words, wrong answers are likely to look right, while at the same time conceptual errors betray a lack of mathematical understanding. I take this to be rough evidence of the learning curriculum of primary school math.

Schoenfeld (1985) has observed a high school geometry class where students display the same general characteristics as Resnick describes for elementary school arithmetic learners. He characterizes the students as naive empiricists who plunge into geometry problem solving with straight edge and compass in constant play, without planning, without making sure they understand the problem, believing that mathematical proof is irrelevant. They do not bring their mathematical resources to bear, have no control over the process and believe themselves unable to invent or discover procedures (because they are not mathematical geniuses). Schoenfeld addresses the question of how the curriculum of teaching has unintended consequences for what children learn about math in classroom lessons (1985, chap. 10; 1988). Well-taught lessons by well-meaning teachers aimed at preparing students to successfully pass state and national standardized examinations lead to routinized procedures at the expense of understanding. Lessons place emphasis on the form of presentation of results at the expense of mathematical argumentation. Students expect problems to take less than 2 minutes to solve and they believe that if they can't solve a problem in about 10 minutes they will never be able to do so. They believe that mathematics is to be received not discovered, and that it is a body of knowledge rather than a form of activity, argumentation, and social discourse. Schoenfeld concludes that math is *taught* as what experts know to be true rather than as a process of scientific inquiry (what mathematicians might be said to do). The decomposition of skills – a major structuring device in math curricula – strips problem-solving activity of any relation with mathematical practice. And all this is done in the name of preparing students to do geometry constructions so automatically that they will be sure to pass the New York state regency exams.

Math practice in school classrooms

In an ethnographic study of math lessons in a bilingual Spanish/English third-grade classroom it was possible to look closely at the process of development of faulty math practice in children's everyday classroom activity. My collaborator, Michael Hass, focused on a group of 11 children, the "upper" math group. The children brought to a three-week unit on multiplication and division facts almost as much knowledge as when they finished. They could solve, on average, half of the problems on a 40-problem test given before and after the unit (Hass, n.d.). There were differences in pretest scores between children in the group. But the performances of the less successful converged over time with those of the more adept, so that all finished with roughly the same level of performance on the final test. When these findings are discussed with colleagues, this capsule summary provokes a variety of diagnoses, typically, that the teacher must not be teaching effectively, or there is something wrong with the testing procedure, or individual children must have learning difficulties, be poorly motivated to learn, or have insufficient mental capacity to advance more rapidly. In contrast to these explanations, which focus on teaching/transmission and individual motivation, we sought an explanation in the everyday practice of the children (which includes the teacher's participation in and effects on learning activity as well). Hass discovered, by following the children's activities closely, that in the three-week period the children were deeply engaged in math work during individual work time (about 75% of class time), but invested minimal attention and involvement in ongoing activity during the teacher's instruction sessions (about 25% of class time). During the three weeks the children gave no evidence of having adopted *any* of the specific strategies demonstrated by the teacher during periods of general instruction.

The children sat around a table for individual work and the teacher moved about between their table and two others helping children, or she sat at her desk checking workbook exercises as they finished their assignments. There was a great deal of interaction among the children at the table. (The three who interacted least were the least able in math. One improved sharply after being placed between two highly interactive students who drew him into much greater participation.) The children began their group work sessions by making sure they agreed on what they were supposed to do. They coordinated the timing of their activity so as to work on approximately the same problems at the same time. They asked each other for help and helped each other without being asked. They collaborated and invented procedures. They discovered that the multiplication table printed in their book could be used to solve division problems, an opportunity for mathematical discussion of which the teacher was unaware. Each of the 11 turned in nearly errorless daily practice assignments. On the rare occasions when one of the students consulted the teacher for individual help, the information gleaned in the interaction quickly spread around the table. Essentially all problems were solved using counting and regrouping strategies. These were not presented in lessons and were not supposed to be in use.

The children had unintended opportunities to practice the problem-solving methods they invented or brought with them to the classroom. But they employed them so as to produce the appearance of having used the teacher's procedures, for which she took a correct answer as evidence. The children produced correct answers to problems that had been designed to inculcate a particular way to carry out arithmetic operations that they did not use. Interviews with the teacher suggested that she was unaware of the interactive math activity of the children; the children when interviewed individually reported that they consulted the teacher when they had difficulty solving problems. In sum, the teacher, text, and exercise books prescribed in detail how the children should act – what their everyday practice of math should be – while the children produced a different practice. When the teacher prescribed specific new procedures for carrying out multiplication and division operations, the children did not adopt the prescribed practice. The children did not take the risk of failing to get the answer right, but engaged in familiar processes of arithmetic problem solving instead, developing their practice of learning math in the classroom cautiously, out of known quantities. This was aimed at success or at least survival in the classroom – a specialized collection of activities – rather than being focused on deep understanding of mathematics. The dilemmas that seemed to motivate this practice were ones about performance and blame avoidance. Further, by working out answers using their own techniques and then translating them into acceptable classroom form on their worksheets, the children generated a powerful categorical distinction for themselves between "real" and "other" math. It is not necessary to search beyond the classroom for the generation of this distinction.

Other research supports the claim that the classroom promotes a working repertory of mathematical practices that are not taught, but that are brought into play in order to produce proper appearances of successful problem solving. Brenner (1985) carried out research in Liberia on primer, first-, and fourth-grade arithmetic classes in Vai schools in Grand Cape Mount County. The Vai arithmetic procedures and number system (which tallies at 5, 10, and 20) are different from those taught in Vai schools, where English is the language of math instruction, old "new-math" textbooks are used, and a base-10 number system is taught. The children routinely develop a *syncretic* form of Vai and school-taught arithmetic, and become increasingly skilled in its use over time, although it is never taught. Presumably the urge to manufacture a successful performance in the classroom is important there as well. In short, the work of Schoenfeld, Hass, and Brenner, among others, suggests that the problems that genuinely engage even enthusiastic math learners in school classrooms are, at an important level, dilemmas about their performance rather than mathematical dilemmas. These give shape to learners' everyday mathematical activity in the classroom as they strive to succeed and in the process generate appearances of understanding.

I have argued that problem solving in general (and thus in school) is dilemma-motivated. Ongoing activity in school appears to be shaped by, and shapes in turn, whatever issues are lively and problematic for learners. Teachers cannot make math the central ongoing activity by decree (or lesson plan); math will be problematic in substantive ways only when the central dilemmas of ongoing activity are mathematical ones. Where mathematics learning is consistently the official activity but not the central dilemma, then learners in most U.S. schools should be expected to generate a veneer of accomplishment through activity of a dependable and effective kind, in ways teachers do not teach or intend.

Conclusions

It is time to sketch a more general theoretical description of understanding-in-practice. Ortner (1984) has pointed out that although 20 years ago socialization, or cultural transmission, was viewed as the central mechanism for the reproduction of social systems, today there is some consensus around the view that everyday practices "embody within themselves, the fundamental notions of temporal, spatial and social ordering that underlie and organize the [sociocultural] system as a whole" (1984:154). Understanding-in-practice looks like a more powerful source of enculturation than the pedagogical efforts of caregivers and teachers. Social practice theory argues that knowledge-in-practice, constituted in the settings of practice, based on rich expectations generated over time about its shape, is the site of the most powerful knowledgeability of people in the lived-in world. The encompassing, synthesizing intentions reflected in a theory of understanding-in-practice make it difficult to argue for the separation of cognition and the social world, the form and content of learning, or of learning and its "applications." Internalization is a less important vehicle for transmission of the experience the world has to offer, in this view, than activity in relation with the world.

This theoretical perspective and the research on everyday math practices in kitchens and schools together challenge the privilege accorded school settings as sites of universally applicable knowledge that alumni should expect to take out into the world and substitute for their everyday practices in order to improve them. School math at its best looks no less mathematically powerful from this vantage point, but it looks powerful in specialized ways, as a practice with conventions, occasions, organization, and concerns of its own. Further, the notion that school is not part of "real life" is inaccurate as well as pejorative in its connotations about the significance of schooling; so is the notion that everyday math should be replaced by "real" math. The latter assertion involves a misanalysis of the notable disjunctions between school math algorithms and the generative assembly and transformation of quantitative relations in everyday life. These misunderstandings and conflicting evaluations of social situations and knowledge-to-be-learned must surely cause students both apprehensions and misapprehensions, and contribute to the general sense that schools fail to educate children in meaningful ways.

There is a widespread belief that the more schools fail to educate children, the more learning should become the object of concentrated, specialized attention and standardized accountability. Curricula, textbooks, and lessons should make more explicit what is to be learned (cf.

Apple, 1979). Improving teaching under these circumstances is a process of increasing the prescriptive and detailed character of the transmission of knowledge. The curriculum of school mathematics lessons should provide more detailed recipes for activity itself, for example, on placeholding algorithms, and on single arithmetic operations. Mathematics lessons should be organized as specifications of proper practice – algorithms for solving problems anywhere in the world, any time, taught so specifically that if applied correctly they are guaranteed to produce correct answers. The problem is that any curriculum intended to be a specification *of* practice, rather than an arrangement of opportunities *for* practice (for fashioning and resolving ownable dilemmas) is bound to result in the teaching of a misanalysis of practice (as in the third-grade math classroom) and the learning of still another. At best it can only induce a new and exotic kind of practice contextually bound to the "educational" setting (the syncretic Vai math, for instance). In the settings for which it is intended (in everyday transactions), it will appear out of order and will not in fact reproduce "good" practice.

On the other hand, the curriculum of tailoring names tasks without specifying procedures. "Learn to make garments!" would be the prescriptive message at the highest level. "Learn to sew them, then learn to cut them out" would be the prescription at the next level down. At the third level there are no instructions (only a summing up of my observations about what apprentices do). Apprentices observe and experiment until they achieve a first approximation; then they practice. This curriculum shapes opportunities for doing tailoring work. Master tailors spend a lot of time doing what apprentices want to learn to do, where apprentices can see them do it and can also assist their masters in increasingly central ways. It means no one is unclear about the goals of apprenticeship, and also that the process of getting there, one day at a time, has both well-defined goals and an improvisational character.

Learning in school, like all practice, is improvised, but there are two reasons why that practice may not be what the teacher intends to teach. When the teacher specifies the practice to be learned, children improvise on the production of that practice but not the practice itself. And it is not possible to resolve problems that are not, in some sense, their own. The more the teacher, the curriculum, the texts, and the lessons "own" the problems or decompose steps so as to push learners away from owning problems, the harder it may be for them to develop the practice.

"Owning problems" and "understanding" are closely related in a conception in which learners appropriate knowledge into their improvised everyday practice. But different theories of learning have different metaphors for relations between learners and what they are learning. In recent years much of that imagery – (micro)*worlds*, knowledge domains, and problem spaces – has made problems to be solved very large. Researchers have imagined learners moving around inside them, as if the problem contained the learner. The idea of apprenticeship, or learning in practice, reverses this relation by making central the encompassing significance and meaning – understanding – that children have the opportunity to develop *about* things they are learning. In the first of these views, the subject matter is supposed to be the environment of the child – it envelops the learner in a "world." In the latter, the child's understanding (giving significance to, and critical analysis of relations of the subject to other aspects of the life world) encompasses and gives meaning and value to the subject matter, the process of learning it, and its relations with the learner's life and activity more generally. This development seems to me a more interesting long-range goal of education than the acquisition of information. And it serves notice that a theory of learning in practice must expand to include more than one level of learning activity (see, e.g., Engestrom, 1987) at the same time that it includes more than one level of understanding of the subject to be learned in practice.

Given that the development of an understanding about learning and about what is being learned inevitably accompanies learning in the more conventional sense, it seems probable that learners whose understanding is deeply circumscribed and diminished through processes of explicit and intense "knowledge transmission" are likely to arrive at an understanding of themselves as "not understanding" or as "bad at what they are doing" even when they are not bad at it (such seems the fate of the vast majority of the alumni of school math classes). On the other hand, learners who understand what they are learning in terms that increasingly approach the breadth and depth of understanding of a master practitioner are likely to understand themselves to be active agents in the appropriation of knowledge, and hence may act as active agents on their own behalf. This is not a tidy process and it is sure to have unintended consequences different from the present unintended consequences of teaching, but perhaps less counterproductive ones than when the question of understanding is simply not addressed in classrooms, as is now generally the case. Such an improvised, opportunity- and dilemma-based learning process may even be a prerequisite for widespread, self-sustained learning.

Notes

1 Before trying to describe a craft apprenticeship system and illustrate how such a study offers resources for thinking about learning in the context of schooling, I would like to amplify the notion that the research strategy employed here – "looking back" at the sociocultural form, schooling, from a viewpoint located in a different educational "world" – is useful. In my view, one of the hazards facing researchers on cognition, learning, and education is the densely interwoven history and contemporary relations among schooling, cognitive theory, the educational establishment, and the lives of school alumni. They share underlying beliefs about life, learning, and the pursuit of

life-after-school. The everyday character of schooling, its social situatedness, and historical integration with academic theories of cognition and learning are mainly treated as if they did not exist, or worse, did not matter. For this reason, going straight to schools for empirical studies of processes of learning while at the same time trying to reexamine the prevailing theory, is fraught with pitfalls – it should be difficult to tell whether one universal process of learning is being articulated by the academy and instantiated in schools, or whether there is cultural/historical coordination of one set of beliefs about learning in the academy and in schools simultaneously. It seems helpful, in short, to try to understand how learning is organized and what people think about it elsewhere before addressing this question to schooling.

2   A short round of definitions may be in order here. Thus, broad sociocultural *contradictions* (e.g., between eating for beauty and eating for pleasure) are experienced in conflict, as *dilemmas* in the lived-in world (e.g., to diet or to binge, thus to look different in the long run or feel better in the short run). They are embedded in social practice, of which the dieters' philosophies and activities surrounding food would be an example. A *problem* (e.g., calculating protein options while fixing lunch) is a closed-system puzzle. The motivation for problem-solving activity resides in the dilemmas that lead to such activity. Thus motivation (meaning- and action-impelling forces) must be specified to produce an adequate account of problem-solving activity. I shall come back to this in the analysis of math practice in the classroom.

References

Acioly, N., & A. D. Schliemann. 1985. Intuitive mathematics and schooling in understanding a lottery game. Unpublished paper. Recife, Brazil: Universidade Federal de Pernambuco.

Apple, M. 1979. *Ideology and curriculum.* London: Routledge & Kegan Paul.

Bartlett, F. C. 1958. *Thinking: An experimental and social study.* New York: Basic Books.

Bourdieu, P. 1977. *Outline of a theory of practice.* Cambridge: Cambridge University Press.

Brenner, M. 1985. Arithmetic and classroom interaction as cultural practices among the Vai of Liberia. Unpublished doctoral dissertation. University of California, Irvine.

Brown, J. S., A. Collins, & S. E. Newman. In press. Cognitive apprenticeship: Teaching the craft of reading, writing and mathematics. In L. B. Resnick (Ed.), *Knowing, learning and instruction: Essays in honor of Robert Glazer.* Hillsdale, NJ: Lawrence Erlbaum.

Carraher, T., D. Carraher, & A. Schliemann. 1982. Na vida dez, na escola, zero: Os contextos culturais da aprendizagem da matimatica. Sao Paulo, Brazil. *Caderna da pesquisa* 42:79–86.

    1983. Mathematics in the streets and schools. Unpublished manuscript. Recife, Brazil. Universidade Federal de Pernambuco.

Carraher, T., & A. Schliemann. 1982. Computation routines prescribed by schools: Help or hindrance. Paper presented at NATO conference on the acquisition of symbolic skills. Keele, England.

D'Andrade, R. G. 1981. The cultural part of cognition. *Cognitive Science* 5:179–195.

Davydov, V. V., & L. A. Radzikhovskii. 1985. Vygotsky's theory and the activity-oriented approach to psychology. In J. V. Wertsch (Ed.), *Culture, communication, and cognition: Vygotskian perspectives* (pp. 66– 93). Cambridge: Cambridge University Press.

de la Rocha, O. 1986. Problems of sense and problems of scale: An ethnographic study of arithmetic in everyday life. Unpublished doctoral dissertation. University of California, Irvine.

Engestrom, Y. 1987. *Learning by expanding.* Helsinki: Painettu Gummerus Oy.

Giddens, A. 1979. *Central problems in social theory: action, structure and contradiction in social analysis.* Berkeley: University of California Press.

1984. *The constitution of society.* Berkeley: University of California Press.

Hass, M. n.d. Cognition-in-context: The social nature of the transformation of mathematical knowledge in a third grade classroom. Social Relations. University of California, Irvine.

Lave, J. 1988. *Cognition in practice: Mind, mathematics and culture in everyday life.* Cambridge: Cambridge University Press.

n.d. Tailored learning: Apprenticeship and everyday practice among craftsmen in West Africa. Unpublished manuscript.

Lave, J., M. Murtaugh, & O. de la Rocha. 1984. The dialectic of arithmetic in grocery shopping. In B. Rogoff & J. Lave (Eds.), *Everyday cognition: Its development in social context.* Cambridge, MA: Harvard University Press.

Marx, K. 1957 (1887). *Capital.* (Dona Torr, Ed. and Transl.). London: Allen and Unwin.

Murtaugh, M. 1985a. A hierarchical decision process model of American grocery shopping. Unpublished doctoral dissertation. University of California, Irvine.

1985b. The practice of arithmetic by American grocery shoppers. *Anthropology and Education Quarterly* 16(3):186–192.

Ortner, S. B. 1984. Theory in anthropology since the sixties. *Comparative Studies in Society and History* 26(1):126–166.

Resnick, L. B. 1986. Constructing knowledge in school. In L. S. Liben and D. H. Feldman (Eds.), *Development and learning: Conflict or congruence?* Hillsdale, NJ: Lawrence Erlbaum.

Romney, A. K., S. Weller, & W. Batchelder, 1986. Culture as consensus: A theory of culture and informant accuracy. *American Anthropologist* 88(2):313–338.

Sahlins, M. 1976. *Culture and practical reasons.* Chicago: University of Chicago Press.

Schoenfeld, A. H. 1985. *Mathematical problem solving.* New York: Academic Press.

1987. What's all the fuss about metacognition? In A. Schoenfeld (Ed.), *Cognitive science and mathematics education.* Hillsdale, NJ: Lawrence Erlbaum.

1988. When good teaching leads to bad results: The disasters of "well taught" mathematics courses. *Educational Psychologist* 23(2):145–166.

Scribner, S. 1984. (Ed.). Cognitive studies of work. Special issue of the *Quarterly Newsletter of the Laboratory of Comparative Human Cognition* 6(1 & 2).

Scribner, S., & E. Fahrmeier. 1982. Practical and theoretical arithmetic: Some preliminary findings. Industrial Literacy Project, Working Paper No. 3. Graduate Center, CUNY.

9
Mathematics learning in Japanese, Chinese, and American classrooms

James W. Stigler and Michelle Perry

It might at first glance seem misguided to study cultural differences in learning by focusing on schools. Indeed, the surface features of school mathematics are more similar than different when compared across cultures, and even classrooms in different cultures appear to resemble one another in many respects. Yet schooling is a cultural institution, and more detailed analysis reveals the subtle and pervasive effects of culture as it impinges on children's learning of school mathematics – in the curriculum, in the organization and functioning of the classroom, and in the beliefs and attitudes about learning mathematics that prevail among parents and teachers. In this chapter, we will present some of what we have learned about the classrooms in which children learn mathematics in Japan, Taiwan, and the United States.

The decision to compare mathematics learning in Asian and American classrooms is, of course, not arbitrary. We have known for some time now that American secondary school students compare poorly on tests of mathematics achievement with students from many other countries, but especially with students from Japan (Husen, 1967; McKnight and others, 1987; Travers and others, 1985). More recently, Asian-American differences in achievement have been found to exist as early as kindergarten and to be dramatic by the time children reach fifth grade. Stevenson, Lee, and Stigler (1986), for example, studied children from representative samples of fifth-grade classrooms in Sendai, Japan;

Reprinted with permission from *Children's Mathematics*, ed. G. B. Saxe and M. Gearhart, New Directions for Child Development, no. 41 (San Francisco: . Jossey-Bass, Fall 1988).

This chapter was written while the first author was supported by a Spencer Fellowship from the National Academy of Education, and the second author by funds from the Benton Center for Curriculum and Instruction, University of Chicago. Research reported here was conducted in collaboration with Harold Stevenson, Center for Human Growth and Development, University of Michigan, and with numerous other colleagues: Shin-ying Lee, University of Michigan; Chen-chin Hsu, National Taiwan University Medical College; Lian-wen Mao, Taipei Bureau of Education, Taiwan; and Seiro Kitamura, S. Kimura, and T. Kato, Tohoku Fukushi College, Sendai, Japan. The first University of Michigan study was supported by NIMH grants MH 33259 and MH 30567, and the second by National Science Foundation grant BNS8409372.

Taipei, Taiwan; and Minneapolis, USA. On a test of mathematics achievement, the highest-scoring American classroom did not perform as well as the lowest-scoring Japanese classroom, and outperformed only one of the twenty classrooms in Taipei. Explaining differences as dramatic as these presents a challenge to researchers and also to educators who must grapple with the problem of declining mathematical competence in American society.

Where should we look for explanations? The fundamental problem we encounter is that almost every dimension on which we could compare Asian countries with the United States proves to differentiate these societies. Given this enormous confounding of factors, it is almost impossible to tell which are causally related to differences in learning and which are only related by chance. Aside from this limitation, however, there is a great deal to learn by understanding the way cultural and educational resources are marshalled to produce the outstanding achievement – at least in the domain of mathematics – produced by Asian societies. In this chapter we focus on classrooms, because classrooms are where most people learn most of what they ever know about mathematics.

Just sitting in a Japanese mathematics lesson can provide us with important insights, not only about the way mathematics is taught in Japan but also about the way mathematics is taught in the United States. We can illustrate this point with an anecdote. Several years ago we visited a mathematics class in a Japanese elementary school where the lesson was on drawing cubes in three-dimensional perspective. The class was typical by Japanese standards: thirty to forty students at their desks arranged in rows, facing the teacher who was standing at the front of the room. Each student was working in his or her notebook, but there also was a great deal of discussion from desk to desk, and the noise level was rather high. The discussions were not inappropriate, however; rather, they were directed almost completely to the mathematical topic at hand.

Against this background, one child was having trouble. His cube looked crooked, no matter how carefully he tried to copy the lines from the teacher's example. And so the teacher asked this child to go to the blackboard and draw his cube. Standing there, in front of the class, he labored to draw a cube correctly while the rest of the students in the class continued working at their desks. After working for five or ten minutes, he asked the teacher to look at his product. The teacher turned to the class and asked, "Is this correct?" The child's classmates shook their heads and said, "No, not really." After some open discussion of where the problem might lie, the child was told to continue working at the blackboard and try again. This scene continued for the duration of the forty-minute class. As the lesson progressed, the group of American observers began to feel more and more uncomfortable and anxious on behalf of the child at the board. We thought that any minute he might burst into tears, and we wondered what he must be feeling. Yet he did not cry and, in fact, did not seem at all disturbed by his plight. At the end of the class he finally drew a passable cube, in response to which the class applauded.

As we later came to learn, scenes like this are not unusual in Japanese classrooms, and later we will show how this one fits into the broader context of mathematics learning in Japan. For now, we want to focus on the effect the experience had on us, because it exemplifies one of the greatest benefits of cross-cultural research for the study of educational processes. When educational researchers look only at classrooms in their own culture, they become accustomed to many of the most predominant characteristics of those classrooms and thus fail to note the significance of those characteristics. American teachers generally do not call children to the board to display their errors, because they fear the possible damage it might do to the child's self-esteem. Yet nothing drives us to question this aspect of American teaching more than to be confronted with it in a scenario like the one we have described. The anthropologist Melford Spiro (this volume) has described the aim of anthropology as to make the strange familiar and the familiar strange. Nothing could better describe the aim of our research. We hope that our comparisons of Asian and American mathematics education will lead us to question practices that we take for granted and understand practices that we at first find strange.

The information about Japanese, Chinese, and American classrooms we present below comes from two large cross-cultural studies based at the University of Michigan that have investigated academic achievement and its correlates in Japan, Taiwan, and the United States. Data for the two studies were collected in 1979–80 and in 1985–86, and data from the second study are still in the process of being analyzed. Although both of these studies included testing of children and interviewing of parents as part of their designs, we will focus in this chapter on classroom observations. The methods used for observing classrooms differed substantially across the two studies. Yet taken together, they provide us with an integrated view of how mathematics classrooms differ across these three cultures.

Differences in mathematical knowledge

A criticism often voiced in response to our first study was that our test measured mostly computational skills and did not measure abilities that American educators consider to be more important, such as creative problem-solving skills. In our second study we took heed of such criticism by designing tests to sample as wide a variety of mathematical skills and knowledge as possible, thus broadening our understanding of what specific knowledge differences underlie Asian superiority in mathematics achievement. In addition to group tests of computational skills and, for fifth-grade students, basic knowledge of geometry, we constructed ten more tests of mathematics-related knowledge that were administered in two separate individual testing sessions. All of the tests

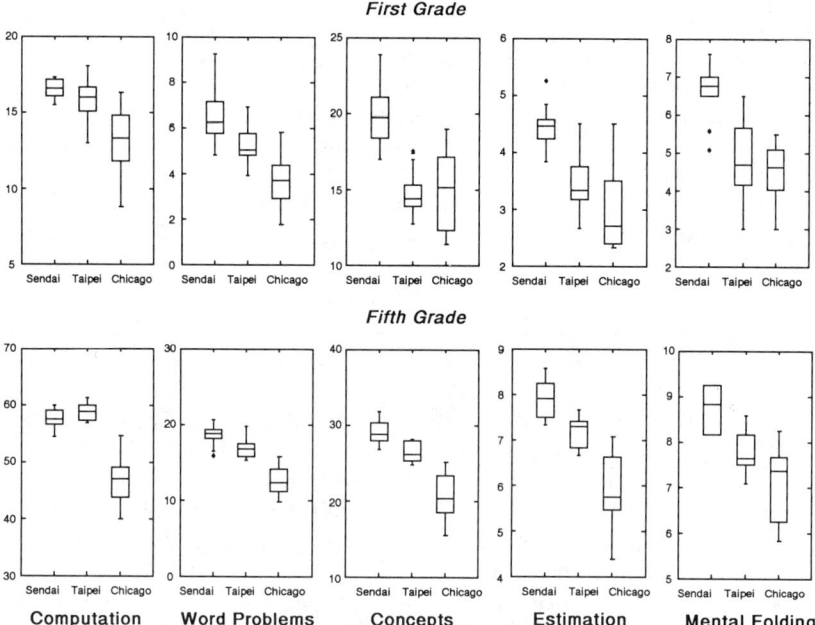

Figure 9.1. Box plots showing distribution of school means of number correct on five mathematics-related tests.

were especially constructed for this study and were judged culturally unbiased by a team of researchers representing each of the cultures being studied. The tests included novel word problems, conceptual knowledge, operations, graphing, estimation, measurement, visualization, mental image transformation, mental calculation, and memory for numbers. A total of 5,524 children across a total of 160 first- and fifth-grade classrooms in the three locations were tested.

Are differences in performance restricted to computational skills, or do Asian students also do better than their American counterparts on tests of other mathematics-related skills? Although we are just beginning our analyses of the test data, the answer is clear: Japanese students, in both first and fifth grades, outscore American students on almost every test we constructed. The pattern of results from Taiwan resembled those from Japan for fifth-graders but were more mixed for first-graders. Let us briefly examine some of these results.

In Figure 9.1 we present box plots (Tukey, 1977) showing the distribution of school means for five representative tests from the battery. These plots are useful because they indicate both median performance (denoted by the center line) and variability across schools in each of the three locations at both grade levels. The five tests presented in Figure 9.1 cover a broad range of topics: (1) a test of computational skill; (2) a test of word-problem solving, including both standard and nonstandard types of problems; (3) an intensive interview designed to tap children's conceptual knowledge of mathematics across a wide variety of domains, including place value, equations, and fractions; (4) a test of estimation skills; and (5) a test requiring students to mentally fold an irregularly shaped piece of paper in accordance with verbal instructions.

At the left-hand side of Figure 9.1 are the results of the test of computational skills. These results replicate those found in our earlier study (Stigler, Lee, Lucker, and Stevenson, 1982), even though the American children were sampled from Chicago instead of Minneapolis. At first grade, the Japanese and Chinese schools both score higher and are less variable than are the American schools, and this pattern is even more pronounced in the fifth grade. Moving to the right, we see a similar pattern for performance on the test of word problems. It is important to note that by the time students reach the fifth grade, there is almost no overlap in the distributions of Asian and American students.

The next three tests presented in Figure 1 – conceptual knowledge, estimation, and mental folding – differ from the first two in that they are made up of questions not typically encountered as part of the mathematics curricula in any of the three locations. Interestingly, they also show a different pattern of results than we saw in the tests of computation and word problems. In first grade, students in Sendai are scoring far higher than are students in either Taipei or Chicago, who are performing approximately equally well. By the time they reach fifth grade, however, the students from Taiwan have passed their American counterparts and are approaching the level of performance attained by the Japanese.

In summary, the Asian advantage in mathematics, at least at the elementary school level, is not restricted to narrow domains of computation but rather pervades all aspects of mathematical reasoning. These findings should provide ample motivation for examining cultural differences in the way mathematics is learned in Japanese, Chinese, and American classrooms.

Methods for classroom observations

FIRST STUDY

The first study was conducted with a sample of first- and fifth-grade elementary school students and teachers in Sendai, Japan; Taipei, Taiwan; and the Minneapolis metropolitan area. In each city, ten representative schools were selected, and within each school two first- and two fifth-grade classrooms participated, yielding a total of 120 classrooms across the three cities. Each classroom was visited forty times over a two- to four-week period. The visits were scheduled to yield a stratified random sample of time across the school day and school week, thus making it possible to estimate the amount or percentage of time that was devoted to various activities. (A full description of the method can be found in Stigler, Lee, and Stevenson, 1987.)

Each visit lasted about an hour and included time for separate observations of teachers and of individual students. We used a time-sampling procedure to observe the target – either teacher or child – for ten seconds, and then to spend the next ten seconds coding the presence or absence of a checklist of categories. This procedure was repeated according to a predefined sequence that counterbalanced order of observation across the teacher and the twelve randomly chosen target students in each class. Across the two- to four-week observation period, each of the twelve children in each classroom was observed for about thirty-three minutes (not including coding time), and each teacher was observed for about 120 minutes.

The student coding system included thirty categories, although coding was eased somewhat by the fact that many of the categories were mutually exclusive. Various aspects of the classroom were coded from the target child's point of view, including the following: whether the class was engaged in academic activities or in transition between activities, what subject matter was being taught, how the classroom was organized and who the leader was of the child's activity, and what kinds of on- and off-task behaviors the child was engaged in.

The teacher coding system contained nineteen categories. These categories described who the teacher was working with, what kinds of teaching behaviors the teacher was engaged in, and what kinds of feedback the teacher was offering to the students. Specific categories from the student and teacher coding schemes will be introduced as the results are presented.

SECOND STUDY

The second study was again conducted in Sendai, Japan, and Taipei, Taiwan. In the United States, however, we decided to move our study to the Chicago metropolitan area, which is far more diverse in population than Minneapolis and thus more representative of mainstream America. In each of the two Asian cities, ten schools were selected to participate in the study. In the Chicago area, twenty schools were chosen to represent the urban and suburban areas that make up Cook County. Twenty rather than ten schools were chosen, because Cook County is more diverse than either of the Asian cities. Within our Chicago sample, we included public and private schools; upper, middle, and lower socioeconomic status neighborhoods; predominantly black, white, Hispanic, and mixed ethnic schools; and urban and suburban environments. As in the first study, two first-grade and two fifth-grade classrooms from each school were selected to participate in the study, yielding a total sample of 160 classrooms in the three locations.

Observations for the second study differed in two important ways from observations conducted in the first study. First, only mathematics classes were observed. Second, detailed narrative descriptions of each class were recorded, yielding a far richer source of information than we had available from the first study.

Each of the 160 classrooms in the mathematics study was visited four separate times over a one- to two-week period, yielding a total of 640 observations across the three locations. Observers, who were local residents of each city, arrived just before teachers began the daily mathematics lesson and observed until the mathematics class was over.

The observers were instructed to write down as much as they could about what was transpiring during the class. Their goal was to record the ongoing flow of behaviors and to include descriptions of all supporting materials (for example, what was written on the blackboard, how many children were working on which problem, and so on). The observers also noted, with marks in the margin, when each minute of time had elapsed. These minute markers were included so that we would be able to estimate the durations of various activities.

The observations produced 640 different narrative descriptions of mathematics classes, in three different languages. Not all observations were of equal quality: the observations varied in both detail and consistency. How were we to code and summarize the data into a form that would be useful in characterizing cross-cultural differences in mathematics teaching?

We first convened a group of bi- and tri-lingual coders to read all of the observations and to summarize their contents in English. In addition, a subset of the observations was translated verbatim into English. From these, we developed a feel for the range of situations we would have to code and some intuitions about cross-cultural differences. We then constructed a coding system that contained some predefined categories but that also included procedures that would preserve detail.

Each observation was divided into segments as the basic unit of analysis. A segment was defined as changing if there was a change in either topic, materials, or activity. Topics were globally defined, including categories such as telling time, measurement, or addition facts. Materials included such items as textbooks, worksheets, the blackboard, or flashcards. Activities, again, were rather molar: examples included seatwork, students solving problems on the blackboard, or teachers giving explanations. The categories were not intended as the full description of the class but rather as a way of organizing the information into a more useful format. As it turned out, there were not large cross-cultural differences in either the average number of segments that comprised a lesson (five to six segments in first grade, six to eight in fifth grade), or the average duration of each segment (seven to eight minutes in first grade, five to six in fifth grade).

In addition, an English language summary was constructed of each segment that would recapitulate in some detail what was going on during the segment. The summaries were standardized somewhat by the use of keywords that would alert us to the presence or absence of certain categories in the classroom. For example, whenever a student was observed asking a question of the teacher, the summary would include the standard keyword "S-to-T," which would facilitate a computer search for all such situations. Our goal was to make the summaries as consistent as possible in style and language.

Time, organization, and disorganization: findings from the objective coding

The results of the first observational study served mainly to differentiate classrooms is the United States, on one hand, from classrooms in Japan and Taiwan, on the other. Very few differences emerged between Chinese and Japanese classrooms. In some respects, one only has to visit one Chinese or Japanese classroom to see vast differences between Asian and American elementary school classrooms. Class size is a major difference: while the classrooms in our Minneapolis sample average twenty-two students in the first grade and twenty-four students in the fifth grade, the classrooms in Taipei average forty-five and forty-eight students at the two grade levels, and those in Sendai, thirty-nine at both grade levels. Most Asian classrooms are arranged with desks in rows facing the teacher, while American classrooms often have desks arranged in groups.

The two dimensions on which the Asian observations differed most from the American ones were time spent in the teaching and learning of mathematics and the level of organization in the classroom.

TIME

Children in Japan and Taiwan spend significantly more time in school than do American children, and this ultimately translates into significantly more time learning mathematics. School is in session 240 days per year in both Japan and Taiwan, compared to only 180 days per year in the United States. Although first-graders in all three cities that we studied spent about thirty hours per week in school, fifth-graders in Sendai spent thirty-seven hours a week in school, those in Taipei, forty-four hours, and those in Minneapolis still only thirty hours.

During academic classes, Chinese and Japanese children at both grade levels spent a much higher percentage of their time engaged in academic activities than did American children. In first grade, American, Chinese, and Japanese children spent 69.8%, 85.1%, and 79.2% of the time, respectively, engaged in academic activities. At the fifth grade the corresponding percentages were 64.5%, 91.5%, and 87.4%. Furthermore, although the percentage increased between first and fifth grade for the Asian children, the percentage actually declined slightly across grade levels for the American children.

The majority of class time in all three cultures was devoted to either reading/language arts or mathematics, and although the total percentage of time devoted to both of these subject matters was similar across the three cultures, the way time was apportioned between the two varied significantly by culture. American teachers at both grade levels devoted more time to reading/language arts and less time to

Table 9.1.   *Number of hours each week spent in language arts and mathematics*

	Country		
	U.S.A.	Taiwan	Japan
First Grade			
Language arts	10.6	10.5	8.8
Mathematics	2.9	3.9	6.0
Fifth Grade			
Language arts	8.2	11.2	7.8
Mathematics	3.4	11.4	7.6

mathematics than did Chinese and Japanese teachers. By the fifth grade, both Chinese and Japanese teachers spent approximately equal time teaching mathematics and reading. American teachers, by contrast, spent almost three times as much time on reading as they did on mathematics.

Calculations based on the hours per week spent in school, the percentage of time spent in academic activities, and the percentage of time those academic activities were mathematics versus reading/language arts allow us to estimate the number of hours each week children in the three cultures spend working on the different subject matters. The results of these calculations are presented in Table 9.1. The cross-cultural differences in the number of hours devoted to mathematics instruction are large, sufficiently large, in fact, that they could go a long way toward explaining the cross-cultural differences in mathematics achievement.

ORGANIZATION

The second dimension that differentiated American mathematics classrooms from those in Japan and Taiwan was the way in which the classrooms were organized. Classrooms in Japan and Taiwan were centrally organized, with most activity under the direct control and supervision of the teacher, while classrooms in the United States were more decentralized in their structure and functioning. Correlated with this difference in type of organization was a difference in the amount of disorderly, off-task behavior present in the classrooms, such that the American classrooms, where there was less direct control by the teacher, also evidenced more off-task behavior.

These differences in type of classroom organization were indexed by several categories in our observational coding scheme. The upper panel of Figure 9.2 shows the level of organization of the classroom as coded in the observations of children. Japanese and Chinese students spent the vast majority of their time working, watching, and listening together as

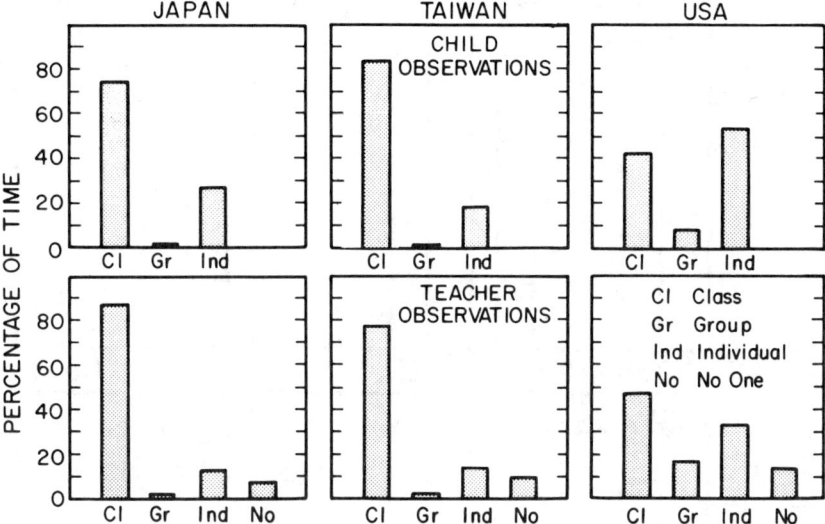

Figure 9.2. Percentage of time spent in various classroom organizations.

a class and were rarely divided into smaller groups. American children, by contrast, spent the majority of their time working on their own and a smaller amount of time working in activities as a member of the whole class. The same picture emerges when teachers are observed (the lower panel of Figure 9.2). American teachers spent more time working with individuals and less time working with the whole class than did Chinese or Japanese teachers. In addition, American teachers were coded as working with no students 13% of the total time in mathematics classes, as opposed to only 6% of the time for Japanese teachers and 9% of the time for Chinese teachers.

The counterpart of these findings is displayed in Figure 9.3, where we see what percentage of the total time in mathematics classes students were part of a teacher-led activity and what percentage they were part of an activity with no leader. In Taiwan the teacher was the leader of the children's activities 90% of the time, as opposed to 74% in Japan and only 46% in the United States. No one was leading the students' activity 9% of the time in Taiwan, 26% of the time in Japan, and 51% of the time in the United States.

Taken together, these findings indicate that classrooms in the Asian cultures are organized more hierarchically than are classrooms in the United States, with the teacher directing energies to the whole class and with students more often working under the direct supervision of the teacher. Because of these differences in organization, American students experience being taught by the teacher a much smaller percentage of time than do the Asian students, even though American classes contain roughly half the number of students.

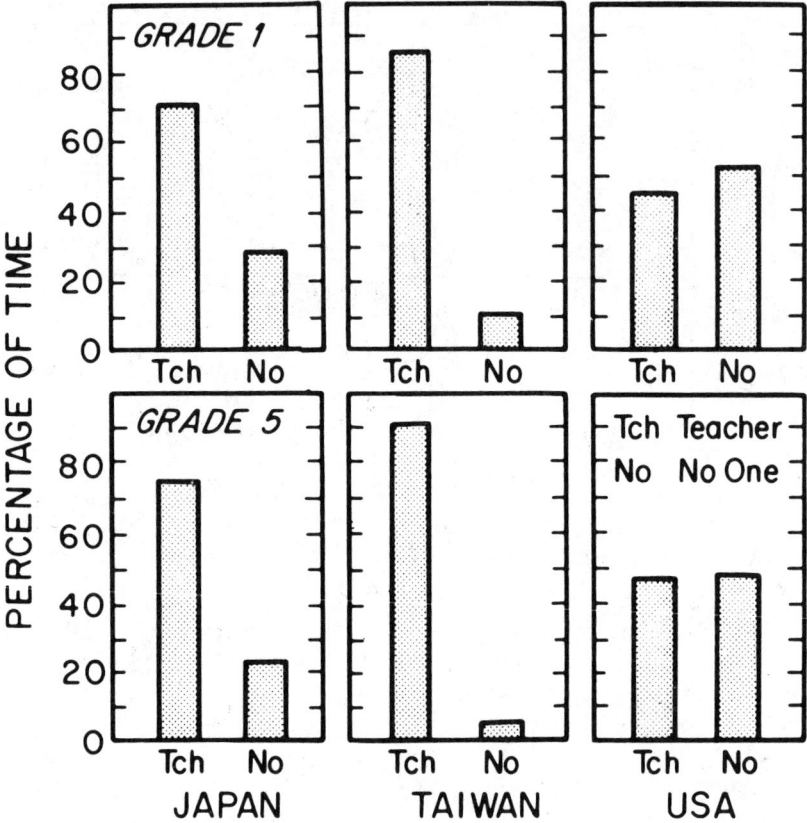

Figure 9.3. Percentage of time students spent in activity led by teacher and by no one.

Associated with the relatively decentralized organization that characterizes American classrooms is a higher level of disorderly behavior. This disorderliness was revealed in our coding of the incidence of inappropriate or off-task student behaviors. If the target child was not doing what the teacher expected him or her to do, he or she was judged as being off-task. Two categories of off-task behaviors were distinguished: those involving inappropriate peer interaction and those the target child engaged in alone. In addition we coded whether or not the target child was out of his or her seat. The results from these observations are presented in Figure 9.4.

There were large cross-cultural differences in the overall percentage of time students spent engaged in inappropriate, off-task activities. Across both grade levels, American students were off-task 17% of the time during mathematics class, as opposed to only 10% of the time for Chinese and Japanese students. Unfortunately, we did not code what students were actually doing but only that they were not behaving in

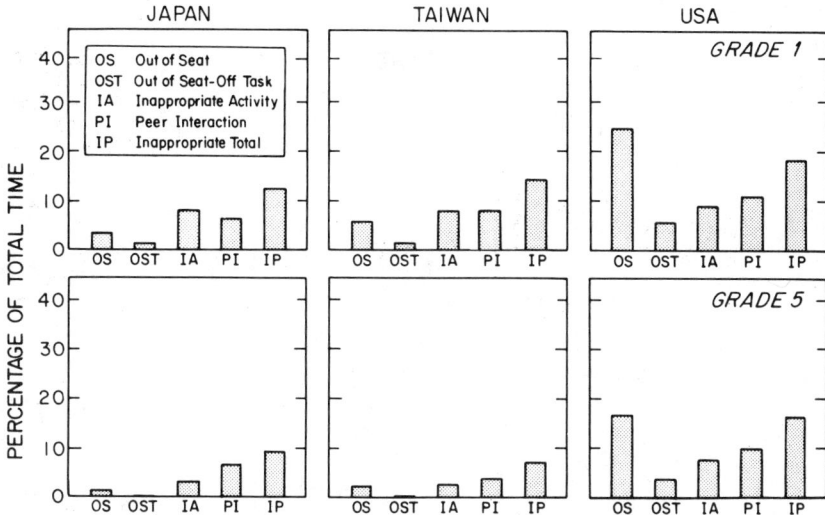

Figure 9.4. Percentage of time spent in inappropriate activities.

accordance with classroom norms as defined by the teacher. Thus, we do not know whether some of the behavior coded as off-task might nevertheless have been oriented toward academic goals.

American students were coded as being out of their seats during mathematics classes 21% of the time, whereas Chinese and Japanese children were out of their seats 4% and 2% of the time, respectively. Of course, being out of one's seat does not necessarily imply that one is off-task, particularly in American classrooms. However, if we look at the percentage of time students were both out of their seats and off-task, the American percentage was five times as high as that in the other two countries (5% versus less than 1% in Japan and Taiwan).

Problem solving, evaluation, and coherence: preliminary ideas from the narrative observations

The data derived from the first observational study is informative, up to a point: we get basic information about how time is spent by students in the three countries and about how frequently classrooms are organized in various ways. The limitation of these data is that we learn very little about how mathematics is actually taught in the three cultures. In contrast, the narrative observations collected in the current study provide us with richly detailed information concerning what happens in mathematics classes in Sendai, Taipei, and Chicago. In the remainder of this chapter we will present some ideas based on preliminary analyses of the narrative records.

Three ways in which classrooms in the three cultures were observed

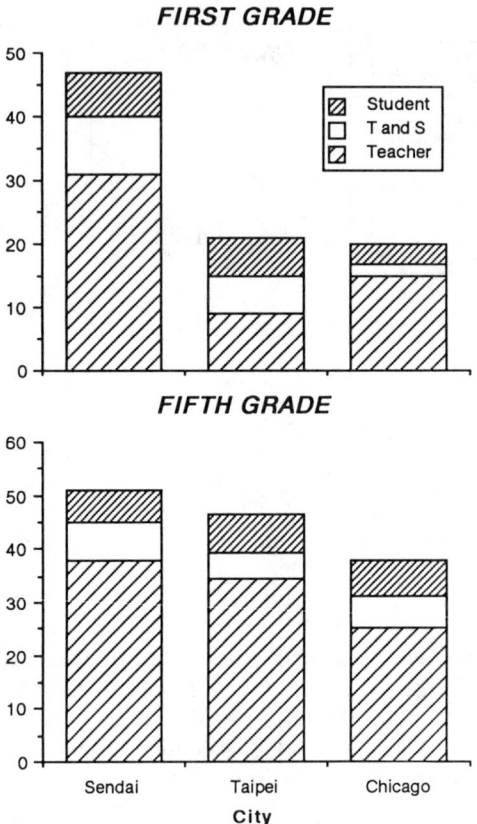

Figure 9.5. Percentage of segments with explanations from teachers only, from students only, and from both teachers and students.

to vary were in the nature of mathematical problem-solving activities, the methods by which student work was evaluated, and the coherence of lessons from the child's point of view.

PROBLEM SOLVING

A major component of mathematics lessons in all three cultures involves learning how to solve, and then solving, mathematical problems. However, the styles of learning and instruction that surround problem solving, as well as the formats in which problems are presented, appear to differ greatly across cultures.

Reflection versus performance. In terms of style, classrooms vary in the degree to which they emphasize performance and practice, on the one hand, versus reflective thinking and verbalization, on the other. Chinese classrooms differ from Japanese classrooms in this regard: The Chinese classrooms are more performance oriented and the Japanese classrooms more reflective. American classrooms are not at all reflective, as are Japanese classrooms, nor do they place a consistent emphasis on performance, as do Chinese classrooms.

One index of reflectivity is simply the amount of verbal explanation, both by teachers and by students, that occurs during mathematics lessons. The percentages of segments that contained verbal explanations by the teacher, a student, or both are presented in Figure 9.5. In the first grade, 47% of all Japanese segments contained verbal explanations, compared to 21% of Chinese segments and 20% of American segments. By fifth grade, the incidence of explanations in classrooms in Taipei and Chicago has increased to 47% and 38%, respectively, but the incidence of explanations has increased in the Japanese segments as well, up to 51%. Clearly, there is more verbal discussion of mathematical concepts and procedures in Japanese classrooms than there is in either Chinese or American classrooms, and this difference is most pronounced in the first grade.

Indeed, when visiting a Japanese mathematics class, one detects a more relaxed pace than occurs in either Chinese or American classrooms. Japanese teachers tell students it is the process of problem solving that matters, not simply getting the correct answer. Japanese teachers thus often try to slow their students down, asking them to think about a problem and how to solve it, then discuss their thoughts with the class, rather than rushing on to solve the problem. Interestingly, Japanese fifth-grade teachers asked their students not to solve but to think about a problem in 7% of all segments, something that occurred in only 2% of the Chinese and American segments.

Chinese teachers, on the other hand, emphasize fast and accurate performance, or getting the right answer quickly. For example, 17% of all Chinese segments were devoted to practicing rapid mental calculation, an activity that was never observed in either the Japanese or American classrooms. It appears that Chinese teachers emphasize "do," the Japanese teachers emphasize "think."

Manipulatives and real-world scenarios. One might expect that the Japanese emphasis on reflection and verbalization would imply less reliance on concrete manipulatives or real-world problems. In fact, however, this was not the case. Both Japanese and Chinese teachers, as we will show, relied more on manipulatives and real-world problem situations than did teachers in our Chicago sample.

The use of concrete and real-world materials during classroom instruction was coded in two categories: (1) concrete manipulatives (for example, presented with eighty discrete objects, children are asked to divide them into four equal groups) and (2) real-world scenarios, which included word problems, dramatic enactments of mathematically solvable real-world problems, or the (relatively infrequent) situation where students are asked to generate a word problem to correspond with a symbolic equation. We assume that segments in which neither manipulatives nor real-world problems were used depended primarily on symbolic mathematical materials for instruction.

The percentages of instructional segments in which problems were presented using concrete manipulatives, real-world scenarios, or both are presented in Figure 9.6. The upper panel of Figure 9.6 shows that in first grade, both manipulatives and real-world scenarios are used more frequently in Taipei than in either Sendai or Chicago and more frequently in Sendai than in Chicago. In the fifth grade (lower panel of Figure 9.6), teachers in all three cultures have increased their use of real-world scenarios while at the same time reducing their reliance on manipulatives. However, there still are large differences between the three cultures on both counts: Sendai shows the largest proportion of segments in which real-world scenarios are used, and Chicago shows the least. Taipei teachers, on the other hand, use more manipulatives in fifth grade than do teachers in the other two locations, whereas Chicago teachers use the least. Thus, although Japanese and Chinese teachers differ in the degree to which they use manipulatives versus real-world content in their teaching of problem solving, both groups of Asian teachers use far more manipulatives and real-world problems combined than do the American teachers.

Children learn not only from the way that problems are presented but also from the type of feedback they receive and the manner in which that feedback is provided. Children are also sensitive to the ways that lessons are structured. Thus, two additional factors that seem to distinguish mathematics classrooms in Japan, Taiwan, and the United States are (1) the way in which feedback is provided to students, and (2) the degree to which students are provided with opportunities to construct coherent representations of mathematics lessons.

EVALUATION

Students' work is evaluated frequently in classrooms. We have found that both the frequency of and the approach to evaluations of students' mathematical solutions differ in the three cities.

Our first analysis reveals the frequency with which children's work is evaluated in the three cities. In first-grade mathematics lessons, 7% of all segments in Chicago were devoted to evaluation, whereas 12% of segments in Sendai and 13% in Taipei were devoted to evaluation. Although evaluation segments occurred more often in fifth grade than in first grade, there were fewer such segments in the fifth grade in Chicago (14%) than in Sendai (17%) or Taipei (18%). Furthermore, although the evaluation that occurs in lesson segments devoted to evaluation is usually public and visible to the whole class, this was less true in Chicago than it was in Sendai or Taipei. Thus, students in Chicago have somewhat less opportunity to have their own work evaluated, and to observe the evaluation of other students' performance, than do students in the two Asian cities.

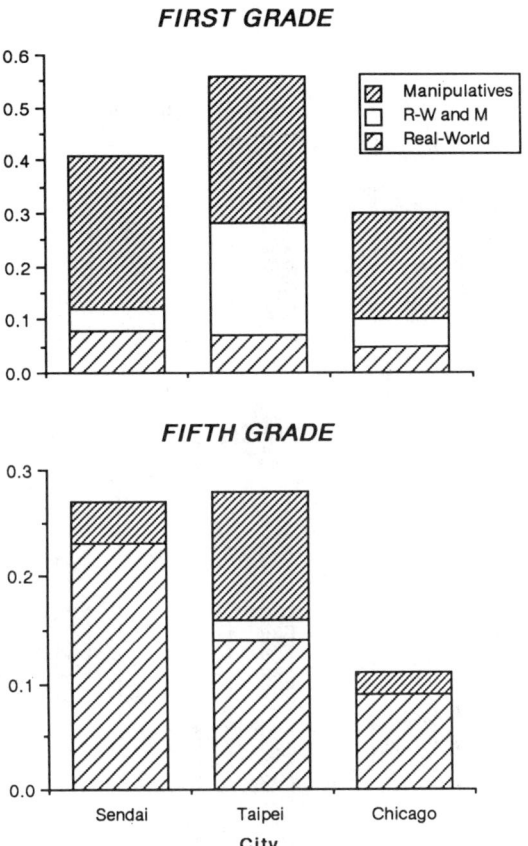

Figure 9.6. Proportion of instructional segments using concrete manipulatives, real-world scenarios, or both.

In addition to the differences in frequency of evaluation, we also have discovered differences in the methods used for evaluating students' work. Each evaluation segment was coded for how the students' answers were treated. In analyses of segments in which evaluation was the primary activity, the three most common methods of evaluation were as follows: (1) displaying a student's erroneous solution and re-working the problem until a correct solution was derived, (2) having students report to the class how many problems in a set of problems were solved correctly (for example, the teacher asks all students who solved all problems correctly to stand up), and (3) praising or rewarding students for their efforts and/or correct solutions. Not all evaluation segments used one of these three methods, but a sizable percentage did. Figure 9.7 presents the percentage of public evaluation segments in each country and grade level that employed each of the three methods. (It

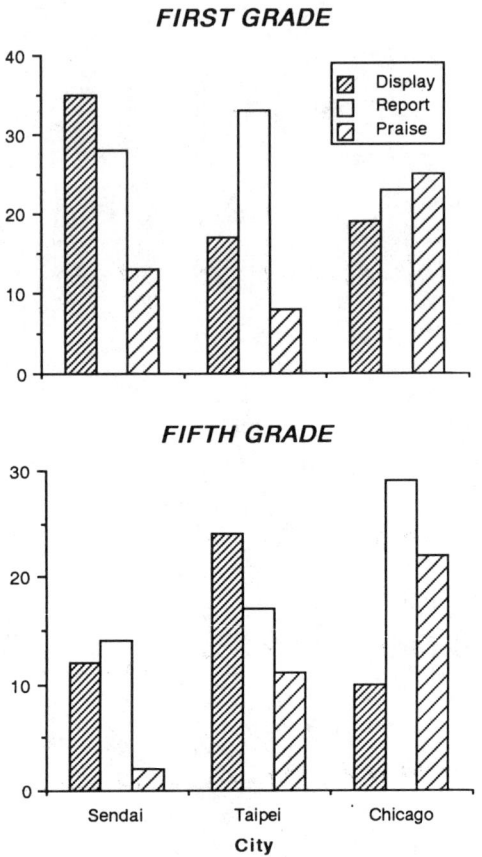

Figure 9.7. Percentage of evaluation segments containing different kinds of feedback.

was only possible to code public evaluation segments, since only public evaluation was visible.)

It is clear from Figure 9.7 that the predominant methods for evaluating students differ for the students in the three cities and also differ from the first to the fifth grade. First-grade Japanese students are frequently evaluated by having their errors displayed to the class. These errors are then discussed, and correct solutions are derived by class members. This type of evaluation occurs in 35% of all first-grade evaluation segments in Sendai but in only 17% of the Taipei and 19% of the Chicago first-grade evaluation segments. The most prevalent type of evaluation in Taipei was reporting to the class the number of problems correctly solved. This occurs in 28% of the Sendai, 33% of the Taipei, and 23% of the Chicago first-grade evaluations. The most prevalent type of evaluation found in the Chicago first-grade segments was praising students. Thus, in the first grade, the Japanese students are revising their incorrect attempts, the

Chinese students are letting the class know how well they performed, and the American students are being told that they have done a good job.

The picture changes somewhat when we examine the evaluations that occur in the fifth grade. Fifth-grade students in Taipei are often evaluated by having their errors displayed to their classmates (in 24% of the evaluation segments), whereas this happens less frequently in Sendai (in only 12% of the evaluation segments) and in Chicago (in only 10% of the evaluation segments). The fifth-grade students in Chicago and in Sendai are evaluated most frequently by announcing how many problems they solved correctly. However, this happens much more in Chicago (in 29% of the evaluation segments) than in either Sendai (in 14% of the evaluation segments) or in Taipei (in 17% of the evaluation segments). And finally, students in Chicago are still receiving more praise (22% of the evaluation segments) than are students in either Sendai (2%) or Taipei (11%).

COHERENCE

This last dimension is also the most speculative and difficult to document. Having read the corpus of narrative observations, we are left with the impression that Japanese classrooms in particular, and Chinese classrooms to some extent, are structured in a more coherent fashion than are American classrooms. We use the word *coherent* very much in the way researchers studying text comprehension use the word. A text is coherent to the extent that it enables or allows the comprehender to infer relations between events (Trabasso and van den Broek, 1985). In like manner, teachers who provide a basis for children to infer reasons for and relations between events provide the basis for coherence in the classroom. Work by Trabasso, Stein, and others has shown that coherence across events in a story has a profound impact on the ease with which the reader can encode, understand, and remember the events of a story (Trabasso and van den Broek, 1985; Stein and Policastro, 1984). Our speculation is that mathematics lessons, too, may be easier to comprehend, and students likely to learn more, when the episodes that comprise the class are coherent.

The analogy between a story and a mathematics classroom is not perfect, but it is close enough to be useful for thinking about the process by which children might construct meaning from their experiences in mathematics class. A mathematics class, like a story, consists of sequences of events related to each other and, hopefully, to the goals of the lesson. What we tend to find in the American observations, unfortunately, are sequences of events that go together much like those in an ill-formed story. If it is difficult for adult observers to construct a coherent representation of the events that constitute a first- or fifth-grade mathematics class, then it surely would be even more difficult for the average child sitting in those classes to do so.

What, specifically, do we see in Asian classrooms that leads us to perceive them as being more coherent? One possibility is the small amount of time, relative to American classrooms, that is spent on transitions from one activity to another and on irrelevant interruptions. In American first-grade classrooms, a total of 21% of all segments contain transitions or irrelevant interruptions, compared to 7% in Sendai and 14% in Taipei. In fifth grade the corresponding percentages are 15%, 3%, and 3%. Rarely is the logical flow of an Asian class broken to pursue less mathematically important business (such as the time-consuming distribution of materials) that may give students the wrong idea about what is important about mathematics.

Another aspect of Asian classrooms that may facilitate coherence is a tendency we observed both in Japan and Taiwan to devote an entire forty-minute mathematics class to the solution of only one or two problems. In such a lesson, students might discuss the features of the problem, solve the problem using alternative methods, discuss and evaluate the alternative solution strategies, model the problem using manipulatives, and so on. The problem thus serves to provide topical continuity across the different segments of a lesson, much as a protaganist's goals and purposes provide continuity across the events of a story.

Assuming that a lesson with fewer problems is more coherent than one with more problems, it is worthwhile to ask whether there is, in fact, a large difference in number of problems presented across Japanese, Chinese, and American mathematics lessons. In a preliminary analysis, we counted the number of problems presented during fifth-grade instructional segments that lasted five minutes (the median length of all fifth-grade segments with ongoing instruction). The distribution of five-minute segments over number of problems presented is shown in Figure 9.8. What we find is that 75% of all five-minute instructional segments in Sendai focused on only one problem, compared to 55% of the segments in Taipei and only 17% of the segments in Chicago.

The devotion of even five minutes to a single problem was relatively rare in American classrooms, not to mention spending an entire class period on only one problem. In no class did we observe an American teacher sticking with a single problem for an entire class. Indeed it appears that American teachers value just the opposite approach. In recent research that examined characteristics of expert mathematics teachers in the United States, it was reported that the expert elementary mathematics teacher can get through forty problems in a single class, whereas the novice teacher may only cover six or seven problems (Leinhardt, 1986; Leinhardt and Greeno, 1986). It would appear that the Japanese or Chinese teacher is striving for a different goal. Or perhaps they are just adapting to a different reality: The value placed on homework in both of these Asian cultures means that repetitive practice can be accomplished at home and class can be reserved for teaching. American teachers must, especially at the first-grade level, accomplish both purposes during the school day.

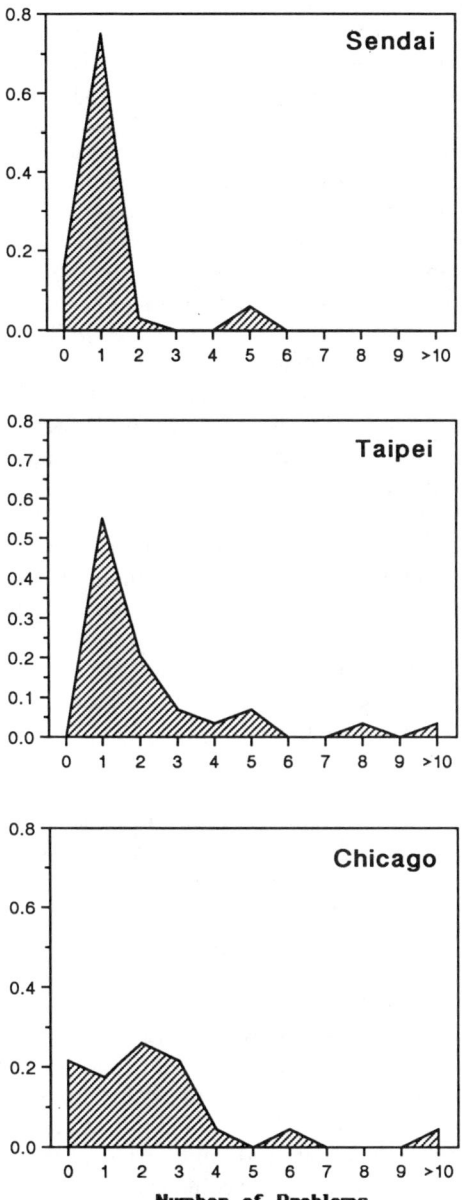

Figure 9.8. Distribution of 5-minute instructional segments by number of problems covered.

It is important to note that sticking to one problem does not imply a boring class that lacks variety. Variety, as indexed by change in segment, is approximately equal across the three cultures. For example, the typical first-grade mathematics class in all three cities consists of five or six segments, each lasting seven or eight minutes. What is different is the nature of the changes that occur from one segment to another. While in Japan and Taiwan segment changes are more often coded because of changes in materials or activities without a change in topic being taught, in American classrooms changes are more often coded because of a change in the topic being taught (also see Berliner and Tikunoff, 1976). In the first grade, changes in segments in Japan were due to a change in topic only 7% of the time, in Taiwan, 16% of the time, and in the United States, 25% of the time. This pattern is even more striking in the fifth grade: changes in segments in Japan were due to a change in topic only 1% of the time, in Taiwan, only 3% of the time, and in the United States, 17% of the time. Thus, the students in our Chicago sample must have had to change gears more frequently than their peers in Taipei and Sendai, within the bounds of a single mathematics lesson. And it is important to remember that changing topics does not mean merely a change in problem but rather a change on the order of starting with measurement and moving to multidigit addition. For example, one first-grade American class started with a segment on measurement, then proceeded to a segment on simple addition, then to a segment on telling time, and then to another segment on addition. The whole sequence was called "math class" by the teacher, but it is unclear how this sequence would have been interpreted by a child. In this case, it seems that it would be impossible for anyone to construct a coherent account of the whole class.

In other cases, where the topic does not change within a lesson, the sequence itself could be construed coherently, but American teachers do little to help the child construct a coherent representation. A good example of this kind of situation is provided by the topic of measurement as it is normally taught in first-grade classrooms. Most American textbooks teach fundamental measurement in the following sequence: First they teach children to compare quantities directly and to say which is longer, wider, and so on. Next, nonstandard units of measurement are introduced, and children are taught to ascertain, for example, how many paper clips long their pencils are. Finally, students are introduced to the concept of standard units and taught to measure objects in inches or centimeters. This is a sensible sequence and could conceivably be taught in a coherent manner.

Let us examine the way in which this sequence is implemented in one American classroom in our sample. In the first segment, the teacher has children examine objects – pencils, crayons, paperclips, chalk, and so on – and compare them to determine which are longer. The teacher then moves the class to the next segment and says:

OK, open your workbooks to page 12. I want you to measure your desk in pencils, find out how many pencils it takes to go across your desk, and write the answer on the line in your workbooks. [Children carry out instructions.] Ok, the next line says to use green crayons, but we don't have green crayons so we are going to use blue crayons. Raise your hand if you don't have a blue crayon. [Teacher takes approximately 10 minutes to pass out blue crayons to students who raise their hands; coded as a transition segment.] Now write the number of blue crayons next to the line that says green crayons. [Teacher then moves on to the third segment.] OK, now take out your centimeter ruler and measure the number of centimeters across your desk and write the number on the line in your workbooks.

What is fascinating about this particular class is that there is absolutely no marking by the teacher of the transition points – the three segments just follow each other as though there were no transition. There is no discussion of how each exercise is important in providing students with an understanding of measurement, no discussion of why units are important or why standard units are important, no discussion of historical development of measurement procedures that could provide more meaning to the sequence of activities, and no discussion of the goals of the class and how each activity relates to those goals. More time is devoted to making sure students have a blue crayon – which is totally irrelevant to the purpose of the lesson – than to conveying the purpose of the three segments on measurement. If we put ourselves in the child's position, what is the likelihood that we would construct a coherent, meaningful account of this particular class?

In Chinese classrooms, and in Japanese classrooms to an even greater extent, we see teachers explicitly pointing out to children the relationships that obtain between different segments within a lesson and between different lessons. For example, one Japanese first-grade teacher was quoted as asking this question of a student at the beginning of a mathematics class. "Would you explain the difference between what we learned in the previous lesson and what you came across in preparing for today's lesson?" To hear a question of this sort posed to a six-year-old would be surprising to most American educators. Perhaps more surprising is that the student was able to answer the question.

As another example, a teacher might draw parallels between a problem solved symbolically and the same problem solved with concrete manipulatives. In both of these examples, the students are given the opportunity to infer coherence across the episodes that constitute their experience in mathematics class. Transitions in the Asian classes often are marked by verbal discussion of the relation between two segments, and classes, especially in Japan, often start with the teacher explaining the goal of the day's class and how the activities relate to the goal. In our narrative data, we found that the Japanese teachers were twice as likely to make explicit reference to connections across episodes than were either the Chinese or American teachers (9% of all segments, compared to 5% and 4%).

In sum, the children we observed in our American sample are faced with a very difficult task: they are required to solve many problems on their own, and often there is no apparent link among the types of problems they are being asked to solve. This clearly differs from the way mathematics classes proceed in Taipei and Sendai. Although the Chinese and Japanese lessons were different on many dimensions, children in both of these cultures were given better opportunities to construct mathematical concepts and also were given more opportunities to get public feedback about whether their constructions were accurate.

Conclusion

Japanese and Chinese elementary school students are learning more about all aspects of mathematics than are their peers in the United States. Although there are many possible explanations for these differences, we have chosen, in this chapter, to focus on classrooms, since classrooms are the context in which most children learn mathematics. What we have found is not surprising, given the cross-cultural differences in achievement: classrooms in Sendai and Taipei differ markedly from those in our American samples on a number of dimensions.

In our first study, which employed a time-sampling objective coding scheme, we found that students in both Sendai and Taipei spend a great deal more time in mathematics class than do American students and that they spend less time during mathematics class engaged in off-task, inappropriate behaviors. We also found that classrooms are organized differently in the Asian cultures. Whereas Asian students spend most of their time working on teacher-led activities as members of a whole class of students, American students spend more time working independently, with contact with the teacher more likely to take the form of individualized or small-group instruction. These differences in organization mean that American students spend much less time in school being attended to by the teacher, if we assume that students working as members of a whole class feel that the teacher is working with them.

Why do we organize our U.S. mathematics classes in the way that we do? Some part of the answer can be tied to cultural beliefs about the nature of individual differences and the nature of learning. In other research conducted by the Michigan group, we have found that American mothers are more likely to see mathematical ability as innately determined than are Asian mothers (Stevenson, Lee, and Stigler, 1986). Because we tend to think individual children are inherently unique in their limitations, we believe that the education appropriate for one child may not be appropriate for another, and thus we tend to emphasize individualized learning. Asian educators are more comfortable in the belief that all children, with proper effort, can take advantage of a uniform educational experience, and so they are able to focus on providing the same, high-quality experience to all students. Our results suggest that American educators need to question their long-held assumption that an individualized learning experience is inherently a higher-quality, more effective experience than is a whole-class learning experience. Although it may be true that an equal amount of time with a teacher may be more effective in a one-on-one situation than in a large-group situation, we must realize that the result of individualized instruction given realistic financial constraints is to drastically reduce the amount of time a teacher can spend with any individual student.

In our narrative observations, preliminary analyses again revealed a number of differences in the way mathematics is taught in Asian and American classrooms. Asian students are given more opportunities for solving real-world problems, and Japanese students, in particular, spend a far greater amount of time than do either Chinese or American students engaging in reflective verbalization about mathematics. We also found a greater reliance on public evaluation of both the products and the processes of students' problem-solving efforts. In Japan the most common form of evaluation involved children putting their incorrect solutions on the blackboard for all to see and then having the whole class discuss the nature of the error and possible ways of correcting it.

This brings us back to the earlier story of the Japanese classroom. We can see that it represents quite well many of the characteristics of mathematics learning in Japanese classrooms: the whole class working together; talking but not off task; one child publicly displaying his failed solution, not to be ridiculed but rather to be corrected by his classmates. How is it possible for this scenario to occur so frequently in Japan but so little in the United States? The answer, again, lies in cultural differences. Not only are children in the United States rarely evaluated in this manner, but it is considered by many cruel to do so. If errors in mathematics are seen as due more to innate ability differences than to educable factors, then it would be regarded as cruel to publicly demonstrate a child's failings, which are no fault of his or her own. It may be that the costs of such a technique, within the context of American culture, outweigh the advantages that may derive from the analysis of incorrect problem solutions. For better or worse, American teachers feel more comfortable praising the student who performs well than discussing the errors that can occur in the course of problem solving. Unfortunately, praise is not a particularly good way to start a deep discussion of mathematics principles and procedures.

The most difficult questions, of course, remain unanswered. These are (1) which, if any, of the differences we have found cause the differences in performance? and (2) which aspects of Asian classrooms, if implemented in the context of American education, would contribute to enhancing the learning of American children? At present we cannot provide answers to these questions, and this kind of survey research will never be able to do so. What we hope to have done is to provide American educators with a picture of classroom learning that is different from our own and which thus may function to train attention back on assumptions about learning mathematics that are implicitly present in American mathematics classrooms. As White (1987) has pointed out, comparisons of education in Japan and the United States provide us not with a blueprint but rather with a mirror that can sharpen our awareness of how we educate our children and how we might do it differently. We hope that the research reported in this chapter will serve this purpose and will inspire the awareness and experimentation that will be required to understand how children in different cultures learn mathematics from classroom instruction.

References

Berliner, D. C., and Tikunoff, W. J. "The California Beginning Teacher Evaluation Study: Overview of the Ethnographic Study." *Journal of Teacher Education*, 1976, 27(1):24–30.

Husen, T. *International Study of Achievement in Mathematics*. New York: Wiley, 1967.

Leinhardt, G. "Expertise in Math Teaching." *Educational Leadership*, 1986, 43(7):28–33.

Leinhardt, G., and Greeno, J. G. "The Cognitive Skill of Teaching." *Journal of Educational Psychology*, 1986, 78(2):75–95.

McKnight, C. C., Crosswhite, F. J., Dossey, J. A., Kifer, E., Swafford, J. O., Travers, K. J., and Cooney, T. J. *The Underachieving Curriculum: Assessing U.S. School Mathematics from an International Perspective*. Champaign, Ill.: Stipes, 1987.

Spiro, M. E. "On the Strange and the Familiar in Recent Anthropological Thought." In J. Stigler, R. Shweder, and G. Herdt (eds.), *Cultural Psychology*. New York: Cambridge University Press, this volume.

Stein, N. L., and Policastro, M. "The Concept of a Story: A Comparison Between Children's and Teachers' Perspectives." In H. Mandl, N. L. Stein, and T. Trabasso (eds.), *Learning and Comprehension of Text*. Hillsdale, N.J.: Erlbaum, 1984.

Stevenson, H. W., Lee, S. Y., and Stigler, J. W. "Mathematics Achievement of Chinese, Japanese, and American Children." *Science*, 1966, 231:693–699.

Stigler, J. W., Lee, S. Y., Lucker, G. W., and Stevenson, H. W. "Curriculum and Achievement in Mathematics: A Study of Elementary School Children in Japan, Taiwan, and the United States." *Journal of Educational Psychology*, 1982, 74(3):315–322.

Stigler, J. W., Lee, S. Y., and Stevenson, H. W. "Mathematics Classrooms in Japan, Taiwan, and the United States." *Child Development*, 1987, 58: 1272–1285.

Trabasso, T., and van den Broek, P. "Causal Thinking and Story Comprehension." *Memory and Language*, 1985, 24:612–630.

Travers, K. J., Crosswhite, F. J., Dossey, J. A., Swafford, J. O., McKnight,

C. C., and Cooney, T. J. *Second International Mathematics Study Summary Report for the United States*. Champaign, Ill.: Stipes, 1985.

Tukey, J. W. *Exploratory Data Analysis*. Reading, Mass.: Addison-Wesley, 1977.

White, M. *The Japanese Educational Challenge: A Commitment to Children*. New York: Free Press, 1987.

PART IV
Cultural selves

10
Adolescent rituals and identity conflicts

John W. M. Whiting

American psychologists have described adolescence as a period during which young people are concerned about who they are. Erikson (1950) has referred to this as the identity crisis. The cross-cultural evidence suggests that the types of crises faced by the developing young man or woman depends on previous experience, especially during infancy. It also suggests that the individual's search for an identity is present and active during childhood as well as adolesence.

The parental generation is concerned with helping their children accept and understand the appropriate adult identity. In some cultures they do so by sponsoring elaborate rituals that often occur around puberty. These rituals include messages that reassure young people who have conflicts and anxieties about their identity. A careful review of the life cycle suggests that these ceremonies serve as a capstone for identity confusions that have their origins in infancy and early childhood.

Identity can be understood as a person's perception of his or her place in the social structure. Am I a male or a female? A child or an adult? – These are two of the most salient conflicts to be solved before a person becomes a full-fledged, competent adult. It is assumed that one's identity is acquired by the process of identification. There are a number of theories about the details of this process. In a paper on learning by identification I proposed a model that specifies some of the psychological mechanisms involved in this process (Whiting, 1960; see also Burton & Whiting, 1961). This has been referred to as the status envy hypothesis. The theory can be summarized as follows: The social structure of any society consists of a number of statuses or social positions, each of which has an attached role and each of which is defined by a set of attributes such as sex, age, occupation, kinship affiliation, and the like. An important feature of each status is its position in the privilege hierarchy. Incumbents of those statuses having high rank are envied by those who have a lower rank. Although the process of identification is the same for males and females, I have decided to limit the discussion to males for the sake of simplicity.

It is assumed that a child learns the status system by observing and cognizing the roles of others, particularly of the members of his immediate household. Those members who are perceived by ego to control resources that are important to him will be envied and preferred as models. He will observe them carefully and imitate them, if he is permitted and physically capable of doing so. Very often a child is forbidden to perform the role of an envied status. For example, when he acts like his younger sibling whom he perceives to occupy a privileged status, he is told not to act like a baby. He may wish to stay up as late as his older sibling, but not be permitted to do so.

Privilege is not the only basis for envy. Power is equally, if not more important. To the child, ego's caretakers are not only privileged but also powerful. The mother, who is usually the chief caretaker or resource mediator, does not always immediately comply with ego's expressed wishes, but sometimes delays or refuses altogether. In some cultures it is even believed that excessive compliance will spoil the child. The status envy hypothesis holds that when a resource mediator withholds desired goods and services from ego it not only frustrates him but also makes him wish to take over the role of the resource mediator. He feels that it would be desirable to gain direct control of the coveted resources rather than having to depend on indirect control. He wishes he could get what he wants without having to ask for it. Again, however, he discovers that he may be unable to do so because he lacks the skill, or he is prohibited from trying. When such is the case, the theory holds, the child will covertly practice the role of the envied status. Such practice is accomplished both in fantasy and play. Children's folktales are filled with the accomplishments of their heroes, be they superman or coyote.

In order to estimate the strength and nature of the initial identifications of the infant, this discussion focuses on variations in the structure of the nuclear family household. Cross-cultural research on various world samples of preindustrial societies has shown that two contrasting styles can be distinguished (Munroe, Whiting, & Hally, 1969; Munroe, Munroe, & Whiting, 1981; Whiting, 1964, 1971; Whiting, & Whiting, 1975). In what are labeled back and hip cultures, the infant is carried in a sling, shawl, or rebozo, or in the mother's arms. While resting, he is held in his mother's lap and at night he sleeps next to her. In the contrasting culture type, an infant spends most of his time in a crib or cradle or is heavily swaddled. He is usually carried in a cradleboard or baby carriage, naps in it during the day, and sleeps in it at night.

I am always more comfortable with a cross-cultural variable if I know how it is distributed over the world. This often leads to some useful insights about the effect of environment on culture. Plotting the "mother–infant closeness" variable on a world map turned out to be particularly instructive: The use of cradleboards and heavy swaddling is concentrated in North America, Patagonia, and the high Andes, Europe, and nontropical Asia. Close body contact and frequent holding and carrying characterize the cultures of tropical South America, sub-Saharan Africa, tropical Asia, and the islands of the Pacific. Eighty-three percent of the societies in the sample lying in the tropics were reported to have close and frequent contact between mother and infant, and 80% of the societies situated in the temperate and frigid zones used heavy swaddling, cradles, or cradleboards (Whiting, 1981). There are, of course, interesting exceptions such as Arctic Inuit mothers, who carry their infants under their parkas, and the Yaghan of Patagonia, who have always been an ethnographic anomaly with respect to their lack of clothing in a cold climate – they do not bundle their infants. However, it seems evident that "packaging" infants is an adjustment to cold climates.

It should be pointed out here that the image of the American Indian mother with a cradleboard strapped to her back is apparently somewhat misleading. According to what data we could find, except when moving camp, the cradleboard and infant were hung from a tent pole or propped up near where the mother was working rather than being strapped to the mother's back. Chisolm (1983), who has made careful observations of Navajo infants, states that they are only carried from the hogan to the pick-up truck.

A crib or cradle is the usual resting place for an infant in European and northern Asian cultures. Modern middle-class America is, of course, a good example of a case that would be coded low on closeness of body contact and frequency of being held or carried. I know of no other culture where a baby is often put to bed in a separate room. Some examples of the back- and lap-type cultures will serve to sharpen the contrast. Konner (1976, pp. 220–222) described the use of the sling by the !Kung San Bushmen of the Khalahari Desert in Botswana:

> From the earliest days of life and throughout the first year, three positions characterize infant posture: (1) awake, held sitting or held standing in the lap of the mother or other caretaker (since there are no chairs, adults were typically sitting on the ground); (2) awake or asleep, in the infant sling at the mother's side; (3) asleep, lying on a cloth on the ground beside the mother. . . . Infants are rarely permitted to lie down while awake. Mothers consider that this is bad for motor development.

While awake, typical African infants spend most of their time in body contact with someone. Charles Super (unpublished field notes) reports that among the Kipsigis, a back- and shawl-carrying culture, in 70% of 593 spot observations of 25 infants under 1 year of age, they were in body contact with a caretaker, and in only 4% were they out of the caretaker's reach (beyond 1 meter). Leiderman and Leiderman (1973) report similar data for 67 Kikuyu infants observed during their first year (972 observations). They were in contact with the mother or another caretaker in 68% of the observations.

Infant care in Eurasia is quite different from Sub-Saharan Africa. In only a few societies is the infant carried in a sling or shawl. Elsewhere, it is moved about in a transportable cradle. The baby carriage or cradle on wheels is a common method in Western Europe. The transportable cradle and also used as a napping place for the infant during the day, and as a sleeping place at night. In crib and cradle cultures, there is far less close contact between mother and infant than in the back and lap culture.

The magnitude of the difference in the frequency of close contact between mother and infant in a cradle culture and a shawl-carrying culture can be estimated by comparing the observational study of Lewis and Ban (1977:340) in Yugoslavia with Super's observations among the Kipsigis. Eighteen 3-month-old Yugoslavian infants and their mothers were observed for 1 hour during the day while they were awake (eyes open). Every 10 seconds note was made if the infant was being touched or held by the mother. By this measure the infant was in direct contact with the mother 27% of the time. This compares with 70% for the Kipsigis. Even when the infant is held in the crib or cradle cultures, he is most frequently separated from the mother by thick clothing. Most of the communication with the mother is in the vocal rather than the kinesthetic mode.

But does it make any difference whether an infant remains physically attached to his mother for a long period after he is born or is immediately transferred to a cocoon of his own? I believe it does. In order to predict the consequences of this difference, several assumptions must be made. The first of these is that calming an infant when he is frightened is one of the most important tasks for an infant's caretaker. Strange and unusual events are frightening to an infant. Such events result in a stress response that includes crying and other signs that the adrenal cortex has been activated. Close body contact has the effect of inhibiting these stress responses. In the framework of ethno-child psychology this is known as comforting a child. This is usually accomplished in our culture by picking the infant up and holding him over one's shoulder. In back and lap cultures, there is a comforting mechanism continually in place, whereas in the cultures in which infants spend most of their time in cribs or cradles, they must cry for help when they are frightened. Although the fright–comfort sequence is, I believe, most important, other drives such as hunger and temperature extremes are also more readily and quickly avoided or satisfied if the infant is on the mother's back, side, or lap than if he is in a crib, cradleboard, or baby carriage at some distance from potential caretakers.

The psychological consequences of the two types can be clearly distinguished. In the close-contact cultures it is as though the infant is not born until he is weaned from his mother's back. He is to all intents and purposes still a part of her. He has a piggyback view of his mother's role. The relationship between infant and mother is one that might be called "symbiotic attachment." A child riding high on the mother's back can see what the mother sees. He hears what she hears. I have previously assumed that this close contact with the mother leads to initial identification with her. This interpretation is contrary to the status envy theory and should be corrected. An infant in close contact with his mother is in the most desired status. Most of his needs are immediately and directly satisfied. There should be little reason to envy his mother.

When he is weaned from her back and lap, however, the situation changes. The resource-mediator that he has previously depended on has gone back on him. His first reaction to this is one of rage. I witnessed a 2-year-old infant in Kwoma, New Guinea, put on a violent show of rage when his mother left him behind for the first time when she went to the swamp to collect sago. Similar scenes are reported in the ethnographic descriptions of other close-contact cultures.

I now believe that in close mother–infant contact cultures, weaning from the back is the beginning of the formation of gender identity. His mother now has a status that is clearly powerful and to be envied. His first reaction therefore is to identify with the mother and try to act out the female role.

> For example, the Kikuku children we observed in the village of Ngeca, Kenya, when weaned from the back at the birth of a younger sibling, are discouraged from attempting to continue to expect help from the mother. They are encouraged to act out and covertly practice the female role. The young boy is encouraged in this role by being asked to be nurturant to his newborn sibling, and to help his mother in housework. As he gets older and has new desires, however, he notices that his father and older brothers control many of the resources that he now covets. This is the sequence that we have inferred from our observation of children between the ages of 2 and 5 observed by our Kikuyu assistants in the village of Ngeca in Kenya. (Whiting & Edwards, 1988)

The weaned child now sleeps with an older sibling rather than his mother. He is now eating adult food. He is frequently cared for and fed by his older siblings. He is also carried by them. As he becomes older he seeks the company of the older children. He shows an increasing preference for same-sex companions. He observes that older boys and his father do not care for infants or do routine housework. He notes that it is customary for men to be served before women and to receive the choicest food. His perception that females are the controllers of resources is called into question by his growing knowledge of privilege and power in the adult world. He begins to recognize, on the basis of his new stereotypes of male and famale roles, that men have the status that he envies.

In this society the perception of the separate worlds of men and women is clear. Men do not sleep with their wives after the birth of a child. They frequently have a room or house of their own. They are usually away from the area where the young children spend their time during most of the daylight hours. When they are present, they are perceived to be waited on by the women. They do not seem to be required to work. The conflict between mothers and their children peaks during the 4- and 5-year age period. When the 4- and 5-year-old boys seek the company of older boys, they are often rejected or dominated by them. When they try to emulate the role of adult males, they are prevented from doing so, confined to the family homestead where they continue to interact with younger siblings and older girls and adult women.

Once they are allowed to leave the homestead, boys are found further from home than their female same-age peers. By 6 or 7 a boy is only required to carry younger siblings if there is no female that can be called on. His mother expects less housework. By now, if his father has a separate house, he sleeps with the older boys and his father. The separation of the worlds of men and women is easy for the young child to see. No one needs to tell him about the relative power of men and women. He begins to doubt his early preference for the female role resulting from his initial identification with his mother. A secondary identification with the male status begins to take shape. He is consequently thrown into a state of gender identity conflict. Our theory holds that the function of the Kikuyu puberty rite is to help resolve this conflict.

When he reaches puberty, a Kikuyu youth is initiated into the next age grade, that of junior warrior. Circumcision is the central feature of the initiation rites. This involves excising the prepuce, which, according to native theory, is feminine and must be removed if one is to become a man (Worthman & Whiting, 1987).

British missionaries were able to convince the Kikuyu elders in Ngeca that these rites were pagan and should be abolished. Despite the fact that the elders no longer sponsored the rites, the present generation of Kikuyu adolescent boys arranged to be circumcised at the local clinic without ceremony. I asked my Kikuyu research assistant who was a student at the University of Nairobi why he did this. He replied in a way that suggested that I had asked a foolish question. "Why, if you are not circumcised, how can you be a man?"

The identity conflict is quite different for the crib and cradleboard infant. Here he is separated from his mother at birth. If he needs help, he often has to cry for it. Although he is unable to care for himself, anyone who hears an infant cry for help is genetically prepared to nurture him (Whiting & Edwards, 1988). Thus although he is unable to directly satisfy his needs, he has dominant control over his social environment. In other words, crib and cradle infant, rather than continuing in a symbiotic relationship with his mother, has one of ambivalent dependency toward her.

It is also the case that the father usually has quite a different status in the crib and cradle cultures than that described for the back and lap cultures. In most crib and cradle cultures, the father, rather than the infant, sleeps with the mother. From the infant's point of view, his parents jointly occupy the most desired status. They are keeping each other warm while he is left in the cold, alone in his crib. He perceives that the privileged status is based on size rather than gender. His father, as well as his mother, is to be envied and emulated.

His caretakers are quite effective in meeting his needs as an infant and he occupies a powerful and desired status. When, with the birth of a younger sibling, independence training begins, however, such is no longer the case. His first response is to envy his younger sibling and regress to an infantile role. His parents do not permit this. Nor is he able to play the adult parental role. He is encouraged to be self-reliant, but he feels abandoned and inadequate.

Again the culture provides a ritual solution to help him in his dilemma. In the crib and cradle cultures of Europe and the Middle East, the child is taught that the Judeo-Christian God is there to take over the parental role. When it is no longer appropriate to ask his real parents for help, he is taught to pray to "Our father who art in heaven." The North American Indians, another culture area of crib and cradle (in this case the ubiquitous cradleboard), believe that guardian spirits rather than a high god are the supernatural caretakers.

The quest for a guardian spirit is widespread among the Indians of North America. Guardian spirits appear to an individual in a dream or vision. Such dreams are believed to be induced by fasting and isolation. Landes (1938) reports for the Southern Ojibwa that the pubescent boy is encouraged to seek a supernatural power who will "adopt him and care for him as a parent or grandparent cares for a child" (p. 4). By isolating himself and fasting, the pubescent boy will arouse pity in the supernatural, which will take him as a protégé, bound to him "by the firmest loyalties that exist in Ojibwa." In the Ojibwa idiom, to "pity" another is to adopt and care for them. Landes continues to describe the vision quest as practiced by the Southern Ojibwa: Beginning around the age of eight, children are encouraged to prepare for the vision quest. They are taught to go without food. Every few years the village decides that the pubescent boys should be sent out to a neighboring island or an isolated spot in the woods, without food or drink. They are visited each morning to learn whether they have been successful in their quest. Boys who are not able to endure the fast and isolation return home and are encouraged to try again when the village plans a new vision quest. Those who are successful have acquired a surrogate parent to replace the parents who have deserted them.

This essay may seem far removed from psychoanalytic theory, but such is not the case. As a graduate student at the Yale Institute of Human Relations, I was convinced that Freud was correct in his assumption that early experiences had a profound and irreversible effect on personality development. Although Freud's formulation was sometimes faulty, there are important continuities over the life cycle. I submit this chapter as evidence that the closeness of mother–infant contact has an effect that culture must try to resolve.

I at first accepted Freud's libido theory, and his formulation of the stages of psychosexual development and his fixation theory. My early cross-cultural research with Irvin Child explored the effect of the socialization of the child in the oral, anal, and sexual stages as presented in Freud's theory of psychosexual development (Whiting & Child, 1953).

We added the socialization of dependency and aggression, two modes of interpersonal behavior.

These interpersonal variables turned out to be more meaningful than Freud's psychosexual variables, and in subsequent research we added training in self-reliance, nurturance, responsibility, and the control of dominance and aggression. The history of the socialization of these behaviors turned out to be more fruitful than the age of weaning or the severity of toilet training. It also became clear that a child's relation to the people in his environment and the child's perception of which of them control the resources that he covets, play a central role in his development. How a child learns his place in the social network of his culture seemed more important than his psychosexual fixations.

The change in orientation led to the development of the status envy theory presented in this chapter. In sum, the child envies and identifies with those individuals who control the resources he covets. He monitors and imitates or covertly practices his perception of their behavior. These envied individuals may not be the same throughout childhood. They vary both with age and with culture types. I find the concept of identity conflict more useful than fixation in understanding the hang-ups that societies produce in individuals during infancy and childhood and try to resolve during adolescence.

References

Burton, Roger V., & J. W. M. Whiting. 1961. The Absent Father and Cross-Sex Identity. *Merrill-Palmer Quarterly of Behavior Development* 7(2):85–95.

Chisholm, J. S. 1983. *Navaho Infancy*. New York: Aldine.

Erikson, Erik H. 1950. *Childhood and Society*. New York: Norton.

Konner, M. J. 1976. Maternal Care, and Development among the !Kung. In R. Lee & I. DeVore (Eds.), *Kalahari Hunters and Gatherers*. Cambridge, MA: Harvard University Press.

Landes, Ruth. 1938. *The Ojibwa Woman*. New York: Columbia University Press.

Liderman, P. H., & B. F. Leiderman. 1977. Economic Change and Infant Care in an East African Agricultural Community. In P. H. Leiderman, S. R. Tulkin, & A. Rosenfeld (Eds.), *Culture and Infancy*. New York: Academic Press.

Lewis, M., & P. Ban. 1977. Variance and Invariance in the Mother-Infant Interaction: A Cross-Cultural Study. In P. H. Leiderman, B. R. Tulkin, & A. Rosenfeld (Eds.), *Culture and Infancy*. New York: Academic Press.

Munroe, R. L., R. H. Munroe, & J. W. M. Whiting. 1981. Male Sex-Role Resolutions. In R. H. Munroe, R. H. Munroe, & B. B. Whiting (Eds.), *Handbook of Cross-Cultural Human Development*. New York: Garland.

Munroe, R. L., J. W. M. Whiting, & David J. Hally. 1969. Institutionalized Male Transvestitism and Sex Distinctions. *American Anthropologist* 71(1):89–91.

Whiting, B. B., & C. P. Edwards. 1988. *Children of Different Worlds*. Cambridge, MA: Harvard University Press.

Whiting, J. W. M. 1960. Resource Mediation and Learning by Identification. In

I. Iscoe & H. Stevenson (Eds.), *Personality Development in Children.* Austin: University of Texas Press.

1964. Effects of Climate on Certain Practices. In W. Goodenough (Ed.), *Exploration in Cultural Anthropology.* New York: McGraw-Hill.

1971. Causes and Consequences of the Amount of Body Contact between Mother and Infant. Paper presented at the annual meeting of the American Anthropological Association, New York.

1981. Environmental Constraints on Infant Care Practices. In R. L. Munroe, R. H. Munroe, & B. B. Whiting (Eds.), *Handbook of Cross-Cultural Human Development.* New York: Garland.

Whiting, J. W. M., & I. L. Child. 1953. *Child Training and Personality.* New Haven, CT: Yale University Press.

Whiting, J. W. M., & B. B. Whiting. 1975. Aloofness and Intimacy of Husbands and Wives. *Ethos* 3(2):183–207.

Worthman, C. M., & J. W. M. Whiting. 1987. Social Change in Adolescent Sexual Behavior, Mate Selection, and Premarital Pregnancy Rates in a Kikuyu Community. *Ethos* 15(2):145–165.

11
Sambia nosebleeding rites and male proximity to women

Gilbert Herdt

Since the early work of Bateson (1936) and Mead (1935), New Guinea cultures – especially in the Eastern Highlands studied by Read (1951, 1952) – have been identified with various initiatory rituals, among which none have proved as symbolically complex or theoretically controversial as those of bloodletting. In spite of considerable cross-cultural variation in the practices, researchers have not only drawn on these data, but have also reached divergent conclusions about their meaning. Furthermore, each of the proposed interpretations implied different slants on the development context of the rites that were seldom explicated, let alone demonstrated. It is remarkable, then, that after these many years of theoretical interest no ethnographer since Read (1965:127–133) had published detailed observations of these ritual behaviors until recently (cf. Lewis 1980; Poole 1982; Tuzin 1980:72–78), and none has systematically described the behavioral experience or cultural context of bloodletting in the male life cycle of a Highlands people. It is these problems – in relation to the cultural structure of nosebleeding and the ritualization of proximity to women throughout the developmental cycle – that I shall examine among the Sambia, a hunting and horticultural people of the Eastern Highlands.

New Guineasts have tended to view bloodletting rites from several analytic perspectives. Read's (1952) emphasis on the social solidarity effected by the cult context of such rites has been widely supported (Berndt 1962; Newman 1965; Strathern 1969). Others have also concurred with Read (1952:13) that bloodletting is a form of "psychological conditioning" associated with the male warrior ethos (Allen 1967;

Reproduced by permission of the American Anthropological Association from *Ethos 10*:3 (Fall 1982). Not for further reproduction.

This study is based on two and one-half years' fieldwork (1974–1976, 1979) among the Sambia of Papua New Guinea. Research support came from: the Australian-American Education Foundation; the Department of Anthropology, RSPS, Australian National University; the National Institute of Mental Health; and the Department of Psychiatry within UCLA's Neuropsychiatric Institute, all of which funding is gratefully acknowledged. I wish also to thank Robert J. Stoller, Donald F. Tuzin, Fitz John P. Poole, and Terence Hays for their helpful comments on an earlier version of this essay.

Hogbin 1970; Mead 1935; Tuzin 1980; Whiting 1941). Meggitt (1964) saw consistent correlations between types of sexual activity (e.g., "lechers" and "prudes"), purificatory cults, and intergroup hostility vis-à-vis affines (cf. Allen 1967:11–12, 52–53). Langness (1967) went further, arguing that "sexual antagonism" – within the warring Highlands environment – arose as a culturally constituted response to deny men's dependence upon women. Lindenbaum (1972, 1976) contended that rites like male bloodletting operate as systemic ecological controls on women and their productivity (cf. Chowning 1980). Langness (1974) further added that the secrecy of cult rituals effects *male* solidarity and power in regulating strategic female domains in which male social control needs "supernatural" aids. Moreover, many New Guineasts have emphasized native ideas that expurgations of maternal substance or "pollution" are needed to develop and maintain masculinity (Bateson 1936:130ff.; Berndt 1965:92–94; Herdt 1981; Hogbin 1970: 103ff.; Lewis 1980; Mead 1935:85; Meigs 1978; Newman 1964; Poole 1982; Read 1951, 1965; Whiting 1941:64ff.). In sum, however, these studies have taken a synchronic viewpoint which stresses the *adult outcome* of ritual experiences for the functioning of social groups and institutions.

Here I take a diachronic perspective on Sambia sexual polarity and ritual that will, I hope, offer fresh questions and answers about ritual bloodletting by attending to the developmental context in which it emerges. Let me begin by stating several analytic points about the Sambia sociocultural system (see Herdt 1981, 1982). The first point concerns a societal imperative: before pacification (1964–1965), Sambia communities needed to create tough, aggressive fighters to fill and replenish the ranks of their warriorhood. Next, I believe that the production of this type of "warrior personality" among males anywhere was not easy or "natural" (Mead 1935 and Schwartz 1973); moreover, its difficulties were exacerbated by the Sambia developmental cycle that results in the presence of too much mother and too little father, thus stunting the male's early separation from his mother in childhood. Last, the accommodation of these early childhood experiences, and core gender identity (see Stoller 1968), to the demanding behavioral environment of adult male character structure, established special, enduring, psychosocial needs for autonomy that could be symbolically sustained through ritual mechanisms – e.g., nosebleeding behaviors – enabling competent adjustment to, and performance of, the adult masculine gender role throughout life. Although these psychosocial needs arose as unintended social consequences of Sambia socialization, their symbolic expression has been culturally transmitted and reproduced to filter those needs. The symbolic structure specifically "filtered out" mother and all that she stood for, and "filtered in" father, aggressively, and ritualized proximity to women; and these "symbolic filters" (Herdt 1981) came to take on a life of their own – as "internal discourse" for the institution and audiences (Foucault 1980:28) of bloodletting. Viewed in this way, the experience of nosebleeding binds the ideological and sensory poles of meaning to the *designata* of dominant symbols (Turner 1967) in Sambia ritual, making the male warrior ethos and world view (Geertz 1973) a dynamic product of a developmental context.

It is obvious and has been well reported (see below) that cutting the body in bloodletting is painful. It is also known that these "mutilation rites" are, throughout New Guinea, first administered forcibly by elders on groups of boys in collective initiation. Bloodletting is often said to be necessary for "male growth," so one can understand, in terms of the native model, why bloodletting should be done until maturity has been achieved. But what motivates those ritual behaviors afterwards, on into old age? Unless one assumes (as I do not) that these painful operations are *intrinsically* pleasurable or satisfying, we must examine the cultural and social psychological factors that compel subsequent adult operations: beliefs, self experiences, and ever present audiences that are sufficiently approving or fearsome to result in the painful repetition of such self-inflicted acts. Here, I think, we anthropologists have still not met the challenge of Bettelheim's (1955:14) old question: What is "the function of mutilations regularly inflicted"? The Sambia material is helpful.

The Sambia ritual cycle of initiations emphasizes four broad developmental themes in males' relationships to women that define the context of nosebleeding throughout the life cycle. They emerge as follows: (1) Boys must be physically separated from their mothers, and then nosebled, to rid them of female pollutants that block "male growth" (a concept that is, however, complex). (2) The behavioral and cultural content of secret rites, especially nosebleeding, is organized violently so as to effect psychological detachment of boys vis-à-vis their mothers and avoidance of all females. (3) This ritual aggressiveness, furthermore, effects attachment to masculine figures through obedience to them as authorities, who train the boys to become warriors – social outcomes that help explain, but also require changes in – the cultural context of nosebleeding ritual following the initiates' social elevation into the upper ranks of the ritual cult hierarchy. (4) After marriage, nosebleeding acts as transformed from being involuntary public rituals to voluntary private events: men must (while alone) induce nosebleeding on each occasion of their wives' menstrual periods, into old age. And they also become initiators. Thus, initiation nosebleedings are a social control mechanism of the male cult which effects the *collective regulation* of boys; whereas among adult men, private nosebleedings become a means of one's autonomous *self-regulation* in contacts with women. The meaning of nosebleeding thus changes with successive ritual initiations; and, among adult men, those layers of meaning (concepts of manhood) are fixed within the developmental transformations in male character structure that enable one's self-regulation to come about. From these points there follows my thesis: psychosocial (and physical) *proximity to women* is the key variable in predicting the occurrence of nosebleeding behavior; changes in the cultural definitions of proximity, at different points in the male life cycle, precisely regulate the shifting temporal sequence, ideological teachings, sociocultural context, and the affective intensity of the bloodletting experience.

Each one of these developmental themes bearing on nosebleeding and proximity to women shall be examined in turn. A related and somewhat disconcerting pattern in the Sambia system will also be tackled. Sambia believe that a boy must be nosebled to "grow" and attain reproductive competence. But once married and fully initiated, men no longer offer that rationale for the private practices – not until middle age, that is. Among those older men, who have long since married once, twice, or more, and reared families, many again begin offering the pat statement that unless they nosebleed themselves they will "stop growing." The thick connotations of that sense of "growth" must be interpreted, since they involve the end point of psychosocial autonomy and contacts with women.

The cultural context

Sambia are a mountain people inhabiting isolated river valleys of the remote Eastern Highlands. They number some 2,000 people dispersed in clusters of small hamlets over a wide region. Men hunt and both sexes garden. Descent is patrilineally based; residence is patrilocal. Marriage is arranged through infant betrothal or sister exchange. Warfare was endemic and destructive among Sambia. It had two forms: the stylized bow-fight among neighboring hamlets and the inter-hamlet war party sent to raid and kill neighboring tribes. Propinquitous hamlets thus inter-married and sometimes warred (cf. Meggitt 1964:219ff.). And every three or four years they joined together in building a great collective cult house to stage bachelorhood initiation (see Herdt 1981).

Relationships between the sexes are sharply polarized along the lines of a misogynist male belief system depicting women as polluting, depleting inferiors a man should distrust and keep distant. Most unrelated, sexually mature women are regarded as potentially contaminating relative to their menstrual and vaginal fluids. But these ideological stereotypes (see M. Strathern 1972) do shift somewhat, according to particular individuals and situations. For example, men fear contamination mostly from their wives, not their sisters. Like Tuzin (1982), I have noted a disparity between male ritual rhetoric and the more steady domestic relationships among the sexes, including spouses. Sambia customarily expect the spouses to cohabit within a single domicile, and this pattern also affects men's ritually constituted misogyny. Nevertheless, one should not wish to push the significance of these constraints too far: men are in full charge of public affairs; women are relegated to heavy, dirty garden work and the polluting business of childbearing; ritual secrecy remains an enduring political and psychological force that suppresses women and children; most men are constantly mindful of female contamination and semen depletion through sexual intercourse; and abusive language, squabbling, and wife-beating, as well as suicides resulting from some such incidents, are pervasive in Sambia life.

The developmental cycle of children thus occurs in the context of open hostility, or at the least, ambivalence, in men's behavior toward their wives. Children are involved in this familial conflict. By custom, infants are exclusively cared for by their mothers; other female caretakers later help out. Fathers remain aloof since both mother and child are regarded as one in their polluting potential, especially following birth; and also because postpartum taboos strictly forbid close interaction among the spouses, since that would lead to sexual intercourse, harming both mother and infant. Boys and girls remain closely attached to their mothers until two or three years of age (and sometimes longer, according to particular circumstances, e.g., widowhood). Girls become their mother's companions, and they continue residing with their parents until marriage, usually around the time of the menarche (about 17–19 years of age). Thereafter, the young women reside with their husbands or parents-in-law, which often removes them to another hamlet. Boys spend more time with their mothers and playmates than they do with their fathers. This style of maternal attachment continues relatively unchanged until first-stage initiation. But boy-initiates are thereafter sanctioned for *any* contact (e.g., talking, looking at, or eating) with women, including their mothers. They reside exclusively in the men's clubhouses with other unmarried initiates and bachelors. Not until ten years and more later, after marriage and the strict deritualization of these avoidance taboos, may youths begin interacting with women again.

Men worry over the effects of the mother's prolonged contact with children, but especially with their sons. This concern is more than ideological rationalization, as one sees in actual case studies (see Herdt 1981). Stated briefly, men regard the attainment of adult reproductive competence as far more problematic for males than females. Maleness is thought to depend on the acquisition of semen – the stuff of "biological" maleness – for precipitating male anatomic traits *and* masculine behavioral capacities (e.g., prowess). Femaleness rests on the creation and circulation of blood, which is held, in turn, to stimulate the production of menstrual blood, the menarche, and final reproductive competence. A girl's menarche is celebrated in secret events that simply recognize socially her "natural" achievements. In girls, who possess a self-activating and functional menstrual-blood organ (*tingu*), maturation is thus viewed as an unbroken process leading from birth and maternal bonding into adulthood. In boys, however, two obstacles block male growth: their mother's pollution, food, and overall caretaking, which at first nurtures but then stifles growth; and their innate lack of semen, since the semen organ (*kereku-kereku*) can only store, not manufacture, semen – the key precipitant of manly reproductive competence. In the native model, then, femaleness is a natural development leading into feminine adulthood; maleness is not a naturally driven process but rather a pesonal achievement of which men wrest control through ritual initiations to ensure that boys attain adult masculine competence.

The Sambia ritual cult channels male development through six successive stages of initiation. The first three initiations are collectively performed by the regional confederacy of hamlets noted above. The cycle begins by constructing the cult house, quickly followed by third-stage initiation, a puberty rite (youths, ages 14–16). These graduated bachelors then assist in the staging of second-stage initiation (boys 11–13 years). Last, both these elevated age-grades join adult men in staging first-stage initiation (boys 7–10 years), creating a new regional set of age-mates. Following third-stage initiation, youths are eligible for marriage; within a year or more, fourth-stage initiation – a marriage ceremony and associated secret rites – can be held inside the hamlet. Later, at the menarche of a particular youth's wife, his fifth-stage initiation will be performed. (Until now and for some months afterwards, the youth continues residing in the clubhouse. Later, the couple will build a separate house, cohabit, and may then engage in coitus.) Finally a year or two later, at the birth of his first child, he is initiated and attains sixth-stage ritual status. After two children are born, he is accorded the cultural status of full manhood (*aatmwunu*). What distinguishes Sambia ritualized masculine development from that of other Highlands initiatory cults is the prolonged institutionalization of secret homosexual fellatio, which is believed vital to the boy's maturation. Men hold that oral insemination is the only means of creating the "biological" changes needed to masculinize boys. It continues for many years, boys being first fellators then fellateds, and later, bisexuals. But, following marriage, custom decrees that homosexual activity halt and that men become exclusively heterosexual (see Herdt 1980, 1981).

The belief system

How shall we take cognizance of the male belief system surrounding blood and female pollution in understanding the significance of secret nosebleeding? Here I wish to simply summarize a larger body of data to orient the following material on ritual behavior.

At various levels of meaning, blood and its secular and ritual *designata*, are identified with the vitality and longevity of women and femaleness. Females, unlike males, are believed to be gifted with an endogenous means of producing blood that hastens the development of female growth, the menarche, and the menses; it is also the provider of womb life for the fetus. The male and female parts in reproduction are clearly defined: a man's semen enters the womb and becomes a pool that eventually coagulates into fetal skin and bone tissue, set within the female blood of the womb. Fetal blood, supplied only by the mother's womb, becomes the circulatory blood needed by all babies and adults.

For all humans, circulatory blood is thought to be an elixir – within limits – that stimulates body functioning and growth, and the ability to withstand sickness or injury. The limits of this idea are embedded in several constructs through which Sambia perceive blood. First, there is a tacit distinction that amounts to the difference between circulatory blood and menstrual-womb blood. Both males and females possess circulatory blood (*menjaaku*); but only females have menstrual blood (*chenchi*), categorized with all female contamination (*pulungatnyi*). Second, Sambia speak of reproductively competent humans (and also trees and animals) as being fluid or "watery" (*wunyu-tei*), not "dry" (*yaalkoogu*), that is, either sexually mature or old and "used up." In females, fluidity stems from having circulatory and menstrual blood, vaginal fluids, and that part of her husband's semen a woman "ingests" through sexual intercourse. Males, by contrast, are fluid only through their original circulatory blood, and later (artificially ingested), semen. Children and old people are "dry" but girls are more fluid than boys; adults – unless sickly or sexually depleted – are fluid. Third, blood is said to be "cold," whereas semen is "hot." Since Sambia see sickness and plagues (*numbulyu-oolu:* "pathway of sickness") as incorporeal active agents attracted to "heat" and repelled by "cold," this temperature difference counts heavily in body functioning: the more blood, the less sickness; the more semen, the greater chance of illness and debilitation. Fourth, menstrual periods are likened to a periodic sickness that rids female bodies of excess *tingu* blood and any sickness that manages to penetrate them. Ironically, then, women bounce back from their periods with greater vitality vis-à-vis this "natural" expurgative function males lack (cf. Mead 1935:106). The female capacities to create and discharge blood are thus *designata* of the structure and functioning of women's bodies, the embodiments of birth-giving, procreative fluidity, and health, so men reckon that these mechanisms account for why women typically outlive men.

Now what matters for ritual nosebleeding is that menstrual-womb blood, although a life-giving female elixir, also represents the sine qua non of lethal fluids for male body functioning. By implication, all male circulatory blood originates from the mother's womb, so the collective initiatory nose-bleedings try to purge it. Other female substances like skin flakes, saliva, sweat, and especially vaginal fluids, are also classified as *pulungatnyi* and are felt to be inimical to men. (Male illness resulting from female sorcery usually hinges on the conviction that a man has incorporated menstrual or vaginal fluids.) But menstrual blood is dreaded most. Children take in these substances through birth, and later, through feeding and touching. Women definitely evince concern not to contaminate themselves or others, especially their children, with menstrual fluids during their periods. Neither their public statements nor activities, however, reveal the intense anxiety easily aroused in men. Contrary to girls, boys are definitely at risk: menstrual-womb blood can thwart the "biological" push into masculine maturity. Men are even at greater risk since menstrual blood, in particular, can penetrate the urethra during coitus, bringing sickness and turning back the manliness that has been so hard won. For this reason, men say, they must remain cautious about contact with their children, too, since the latter may unwittingly transmit (cf. Meigs 1976) and infect men with the traces of their mother's body products.

The most harmful effect of women's *verbal behavior* during child-bearing is pinpointed on the boy's nose which is, next to the mouth, the body's main port of entry. Here, mother's speech and harangues have a lethal power. A woman's airstream emitted while speaking is thought to emerge from her blood-filled caverns. If it is directed – particularly at close range during anger – toward boys, the boys are believed harmed: simply by inhaling those insults and air (cf. Meigs 1978:305), a boy is defiled: the nasal orifice absorbs and stores the contaminants, hence-forth blocking the free movement of circulatory blood and other fluids from the nose throughout the body. (Likewise, women pollute boys simply by lifting their legs in proximity to them, emitting vaginal smells that boys can breathe in; and, for this reason, men keep their noses plugged during coitus, avoiding incorporation of the vaginal smell they describe as most harmfully foul; see also Devereux 1937:515.) Nose-bleeding is *the* critical means of egesting these incorporated materials from the male body, since Sambia practice no other form of bloodletting.

Despite these necessary expurgations, however, nosebleeding is unmistakably risky, even dangerous. The reason is simple: blood loss from cuts or wounds in general is dangerous, a process that, if left unchecked, would rob one of circulatory blood and of life itself. Large cuts are handled as quickly as possible; and even with minor scrapes men are squeamish about placing bindings to stop any blood loss. (The greatest single expense in my fieldwork medical budget was for bandages – for which people constantly asked.) Blood is "vital stuff" (Lewis 1975:203): like ourselves, Sambia view the containment of blood loss as a critical symptom of life-risk and a prognostic indicator for recovery. Birth giving and menstrual bleeding also carry a risk, but one of a different sort, since the female body is thought to "naturally" control blood flow. Thus, even though women use native medicines to reduce menstrual flows, they appear to be relatively unconcerned about their periods. Male nosebleeding is another matter. Nosebleeding is painful and the blood-loss disliked: it is done to remove female conta-minants. Indeed, it is unlikely that Sambia would ever use medicinal bloodletting as did our ancestors, or as do other New Guineans (Barth 1975:139; Williams 1936:342). Here, I think, is a major clue as to the psychosocial difference between nosebleeding, and menstrual periods or medicinal bleeding: one initiates a temporary bleeding inside a ready orifice to remove poisonous female matter, and it is he who rather precisely controls the amount of blood loss (cf. Lindenbaum 1976:57).

These elements of belief, namely women's innate production of blood, its association with reproduction, the contaminating potential of female blood for males, and the riskiness of blood loss, are the background factors that generally influence – color, crystallize, constrain – the actual experience of secret nosebleeding. In their particulars, however, secular beliefs combine with subsequent ritual teachings that are introduced through transitions in the ritual life-cycle. Successive stages of initiation teaching draw' on more secret, explicitly sexual elements, that reinforce the aggressive ethos of the Sambia warriorhood. It is to the system of ritual nosebleeding behaviors that I now turn, describing the emerging contexts of ritual belief in sequence.

Ritual nosebleeding behavior

The nosebleeding (*chemboo-loruptu: chembootu*, nose; *loropina:* a verb meaning to "cleanse and expand") act is the single most painful ritual technique, by common assent of initiates and men alike. (In contrast, mere piercing of the nasal septum is a benign secular ceremony occurring in childhood for both sexes.) That feeling is understandable. Physically, nosebleeding is a penetrating trauma of the nasal mucous membranes. The psychological effect of nosebleeding is enhanced by secrecy; so its forcible administration by men upon boys – and by surprise, at that – turns into a violent assault having effects probably close to producing authentic trauma. Boys themselves often hark back to the nosebleeding with expressions such as "I feared they were going to kill me." The ritual efficacy and subjective dynamics of collective nosebleeding are highly focused on the actual blood flow. The body of assembled initiators *always* concentrate on a generous but controlled blood flow – the sight of which is greeted triumphantly with a unified ritual/war chant. That collective action amounts to a forcible penetration of a boy's boundaries, for, aside from its surprise and ostentatious context, the psychological impact of nosebleeding assumes greater power when it is understood that Sambia place tremendous personal emphasis on the nose, second only to the genitals: the nose is second to none in matters of body appearance, notions of beauty, and their manifestations in gender symbolism.[1]

Sambia recognize two different procedures for nosebleeding that are associated with phratry affiliation. These techniques are hidden from all women and children, and from younger initiates until their ritual revelation at successive initiations. Traditionally, knowledge of the different practices was partially hidden from men of the two opposing phratries of the Sambia Valley, since the procedures are incorporeal property: ritual customs – trademarks – of the respective groups. Following pacification, however, these practices were shared with the opposite sides. Nowadays, men have some choice in the type of nosebleeding utilized in collective or private ritual.[2] The most common technique consists simply of thrusting stiff, sharp cane grasses into the nose until blood flows (cf.

Langness 1974:194; Read 1965:131). The other technique, forcing extremely salty liquid down the nose, is also painful, but there is less severe penetration since no hard projectile is involved. In the latter instance a beastly saline solution is made from soaking water in native vegetal salt that is sponged into the nostrils as the face is held upwards. Blood instantly flows following that action most times, and profusely so, in some cases.

The cane-grass technique was used in the first-stage and third-stage collective initiations by all the Sambia groups in which I observed nosebleeding. That practice is regarded as more dangerous than the water technique, largely due to men's perception that there is always a chance that the cane-grasses might break off and lodge in one's nose, risking death – the prime reason men offer in explaining why Sambia themselves abandoned cane swallowing before pacification. Following third-stage initiation, the choice of bloodletting technique is made on the basis of phratry membership in individually oriented fifth- and sixth-stage initiations. In private nosebleeding, however, personal needs and public glory are also involved; for example, the cane-grass technique is the riskier, more daring routine, and is identified as among the most masculine of activities. Here, men's subjectivity seems to be pinpointed on the need – and pseudorisk – of a physical, hard projectile actually penetrating the nostrils to achieve the painful and desired inward-to-outward effect of blood release. And, to reiterate, that penetrating thrust of cane-grass seems to be necessary for culturally accomplishing the first acts of efficacious nosebleeding within collective initiations.

With this background, I shall describe field observations on the first-stage nosebleeding behavior in detail; because of limited space I will then summarize the data pertaining to later initiatory nosebleeding contexts.

FIRST-STAGE INITIATION

Nosebleeding occurs on the third day of first-stage initiation as but one part of a longer sequence of manly ordeals. It is preceded by purificatory rites, collective dancing, fasting, beating rites, and a state of fatigue born of sleeplessness and constant, frighteningly unpredictable surprises. On the morning of its occurrence, the novices' mothers are sarcastically informed that their sons are to be killed, so women begin a sorrowful wailing – that is genuinely tearful or ritually stylized – according to their personal situations. The novices, too, are threateningly warned to watch out because of what lies in store. Here, the mysterious power of the flutes (heard, not yet seen) comes into play, building on and enfusing the novices' growing expectations about the elders' authority over the supernatural and themselves (see Herdt 1982). The initiates are first taken from their mothers and lodged in the ritual cult-house: several hours later they are removed to the edge-land forest where the unexpected nosebleeding occurs.

Initially, the boys confront a massive vibrating wall of thick green foliage, a fence of young saplings tightly woven together. Pieces of red headband (a ceremonial garment) are tied up in the green mass, while inside (unseen to the novices) a chorus of bachelors shakes the trees, emitting an eerie sputtering sound associated with ritual ordeals. The effect is calculatedly bizarre: from the approaching distance one is made to experience the green mass itself as if blood were dripping from the branches. The novices plunge into that disturbing morass literally tied to the backs of their ritual sponsors, through a small opening at its center. Some scream and cry; some try to escape. But all are carried through the barricade into a muddy inner chamber, that leads only one way – into a cagelike passageway of naked saplings, tied together like a fence on both sides.[3] (The passage space was barely wide enough for me to walk through.) Lined up, outside and next to the passageway, are numerous warriors holding wild ginger stalks; and as the sponsor/initiate pairs walk the gamut of the enclosure they are pounded on their legs and backs. Most of the boys cry; indeed, by the time they exit into the forest clearing (20 feet away), many look terrified. Several cry out for their mothers as the all-male audience looks on.

The initiates are then grouped around the ritual site of a small brook flowing down from a thicket. A huge crowd of men assemble, fencing in the initiates. The nosebleeders themselves take center-stage: several of them are wearing upturned pig's-tusk noseplugs (worn with the tusk points turned upwards only at war and during these rites). The men are serious; and even as their tense bodies strain forward to convey that posture some of the men actually grimace. A ''strong'' man, a former war-leader, steps forward and silently plunges cane-grasses down his own nose: in full view of the initiates blood streams down his face into the water. Somewhere, still out of sight, the flutes hauntingly serenade his feat. The men all respond with a piercing ritual/war chant: a signal that they want more.

The first boy is quickly grabbed. He struggles and shouts but is held down by three men. None of us can catch his breath before the initiator rolls up cane-grasses and, as the novice's head is held back, pushes them down repeatedly into the boy's nose. Tears and blood flow as the boy is held, and relaxed forward, over the water. Next, one and then another boys' is grasped and bled. One lad tries to run away but is grabbed: as a punishment he is next bled harder and longer than the others. The next initiate resists fiercely, so four men lift him up off the ground and, while there suspended, he is nosebled. Another boy is penetrated until blood flows profusely; and after each instance of this, the collectivity of men raise the ritual/war chant time and again.

Many of the previous first-stage initiates (from an initiation held several months earlier) were also nosebled again. They stood in the wings of the group. Some resisted; others did not. But few of them resisted as fiercely as the new novices. Soon the act became almost mechanical for the initiators – the boys' clansmen, cross-cousins, and matrilateral kin.

The reactions of the boys, however, are the opposite. At first the new novices do not resist much. But after several boys defied the bleeders, others resist more. Some struggle and cry; some must be forcibly bled. The men have little pity for the lads. Those who resist are even more severely dealt with by prolonging the action and thereby brutalizing it. All of the novices (they numbered 42) are bled. Afterwards, the boys remain standing over the stream to let the blood flow. The water ensures that women will not later discover any signs of blood, and it also allows the boys to wash themselves off. Then sponsors (who did not serve as bleeders) dab the boys' noses with ferns wiping the face clean of any remaining traces of blood. An elder collects the leaves.[4]

Following the bleeding, the boys were lined up by the stream for the ritual teaching. The rhetoric described the nosebleeding as punishment for the insubordination of novices toward their fathers and elders. Pollution was also mentioned. Merumie (a respected fight leader and shaman) did the rhetorical teaching; he began by telling the novices that they must learn hospitality:

> If a man visiting your hamlet comes and asks you for water, you must offer him some. You must not hide your water vessels. He ought to be given water; if there is none, you must go and fetch some, even if it is dark and raining.

Next he reprimanded the boys, saying that when they were children they made "bad talk," sassing ritual initiates. He further asserted that if the boys defied or disregarded their elders' instructions to fetch water or betel nut, they would be nosebled again, as punishment. For those acts, Merumie said, "We now pay you back." The boys are told they must "change their ways."

Merumie then lectured the boys on their mothers' harmful effects and the value of letting blood:

> You [novices] have been with your mothers...they have said "bad words" to you; their talk has entered your noses and prevented you from growing big. Your skins are no good. Now you can grow and look nice.

A teaching about warrior aggressiveness was also performed until the first-stage initiation in 1973, at which time it was abandoned.[5] Elders stressed that nosebleeding could help novices become more fearless during warfare. Boys were told to be "strong" and unafraid on the battlefield. They were upbraided: having been nosebled themselves, henceforth they must not fear the sign of their age-mates' or comrades' spilled blood on the battlefield. In fact, elders stressed, the sight of blood itself was to have been regarded as a challenge – to seek revenge against the responsible enemies for the loss of blood on one's own side.

SECOND-STAGE INITIATION

Nosebleeding is not performed at this event, several years later. (Likewise, no nosebleeding occurs at fourth-stage initiation.) Boys do not know that, of course, until afterwards: in each subsequent initiation they are always left wondering about that fearsome possibility until the last. Men say that the initiates, having been bled once and long separated from their mothers, are protected by other external "cleaning" rites, like those which painfully scrub the body through use of stinging-nettles. However, individual second-stage initiates may be bled at the behest of their clansmen during subsequent first-stage nosebleeding rites. In addition, and somewhat inexplicable at that, men say that the boys, who are fed pandanus fruit (ending a taboo imposed earlier at first-stage initiation), are spurred enough by its ingestion and the smearing of its crimson juice on their skin to further "grow them." Women are expressly forbidden to see those events – which secrecy also seems to help offset the need for another nosebleeding till the following initiation.

THIRD-STAGE INITIATION

This event is the last collective initiatory performance of nosebleeding performed on boys as a regional set of age-mates. Later instances are individually oriented rites. This may be one reason the context is severe, almost cruel, in its violence and physical threats. This time, however, there is a greater element of voluntary action on the part of the youths, who, having attained puberty, are accorded the status of "young men" to be betrothed. As new warriors they are expected to be brave, self-disciplined, and emotionally steadfast, even though some cannot live up to that demand. After two days of the initiation (which lasts a week), youths are assembled on a signal (not dragged into line on their ritual sponsors' backs as occurred the first time). Many of them (they told me later) suspected they were to be nosebled. While lined up, military fashion, they are thus "attacked" by older men. A line of warriors, soot-blackened and garbed "like ghosts, like enemies," encircle them, plucking bows and arrows, hooting, shouting, and feigning an ambush. There, on a hidden hillside (away from the hamlet women), without a stream, they are grasped by sponsors and men and forcibly nosebled again (cf. Newman and Boyd 1982; Tuzin 1980). Although youths are not supposed to flinch, struggle, or cry, some of them do: the terror of the experience is greater than the stamina of certain individuals to passively submit to nasal penetration. (See Table 11.1 on the bilaterality of choice in this situation.) No stream should be needed for that reason: if the youths are "manly enough" they will effortlessly and with sober-faced calm allow themselves to be neatly nosebled. Their blood should carefully fall into leaves provided for their own cleansing and disposal.

The teachings of third-stage nosebleeding convey to youths, for the first time, some dangers of sexual contact – physical intimacy – with women. But that is *not* why elders tell them they were bled: after all, initiates must strictly avoid women, so the thought of illicit heterosexual intercourse is not even mentioned. Instead, youths are warned about three things: first, they must be vigilant and always ready for enemy attack; second, sexual contact with women will debilitate and make them vulnerable to death in battle; and third, they must avoid women and know that death from the angry husband and his cohorts awaits adulterous transgressors. The first element is graphically impressed on the novices by the mock attack of men posing as tribal "enemies" who administer the nosebleeding. The second element is left ominously vague, for the future. The third aspect is sanctioned by, and indexed toward, the flutes, whose cries – during the ritual – are said to represent a woman's sensuous moans as she adulterously copulates with an unwary youth. The unsuspecting youth will be killed by the cuckold and his age-mates, elders warn: obey us or suffer that fate. In other words, nosebleeding is here explicitly used as a powerful social sanction to constrain the youths' sexuality, ruling out premarital heterosexuality and ruling in homosexual activities. Indeed, it is the youths' first act of being a homosexual inseminator, at the conclusion of third-stage initiation, that is culturally regarded as an essential confirmatory act towards attaining manhood.

FIFTH-STAGE INITIATION
These events are triggered by the occurrence of menarche for the youth's young wife. Nosebleeding is its final ritual. The novice and his married age-mates engage in days of collective hunting in the forest (for possum-meat prestations bestowed on the wife's cognatic kin) while adhering to strict ingestion taboos. Bloodletting then becomes the focus of essential teachings that finally reveal the full dangers of genital-to-genital intercourse, vaginal pollution, and the subsequent dangers of wives' menstrual periods.

The novice himself is first to be nosebled as his elders and cohort look on. There is absolutely no question here of voluntary submission to the act: the youth is expected to be willing, even eager to be bled; most youths remained unflinching and frozen during the actual procedure. Any sign of fear or reticence is regarded as unmanly and inappropriate, and my observations have revealed no visible reticence. Either cane-grasses or the saline solution are acceptable techniques depending on one's phratry identification; but that decision is a matter for elders, not youths, to decide. Older men actually nosebleed the youth. Afterwards, when blood flows, the characteristic ritual/war chant is raised by the whole chorus of men. The novice's age-mates are then bled too. Older men may choose to bleed themselves or to be bled. (Younger initiates, of course, are excluded from this secret ritual advancement.) Older middle-aged men, particularly graying elders, do not usually take part, and nothing is said about this. (I have, however, seen several such men on occasion spontaneously ask to be bled.)

Elders emphasize the youth's erotic/procreative relationship to his newly menstruating wife in the following teachings. More than at fourth-stage initiation, ritual knowledge of purificatory techniques is taught so youths can protect themselves against the lethal effects of female sexual contact. Examples: special leaves may be eaten and muds smeared on the skin to strengthen the body; other leaves can be used to plug the nose; and tree bark can be chewed (and later spit out) during coitus to eliminate from one's mouth traces of female body odors and breath. The youths are especially warned to be conservative in all ways about heterosexual intercourse, and they are taught how to replace depleted semen "lost" to their wives (see Herdt 1981:249). Once again, the youths are enjoined not to be adulterous and they are warned of the fatal consequences if that rule is broken. And all of these warnings are set within the ritual prescription that, henceforth, the young man must take personal responsibility for privately nosebleeding himself alone in the forest after each of his wife's menses (regardless of whether he recently had coitus): that deadly blood must be avoided and eliminated at all costs, with scrupulous measures taken before and after each menses to avoid its contagious power.

Fifth-stage teachings also explicate a theme of hostility to women that was earlier implicit. This theme concerns making men responsible, autonomous warriors, by re-directing onto women some responsibility for the "pain of nosebleeding." It is an unmanly sign of weakness (*wogaanyu*) for the youth to sit idly by while his wife menstruates. Since she is "reproductively active," elders say, a man must be "ritually active" in a way germane to her body's release of menstrual blood into his world. Men add that *they* have no other orifice with which to bleed except that of the nose. Elder authorities challenge that since the youth now has (a sexual relationship with) a wife, he must prove himself stronger, manlier, on the battlefield. That message is then referred back ominously to domestic life: since it was *because* of the wife's harmful menses that the youth had to "feel pain," he must never forget his suffering on her account. She must bear responsibility for his pain; she must learn to respect him for the warriorhood ordeals he has endured to be fully masculine for her. So, if a wife is sassy or insubordinate, or under any hint of suspicion that she is being unfaithful, a man must not spare the rod in demonstrating his ownership and power over this creature who is responsible for his smarting nose.

SIXTH-STAGE INITIATION

This nosebleeding occurs in conjunction with the birth of a man's first child. The rite again follows ceremonial hunting and other purificatory rites. It confirms final initiation into the male cult hierarchy, although the rites and feasting are repeated again for the next birth or two – confirming full status as a masculine person. The teachings center on the birth fluids and their polluting potential, and a man's need to adhere to postpartum taboos by keeping distant from the mother/infant pair. The nosebleeding behavior is somewhat different: as competent manly adults, men are now autonomous and responsible for the maintenance of their own health. Indeed, the behavioral shift from being bled by others to bleeding oneself may actually occur in this initiation since novices have a choice with regard to nosebleeding themselves. (This choice also applies to the initiate's age-mates, who are also bled.) What matters is the greater stoic demand to self-consciously nosebleed oneself as a secret masculine response in defending against the immediate danger at hand: one's own wife's birth contaminants released into the close quarters of the hamlet environs. Following this initiation, most men do not nosebleed themselves again until (some two to two and one-half years later) they resume coitus with their wives following the child's breast-weaning. Whether induced by oneself or others, then, this nosebleeding is a "voluntary" act applauded again by the ritual/war chant accompanying the released blood.

PRIVATE NOSEBLEEDING ACTS

I have already mentioned the normative injunction that a man is personally responsible for "cleansing" his body through nosebleeding after each of his wife's periods. Here I shall simply sketch the context of those private rites that follow after fifth-stage initiation and into old age.

Private nosebleedings are highly personal acts performed alone. The morning on which a man's wife disappears to the menstrual hut (and she will never even mention this to her husband or other men), the husband also quietly leaves the hamlet compound for his own forest preserve. There he nosebleeds himself with respect to the ritual procedure of his phratry. He ingests certain leaves and tree "milk-saps," and also rubs the "milk-saps" on his body to "strengthen" it at those points he contacted his wife (i.e., penis, abdomen, navel, etc.) during coitus. Then he smears red mud on his torso and limbs. This oddly sympathetic body-painting obviously communicates to the community that he has done *something secret* in the forest; men themselves say the red mud merely "hides" the underlying white tree-sap smeared on the skin from the probing eyes of women and children. (The full significance of meaning surrounding that egested blood, the white "milk-sap" and red ochre, is complex and will be examined elsewhere.) Here, of course, we have arrived at the final regime of bloodletting behavior, and one in which the action *is* completely private, is "voluntary," self-induced, and is performed – or so one thinks – for the independent audience of oneself. At the same time, though, private nosebleeding depends on personal initiative and is publicly unobserved, so we should thus expect individual variation in its behavior and experience.

This latter point raises difficult questions about the experience of adult bloodletting – a subject that constitutes a fascinating "internal discourse" in male life precisely because it is so much avoided. Most men are timid and tight-lipped about private nosebleeding, even among their peers. Younger men even evince some embarrassment about it. Such reticence seems striking and puzzling, for among their cronies men will sooner or later touch on their night's dreams, and wet dreams, body fluids (both male and female), sexual conquests or needs and even, with repugnance, female contaminants – all ritual domains except personal bleeding. (To get detailed information, I had to elicit personal accounts from informants, and usually while alone with them.) The silent message seems to be that a powerful, but vulnerable, piece of the self is secreted in that private act – an idea to which I shall later return.

What emerges from ritual rhetoric and private conversations is the view that private nosebleeding is both burdensome and painful, necessary and cathartic. All adult men are believed to regularly let blood as described above, but their emotionality differs somewhat. The fight leaders and self-conscious elders are undemonstrative and matter-of-fact about their bleedings; younger newlyweds are more exuberant, but also more squeamish. Weiyu, a close, married informant in his early 20s, deplores the fierce pain of nosebleedings; grudgingly submits to it only when absolutely unavoidable, in public, where he uses cane-grass on himself; but in private he uses the salt solution because it is less dangerous. Imano, an older, quieter, comfortable man, about 30 years old, who has two wives and definitely enjoys coitus with them, is also known as a faithful nosebleeder; he feels that the bloodlettings keep him healthy, and he generously lets blood in regular synchrony with his wives' periods. Sambia men thus engage in private bleeding for many years, till they halt coitus or their wives undergo menopause and stop having periods. In between, one hears many comments about the value of nosebleeding, but the earlier idioms about "male growth" disappear. Then, among seniors in their late 30s and 40s, men again offer, in explanation of their own continuing bloodletting, the pat remark: "I am still growing."

Men are quite explicit about the conscious intent of that idea. My informant, Tali, for instance, has said: "The woman expels her blood and you, her husband, must also expel it. If you don't, your stomach will become no good, it will swell up..." (cf. Meigs 1976). For that reason, he noted, "Old men continue nosebleeding until their wives stop menstruating." Unless they do, he said, they "won't grow anymore." And here is Weiyu:

> It's [menstrual blood] not men's blood, but the bad talk and menstrual blood of a man's "sickly" wife. It [blood] doesn't belong to us, it belongs to the women.... We say their [women's] blood and bad words enter our skin and lodge there, so we expel it [blood] from the nose.
> G. H.: But what can you replace the blood with?
> Weiyu: Nothing. We don't replace it. It's the contamination (*pulungatunyi*) of women, we expel it, that's all; it shouldn't be replaced.

But eventually, as Tali said elsewhere, "Old [i.e., senile] men don't [need to] perform nosebleedings on themselves; his [sic] skin is fastened to his bones; [He thinks to himself:] 'I won't grow anymore.'" To understand that belief and the developmental transformations that lead to its expression in adult behavior, I must interpret the whole system of ritual nosebleedings that shape male character.

Ritual transformations in male character structure

Although it seems clear that forcible bloodletting – administered collectively on boys – eventuates in the adult social outcome that men will voluntarily and, in private, let their own blood, the psychosocial mechanisms underlying this shift remain implicit. Nor is it clear why ceremonial bloodlettings throughout New Guinea involve extensive "ritual violence" (Tuzin 1982), "male dominance" (Langness 1974), or "ritual aggression" (Berndt 1962), and even, as among the Gahuku (Read 1965:129), "ritual exhibitionism...of the sexual aspects of male strength." To understand these issues in the Sambia material I shall analyze the above data with reference to several theoretical perspectives that help account for the influence of forcible nosebleeding on male personality development. Four developmental themes involving nosebleeding as cultural and behavioral controls on proximity to women (see Table 11.1) will be examined: (1) maternal detachment, (2) ritual aggression and obedience, (3) ritual reversals, and (4) heterosexual autonomy.

Maternal detachment

The great impetus of Sambia initiation concerns the physical separation of boys from women and children, followed by their irreversible insertion into exclusive male associations. This dual process is well-known from the literature (Allen 1967; Poole 1982; Whiting, Kluckhohn, and Anthony 1958). But, with few exceptions (Roheim 1942; Tuzin 1980), writers have tended not to view the behavioral experience of initiation in the context of the nature of the boy's tie to his mother (Bowlby 1958). In New Guinea societies like that of the Sambia this tie amounts to an "exclusive attachment" (Bowlby 1969) to mother and the female domain. Initiation is the most radical means of breaking that bond in order to subjectively create a new identity in the boy. This conclusion – which is no news to New Guineasts – is novel only in its psychosocial stress: boys must be traumatically detached from their mothers and kept away from them at all costs, otherwise the desired identity transformation cannot take place.

The severity of this ritual detachment remains a measure of the qualitative strength of the mother/child bond in traditional Sambia life before pacification. Admittedly, the data to support this view are retrospective and, at best, thin (but see Mead 1935; Whiting 1941). Nor does space allow an extended presentation of ethnographic material on post-pacification Sambia (cf. Herdt 1981). But even today, from birth on, Sambia infants still experience profound and constant sensual involvement with their mothers, not their fathers, for several years and more. Babies are attached to their mothers, who meet their basic biosocial needs – food, warmth, cleanliness, stimulation, quieting, protection. In the warring environment, fathers were removed from their infants for

Table 11.1. *Cultural and behavior characteristics of nosebleeding rites in the male life cycle*

Initiation stage	Focus of ritual teachings				Behavioral context: audience			Physical and societal constraints			
	Physical growth	Mother's pollution of ego	Warrior's aggres-siveness ethos	Wife's pollution of ego	The directing authorities	Collective ritual	Solitary private ritual	Voluntary nose-bleeding	Involuntary nose-bleeding	Other-induced bleeding	Self-induced bleeding
First Stage (7–10 years)	X --- X ---- X				Elders	X				X ---- X	
Second Stage (11–13 years)											
Third Stage (14–16 years)			X		Elders	X			X ---- X ---- X (Bilateral)		
Fourth Stage (16 years +)											
Fifth Stage (16–20 years)			X ---- X		Elders Peers	X		X			X
Sixth Stage (20–30 years)			X ---- X		Elders Peers	X		X		X --- X (Optional)	
Wife's Menses	X (Old age)		X ---- X		Self	X --- X					X

long periods. They are still weakly involved in infant-caretaking, on an hour-by-hour basis, compared to mothers or older siblings. The polarity of the sexes – in the division of labor, domestic discord, and in ritual arenas – exacerbates the struggle for security in the child's developing sense of self. Were this a different historical tradition the outcome might be left to chance. But not so for Sambia who believed – can it be felicity? – that boys do not "naturally" mature, become manly, unless powerful collective responses place boys into firm masculine gender roles that deny and override mother's influence, feminine attributes, and identity-signs in the boy (see Stoller and Herdt 1982).

Initiation begins with boys being taken from their mothers in a way that guarantees anxiety in the novice. They are kept in the dark about whether or not they will be initiated. It is true that most boys "know" (at some level of awareness) that they will be initiated eventually. It is also true that initiation is associated with male pride and glory, that is, parading in ritual regalia, and that it is boys' only means to "grow up": parents and others communicate attitudes of this sort, overtly or covertly, according to the family situation. But remember that Sambia boys are only 7–10 years old, that initiation is designed as a surprise, and that its symbolic messages are coded to create anxiety in the boy's wrenching from hearth and family: feelings of loss arising from the irreversible awareness that the initiate may never again "be with" – touch, hold, talk to, eat with, or look at – his mother.

First-stage rituals make use of this traumatic reaction in precise ways designed to radically resocialize the boy. Both parents are removed from the scene; a substitute ritual sponsor is introduced; boys undergo days of ordeals, hunger, thirst, sleeplessness, fatigue, and alarming surprises – including great revelations (e.g., about the flutes and ritual fellatio). Thus, following physical separation, a different form of attachment – "anxious attachment," in Bowlby's (1971:196–197, 201–203) terms – is stimulated. It arises from fear and inability to predict what will happen next, while being denied access to one's protective attachment figure, mother. *De*tachment results: despair, crying, searching behavior, including depression or its suppressed counterpart, anger (see Poole 1982). Sambia rituals play upon such feelings by making familiar persons or surroundings seem alien, bizarre, and even terrifying. (Róheim [1945:249] referred to such a process as "separation anxiety.") In the wake of these experiences new *male* attachment figures and sentimental bonds are introduced. The ritual sponsor, for instance, is the primary guardian and maternal substitute; and boys who called for the parents, who sobbed or clung to their sponsors, for example, in nosebleeding, were carried, and offered solace and comfort, by their sponsors. Sharing in ordeals also forges lasting ties between novices as age-mates (Turner 1967), and this peer group identification also tends to mitigate maternal loss and detachment.

Forcibly inserted into secret male rites – in this mood stage – nose-bleeding thus becomes a most powerful means for penetrating inside a boy's body and identity. Mother is removed; blood becomes a sign *of* and *for* her, in the all-male context. Further, cutting the nose releases *mother's* blood: in ritual experience this blood is not simply a "symbol" of female essence – it *is* isomorphic with one's (incorporated) female-ness and what that means – womb, nurturance, mother's goodness, softness and curses, and the femaleness that cannot become maleness. Ritual attempts to identify all those aspects as contained within the part of self which is removed with the blood. For as Marilyn Strathern (1979) has argued, New Guinea societies often make the body/skin surface an analog of what we call the "self." Nosebleeding violates one's body boundaries, removing the "female" blood, so that one's body (self) literally becomes an object of reclamation by the ritual cult. It is only the completion of this act that paves the way for appropriate homo-sexual fellatio, which "fills up" boys' insides with semen – "biological maleness" – "displacing" the female essences.

But the critical experiential precedent is this: a male learns to nose-bleed in order to eliminate femaleness from his body – an act which for boys separates "me" from mother and all femaleness – and this act in time becomes a sign to the self that one's identity is clearly male.

Ritual aggression and obedience

Forcible nosebleeding belongs to a power play. Viewed in developmental perspective, nosebleeding is one of many social control mechanisms used to create and maintain the social hierarchy of the ritual cult. The hamlet-based warriorhood, into which boys are conscripted, supports this cult hierarchy. Elders are at the top of the ritual status ladder. Fully initiated married men dominate over bachelors, who dominate initiates. Women and children are excluded from cult rites, to which they are nonetheless politically subordinated. Men (including the boys' fathers) utilize initiation to separate boys from their mothers and natal house-holds, thereafter ensuring masculine gender differentiation, conformity to adult male gender role norms, and the maintenance of cult secrets. Initiation thus effects immediate and total *physical separation* from all females. But what about the latter nosebleedings, for example, those at third-stage initiations? Why is it necessary to violently nosebleed youths years after they have been detached from their mothers, have avoided women, and have conformed to ritual conventions as residents of the men's clubhouse?

To answer this question we must understand the political context of ritual domination. The presence of a cult-based warriorhood in every Sambia hamlet is a function of certain societal imperatives that clan elders direct. These imperatives can be briefly stated as follows: (1) per-petuation of socioeconomic stability in the community; (2) requiring control and expropriation of the products of women's bodies and labor, that is, sexual services, babies, breast milk, garden food, and domestic services (cooking, baby-sitting); (3) authority over sons, whose allegiance as ritual supporters and young warriors is vital for the maintenance of elders' authority and hamlet defense; and (4) control over female children – daughters, sisters, nieces, cousins, granddaughters – who are needed as a commodity to obtain future wives for the bachelors, whom elders control further by abrogating all responsibility for exchanging these females and arranging marriages for youths. The eventual success of all these political moves, however, is bound up with first separating boys from the female realm, and making them dependably fierce warriors – obedient to "the cult" – in the persons of the elders: "agents of external authority" (Milgram 1974:62).

Seen in symbolic terms, this latter requirement is by no means easy or "natural." If we cast Sambia relationships in the conceptual paradigm of Bateson's (1936, 1972) ideas about "complementary" versus "symmetrical" ties, elders are faced with a dilemma that initiation resolves. As uninitiated boys, males are in complementary relationships to their mothers, who are their primary superordinates. Initiation transfers this relationship to elders and bachelors: boys become their subordinates. Initiates are removed from direct interaction with females. Age-mates take up symmetrical relationships with one another, matching masculine performances in hunting and fighting. Even ingesting semen becomes a "race" between initiates to see who grows faster. By puberty, then, bachelors are superordinates of initiates but subordinates of elders. Women are tantalizingly nearby but still stringently roped-off and out of reach. Here is where ritual violence is reintroduced and must be perpetuated.

Nosebleeding, periodically performed as a secret surprise of later initiations, is the most powerful social sanction for reinforcing boys' obedience to authority. Next to threats of death (which are also used), nosebleeding can be seen as an act of raw aggression (Tuzin 1980:74) over budding youths.[6] This domination comes first in late childhood, when boys would be prone to sexual experimentation; it comes next at puberty – when a powerful inhibitor is again needed to ensure heterosexual repression. As a kind of "symbolic castration" (or perhaps even "phallic aggression": Vanggaard 1972:101–112) violent bloodletting is a very efficient but traumatic means of funnelling youths' sexual and aggressive impulses along a particular developmental line – away from women, and elders, respectively – toward initiates (fellators) and enemies. Adjustment to ritual cult life takes that form: being involved only in homosexual relationships, avoiding all heterosexual impulses and contacts with women until marriage; and performing as efficacious hunter-warriors, directed by war leaders and elders. Ritual beliefs about the deadly contaminating power of women's bodies, with their greater depleting power compared to boy-fellators, further rationalizes youths' fears and avoidance of women.

In short, under the most powerful conditions of collective initiation, ritual aggression is used to instill fear and obedience of male authorities and cult conventions, bravado in fighting performance, and avoidance and fear of women.

Ritual reversals

A dramatic transformation occurs in nosebleeding behavior between first initiation and the attainment of adulthood years later: the shift from being forcibly nosebled to "voluntarily" bleeding oneself. This reversal involves many other changes – psychosexual and cultural, as well as sociopolitical advancements in ritual roles and statuses. On the surface, this shift suggests fundamental alterations in one's behavior, from being a helpless (not passive) victim of violent nosebleeding assaults, to becoming a victorious initiator fully in charge of his own ritual actions and bodily functioning. Psychodynamically, however, self-bleeding requires developmental changes in character structure that Sambia identify with the esteemed traits of the proven warrior. Being a trustworthy cult member and being self-controlled in proximity to women are among these traits. Here, we must be chiefly concerned with identity transformations that are psychologically entailed by cultural and contextual shifts in the performance of nosebleeding itself. (The gross characteristics of these changes are represented in Table 11.1.)

First there are changes in the societal constraints governing the cultural context of nosebleeding. The general rule is: the more immature and less obedient the initiate is to male authority, the more violence accompanies bloodletting. At the start of the ritual cycle, the greatest force is used, implying that only males who must be forcibly separated from women require physical assaults. Thereafter "voluntary" choice enters into bleeding. From third-stage initiation on, one *should* stoically submit to the ordeal others perform on oneself. The cult standard is clear: the *manliness* of one's identity is judged by the initiate's willingness and capacity to be bled without fear or other "female" emotions. This reversal occurs simultaneously with performative acts that signify one's accountability to all ritual conventions – and without others having to regulate the initiate's activities – as, for instance, with new novices who are distrusted. From the start to the finale of ritual transitions it is the initiate's relationships to women that are most visible and scrupulously monitored in this respect. A novice's avoidance of all females is watched at first. The youth's continuing avoidance, his abstinence from premarital heterosexual contacts, and his patient obeisance to his elders in regard to his eventual marriage contract are next. Later, the signs of self-accountability in a married man are judged by his ritual regulation of sexual relations with his wife, and by his adherence to postpartum taboos, purifications, nosebleedings following coitus, and refraining from adultery.

Second, there are changes in the cultural beliefs surrounding nosebleeding. The general theme of ritual rhetoric stresses the dual ideas that the creation and preservation of maleness ("growth") goes hand in hand with becoming an aggressive warrior. Ideologically, first-stage nosebleeding is a punishment for boys' childish insolence to men; represents the idea that mothers' blood has blocked boys' masculinization; and embodies the notion that boys must become tough and learn to master their fear of blood on the battlefield. Initiates, here as always, are made beholden to their elders for ensuring their masculine "growth." Following puberty, however, the concern with "growth" turns upon the fear of menstrual contamination. Rhetoric about "mother" is dropped. Instead, from fourth-stage until old age, beliefs about female contamination are transferred from mother onto men's wives, only sexual intercourse – not mere nurturance – becomes the perceived danger that thwarts maleness.

Throughout this transformation the only elements that remain constant are women as dangerous and the cultural beliefs about the aggressive warrior's ethos. Repeated nosebleedings not only condition one to the sight of blood, but their initial traumas are supposed to be converted into bold prowess – leading and killing in battle without compunctions. The social significance of this aggressive stance is, without doubt, later inserted into domestic life too: one who is an accomplished killer is to be feared by his wife and respected by peers. Consequently, elders constantly stress the initiates' obedience to authorities as well. Nosebleedings are chronologically timed in the life cycle to ensure that elders retain social control over bachelors – after puberty – until such time that youths are married and thereby become adult members invested in the cult. Then, of course, they can be relied upon for perpetuation of established controls over women and initiates.

Third, a number of highly structured and ritually organized reversals in sexual behavior are correlated with the meaning of bloodletting acts as various levels of significance. Ultimately, all these transformations bear upon physical proximity to women. Sexually, these changes issue from first being a passive homosexual fellator to being a dominant fellated; thereafter sexual behavior switches from exclusive homoerotic contacts to brief bisexual encounters – secret fellatio with boys and private fellatio with one's bride – and then, finally, to exclusive heterosexual relationships in marriage. (For details, see Herdt 1981. Some rather complex symbolic interchanges of blood and semen, also involved in this structure, are examined elsewhere.) Moreover, several important symbolic attachments to ritual agents – such as the fantasied female hamlet-spirit animating the ritual flutes – are fostered as transitional objects in boys' identity changes from childhood to manhood, which attachments lend transitional homosexual practices their own excitement (cf. Herdt 1982). Changes in nosebleeding behavior then, from one ritual stage to the next, are followed by new sexual rights and duties – the final form of which I set out below.

Last, the composition of the nosebleeding ritual audience undergoes symbolic changes of various sorts. At first-stage initiation, novices are classed together against all older males. As age-mates, these boys are placed in symmetrical relationships with one another, nosebleeding and doing other acts with which their masculine performance is compared and judged. They are made subordinates of all elder males, who substitute for the boys' superordinate mothers in complementary relationships to initiates. Boys' fathers are in the audience of initiators; physical presence here counts as a primary sign of the politico-ritual division between fathers and sons. Nevertheless, both generations are made privy to the all-male secret rites, compared to the mothers – who are left wailing helplessly behind in the village. But mother is symbolically inserted into the context – through the *designata* of nose blood, "female contamination" – which invidiously links boys and women. Never again is that comparison made. In subsequent nosebleedings, then, mother is a part of the distant background whereas father becomes an emerging ritual teacher; and one's peers and adult men emerge as the key audience. The ritual sponsor's role declines after marriage until it is perfunctory. Elders remain prominent until adulthood, since they sanctify ritual teachings, but they, too, increasingly take a back seat as their physical power wanes. After puberty, moreover, the frightening attacks halt: no reason to remind bachelors who are one's enemies, for they are identified with other groups who kill (whose initiates drain off one's semen and whose women – potential wives – can pollute and sorcerize), not just nosebleed bachelors, as their elders do to "help" them.

The final transformations occur following marriage and fatherhood. One's wife now displaces mother as the focus of contaminated blood that must be expelled due to sexual contacts. But the bloodlettings are self-induced and private, acknowledging the marital bond and the particular periodicity of men's wives. Men do not perform for their peers or compete with them in bloodletting. They are, obviously, competing now with their wives, but this symmetrical "contest" is solitary and secreted in a very special sense. That mode of self-control concerns my final argument.

Heterosexual autonomy

Sambia manhood rests on the above ritual transformations – the fusion of which is necessary for, and "carried" in, the psychosocial elements of painfully performing private bloodlettings on oneself. That act, to reiterate, represents marriage and fatherhood: full manhood. It signals also the "acceptance" (socialization, internalization, habitualized reinforcements, etc.) of masculine rhetoric, secret beliefs, and comportment regarding self and significant others; in a word: self-autonomy. Two pervasive cultural assumptions must be kept in mind. First, it is in a man's own willingness to bleed himself that Sambia recognize the finishing-off of the phallic warrior. Second, only men who are married and having sex with their wives privately bleed themselves. (Analogically, then, Sambia "read" private bloodletting as meaning that one is engaging in heterosexual coitus, the most privileged sexual act.) Most of all, we must analytically underline the context of these assumptions: once again – for the first time in years following maternal separation – the individual man is placed alone in an intimate relationship with a woman.

Contained within the passages leading to this heterosexual union we can see several remarkable contradictions in masculine experience. Full masculine adulthood is denied without marriage. Children – heirs – are necessary for full personhood. Cohabitation and coitus are thus necessary for social esteem and the "reproduction" of the family and society. Ironically, physical and especially sexual proximity to women is the key threat to masculine health and vitality: it saps one's semen and "paints the penis" with female contaminants. And what about heterosexual pleasure? While most men regard coitus with some trepidation, and the act itself is laden with shame (see Herdt 1981:164ff.), Sambia men generally regard it as intensely exciting and pleasurable (and no less so *because* it is dangerous).[7] Mixed in all these contradictions is also the great imperative that one must not become too intimate for fear of revealing ritual secrets – including previous homosexual activities – and of losing control over one's wife and children.

There is another dynamic which we can see as a dilemma but which Sambia themselves unself-consciously act upon. The ritual rhetoric regards women as men's inferiors. Men are supposed to be "on top" – in complementary dominating relationships with women – in domestic interaction, in economic routines, in ritual, and in sex. (Never mind that women don't always or easily bow to men in public.) However, after marriage, men's private nosebleeding acts amount to quite a different symbolic pattern: symmetrical responses to their wives' periods. On the one hand, men define the husband/wife relationship as complementary: men hunt, women garden; the more *womanly* a wife becomes – producing babies and garden food – the more *manly* the husband is perceived (as genitor). But, on the other hand, ritual convention requires that a man match his wife's "natural periods" with "cultural periods" of nosebleeding. Otherwise, he is seen as *wogaanyu* (weak, feminine). The implicit idea is that a woman's periods are evidence that she is still growing, is still fluid, not dry or "used up." She must not "win" over her husband, Sambia say. As an instance of the "Jones effect," private nosebleeding matches female with male "growth" in terms of an equivalent (not identical) act. (Sambia do not say nosebleeding is the same as menstruation: cf. Bettelheim 1955:177–178; Hogbin 1970; Lewis 1980:128–131; Lidz and Lidz 1977; Róheim 1945:169–171; 1949:321–322.) Regular nosebleedings thus ritually frame the marital relationship as special compared to symmetrical peer ties or other complementary relationships (subordination to elders; dominance over initiates, and dominance over wives in public). In short, the marital bond is the one enduring relationship that has both symmetrical and complementary aspects because of regular "bleedings" in both spouses.

My point is that private nosebleeding is the key ritual context in which men live these contradictions. Custom demands that men live with their wives, have sex, rear children, and yet avoid interpersonal closeness, that is, they should stay aloof (Whiting and Whiting 1975). In both public and private situations, in sex and in battle, the ritual cult depends upon a man's personal control – autonomy, vigilance, self-regulation – as well as hostility (aggressiveness) toward wife and enemies, real or potential. Of course men do not treat their wives as real enemies; and in some Sambia marriages one finds expressions of care, respect, and, in this sense, love. But the rhetoric of ritual discourse ignores these complications (Faithorn 1976) by expecting visible aggressiveness in one's stance towards the world. By culturally structuring proximity to women in terms of systematic bleeding, the ritual cult has ensured that even in adulthood men will sustain these expectable contradictions. Privately, men nosebleed to eliminate their wives' femaleness from their bodies. This act compulsively repeats, time after time, the separation of the male "me" from other aspects of self (conscious, unconscious): mother, wife, father, elders, one's earlier identities. Its affects – fear, disgust, phobic reactions to red fluids, shame – suggest that bloodletting experience has unconscious elements that utilize "conversion-reaction" as a culturally constituted defense mechanism (Spiro 1965) in the service of ego. Its solitariness (Freud 1907:19) also allows for the ripe experience of personal, not just collective, fantasies. For instance: that one's noseblood (can it be otherwise?) contains some part of mother (circulatory blood). Private nosebleeding signifies to the self that one is still male and masculine despite heterosexual union. It thus aids heterosexual virility and maintains controlled proximity in a double sense: to one's wife and to one's secret ritual (secret identity).

But what about the anomaly of old men still "growing"? This complex problem requires an answer that is both symbolic and psychological. First there is a semantic point: what does the native concept of "growth" mean? I hope it is clear that for Sambia its connotations extend beyond mere physical maturation (though the natives often couch their answers in this form when responding to elicited questions).[8] *Male* "growth" entails "strength" (*jerungdu:* another thick idea), personality traits such as aggressiveness and autonomy, as well as attitudes and behavioral acts involving interpersonal ties. On these grounds "growth" has a psychological sense that is similar to our own concept of "separateness" (see Mahler 1963 on separation-individuation). We must remember that boys' first experience with "growth" is what *elders* collectively teach. So when men say, in middle age, that they are now *privately* nosebleeding because they are still growing – and their situation involves physical, erotic, and psychological proximity to their wives – then we may postulate a psychosocial conflict requiring painful ritual acts which relieve that conflict. Psychologically, I think, the resurrection of the notion of "growth" to account for their bloodletting, despite their age, social respect, wives and children, seems to suggest there is a characterological identity conflict in Sambia males that never really goes away, it just lies dormant for a time. Symbolically, growth-through-nosebleeding is always available as a sign for elders to again clarify the separateness of their body boundaries and sense of self as being clearly masculine.

From this viewpoint there is no puzzle about why elders say they must still nosebleed to "grow." Their own physical powers are waning. Death is ahead. They have outlived some of their peers and enemies, but their wives are still there. And they still menstruate until menopause. They still engage in sex and perhaps – as some of them say – they enjoy it more. (Hors d'affaire?) But their fighting days are long gone and their hunting is negligible. They garden, visit, spin tales, and still direct ritual. In short, their phallicness is defused, they are more with their wives – upon whom they become increasingly dependent – and the old boundary between the masculinity and femininity in the marital bond grows fuzzy. The main result is that they may slip into a new complementary relationship, subordinated to their wives as they were once dominated by their mothers. Nosebleeding is still a ready means to defend against this loss of autonomy in old age, for it is the best revitalizing act available. It also serves as a sign – to self and community – that the elder is still sexually active and is symmetrically matching his wife's periods.

Conclusion

The violence of Sambia initiation is tied to the exigencies of its behavioral environment, which was defined by constant war. Nosebleeding, regularly inflicted, is but one of the mechanisms that requires and creates an especially aggressive kind of masculinity, whose model – the idealized phallic warrior – was suited to this environment. Moreover, the rites are the most powerful regulator of male interaction with females. Consecutive initiations effect both these outcomes: males begin as infants long sheltered in their mother's world, but they must wind up as warriors capable of killing, perpetuating painful initiations, and living and copulating with potentially hostile women. The contrast between those two countervailing developmental epochs is the difference between being traumatically conscripted into the ritual cult versus internalizing its "inalienable" fierce temperament (Mead 1936:265); between being forcibly bled versus painfully bleeding oneself. However much boys resist this psychosocial transformation, they cannot be allowed to circumvent it, for individual and community survival depends upon its successful outcome.

The degree of ritual violence and radical resocialization which characterizes Austro-Melanesian cults like that of Sambia are measures of the profound psychosocial obstacles against which men must work to initiate boys. The scale of institutionalization and affective intensity of bloodletting rites are correlated with a configuration of fragile family dynamics virtually unmatched elsewhere in the tribal world (except, perhaps, the Amazon basin: see Murphy 1959). The effects of warfare arrangements on the family can be seen in intense, prolonged maternal attachment, and distance from father. And too little father and too much mother inhibit a boy's easy, rapid, conflict-free transition into the warrior mold. (Read [1952] was correct: aggressiveness is not an easy condition for humans to *create and sustain*. Freud [1930:34, 50] should have visited New Guinea.)

The corresponding developmental issues are twofold. First, how to check boys' earliest pre-Oedipal identifications and wishes to merge with, and depend upon, their mothers (Mahler 1963). Thus, the "primary femininity" in a boy's core gender identity (Money and Ehrhardt 1972; Stoller 1977) must be drastically halted, for Sambia scarcely allow softness in men. Second, how to get boys to *primarily* identify with their fathers, with masculinity and the cult at large, thereby forcing them to conform to the psychosocial (and Oedipal) demands of war, ritual, and "hostile" women. No exceptions to universal initiation are allowed (cf. Barth 1975:47), which mocks the naïveté of early armchair writers regarding personal choice in ritual.[9] In short, a fierce "push" and a pride-filled "pull" by the men's organization are needed to effect maternal detachment and masculinization in boys (Lidz and Lidz 1977; Stoller and Herdt 1982). Repeated nosebleeding is essential to the culturally desired outcome.

It is the precise psychocultural definition of proximity to women, at each point in the life cycle, that governs the vicissitudes of Sambia nosebleeding. Let us accord full recognition to the native point of view: being in closeness to women is a social problem of magnitude at various levels – political, sexual, psychological, ritual. For males, female proximity always remains a power-laden issue; it embodies the culture dilemma mentioned before; it involves conflict, domestic and ritual, intrapsychic and interpersonal – as seen most dramatically in initiations – where nosebleeding mediates between individual "life crises" and the social order.

How does nosebleeding regulate proximity? There are four domains of constraints based on ritual custom and belief. (1) *Symbolic identifications:* nearness to women is believed always to impart femaleness to males, and hence, pollution (demasculinization). In ritual, boys are identified with mothers, and husbands with wives. The rule is: female contacts make one less masculine, so avoid them. Later, symbolically, one must match one's wife's periods with private bleedings to ensure that he is as clearly male and as productively masculine as she is productively feminine. (2) *Cultural timing:* enforced nosebleeding checks personal choice at critical junctures in attachments to women: separation from mother; puberty and sexual maturation; marriage and cohabitation; birth and postpartum "distance"; and encroaching agedness, which threatens overdependence on one's wife. (3) *Sexual access:* nosebleeding is the greatest sanction supporting boys' female avoidance behavior, youths' taboos on premarital heterosexuality and adultery, homosexual practices, and men's self-regulation in sexual activities with their wives. (4) *Secret identity:* nosebleeding experience, concealed by ritual secrecy, appropriates a vulnerable piece of the self that is primarily feminine and thus must be bounded and kept hidden from women. This last point means that nosebleeding is not only a culturally constituted bundle of defense mechanisms (cf. Bettelheim 1955; Stephens 1961; Whiting, Kluckhohn, and Anthony 1958). It is also a creator of that complex experience: selfhood.

Seen this way, nosebleeding is a *system of identity contexts* which layer upon one another in the life cycle. Each successive initiation introduces changes in the bloodletting act – roles, scripts, signs, and audiences which unfold and transform the social organization of experience. To balance childhood experience against the demands of adult roles (with all that entails) constitutes the "internal discourse" of private nosebleeding for men. This discourse concerns the objective dilemma that one live and be sexually intimate with a woman while staying aloof from her, being secretive, fierce, and manipulative, according to warfare and ritual designs (initiate sons, trade daughters in marriage). The formula of self-bleeding ensures this touchy holding pattern. That solitary act subsumes layer upon layer of past experience and identity. Its audiences include the inner representations or fantasied "voices" of mother and father, one's earliest objects; as well as one's elders and peers present through memories of past initiations, with their trauma, separations, violence, cutting of flesh, manly pride, respect, and autonomy. The ritual cult thus reinserts itself, time and again, into the self and the marital relationship. And this is how it must be: enjoying women and sexual release in coitus is a self-initiated threat to manhood. Bloodletting becomes a habitualized style for checking one's affections and lust, one's self-doubts about being alone with, and inside of, a woman again. It is humanly impossible for men, without coitus, to create children and reap the rewards of hard-won sexual access and manhood, but they take their lives into their own hands each time they do so. Private nosebleeding therefore enables a man to maintain lifelong proximity to his wife – with some intimacy – by serving as a sign that he is separate and potent (it keeps him "heterosexually masculine") and a vigorous warrior. This thick compound of meanings is embodied in the adult sense: "I am still growing."

If my interpretation is correct, then we should expect that the end of warfare will bring an end to nosebleeding. As a system of identity contexts, bloodletting is a part of the behavioral environment that included war and other material consequences of the sociocultural system and family arrangements. Pacification has indeed changed the whole system; but the parts of the system are not changing in equal measure. In fact, cane-swallowing was abandoned first, the warriorhood aspect of nosebleeding teachings was halted in 1973, and finally, nosebleeding iteslf was entirely dropped from the most recent Sambia initiations in the late 1970s. Family arrangements are changing slowly, although there are no longer the tremendous pressures on males to always be seen as fierce warriors. Initiation persists (cf. Gewertz 1982). Men, reared with war, still privately bleed themselves. But, in another generation, nosebleeding will only be known as social history to the Sambia.

Notes

1 The generic term for nose is *chembootu*; the penis is called *laakelu*; the glans penis is *laakelu chembootu* – which male idiom jokingly labels "that no good man down there (i.e., the pubic area) without teeth." Nose and penis associations like this one are not only consciously genderized in everyday discourse (see Herdt 1980:61–62) but unconsciously elaborated in individual dreams and cultural products like ritual symbolism and folklore.

2 This report represents the ethnographic present of 1974–1976, when these data were mostly collected. Sambia say that they stopped practicing cane-swallowing (cf. Berndt 1965:84: Salisbury 1976:62) of their own volition shortly before pacification (about 1964–1965). Pacification has brought formerly hostile Sambia hamlets close together, social changes that have also resulted in sharing certain clan or phratry ritual secrets (e.g., about nose-bleeding) with affines or age-mates, creating more choice in these matters. During fieldwork in 1979, I noted that most Sambia men still privately nosebled, according to their own self-reports. In contrast, however, those same men say that cane-swallowing was simply *too* dangerous, painful, and messy (they feared that the canes would break off in their stomachs and kill them); nosebleeding is much preferred.

3 It is with the imagery of ritual paraphernalia like this – "blood raining down," a dark cavernous entrance, and a tight narrow passageway leading into a flowing stream (where blood is expelled) – that Jungians delight in inter-preting womb and birth symbolism: "unconscious universal archtypes." But notice, too, that the ritual site, like a good Hollywood director's stage set, is constructed so that its subliminal perceptual effects build mystery, sanctity (Freud 1964:67), and fear, experiences that heighten and funnel subjective excitement along this particular line to a psychosocial outcome: trauma (for the novice) or triumph (for the initiation). I am indebted to Robert J. Stoller for this suggestion.

4 These bloodied leaves have but one, dramatic use, vis-à-vis older men's harangues of women somewhat later, back at the dance-ground site. The initiates' mothers are cursed for their "bad" treatment (e.g., cursing) of the boys, which is said to have thwarted masculine growth and required that men "kill" the boys. The red-stained leaves are held up as evidence of the boys' deaths. On one occasion I witnessed a remarkable display at this time: a young man, holding some of the bloody leaves, became excited and agitated and, quite beside himself, ran up to and assaulted one of the mothers nearby, forcibly stuffing some of the leaves in her mouth. He fled, and immediately a large group of women turned on the men denouncing the assault. This anecdote graphically illustrates how the nosebleeding context – for one adult initiator, at least – precipitated a flurry of aggressive behavior that was permitted to be directed towards a boy's mother.

5 Elders say that this warriorhood aspect of first-stage nosebleeding teaching

was abandoned in the early 1970s because it was anachronistic. Its counterpart in third-stage rites, however, is still taught. This seeming descrepancy involved the fact that third-stage initiates are older – they still remembered warfare – and, moreover, the bachelors are required to socially perform as warriors, even though war is gone.

6 I think that workers have tended to play down the subjective terror of this experience, for Sambia males are virtually unanimous in expressing the feeling that they believed they were to be killed on the spot at nosebleeding, and one finds similar reports elsewhere, spread between Australia (for example, Howitt 1884: 451n.) and New Guinea (cf. Read 1965:132; Watson 1960:144–145). Tuzin's (1980:74ff.) important work is the best and most recent exception to this omission.

7 Here are several clues about why men avoid discussing private nosebleeding. Private bleeding means you are engaging in coitus. Since coitus is shameful (even when men privately discuss sex with their cronies they tend to intellectualize, rather than refer to personal experience) private bleeding is tinged with shame. (See Whiting's [1941:64] related anecdote.) I suspect that men's heterosexual excitement is another factor, since sexual desire for women implicates loss of control, and intimacy, two areas that I have stressed above. (See also Tuzin 1980:76.)

8 Perhaps we should carefully examine again the connotations and contexts in which ideas about male "growth" are cited in Highlands societies (cf. Meigs 1976:399; Read 1951:162; Salisbury 1965:61).

9 "Teenagers in pre-literate societies are probably relatively more able to meet adult tasks than are adults in our society; hence they feel less dependent on or overawed by adults. These adolescents would certainly be able to resist rites inflicted on them by the old men if they wanted to do so" (Bettelheim 1955: 92). Clearly, we can see Oedipal dynamics at work in the fierceness of initiation, both for fathers and sons. Indeed, it could be argued (Róheim 1942) that it is not until men fully act as initiators for their sons that they have attained the status of manly persons. How valid is Reik's (1946) contention that these fathers are mainly motivated to traumatize their sons out of hostile, Oedipal wishes? We still do not know, of course; though whatever their intrapsychic motives, there remains plenty of other, socially sanctioned reasons, for allowing men to believe they are acting out of necessity for the welfare of themselves and their sons. Nevertheless, there is far too much violence, trauma, and even genital threats in penis bleeding (see, for instance, Salisbury 1965:56ff.; Tuzin 1980:69–70) such that we should dismiss the Oedipal argument out of hand (cf. Bettelheim 1955; Langness 1974:204–205; Lidz and Lidz 1977:29; Stephens 1961; Young 1965).

References

Allen, Michael R. 1967. *Male Cults and Secret Initiations in Melanesia.* Melbourne: Melbourne University Press.

Barth, Frederik A. 1975. *Ritual and Knowledge among the Baktaman of New Guinea.* New Haven: Yale University Press.

Bateson, Gregory. 1936 (1958). *Naven.* Stanford: Stanford University Press. 1972. *Steps to an Ecology of Mind.* Scranton, Pa.: Chandler.

Berndt, Ronald M. 1962. *Excess and Restraint.* Chicago: University of Chicago Press.

1965. The Kamo, Usurufa, Jate and Fore of the Eastern Highlands. *Gods, Ghosts and Men in Melanesia* (P. Laurence and M. J. Meggitt, eds.), pp. 78–194. Melbourne: Melbourne University Press.

Bettelheim, Bruno. 1955. *Symbolic Wounds, Puberty Rites and the Envious Male*. New York: Collier Books.

Bowlby, John. 1958. The Nature of the Child's Tie to His Mother. *International Journal of Psychoanalysis* 39:350–373.

1969. *Attachment and Loss*, Vol. 1: New York: Basic Books.

1971, *Attachment and Loss*, Vol. 2, New York: Basic Books.

Chowning, Ann. 1980. Culture and Biology among the Sengseng of New Britain. *Journal of the Polynesian Society* 89:7–31.

Devereux, George. 1937. Institutionalized Homosexuality of the Mohave Indians. *Human Biology* 9:498–527.

Faithorn, Elizabeth. 1976. Women as Persons: Aspects of Female Life and Male–Female Relations Among the Kafe. *Man and Women in the New Guinea Highlands* (P. Brown and G. Buchbinder, eds.), pp. 86–95. Washington, DC: American Anthropological Association.

Foucault, Michel. 1980. *The History of Sexuality* (Robert Hurley, trans.). New York: Vintage Books.

Freud, Sigmund. 1907 (1963). Obsessive Acts and Religious Practices. *Character and Culture*, pp. 17–33. New York: Collier Books.

1930. *Civilization and Its Discontents* (J. Strachey, trans.). New York: Norton.

1964. *The Future of an Illusion*. Garden City: Doubleday/Anchor Books.

Geertz, Clifford. 1973. Ethos, World View, and the Analysis of Sacred Symbols. *Interpretation of Cultures*, pp. 126–141. New York: Basic Books.

Gewertz, Deborah. 1982. The Father Who Bore Me. The Role of the *Tsambunwuro* during Chambri Initiation Ceremonies. *Rituals of Manhood: Male Initiation in Papua New Guinea* (G. H. Herdt, ed.), pp. 286–320. Berkeley: University of California Press.

Herdt, Gilbert H. 1980. Semen Depletion and the Sense of Maleness. *Ethnopsychiatrica* 3:79–116.

1981. *Guardians of the Flutes: Idioms of Masculinity*. New York: McGraw-Hill.

1982. Fetish and Fantasy in Sambia Initiation. *Rituals of Manhood: Male Initiation in Papua New Guinea* (G. H. Herdt, ed.), pp. 44–98. Berkeley: University of California Press.

Hogbin, Ian. 1970. *The Island of Menstruating Men*. Scranton, Pa.: Chandler.

Howitt, A. W. 1884. On Some Australian Ceremonies of Initiation. *Journal of the Royal Anthropological Institute* 13:432–459.

Langness, L. L. 1967. Sexual Antagonism in the New Guinea Highlands: a Bena Bena Example. *Oceania* 37:161–177.

1974. Ritual Power and Male Domination in the New Guinea Highlands. *Ethos* 2:189–212.

Lewis, Gilbert. 1975. *Knowledge and Illness in a Sepik Society*. London: Athlone Press.

1980. *Day of Shining Red*. Cambridge: Cambridge University Press.

Lidz, Ruth W., and Theodore Lidz. 1977. Male Menstruation: A Ritual Alternative to the Oedipal Transition. *International Journal of Psychoanalysis* 58:17–31.

Lindenbaum, Shirley. 1972. Sorcerers, Ghosts, and Polluting Women: an Analysis of Religious Belief and Population Control. *Ethnology 11*: 241–253.

——— 1976. A Wife is the Hand of Man. *Man and Woman in the New Guinea Highlands* (P. Brown and G. Buchbinder, eds.), pp. 54–62. Washington, DC: American Anthropological Association.

Mahler, Margaret S. 1963. Thoughts about Development and Individuation. *Psychoanalytic Study of the Child 18*:307–327.

Mead, Margaret. 1968 (1935). *Sex and Temperament in Three Primitive Societies*. New York: Dell.

Meggitt, Mervyn J. 1964. Male-Female Relationships in the Highlands of Australian New Guinea. *American Anthropologist 66*:204–224.

Meigs, Anna. 1976. Male Pregnancy and the Reduction of Sexual Opposition in a New Guinea Highlands Society. *Ethnology 25*:393–407.

——— 1978. A Papuan Perspective on Pollution. *Man 13*:304–318.

Milgram, Stanley. 1974. *Obedience to Authority, An Experimental View*. London: Tavistock.

Money, John, and Anke Ehrhardt. 1972. *Man, Woman, Boy, Girl*. Baltimore: Johns Hopkins University Press.

Murphy, Robert F. 1959. Social Structure and Sex Antagonism. *Southwestern Journal of Anthropology 15*:89–98.

Newman, Philip. 1964. Religious Belief and Ritual in a New Guinea Society. *American Anthropologist 66*:257–272.

——— 1965. *Knowing the Gururumba*. New York: Holt, Rinehart & Winston.

Newman, Phillip, and David Boyd. 1982. The Making of Men: Ritual and Meaning of Awa Male Initiation. *Rituals of Manhood: Male Initiation in Papua New Guinea* (G. H. Herdt, ed.), pp. 239–285. Berkeley: University of California Press.

Poole, John Fitz P. 1982. The Ritual Forging of Identity: Aspects of Person and Self in Bimin-Kuskusmin Initiation. *Rituals of Manhood: Male Initiation in Papua New Guinea* (G. H. Herdt, ed.), pp. 99–154. Berkeley: University of California Press.

Read, Kenneth E. 1951. The Gahuku-Gama of the Central Highlands. *South Pacific 5*:154–164.

——— 1952. Nama Cult of the Central Highlands, New Guinea. Oceania 23:1–25.

——— 1965. *The High Valley*. London: George Allen and Unwin Ltd.

Reik, Theodore. 1946. *Ritual: Four Psycho-Analytic Studies*. New York: Grove.

Róheim, Geza. 1942. Transition Rites. *Psychoanalytic Quarterly 2*:336–374.

——— 1945. *The Eternal Ones of the Dream*. New York: International University Press.

——— 1949. The Symbolism of Subincision. *American Imago 6*:321–328.

Salisbury, Richard F. 1965. The Siane of the Eastern Highlands. *Gods, Ghosts and Men in Melanesia* (P. Lawrence and M. Meggitt, eds.), pp. 50–77. Melbourne: Melbourne University Press.

Schwartz, Theodore. 1973. Cult and Context: the Paranoid Ethos in Melanesia. *Ethos 1*:153–174.

Spiro, Melford E. 1965. Religious Systems as Culturally Constituted Defense Mechanisms. *Context and Meaning in Cultural Anthropology* (M. E. Spiro, ed.), pp. 100–113. New York: Free Press.

Stephens, W. N. 1961. A Cross-Cultural Study of Menstrual Taboos. *Genetic Psychology Monographs 64*:385–416.

1962. *The Oedipus Complex: Cross-Cultural Evidence.* New York: The Free Press.

Stoller, Robert J. 1968. *Sex and Gender, Volume I: On the Development of Masculinity and Femininity.* New York: Science House.

1977. *Perversion: The Erotic Form of Hatred.* London: Quartet Books.

Stoller, Robert J., and Gilbert H. Herdt. 1982. The Development of Gender Identity: A Cross-Cultural Contribution. *Journal of the American Psychoanalytic Association* 30:29–59.

Strathern, Andrew J. 1969. Descent and Alliance in the New Guinea Highlands: Some Problems of Comparison. *Proceedings of the Royal Anthropological Institute of Great Britain and Northern Ireland for 1968*, pp. 37–52.

Strathern, A. Marilyn. 1972. *Women in Between*, London: Seminar Press.

1979. The Self in Self-Decoration. *Oceania* XLIX: 241–257.

Turner, Victor. 1967. Betwixt and Between: the Liminal Period in Rites de Passage. *The Forest of Symbols*, pp. 93–111. Ithaca: Cornell University Press.

Tuzin, Donald F. 1980. *The Voice of the Tamberan: Truth and Illusion in Ilahita Arapesh Religion.* Berkeley: University of California Press.

1982. Ritual Violence among the Ilahita Arapesh: The Dynamics of Religious and Moral Uncertainty. *Rituals of Manhood: Male Initiation in Papua New Guinea* (G. H. Herdt, ed.), pp. 321–355. Berkeley: University of California Press.

Vanggaard, Thorkil. 1972. *Phallos.* New York: International University Press.

Watson, James B. 1960. A New Guinea "Opening Man." *The Company of Man* (J. B. Casagrande, ed.), pp. 127–173. New York: Harper and Row.

Whiting, John W. M. 1941. *Becoming a Kwoma: Teaching and Learning in a New Guinea Tribe.* New Haven: Yale University Press.

Whiting, John W. M., R. Kluckhohn, and A. Anthony. 1958. The Function of Male Initiation Ceremonies at Puberty. *Readings in Social Psychology* (E. E. Maccoby, T. M. Newcomb, and E. L. Hartley, eds.), pp. 359–370. New York: Henry Holt.

Whiting, John W. M., and Beatrice B. Whiting. 1975. Aloofness and Intimacy of Husbands and Wives: a Cross-Cultural Study. *Ethos* 3:183–207.

Williams, F. E. 1936. *Papuans of the Trans Fly.* Oxford: Clarendon Press.

Young, Frank W. 1965. *Initiation Ceremonies: A Cross-Cultural Study in Status Dramatization.* Indianapolis: Bobbs-Merrill.

12
On self characterization

Vincent Crapanzano

The finished man among his enemies? –
How in the name of Heaven can he escape
That defiling and disfigured shape
The mirror of malicious eyes
Casts upon his eyes until at last
He thinks that shape must be his shape?
And what's the good of an escape
If honour find him in the wintry blast?
    Yeats, "A Dialogue of Self and Soul"

In this chapter I develop several ideas about the self, the other, and their characterizations that have received preliminary formulation in some of my previous publications, particularly those on life history (1977, 1980), transference and countertransference (1981), dialogue (n.d.), and the relationship between self and desire (1982). In these papers I adopted a radically dialectical approach to the self. I argued that self-awareness arises when the ego – my most primitive prereflexive term – views himself, herself, or more accurately (since gender attributions require minimal self-reflection) itself (understood in a pregender way) from the vantage point of the other. Unlike Hegel ([1807] 1977), George Herbert Mead (1964), and Jean-Paul Sartre ([1943] 1956, [1952] 1964), however, I maintained that the dialectical movement is continuous; that the characterizations, or the typifications, of the other are subject to (a) conventional constraints embedded in language (understood broadly, as in the German *Sprache*), (b) desire (itself articulated through and constrained by language), and (c) the resistance of the other, resistance being understood in phenomenological terms as the most elementary criterion of the real. I maintain further that the arrests of the dialectical process through desired characterizations and typifications of the other (and therefore the self) mask, ideologically as it were, the continuous movement of self and other constitution. Put simply: One casts the other (subject to conventional constraints and resistance) in order to cast oneself. And, I hasten to add, one casts oneself in order to cast the other. The movement is complexly circular, and any description of it – whether expressed in narrative form (as in Hegel's tale of the master and the slave or Sartre's of Jean Genet) or theoretically (as in Mead's, Sartre's or, for that matter, Lacan's [1966] formulations) – insofar as a description has to begin somewhere, suggests a determinable beginning to the movement and a *reality* to the arrests. In other words, exposition confirms the ideological masking of circularity and the play of desire and language with resistance – the real.

I do not wish to deny the existence of arrests in the dialectical process. They may be understood in terms of an internalization of significant figures, or images, in the subject's biography, in terms of more or less culturally sensitive maturation processes, of the inevitable emergence of archetypical orientation points, of a response to conditioned typifications and generalizations of the other, or of some sort of psychophysiological entropy. Such formulations – we recognize them as *our* psychologies – serve to reinforce our own cultural understanding of the self as having evolved or developed into a more or less consistent, a particular, perduring entity, which may yet be subject to conflict, splitting, and fragmentation as well as to amalgamation, cohesion, and growth. Here, I am striving to discuss the self at what can be called, *faute de mieux*, a prepsychological level; that is, I am seeking a formulation that will enable us to understand the grounding of our psychologies and provide, if not a metalanguage, then a nonpsychological vantage point for their viewing.

Strictly speaking, I can only evoke the possibility of such groundings, vantage points, and metalanguages; for, insofar as I write in the same language as the psychologies, I am bound to fail. My horizon is as encompassed by the same language as the psychologies themselves. There can, in my view, be no truly external vantage point, no transcendental ego, no real possibility of a transcendental reduction, or epoché. There can only be the evocation of such transcendencies, which have themselves, ironically, to be seen as possibilities within our encompassing language. Such possibilities are facilitated by our peculiar narrative conventions (the omniscient narrator or, for that matter, reader), by our theologies (an omniscient deity – itself perhaps a refraction of our narrative presumption), and by such long-standing tropes as the traveler.

The traveler, today embodied with suspiciously forceful empirical certainty in the anthropologist (though more accurately in the "anthropologist"), has had considerable philosophical currency (Van den Abbeele, 1984). (How often do our students, if not we ourselves, read, say, Lévi-Strauss's *Tristes Tropiques* as though we were reading about Lévi-Strauss and not about "Lévi-Strauss," the character that Lévi-Strauss creates in his tale?) Spanning worlds, translating without *really* translating, explaining without *really* explaining, describing without *really* describing, doomed less tragically than comically to failure, the traveler may be from the West – the hero who bursts forth – or like Montesquieu's Usbek or our "man-from-Mars," he may be from some distant, exotic place. It is they – the traveler, the anthropologist, the man-from-Mars, or what they have or are deemed to have said – that provide at least the illusion of a transcendent vantage point for self-reflection (Crapanzano, 1987a). As an anthropologist, I suppose I am acting here – I hesitate – true to trope.

Dialectical models of self-constitution have tended to conceptualize the process in dyadic terms, as between ego and alter, the potential master and slave, or self and other. This process (regardless of the actual number of participants) has, however, to be understood in triadic terms (Crapanzano, 1980, 1982; n.d.). (Suggestions of this triadic dimension to the dialectical process are to be found in Sartre's [1956] discussion of the other in *Being and Nothingness* and Lacan's [1966] analysis of the *Autre, autre*, and *petit a*.) Insofar as the self is an arrested moment in a continuous dialectical movement and insofar as such arrested moments depend upon language, the constitution of "self" requires a guarantor of meaning or, at least, of the conventions of meaning, that permits, within limits, the play of desire. I have called this guarantor, in the spirit of Peirce ([1931] 1974), the Third, but my understanding of it is only tangentially Peircean. The Third is not a real or imaginary being but a function that can be embodied in real or imaginary beings, in fathers, mothers, kings, presidents, totems, ancestral effigies, fetishes, anatomical parts, or the eye, as, for example, in Victor Hugo's *La Conscience*:

Il vit un oeil, tout grand ouvert dans les ténèbres,
Et qui le regardait dans l'ombre fixement.

Indeed – in conscience itself. More abstractly, the function of the Third may be symbolized by such notions as the law, convention, culture, language, tradition, tact, the establishment, the church, reason, or the Lacanian *nom de pére* – the name, the no, of the father. It may be conceived as the (absent) interlocutor in those silent but forceful secondary, or shadow, dialogues that accompany any primary dialogue (e.g., the dialogue between the student of anthropology who engages silently with his mentors back home and all they symbolize as he converses with his friends in the field) (Crapanzano, 1987b).[1] The institutionalization, ritualization, and the internalization of the representations – the embodiments and symbolizations – of the Third mask the instability of these representations, projecting an altogether illusory stability that is perhaps (and I am being facetious) only now coming apart in this supposed postmodern era. The representations of the guarantor of meaning are themselves implicated in the dialectical play of desire, convention, and resistance, becoming, as it were, the ultimate stake in the negotiations between ego and alter. Who has the fetish has the power!

My approach to the self, in this discussion at least, is dialectical in a structural, and not in a phenomenological, sense. My concern is not with the experience of the self, though at times I will be concerned with descriptions of that experience but with the complex linguistic processes by which self-reflection is borne. My emphasis will not be on the sentence as a maximal unit but on verbal exchanges I call dialogues that are "bathed" to varying extents in what Henry James ([1905] 1984:134), who never thought much of pure dialogue, calls a medium – "that distillation of the natural and social air."

The Western propensity to confuse the experience of the self, the notion of the self, and self characterization reflects if not the structure of our language then the assumptions we make about them and what they can and cannot do. I refer here specifiically to our tendency to view language unifunctionally, in essentially referential terms (Silverstein, 1976; 1979; 1985), and to an ambivalent attitude we take to the relationship between the word and the object it denotes. The word may either be reflective of – "true to" – a reality out there, say, the self, or it may create, delineate, or in some other way determine that reality. We have, accordingly, an empiricist view of the self, as existing independently of its linguistic designation or a linguistically determined, a naively Whorfian, view of the self, as found, for example, in Berger and Luckmann's (1967:178) contention that a psychology "tends to realize itself forcefully in the phenomena it purports to interpret."[2]

It is tempting to assert that through the arrests in the dialectical processes the self is transformed into a "self," but such an assertion oversimplifies a much more complicated linguistic, and interpretive, process. The arrests would then simply afford an act of self-nominalization from the vantage point of a fixed alterity supported by a monumental guarantor of meaning. The self, like the other, would become an object of reference – of labeling or typification – without regard to the dialogical horizons in which the referencing, the naming, occurred, and the rhetorical and pragmatic features of that dialogue.

Typification – characterization – has, of course, been understood referentially, as giving a role, a name, or a label to the individual in question. Berger and Luckmann (1967:30–31) write, for example: "The reality of everyday life contains typificatory schemes in terms of which others are apprehended and 'dealt with' in face-to-face encounters. Thus I apprehend the other as 'a man,' 'a European,' 'a jovial type,' and so on." Such typifications are thought to be diagnostic: that is, to be based on "inherent" referentially describable – essential(-ized) – features of the typified individual, and as such, to be subject to empirical verification. Consider, for example, the diagnostic criteria for Martland's traumatic encephalopathy, that is, for being punch drunk. They are described in a standard psychiatric textbook (Noyes and Kolb, 1963: 190) as follows:

> The patient shows an insidious impairment of skill, a slowing of muscular action, a little uncertainty in equilibrium, slight confusion, and deteriorioation in attention, concentration, and memory. Speech becomes thick and hesitating. The patient "continuously simulates a person who is just a little drunk." Most patients are voluble and euphoric. Confusion and defects of memory become more marked, and intellectual impairment continues to a disabling degree. The

tremor, propulsive gait, and mask-like facies of parkinsonian syndrome appear.

Similar criteria can be elicited for any role player, personality type, or character.

I should like to suggest that the criteria upon which typifications or characterizations of self and other are based refer less to inherent, referentially describable and essentialized features, or traits, of the individual to be typified than to pragmatic features of the verbal transactions (and their accompanying behavior) in which the typifier, if not as an actual participant then as a witness, is engaged with the typified. In other words, typifications and characterizations are essentializations of pragmatic features, of *Gestalten*, of the encounter that are ascribed to the individual to be typified.[3] As such, they are metapragmatic ascriptions; they are not expressed, however, in linguistic terms but metaphorically, we might say, in highly conventionalized social-dramatistic or character-personality terms. I call them metapragmatic ascriptors and, in this chapter, I am concerned with those that "describe" pragmatic features in character-personality terms.[4] Like all metapragmatic characterizations, metapragmatic ascriptions are formulated, inevitably, in referential terms that are organized into (folk) psychologies and characterologies that ignore, if they do not deny, their pragmatic basis.[5]

Such psychologies promote the illusion of a primary, referentially describable basis for their attributions and, as such they not only ground a static, naively empirical view of their subject (one that denies the "creative" dimension of the word) but they also support the conventional arrests, the hypostasizations, and reifications of individual self-articulations.[6]

Let me clarify. Given the propensity to view language in unifunctional – in semantico-referential terms – and to understand other functions of language as secondary to, or derivative of, those semantico-referential functions (Silverstein 1976; 1985), context-dependent, or pragmatic, meaning, as opposed to context-independent, semantic meaning, has been underplayed. (I should note that the privileging of semantic meaning ties in well with an "otherworldly" epistemological tradition, going back at least to Socrates, that gives preference to decontextualized or decontextualizable – pure – knowledge.) Context is itself both intra- and extralinguistic, proximate, and distant, and determined in any utterance by indexical locutions that not only point to relevant features of the speech situation but invoke implicitly the appropriate frames for understanding and interpretation. Such indexicals (such as the deictics *this* and *that*, *here* and *there*, *then* and *now*) have referential content – Silverstein (1976) calls them "referential" indexes – or they may be devoid of referential context – Silverstein's "pure" or "nonreferential" indexes. A shift from "here" to "there" in response, say, to the question "Where is the key?" changes the referential content of the sentence "Here is the key" in a way in which a change from "O *moço*" to "*O Seu*"

– from a vocative expression used to address in Brazilian Portuguese a man inferior to the speaker to one denoting equality or superiority – does not involve a change in referential content. The "same" man is being addressed, although of course it changes the social context of the utterance dramatically. Such pure indexicals are very context-creative. There is, I should add, a pragmatic dimension to all referential locutions, although their pragmatic force may be highly attenuated.

Statements about language may be metareferential (metasemantic) or metapragmatic. A metareferential statement refers to the semantic meaning of an expression: " 'Sydenham's chorea' refers to an infectious encephalitis involving both the cortex and basal ganglia"; "By 'those others' he meant the possessing spirits he could not name without endangering himself." Metapragmatic statements refer to the pragmatic features of an utterance: " 'Here,' like 'there' is a spatial deictic"; "Have you noticed that whenever that old Italian peasant wants something from him she calls him *sua eccellènza.* "[7] Both metareferential and metapragmatic utterances are themselves referential, although they are not without a pragmatic dimension (as should be clear from the examples I have given above – examples that cast me in a certain way). The referentiality of metapragmatic utterances facilitates their incorporation into theoretical and ideological orientations that are based upon a referential understanding of language (Crapanzano, 1981). Indeed, where there is a privileging of the referential function of language, the pragmatic function tends to be referentially masked. Although it is uncovered by such interpretive strategies as Marxism (as "mystified class markers") or psychoanalysis (as "unconscious desires"), these pragmatic functions are understood – reified even – referentially. But, perhaps too simply, such totalizing hermeneutical systems, but others as well, tend to confuse the referentiality of metapragmatic statements with the primary referentiality of an utterance or, on occasion, the referentiality of metareferential statements.

Metapragmatic ascriptors express in referential language pragmatic features of verbal transactions. Such features are "summarized" metapragmatically in socially conventional, more or less precise characterological and psychological terms. They make use of scientific or scientific terms: "John is an introvert"; "Susan is paranoid"; "Peter is schizy." Or they may make use of more common folk psychological expressions: "John's not much of a joiner"; "Susan, well, she sees herself as a victim"; "Peter is timid"; "Susan is suspicious"; "Peter is distracted." More often, it would seem, such characterizations are less precise, more discursive, and shift from idiom to idiom. They may have what I would call a referential-pragmatic lead-in: "John, well he doesn't say much; he kind of keeps to himself; I guess he's real timid." "Susan thinks everybody hates her. You smile at her, and you'd think you'd stabbed her in the back; she's a real creep." "Now, Peter, you got to understand him; he's real hard to know – kind of unpredictable; sometimes he's with you and sometimes he's way off in left field; yeah, I guess you'd have to say he's got a screw loose; he's a real nut, but likable." Often such characterizations are accompanied by examples of behavior that support the characterizations. Such examples are conventional paraphrases of events that occurred or are likely to have occurred; pragmatically, they serve to support the ultimate, referential characterization. (I should add that such characterological summations, referential as they are, may serve, pragmatically, to put a stop to the characterizing discourse or to shift it to the interlocutor.) Rarely in such characterizations are ego's self characterizations accepted as referentially adequate.[8] Notions of character, personality, and self are, I believe, meta-metapragmatic. They are referential abstractions of referentially expressed, and pragmatically persuasive, metapragmatic statements. Hence, when we talk about the notion of self prevalent in a particular society, we are talking about abstractions of metapragmatic ascriptions and descriptions, which if current in the society, and not just an outsider's abstraction, feed back on the metapragmatic vocabulary and indeed highlight those pragmatic features of the primary discourse that are ideologically relevant.

The illustration of this process presents us with considerable, if not insurmountable, difficulties. Much of the characterization that takes place, if it is articulated at all, is articulated silently in those shadow dialogues of which I have spoken. They afford the vantage point for the reflective stance required for such a characterization. (Most often such characterizations are not only post dictionem but occur in another conversation with another interlocutor.) Of course such reflective moments may well be triggered by various rhetorical strategies within the primary discourse. Among these are metalinguistic and what, for a better term, I call quasi-metalinguistic locutions or hedges, such as "as it were," "so-to-speak," "if I may say" – expressions that cause a reflective pause in the primary discourse without the speaker's actually making an explicit metalinguistic comment ("Oh dear, what nonsense I am talking") but rather suggesting a reflective understanding of the meaning of the following expression that is left to the interlocutor to determine (if it is to be determined at all [Sweetser 1987; Kay 1987]). They serve as well to cast the speaker as someone "sensitive to the nuances of language," "cautious," "bright," or indeed "indecisive," and his interlocutor as someone capable of appreciating his sensitivity, caution, brightness, or indecisiveness. They create a complicity between the speaker and his audience.

If characterizations are made in the primary discourse, they often change the direction or the level of discourse. They draw attention in characterological or personality terms to the self-constituting dimension of the primary discourse, and – this is most important for herein lies very considerable rhetorical power – they evoke the existence of other possible, more privileged, "truer" understandings (rooted, I would argue, in the secondary dialogues) that are somehow external to, and conventionally masked by, the primary discourse – understandings that are placed, in our culture, in that always mysterious, and potentially threatening place: the mind of the other. Stated, such characterizations shift the established hierarchical or egalitarian relationship between the speaker and his interlocutor in dramatic ways that may require some sort of redressive maneuvering to restore the "original" relationship. They may, of course, be redressive of some previous disturbance in the established relationship.

As a first illustration of this process of characterization, let me quote from *Alice in Wonderland*. Alice has come to the little house where the Duchess lives. She wants to enter – one supposes. She approaches the door timidly and knocks. The Frog Footman, who is sitting at the door, tells her it is no use knocking because there is too much noise inside for anyone to hear her knock.

> "Please, then," said Alice, "how am I to get in?"
>
> "There might be some sense in your knocking," the Footman went on, without attending to her, "if we had the door between us. For instance, if you were *inside*, you might knock, and I could let you out, you know."
>
> He was looking up into the sky all the time he was speaking, and this Alice thought decidedly uncivil. "But perhaps he can't help it," she said to herself, "his eyes are so *very* nearly at the top of his head. But at any rate he might answer questions. – How am I to get in?" she repeated, aloud.
>
> "I shall sit here," the Footman remarked, "till tomorrow –"
>
> At this moment the door of the house opened, and a large plate came skimming out, straight at the Footman's head; it just grazed his nose, and broke to pieces against one of the trees behind him.
>
> "– or next day, maybe," the Footman continued in the same tone, exactly as if nothing had happened.
>
> "How am I to get in?" asked Alice again, in a louder tone.
>
> "*Are* you to get in at all?" said the Footman. "That's the first question, you know."
>
> It was, no doubt: only Alice did not like to be told so. "It's really dreadful," she muttered to herself, "the way all the creatures argue. It's enough to drive one crazy!"
>
> The Footman seemed to think this a good opportunity for repeating his remark, with variations. "I shall sit here," he said, "on and off, for days and days."
>
> "But what am *I* to do?" said Alice.
>
> "Anything you like," said the Footman, and began whistling.
>
> "Oh, there's no use in talking to him," said Alice desperately: "he's perfectly idiotic!" And she opened the door and went in. (Carroll [1865; 1871] 1960:80–82.)

This playful passage is deceptively simple. The Footman does not seem to engage Alice as a person (despite his "*you know's*," impersonal and conventional as they are). At first he is caught up in the logic of knocking and entering and then in his stubborn assertion of remaining seated. He shows no wonderment; he makes no characterizations; he seems oblivious to their very possibility. Alice is, however, immediately disturbed by his "uncivil" (from *civis*, citizen) manner, as she calls his behavior, and although she tries to justify it (as a civil person might confronted with incivility) on the basis of his ophthalmic anatomy ("his eyes are so *very* nearly on the top of his head"), she cannot excuse his refusal "to answer questions." Note that Alice says to herself not "to answer my questions" but more impersonally "to answer questions." Is the "my" precluded by the Footman's contextual disengagement, his indifference to Alice, leaving her no choice but to reassert her *I* in repeating, "How am I to get in?" Have we here, incidentally a pun, the ocular eye of the Frog Footman with Alice's pronominal "I"? Clearly, if the Footman's eye/I is on top of his head, he cannot relate – see/speak – to Alice. Alice's repetition of the question produces a stubborn, almost echolalic "I" in the Footman: "I shall sit here till tomorrow." So caught up is he in this pronouncement, so unmindful of his situation, that the progression of his pronouncement is unaffected even by the plate thrown from the house that grazes his nose. He continues to speak "exactly as if nothing had happened." Finally, after Alice asks yet again how she is to get in (is she only referring to the Duchess's house or also to the Footman's discourse, mind, attention, or engagement?), the Footman answers her in an altogether unpleasant manner: "*Are* you to get in at all? That's the first question, you know." (The narrator chooses, for the first time in the passage, to characterize Alice's feelings rather than to allow her to express them: "It was no doubt: only Alice did not like to be told so.") Muttering to herself, she characterizes the Footman: he is dreadfully argumentative. Note the partly communicative externalization of this first characterization. A response follows impersonally – from an unclear vantage point (Alice's? the narrator's? whose?). It is a semi-objective entry into the mind of the Footman: "The Footman seemed to think this a good opportunity for repeating his remark." Alice asks (Lewis Carroll stresses Alice's *I*): "But what am *I* to do?" The Footman responds indifferently: " 'Anything you like,' he said and began to whistle." Whistling is a sort of analogue to his previous disengaged utterance. Alice is left desperate. "Oh, there is no use in talking to him. He is perfectly idiotic." And she opened the door and went in to the Duchess's house.

We can read this entire passage as a play on the gap between conventional behavior and talk – the signifying chain – and reality – the signified – or as a display of the failure of the pragmatic features of an utterance to engage with its context, creating thereby the highly impersonal, autonomous, dreamlike quality of Alice's wonderland. But, for our purposes, what are important are the pragmatic bases for Alice's characterizations. They seem to result from a failure in the self-constituting process. Alice is never really acknowledged by the Frog Footman in her particularity; at most she is a stimulus for his cogitations, their expression, and his willfulness. She herself is unable to address the Footman with the indexical second person pronoun, a "you," but has to refer to him with the third person, anaphoric pronoun, a "he." It is as though she is conversing with another (who may just happen to be embodied in the Footman if he should happen to overhear her mutterings) in another dialogue just as the Footman's "you" in, say, "you know" could be addressed to anyone – and not just Alice. Her verbal transactions with the Footman become a text, for her, that serves – one hopes – to engage another interlocutor (the reader perhaps) in her self-constitution – in a pragmatically resonant dialogue.

Before pursuing the implications of such secondary dialogues that are embedded in a literary text that is written in the third person, affording, thereby, certain metapragmatic – psychological or characterological – possibilities not afforded in everyday discourse, let me give a second example, this time, an ordinary conversation between two teenage girls whom I will call Christine and Peggy.

C. "You know it was really weird. Here I was in this scary movie with Tommy. He was practically a stranger. I couldn't keep my eyes open, but he just sat there – so cool. I really hated him."

P. "Yeah, I know what you mean. He isn't phased by anything."

C. "He's really cool."

P. "Antarctic."

C. "No, he's really a nice guy – kind of sweet. I didn't really know him until then. I got so worked up. I kept seeing the hitcher behind every parked car we passed."

P. "Oh, God."

C. "Well, I'm not really the scared type, but I kept shutting my eyes in the movies and then...."

P. "Peeking. Yeah, I know what you mean. I do it all the time. It's, like, cheating but...."

C. "Anyway I got myself so hyper that Tommy had to calm me down – until two in the morning."

P. "What'd your father say? He's so strict."

C. "He didn't say anything. He must have fallen asleep."

P. "Ooh, fresh. Are you going to see him again?"

C. "Maybe."

P. "Come on."

C. "Well, maybe on Friday. It's not sure yet. Come on, you've got Rob."

P. "Yeah, but...."

C. "Well, Tommy's not your type. You need someone more outgoing. Me, I like the quiet type – cool and confident."

P. "Rob's cool and confident."

C. "Yeah, but he's outgoing. You need that kind of guy. You're his type. He's got such awesome eyes. Do you think Tommy's my type?"

P. "You're both kind of. . . . Well, you're, like, wild, and he's calm and cool."

C. "Yeah, I got you. I guess I am kind of wild."

We see in this exchange dramatic, at times almost desperate, shifts in alignment – in what Erving Goffman ([1979] 1981) would call footing – as Christine and Peggy choreograph their relationship – their identities. The stakes are high and unlike Alice's abortive attempts to "reach" the Frog Footman, the two girls are fully engaged. Peggy and Christine as well as Tommy, Rob, and Christine's father who are figures in the conversation are all, at one point or another characterized. Tommy is the central figure. Christine casts him as "practically a stranger," "cool," "a nice guy," "kind of sweet," "quiet," "cool and confident." Peggy repeats Christine's characterizations. She says Tommy "isn't phased by anything." When she exaggerates Christine's characterization of Tommy as "cool," with an "antarctic," however, Christine immediately corrects her: "No, he's really a nice guy – kind of sweet." Christine is, from the start, in the dominant position. She speaks more and continually centers the conversation on herself. (She uses a total of 22 first-person locutions, "I," "my," "mine," or "me" to Peggy's 4; she uses 5 second-person locutions to Peggy's 4.) Peggy can do little more than echo her. When Peggy tries at one point to turn the conversation to herself – "Peeking. . . . I do it all the time. It's like cheating but . . ." – Christine immediately refocuses the conversation on herself and (her) Tommy. She characterizes herself both directly, "I'm not the scared type," and indirectly, "I couldn't keep my eyes open." Peggy never characterizes herself and she accepts Christine's characterization of her. When Peggy does ask Christine directly whether or not she is going to go out with Tommy again, Christine hedges. Why? We do not know. Did Tommy ask her out? She does use the hedging, however, to her advantage. She points out Peggy's possible envy. (We do not know how Peggy looked; she may of course have stimulated such a remark.) "You've got Rob" Christine says, and tells Peggy that Tommy is not her type, restoring thereby her dominant footing. (Peggy may have initiated this through her expression.) Peggy needs someone outgoing, according to Christine; Christine herself needs someone "quiet," "cool," and "confident." Hurt, Peggy insists that Rob is "cool and confident." A serious break between the two girls is imminent. Christine quickly restores the relationship by telling Peggy that Rob, outgoing and with "awesome eyes," is her type, and then with vulnerable hesitation, she asks Peggy if Tommy is her type. Peggy's answer is a stroke of diplomatic genius. She hesitates (complementing Christine's hesitation), she calls Christine "wild" (a term of flattery here), and partly echoes Christine's characterization of Tommy as "cool and confident" with "cool and calm." Christine has no choice but to agree to Peggy's characterization of her. "I guess I am kind of wild." Despite Peggy's dominant position as characterizer of Christine at this moment, Christine remains the center of conversational attention. Does Peggy's characterization of Christine as "wild" reflect the "wildness" of her conversation – in the absence of a cooling and calming Tommy?

With varying degrees of intensity and articulation the constituting of self and other occurs in all verbal transactions. Alice's encounter with the Frog Footman comes as close to being a limiting case as do some of the conversations that occur, or perhaps do not occur, in Beckett's novels, plays, and monologues. (Conversation, it should be remembered, comes from *versari*, to be situated or occupied, and *cum*, with.) Self characterizations and characterizations of one's interlocutor are probably not all that frequent in most ordinary conversations, and when they occur, as I have noted, they usually involve some sort of change in the level of discourse and in the footing of the participants. Alice characterizes the Footman in the third person; Christine's self characterizations – "I'm not the scared type" – and her demand to be characterized by Peggy are complex strategies for focusing the exchange. It would seem that their pragmatic function here, as in many similar conversations, overrides whatever semantic value the characterizations have. Indeed, we often ignore a person's self characterizations, particularly when they are expressed in the present tense, or regard them not as accurate descriptions but symptoms of the person's character.[9]

Characterizations occur in various types of psychotherapy to produce, for example, insight or a reaction, in certain job interviews, particularly those that measure stress ("You are a bitch"), in amorous conversations ("You're a love"), and in auditions ("You'll never be a Hamlet"). Often the characterizations are given to produce an effect (insight, catharsis, stress, anger, humility, delight, love). There may of course be a good deal of characterizing third parties, as in Christine and Peggy's conversation. Here, too, these third-party characterizations, however accurate diagnostically, serve pragmatic purposes. They may figure in a drama of self-constitution as they did for Christine and Peggy.

Retrospective and third-party characterizations demand a level of articulation that does not necessarily occur in the shadow dialogues – the mentation and cogitation – that occur along with the primary self-constituting discourse. Indeed, many of the retrospective and third-party accounts describe or conventionally paraphrase these secondary dialogues. Narratives, in the third person, for example, have conventions for describing these contemporaneous (usually immediately reflective) shadow dialogues, or the co-occurring thoughts and perceptions. These conventional descriptions, which often obscure even the retrospective dimension of immediate reflection, are not particularly well-developed in the passage from *Alice in Wonderland* we have considered, but they are there. "Alice did not like to be told to." "The Footman seemed to think this a good opportunity for repeating...." Such descriptions, at least in the realist novels of the 19th century (but also in Virginia Woolf and a good deal of James Joyce) are expressed in well-formed sentences – descriptions that promote, if I may use the word, an *interiority*, an independence of mind, and an articulateness of thought that seems coordinate with an ideology of individualism. Often, particularly in the 19th-century novel – in Trollope, the early George Eliot, and even Jane Austen – such descriptions promote an illusion of an omniscient capacity that is ironically undermined by a failure of (moral) character that hides from itself its ignorance or presumes an irrealistic extension of its knowledge. Later in the century, in novels like Eliot's *Daniel Deronda* and in *Doppelganger* tales, the limits of lucidity are probed, the moral-and-cognitive (literary) self is sundered, and the resultant black hole – the point of nonlucidity – located now within the self, is given (an institutionalized) expression (and the possibility of at least partial correction) in the development of psychoanalysis and its "discovery" of the unconscious. Such a view articulates an individuality that is somehow "independent" of the dialogical – the transactional – dimension of human social life, although, I hasten to add, some privileged (most often parental and sometimes traumatic) transactions from early childhood are incorporated, in a primitive, petrified, form, within the individual's character or self.

In chapter 5, volume 2 of Jane Austen's *Emma* ([1816] 1972), the heroine Emma Woodhouse, "handsome, clever, and rich, with a comfortable home and happy disposition," meets for the first time, Mr. Frank Churchill. He is the son by a previous marriage of a Mr. Weston who has recently married Emma's former governess, Miss Taylor. Emma had a hand in arranging this marriage. It will be remembered that unlike Jane Austen's other heroines, Emma has shown little concern for her own marriage. She is, in Sir Walter Scott's (1815) words, bent "on forging wedlock-fetters for others." Frank Churchill is unknown in Highbury – he was taken in by Mr. Weston's wealthy in-laws when he was a child – although he is the subject of considerable speculation in this quiet community whose members, at least those of the middle class of whom Austen writes, escape through "the little event" from what seems to be a life of consummate boredom. Frank has been expected for a considerable time, so considerable a time that, to some of Emma's set, his failure to visit his father and his father's new life intimate a flaw in his character. Mr. and Mrs. Weston do not conceive of this possibility. They should like to engage Frank's interest in Emma and Emma's in Frank. Despite herself, Emma is curious about Frank.

Emma opens the door to the parlor and discovers two gentlemen sitting with her father. They are Mr. Weston and his son. Frank had arrived earlier than expected, and Mr. Weston hastened to bring him to visit Highbury's most distinguished family.

> The Frank Churchill so long talked of, so high in interest, was actually before her – he was presented to her, she did not think too much had been said in his praise; he was a *very* good looking young man: height, air, address, all were unexceptionable, and his countenance had a great deal of spirit and liveliness of his father's; he

> looked quick and sensible. She felt immediately that she should like him; and there was a well-bred ease of manner, and a readiness to talk, which convinced her that he came intending to be acquainted with her, and that acquainted they soon must be. (p. 128)

Emma is pleased with Frank's "eagerness to arrive, which had made him alter his plan, and travel earlier, later, and quicker, that he might gain a half a day" (p. 128). Mr. Weston is, of course, exultant at his son's early arrival, remarking that an early arrival gives such pleasure that it is worth the little extra exertion needed. Frank gently corrects his father's observation, "It is a great pleasure, where one can indulge in it, although there are not many houses that I should presume on so far; but in coming *home* I felt I might do anything" (p. 128).

> The word home made his father look on him with fresh complacency. Emma was directly sure that he knew how to make himself agreeable; the conviction was strengthened by what followed. He was very much pleased with Randalls, thought it a most admirably arranged house, would hardly allow it even to be very small, admired the situation, the walk to Highbury, Highbury itself, Hartfield (the Woodhouse home) still more, and professed himself to have always felt the sort of interest in the country which none but one's *own* country gives, and the greatest curiosity to visit it. That he should never have been able to indulge so amiable a feeling before, passed suspiciously through Emma's brain; but still, if it were a falsehood, it was a pleasant one, and pleasantly handled. His manner had no air of study or exaggeration. He did really look and speak as if in a state of common enjoyment. (p. 128)

After talking about "subjects in general" that "belong to an opening acquaintance," Frank "contrived to find an opportunity, while their two fathers were engaged with each other, of introducing his mother-in-law, and speaking of her with so much handsome praise, so much warm admiration, so much gratitude for the happiness she secured to his father, and her very kind reception of himself, as was an additional proof of his knowing how to please – and of his certainty thinking it worth while to try to please her" (p. 129). Frank Churchill's praise of Mrs. Weston continues; he comes near to "thanking Emma for Mrs. Taylor's merits, without seeming quite to forget that in the common course of things, it was rather to be supposed that Miss Taylor had formed Miss Woodhouse's character, than Miss Woodhouse Miss Taylor's" (p. 129).

> "Elegant, agreeable manners, I was prepared for," said he; "but I confess that, considering every thing, I had not expected more than a very tolerably well-looking woman of a certain age; I did not know that I was to find a pretty young woman in Mrs. Weston."
>
> "You cannot see too much perfection in Mrs. Weston for my feelings," said Emma; "were you to guess her to be *eighteen*, I should listen with pleasure; but *she* would be ready to quarrel with you for

using such words. Don't let her imagine that you have spoken of her as a pretty young woman."

"I hope I should know better," he replied; "no depend upon it, (with a gallant bow), that in addressing Mrs. Weston I should understand whom I might praise without any danger of being extravagant in my terms."

Emma wondered whether the same suspicion of what might be expected from knowing each other, which had taken strong possession of her mind, had ever crossed his; and whether his compliments were to be considered as marks of acquiescence, or proofs of defiance. She must see more of them to understand his ways; at present she only felt they were agreeable. (p. 129)

Emma notices the attention Mr. Weston is paying to her exchange with Frank Churchill, and she is "most comfortable" in her father's "perfect exemption" from any penetration of what may be transpiring between them. (He is, again in Sir Walter Scott's words, "a silly valetudinarian.")

The two visitors soon leave, Mr. Weston for the local inn, where he has some business, and his son to visit Miss Jane Fairfax, whom he feigns to know but slightly. "Emma remained very pleased with this beginning of the acquaintance, and could now engage to think them all at Randalls [the Weston's house] any hour of the day with full confidence in their comfort" (p. 131).

This passage is more complex than the two others we have considered. The novel's "every sentence, almost every epithet," Reginald Farrer wrote in the *Quarterly Review* in 1917, "has its definite reference to equally unemphasized points before and after in the development of the plot." The passage I have chosen is, in fact, pivotal in the unfolding of both plot and character. There are intimations of Frank's (for want of a better word) duplicity and Emma's misapprehension – her *méconnaisance* that, ironically, like all *méconnaissance* requires a *connaissance*, a subliminal knowing – of Frank, herself, and her relationship to Frank that is self-masked in her exquisitely commanded characterization of Frank, Mr. Weston, and her father as well as in her studied self-observation. What is of interest to us, however, is the manner in which the characterizations are conveyed. The novel is written in the third person but, as Wayne Booth (1961) has observed, written largely, though not completely, through the eyes of Emma herself. The passage contains both direct quotation and various modes, less of indirect discourse, than free-form quotation (*erlebte Rede*) of both conversation and thinking. At the simplest level this narrative technique permits the expression of the (putative) simultaneity of Emma's (silent) perception and thought and the discourse she is participating in or witnessing. Thus, as Emma hears Frank Churchill use the word "home" for his father's house Randalls – "but in coming *home* I felt I might do anything" – we follow Emma's contemporaneous, though silent, observation of Mr. Weston – "his father looked at him with fresh complacency"

– and Emma's conviction (a characterization) that Frank Churchill "knew how to make himself agreeable." There are numerous instances of this technique throughout the passage, and they make use, as we shall see below, of complex shifts of sometimes ambiguous vantage points.

What is striking about Emma's or the narrator's observations that lead to explicit or implicit characterizations is that they are less concerned with the referential function of the discourse, quoted or paraphrased, than with its pragmatic dimension – with its context-producing, its self- and other-constituting effectiveness. Emma's interest in Frank's use of "home" is not referential – he could have used any number of other terms for Randalls – but with its pragmatic implication. "Home" operates here rather like an honorific; it is a meta-pragmatic shift that gives an intimate and personalized, a homey, familial quality to Randalls and to Frank Churchill a certain filial sensitivity that produces in his father "a fresh complacency." For Emma, it renders Frank if not "agreeable" then capable of making himself agreeable. Emma's characterization of Frank is based here on the pragmatic function of "home" and her characterization is, as it were, metapragmatic. Her conviction is strengthened, we are told, by what follows. Frank professes an exaggerated admiration for Randalls, Highbury, and Hartfield as well as that interest "in a country which none but one's *own* country gives." Note the author emphasizes "own." It is again, I submit, the pragmatic features of Frank's descriptions that lead Emma to a passing "suspicion" that he might have indulged himself in the pleasures of home and Highbury earlier if his feelings were so heartfelt and to her dismissal of that suspicion: "but still if it were a falsehood, it was a pleasant one, and pleasantly handled." Emma makes similar observations on the basis of Frank Churchill's "handsome praise" and "warm admiration" for Mrs. Weston and the gratitude he claims to have "for the happiness she secured to his father, and her very kind reception of himself." He understood what would be welcome; he could be sure of little else. When Frank speaks of his stepmother's youth, however, Emma corrects him sharply ("Don't let her imagine that you have spoken of her as a pretty young woman"), forcing him to take account of himself ("I hope I should know better") and to extricate himself from this indiscretion through a gallant bow and an ever more gallant bit of flattery: "No, depend upon it, that in addressing Mrs. Weston I should understand whom I might praise without any danger of being thought extravagant in my terms." Such flattery that calls attention, implicitly, to its own artifice risks drawing Emma into an intimate but always insecure complicity – a sort of double-bind of the sophisticate – that can only perpetuate the artifice (and ultimately the insecurity) upon which it is built. Emma wonders – she can no longer be sure – "whether the same suspicion of what might be expected from their knowing each other, which had taken strong possession of her mind, had ever crossed his." She wonders whether "his compliments were to be considered as marks of acquiescence, or proofs of defiance." Caught in this hermeneutic impasse, Emma, rather more practical than she sometimes gives on, concludes that "she must see more of them to understand his ways." (The "them" refers back to "compliments.") But she finds them agreeable.

Much, though not all, that transpires in Emma's Highbury is seen through Emma's eyes. Jane Austen's narrative technique permits her, as I have noted, to report conversation and to describe the accompanying thought and perceptions of her heroine. A *simultaneity* is conventionally produced that is diegetic – "internal" to the narrative – and does not seem to be disturbed by the temporal progression, the sequentiality, of the narrator itself. In the passage we have been discussing, many of the paraphrases of Emma's thoughts and perceptions appear to arise from Emma's own unmediated vantage point. "Emma was directly sure that he knew how to make himself agreeable." "He did not advance a word of praise beyond what she knew to be thoroughly deserved by Mrs. Weston; but undoubtedly he could know very little of the matter." "Emma wondered whether the same suspicion of what he expected. . . ." (All of these examples are or approximate indirect discourse.) Other paraphrases, however, seem to arise from an external, objectivistic – the narrator's – vantage point, giving the distance that Wayne Booth maintains keeps Emma a sympathetic figure. "Their subjects in general were such as belong to an opening acquaintance." "But when satisfied on all these points, and their acquaintance proportionately advanced, he contrived to find an opportunity, while their two fathers were engaged with each other, of introducing his mother-in-law." The objectivity of such passages – their apparent source in a distinct and separate narrator – is suggested less grammatically than by a coloring, a tonality (through choice of words and turns of phrase) that does not fully coordinate with the coloring and tonality we would expect from Emma as we come to know her. (We should note that the novel begins from the perspective of the narrator and only slowly introduces Emma's perspective.) When we read these objectivistic passages carefully, however, we often find it difficult to determine exactly where Emma's consciousness ends and the narrator's begins. There is, here as in other novels and stories, I believe, a blurring that has been denied all too frequently by those critics who insist upon neat and discriminate vantage points. They fail, I believe, to take into account the submerged dialogical relationship between a character's vantage point and that of the narrator – and the possibility of blurrings that can, and do inevitably, occur.

Such a dialogical relationship is apparent in the following lines. [1] That he should have been able to indulge so amiable a feeling before, passed suspiciously through Emma's brain; [2] but still if it were a falsehood, it was a pleasant one, and pleasantly handled. [3] His manner had no air of study or exaggeration. [4] He did really look and speak as if in a state of no common enjoyment. (p. 128)

The passage begins from the vantage point of the narrator as indicated by "passed suspiciously through Emma's brain." The Emma we have come to know (stylistically at least) would not be given to such a neuro-anatomical figure to describe her own thoughts and perceptions. The second sentence places us within Emma's purview. (Its transitional status, bridging the objectivism of the first sentence with the subjectivism of the third and fourth sentences, is suggested by both the use of the argumentative "but still" and by the semicolon that divides it from the first but not the third sentence.) The third and fourth – declarative – sentences are clearly articulated from Emma's perspective. They state a fact – a characterization – with certainty. There is within this sequence of sentences, I submit, a submerged dialogical progression. From the vantage point of an absent interlocutor, expressed through the objectivistic language of the first sentence, Emma is, so to speak, made to perceive something not particularly agreeable. The second sentence is a response to this undesirable perception. It is argumentative "but still." The third and fourth sentences are assertions that conform less to the "objective fact" (the facts described from a narrator's point of view) – Frank Churchill's duplicitous flattery – than to Emma's desired picture of Frank Churchill. But even in these two sentences there is a responsive dimension indicated by the negatives ("no air of study or exaggeration," "no common enjoyment," as well as by the "really" in the fourth sentence). "He did really look and speak as if...."

Similar, submerged dialogical progressions can be seen in other passages. Let me quote, once more, the following one:

> Emma wondered whether the same suspicion of what might be expected from their knowing each other, which had taken strong possession of her mind, had ever crossed his; and whether his compliments were to be considered as marks of acquiescence, or proofs of defiance. She must see more of them to understand his ways; at present she only felt they were agreeable. (p. 129)

Here, the dialogical progression appears to be internal. Caught in a hermeneutical impasse, Emma converses with herself, or more accurately, with, we might say, an internalized interlocutor – a sort of alter ego. She affirms her stance in the last two sentences in response to a not fully articulated perception of a possibly undesirable aspect of Mr. Frank Churchill. But even in this "internal dialogue" we recognize at least a vestigial identification of the silent, internalized dialogical partner with the narrator; this is suggested, again by a neuroanatomical figure, "which had taken strong possession of her mind."

It is ironic that the very figures "brain" and "mind" that reveal the submerged dialogue between Emma and the narrator are precisely the figures that serve to mask the dialogical nature of the self. "Brain" and "mind" are, in the West, two of the most preeminent *loci* in the self. They connote independence, autonomy, particularity, originality, individuality, and thinghood. Like mind and brain, the self is conceived as somehow independent of the other – of social transactions; and yet, as we know, this independence is always in question. Psychologies, like the psychoanalytic, have to be conceived as compromises between two contradictory ideological positions: the self (psyche, soul, mind) as somehow independent – a position symbolically affirmed by a series of often crude physical and physiological metaphors – and the self (psyche, soul, mind) as a product of social interaction. In psychoanalysis social interaction is primarily restricted to the internalization of parental norms and values during a relatively restricted period in the individual's development; thereafter, barring traumatic and other exceptional experiences, the individual's self, now formed, seems removed from the influences of social interaction.[10] Such a position conforms. I believe, to a prevalent ideology of individualism that has, yet, to take into account human sociality.

The position I am taking here is, as I noted earlier, prepsychological. What I have tried to do is to look at those processes embedded in verbal transactions that are articulated – or masked – in current (folk) psychologies in the West. The constitution of self and other is, I suggest, the result of momentary arrests in a continuous dialectical movement; such arrests result from the interplay of desire, resistance, and symbolic (linguistic) constraints. In their articulation they conform to prevalent ideological orientations, including (folk) psychologies, characterologies, and theories of language that are themselves undoubtedly grounded in particular socioeconomic arrangements. Traditional dialectical approaches to the self have either ignored the role of language or have accepted a purely referential understanding of language. Typification in such theories is simply a naming or a labeling. Such theories of typification mask rather more complex linguistic processes that occur in this dialectical movement. The characterizations of self and other, at least, are based upon the pragmatics of dialogue exchanges; they are, as such, metapragmatic characterizations of these pragmatic processes – cast not in the idiom of language but figuratively, if you will, in folk psychological and characterological terms. Insofar as metapragmatic characterizations are necessarily expressed in referential terms, there is a marked tendency for the referentiality of such metapragmatic characterizations to cover over their pragmatic basis as they are integrated into referentially elaborated and understood theories of self, character, and personality. Such theories figure, as representations of what I have called the Third, the guarantor of meaning and convention, presumed necessary for any "meaningful" verbal exchange, in the pragmatic movement upon which self characterizations are made.

Benveniste (1966) and other students of pragmatics have argued that first- and second-person pronouns are indexicals, that they differ from third-person anaphoric pronouns, which refer back to some antecedent noun – ultimately, in the case of human beings, to a proper noun. I myself (1982) have suggested that the first- and second-person pronouns, when viewed within a dialogical context, do have an anaphoric potential; they relate back to previous occurrences of the I (understood in opposition to the you) and refer forward to their future occurrences (again in opposition to the you). There is, if I may speak figuratively, an inherent instability in this process; for the I to be more than a mere index of the instance of discourse, it requires a reduction of the you to an anaphoric pronoun, ultimately to a noun, a proper noun. (The converse would be equally true.) Such a reduction, if successful, would negate the very dialogue (between I and you) upon which the I seeks its constitution (its referentiality); for, there can be no dialogue between an I and a he or she (Alice, notwithstanding). It is here, perhaps again, that the function of the Third prevails, for it can support the referential conventions of language that mask the pragmatically induced instability of dialogical exchanges. Herein lies its power whether internalized as conscience or externalized in some figure of authority – law, reason, king, or fetish.

Notes

1 I cannot elaborate on secondary, or shadow, dialogues here. They are a model for thought that accompanies primary dialogues. I am, of course, indebted to theorists who haved conceived of thought as inner speech (Vygotsky [1934], 1962; Wertsch, 1985) or more specifically as dialogue (Voloshinov, 1973; Emerson, 1983). The interlocutors in such secondary dialogues are unstable and highly symbolic (despite whatever fantasized determinations they may have). They may be, within these terms, determinate, as for example, when one maintains an inner conversation with an enemy or when suffering from what Diderot called *esprit d'escalier*; or indeterminate – a sort of unspecified, generalized partner of the sort that psychoanalysts would see as an introject of important (parental) figures in one's biography; or they may be abstract like "the voice of conscience."

2 There are, to be sure, all sorts of intermediate positions between the empirical and the Whorfian ones.

3 I am indebted to Michael Silverstein for this formulation.

4 I use the word "ascriptor" to stress a certain presumption in such characterizations – a presumption that has moral and political force. Although I do not wish to engage in the debate between descriptivists and ascriptivists (see Geach, 1960, for example) which is only tangential to my argument, I do want to call attention to the fact that characterizations of *self and other* are rarely "neutral," empirically verifiable, descriptions; they figure within the plays of power and desire that occur in every verbal exchange and are thus morally and politically resonant ascriptions.

5 In my paper "Text, Transference, and Indexicality" (1981), I argued that attributions of transference and countertransference during psychoanalytic sessions were based on pragmatic features of the sessions. A certain free play was afforded by the conventions of exchange: One could be both "patient," however socially characterized, and, say, "son" or "daughter"; one could be both "psychiatrist" and "father." Both roles – in fact more complex, multiple roles – were constantly being negotiated as were (and here I am elaborating my argument slightly) the rules of relevance and interpretation;

that is, what, and how what, should be interpreted. Such interpretations of the pragmatic features of the exchange were cast in a language, by the psychoanalyst at least, that masked their pragmatic basis. Although meta-pragmatic, they were expressed in a referential language that was identical to the (meta-) language in which symbolic processes (in dreams, for example) were described.

6 I should note that the static, empirical view also provides the basis for those critical views that assert the creative dimension of language so strongly that any empirical certainty, other than at the level of language, is precluded.

7 Natural languages, as Silverstein (1985:225) points out, have "to a certain extent" their own pragmatic metalanguage – a built-in metapragmatic function (e.g., ways about talking about talk in a purposive way). They may also have more complex "indexical-denotationals" that "denote by virtue of instantiating an indexable configuration of speech-event components" (e.g., in certain illocutionary predicates). Both metapragmatic functions – the built-in and the instantiated – can be rendered more explicit metaprag-matically – in a virtual way, as in the examples I have given. Considerably more research is required to discover how metapragmatic functions are rendered explicit both linguistically and metaphorically in nonlinguistic terms.

8 When someone says for example, "I am timid" or "I am an introvert" only a naive interlocutor would accept such self characterizations at face value. The sophisticated interlocutor might use them as evidence for whatever charac-terization he might make in roughly the following way. X is the sort of person who says "I am timid" or "I am an introvert" in context B when talking to Y. In other words, the referentiality of such characterizations is less diagnostic than its pragmaticity. (See the ensuing discussion in the text.)

9 See note 8. The acceptability of self characterizations is, in fact, considerably more complicated than I have indicated here. It depends, in part, on the distance that the speaker creates between himself in some seemingly extra-discourse sense and himself in an intradiscourse sense – between what Erving Goffman ([1979] 1981) would call the "animator" of the statement and the "figure" in the animator's statement. There seems to be some sort of splitting between the I of any utterance that indexes the speaker as outside, independent, and somehow master of the utterance and the I that is indexed as internal to, controlled by, and qualified through the utterance – through predication, style, and attribution. See Silverstein (1985:225) for an elabora-tion of the functional laminations of pronomial usage. He notes, for example, that the subjects *I* and *you* pick out are characterized as parts of the speech situation indexed in and by the pragmatics of use, independent of the fact that these objects are also the referents of the expression *I* and *you*. A self characterization in the present tense uttered with irony may on certain occasions be taken at face value while the same self characterization, in the same tense, uttered on an identical occasion in a nonironic, serious mode would be completely unacceptable. Self characterization in the past tense or in narratives of the past are at times acceptable at face value within their explicit or implicit narrative context in part at least because of the "distance" between the speaker and the I embedded in his discourse. Other conventions are probably operative as well. A reader of *Heart of Darkness* – or Marlowe's silent audience – might accept Marlowe's characterizations of himself as a younger man trying to find a job on an African steamer by

"worrying" his Continental relations. "I am sorry to own I began to worry them. This was already a fresh departure for me. I was not used to get things that way, you know. I always went my own road and on my own legs when I had a mind to go. I wouldn't have believed it of myself" (Conrad [1899] 1971:8). But, pragmatically, by characterizing his past self in this rhetorically and stylistically complex passage, with its avowals and disavowals, its pleas to an audience, etc., Marlowe is in fact casting his present self – as an old tar, a storyteller, an adventurer with an introspective bent. Sophisticated interlocutors have to ask: What kind of a man is Marlowe such that he would characterize himself as a young man in the way he does?

10 Depth metaphors in psychoanalysis and other psychologies often serve to mediate or even to fudge theoretical contradictions, at least at the deepest level.

References

Austen, Jane. [1816] 1972. *Emma*. New York: Norton.

Benveniste, Emile. 1966. *Problèmes de Linguistique Générale*. Vol. I. Paris: Gallimard.

Berger, Peter, & Thomas Luckmann. 1967. *The Social Construction of Reality: A Treatise in the Sociology of Knowledge*. New York: Anchor Books.

Booth, Wayne. 1961. *The Rhetoric of Fiction*. Chicago: University of Chicago Press.

Carroll, Lewis [Charles Lutwidge Dodgson]. [1865; 1871] 1960. *The Annotated Alice: Alice's Adventures in Wonderland and Through the Looking Glass*. New York: Bramhall House.

Conrad, Joseph. [1899] 1971. *Heart of Darkness*. New York: W. W. Norton.

Crapanzano, Vincent. 1977. The Life History in Anthropological Field Work. *Anthropology and Humanism Quarterly* 2:3–4.

1980. *Tuhami: Portrait of a Moroccan*. Chicago: University of Chicago Press.

1981. Text, Transference, and Intexicality. *Ethos* 9:122–148.

1982. The Self, the Third, and Desire. In Benjamin Lee (ed.), *Psychosocial Theories of the Self* (pp. 179–206). New York: Plenum Press.

1987a. Editorial, *Cultural Anthropology* 2 (2): n.d. Hidden Dialogues.

1987b. Hidden Dialogues. Paper delivered at American Anthropological Association meetings.

Emerson, C. 1983. The Outer Word and Inner Speech: Bakhtin, Vygotsky, and the Internalization of Language. *Critical Inquiry* 10(2):245–264.

Farrar, Reginald. 1917. Jane Austen, *ob* July 18, 1917. *Quarterly Review 128*: 23–25.

Geach, P. T. 1960, Ascriptivism. *Philosophical Review* 69:221–225.

Goffman, Erving. [1979] 1981. Footing. In *Forms of Talk* (pp. 124–159). Philadelphia: University of Pennsylvania Press.

Hegel, G. W. F. 1977. *Phenomenology of the Spirit*. [1807] (A. V. Miller, Trans.). Oxford: Oxford University Press.

James, Henry. [1905] 1984. The Lesson of Balzac. In *Literary Criticism: European Writers and the Prefaces* (pp. 115–139). New York: Library of America.

Kay, Paul. 1987. Linguistic Competence and Folk Theories of Language: Two English Hedges. In Dorothy Holland and Naomi Quinn (Eds.), *Cultural*

Models in Language and Thought (pp. 63–67). Cambridge: Cambridge University Press.

Lacan, Jacques. 1966. *Ecrits*. Paris: Seuil.

Mead, George Herbert. 1964. *On Social Psychology*. Chicago: University of Chicago Press.

Noyes, Arthur P., and Lawrence C. Kolb. 1963. *Modern Clinical Psychiatry*. 6th ed. Philadelphia: W. B. Saunders.

Peirce, C. S. [1931] 1974. Principles of Philosophy. In *Collected Papers*, Vol. I (pp. 3–363). Cambridge, MA: Harvard University Press.

Sartre, Jean-Paul. [1943] 1956. *Being and Nothingness: An Essay in Phenomenological Ontology*. (Hazel E. Bornes, Trans.). New York: Philosophical Library.

——— [1952] 1964. *Saint Genet: Actor and Martyr*. (Bernard Frechtman, Trans.). New York: Mentor.

Scott, Walter. 1815. Review of *Emma*. *Quarterly Review 14*:188–201.

Silverstein, M. 1976. Shifters, Linguistic Categories and Cultural Description. In Keith Basso and Henry Selby (Eds.), *Meaning in Anthropology* (pp. 11–55). Albuquerque: University of New Mexico Press.

——— 1979. Language Structure and Linguistic Ideology. In P. Clyne, W. Hanks, & C. Hofbauer (Eds.), *The Elements: A Parasession on Linguistic Units and Levels* (pp. 193–247). Chicago: Chicago Linguistic Society.

——— 1985. The Functional Stratification of Language and Ontogenesis. In James V. Wertsch (Ed.), *Culture, Communication and Cognition: Vygotskian Perspectives* (pp. 205–235). Cambridge: Cambridge University Press.

Sweetser, Eve E. 1987. The Definition of *Lie*: An Examination of the Folk Models Underlying a Semantic Prototype. In Dorothy Holland & Naomi Quinn (Eds.), *Cultural Models in Language and Thought* (pp. 43–66). Cambridge: Cambridge University Press.

Van den Abbeele, Georges Y. 1984. Cartesian Coordinates: Metaphor, Topography, and Presupposition in Descartes. In Bernard Beugnot (Ed.), *Voyages: Récits et Imaginaire* (pp. 3–14). Paris: Biblio 17.

Voloshinov, V. N. (Bakhtin, M. M.) [1929] 1973. *Marxism and the Philosophy of Language*. (L. Matejka & I. R. Titunik, Trans.). New York: Seminar Press.

Vygotsky, L. S. [1934] 1962. *Thought and Language*. Cambridge, MA: MIT Press.

Wertsch, James V. 1985. *Vygotsky and the Social Formation of Mind*. Cambridge, MA: Harvard University Press.

PART V
Cultural conceptions of psychoanalysis

13
Stories from Indian psychoanalysis
CONTEXT AND TEXT

Sudhir Kakar

For a richer understanding of the stories from Indian psychoanalysis, they first need to be placed in a framework, provided with a context for their text. This context is itself a story, the story of psychoanalysis in India, which can be fascinating from many points of view.

First, this story holds an epistemological promise in helping us to resolve a perennially vexing issue, namely, the persistent doubt with regard to the universality of psychoanalytic findings. For many contemporary social scientists the question of whether a theory of mental life – originating in the treatment of neurotics from the Viennese Jewish milieu of the early 20th century and confirmed, if that, by scattered case histories of middle-class patients from the Western world – can ignore the cultural relativism of its postulates as resolutely as psychoanalysis has done, is today almost rhetorical. Their suspicion that psychoanalytic theory is limited by its origins has by now hardened into a doubt that refuses to accord validity to psychoanalytic interpretations of non-Western myths, folklore, and rituals as evidence for the transcultural truth of psychoanalysis. What they demand is evidence of a more direct kind from within the non-Western culture itself. An account of clinical practice of psychoanalysis in India, of stories from Third World consulting rooms just might provide this sort of evidence, even when one must admit that such evidence can never be conclusive. Doubts as to the adequacy of the method by which the evidence is collected and the objectivity of the collectors are bound to persist.

The second interesting facet of the Indian psychoanalytic story has to do with the curiosity surrounding the practice of an esoteric art among people whose metaphysical assumptions concerning the nature of man, society, and the world are quite different from those governing societies in which psychoanalysis has been traditionally practiced. To formulate this curiosity in questions: What are the goals pursued by an analyst in India, where individualism stirs but faintly and where the subordination of the individual to the superordinate family interests and relationships is a preeminent value? Can the bitterly contested charge leveled against Japanese psychoanalysts more than 30 years ago – namely that they do

Part of this paper has appeared as "The Maternal–Feminine in Indian Psycho-analysis" in the *International Review of Psychoanalysis*, copyright the Institute of Psychoanalysis, London.

not try to free the individual but endeavour to adjust him to his environment – also be raised against their Indian counterparts, whose patients too must function in a similar (though not identical) familial milieu? How does the analyst and the patient conceive of their joint endeavor in a culture that considers boundaries to be obstacles and autonomy a curse, and where, for instance, one patient's relatives described the symptoms of his chief complaint as follows: "He is very stubborn in pursuing what he wants without taking our wishes into account. He thinks he knows what is best for him and does not listen to us. He thinks his own life and career are more important than the concerns of the rest of the family." These are, however, questions I have discussed elsewhere and therefore will remain out of the purview of the present paper.[1]

Another exciting aspect of Indian psychoanalysis is less epistemological than literary. It lies in the pleasures of the narrative, its metaphoric richness, and the delights of connotation. In a particular case, the narratives of the inner world of Indians promise the satisfaction of that extra degree of curiosity that is aroused by the lives of people whose culture and history are vastly different from those of Europeans and other Westerners who have thus far been the protagonists of psychoanalytic dramas.

Yet at the very outset I must confess that this essay can only partly fulfill the varied expectations its title holds out. As we shall see later, the nature of the psychoanalytic enterprise and its epistemological status preclude the possibility of resolving the universal-versus-relative question in any conclusive manner. The literary pledge, too, cannot be quite redeemed. In part, this is due to shortcomings in my own narrative skills and in part to the fact that psychoanalytic case histories have certain inbuilt limitations. They must necessarily lack the concreteness, characteristic of literary narratives, that is required for describing what Oliver Sacks calls the melodic and scenic nature of inner life.[2] To enrich case histories with the self-same persistency of telling detail found in fictional lives is to invite the danger of violating trust and breaching the ethic of the consulting room. Tales from the couch are fated to remain vignettes, stunted stories always falling short of their true potential.

Analogous to the working method of the classical analyst who proceeds from the surface to the depths, I, too, would like to go about my task by starting from the context and form of Indian psychoanalysis before going on to its text. Thus I begin with some generalizations on the inner world of Indian patients. I realize, of course, that whereas the first part of my agenda may be relatively noncontroversial, the implications of the second part – namely that each patient is not just a unique individual and that many patients who belong to a distinctive cultural configuration share certain dominant fantasies – will arouse skepticism in some of my colleagues. At the moment, I can only plead for a suspension of disbelief till I have completed the presentation of my assumptions and evidence.

The historical context of Indian psychoanalysis is inseparable from the life and work of Girindrashekhar Bose.[3] Born in 1886, Bose was the son of the chief minister of a small princely state in Bengal. Although he studied medicine and practiced as a physician in Calcutta after graduating in 1910, Bose's abiding intellectual passion was abnormal psychology. He learned hypnosis and by 1914 he had begun to treat patients suffering from mental disorders by a technique closely akin, as he says, to Freud's original method, presumably the use of hypnosis, suggestion, pressing and questioning to recall memories and encourage associations. He had already developed some of his psychological ideas, including the basic elements of his theory of opposite wishes – namely that for every expressed wish there is an opposite wish working in the unconscious – before the first English translations of Freud's writings reached Calcutta and made a strong impression on the young Bengali doctor's mind. A man of great energy and a good deal of originality, Bose immersed himself further in his psychological studies and in 1921 received the first Doctor of Science degree in psychology awarded in India. Steeped in Hindu philosophy and the Indian cultural tradition, Bose had many other firsts to his credit: he held the first professorship of psychology at the University of Calcutta, he was a founder of the Indian Psychological Association, and, for us the most important first of all, he was the architect of the Indian Psychoanalytic Society.

The founders' meeting of the society took place in 1922 with Bose in the chair. Of the 15 original members, 9 were college teachers of psychology or philosophy, 5 – including 2 Britishers – belonged to the medical corps of the Indian Army, while the professional affiliation of the remaining member is intriguingly listed as "Secretary of the Jute Balers Association."[4] In the same year, Bose wrote to Freud in Vienna. After expressing sentiments of respect and admiration for the master's work, he informed him of the formation of the Indian society. Freud was pleased that his ideas had spread to such a far-off land and asked Bose to write to Ernest Jones, then president of the International Psychoanalytical Association, for membership of that body. Bose did so and the Indian Psychoanalytic Society with Bose as its first president, a position he was to hold till his death in 1953, became a full-fledged member of the international psychoanalytic community. Although psychoanalysis attracted some academic and intellectual interest in the thirties and forties, mostly in Calcutta, the number of Indian analysts was still 15 in 1945, when a second training center, under the leadership of an Italian, E. Sevadio, was started in Bombay.

Cut off from the thrust and parry of debate, controversy and ferment of the psychoanalytic centers in Europe, dependent upon not easily available books and journals for outside intellectual sustenance, Indian psychoanalysis was nurtured through its infancy primarily by the enthusiasm and intellectual passion of its progenitor. In the informal meetings of 8 to 10 people held on Saturday evenings at the president's house – the house was to become the headquarters of the Indian society after Bose's death – Bose read most of the papers and led almost all the discussions. Without the benefit of training analysis himself, it was Bose who "analyzed" the other members in a more or less informal manner and otherwise endeavored to keep their enthusiasm for psychoanalysis alive.

From my own experience of psychoanalytic institutes in different countries, I would venture to say that practicing psychoanalysis is not unlike performing Indian classical music. The basic musical vocabulary may be shared, yet each *gharana* or school has a specific, traditional way of elaborating and performing a *raga*. The musician has learned this traditional way through personal instruction over many years from his teacher who, in turn, has learned it from his teacher, and so on. Similarly, the way we practice psychoanalysis is essentially learned from our own training analysis and can often be traced to a particular psychoanalytic *gharana*. Such a *gharana* is not to be confused with a self-conscious school advancing a divergent theoretical position. All it means is that the practitioners belonging to a *gharana* share a particular style of psychoanalytic "performance." Coterminous with a training institute or even with a national boundary, the *gharana's* original teacher can often be traced back to the first generation of analysts.

In any event, because of its relative isolation, Indian psychoanalytic practice has been decisively marked by the stamp of the first Indian analyst. Essentially, Bose's method is derived from the psychiatric practice of his pre-Freudian years, his theory of opposite wishes, and his readings of Freud's writings on analytical technique. In a short communication to the *International Journal of Psychoanalysis* in 1931, he described it as follows:

> In contrast with the active therapy and the forced fantasy method of Ferenczi, the method has the following salient features. In suitable cases the patient is first asked to give his free associations to determine the nature of the repressed wish active at the time. He is then *ordered* to build up wish fulfilment and fantasies with reference to the repressed wish, ultimately taking up the roles of the subject and the object in the wish-situation. (Italics mine)[5]

The patient was further instructed to repeat this at home and to report the resultant fantasies in the next analytic hour. In the session the patient reclined in an easy chair with his eyes closed, the analyst sitting at the back diligently taking notes of what he or she said. These detailed notes were more than an aide-memoire for the analyst. They were actively used in the process of analysis for breaking down resistance. "The record is of value also in removing the resistances of the patient who may be denying some of his former statements in spite of the assertions of the analyst to the contrary. A reference to notes brings about a conviction of the truth of interpretations much more."[6] As late as in 1966, the brochure published on the occasion of the silver jubilee celebrations of Lumbini Park, the mental hospital run by the Indian society, in its photographic illustration of an analytical session, shows a patient sitting, with his eyes closed, on a folding canvas chair while the analyst behind him is bent over a notebook writing down his utterances.

The actively didactic stance of the Indian analyst, as he engages in a lively interaction with the patient, fits more with the model of the guru–disciple than the doctor–patient relationship. In an earlier paper, I have pointed out some of the reasons for this greater activity on the part of the Indian analyst: an absence in the Hindu philosophical and literary tradition of life-historical introspection so that the patient may have to be taught the kind of "psychological mindedness" needed for successful psychoanalysis; the traditional child-rearing practices and ideology of social relations, which emphasize a demonstratively close "symbiotic" mode of relating with significant others, expectations from which the analyst is not immune; the dominant Indian idiom in which words are only a small part of interpersonal communication, where the patient often craves for eye contact and seeks to complement the spoken communication with facial expression, hand gestures, and bodily movement.[7]

When Bose instructs the patient on the direction his fantasy should take, he is not far removed from some of the meditative procedures used in the Hindu psychophilosophical schools of self-realization. Tantric visualization such as *nyasa* or the *yoganidra* of Raja Yoga come immediately to mind. They are techniques with which Bose, through his deep study of the Yogas, was thoroughly familiar.

Well into the 1940s, the published work of Indian psychoanalysts shows a persisting concern with illuminating Indian cultural phenomena as well as registering the "Indian" aspects of their patients' mental life. We thus come across papers on the Hindu psychology of expiation, on the interpretation – in the light of *Totem and Taboo* – of *prasad*, that is, the food remains of a god or a superior person.[8] There are studies of Indian sculptural motifs such as the *lingam, ardhanarishwara, Mahisasuramardini* as representing various aspects of the Oedipal situation, and of the Hindu family in the light of psychoanalytic theory. We encounter scattered comparative observations such as "The Indian paranoic often turns to religion."[9] Mythological allusions to Hindu gods and goddesses like Shiva or Kali regularly crop up in case history reports where the mythology appears to be used by the patient for both defensive and adaptive purposes. Thus, for instance, T. C. Sinha, a student of Bose and later himself a president of the Indian society, reports the case of a 16-year-old youth whose intense passive homosexual wishes were accompanied by the fear of pregnancy.[10] He countered the analyst's reassurance that men could not become pregnant by referring to the example of the mythical Yuvanasva. Although he had a hundred wives, the king Yuvanasva had no son and approached sages for a remedy. Taking pity on him, they performed a special ritual. A jug of water was made potent by recitals of mantras to be given to the queens to make them pregnant. Unknowingly, Yuvanasva drank of this water and after 10 months gave birth to a child who came out of his body by bursting open the right side of his stomach. To protect himself from Yuvanasva's mythical fate, the patient now developed the fantasy of having his own penis inside his anus.

Yet another patient, in the first published case history from the annals of Indian psychoanalysis, weaves Hindu philosophical ideas and sexual beliefs in the elaboration of his neurosis. Sounding like a parody of Gandhi, the patient is a married young man and the father of several children.

> He is of religious bent and his ideal in life is to attain what has been called in Hindu literature *jivanmukti*, i.e., a state of liberation from worldly bondages and a perfect freedom from all sorts of passions whether bodily or mental. The possibility of the existence of such a state and of its attainment is never doubted by the patient as he says he has implicit faith in the Hindu scriptures which assert that the realization of *brahma* or supreme entity, results in such a liberation. [He believes] that the only thing he has to do is to abstain from sex of all sorts and liberation will come to him as a sort of reward. . . . Since one pleasure leads to another it is desirable to shun all pleasures in life lest they should lead to sex. The patient is against forming any attachment whether it be with his wife or children or friends or any inanimate object. He is terribly upset sometimes when he finds that in spite of his ideal of no-attachment and no-sex, lascivious thoughts of the most vulgar nature and uncontrollable feelings of love and attraction arise in his mind. . . . In spite of his deep reverence for Hindu gods and goddesses filthy sexual ideas of an obsessional nature come into his mind when he bows before these images.[11]

By the 1950s, however, the interest in comparative and cultural aspects of mental life as well as the freshness of the papers written by the pioneering generation of Indian psychoanalysts was totally lost. In the last 25 years, Indian contributions, to judge from the official journal of the Indian society, have been neither distinctive nor original. Even the best papers are little more than status reports on global analytic concepts or introductions to the theories of a few selected post-Freudians such as Klein or Bion.

Here I can only speculate on the reasons for this total divorce of Indian psychoanalysis from Indian culture and society. Psychoanalysis, in the sense of psychoanalytic concepts and theories that gain a large number of adherents among analysts at a given time and subsequently shape their clinical observations, is not completely independent of the historical situation of the analyst and his patients. Freud's postulation of the death instinct and increasing interest in the problems of human aggression after the carnage of World War I, and the magnified importance of object-relations theories after the reassertion and renaissance of the values of the counterenlightenment in Western societies since the later 1960's, are only two instances of the influence of the historical *zeitgeist* on psychoanalytic theorizing and practice.

In India, the last 40 years have witnessed an ever-increasing pace of modernization and industrialization. The country has entered into the world market, both economic and intellectual, in a big way. That market is dominated by the First World. There has been a phenomenal rise of an urban, educated middle class to which normally both the Indian analysts and their patients belong. A consequence of these related processes has been the uncritical acceptance by the middle class, itself the child of modernization, of Western intellectual models (of which Marxism is also one) with claims to universality. It is perhaps no accident that in Bombay – the most western of Indian cities, both geographically and spiritually – the younger generation of psychoanalysts are adherents of the Kleinian school which, with its focus on the universal aspects of the object – "good" and "bad" breasts, "good" and "bad" penises and so on – is perhaps the most universalistic of the many "relational" theories. But even in more traditional Calcutta on the eastern seacoast, any critical engagement with received theory has by now almost disappeared. This, we shall see later, was not true of the early period of psychoanalysis in India. If psychoanalysis is any kind of illustration for the rest of Indian intellectual life, then it seems that when India entered the world market on a truly big scale after Independence, the Western colonization of the Indian mind paradoxically became greater than was the case when the country was still a British colony.

The absence of the cultural idiom in case histories today, such as the patient's use of Indian mythology, are then not only due to a presumed increase in mythological illiteracy as a consequence of the modernizing process. It may well also be due to the patient's sensing the analyst's disinterest in such material because of his commitment to "deeper," universalistic models. Far from the intellectual founts of his professional existence, practicing in a culture indifferent to psychoanalytic ideas and hostile to its view of the person, the Indian analyst tends to idealize analytic "gurus" in distant, presumably more receptive lands and to accord analytic theories greater validity than they in fact might possess. This can unwittingly result in an amplified need for what Donald Spence has called "narrative smoothing." Only the self-confidence arising from the passion of genesis, as in the case of Bose in the early years of Indian psychoanalysis, can provide bulwarks against such needs, namely, the various ways in which reported clinical data come to seem in full agreement with received theory.[12]

My first impression of the text of Indian psychoanalysis – that is, the content of Indian case histories in comparison with Western ones – is the fluidity of the patients' cross-sexual and generational identifications. In the Indian patient the fantasy of taking on the sexual attributes of both the parents seems to have a relatively easier access to awareness. Bose, for instance, in one of his vignettes, tells us of a middle-aged lawyer who, with reference to his parents, sometimes

> took up an active male sexual role, treating both of them as females
> in his unconscious and sometimes a female attitude, especially

towards the father, craving for a child from him. In the male role, sometimes he identified himself with his father and felt a sexual craving for the mother; on other occasions his unconscious mind built up a composite of both the parents toward which male sexual needs were directed; it is in this attitude that he made his father give birth to a child like a woman in his dream.[13]

Another young Bengali, whenever he thought of a particular man, felt with a hallucinatory intensity that his penis and testes had vanished altogether and were replaced by female genitalia. While defecating he felt he heard the peremptory voice of his guru asking, "Have you given me a child yet?" In many of his dreams, he was a man whereas his father and brothers had become women. During intercourse with his wife he tied a handkerchief over his eyes as it gave him the feeling of being a veiled bride while he fantasised his own penis as that of his father and his wife's vagina as that of his mother.[14]

Before proceeding to propositions on Indian mental life from case histories, of others as well as my own, I must first address a crucial epistemological issue. In its most general form, I am referring here to the doubts concerning the adequacy of the psychoanalytic method and the clinical situation in yielding verifiable data, doubts that have been forcefully reiterated by Grunbaum in recent years.[15] Somewhat more specifically, I am alluding to the suggestibility problem, namely, the suspicion that overtly or covertly the analyst is suggesting to the analyst and what to produce in his associations, which will then provide the basis for interpretation. To pinpoint the issue even further in our context, many may have grave reservations about the content of the clinical material elicited by the active, didactic stance of the Indian analyst, a stance to which the analytic method of Bose has greatly contributed. One can legitimately wonder if the analyst's activity does not come perilously close to what a lawyer is forbidden to do in the courtroom, namely, "lead the witness," increasing the chances of suggestion and thus adulterating the clinical data beyond salvation.

We know that ever since Freud, who was seriously concerned about the suggestion problem, analysts have tried to make sure that analytic technique, in contrast to other psychotherapies, minimizes suggestion to an extent where it can no longer be regarded as an alternative explanation. As Edelson reminds us, interpreting the defense rather than suggestions about what the patient is defending against, interventions calling attention to the patient's habitual way of resolving ambiguities in life and in the analytic situation, pointing out the context in which the analysand has difficulties in saying what he has on his mind, and calling attention to what needs further explanation – these constitute the bulk of analytic interventions in the clinical situation.[16] These are relatively free from the taint of suggestion. Heightened didactic activity on the part of the analyst thus need not be ipso facto suggestive. The analyst can exhort, encourage, and interact as much as is demanded by the context in which he operates as long as he refrains from suggesting the contents of a defense or of an unconscious conflict until the patient himself discovers them in some form or other. The *public* record of raw data in psychoanalysis being notoriously limited, we have no way of knowing whether the pioneers of the Indian *gharana* (or, for that matter, of any other school) rigorously followed the discipline of the analytic technique. We have also no overriding reason to doubt that they did not.

In my own work, 50 years after Bose's contributions, of which I was quite unaware until recently, I am struck by the comparable patterns in Indian mental life that we observed independently of each other, and this in spite of our different emotional predilections, analytic styles, theoretical preoccupations, geographical locations, and historical situations. Such a convergence further strengthens my belief, shared by every practicing analyst, that there is no absolute arbitariness in our representation of the inner world. There is unquestionably something that resists, a something that can only be characterized by the attribute "psychical reality," which both the analyst and the analysand help discover and give meaning to. Yet honesty compels one to add that for many of us this conviction is maintained in the face of recurrent doubt. As Derrida reminds us, Freud himself confided to Fliess in 1897 that there is no "index of reality" in the unconscious and that it is impossible to distinguish between truth and a fiction "invested with affect." He could only carry on and propose his work as scientific – in the classical sense – by reintroducing the boundary between *Wahrheit* and *Dichtung* in inner life,[17] distinctions we no longer need to make in quite the same way. Like the quantum universe of physics, the universe of psychoanalysis too is of interconnection, of nonseparability, and it is precisely the analyst's participation that makes it impossible to speak of either the absolute subjectivity or absolute objectivity of the discipline.

Bose's observations, which were based on his treatment of six hundred cases, are succinctly outlined in a letter to Freud dated April 11, 1929:

> Of course I do not expect that you would accept offhand my reading of the Oedipus situation. I do not deny the importance of the castration threat in European cases; my argument is that the threat owes its efficiency to its connection with the wish to be female [Freud in a previous letter had gently chided Bose with understating the efficiency of the castration threat]. The real struggle lies between the desire to be a male and its opposite, the desire to be a female. I have already referred to the fact that castration threat is very common in Indian society but my Indian patients do not exhibit castration symptoms to such a marked degree as my European cases. The desire to be a female is more easily unearthed in Indian male patients than in European. . . . The Oedipus mother is very often a combined parental image and this is a fact of great importance. I have reason to believe that much of the motivation of the "maternal deity" is traceable to this source.

Freud's reply is courteous and diplomatic: "I am fully impressed by the difference in the castration reaction between Indian and European patients and promise to keep my attention fixed on the opposite wish you accentuate. The latter is too important for a hasty decision."[18]

In another paper, Bose elaborates on his observations and explains them through his theory of opposite wishes:

> During my analysis of Indian patients I have never come across a case of castration complex in the form in which it has been described by European observers. This fact would seem to indicate that the castration idea develops as a result of environmental conditions acting on some more primitive trend in the subject. The difference in social environment of Indians and Europeans is responsible for the difference in modes of expression in two cases. It has been usually proposed that threats of castration in early childhood days, owing to some misdemeanour [are] directly responsible for the complex, but histories of Indian patients seem to disprove this.[19]

Bose then goes on to say that although the castration threat is extremely common – in girls it takes the form of chastisement by snakes – the difference in Indian reactions to it are due to children growing up naked till the ages of 9 to 10 (girls till 7) so that the difference between the sexes never comes as a surprise. The castration idea that comes up symbolically in dreams as decapitation, a cut on a finger, or a sore in some parts of the body has behind it the "primitive" idea of being a woman.

It is the ubiquity and multiformity of the "primitive idea of being a woman" and the embeddedness of this fantasy in the maternal configurations of the family and the culture, that I would like to discuss in my own observations. As one might have guessed by now, the hegemonic narrative of Hindu culture is neither that of Freud's Oedipus nor of Christianity's Adam, but of Devi, the great goddess, especially in her manifold expressions as mother in the inner world of the Hindu son. In India, at least, a primary task of psychoanalysis, the science of imagination or even (in Wallace Stevens' words) "the science of illusion," is to grapple with *Mahamaya* – "the Great Illusion" – as the goddess is also called. I would like to begin my exposition with the first 15 minutes of an analytic session.

The patient is a 26-year-old counselor in a school who has been in analysis for 3 years. He entered analysis not because of any particular personal problems but because he thought it would help him professionally. In this particular session, he begins with a fantasy he had while he was in a bus. The fantasy was of a tribe living in the jungle, which unclothes its dead and hangs them on the trees. M., the patient, visualized a beautiful woman hanging on one of the trees. He imagined himself coming at night and having intercourse with the women. Other members of the tribe are eating parts of the hanging corpses. The fantasy is immediately followed by the recollection of an incident from the previous evening. M. was visiting his parents' home, where he had lived until recently, before he married and set up his own household. This step was not only personally painful but also unusual for his social milieu, where sons normally brought their wives to live in their parental home. His younger sister, with her 3-year-old son, was also visiting at the same time. M. felt irritated by the anxious attention his mother and grandmother gave the boy. The grandmother kept on telling the child not to go and play out of the house, to be careful of venturing too far, and so on. On my remarking, that perhaps he recognized himself in the nephew, M. exclaimed with rare resentment, "Yes, all the women [his mother, grandmother, his father's brother's wife, and his father's unmarried sister who lived with them] were always doing the same with me."

Beginning with these 10 minutes of a session, I would like to unroll M.'s conflicts around maternal representations and weave them together with the central maternal configurations of Indian culture. Because of this particular objective, my presentation of further material from M.'s analysis is bound to be subject to narrative smoothing. A case history, although it purports to be a story that is true, is actually always at the intersection of fact and fable. However, its tale quality arises less from the commissions in imagination than from omissions in reality.

Born in a lower middle-class family in a large village near Delhi, M. is the eldest of three brothers and two sisters. His memories of growing up, until well into youth, are pervaded by the maternal phalanx of the four women. Like his mother, who in his earliest memories stands out as a distinct figure from a maternal-feminine continuum, to be then re-absorbed in it, M. too often emerges from and retreats into femininity. In the transference, the fantasies of being a woman are not especially disturbing; neither are the fantasies of being an infant suckling at a breast, which he has grown onto my exaggeratedly hairy chest. One of his earliest recollections is of a woman who used to pull at the penises of the little boys playing out in the street. M. never felt afraid when the woman grabbed at his own penis. In fact, he rather liked it, reassured that he had a penis at all, or at least enough of one for the woman to acknowledge its existence.

Bathed, dressed, combed, and caressed by one or the other of the women, M.'s wishes and needs were met before they were even articulated. Food, especially the milk-based Indian sweets, were constantly pressed on him. Even now, on his visits to the family, the first question by one of the women pertains to what he would like to eat. For a long time during the analysis, whenever a particular session was stressful, because of what he considered a lack of maternal empathy in my interventions, M. felt compelled to go to a restaurant in town where he would first gorge himself on sweets, before he returned home.

Besides the omnipresence of women, my most striking impression of M.'s early memories is their diurnal location in night and their primarily tactile quality. In part, this has to do with the crowded, public living arrangements of the Indian family. Here, even the notions of privacy are absent, not to speak of such luxuries as separate bedrooms for parents and children. Sleeping in the heat with little or no clothes next to one of his caretakers, an arm or a leg thrown across the maternal body, there is one disturbing memory that stands out clearly. This is of M.'s penis erect against the buttocks of his sleeping mother and his reluctance to move away, struggling against the feelings of shame and embarrassment that she may wake up and notice the forbidden touch. Later in adolescence, the mothers are replaced by visiting cousins sharing mattresses spread out in a room or on the roof, furtive rubbings of bodies, and occasional genital contact while other members of the extended family are in various stages of sleep.

Embedded in this blissful abundance of maternal flesh and promiscuity of touch, however, is a nightmare. Ever since childhood and well into the initial phases of the analysis, M. would often scream in his sleep while a vague, dark shape threatened to envelop him. At these times only his father's awakening him with the reassurance that everything was all right helped M. compose himself for renewed slumber. The father, a gentle, retiring man, who left early in the morning for work and returned home late at night, was otherwise a dim figure hovering at the outskirts of an animated family life.

In the very first sessions of the analysis, M. talked of a sexual compulsion that he found embarrassing to acknowledge. The compulsion consisted of traveling in a crowded bus and seeking to press close to the hips of any plump, middle-aged woman standing in the aisle. It was vital for his ensuing excitement that the woman gave her back to him. If she ever turned to face M., with the knowledge of his desire in her eyes, his erection immediately subsided and he would hurriedly move away with intense feelings of shame. After marriage, too, the edge of his desire was often at its sharpest when his wife slept on her side with her back to him. In mounting excitement, M. would rub against her and want to make love when she was still not quite awake. If, however, the wife gave intimations of becoming an enthusiastic partner in the exercise, M. sometimes ejaculated prematurely or found his erection precipitately shrivel.

It is evident from these brief fragments of M.'s case history that his desire is closely connected with some of the most inert parts of a woman's body, hips and buttocks. In other words, the desire needs the woman to be sexually dead for its fulfillment. The genesis of the fantasy of the hanging corpse with whom M. has intercourse at night has at its root the fear of the mother's sexuality as well as the anger at restraint on his explorations of the world. However, my choice of M.'s case is not dictated by the interest it may hold from a psychoanalytical perspective. The choice, instead, has to do with its central theme – namely, the various paths in imagination that M. traverses in the face of many obstacles to maintain an idealized relationship with the maternal body. This theme and the fantasized solutions to the disorders in the mother–

son relationship are repeated again and again in Indian case and life histories. Bose's observation on the Indian male patient's "primitive" idea of being a woman is then only a special proposition of a more general theorem. The wish to be a woman is one particular solution to the discord that threatens the breaking up of the son's fantasized connection to the mother, a solution whose access to awareness is facilitated by the culture's views on sexual differentiation and the permeability of gender boundaries. Thus, for instance, when Gandhi publicly proclaims that he has mentally become a woman or, unaware of Karen Horney and other deviants from the orthodox analytic position of the time, talks of man's envy of the woman's procreative capacities, saying "There is as much reason for a man to wish that he was born a woman as for woman to do otherwise," he is sure of a sympathetic and receptive audience.[20]

In the Indian context, this particular theme can be explored in individual stories as well as in cultural narratives we call myths, both of which are more closely interwoven in Indian culture than is the case in the West. In an apparent reversal of a Western pattern, traditional myths in India are less a source of intellectual and aesthetic satisfaction for the mythologist than of emotional recognition for others, more moving for the patients than for the analyst. Myths in India are not part of a bygone era. They are not "*retained* fragments from the infantile psychic life of the race," as Abraham called them, or "*vestiges* of the infantile fantasies of whole nations, secular dreams of youthful humanity," in Freud's words.[21] Vibrantly alive, their symbolic power intact, Indian myths constitute a cultural idiom that aids the individual in the construction and integration of his inner world. Parallel to patterns of infant care and to the structure and values of family relationships, popular and well-known myths are isomorphic with the central psychological constellations of the culture and are constantly renewed and validated by the nature of subjective experience.[22] Given the availability of the mythological idiom, it is almost as easy to mythologize a psychoanalysis, such as that of M., as it is to analyze a myth; almost as convenient to elaborate on intrapsychic conflict in a mythological mode as in a case historical narrative mode.

Earlier in the chapter, I advanced the thesis that myths of Devi, the great goddess, constitute the hegemonic narrative of Hindu culture. Of the hundreds of myths on her various manifestations, my special interest here is in the goddess as mother, and especially the mother of the sons, Ganesha and Skanda. But before proceeding to connect M.'s tale to the larger cultural story, let me note that I have ignored the various versions of these myths in traditional texts and modern folklore – an undertaking that is rightly the preserve of mythologists and folklorists – and instead picked their best-known popular versions.

The popularity of Ganesha and Skanda as gods – psychologically representing two childhood positions of the the Indian son – is certainly undeniable. Ganesha, the remover of obstacles and the god of all beginnings, is perhaps the most adored of the reputed 330 million Hindu gods. Iconically represented as a pot-bellied toddler with an elephant head and one missing tusk, he is proportionately represented as a small child when portrayed in the family group with his mother Parvati and father Shiva. His image, whether carved in stone or drawn up in a colored print, is everywhere: in temples, homes, shops, roadside shrines, calenders. Ganesha's younger brother, Skanda or Kartikkeya, has his own following, especially in South India, where he is extremely popular and worshiped under the name of Murugan or Subramanya. In contrast to Ganesha, Skanda is a handsome child, a youth of slender body and heroic exploits who in analytic parlance may be said to occupy the phallic position.

Ganesha's myths tell us one part of M.'s inner life while those of Skanda reveal yet another. Ganesha, in many myths, is solely his mother Parvati's creation. Desirous of a child and lacking Shiva's cooperation in the venture, she created him out of the dirt and sweat of her body mixed with unguents. Like M.'s fantasies of his femininity, Ganesha too it not only his mother's boy but contains her very essence. Even when indubitably male like Skanda, M. is immersed in the world of mothers that an Indian extended family creates for the child. Skanda, like M., is the son of more than one mother; his father Shiva's seed, being too powerful, could not be borne by one woman and wandered from womb to womb before Skanda took birth. M.'s ravenous consumption of sweets to restore feelings of well-being has parallels with Ganesha's appetite for *modakas*, the sweet wheat or rice balls that devotees offer to the god in large quantities "knowing" that the god is never satisfied, that his belly empties itself as fast as it is filled.[23] For like the lean M., the fat god's sweets are a lifeline to the mother's breast; his hunger for the mother's body, in spite of temporary appeasements, is ultimately doomed to remain unfulfilled.

In the dramatization of M.'s dilemma in relation to the mother, brought to a head by developmental changes that push the child toward an exploration of the outer world while they also give him increasing intimations of his biological rock-bottom identity as a male, Ganesha and Skanda play the leading roles. In a version common to both South India and Sri Lanka, the myth goes as follows:

A mango was floating down the stream and Uma (Parvati) the mother, said that whoever rides around the universe first will get the mango. [In other versions, the promise is of *modakas* or wives.] Skanda impulsively got on his golden peacock and went around the universe. But Ganesha, who rode the rat, had more wisdom. He thought: "What could my mother have meant by this?" He then circumambulated his mother, worshiped her and said, "I have gone around my universe." Since Ganesha was right his mother gave him the mango. Skanda was furious when he arrived and demanded the mango. But before he could get it Ganesha bit the mango and broke one of his tusks.[24]

Here Skanda and Ganesha are personifications of the two opposing wishes of the older child on the eve of Oedipus. He is torn between a powerful push for independent and autonomous functioning, and an equally strong pull toward surrender and reimmersion in the enveloping maternal fusion from which he has just emerged. Giving in to the pull of individuation and independence, Skanda becomes liable to one kind of punishment – exile from the mother's bountiful presence, and one kind of reward – the promise of functioning as an adult, virile man. Going back to the mother – and I would view Ganesha's eating of the mango as a return to and feeding at the breast, especially since we know that in Tamil Nadu the analogy between a mango and the breast is a matter of common awareness[25] – has the broken tusk, the loss of potential masculinity, as a consequence. Remaining an infant, Ganesha's reward, on the other hand, will be to never know the pangs of separation from the mother, never to feel the despair of her absence. That Ganesha's lot is considered superior to Skanda's is perhaps an indication of Indian man's cultural preference in the dilemma of separation-individuation. He is at one with his mother in her wish not to have the son separate from her, individuate out of their shared anima.[26]

For M., as we have seen, the Ganesha position is often longed for and sometimes returned to in fantasy. It does not, however, represent an enduring solution to the problem of maintaining phallic desire in face of the overwhelming inner presence of the Great Mother. Enter Skanda. After he killed the demon Taraka who had been terrorizing the gods, Parvati became quite indulgent toward her son and told him to amuse himself as he pleased. Skanda became wayward, his lust rampant. He made love to the wives of the gods and the gods could not stop him. On their complaining to Parvati, she decided to take the form of whatever woman Skanda was about to seduce. Skanda summoned the wife of one god after another but in each saw his mother and became passionless. Finally thinking that "the universe is filled with my mother," he decided to remain celibate forever.

M., too, we saw, became "passionless" whenever in the bus the motherly woman he fancied turned to face him. But instead of becoming celibate, he tried to hold on to desire by killing the sexual part of the mother, deadening the lower portion of her trunk, which threatened him with impotence. Furthermore, the imagined sexual overpowering-ness of the mother, in the face of which the child feels hopelessly inadequate, with fears of being enveloped and swallowed by her dark depths, is not experienced by M. in the form of clear-cut fantasies but in a recurrent nightmare from which he wakes up screaming. Elsewhere, I have traced in detail the passage of the powerful, sexual mother through Hindu myths, folk beliefs, proverbs, symptoms, and the ritual worship of the goddess in her terrible and fierce forms.[27] Here, I shall narrate only one of the better-known myths of Devi, widely reproduced in her ironic representations in sculpture and painting, in order to convey through the myth's language of the concrete, of image, and symbol, some of the quality of the child's awe and terror of this particular maternal image.

The demon Mahisasura had conquered all the three worlds. Falling in love with the goddess, he sent a message to make his desire known to her. Devi replied that she would accept as her husband only someone who defeated her in battle. Mahisasura entered the battle field with a vast army and a huge quantity of fighting equipment. Devi came alone, mounted on her lion. The gods were surprised to see her without even armor, riding naked to the combat. Dismounting, Devi started dancing and cutting off the heads of millions and millions of demons with her sword to the rhythm of her movement. Mahisasura, facing death, tried to run away by becoming an elephant. Devi cut off his trunk. The elephant became a buffalo and against its thick hide Devi's sword and spear were of no avail. Angered, Devi jumped on the buffalo's back and rode it to exhaustion. When the buffalo demon's power of resistance had collapsed, Devi plunged her spear into its ear and Mahisasura fell dead.

The myth is stark enough in its immediacy and needs no further gloss on the omnipotence and sexual energy of the goddess, expressed in the imagery of her dancing and riding naked, exhausting even the most powerful male to abject submission and ultimately death, decapitating (i.e., castrating) millions of "bad boys" with demonic desires, and so on. The only feature of the myth I would like to highlight that is absent both in M.'s case vignette and in the myths narrated so far, is that of the sword- and spear-wielding Devi as the phallic mother. In the Indian context, this fantasy seems more related to Chasseguet-Smirgel's notion of the phallic mother being a denial of the adult vagina and the feelings of inadequacy it invokes rather than allowing the traditional interpretation as a denial of castration anxiety.[28] In addition, I would see the image of the goddess as man-woman (or, for that matter, of Shiva as *ardha-narishwara*, half man–half woman) as incorporating the Indian boy's wish to become a man without having to separate and sexually differentiate from the mother, to take on male sexual attributes while not letting go of the feminine ones.

The myth continues that when Devi's frenzied dancing did not come to an end even after the killing of the buffalo demon, the gods became alarmed and asked Shiva for help. Shiva lay down on his back and when the goddess stepped on her husband she hung out her tongue in shame and stopped. Like M.'s gentle and somewhat withdrawn father who was the only one who could help in dissipating the impact of the nightmare, Shiva too enters the scene supine yet a container for the great mother's energy and power. In other words, the father may be unassuming and remote, yet powerful. First experienced as an ally and a protector (or even as a covictim) the father emerges as a rival only later. The rivalry too, in popular Indian myths and most of my case histories, is less that of Oedipus, the power of whose myth derives from the son's guilt over a fantasized and eventually unconscious parricide. The Indian context stresses more the father's envy of what belongs to the son including the mother – and thus the son's persecution anxiety – as a primary motivation in the father–son relationship. It is thus charged with the dread of filicide and with the son's castration, by self or the father, as a solution to the father–son competition. Shiva's beheading of Ganesha, who on the express wish of his mother stood guard at her private chambers while she bathed, and the replacement of his head by that of an elephant, and the legends of Bhishma and Puru, who renounced sexual functioning in order to keep the affections of their father intact, are some of the better-known illustrations.[29] But the fate of fathers and sons and families and daughters are different narratives – stories yet to be told, texts still to be written.

Cultural ideas and ideals, then, manifested in their narrative form as myths, pervade the innermost experience of the self. One cannot therefore speak of an "earlier" or "deeper" layer of the self beyond cultural reach. As a "depth psychology," psychoanalysis dives deep, but in the same waters in which the cultural river flows. Preeminently operating from within the heart of the Western myth, enclosed in the *mahamaya* of Europe – from myths of ancient Greece to the "illusions" of the enlightenment – psychoanalysis has had little opportunity to observe from within, and with empathy, the deeper import of the myths of other cultures in the workings of the self.

The questions relating the "how" of this process are bound up with the larger issue of the relationship between the inner and outer worlds, which has been of perennial psychological and philosophical interest. It is certainly not my intention to discuss these questions at any length. I would only like to point out that, apart from some notable exceptions (such as Erik Erikson, who held aloft a vision of a "psychoanalysis sophisticated enough to include the environment"), the impact of culture on the development of a sense of identity – construction of the self, in modern parlance – has been by and large underestimated.[30] Freud's "timetable," in which culture enters the psychic structure relatively late in life as "ideology of the superego,"[31] has continued to be followed by other almanac makers of the psyche. Even Heinz Kohut, as Janis Long has shown, does not quite follow the logical implications of his concept of "self object".[32] These are, of course, the aspects of the other that are incorporated in the self and are experienced as part of one's own subjectivity. Kohut, too, follows Freud in talking of a "culture selfobject" of later life, derived in part from cultural ideas, which helps in maintaining the integrity and vitality of the individual self.[33] Yet the idea of selfobject that goes beyond the notion of a budding self's relatedness to the environment to the environment's gradual transmutation into *becoming* the self, implies that "*what* the parents respond to in a developing child, *how* they respond and what they present as idealizable from the earliest age"[34] – surely much of it a cultural matter – will be the raw material for the child's inner construction of the self. In other words, a caretaker's *knowing* of the child, a knowing in which affect and cognition are ideally fused, is in large part cultural and forms the basis of the child's own knowing of his or her self. The notion that the construction and experience of the self are greatly influenced by culture from the very beginning does not imply that there is no difference between individual faces and cultural masks, no boundary between inner and outer worlds. The tension between the two is what gives psychoanalysis and literature much of their narrative power. All I seek to emphasize here is that this boundary cannot be fixed either in time or psychic space. It is dynamic, mobile, and constantly subject to change.

Notes

1 Sudhir Kakar, "Psychoanalysis and Non-Western Cultures," *International Review of Psychoanalysis*, vol. 12 (1985):441–448.

2 Oliver Sacks, *The Man Who Mistook His Wife for a Hat* (New York: Harper and Row, 1987), p. 148.

3 For details of Bose's life, see T. C. Sinha, "Psychoanalysis in India," in *Lumbini Park Silver Jubilee Souvenir* (1966), pp. 617–677; and Sinha, "Lumbini Park," in ibid., p. 36.

4 The notice of the meeting is in the archives of Indian Psychoanalytic Society in Calcutta.

5 G. Bose, "A New Technique of Psychoanalysis," *International Journal of Psychoanalysis* vol. 12 (1931):387–388.

6 G. Bose, "A New Theory of Mental Life," *Samiksa*, vol. 2 (1948):108–205.

7 Kakar, "Psychoanalysis and Non-Western Cultures."

8 The papers are S. Sarkar, "The Psychology of Taking Prasad"; M. N. Banerji, "The Hindu Psychology of Expiation"; R. Haldar, "Study of Indian Sculptures in Light of Psychoanalysis"; M. N. Banerji, "Hindu Family and Freudian Theory." The original papers are not available but brief summaries can be seen in the reports from the Indian Society in the *International Journal of Psychoanalysis* for the years 1932, 1933, and 1944.

9 G. Bose. "The Paranoid Ego," *Samiksa*, vol. 2 (1948):1–20.

10 T. C. Sinha, "Some Psychoanalytic Observations on the Siva Linga," *Samiksa*, vol. 3 (1949).

11 G. Bose (1938), "All or None Attitude in Sex," *Samiksa*, vol. 1 (1947):14.

12 Donald P. Spence, "Narrative Smoothing and Clinical Wisdom," in T. Sarbin (ed.), *Narrative Psychology* (New York: Praeger, 1986).

13 G. Bose, "A New Theory of Mental Life," p. 158.

14 Bose, "The Genesis and Adjustment of the Oedipus Wish," *Samiksa*, vol. 3 no. 1 (1949):222–240.

15 A. Grunbaum, *The Foundations of Psychoanalysis: A Philosophical Critique* (Berkeley: University of California Press, 1984).

16 M. Edelson, *Hypothesis and Evidence in Psychoanalysis* (Chicago: University of Chicago Press, 1984), pp. 130–131.

17 J. Derrida, "My Chances/*Mes Chances*," in T. Sarbin (ed.), *Taking Chances: Derrida, Psychoanalysis and Literature* (Baltimore: Johns Hopkins University Press, 1984), pp. 1–32.

18 T. C. Sinha, "Psychoanalysis in India", p. 66.

19 G. Bose (1926), "The Genesis of Homosexuality" *Samiksa*, vol. 4, no. 2 (1950):74.

20 M. K. Gandhi, *To the Women* (Karachi: Hingorani, 1943), pp. 194 and 28–29; Karen Horney, "The Flight from Womanhood: The Masculinity Complex in Women As Viewed by Men and Women," in *Feminine Psychology* (New York: Norton, 1967).

21 Karl Abraham, *Dreams and Myths: A Study in Race Psychology* (New York: Journal of Nervous and Mental Health, 1913), p. 72; S. Freud, "Creative Writers and Daydreaming," *Standard Edition of the Complete Psychological Works of Sigmund Freud*, vol. 9 (London: Hogarth Press, 1953), p. 152.

22 Gananath Obeysekere, *Medusa's Hair: A Study in Personal and Cultural Symbols* (Chicago: University of Chicago Press, 1981).

23 Paul B. Courtright, *Ganesa* (New York: Oxford University Press, 1986), p. 114.

24 G. Obeyesekere, *The Cult of Pattini* (Chicago: University of Chicago Press, 1984), p. 471.

25 Margaret T. Egnor, *The Ideology of Love in a Tamil Family*, unpub. (Geneva, NY: MS, Hobart and Smith Colleges, 1984), p. 15.

26 S. Kakar, "Psychoanalysis and Anthropology: A Renewed Alliance," *Contributions to Indian Sociology*, vol. 21, no. 1 (1987):88.

27 S. Kakar, *The Inner World: A Psychoanalytic Study of Childhood and Society in India* (Delhi: Oxford University Press, 1978).

28 J. Chasseguet-Smirgel, "Feminine Guilt and the Oedipus Complex," *Female Sexuality*, ed. Chasseguet-Smirgel (Ann Arbor: University of Michigan Press, 1964), pp. 94–134. For traditional views, see S. Freud, "Fetishism," *Standard Edition* 21 (1924), and "Splitting the Ego in the Process of Defence," *S.E.* 23 (1940). See also R. C. Bak, "The Phallic Woman: The Ubiquitous Fantasy in Perversions," *The Psychoanalytic Study of the Child*, vol. 23 (1967):15–16.

29 Sudhir Kakar and John Ross, *Tales of Love, Sex and Danger* (New York: Basil Blackwell, 1987).

30 Erik H. Erikson, *Childhood and Society* (New York: W. W. Norton, 1950).

31 S. Freud, "New Introductory Lectures on Psychoanalysis," *Standard Edition of the Complete Psychological Works of Sigmund Freud*, vol. 22 (London: Hogarth Press, 1953), p. 22.

32 Janis Long, "Culture, Selfobject and the Cohesive Self," paper presented at a meeting of the American Psychological Association, August 1986.

33 Heinz Kohut, *Self Psychology and the Humanities*, ed. D. Strozier (New York: W. W. Norton, 1985), pp. 224–231.

34 Long, "Culture, Selfobject and the Cohesive Self," p. 8.

14

The cultural assumptions of psychoanalysis

Takeo Doi

I have decided to use as a point of departure for this discussion a quotation from Freud that clearly indicates that he was aware of the cultural context in which psychoanalysis was born and is practiced. In discussing the cross-cultural insights into psychoanalysis, I consider Freud's ideas first because psychoanalysis is, after all, his brainchild. Surely there is nowadays increasing diversity in psychoanalytic theory and practice, but Freud is "still our lost object, our unreachable genius, whose passing we have never properly mourned," the "father who doesn't die," as Dr. Wallerstein aptly put it in his presidential address, "One Psychoanalysis or Many," at the 1987 International Congress of Psychoanalysis. In plain language, one might just as well say that the ghost of Freud is still uniting the entire body of psychoanalysts, if not hovering over them. Perhaps this is as it should be, but I feel there is something in Dr. Wallerstein's remark that deserves our further consideration, and I shall come back to it at the end of this chapter. At any rate, I discuss psychoanalysis only to the extent that it is still dominated by Freud's original thinking.

Now the quotation from Freud that I want to use is in his essay, "The Future Prospects of Psychoanalytic Therapy." As its title suggests, the paper has an exuberant tone, promising a substantial improvement in therapeutic prospects of psychoanalysis. According to Freud's reasoning, the improvement will come from three directions: advances in knowledge and technique, increased authority of the psychoanalyst, and the general effect of psychoanalytic enlightenment of the general population. What I would like to quote is the beginning of the paragraph that introduces the discussion of increased authority of the psychoanalyst:

> I have said that we had much to expect from the increase in authority which must accrue to us as time goes on. I need not say much to you about the importance of authority. Only very few civilized people are capable of existing without reliance on others or are even capable of coming to an independent opinion. You cannot exaggerate the intensity of people's inner lack of resolution and craving for authority. The extraordinary increase in neuroses since the power of religions has waned may give you a measure of it. (1910b:146)

This passage is interesting on several points. First of all, Freud is surprisingly forceful in acknowledging the necessity of authority for human beings. In fact his statement is made in such general terms that it could refer even to himself or other like-minded people who otherwise would not deign to depend on others. Implicit here is his recognition that the authority is there primarily to sustain people. In other words, there seems to be a reciprocity between the exercise of authority and the people's need. Again noteworthy is his suggestion that the contemporary increase in neuroses is related to the decline of authority of religion. Would it not follow then that if psychoanalysis purports to cure neuroses, it somehow takes the place of religion with regard to authority, even though it won't be just a substitute for religion? At any rate, it seems to me that his expectation of increased authority for the future psychoanalyst would be realized only in such a context. That is to say, authority removed from religion would be added to psychoanalysis.

I hope in reasoning like this I am not too far from what Freud actually might have thought of. However, he did not pursue this line, as obviously he did not want psychoanalysis to be associated with religion even remotely. Thus, right after the quoted passage, he changed to a related thought that society was not kindly disposed toward psychoanalysis at the beginning because it was too novel and will never embrace it wholeheartedly because it takes society to task for causing neuroses. Will his expectation of increased authority for the future psychoanalyst come to nothing, then? To this quandary he offers the following consolation: "And yet the situation is not so hopeless as one might think at the present time. Powerful though men's emotions and self-interest may be, yet intellect is a power too – a power which makes itself felt, not, it is true, immediately, but all the more certainly in the end" (1910b:147). Now it will be very interesting to examine his reasoning so far. At the beginning he seems to covet authority for psychoanalysis. On second thought, he doubts its feasibility. Then he ends up espousing the cause of pure intellect for psychoanalysis. If that is his reasoning, did he give up the claim to authority for psychoanalysis? He does not say so, leaving the question of authority up in the air for the moment. But when one comes to the very end of this essay, it becomes clear that he really did not let go the claim to authority completely, because he seems to be setting hopes on the turnabout of social authority as a result of the enlightenment of the whole population by psychoanalysis. All in all, will it be too much to say that Freud's attitude toward authority was rather ambiguous, if not clearly ambivalent?

I think this way of thinking sheds a new light on the nature of psychoanalytic therapy as Freud conceived it. For there is reason to believe that not only could Freud not assume authority for the psychoanalyst for the time being, but evidently he even postulated that the psychoanalyst should not play the role of authority in the way religion did for the faithful. True, the psychoanalytic relationship is not symmetrical, since "it presupposes the consent of the person who is being analyzed and a situation in which there is a superior and a subordinate," as Freud put it (1914:49). But this superior position of analyst does not entail authority in the usual sense of the word as it appears, for instance, in the previously quoted passage from Freud; rather, it corresponds to that of expert, since the main task of the psychoanalyst is to assist the patient in interpreting his mental state. In other words, the analyst is very much task-oriented and will hardly cater to the patient's dependency need. Still, one might protest that the discretion on the part of the analyst will not prevent people from looking up to him as authority, which certainly is the case. But, then, since he is supposed not to nurture and sustain people, his authority would be a very impersonal one, indeed, like that of an efficient bureaucrat. In other words, he would appear even as an authoritarian figure at times. This is exemplified by none other than Freud, and I shall cite his treatment of Dora as an example to explain my point.

First, a brief outline of the case is in order. Dora, an 18-year-old girl, was brought to Freud by her father because of a suicide note she left on her desk. The turn of events that led up to this outcome was rather ugly, to say the least. She was nearly seduced by a friend of her father's, when her father himself was having an affair with the friend's wife. The seducer denied the fact of seduction and she entreated her father to sever the relationship with his friend's wife. But his having refused to comply with her wish finally drove her to suicidal thoughts. Now I don't know if Freud felt sympathy for the poor girl. If he did, it was not recorded. What was recorded is that he worked intensively on her assumed infatuation with the seducer, utilizing thereby dream interpretation extensively. One day, 3 months after the treatment started, when he expressed satisfaction at the result of dream interpretation, she replied "in a depreciatory tone": "Why, has anything so very remarkable come out?" Then at the following session all of a sudden she announced her decision to terminate the treatment on that very day. Freud was not visibly shaken by her unexpected move and said, "You know that you are free to stop the treatment at any time. But for today we will go on with our work" (1905:105). So the hour was spent as usual. Shouldn't one be amazed by his aloofness? I believe, however, that contrary to his seeming calmness, he was deeply disappointed by the abrupt termination of her treatment. This is borne out by the fact that he explains at some length his afterthoughts of why he did not urge her to stay on in treatment, that is, why he let her go, and, furthermore, by what happened afterward. Namely, when she returned to him 15 months later asking for help because of a minor symptom, be dismissed her, saying that he had nothing to offer her this time and would "forgive her for having deprived [him] of the satisfaction of affording her a far more radical cure for her troubles" (1905:122). Don't you think that Freud was very authoritarian in all this? My point is that, busy as he was forgiving Dora's alleged offenses, he was totally deaf to her cry for help. I should say, however, that he is not to blame for this, after all, because this would have been inevitable if psychoanalytic therapy consisted in only giving the kind of service an expert could give.

Please don't take me wrong on this matter. I am not saying that Freud always behaved like this toward his patients. On the contrary, he is known to have been very cordial, even collegial, especially if the analysand was someone who wanted to learn from him. But apparently he could have become authoritarian when provoked. And I should think this stems mainly from Freud's ambivalence about taking the role of authority vis-à-vis those who crave it. Another example to prove this point can be found in his analysis of religion, as set forth in his essay, "The Future of an Illusion." He argues there that religion is an illusion because it is based on wishful thinking and converts helplessness into an unrealistic belief that one is taken care of by a beneficent Providence. Against such an illusion he contrasts the attitude of those who "admit to themselves the full extent of their helplessness and their insignificance in the machinery of the universe." He compares their positions to that of "a child who has left the parental house where he was so warm and comfortable." Then he insists, "But surely infantilism is destined to be surmounted" (1927:49). In other words, he disapproves of religion precisely because it serves as authority for those who desperately need help. To this argument of his I would say that the feeling of helplessness is surely attended to in religion, but that it will never be eliminated thereby; if anything, it will be cultivated or even refined, whereas it is more likely to be downgraded or blotted out by psychoanalysis, which presupposes that one should surmount "infantilism." No wonder that Freud sounds authoritarian or authoritative, or even pontifical, in explaining away religion in the name of rationality – by so doing he succeeds in brushing aside dependence and helplessness out of his personal view.

I think you can see that I am putting authority and dependence together as a set. That is to say, authority presupposes dependence, just as dependence presupposes authority. Evidently Freud could see that relationship very well, as the above-quoted passage clearly indicates. However, since he was ambivalent about authority, he couldn't tolerate dependence, and thus he ended up being authoritarian. This is my critique of Freud in a nutshell, and formulated like this it would look very simple, almost self-explanatory, as though anybody could have thought it out. However, in my case it was cross-cultural experiences that led me to arrive at this critique. Therefore, I would like to convey the essence of those experiences in the following paragraph.

After I first went abroad to study in the United States, I was immediately struck by the different way that people relate to one another in Japan and the United States. I realized that the difference lies in the tolerance for dependent relationships in Japan and the lack of tolerance in the United States, a fact that is borne out by the existence of a special vocabulary in Japanese to express various phases of emotional dependence. I don't want to go into details on the matter of language here. Suffice to say that the word *amae*, which plays a pivotal role in the vocabulary, originally refers to infant psychology in that it indicates what an infant feels toward its mother when it wants to come close to her and is accepted by her. This observation made me think two things. One, the dependent relationships that the Japanese seem to enjoy are the extension of dependency toward parents. Two, the theme of *amae* is relevant to psychoanalytic theory as it supplies a conceptual tool for developmental psychology. Thus in the light of this insight I came to review the concepts Freud invented to account for infant psychology, especially narcissism and omnipotence. (For more detailed discussion of my view, see Doi, 1962, 1963, 1964, 1969.)

Next, let me quote the pertinent passages from Freud in order to comment on them.

> The primary narcissism of children which we have assumed and which forms one of the postulates of our theories of the libido, is less easy to grasp by direct observation than to confirm by inference from elsewhere. If we look at the attitude of affectionate parents toward their children, we have to recognize that it is a revival and reproduction of their own narcissism, which they have long since abandoned. (1914: 90–91)

> The situation is that of loving oneself, which we regard as the characteristic feature of narcissism. Then, according as the object or the subject is replaced by an extraneous one, what results is the active aim of loving or the passive one of being loved – the latter remaining near to narcissism. (1915:133)

> This extension of the libido theory . . . receives reinforcement . . . from our observations and views on the mental life of children and primitive peoples. In the latter we find characteristics which, if they occurred singly, might be put down to megalomania: an overestimation of the power of their wishes and mental acts, the "omnipotence of thoughts," a belief in the thaumaturgic force of words – "magic" – which appears to be a logical application of these grandiose premises. In the children of today, whose development is much more obscure to us, we expect to find an exactly analogous attitude toward the external world. (1914:75)

In the first quotation Freud is clearly begging the question. Because it is much more reasonable to think of the attitude of affectionate parents as a revival and reproduction of their own, still-continuing desire to be loved and cared for, rather than to derive this desire from the hypothetical concept of primary narcissism. The second quotation repeats the same idea as the first in a different form, but there is added an interesting thought that relates the desire to be loved closely to narcissism. I think the expression "narcissistic gratification," which came to be widely used, originally stems from this idea of Freud's. The third quotation applying the concept of omnipotence to the psychology of children may be descriptive, but I can't help feeling that its description is a bit comical, if not derisive, because actually in all cases of so-called omnipotence of thought the person so described is often fearful, at least objectively quite helpless. Thus one can say that the terms of narcissism and omnipotence actually serve to hide or explain away the bottom fact of human dependence and helplessness.

To do justice to Freud, it is not that he was not cognizant of human dependence and helplessness in infancy. He even noted in his later work that this fact of dependence and helplessness "establishes the earliest situations of danger and creates the need to be loved" (1926:155). As a matter of fact, I wonder if it would not be too wide of the mark to equate the need to be loved he mentions here with *amae*. But it is true nonetheless that he really wanted to get rid of dependence and helplessness if possible at all, as was manifest in the argument he developed in "The Future of an Illusion." In this connection it would be worthwhile to remember that the term "omnipotence" was primarily used to refer to the Judeo-Christian God. Also, even though the term "narcissism" was taken from Greek mythology, the concept of loving oneself that it indicates may evoke a godlike quality as it predicates the original state of being as that of complete self-sufficiency. It is then conceivable that Freud could apply with impunity to human psychology the concepts originally reserved for God precisely because the power of religion was waning in Western societies.

You can now see that beginning with the cross-cultural experiences and explaining how they made me reexamine some of the concepts Freud invented I have now come full circle and arrived at the same critique of Freud I set forth first. Namely, his ideas clearly reflect the intellectual climate of Western societies around the turn of the century. In fact, Freud's ambivalence about authority and dependence can be better understood against this background, since both authority and dependence have been closely tied up with Christianity in Western societies. That is to say, if Christianity loses its credibility, both authority and dependence also have to become suspect. Thus Freud felt it necessary to explain them away or else to posit them somehow inside the individual psyche. The result then has been, as we know, a beautiful intellectual construct of libidinal development from primary narcissism onward. The only trouble with this construct, however, is that it tends to be a closed system.

To turn our eyes to the Japanese scene, it of course is entirely different from what prevails in the West. For the world of *amae* is an everyday phenomenon and the Japanese are more likely to be deferential toward authority than not, as they have very few hang-ups about authority. As you know, Japan was never converted to Christianity as a nation, hence cannot be affected by the decline of its influence. In other words, inherent in the Japanese psyche is the polytheistic and animistic ethos and to that extent it is immune from Western secular rationalism. In this connection I would like to mention the question I am often asked by Americans, that is, "Why is psychoanalysis not popular in Japan?"

The usual answer I give to them is as follows. "Can you tell me why it became popular in the United States? If you can, then I can tell you why it didn't in Japan." So what I really want to say is that psychoanalysis cannot take root in Japan unless it sheds its cultural bias. But surely it works beautifully with the Japanese if it is prepared to deal with authority and dependence as something truly to be reckoned with. In order to avoid misunderstanding, let me say that I am not suggesting that authority and dependence do not count for the Western patients. They do, as a matter of fact. All I am saying is that there has been a silent conspiracy between psychoanalysis and Western culture in general, at least until recently, in neglecting those issues. But surely this neglect cannot go on forever.

Now in conclusion I will go back to Dr. Wallerstein's remark, as I promised in the beginning. He said in effect that Freud can still function as a rallying point for all divergent schools of psychoanalysis since he is "our lost object," the "father who doesn't die." This appellation of Freud may be a quite appropriate one. But what puzzles me is that it does remind us of Freud's own definition of God. Namely, he stated that "a personal God is, psychologically, nothing other than an exalted father" (1910a:123). Then, by the same logic, should we think that Freud is a personal God for us psychoanalysts if he is a "father who doesn't die"? This surely sounds awkward. Or should I perhaps say, God forbid? There is of course no denying that Freud was a great genius. He created a new method of investigation and thus became the founder of psychoanalysis. We learned a great deal from him and shall continue to do so for many days and years to come. But if we take him for "father who doesn't die," psychoanalysis might become a substitute religion. Then, as such, Freud's remark that "young people lose their religious belief as soon as their father's authority breaks down" (1910a, p. 123) would come to apply to psychoanalysis as well. In order to make this point clear, let me once more recapitulate what we have discussed so far. According to what Freud stated in the essay I first introduced, the psychoanalyst could not and should not assume authority. But if he comes to identify with Freud as a "father who doesn't die," is he not assuming authority surreptitiously or simply borrowing Freud's authority? But we have to remember that Freud's authority is not to sustain people, as it does not go beyond that of an expert. In other words, it does not stay put and one knows not when it falls. Therefore, the analyst who rests on Freud's authority is bound to fall when Freud falls. I am afraid that is why contemporary psychoanalysis is losing the advantages it was once thought to possess.

References

Doi, T. 1962. *Amae*: A key concept for understanding Japanese personality structure. In Robert J. Smith & Richard K. Beardsley (Eds.), *Japanese culture: Its development and characteristics*. Wenner-Gren Foundation for

Anthropological Research.

1963. Some thoughts on helplessness and the desire to be loved. *Psychiatry* 26:266–272.

1964. Psychoanalytic therapy and "Western man": A Japanese view. *Int. J. Social Psychiatry*, Special edition, No. 1, 13–18.

1969. Japanese psychology, dependency need and mental health. In W. Caudill & T. Lin (Eds.), *Mental health research in Asia and the Pacific*. Honolulu: East-West Center.

Freud, S. 1905. Fragments of an analysis of a case of hysteria. *Standard edition of the complete works of Sigmund Freud*, vol. 8. London: Hogarth Press, 1953.

1910a. Leonardo da Vinci and a memory of his childhood. *Standard edition of the complete works of Sigmund Freud*, vol. 11. London: Hogarth Press, 1953.

1910b. The future prospects of psychoanalytic therapy. *Standard edition of the complete works of Sigmund Freud*, vol. 11. London: Hogarth Press, 1953.

1914. On narcissism: An introduction. *Standard edition of the complete works of Sigmund Freud*, vol. 14. London: Hogarth Press, 1953.

1915. Instincts and their vicissitudes. *Standard edition of the complete works of Sigmund Freud*, vol. 14. London: Hogarth Press, 1953.

1926. Inhibitions, symptoms and anxiety. *Standard edition of the complete works of Sigmund Freud*, vol. 20. London: Hogarth Press, 1953.

1927. The future of an illusion. *Standard edition of the complete works of Sigmund Freud*, vol. 21. London: Hogarth Press, 1953.

Wallerstein, R. 1987. One psychoanalysis or many. *Int. J. Psycho-Anal.* 69: 5–21.

15
Infant environments in psychoanalysis
A CROSS-CULTURAL VIEW

Robert A. LeVine

Freud was an avowed Darwinian, but the relationship between his theory and evolutionary biology is still being debated. Similarly, psychoanalysis is a developmental psychology, yet its connections with direct observations of child behavior remain problematic. This chapter examines certain psychoanalytic assumptions regarding the environments of infants in the light of direct observations made in culturally diverse human populations. Its aim is to provide a more secure base for a psychoanalytic contribution to the understanding of early experience and development and their place in human adaptation.

In 1937 Heinz Hartmann presented to the Vienna Psychoanalytic Society his attempt to ground psychoanalytic ego psychology in a set of sophisticated assumptions concerning the biology, psychology, and sociology of individual development. Published two years later in German and two decades later in English, Hartmann's *Ego Psychology and the Problem of Adaptation* (1958) bridged many gaps between psychoanalysis and the biological and social sciences and influenced subsequent theory within psychoanalysis and to some extent outside it. One of its most influential concepts is "the average expectable environment of the child." Hartmann did not specify what he meant by this nor did he state unequivocally whether it was supposed to be universal for all humans or variable across cultures. His strongest statement on the universal side was the following:

> Strictly speaking, the normal newborn human and his average expectable environment are adapted to each other from the very first moment. That no infant can survive under certain atypical (on the average not expectable) conditions and that traumata certainly are integral to typical development, do not contradict this proposition. (Hartmann, 1958:51)

On the other hand, Hartmann conceived of this state of adaptedness as being limited to the first few months of life, and – keeping the door open for more environmental influence than could be demonstrated at the time – he sometimes used the term "average expectable" to refer to situational diversity in standards of adaptation or mental health (e.g., 1958:23, 76).

As a developmental concept, Hartmann's average expectable environment is usually interpreted as a pan-human requirement for normal development, with the following features:

1. *Preadaptation.* The human infant is prepared by its genetic inheritance to anticipate a specific range of environmental stimuli that facilitate the development of normal ego functions, the prerequisites for adaptive capacities.
2. *Variation.* Within the genetically specified range, a variety of early environmental patterns of stimulation can act as "releasers" for normal developmental patterns (Hartmann, 1958:35).
3. *Limits.* Outside that range of environments, the development of ego functions will not proceed normally, and pathologies of ego development, leading to maladaptive outcomes, will result. Thus mental health is at stake in the maintenance of an average expectable environment for infants and young children.

Because Hartmann failed to specify the environmental range required for normal development, the implications of an average expectable environment for research and clinical practice are dependent on the interpretation and theoretical position of the investigator. The concept is, first of all, consistent with Freud's ([1905] 1953) theory of psychosexual development, in which each stage requires (i.e., "expects") drive gratification within an optimal range in order to prevent potentially pathogenic fixation; excessive deprivation or excessive gratification leads to vulnerability. Thus the Hartmann formulation can be seen as providing theoretical elaboration and support for the kind of environmental influence posited in Freud's libidinal stages. Although Hartmann is quite clear that his focus is on ego development rather than the development of the sexual drive, his concept is sometimes interpreted as a restatement and defense of Freud's position.

Second, the evolutionary basis of the average expectable environment can be seen as needing theoretical amplification. Bowlby's (1969: 91) model of the "environment of evolutionary adaptedness" specifies the Hartmann concept in terms of survival risks to infants (particularly predation) in early hominid populations on the African savannahs, translated by natural selection into a genetic preparedness for attachment on the part of human infants and mothers. This model, currently influential in child development research, removes the average expectable environment from the field of direct empirical assessment and makes it a theoretical assumption to be tested only through its derived propositions.

A third approach is to conduct empirical research on the environments of children in contemporary human populations to discover what conception of an average expectable environment the data support. This seems to be what Hartmann had in mind when he stated: "Yet methodology warns us that, in a realm which is more amenable to direct observation than to reconstruction from the psychoanalysis of adults, we should avoid making assumptions which clash with observations of behavior" (1958:52).

Although Hartmann left the foci of observation open in this early monograph, his later seminal writings with Ernst Kris and Rudolph Loewenstein (Hartmann, Kris, & Loewenstein, 1964) provide indications of what he thought they should be:

> As the child learns to distinguish between himself and the mother, he develops understanding for her communications. Little is known about the detailed processes by which this understanding is established; reactions to the actual handling of the child by the mother, to touch and bodily pressure, certainly play a part; gradually, the understanding of the child for the mother's facial expression grows. It seems probable that experiences concerning emotive processes and expressive movements in the infant himself form the basis or are a necessary condition for the infant's understanding of the mother's expression. . . . But the cognitive side of the process, the understanding of signs of communication, is part of the libidinal tie existing between the two. (Hartmann et al., [1946] 1964:39)

> We have mentioned before that clinical observations suggest that even the formation of the ego. . . seems to be dependent on, among other factors, the nature of the earliest object relations, as studied recently in the vicissitudes of the mother–child relation. There is no doubt that cultural differences may be responsible for similar variations. In fact, we expect that in the not-too-distant future anthropologists will utilize propositions in this area in describing psychological phenomena related to certain types of difference between cultures. (Hartmann et al., [1951] 1964:94)

These comments indicate that the study of mother–infant communication, in our own and other cultures, represents the direction Hartmann was recommending when he suggested that direct observations should replace a priori assumptions concerning the average expectable environment of the child. In the next section I present some results from observational studies of mother–infant communication in diverse cultures.

Variations in mother–infant communication

For more than a decade my research group at Harvard has been investigating infant care and mother–infant interaction in culturally diverse settings, including East Africa, Western Europe, the United States, and Mexico (Richman et al., 1988). Our research program has been organized around naturalistic home observations of mother and child conducted during the daytime and providing an opportunity to assess the frequency of gross categories of maternal behavior at several points during the first 2 years of life. This method does not capture what

Table 15.1. *Maternal behavior to infant, expressed as a proportion of her total observed behavior, in samples of Gusii (Kenya) and the U.S. middle class (Boston)*

	Gusii				United States			
	3–4 months (n = 9)		9–10 months (n = 17)		3–4 months (n = 9)		9–10 months (n = 9)	
	Mean	S.D.	Mean	S.D.	Mean	S.D.	Mean	S.D.
Talk	.11	.08	.14	.08	.25	.08	.29	.07
Look	.12	.06	.12	.06	.40	.17	.43	.19
Hold	1.00	.17	.88	.51	.54	.16	.25	.09

happens at night nor does it assess the meaning and impact of the observed behavior, but its comparative data on some basic parameters of the infant environment are useful points of departure for exploring the broader and deeper contexts in which the behavior is embedded. In what follows, I present some of our observational data on maternal behavior, provide contextual interpretations from the mother's perspective, and then speculate on a contextual interpretation from the perspective of the infant. Later sections discuss the implications of this analysis for conceptualizing the average expectable environment of the child and for psychoanalytic theories of development.

The data presented (Table 15.1) have been selected from an analysis by Amy Richman (1983; Richman et al., 1988) that compares maternal behavior in samples drawn from two culturally diverse populations, the Gusii of Kenya and the middle class of Boston in the United States.

The Gusii are an agricultural people totaling about one million who are located in the fertile highlands of southwestern Kenya. They have one of the highest birth rates in the world; the average woman bears close to 9 children, with a median of 10. Gusii infant mortality, on the other hand, is quite low for Sub-Saharan Africa, probably about 80 per 1,000 live births, and even declined during the 1970s (Hobcraft, McDonald, & Rutstein, 1984; Moseley, 1983). Their high fertility and relatively high rates of child survival represent the achievement of indigenous goals to Gusii parents.

The children in the Gusii sample were large at birth and healthy during the first year by American pediatric standards, and they also performed above the U.S. norms on the Bayley infant tests during that time (LeVine et al., in press). Thus these are, in biomedical terms, normal and healthy infants being raised in reproductively successful parental environments. The same could be said for the children of the American sample, drawn largely from upper middle-class suburban families who chose to have fewer children. Since none of the Gusii infants were first-borns, we selected for comparison American infants who were second- or third-borns, so that differences in maternal behavior by birth order of the child would not constitute the main source of cross-cultural variation. (It is noteworthy nonetheless that first-borns and only children make up about half of all contemporary American children and about 11% of Gusii children.)

Table 15.1 shows that the American mothers devoted about twice as much of their observed behavior to talking to, and more than three times as much to looking at, their infants as the Gusii mothers at the age of both 3–4 months and 9–10 months, while the Gusii mothers held their babies almost twice as much at 3–4 months and more than three times as much at 9–10 months. These figures are surface indicators of divergent styles of infant care, reflecting first of all routine practices organized by custom.

American customs include the use of a plastic seat that holds the infant safely and comfortably facing the mother without physical contact. Another contemporary American custom is the mock conversation, in which a mother engages the baby in an extended verbal "exchange," attempting to elicit a smile, vocalization, and motoric response, usually by repeating questions in a high-pitched voice, interpreting the baby's subsequent babbles as answers to her questions, and maintaining the conversational format by providing imaginary verbal responses as if they were being spoken by the infant. In the mock conversation, the mother looks at and talks to the baby, and the infant seat puts the baby in position for this kind of interaction. In this context, the American mothers treat their infants as distinct individuals, physically separated and capable of engaging in communicative exchange at a distance.

The Gusii mothers follow a different set of customs, in which infants are held by the mother or a child nurse – in the arms, on the lap or strapped onto the back – when they are not sleeping, and often when they are, until about 15 months of age. There are no infant seats or other holding devices; the caregiver's body provides protection and comfort most of the time. Routine practices include feeding and shaking in response to infant crying, but no efforts at extended conversational exchange or other forms of excitement. The customary goal is to keep infants warm, nourished, protected, and quiet, not to stimulate adult conversation, and this is implemented in a setting of physical contact between caregiver and infant.

These customs constitute the contexts of routine mother–infant interaction in the two samples and suggest that the quantitative difference in proportion of observed maternal behavior is merely a symptom of more profound divergence in infant environments. To uncover that divergence we require additional contextual information concerning both mother and child.

Maternal behavior in a particular setting can be interpreted in at least two ways: as a utilitarian pursuit of adaptive goals, given certain environmental contingencies, and as symbolic action, given certain meanings embedded in prevailing cultural models of the mother–infant relationship.

A *utilitarian interpretation*

In utilitarian terms, the American and Gusii mothers can be seen as operating on different time-energy budgets related to the socioeconomic and demographic contexts of their lives. The U.S. mothers, with two young children, were not currently employed outside the home or were employed only part-time; husbands' employment provided an adequate family income. The Gusii women, on the other hand, although many of them had employed husbands too, were expected to provide their childrens' food through labor-intensive agriculture and manage a home with several children; their work load was much greater than that of the American women.

The different styles of behavior observed are congruent with the notion that the Gusii mothers are just too busy to behave toward their infants as the Americans do. The mother's visual and verbal attention is a scarce resource, needed for all the tasks in her life; if she invests it in social interaction with her infant, it is subtracted from other areas where it may be urgently needed. The Gusii mothers, with so many burdens in addition to infant care, do not have the leisure time for mock conversations with an infant; furthermore, they have a style of interacting with infants that is addressed to the infant's basic physical needs while leaving their own visual and verbal attention free for other tasks. Indeed, Gusii mothers were frequently observed holding an infant or breast-feeding while performing other tasks. In these terms, then, differences in the total work load and time-energy budgets of American and Gusii mothers account for the observed differences in their behavior toward infants.

The demographic situations of the two samples of mothers provide other utilitarian bases for explaining their behavioral differences. Although the Gusii maternal and child health situation has improved greatly and is relatively good by African standards, the infant mortality rate still runs about eight or ten times that of middle-class America, and it is not hard to imagine that Gusii mothers are primarily concerned with minimizing survival risks to their infants, particularly during the first year, and tend to give social interaction with the baby much lower priority. Observing Gusii mothers at home and in the pediatric clinic strongly supports the notion that they (and the fathers) are concerned with the vulnerability of their infants to disease and injury. For the American mothers, on the other hand, a low infant mortality rate and accessibility to modern medical services reduces the survival concern and permits play and social interaction with the baby to make a stronger claim on their behavior.

Fertility is another demographic parameter that distinguishes Gusii from the United States: The average Gusii woman has about five times as many children during her life as the average middle-class American, and mothers in each sample know what level of fertility they can expect in the future. For the Gusii women this fate is not simply imposed; they *want* many children, to share the work load when young and provide their mothers with support and security when they grow up. Anticipating that they will give birth again within two or three years, Gusii women are keenly aware that their limited time-energy allocation for child care will be concentrated on the new infant; giving too much visual and verbal attention to any particular infant, except the last one, would be arousing expectations for future maternal attention that could not be met. That might mean raising a demanding child who would interfere with the smooth operation of the household and the birth succession associated with it. This kind of calculus, which is regarded as common sense by Gusii women, appears to be absent among the Americans, who have already decided to have only two or three children anyway, on the assumption that every child needs a great deal of attention throughout the preschool years and that it is natural for children to call attention to their felt needs. The difference in assumptions about fertility and claims on maternal attention is also consistent with the observed behavioral differences between Gusii and U.S. mothers.

These several utilitarian considerations, covering maternal work load, infant mortality, and fertility, all act as environmental pressures to which the observed patterns of maternal behavior can be seen as responsive. In other words, their culturally distinctive styles of mother–infant interaction can be interpreted as adaptive strategies for maximizing desired benefits while mimimizing costs or risks in a particular environmental setting. The Gusii mothers bear offspring in an environment high in risks to infant survival and in the maternal work load, but the incentives for child-bearing are also high. Thus their strategy is to bear many children, minimizing the risks to their survival during the infancy period and realizing the anticipated gains from compliant workers when children are older. The American mothers bear offspring in an environment low in risks to infant survival and – for the mothers in our sample – relatively low in the maternal work load, and in which incentives favor raising a few children capable of competing in school and the labor market when they get older. Thus their strategy is to have a few children and allocate to each a great many resources believed to improve the child's life chances, including social attention from the mother during infancy. In these terms, the differences displayed in Table 15.1 can be attributed to the divergent adaptive strategies of the two samples of mothers.

A cultural interpretation

A cultural analysis points to other contextual information on the Gusii and American mothers. Their cultural models of the mother–infant relationship are influenced by the wider codes of communicative conduct prevailing in their respective communities, for example, their assumptions concerning what an adult conversation is and ought to be. Gusii norms of adult conversational interaction do not include mutual gaze or even the en face position that facilitates visual contact, and adults are often to be seen conversing side by side or at right angles to one another without attempting eye contact. This seems to be due to the fact that the operative ideals of interaction are organized around the avoidance (*ensoni*) and respect (*obosiku*) norms that apply to persons of adjacent generations; that is, classificatory "children" must act severely restrained in the presence of their classificatory "parents" in order to pay them appropriate respect, and this involves avoiding their gaze when conversing with them. Although these norms do not specifically apply to persons of the same or alternate generations, who are permitted mutual familiarity and even obscene joking, eye contact remains relatively rare. My interpretation of this is that the basic meaning of eye contact given by the avoidance norms, namely a disrespectful intimacy, is canonical in Gusii relational thought, permeating other relational contexts and leading to visual aversion.

In the case of Gusii mothers with their infants, the prevalent cultural model does not portray them as conversational partners at all, in contrast to their American counterparts, as I have already indicated. When they do interact, the mothers cannot be expected to engage in frequent eye contact with their infants, since they do not do so with other persons in their lives. In addition, however, a mother is aware that her interaction with the child will eventually (i.e., from puberty onward) be structured by the avoidance norms and that even before that happens, she will expect the respect due a mother as the manager of the domestic work force. By keeping her gaze averted during interaction with the infant, even when the latter is looking at her, the mother acts to prevent the child from becoming disrespectful and to maintain the hierarchical order of the home.

However, mutual gaze may mean something other than disrespect when a Gusii mother gives her infant the kind of visual and verbal attention that is frequent among American mothers; it may mean that she is taking pleasure and pride in the child. To the Gusii, a display of pleasure in one's own good fortune is an open invitation to the jealousy and destructiveness of others less fortunate, even when they are not present. Children are particular targets for the witchcraft of envious neighbors. Thus a Gusii healer showed me the medicine he had for children who do well in school, to protect them from the dangers their good fortune would inevitably attract. Gusii women do not make a display of their love and attachment to their babies for the same reason they do not announce that they are pregnant.

This interpretation, that Gusii mothers infrequently look at and talk to their babies to prevent arousing envy in others, raises the possibility that they do look at and talk to their babies when others are not present

– that is, when we could not observe them. This possibility cannot be entirely ruled out, but it is not as serious a threat to the validity of our observational data as it might seem. One reason is that Gusii mothers spend a great deal of time in settings as public as the ones in which we observed them at home, with neighbors present who might be suspected of witchcraft. Thus the amount of time when they consider themselves truly alone with the baby is relatively small, though of course not necessarily unimportant. Furthermore, in the case of pregnancy, our Gusii informants reported that they did not divulge the news to anyone even in the immediate family, for fear that they could be seen as flaunting their good fortune, although no one was present who was thought likely to be jealous. This suggests that their suppression of behavior interpretable as a display of personal pride is not dependent on the actual social conditions of observation; from their point of view the danger is ubiquitous. Insofar as this applies to playing with one's baby, and we believe it does, such behavior would be inhibited most of the time.

A final cultural meaning that must be mentioned (more briefly here than it deserves) concerns the models of virtue that guide mothers in the socialization of their children, even during infancy. Middle-class American mothers typically want alert, active, responsive, talkative and independent children, and they look for precursors of these qualities to reinforce during infancy. Gusii mothers, although their primary goals for the first year of life are growth and survival rather than behavioral or psychological development, typically prefer respectful children who are attentive to adult commands without being talkative or attention-seeking. In infancy they try to cultivate a quiet, easily soothed baby who will fit easily into the domestic hierarchy of the household under the daytime care of siblings as young as 5 years of age. Mothers assume that the sibling group will socialize each toddler with only occasional maternal intervention. This model of child development helps explain why, when Gusii mothers were asked why they do not play with or teach their infants more than they do, their typical response was that this was something for the other children, not the mother, to do.

This overview of the contexts of maternal behavior in the two cultures shows that, whether examined in terms of adaptive strategies or cultural models and meanings, a contextual approach indicates even greater divergence in the average environments of infants than the quantitative observational evidence captured. The key question is what difference this makes to infants.

From the infant's perspective

Investigating the contexts of an infant's experience is necessarily more speculative, since infants cannot be interviewed like their mothers, nor can we assume they share the cultural ideas that are guiding interaction around them. Nevertheless, if there is one conclusion we can draw from infant research of the last 30 years, it is that infants are capable learners at birth and thus are processing environmental information from the start. What can we say about how Gusii and American infants experience their environments during the first year of life? Here I shall try to describe the normal patterns of visible excitement in their temporal and social contexts for the Gusii and American infants. By patterns of excitement I mean states of emotional and motoric arousal, at one pole, and states of comfort, reduced alertness, and sleep, at the other. By the temporal context I mean its typical length and place in the diurnal cycles of sleep and wakefulness over 24 hours. By the social context I mean the interpersonal conditions associated with excitement and its diminution. My assumption is that these patterns constitute learning routines for infants from which they acquire their earliest social expectations.

Bouts of positive excitement in infants are longer and more frequent among Americans than among Gusii, since American mothers attempt to arouse a positive affective and motoric response in the context of a mock conversation and other play routines. Gusii mothers rarely engage infants in this kind of arousal, although sometimes older children do so. On the whole, it can be assumed that positive excitement, particularly as elicited by the mother, is much more characteristic of American than of Gusii infants (Dixon et al., 1981).

This does not mean that middle-class American infants are kept in a continual state of positive excitement. On the contrary, their typical diurnal cycle is divided into lengthy periods of solitary sleep undisturbed by social stimuli, and periods of waking in which, in addition to eating and bathing, they are the centers of exciting social attention from mother and others in the family. This sharp contrast between isolated sleep and socially exciting wakefulness is heightened by the custom of putting babies to sleep in their own beds in their own rooms, on the one hand, and the custom of engaging them in extended play routines, on the other. It gives infants training in self-comforting as they get to sleep and also builds an expectation for social attention and positive emotional excitement whenever they are awake.

For the Gusii infant the rhythms of interpersonal experience and its association with excitement are radically different. The infant is never isolated, asleep or awake, and is often in physical contact with a caregiver's body in both states. At the same time, the infant is hardly ever the center of social attention and rarely engaged in positively exciting emotional interaction. Even when awake, the infant is soothed, and even when asleep, she is with others. The peaks and valleys of excitement, arousal, and stimulation observable in the American case are largely missing from the experience of Gusii infants; so is the sharp contrast in social density between sleep and waking. Gusii infants learn to fall asleep in the midst of family interaction, and they come to expect that they will be watching others interact without receiving attention themselves. That this is a very different environment for the acquisition of the first emotionally significant relationships seems obvious.

Average expectable environments

There is little doubt that the interpersonal experience of Gusii infants deviates in overall shape and direction, as well as in many specific elements, from what is average and expectable for their counterparts in Boston. This is not an isolated finding; a growing number of infant observation studies in diverse settings indicate cross-cultural variations in maternal behavior during the first year of life. For example, a recent report by Tronick, Morelli, and Winn (1987) on infant care among the Efe Pygmies of the Ituri Forest in Zaire reveals that babies are held and breast-fed by numerous women in the community from birth onward. It is noteworthy that differences in early environments, particularly patterns of mother–infant communication, are found not only in comparisons between Western industrial societies and non-Western agrarian or foraging populations but also in cross-cultural comparisons made *within* Melanesia, *within* Western Europe, or *within* United States metropolitan areas (Richman et al., 1988).

I have emphasized variation in maternal behavior during the first year of life only because that is the period usually thought to be dominated most by universal phylogenetic influences on mother–infant interaction. During the second year, however, cultural differences in the child's environment as organized by parents with divergent priorities are even more manifest. Once the child can walk and talk, cultural meanings of the toddler's mobility and ability to make verbal demands lead to different parental responses. American middle-class parents, for example, tend to value exploration, talkativeness, and reciprocal verbal exchange at this age, but in many other cultural settings these child behaviors are considered inappropriate or dangerous for a young child. As we get more and better-quality data on the environments of children during the first 3 years in far-flung populations, the evidence of diversity linked to particular social and cultural conditions grows stronger.

Many of the environmental conditions of young children observed to be statistically average, culturally valued, and socially expectable in other cultures are ones that would be considered prognostic of abnormal development by psychoanalytic clinicians in our own. Mahler, Pine, and Bergman (1975) and Kohut (1977), for example, have emphasized the importance for normal development of maternal support for the infant and toddler's autonomy, separation, and individuation. By their standards, the environments of Gusii, Japanese (Doi, 1981), and Hindu Indian (Kakar, 1978) children are abnormal, certainly beyond the average expectable environment that appears to promote normality in a Western context. Are these non-Western peoples to be classified as pathological in their development or is an average expectable environment specific to a culture?

Anthropologists interested in human development have raised this question, in one form or another, for at least the past 50 years. Psychoanalysts have often responded by discounting the evidence of variation, asserting that ethnographic accounts are focused on the *interpersonal* environment rather than on the child's inner psychic reality. But Hartmann, who formulated the concept of an average expectable environment, called for direct observation of mother–infant communication, including emotional expressions, as a privileged means of probing the child's earliest experience. And more recent psychoanalytic theorists and investigators of child development such as Bowlby (1969), Kohut (1977), Mahler et al. (1975), and Stern (1985) have given the observable interpersonal environment of the normal infant a central place in their formulations.

Thus observations of interpersonal behavior during the early years cannot be discounted in psychoanalysis. Ethnographic observation is, so to speak, just what the doctors ordered. The next step is to revise the psychoanalytic theory of development in terms necessitated by the evidence of variation in human infant environments.

One hypothesis worth investigating is that the level and patterning of excitement in the first and second years of life influence the child's activity level, attention responses, learning of cognitive and language skills, and emotional vulnerability to interpersonal discontinuities (e.g., separations and losses) during that period and in the ensuing years. This hypothesis predicts, for example, that the average American toddler will be more active, "engaged," talkative, and responsive to explicit teaching routines than her Gusii counterpart, but also more demanding and more sensitive to parental moods, emotional inconsistencies, and other disruptions in the affective context of family life.

Indirect evidence supports the general picture of Gusii toddlers as quiet and undemanding compared with American children. American observers in the 1970s as in the 1950s were surprised at how "subdued" Gusii children were in the 2- to 3-year-old range, rarely talking, moving vigorously, playing noisily or creating disturbances. The finding from the Six Cultures Study (Whiting & Whiting, 1975, p. 64), based on data collected in the 1950s, that the American children aged 3 to 11 years showed about three times the proportion of attention-seeking that their Gusii counterparts did, suggests that the older Gusii children are also relatively undemanding. They have learned the lesson that children should comply with the commands of their elders rather than initiate activity on their own. Furthermore, when Gusii mothers (in the 1970s) were asked to name children they would consider excessively active by their standards (there is no single word for hyperactivity in the Gusii language), they mentioned children whom the American observers estimated to be *less* active motorically than the average American child. Finally, the word *omokwani*, which simply means "a talker" or "talkative," is usually applied by Gusii adults to a child regarded as talking too much rather than one whose verbal facility is a source of parental pride. Our overall impression is that the pattern of early experience typical of Gusii infants produces toddlers who are much less active motorically and verbally and much less demanding or attention-seeking than their American counterparts. This reflects the divergent priorities of parents in the two cultures and is associated, according to this hypothesis, with different benefits and costs.

On the benefit side, the Gusii child may be protected by a less exciting early social experience from the expectations for parental attention and the inevitable disappointments that Kohut and other psychoanalysts have emphasized in accounting for personality disorders. In other words, although Gusii infant care seems cognitively and emotionally understimulating from an American viewpoint, the lower expectations for interpersonal excitement that it engenders may buffer the child emotionally against subsequent failures of responsiveness in the caretaking environment, thereby reducing some of the risks of psychological casualty familiar in the United States. The socially exciting infant experience of American children, according to this view, leaves them more emotionally dependent on a rewarding and motivating attachment to particular adults and thus more vulnerable to emotional upset than Gusii when stable relationships are disrupted by parental death or depression, family conflict or breakup, or discontinuities in caregiving. Gusii parents see the benefits in terms of compliant children who are easily managed, know their place in the domestic hierarchy, and learn to perform appropriate tasks obediently and responsibly. Protection from psychic trauma would not be a benefit they would think of, but Gusii mothers believe that keeping infant expectations for adult attention low prevents young children from becoming morally "spoiled" (*ogosaria*), that is, demanding and cranky, which can lead to conceit and arrogance. From the parents' point of view, Gusii infant care provides the child with expectations that are realistic and morally appropriate.

The psychic costs resulting from Gusii patterns of infant and child care begin with the fact that parents provide little explicit support for the young child's self-assertion and pride in personal accomplishment. Mothers and fathers eschew praise for a child of any age as fostering conceit, and there is a decrement in the amount of adult attention Gusii children receive during the second and third years of life, just when their competence in language and other domains of social behavior is being rapidly acquired. (This is due to the mother's sense that an 18-month-old infant of normal physical growth and motor development no longer needs her attention as much as before and can be taken care of by, as well as learn more effectively from, older siblings and other children.) Psychoanalytic self psychology as formulated by Kohut (1977) would predict that individuals who receive no parental praise and no support for initiative and self-assertion during the early years would grow up lacking "normal" self-esteem and would experience anxiety about personal accomplishment.

Applying this formulation to the Gusii without taking into account what constitutes normal self-esteem in their social world would almost certainly overestimate the severity of the deficit or pathology resulting from this pattern of early experience, forecasting that Gusii adults would be severely impaired in the self-cohesion or ego functions necessary for adaptive action. Contrary to such a prediction, most Gusii adults not only do act adaptively but are clearly ambitious and goal-oriented strivers. Yet the contents of their preoccupations *are* predictable from Kohut's model: The Gusii men and women we worked with were extremely anxious about being publicly recognized for special accomplishment or good fortune, exaggerating the destructive power of their neighbors' jealousy and going to great lengths to postpone public awareness of any advantage gained by themselves, their children, their family. Since many advantages (e.g., fertility, academic achievement, employment) cannot be concealed for very long (particularly from interested gossips in a small community), they sought protection in a variety of defensive strategies: the use of rhetorical devices such as understatement and disavowal of intentionality in conversational discourse (S. LeVine, 1979:358), magical medicines that strengthen one's body against malevolence or strike back against it, alcohol consumption affording the subjective experience of enhanced potency, and permanent emigration to places beyond the reach of jealous neighbors and kin.

The conclusion we draw from these widespread patterns (to be described in detail in future publications) is that Gusii men and women tend to feel extremely vulnerable to the imagined jealousy of others when they contemplate receiving any potentially invidious distinction. This sense of vulnerability betokens a lack of what Americans would call self-confidence; it does indeed suggest less self-esteem, or a weaker positive self-regard, than would be personally valuable for Gusii adults in their current lives. But their current lives are being lived in a newly competitive environment – of land scarcity, academic competition, the scramble for paid employment and the advent of cash and consumer goods – that generates new situations in which invidious social comparisons are more difficult to avoid than they once were.

In the past, it can be argued, a Gusii adult needed less self-esteem, because basic subsistence resources were available without competition, patriarchal rule kept competitiveness in check, and a traditional code of routine and ritual conduct covered most social situations a person was likely to face, endowing behavior with a legitimacy that made people feel safe. Following traditional scripts for social life afforded community protection (including concealment) for individual striving, but socio-economic change has eroded that protection, throwing individuals onto their personal resources for the feeling of safety in social life. In the face of more urgent and less regulated competition spreading around them, Gusii adults feel increasingly threatened and are unable to give themselves the sense of safety they once derived from a coherent community structure, thus turning to the more desperate, relatively ineffective, measures mentioned earlier. Lacking the security once provided by community structure, many find their personal capacities inadequate to the restoration of their own psychological well-being.

This analysis brings us to an old and fundamental question in the study of psychosocial development, namely: Is there a complementarity in structure between the psychic order of the individual and the social order of the community such that certain necessary functions can be fulfilled through mental *or* social organization? Do some societies rely more heavily on customary, institutionalized social organization and others on internalized mental organization (personality structure) for the fulfillment of functions that are necessary for human adaptation? And, to push the matter farther, can the world's peoples be divided into those who rely on psychic organization and those who rely on social organization for the fulfillment of the basic ego functions such as defense? Framing the problem as it often appears in psychoanalytic discussion: Does this division coincide with a gap between "civilized peoples" (i.e., Westerners) who are highly individuated, have sharp ego boundaries and self-structures that give them narcissistic supplies adequate for modern life, and "uncivilized peoples" (like the Gusii) with less individuation, blurred ego boundaries and self-structures adequate only to collective functioning in premodern social life? To a contemporary anthropologist, this question smacks of the Eurocentric social evolutionism that was long ago rejected by our discipline. Nonetheless, it has been implicated in every psychoanalytic formulation regarding cultural variation since *Totem and Taboo* (Freud, [1913] 1953) and bears directly on assumptions regarding average expectable environments (see Hartmann et al., [1951] 1964:94–96).

Personal autonomy and social organization

In modern psychoanalytic theory there is an emphasis on autonomy and individuation as goals of normal personality development that cannot be relinquished without pathological consequences. Dependent and symbiotic relationships are seen primarily as necessary aspects of early life, especially the mother–infant relationship; development proceeds through separation and individuation toward an internal psychic structure that regulates defensive and adaptive processes. This structure is reflected in and protected by a sharply bounded representation of self-encompassing distinctive personal attributes, inner standards of evaluation, and a strong differentiation of subjective experience from external reality (essential to adaptive reality testing). Disruption of this line of development, or regression to an earlier symbiosis, is viewed as leading to psychiatric symptoms and defects in character and cognition (Hartmann et al. [1946] 1964; Mahler et al., 1975; Kohut, 1977). An example of such disruption that has influenced thinking in this field is the group of traumatically separated Jewish refugee children who became symbiotically attached to each other (A. Freud and Dann, 1951); in that case, both the pathogenic conditions and the pathological consequences are indisputable.

In many non-Western cultures, however, adult relationships that appear symbiotic and may be symbiotically experienced – in-kin, community and patron–client relationships, for example – are fostered by cultural values and institutional demands. Individuals regularly find gratification in these relationships without indication of pathology and without impairment of the reality-testing capacities required for successful adaptation in their environments. As any anthropologist who has lived in a well-functioning non-Western culture can testify, the relative lack of autonomy and individuation where we would expect it is found in persons with a strong reality orientation and ability to use secondary process (i.e., rational) thinking. (That is how these populations have survived.) This presents a problem for psychoanalytic theory.

The significance of this problem is illustrated in most acute form by the case of Japan, a non-Western but "civilized" society. Japanese achievements in advanced technology, industrial productivity, and mass scientific education – as well as the control of urban crime and air pollution – are among the generally acknowledged wonders of the modern world. It is quite clear, however, that the Japanese have achieved all this through a different route than that taken in Europe and America, one in which autonomy and individuation have been subordinated to collective and dyadic types of regulation and which permitted forms of dependency, emotional symbiosis and interpersonal control that seem bizarre in Western eyes (Doi, 1981; Rohlen, 1974). The shaping of behavioral development in infancy, as later, is toward interdependence rather than independence (Caudill & Weinstein, 1969; Lebra, 1976). Western-style self-reliance is neither valued nor practiced by the majority, and it is socially and personally acceptable to make radical sacrifices of one's individuality – as a Westerner would view it – for the satisfaction of one's current emotional needs and long-range goals. This culturally organized pattern of personal development may influence the form and contents of psychiatric symptoms (Doi, 1981; Lebra, 1976:215–231), but it is also deeply involved in social adaptation, educational and economic achievement, and social control. Making sense of this phenomenon – that is, a strongly interdependent self-representation accompanied by scientific reality testing, successful social adjustment, and a high level of cultural achievement – is a major challenge to the study of ego development. We need a model of cultural variation in the autonomy of ego functions that does not rest on assumptions imported from the study of psychopathology. I conclude this discussion with a new way of comparing ego functions and their relations to the self based on the assumption that autonomy (in the sense of self-regulation), as cultural ideal and individual accomplishment, is specific to a behavioral domain rather than a general structural property of the individual personality.

The expectation that a particular ego function will become self-regulated, that is, organized as intrapsychic rather than interpersonal structure, varies from one society to another in accordance with the cultural models of a people and their priorities for the development of competence in their children. This cross-cultural variation is not hap-hazard but is closely related to the requirements for adapting to its institutional environment, which entail greater internalization for some ego functions, less for others, and concomitant variations in self-representation.

Our comparison of the Gusii with Americans can illustrate this point. In a traditional Gusii community (before 1908), occupations (apart from part-time healers) were specialized only by age and gender, so that each person performed most of the tasks appropriate to his or her gender at an age-appropriate time of life. A large proportion of the culture's sub-sistence technology was mastered by each individual, and an impressive amount of survival-relevant information was stored in the memory of each adult. Each family was virtually self-sufficient in food production and processing, house building, and basket making (cooked food was eaten out of baskets), and only partly dependent on others for military defense, clothing (made from cowhide), medicine, and healing. Each child was expected to acquire the full range of skills and practical knowledge involved in providing food (through cultivation, animal husbandry, and the necessary processing tasks) and shelter and in other adaptive domains such as the use of wild plants as medicine and poisons, local geography and transportation, child care, disposal of the dead. This meant that, in the absence of specialists, each adult was expected to have a repertoire of competence encompassing most of the adaptive skills required for subsistence in the Gusii habitat. Without writing, the knowledge involved had to be kept in memory, and most Gusii individuals did in fact know most of the survival skills passed down by tradition.

Compare this degree of subsistence competence with that of the average contemporary American. Although we take justifiable pride in the advanced technology and specialized institutions that provide our high standard of living, our reliance on these external systems makes us incomplete persons in terms of adaptive competence in a way that was not true of the Gusii. Most of us do not understand the apparatus on which our lives depend, are helpless without it, and are usually in-capable of repairing it or providing substitutes without the help of specialists. In our own specialized division of labor, it is only collec-tively, not as individuals that our adaptive skills surpass those of Africans and other nonindustrial peoples. At the individual level, we have *less* comprehensive mastery of the techniques through which our survival needs are met than they have of the techniques that enable them to survive. For us, the techniques are encoded not in our indivi-dual egos but in external institutional systems in which we function as peripheral, often passive, receivers rather than central participants. The great efficiency of this arrangement notwithstanding, functions that are elsewhere part of the individual ego and symbolized in the self-representation are yielded by us to a collectivity. Autonomy has been lost. In subsistence adaptation, then, it is we "individualistic" Westerners who cling to our interdependence and readily sacrifice the development of self-regulated individual competence for the benefits of a collective system.

In other areas of ego functioning, members of nonindustrial societies tend to rely more heavily on an external institutional system. In the enforcement of moral standards, for example, the Gusii believe in corporate responsibility for wrongdoing and operate as a moral community to see that justice is done. This is not to say that they have no concept of individual responsibility or individual interests that conflict, but they do not expect the individual to police his own behavior without social support or to receive punishment for wrongdoing by himself. Similarly, cultural beliefs and ritual provide institutionalized defenses to which persons can turn in times of stress; they are not expected to suffer alone or work out individualized solutions to the alleviation of their own suffering.

The apparently greater reliance of nonindustrial peoples on group process and institutional devices in moral control and coping with stress has led some psychoanalytic observers to conclude that they have collective egos and are unable to differentiate self from others. It seems clear in the context of this Gusii–American comparison, however, that *all* peoples depend more on external institutional devices for some ego functions and operate more self-reliantly in other areas. Nonindustrial peoples who live in small face-to-face communities and have not been integrated into an urban economy foster the development in their children of internalized ego capacities relevant to subsistence but encourage interdependence in the domains of social control and stress adaptation. Western industrial societies, on the other hand, value individual self-sufficiency with respect to morality and the management of suffering but foster interdependence in subsistence activities.

At the extremes, this variation can be seen in terms of sociocultural evolution: The development of large-scale, highly differentiated societies based on industrial technology and bureaucratic organization has entailed an economy in which most persons do not participate in primary subsistence activities and a division of labor in which no individual can master more than a fraction of the skills involved. The mass migration required for this urban-industrial transformation has tended to destroy the stability and homogeneity of the face-to-face groups in which moral control and the alleviation of stress could be collectively organized; in place of such groups there arise ideologies fostering inner controls, individualized coping mechanisms, and distinctive personal standards of belief, value, and taste.

Historical tendencies of this sort are anything but uniform. Industrialization and urbanization in some places, notably Japan, has been possible with less disorganization and mixing of populations and hence greater retention of traditional styles of social relationship, morality, and defensive process in the industrial era.

These shifting requirements for self-sufficiency and internal structure in specific areas of ego functioning are accompanied and organized by transformations in the representation of self. The development of a particular competence takes on a different meaning and comes to play a different part in the regulation of self-esteem. The skills involved in agriculture, sailing, or horsemanship among African cultivators, Pacific islanders, or Bedouin Arabs, respectively, are acquired early in life and regarded as minimal requirements for the self-esteem of a mature man; to lack them is to be defective. The same competence in a member of a modern industrial society is regarded as a distinctive accomplishment in which he can take a pride reserved for activities that set him off from others, representing effective pursuit of his own ideals of optimal development or competitive advantage in invidious comparisons. Thus the same skill can vary cross-culturally in meaning according to its role as a minimal requirement for normal self-esteem or a mark of specialness acquired to attain an ideal standard.

Conclusions: parents and expectable environments

This brings us back to the average expectable environment of the child. Parents construct learning environments for their children that foster the acquisition of skills and virtues valued in their community. Parents and community, in accordance with local cultural models, expect the child to develop a capacity for greater autonomy (self-sufficiency or self-regulation) in some domains and less in others. Americans expect a boy to learn to clean his room, while the Gusii expect a boy to learn how to build his new house. In that respect, the Gusii youth becomes more self-sufficient. But the traditional Gusii son was expected to consult both parents in the choice of a wife and to bring her home to his mother for help in setting up their household, while the American youth is expected to make his own marital choice and set up an independent household. In this domain, the American is more autonomous.

Psychoanalytic models have treated personal autonomy as if it were one piece, a necessarily unitary attribute of the self-representation, encompassing the individual's relationships to all aspects of reality, including the world of social objects. But no culture, Western or non-Western, expects a child to become autonomous in all respects, that is, to internalize fully the skills involved in adaptation. Each culture, as an average expectable environment for learning and adaptation, embodies a distinctive profile of more *and* less internalized capacities. It is possible to forgo early psychosocial separation and individuation as we know it in the West and acquire a strong capacity for reality testing and self-regulation in other aspects of life. The divergent development of the Gusii and Americans cannot be characterized simply in terms of how much internalization is expected or how sharp is the typical boundary experienced between self and other.

Gusii parents organize a learning environment for their children that involves little maternal excitement or stimulation during infancy by

American standards and that provides little praise as the child grows older and discourages talking to and seeking attention from adults. This is consistent with a traditional family and community environment organized as an age hierarchy that emphasizes respect and compliance from the young and fitting into one's proper place in the hierarchy. From the Gusii viewpoint, American young people would be considered unacceptably conceited and arrogant, owing to their different early experience. The experience of the Gusii child, then, is good training for adult social participation in the environment as it was organized in the past, in which assertiveness and social visibility were reserved for elders. In recent decades, however, the decay of indigenous authority and the introduction of new forms of competition and social comparison in Gusii communities have elicited more self-assertion and exposed young adults to a more openly competitive atmosphere than they can tolerate without great anxiety. The pattern of early experience that prepared Gusii children for the older environment leaves them feeling excessively vulnerable as adults nowadays, unable to give themselves in adulthood the emotional support for initiative and accomplishment that American children typically get from their parents in the early years and eventually internalize. Although they may well be protected from the pathologies of disappointment and disillusionment that afflict contemporary Americans raised by parents who raise more hopes than they can fulfill, the Gusii seem to lack the positive self-regard they now need to cope with a new expectable environment.

This example suggests that the average expectable environment of the child varies from one culture to another and from one historical period to another within the same community – without producing severe impairment of ego function. Customs of infant and child care tend to give children psychological preparation for social participation in an existing social order that generates specific expectations; as the social order changes, so do the expectations, and after a lag, child rearing changes accordingly.

References

Bowlby, J. 1969. *Attachment*. New York: Basic Books.

Caudill, W., & H. Weinstein. 1969. Maternal care and infant behavior in Japan and America. *Psychiatry* 32:12–43.

Dixon, S. et al. 1981. Mother–infant interaction among the Gusii of Kenya. In T. Field, S. Sostek & P. Vietze (Eds.), *Culture and early interactions*. Hillsdale, NJ: LEA.

Doi, T. 1981. *The anatomy of dependence*, 2d ed. New York: Harper & Row.

Freud, A., & S. Dann. 1951. An experiment in group unbringing. *Psychoanalytic Study of the Child* 6:127–169.

Freud, S. [1905] 1953. Three essays on the theory of sexuality. *Standard edition of the complete psychological works of Sigmund Freud*, Vol. 7. London: Hogarth Press.

⸺ [1913] 1953. *Totem and taboo, Standard edition of the complete psychological works of Sigmund Freud*, Vol. 13. London: Hogarth Press.

Hartmann, H. 1958. *Ego psychology and the problem of adaptation*. New York: International Universities Press.

Hartmann, H., Kris, E., & Loewenstein, R. 1964. Papers on psychoanalytic psychology. *Psychological Issues 4*. Monograph 14.

Hobcraft, J., McDonald, J., & Rutstein, S. 1984. Socioeconomic factors in infant and child mortality: A cross-national comparison. *Population Studies 38*:193–223.

Kakar, S. 1978. *The inner world: A psychoanalytic study of childhood and society in India*. Delhi: Oxford University Press.

Kohut, H. 1977. *The restoration of the self*. New York: International Universities Press.

Lebra, T. 1976. *Japanese patterns of behavior*. Honolulu: University of Hawaii Press.

LeVine, R., Brazelton, T. B., Dixon, S., Leiderman, P. H., LeVine, S., Richman, A. et al. In press. *Omwana: Infants and parents in a Kenya community*. New York: Cambridge University Press.

LeVine, S. 1979. *Mothers and wives: Gusii women of East Africa*. Chicago: University of Chicago Press.

Mahler, M., Pine, F., & Bergman, A. 1975. *The psychological birth of the human infant*. New York: Basic Books.

Moseley, W. H. 1983. Will primary health care reduce infant and child mortality? A critique of some current strategies with special reference to Africa and Asia. Paper presented in IUSSP Seminar on Social Policy, Health Policy and Mortality Prospects, Paris. Paris: Institut National d'Etudes Demographiques.

Richman, A. 1983. Learning about communication: Cultural influences on caretaker–infant interaction. Unpublished doctoral thesis, Harvard Graduate School of Education, Cambridge, MA.

Richman, A., LeVine, R., New, R., Howrigan, G., Welles, B., & LeVine, S. 1988. Cultural differences in mother–infant interaction: Evidence from a five-culture study. In R. LeVine, P. Miller, & M. West (Eds.), *Parental behavior in diverse cultures*, New Directions for Child Development. San Francisco: Jossey-Bass.

Rohlen, T. 1974. *For harmony and strength: Japanese white-collar organization in anthropological perspective*. Berkeley: CA: University of California Press.

Stern, D. 1985. *The interpersonal world of the infant: a view from psychoanalysis and developmental psychology*. New York: Basic Books.

Tronick, E., Morelli, G., & Winn, S. 1987. Multiple caretaking of Efe (Pygmy) infants. *American Anthropologist 89*:96–106.

Whiting, B., & J. Whiting. 1975. *Children of six cultures*. Cambridge, MA: Harvard University Press.

PART VI
Cultural domination and dominions

16
Male dominance and sexual coercion

Thomas Gregor

Without an understanding of the seamy side of sexuality there is no understanding of politics.

Norman O. Brown, Love's Body

The entire matter of gender relationship is so caught up in the politics of social change that it is hard to look at issues such as "dominance" or "sexual coercion" dispassionately. I will try to do so, using information from a variety of societies and focusing on one culture, that of the Mehinaku Indians of Brazil. My intention is to explore the ways in which sexual coercion functions as both symbol and substance of male dominance. This is not a novel idea. But it is one whose significance has not been adequately explored from a comparative perspective. Moreover, it is of importance to a general theory of gender and human development. The inherent asymmetry of sexual coercion creates two radically different male and female worlds. A woman who matures in a society where coercion is prevalent will come to see herself as simultaneously sexual and vulnerable. A male's self-concept will also reflect an alternately aggressive and protective relationship to women. Ultimately, in this setting, gender relationships will be eroticized in ways that intertwine sexuality, interpersonal control, and community level politics. The process is observable in large, complex societies such as our own. It is even more visible in small-scale societies such as the Mehinaku, where sexual coercion is relatively frequent and gang rape is built into religion and justified by supernatural sanctions.

The question of dominance. The concept of male dominance as a cultural universal was once unquestioned. Today, it is challenged on the grounds that it fails to describe relationships in small-scale communities where the private life of the family merges with the public life of the community; that it does not properly balance the domestic authority of women with the public power of men; and that it is a culture-bound concept derived from our sexist, competitive, and stratified society.

I believe otherwise. I am particularly convinced that the issues of gender politics are sufficiently universal to be relevant to all human societies. But the criticism has substance in that it forces us to rethink what we really mean by "dominance." I see the concept as referring to control, evaluation, and exclusion. A society is "male dominated" when women's conduct is by and large controlled by men; when women are regarded as men's intellectual, moral, or spiritual inferiors; and when women are excluded from what are seen as the religious and political centers of the society. Sherry Ortner, who proposes similar criteria, believes that all societies are patriarchies: "I would flatly assert that we find women subordinated to men in every known society. The search for a genuinely egalitarian, let alone matriarchal, culture has proved fruitless" (1974:70). I suspect that Ortner is correct, although it would be difficult and probably pointless to keep a score card for each culture. It makes more sense, when studying a particular society, to examine the ways in whch the genders interact along the dimensions of control, evaluation, and exclusion.

In all probability, the origins of gender inequality reach back to the earliest period of human evolution. At this time, perhaps as much as three million years ago, our hominid ancestors' upright stature and bipedal locomotion made it possible to collect food over a large range, to carry it back to a home base, and to share it with immature offspring and lactating females or females in an advanced stage of pregnancy. In the course of further evolution, the increasing immaturity and dependence of the newborn infant (whose brain size at birth among humans is only 20% of what it will be at maturity) provided an additional basis for a division of labor that linked females to child rearing and other domestic tasks. Thus the facts of life established an initial biological impetus for a division of labor that associated males with extradomestic activities, with subsistence resources such as animal protein that could be distributed to the community as a whole, and, as a consequence, with leadership roles. Simultaneously, women's domination of the nursery set the stage for a masculine personality that would greatly exaggerate the intensity of gender conflicts in adult life. The division of labor and its biological underpinnings are the bedrock of gender inequality.

With the development of culture, the pattern is amplified far beyond what might have been predicted from biology alone. In contemporary cultures, the institutions that perpetuate gender inequality are varied, but I see two modes of male dominance that are of particular interest because they appear and reappear in somewhat different guises in societies at different levels of technology and social complexity. The first, in its purest form, is that of the seclusion of women or "purdah," which is characteristic of the circum-Mediterranean area and the Near East, in which women are restricted by codes of sexual modesty. The mechanisms of purdah include veiling, chaperonage, proof of virginity at marriage, and in extreme cases, clitoridectomy and infibulation. So effective is women's exclusion from the public life of their communities in such cultures that as political actors they are virtually "nonpersons."

My own field research as an anthropologist has been among societies that achieve male dominance through what I call the "men's house complex" (Gregor, 1979), which I regard as a second major institution of patriarchy. The men's house complex is typical of small sedentary societies of the type found frequently in lowland South America and New Guinea. In this pattern, a men's house, serving as a club or temple, is tabooed to women. Within are cult objects such as sacred flutes, trumpets, bull-roarers, and other objects that the women can see only at pain of beatings, death, or gang rape. The men conduct secret rituals within their retreat, and thereby exclude women from the social and religious center of society.

Purdah and the men's house complex are mirror images of one another. The former ensures gender inequality by confining women to their homes and domestic roles. The latter achieves the same effect by walling off a symbolically important area for men only. Industrial societies, which on the face of it appear to be beyond these devices, in fact borrow heavily from both, providing men with protected all-male retreats (exclusive clubs, sports teams, military organizations) and isolating women with a sexual ideology that primarily assigns them to the domestic arena. We have much to learn, therefore, from the operation of these systems at simpler social levels.

Men's cults and sexuality. Of the two patterns, the "men's house complex" is historically the most ancient. Appearing among the world's simplest societies and making use of myths and ritual devices whose origin predates the settlement of the New World, men's cults are among the oldest of the institutions of patriarchy. They are primitive in another sense as well. The ideology of societies with men's cults is often redolent with sexual imagery that explains the cult's origin, and portrays extreme tension in the relationship of the sexes. The recurrent themes include charter myths, which assert that ancient matriarchs once controlled the cult but were tricked or forced into giving up the sacred instruments that were the basis for their power.[1] Myths and hygienic practices and precautions associate feminine sexuality with danger. Contact with women prevents boys from growing up into men, stunts growth, makes hunters improvident, and in general subverts the performance of the male role. In rituals the men may symbolically menstruate from wounds made in their ears, noses, and genitals; "give birth" to initiates; and metaphorically equate female sexual anatomy with their own body parts and ornaments. The sexualized culture characteristic of men's cults expresses a tension between the sexes and the universal conflicts associated with masculinity. Indeed, the data that are emerging from studies in Amazonia and New Guinea are almost textbook illustrations of the psychodynamics of masculine insecurity. The richness of the data is so compelling that psychoanalytic agnostics come back from the field as converts.

There are a number of reasons why societies with men's cults are fertile ground for the development of a sexualized culture. In the main, such societies are small, homogeneous communities where the individual (and his conflicts) can have an impact on the expressive culture of the community. They are unstratified, so that the cohesion of men versus women is not blurred by other modes of allocating social position. And they are characterized by a division of labor that divides men and women into separate, cooperating groups (see Murphy, 1959). In this "genderized" setting it is understandable that sexual coercion and rape are the mechanisms by which men punish women and defend the barriers of the cult.

Sexual coercion

WHAT MAKES COERCION POSSIBLE?
Biological differences between the sexes. By sexual coercion I mean the access to female sexual services through threats, intimidation, or force. In theory, men could also be sexually coerced, but both the biology of the sexual act and the fact of greater male strength make this unlikely. This observation seems self-evident, but it is not trivial. All too often anthropologists make use of a conception of humankind in which culture is assumed to play an overwhelming role in development. When sexual dimorphism is discussed in relation to gender it is frequently minimized. It is often pointed out that men exceed women in stature by less than 9%, and that women in our society achieve less than their full physical potential because they are discouraged from participating in sports. But in fact the disparity between the sexes in strength is substantial, and unlikely to be significantly modified by more equal participation in vigorous activity. Women, on average, have 80% of the leg strength of men and, what is more crucial for aggressive physical encounters, only 56% of the strength of the shoulders, arms, and hands. In all societies women mature in a world where men are physically stronger and can forcibly control them.[2] In the setting of small-scale technologically simple societies, such as those with men's cults, physical strength is a crucial measure of a man. The fact that men can over-whelm women in violent encounters is recognized in such societies and looms large in gender politics.

Coercion, sexual arousal and the dissociative nature of male sexuality. Sexual coercion is possible because of the male ability to dissociate the sexual act from the context of a positive or even a neutral relationship. Hence some men can achieve erection and orgasm in the course of beating and murdering a woman. The fact that men can sexually function in the midst of such acts is linked to their susceptibility to visual stimuli, their ability to symbolically transform the meaning of the act, and (relative to women) a low threshold of arousal. Whether women are generally capable of achieving the requisite degree of dissociation for a similar act in which they would be similarly sexually aroused is uncertain. It is interesting to note, however, that the practitioners of what may be the purest form of the dissociative ability, such as fetishlike pre-occupation with the opposite sex's shoes and undergarments, are almost invariably male (Greenson, 1968:370–71).

Why men rape. The dissociative potential of male sexuality is particularly important given the question of motivation for rape. In contemporary feminist thinking on the subject, rape is seen as a politically motivated form of assault designed to degrade and brutalize women. Hence rape is said to be a "pseudosexual act" motivated by hostility and the desire to keep women subordinate to men. Hence we are told that "the rapist is not expressing a sexual need but rather his need to feel powerful – to dominate and control in a sexual context" (Ehrhart & Sandler, 1985: 17). This thesis had its inception in 1975 with the publication of Susan Brownmiller's popular book *Against Our Will.* "From prehistoric times to the present," claimed Brownmiller, "rape has played a critical function. It is nothing more or less than a conscious process of intimidation by which *all* men keep *all* women in a state of fear" [italics are the author's] (1975:15). The evidence supporting this contention was thin,[3] and the hypothesis itself astoundingly counterintuitive. Nonetheless, the notion that rape is a political rather than personal or sexually motivated act is now well established in feminist thought. The extent to which this idea has penetrated the psychiatric establishment is revealed in a recent survey, which found that 27% of the psychiatrists responding believed that rape is fundamentally rooted in "our male dominated society" (Current Thinking on Rape, 1978). This perspective has even influenced the design of rehabilitation programs for rapists, who are now urged to "rethink their stereotyped notions of femininity" (Ellis & Beattie, 1983).

The most persuasive studies of rape in our own society take the perspective that the motives of rapists are complex and multidetermined. At times their intentions are clearly sexual in character (see Symons, 1979:282), but occasionally they may be commingled with issues of dominance and aggression that move the act closer to Brownmiller's view of the nature of rape. The clearest example of this pattern in our own and other societies is group rape. To date, group or "gang" rape has been only minimally studied, despite increasing awareness that it is a surprisingly common form of sexual coercion. Menachem Amir's study in Philadelphia shows that of the 646 cases examined, 43% involved group (two persons or more) rape (1971:200). The vast majority of these assaults were by lower-class youths, many of whom had substantial arrest records. More recent data, however, has shown that gang rape may also be conducted by more advantaged individuals without criminal backgrounds. The Project on the Status and Education of Women identified 50 incidents of gang rape on college campuses. These incidents, many of which occurred in fraternities, were only a small proportion of the actual total. On at least one campus it was estimated that gang rape was occurring at least "once per week" (Ehrhart & Sandler, 1985:2).[4]

According to Amir's Philadelphia study, group rape differs from individual rape in that it is more likely to be violent, the level of violence is more intense, and the victim has a greater chance of being subjected to severe sexual humiliation (1971:218–219). Above all, Amir's study, as well as the rest of the admittedly sparse literature on gang sex, calls attention to the group dynamic that is present in such assaults. The pattern of leadership and followership within the group, the camaraderie of the men, and the presence of the group as an audience to the sexual acts creates an entirely new situation in which the heterosexual needs of individuals are only secondary. Blanchard (1959), on the basis of psychodynamic interviews and psychological testing of two gangs of particularly brutal rapists, concludes that the "rape experience was largely a relationship between the boys rather than between any of the boys and the girl involved" (1959:263). Gang rape, in Blanchard's study, expressed the rapists' latent homoerotic and voyeuristic motives, which the group leader maintained and directed (1959:266). At the same time, the brutality of the act expressed the assailants' need to dramatically prove their own masculinity to the group. The deliberately sadistic character of gang rape noted in Amir's Philadelphia study is in accord with this interpretation.

These findings regarding individual motivation suggest that the feminist perspective on rape needs to be modified, even in the case of gang rape. Rapists assault women because of a complex mixture of motives, some of which are sexual in character, and some of which reflect personal insecurity and the dynamics of the group to which they belong. I have yet to see substantial evidence that gender politics is truly central to the motivation of rapists. Those who are interested in the prevention of rape might do well to put efforts into deterrence and incarceration of rapists rather than "overcoming their stereotypes about women." Nonetheless, the feminist interpretation of sexual coercion reaches a fundamental truth. Whatever the motivations of the rapists, the implications for gender politics are far-reaching. In a rape-prone society women are socialized in an environment that is dangerous and unpredictable. They are effectively barred from public areas where they are vulnerable to assault. They become dependent on men for protection and redress. Even though rape may have complex and varying motivations, it will profoundly affect the way men and women relate to one another.

Cross-cultural studies and the correlates of coercion. As is the case of sexual behavior in general, sexual coercion is underreported in the ethnographic literature. We know relatively little of its incidence, symbolism, and social meaning in non-Western societies. Rape, which is easier to document than the more subtle forms of sexual coercion, appears to be very common in 19% of a representative sample of cultures examined by Peggy Sanday (1981). These "rape-prone" societies frequently had men's houses or exclusive male activities taboo to women. Rape was at times associated with rituals in which boys were initiated into the adult male group. Violence is common in the rape-prone society, and boys are inculcated in hyper masculine values of toughness and aggression. Cross-culturally, the intensity of interpersonal aggression and warfare is positively associated with the frequency of rape (Sanday, 1981:15,23).

Cross-cultural research has been least successful in correlating the incidence of rape with psychological variables. Specifically, the composite measures of sex anxiety designed by Minturn, Grosse, and Haider (1969) and Whiting and Child (1953) do not show significant correlations with either the incidence or attitudes toward rape. Sanday, using a larger and more detailed sample, found little significant relationship between sexual repression, or the relationship of parents and children with the incidence of rape (1981:24). Although it is risky to use negative evidence from cross-cultural research, the implication is that rape does not necessarily require sexually pathological personalities. Data from our own society support this conclusion. The typical convicted rapist is not an appealing individual in terms of his poor impulse control and propensity to violence, but he is not distinguished from the rest of the prison population by a sexually definable pathology.

The relative lack of information on sexual coercion and rape in the ethnographic literature makes it difficult to generalize about its broad human significance. The Mehinaku Indians are a particularly good focus for research in this area, since sexual coercion and gender politics are a fact of life, and are issues with which the villagers themselves are deeply concerned.

Mehinaku sexual coercion

The Mehinaku are a small tribe of 125 Arawakan-speaking Indians living along the headwaters of the Xingu River in Central Brazil. Before describing their pattern of sexual coercion, it is well to post a note of caution. The data, by their nature, dramatically emphasize the disjunctive and antagonistic side of Mehinaku human relationships. Coercion, however, is only one dimension of an account of Mehinaku gender. As in our own society, Mehinaku gender relations are bimodal in character, having associative as well as oppositional features. Mehinaku sexual relationships are often mutually rewarding, and marriages are frequently enduring alliances marked by deep affection and respect. Men and women are firmly united through the division of labor and the network of kinship. Moreover, overt sexual coercion almost never occurs in the context of marital relationships, and rape is not a frequent event within the village (see Gregor 1985:23–38 for an account of the associative side of Mehinaku gender relations). Nonetheless, there are also significant differences in sexual behavior between the Mehinaku and ourselves. By our standards Mehinaku are remarkably free sexually. The villagers engage in numerous extramarital affairs to the point where the intrigue of sexual relationships is a principal topic of gossip. One man claimed to be engaged in no less than 10 extramarital affairs at the time of my most recent trip. "Good fish get dull," say the villagers, "but sex is always fun." There is, however, a bittersweet quality to this fun, since erotic relationships are fraught with sexual anxieties and, surprisingly, frustration. Even though the men have many sexual partners the frequency of sex is far lower than they wish. "Women," they say, "are stingy with their genitals."

The perceived scarcity of sex is in part a consequence of a developmental pattern in which a Mehinaku woman is taught to devalue herself. From an early age she is told (mainly by the men) that she is "just a girl." She cannot learn the basic myths because the words "will not stay in her stomach." She is mainly fit to gossip, and in fact the term for a gossip of either sex is "woman mouth." She learns that her genitals are unattractive, and she is taught to comport herself modestly, so that no one will see her inner labia. If she is young and attractive, the men may shout aggressive remarks from the security of the men's house as she walks across the village plaza.

At the time of her first menses she is secluded and takes medicines to staunch the flow of contaminating blood. Each month she must throw away food or water that the blood may have magically polluted. Men who are sick or ritually vulnerable will have to leave her house to avoid the contamination. A Mehinaku woman is therefore regarded as dangerous, sexually alluring, and yet at the same time, faintly ridiculous.

The result of these experiences, which are compounded by fear of pregnancy, may be a partial sexual anesthesia. "Women do not like sex" complains one of the men, "and so we must pay for it or take it." Paying for sex is done with gifts, which are labeled by a special term, *yamala*. Quintessential *yamala* are fish, and a woman who is sexually active can count on a small but steady supply of fish from her lovers throughout the year. Ideally, she reciprocates with gifts of spun cotton, but it is generally recognized that the scarcer commodity is female sexuality. Women's gifts are therefore less frequent than men's.[5]

"Dragging women off": individual rape. When there are no fish available a few of the men resort to coercion. According to those who have spoken to me, the techniques vary from importuning to threats and physical aggression. The most common method is to plead extreme desire. A man who is sexually frustrated, it is believed, is in a state of danger and vulnerability and is likely to have a serious accident or illness. A woman who frustrates a man thereby shoulders some of the responsibility for what may happen to him. This possibility puts the onus of a rejection on the woman and encourages acquiescence.

A more aggressive method of extorting sex is to hint that the woman will be a victim of sorcery if she does not comply. The villagers believe that all deaths in the community are caused by witchcraft, so even a veiled suggestion of sorcery is taken seriously. According to the women, only one of the men regularly makes use of threats. As one of his victims explained to me. "He is a witch, so I don't dare say 'no.' When I pull away from him he says: 'What? Do you hold your genitals so dear? You will die later, I will kill you later!' He is a witch, and therefore I am afraid!"

The most aggressive technique of coercing sexual relations is rape. The term used is "aantapai," literally, "dragging off." Normally, when a man solicits a woman for sexual relations, he takes her by the wrist and firmly leads her off the path to a so-called alligator place,[6] which he uses for his assignations. If she resists, he can drag her off and rape her. A strong woman may fight back, and a few of the men offer the possibility of resistance as a reason for not raping women. According to my informants, only one villager ever used rape as his preferred method of gaining sexual services. This so-called *metalawaitsi*, or "joker," usually approached women who were alone, but he was not above "dragging away" a woman from the company of her friends. The "joker" is long deceased, but what was truly remarkable about his career is that there were no effective sanctions to restrain his conduct. So long as he confined his assaults to unmarried women (who are the primary targets of rape) he had little to fear from the other men. As one of the villagers explained to me, it is "so much the better" if an unmarried woman has sex, even if she is reluctant.

Motivation and meaning. Dragging off a woman and raping her occurs very rarely. More frequently, the men report that they simply "pull hard." Women submit both because serious resistance may raise the level of violence, and because they are not entirely unwilling. An act of what we might call rape is thereby a mixture of consent and refusal that is not easy to categorize in our somewhat legalistic terms. We can understand the pattern more fully by realizing that the cost of rape to the Mehinaku women is far less than what it can be in our culture. An act of sex, forced or otherwise, is not endowed with anything like the emotional significance it receives in our society. An unmarried woman is unashamed of her sexual activity, and is not restrained by her kinsmen. "Fathers and brothers," as one informant explained, "do not care who their daughters and sisters have sex with." Consequently an act of sexual relations or an act of coercion is not entangled with honor or shame. Perhaps it is for this reason that the impact of rape is less than in our own society, where the clinical literature documents what is called "the rape trauma syndrome," including sleep disorders, a sense of numbness and flattened affect, a tendency toward self-blame, impairment of memory, and an inability to rid oneself of obsessive anxiety: "It is the first thing I think of when I wake up in the morning" (Burgess & Holmstrom, 1985:50). Severe trauma appears to be missing among Mehinaku victims of rape, whose responses seem to be less a sense of personal violation than anger.[7]

Men "drag women off," according to village men and women, "because they want to have sex with them." The sexual motivation attributed to the men is confirmed by at least one of the individuals who has performed the act: "If women wanted sex the way I want sex I would not drag them off." At times, the men's motivation appears more complex, and the act takes on overtones of punishment. One man, for example, after emphasizing his sexual interest in a woman he had coerced, admitted that he was "paying her back" for having rejected him. The point of these illustrations is that although rape has substantial implications for Mehinaku gender inequality, it would be an error to confuse the men's motivations with the impact that the act has on the society.

Gang rape: "being sexed by many persons." The term for gang rape, "being sexed by many persons"[8] is linguistically differentiated from "being dragged off," and it is in fact an act with vastly different motivations and outcomes. Gang sex occurs legitimately for only one reason: A woman sees the sacred flutes.[9] The men's house, in the center of the village, is at once a temple and club house. Inside are hung various musical instruments and cult objects that are taboo to the women. The most prominent of these are the sacred flutes, called Kowka. Played periodically by trios of musicians, they are the major symbol of masculine control of the community. Any woman who would enter the men's house, or even so much as glance at the flutes that are stored inside, would be taken and gang-raped by all of the villagers other than her closest kin. The last gang rape in the village occurred more than 40 years ago and none of the participants is alive today. Nonetheless, there have been more recent rapes in other neighboring Indian communities. All of these events are recalled and are recounted by the villagers as vivid cautionary tales of what can happen to any woman who sees the sacred flutes.[10]

In none of the historical cases of gang rape that I have recorded has a woman ever deliberately intruded on the men's house or intended to see the flutes. Instead, as in the case among the Mehinaku, she blundered onto the plaza as the musicians were playing outside of the men's house. The subsequent events are typical of other cases of gang rape in terms of the sequence of activities, the men's justifications of the act, and the emphasis on the woman's degradation. The rape itself is ritualized in that it occurs while the flutes are being played. The narrator of this account, a man in his early 40s, has never participated in a gang rape. Like the other village men, however, he is conversant with the event. Whether the details are factually true is less important than that the story is now a part of the villagers' oral history of gender relationships.

> The men whooped: "Hoooo waaaa! Kowka will have sex, Kowka will have sex, Kowka will have sex! It is not good that a woman has seen us. A woman must not see Kowka! The Spirit might kill us if a woman saw Kowka and we did not have sex with her. We must have sex with her."

> "Later," said the chief, "when it is dark you all may have sex with her. That has always been our tradition. It is not good to have seen

Kowka. Kowka is forbidden! The women may not see it! Only the men may see it, by themselves, without the women. Even little girls do not see the flutes."

All of the women were saddened. They were not happy. "Alas," said the woman [who had seen the flutes]. "I will be raped." Yes, she would be raped. The men were happy. They were waiting for her. The old men put medicine on their penises. The old ones put on kaipyalu [tiny stinging ants] to make their penises sensual.

They tied on their belts around their heads. That is Kowka's custom. To hide their faces from the woman. So that the woman would not see the faces of her kin. Her kin who would have sex with her. Her [classificatory] older brothers who would have sex with her. Her distant mother's brothers who would have sex with her. "Aka, aka!" She shouted, she screamed. . . . She was raped! She was raped! She hid her face with her hands, she cried. The Mehinaku whooped: "Hu waaa!" The chief spoke: "It is over, it is good, the tradition is good, it makes the women afraid of us, afraid of our having sex with them," he said.

The men went to bathe to clean themselves. There was no one left who was not bathing. They were cleaning themselves of their own semen. They had been covered with each other's semen from having sex with the woman.

The woman was weak and in pain. She went to the stream and washed herself with soap, she washed her arms, her legs, her vagina, her head which was all covered with the dirt. Then she went back to her house and took to her hammock. She hurt, her vagina hurt her. She was sick, for the penises had hurt her. The semen had hurt her. After several months she died. The men's penises had killed her.

That is why all of the women are afraid of us. It is still that way, when Kowka is being played. "Ah," a woman will say, "is that Kowka being played? No, don't let Kowka come here." They are afraid of the men's penises! So they just stay in their houses.

The question of sexual motivation. Gang rape is perceived by the villagers as a sexual act. They attribute sexual motivation to those who participate ("they have erections, they have orgasms, they are fiends for sex"), and they explain that gang rape was established by the villagers ("the sex fiends of ancient times") for their sexual enjoyment: "Gang rape is our tradition. . . . The Sun [a culture hero] did not make that tradition. We did it, we made that tradition, we made it, the Mehinaku, by ourselves. We did it so that we would not be frustrated [and thereby magically endangered] over sex." Nonetheless, gang rape transforms the meaning of the sexual act. In all my accounts, the men deny that they themselves would be sexually motivated, even if they attribute such desire to other men. They emphasize that the woman was "dripping with semen" (a contaminating fluid) and that some of the men were unable to achieve an erection because of the "foulness" of the women's vagina.

My informants also deny that voyeurism plays any part in gang rape. They point out that the act occurs in semidarkness, and they are at pains to emphasize that it is aesthetically repelling. Nonetheless, voyeuristic motives should not be ruled out, since the men invariably dwell on the lurid nature of the scene. Gang rape, more than in any other Mehinaku activity, is an opportunity for the participants to openly observe each other's sexual behavior.[11]

The issue of homosexual motivation in Mehinaku gang rape is difficult to resolve with the data that are available to me. Certainly, as in the account above, the men are acutely aware of the potential for sexual intimacy with one another: "The men went to bathe to clean themselves. . . . they were cleaning themselves of their own semen. They had been covered with each other's semen from having sex with the woman." Moreover, there is evidence of masculine insecurity and even a degree of feminine identification at the core of the Mehinaku male personality (Gregor, 1985:184ff.). Perhaps because of possible homosexual overtones, gang sex is suffused with ambivalence and uncertainty for the men. It is noteworthy that in the description above, as is true of my other accounts of gang rape, some of the men had to resort to magical methods of inducing an erection, and some could not bring themselves to participate. The entire experience was in many ways unattractive, and tainted, as we shall see further on, with a sense of moral uncertainty. If there is a sexual payoff, it is at best what the villagers call: "inferior, worthless sex."

Symbolism and meanings. As a symbol, gang rape fuses sexuality, violence, domination of women, and group cohesion. Leadership is central to this process. In none of my oral histories of gang rape is the act a spontaneous group assault on a woman who has seen the flutes. Rapes are planned events in which a leader marshals support for the assault and legitimizes the occasion with references to ancient tradition. The leader, as in the instance of the chief in the above narrative, gives meaning to the act and justifies it to the entire village. His comments are intended for all of the village women, for they are all seen as potential transgressors. The women are aware that the message is meant for them and "all of them [are] saddened."

The content of the message is clear from the brutal treatment of the victim. Moreover, the main instrument of torment is the penis, which is depicted as an "angry" weapon that injures and sickens its victim: "She was sick, for the penises had hurt her." Above all, the narrator emphasizes that it is the penis that the women fear: "The tradition is good, it makes the women afraid of us, afraid of our having sex with them [it is the penis that makes] all of the women afraid of us. . . . They are afraid of the men's penises! So they just stay in the houses." Among the Mehinaku, the houses are primarily feminine territory, while the public regions of the village are associated with the men. Keeping the women "in the houses" is a metaphor for keeping them under control and in their place.

Gang rape is an effective method of male dominance because in contrast to individual rape, the impact is socially and personally catastrophic.[12] The basis for the trauma includes the issues of personal violation and public humiliation that are well established in the clinical literature in our own society. Among the Mehinaku, the trauma is perhaps even more intense owing to specific features of the villagers' culture. When the village women explain their horror of gang rape they emphasize that they are physically exposed. Although unclothed by our standards, Mehinaku women normally sit, walk, and generally comport themselves (even in the act of sexual relations) so that their inner labia are not visible. The vagina, which is regarded as unattractive, is metaphorically equated with snails, clams, rotten fruit, and other bad-smelling, mushy objects in mythology and ordinary speech. In the women's accounts of gang rape they emphasize that the victim is held, sometimes off the ground, so that her legs are spread wide apart and her genitals visible to all of the men.

Gang rape is also traumatic because of the volume of semen. Semen is a source of new life, but it is also a magical and powerfully contaminating fluid. A villager walking through the bushes near the community suddenly experiencing a sharp pain in his leg may attribute it to semen left on the ground after a couple's assignation. Women especially do not like semen, and claim that even in ordinary sexual relations it can cause sickness. In every one of my descriptions of gang rape, the narrator calls attention to the vast quantities of semen. The woman is "filled with semen," "drips with semen," is "befouled with semen." In every case after she is raped she goes to bathe. But the contamination does not wash away so easily. She sickens and dies, she gives birth to twins (in itself an horrendous event) or in one instance an "oversized" baby that was killed as soon as it was born "because it had too many fathers."

Long after the rape, she is an object of disgust. She is repulsive to others because of the semen, and because of what has happened to her. More subtly, she is a reminder to the women of what can happen to them and is thereby an object of contagion. Like a pariah, one of the women explains, a woman who is raped cannot be touched:

> If the men have sex with us there is a lot of semen. We are covered with semen. It is disgusting. We cannot make manioc bread, we cannot make porridge or fish stew or get water from the stream. We are made disgusting. Disgust falls upon us. No one will come near us: "You are disgusting," they will say. We are disgusting to everyone. We are disgusting to ourselves. We get sick, sick, and by the time a month goes by we die.

In fact, however, the contamination eventually wears off and the victim can gradually reenter community life. But what makes her experience very different from the victim of gang sex in our own society is that the rapists are her kinsmen, her residence mates, and her extramarital paramours. In my accounts the men wore masks during the rape: "They tied on their belts around their heads...to hide their faces from the woman. So that the woman would not see the faces of her kin. Her kin who would have sex with her." It is doubtful, however, that the mask would keep the woman from recognizing her assailants. If a victim of rape is to survive in the community, she must maintain daily relationships with the same men who tormented her.

Rape and fear. As a symbol of male domination, gang rape is effective. The fact that gang rape is rare and that no Mehinaku woman has been raped for more than 40 years is of small consequence. The cult of the sacred flutes and the possibility of rape transform the relationship of the sexes. Women are frightened of men. They avoid the center of the village, they cast their eyes away from the men's house, and they fear the spirit of the sacred flutes.

The women's fears are reflected in anxious dreams. In nightmares the village women depict themselves as the victim of the men's aggression. In 6 of 109 dreams I collected from 18 of the village women, the assault was explicitly sexual (Gregor, 1981). Collectively, these dreams were among the most anxiety-charged in the sample. A few were highly bizarre in character, as when a woman was chased by a man who turned into a snake, or by a "savage Indian with a two-headed penis." The threat of male violence is pervasive, and torments the women in their unconscious life.

The women have very little hope of change. Although they believe in the spirit of the sacred flutes, they do not believe that the men would die if a woman who had seen the flutes remained unmolested. Gang rape persists, they claim, primarily because the men are physically stronger than they are. Hence women who objected would achieve nothing: "They would just make the men angry. The men would pay no attention if we were to say: 'don't rape us.' We would be thrown right down on the ground if we said something like that. We are afraid of the men. They are stronger than us, and that is why they can do as they please."

Moral ambivalence. The women are victims of rape, but the men also pay a price. At the simplest level, they worry about their female kin. They instruct their daughters to avoid the flutes, and express concern for their wives, sisters, and mothers. As in the case of the women, their concerns follow them into their dream life. One of the men recounted a particularly distressing dream in which he tried to defend his mother from rape after she had inadvertently seen the flutes. The dream was so malign that the informant believed it had been deliberately produced by witchcraft:

"Don't you leave the house" [I said to my mother]; I locked her in. I locked the door. I wanted my mother here in the house. Petala tried to get in and broke down the door. He started to drag mother off. "I'll club you" I shouted. I struck him with a hoe: Tuk! I hit him hard, on the back of the head. More men broke in. Mother was crying hard. I ran after Malu and struck him on the arm. I struck Kupate on the hand with my hoe and I heard the bone crack. I struck Atusa on the shoulder and on the back of the neck with a club. Itsi alone raped my mother. I stuck him as he had sex with her: tak! He died in my dream.

I went outside and fought many people. I clubbed many of them. They fled from me. I was like a soldier, like Lieutenant Carlos [a pseudonym for a Brazilian army officer alleged to have killed many people; the Mehinaku names are also fictitious]. In my hand I held a gun and I shot many people: My ammunition ran out. I grabbed a knife and I stabbed people. And then it was over.

The men's distress goes beyond concern for their female kin. At heart, and despite protestations to the contrary, I do not believe they are entirely comfortable with the tradition of the sacred flutes. In poignant myth, the men tell of a village girl who dressed as a man, crept into the men's house at night, and played the flutes better than any male. Discovered by the villagers she was placed in a pit in the men's house: "The men wanted her to suffer, to die, to be buried alive." For ten days she drank her own urine and ate her own feces until her lover dug her up and took her to a distant tribe. There she prospered and even managed to kill one of the men who had buried her. In mythology, if not in real life, affection for a woman may triumph over a harsh law.[13]

The men as individuals also seem ambivalent about rape. Only one man in the village told me he would denounce a close kinswoman for having seen the flutes, and many of the men said that if they were the only man to see the transgression they would not report it. The men were also careful to explain that they did not personally desire to gang-rape women. It had to be done because the spirit of the flutes would otherwise kill the men; it was acquired by tradition since it had been done before by the Mehinaku grandfathers; and it was politically necessary since the women should be "frightened." I am aware of only one man who totally rejects these rationalizations and regards gang rape as wrong and abusive. His perspective may be idiosyncratic, and is possibly based on his contact with the outside world. It is, however, perhaps comforting to conclude our description of Mehinaku sexual coercion with a quotation from this individual, a man in his 30s and the father of three small children:

No! I don't think gang rape is good. Only in the past was this good. It was those headless, faceless idiots of long ago, of mythic times, that did this. It was the sex fiends of ancient times. I feel sympathy for a woman who has seen the flutes. A man who is a good man does not participate in raping her. If he is a good man he says to her "I am sorry that it happened; alas for you!" A man who does not feel pity is a sex fiend, an unbathed, headless fool.

Male dominance and sexual coercion

The Mehinaku data reveal a number of points in common with our own American experience. Above all, the payoff for sexual coercion is a complex amalgam of sexual desire and many other motivations. As is often the case in our own society, individual rape appears to be part of a pattern in which the rapist "takes what he could not otherwise have." This is the Mehinaku villagers' own explanation for rape, and I think it would be a mistake to look much further. In all societies, men and women have somewhat different sexual agendas with respect to one another, and it is expectable that men, for whom sexual relations are a low-cost and highly motivated activity, will maximize sexual encounters. Coercion will occur in an institutional setting such as that of the Mehinaku, where it is tolerated and where it occurs at a substantially lower cost to the women than in our own society. Admittedly, the men's motivations are at times less clearly sexual, as in the case of a revenge rape, or a rape based on sexual frustration. But in general, it would be an error to look far beyond sexual motivations in individual cases of Mehinaku rape and sexual coercion.

The case of institutionalized Mehinaku gang rape is more complex. Here, as in our own society, the rapists' relationship to each other is as important as is their orientation toward the woman. Male cohesion, group leadership, and support of masculine traditions are part of the pattern. Hostility toward women and the desire to sadistically punish them must also be included in the men's emotional payoff, since, as the men well know, the event is catastrophic for the victim. More obscure sexual motivations of the sort found among group rapists in our own society (notably homosexuality and voyeurism) are also conceivably a part of the picture. As in the case of our own society, however, these undercurrents are muted, in that they are not a conspicuous part of the descriptions and oral histories I have collected of the act.

What is abundantly clear from the Mehinaku data, however, is the massive impact of sexual coercion on the women and its relationship to male dominance. Rape and sexual coercion, from the woman's point of view, is a powerful symbol of dominance because it is an ultimate act of control. Forced sex, and especially gang rape, is an invasion of the woman's body and its most intimate functions. It is a challenge to body boundaries, to ego structure and to self-definition. At the same time, the status of being a victim is itself degrading. When, as among the Mehinaku and many other societies with men's houses, gang rape is built into religion and supported by supernatural sanctions, it is an ultimate symbol of patriarchy. It at once expresses the subordinate status of women and the solidarity of the men. It is the sanction by which men as a group keep women as a group from participating in the religious and political system as equals. It expresses the men's loyalty to one another, and their willingness to betray the ties of affection, kinship, and economic dependence that link them to the woman. It is an overwhelming and supremely effective symbol of gender inequality.

Notes

1 See Bamberger (1974) for a discussion of the recurrent themes in diverse cultures.
2 My comments derive from the discussion of these issues found in Veevers and Adams (1982).
3 Brownmiller supported her position by pointing out that frequency of rape increases at the time of war and therefore was an instrument of political violence; that old and unattractive women are sometimes the victims of rapists; that some rapists admitted to hating women in general; and that psychologists have been unable to find differences between rapists and the general population of males. However, rape occurs during war primarily because of the lower probable cost of the act to the rapist; rapists generally prefer attractive victims; and there are substantial psychological differences between rapists and males in general in terms of their impulsiveness and propensity for violence (see Symons, 1979:280ff.).
4 In some instances, according to the authors, gang rape had become a normal fraternity activity, planned well in advance: "Some fraternities, in 'invitations' for their parties, even advertise the event with 'playful' euphemisms such as 'gang bang' or 'pulling train' (which refers to the men lining up like train cars to take turns). Far from viewing this behavior as rape, they seem to regard it as 'normal' party behavior" (1985:2).
5 The same pattern seems to prevail cross-culturally. Where lovers exchange gifts, the woman's gift is of lower value (Symons, 1979).
6 The term refers to the alligator's notorious ability to lie in wait for its prey (metaphorically, in this case, the village women) and to its highly sexual role in Mehinaku mythology.
7 Vern Carroll reports that among the Polynesian women he studied, being raped is not a serious issue (1976). I would not say the same of Mehinaku women, but the act does appear to be less significant to them than it is to women in the United States.
8 The term for ordinary sexual relations in Mehinaku is "aintyawakapai." The word for gang sex is "aintyawakakinapai." The medial form, "kina," converts the verb to a passive form while suggesting that a multitude is engaged in the action. "Being sexed by many persons' is perhaps the best translation of this term.
9 Among some other tribes with a similar "men's house pattern" women may be raped for a variety of offenses, including acting out of role. Robert Murphy (1974) reports that Mundurucu women who had returned from the mission school or who acted in an unfeminine manner were subject to rape. Among the Mehinaku, rumors occasionally circulate that such women have seen the flutes (see Gregor, 1985:110). Even though these tales are not likely to be acted on, they are a powerful sanction that enforces conformity to the female role.

10 My data on gang rape come from one informant who witnessed but did not participate in the last rape in the Mehinaku village, and from many of the men who provided me with oral histories of rapes. In the course of these descriptions I asked my informants to explain what they believed the motivations of the participants to have been, and what their own would be if they were to take part in a gang rape in the future.

11 All of the Mehinaku, from the furtive safety of the bushes around the village, have almost certainly seen couples having sexual relations. Gang sex, however, allows them to see sexual anatomy and activity in a way they never have before.

12 In theory, we can imagine a society where gang rape does not have a catastrophic impact on women. The Canela of Brazil are a candidate, for we are told that a woman who is raped "eventually learns to like to give herself in these group situations which take place in a spirit of gaiety" (Crocker, 1974: 187). Among the Mehinaku, rape is far more traumatic.

My description of the social and psychological impact of rape on Mehinaku women has greatly benefited from my discussion of the topic with Emiliene Ireland, who has studied the Waura, a neighboring tribe with a similar language and culture.

13 See Gregor (1988) for the full narrative of the myth and its analysis in terms of moral ambivalence regarding gang rape.

References

Amir, Menachem. 1971. *Patterns in Forcible Rape*. Chicago: University of Chicago Press.

Bamberger, Joan. 1974. The Myth of Matriarchy: Why Men Rule in Primitive Society. In *Women, Culture and Society*, Michelle Z. Rosaldo & Louise Lamphere (Eds.), pp. 263–280. Stanford: Stanford University Press.

Blanchard, W. H. 1959. The Group Process in Gang Rape. *Journal of Social Psychology* 49:259–266.

Brownmiller, Susan. 1975. *Against Our Will: Men, Women and Rape*. New York: Bantam Books.

Burgess, Ann W., & Linda L. Holmstrom, 1985. Rape Trauma Syndrome and Post Traumatic Stress Response. In *Rape and Sexual Assault*, Ann W. Burgess (Ed.), pp. 46–69. New York: Garland.

Carroll, Vern. 1976. Rape on Nukuoro: A Cultural Analysis. *Michigan Discussions in Anthropology* 1:134–147.

Crocker, William H. 1974. Extra-marital Sexual Practices of the Ramkokamekra-Canela Indians: An Analysis of Socio-cultural Factors. In *Native South Americans: Ethnology of the Least-Known Continent*, Patricia J. Lyon (Ed.). Boston: Little-Brown.

Ehrhart, Julie K., & Bernice R. Sandler, 1985. Campus Gang Rape: Party Games? Project of the Status and Education of Women. Washington, DC: Association of American Colleges.

Ellis, Lee, & Charles Beattie. 1983. The Feminist Explanation for Rape: An Empirical Test. *Journal of Sex Research* 19:74–93.

Gregor, Thomas. 1979. Secrets, Exclusion and the Dramatization of Men's Roles. In *Brazil: Anthropological Perspectives*. Maxine L. Margolis & William E. Carter (Eds.), pp. 250–269. New York: Columbia University Press.

1981. A Content Analysis of Mehinaku Dreams. *Ethos 9*:353–390.

1985. *Anxious Pleasures: The Sexual Lives of an Amazonian People.* Chicago: University of Chicago Press.

1988. "She Who Is Covered with Feces": The Dialectics of Gender among the Mehinaku of Brazil. In *Dialectics and Gender: Anthropological Approaches*, Richard R. Randolph, David M. Schneider, & May N. Diaz (Eds.), pp. 80–90. Boulder and London: Westview.

Greenson, Ralph R. 1968. Dis-identifying from Mother: Its Special Importance for the Boy. *International Journal for Psycho-analysis. 49*:370–374.

Minturn, L., Grosse, M., & S. Haider. 1969. Cultural Patterning of Sexual Beliefs and Behavior. *Ethnology 8*:301–318.

Murphy, Robert F. 1959. Social Structure and Sex Antagonism. *Southwestern Journal of Anthropology 15*:89–98.

1974. Deviance and Social Control II: Borai. In *Native South Americans*, Patricia J. Lyon (Ed.), pp. 202–208. Boston: Little Brown.

Ortner, Sherry B. 1974. Is Female to Male as Nature is to Culture? In *Women, Culture and Society*, Michelle Z. Rosaldo & Louise Lamphere (Eds.), pp. 67–87. Stanford, CA: Stanford University Press.

Sanday, Peggy R. 1981. The Socio-Cultural Context of Rape: A Cross-Cultural Study. *Journal of Social Issues 37*:5–27.

Sexual Survey no. 11. Current Thinking on Rape. *Medical Aspects of Human Sexuality 12*:125–128.

Symons, Donald. 1979. *The Evolution of Human Sexuality*. New York: Oxford University Press.

Veevers, Jean E., & Susan Adams. 1982. Bringing Bodies Back In: The Neglect of Sex Differences in Size and Strength. Paper presented at Canadian Sociology and Anthropology Association Meetings, Ottawa.

Whiting, J. W. M., & I. L. Child. 1953. *Child Training and Personality*. New Haven, CT: Yale University Press.

17
The children of Trackton's children
SPOKEN AND WRITTEN LANGUAGE IN SOCIAL CHANGE

Shirley Brice Heath

The brief finale of *Middlemarch*, the celebrated tale of families in a Victorian community, opens with these lines:

> Every limit is a beginning as well as an ending. Who can quit young lives after being long in company with them, and not desire to know what befell them in their after-years? For the fragment of a life, however typical, is not the sample of an even web.

George Eliot then capsules in a few pages the lives of Middlemarch's young families as they lived them out beyond the period of time covered in the novel's preceding chapters. Eliot's reminder that any novel is reduction and selection pertains, of course, as well to ethnography. We feel the fragmentary nature of such accounts most especially perhaps when they have focused on children, and after we have closed the pages of such works, we cannot easily quit these young lives, knowing that the ethnographic present never remains as it is described, and we wonder what followed in the after-years.

Such curiosity applies especially to the young of groups known to be in the midst of rapid social change when the anthropologist chooses to write a description of their lives. This chapter looks in on such a community – southern black working-class families described initially during the turbulent years of the 1960s and 1970s. *Ways with Words: Language, Life, and Work in Communities and Classrooms* (1983) gives ethnographic accounts of how the children of two working-class communities in the southeastern United States learned to use language at home and school between 1969 and 1977. One community was Roadville, a group of white families steeped for four generations in the life of the textile mills, but set by the end of the 1970s on a path toward suburban living and careers in small businesses, education, and service industries. The other community was Trackton, a collection of black families traditionally bound to farming but seemingly inextricably tied to life in the textile mills by the end of the 1970s. Within five years after and end of the fieldwork in these two communities, neither existed any longer as a geographical entity. Roadville's families had moved into

I wish to acknowledge the helpful comments of Peggy Miller, of the Department of Education, University of Chicago, on this chapter.

either the largest towns of the region or to the suburbs of cities of the South, and the children of focus in the ethnography were either continuing their education or settling into their first jobs, planning ahead for homes and the beginning of their families. Trackton's families had become scattered, dispersed by the radical upheaval of the economic recession of the early 1980s, with its concomitant severe reduction in the number of textile mills in the Piedmont region of the Southeast. The children of two of the Trackton children introduced in the 1983 ethnography are the subject of this study. We look in on their lives, in one instance, in a high-rise low-income housing unit in Atlanta, and, in the other, in temporary housing in what is currently called "a black slum area" across town from the former neighborhood of Trackton.

The epilogue of *Ways with Words* reminded readers that the dramatic and widely varying social changes taking place for blacks in different geographic regions and economic settings following the War on Poverty and Black-Is-Beautiful movements of the 1960s and 1970s made it especially necessary to recognize that research on black cultures would increasingly be a study in diversity. There is no single black experience. In the geographic region of Trackton, the 1970s proved a time of apparent economic advancement for those blacks who worked in the textile mills. Both males and females had begun to work in the mills before finishing high school, because the mill offered "good pay." Their parents, often combining work on one shift at the mill with part-time domestic work or local construction jobs, sought to rent better housing, buy a place of their own or purchase their first car. But the recession of the early 1980s, accompanied by the dissolution of many of the small local textile mills and the closings or consolidations of the mills of several national textile corporations in response to foreign competition, wiped out the mills as the source of a secure economic future. The erosion by inflation of Trackton families' low wages even during periods of employment made saving impossible. The work opportunities available in the early 1970s through community-based employment provisions of the model cities program, and later the Comprehensive Employment and Training Act (CETA), were short-lived, and after 1981 essentially no new public job programs for the young black poor existed. Those who turned to the aid for families with dependent children program (AFDC) found benefits much lower in real terms than they had been a decade earlier; increased stringency rulings forced fathers to remain "absent" members of what had become single-parent households and proscribed help to mothers from their older children living out of the household. In the 1960s and 1970s, Trackton families had chosen to remain independent of "the projects" of public housing and to rent instead small frame two-family units from absentee black landlords. By 1984, all of the "old-time" Trackton residents had given up hope of independence: Those with grown children moved about, taking turns staying with each child for short periods; families with young children moved to cheaper temporary housing in the older part of town and put their names on the waiting list for public housing. Women who had in earlier days worked as domestics for some white families found when they inquired about such jobs in the mid-1980s that these families had engaged professional cleaning services and put their preschoolers in cooperative play groups or nursery schools. Men who had previously always been able to "pick up" local seasonal agricultural work found the farms and orchards of past years either closed or dependent on machinery for most harvesting tasks. Trackton's proud independent families, intent on "gettin' on" and full of the ideology of "changin' times" in the 1960s and 1970s, met daily in the mid-1980s poverty and dependency that allowed neither time nor inclination for considering the meaning of black movements, Martin Luther King's dream, or the promises of bygone interracial human relations councils.

It is customarily not the anthropologist, but the policy analyst or sociologist, who speaks of the effects of national policy shifts and global economic directions on the lives of members of sociocultural groups set apart in American society by ethnic, racial, geographic, or class boundaries. In 1987, several public figures who were also social scientists published reports of the resulting failed education, family dissolution, and increased percentage of children in poverty (Coleman & Hoffer, 1987; Edelman, 1987; Lefkowitz, 1987; Moynihan, 1987). The central focus of most of these studies was the dysfunctional nature of families and the impoverishing effects of changed social policies, tax laws, and the inadequacy of minimum-wage employment to sustain even very small families (e.g. in 1987 a full-time minimum-wage job provided 75% of the amount specified as poverty level for a family of three). These reports and the prediction from many that the major issue of the next presidential term would be social problems – especially the poverty of children – led me to turn again to the work of anthropologists who studied minority cultures in the United States during the 1960s and 1970s. If we look, for example, at the studies of black communities, most reports, including my own (published in 1983 but based on fieldwork carried out between 1969 and 1981), described intact sociocultural groupings whose cultures were not "deficient," but variant and certainly equivalent in their way to the mainstream pattern. Legacies of African norms and social organizational adaptations to slavery had given black communities not only identifiable value systems and socialization processes, but also cultural ideologies they believed to be of their own creation and definition and of sufficient strength to enable them to push ahead. Key individuals – both nationally and locally – reinforced the significance (as well as the mystification) of these ideologies by linking them to a continued faith in education, the future of their youth, the centrality of religious conviction, and the power of the bonds of brotherhood and sisterhood among blacks.

But by the late 1980s the image both within and beyond many black communities had become largely one of poverty, dissolution, and strife.

Nearly half of all black children lived in poverty, most of these in households headed by a mother under 25 years of age who had neither the education nor self-image to look for or to secure and sustain employment. Nearly 30% of the children entering school in inner cities in the fall of 1987 were born to school dropouts who were themselves still of school age. Moreover, the social scientist/public policy reporters of 1987 argued that although most of the publicity pointed to minority cultures, especially blacks, the trends for blacks foreshadowed those for whites: Between 1969 and 1984 the white child poverty rate went up two-thirds, while the black rate increased only one-sixth (Edelman, 1987:23–33). Relatively few anthropologists have studied closely the everyday-life meanings of these figures and trends among either minority or white communities in the United States. Yet long-term fieldwork in a single region or community builds the basis for continuing ties, and a close look at Trackton families – and especially the young unwed mothers of the late 1980s who were among the children of Trackton in the 1970s – offered me an opportunity to look behind the statistics currently put forward by policy makers to support the agendas for social change of the 21st century (Foster et al., 1979).

This chapter takes up three issues. The first is the question of the extent to which the meanings of cultural membership, played out in numerous texts by Trackton adults for and with their children during my earlier fieldwork, were retained and understood by the young sufficiently to be carried into their socialization practices with their own children. The collective shared and public symbols of Trackton seemed in the 1970s to be elaborated and highly interdependent; through nearly a decade of life with community members, I had seen them persevere in their ideas and values and enforce the sharing of ties to the collective indentity of their own community and black membership. Their everyday narratives and – of special interest to me – their verbal and nonverbal patterns of language socialization with their young, had seemed to fix and stabilize the identity of individuals as members of their own group and as outsiders to others' cultural groups. From their church services and joking rituals to their habits of jointly reading newspapers and retelling stories, they both performed and commented upon their performances of criss-crossing and redundant themes, as they alternately insulated themselves against the otherness of communities beyond them and yet admitted sometimes the need to build bridges to outside institutions that could secure predictable connections when they needed public services, commercial exchanges, and education. But in a totally different spatial setting, without family members or national media to replay either public or intimate symbols of community membership and black pride, would the cultural symbols and texts of their childhood be sufficiently sustained for adaptation in the socialization of a new generation?

This query leads to a second: What are the resources for adaptation within different symbols or cultural texts? and what difference does the degree of time spent with local community-created and sustained symbols, as opposed to mass-produced ones, make to the vitality of one's identification as a member of any sociocultural body? Much has been written about the nature of adaptation, and radically different types of evidence have been used to determine whether aspects of human behavior can be interpreted as strategies of individuals to promote their fitness in specific social and cultural contexts (Mulder, 1987). During the 1960s and 1970s, social historians and anthropologists of Afro-America agreed that numerous patterns of language use, male–female relations, and parent–child bonding evolved during the decades of slavery and promoted the preservation of blacks under slavery in the New World (Levine, 1977; Whitten & Szwed, 1970). Considerable disagreement has followed, however, on the extent to which the particular habits that made positive contributions under slavery, and within a society rigidly divided along occupational and educational lines, now serve negative ends. Currently, America's postindustrial society, so highly dependent on literate-based communication, holds to the ideal of the nuclear family and the value of multiplex linkages to institutions beyond the family. In a climate of these values, black oral traditions, extended real and fictive kin linkages, and primary ties beyond the family centering in religious affiliations may well confer disadvantages (Black Family Summit, 1984; Blau, 1981; Ogbu, 1981).

My third concern relates specifically to the comparative differences between the socialization of Trackton's children in the 1970s and the children of those children in the late 1980s. Language socialization is a lifelong process in which individuals learn to communicate competently across contexts and experiences. The rate of change and conditions of change are crucial here. This concern derives from both the current debates over the relative places of orality and literacy and my own efforts to consider the cross-cultural contexts of a dependence on written artifacts for oral performances, often taken to be the fundamental forms of cultural knowledge. Perhaps, naively, the epilogue of *Ways with Words* suggested that language socialization patterns lay deeply embedded within certain cultural frames, such as family loyalties, space and time orderings, problem-solving techniques, and preferred patterns of recreation – all resistant to externally imposed social changes. Hence, habits of language socialization were likely to change only very slowly and in concert with shifts in these broader activities, values, and organizations.

Language socialization in Trackton

Any study of language socialization carries the goal of understanding both how language is used to socialize the young to become competent members of their cultures and how youngsters learn to use language as part of the totality of social understandings they must gain. "Language socialization research looks for world view–language connections as expressed through forms and functions of language use. It looks for cultural information not only in the content of discourse but in the organization of discourse as well" (Schieffelin & Ochs, 1986). Talk, as well as talk about talk, nonverbal reinforcements of spoken and written language, written artifacts, and the activities and role regulations that frame all of these become the texts that those who study language socialization attempt to study.

In the years of fieldwork in Trackton, adults of the community talked of their children "comin' up." On the porches of their small two-family units and on the plaza that fronted them, they surrounded their youngsters with the talk and activities of children and adults in the midst of everyday activities. They valued children's early nonverbal displays that indicated they had been watching and learning from life around them. They encouraged independent – sometimes even physically dangerous – ventures by young children. In contrast to the assertions of the bulk of studies of parents interacting with young children acquiring language, they did not simplify their talk to children or even feel the need to address them directly. They did not have special routines of question-and-answer displays or baby-talk games, and they did not offer the labels for items of the environment to their children. Instead, they expected that children would learn to talk "when they need to," and to judge when and to whom to give information and to be "wise" and cautious about answering "foolish" questions. Their philosophy of "what's done is done" seemed to keep them from asking children to recount verbally what they had done or were currently doing, unless adults believed children had information adults needed. The display of knowledge through talking about what was done could invite ridicule or punishment, unless offered as a poetic, clever, entertaining, and quasi-fictional narrative that could be jointly constructed by initiator and audience. (For some indication of the sharp contrast between these views and those held by mainstream families, see Heath, in press-a, and Ochs & Schieffelin, 1984.)

As soon as they could toddle, boys became public objects of verbal teasing, and successful verbal retorts could command attention from spectators on several porches. They learned a string of alternative ways of expressing similar meanings as well as alternative ways of performing the same utterance – always a well-formed short sentence with a variety of semantic values and contexts for interpretation. Adults and older children played different roles at different times with toddlers, who were expected to adapt, coperform, and learn that roles did not rest in a single individual, but in widely distributed types of performances across the community. Of children, especially boys, adults said: "Gotta watch hisself by watchin' other folks."

Girl babies entered the same general world as boys of swirling multiparty talk, shifting roles, and widely distributed functions of child caring. As toddlers they did not enter the public stage for the same kind of teasing as boys, although they watched their male peers undergo such public immersions. Carried about on the hips of older girls, they entered their games and banter, talked to themselves replaying conversations about them, and acted out fussin' routines with their dolls, and, throughout the preschool years, with younger children. All infants and young children accompanied adults to church services, and as they grew older, the girls took part in junior choirs and summer choir trades arranged among black churches during summer revival meeting times.

As they began to attend school, Trackton boys and girls spent some after-school time outside the community, but the neighborhood worried considerably about the whereabouts of young girls. Although accepted as inevitable, early pregnancies were the reason given for trying to keep young girls close under the watchful eye of adults. Yet the community valued children as children, not as the offspring of a combination of particular individuals; thus, although the pregnancy was protested, the child was not, and, from 1969 through 1986, no girl in Trackton completed the teenage years without having at least one baby. The particular father or mother mattered little in the 1970s; the neighborhood seemed glad to have a child. Almost invariably, the baby became part of the family under the fulltime care of the mother of the teenager, who returned to high school and the usual social life of other teenage girls.

Two of these teenage mothers provide the cases for discussion here. The first is Zinnia Mae, the middle daughter of a blind diabetic mother. A large girl who was a favorite target of the taunts of peers in the neighborhood and at school, she had her first child at age 14. Trackton judged her situation as especially unfortunate, because her mother was not able to keep her baby, and the boy's father's family never took any interest in the baby. The child went to the oldest sister who lived across town and took the baby into her household to raise and to become her own. Zinnia Mae returned to school, but at 16, the legal age for "quitting" school, she and a girlfriend unknown within Trackton ran away to Atlanta, where Zinnia Mae had three more children, a girl and twin boys, within the next two years.

The second case is that of Sissy, the next to the oldest child in a family of five children. Within Trackton, her household, headed by a strong-minded mother held in high respect by the community, served as a collecting place for other children of the neighborhood during the 1970s. Her mother, Lillie Mae, worked intermittently in several textile mills, and her father supplemented his work on a construction crew with second-shift work at one of the mills. In 1981, after failing in repeated attempts to get steady mill work, he left the family, and Lillie Mae had to move to temporary housing and put her name on the waiting list for public housing. The oldest child in the family, Tony, finished four years at a small college within the state, and after two years of living at home and helping his mother with contributions from the local part-time work he could find, he took a computer training course, found a job within state government, and left home. Between 1982 and 1987, Lillie Mae and the four children at home lived on her welfare check, occasional small checks coerced from the children's father when authorities could find him, and, since Tony left home, the few secret supplements he could send from time to time. Local public housing officials explained the delay in her obtaining public housing by telling her that her family was "too big" for their available units. Sissy became pregnant during her junior year in high school, dropped out of school briefly to have the baby, gave over care of the baby boy, Denny, to her mother, returned to graduate from high school, and continued to live at home while attending a local technical school part-time. For a while, she worked part-time at a local fast-food restaurant, but her wages threatened the larger welfare check her mother received, and she was forced to quit. The baby's father and his family took care of the baby on one weekend every 6 weeks or so, and they bought him presents and some supplies on these visits.

The move to urban life

The high-rise public housing apartment unit in which Zinnia Mae and her three children live looks like any of thousands of others built in American inner cities in the 1960s. The six-story concrete unit in which she lives is only one of eight, each of which covers a city block, in a downtown section of Atlanta. The units surround an internal dirt plot on which parts of swings, see-saws, and tire mazes spring from clusters of dry wiry grass and weeds. Two broken wooden benches that once bordered one side of the plot now stand on one end facing each other and forming a narrow miniature prison that mocks the taller versions that surround it in the form of the apartment units.

Soon after she turned 16, Zinnia Mae and Gloria Sue, a girlfriend who was 17, caught a ride to Atlanta with some young men they met at a local disco. Once in Atlanta, both girls stayed for a while with Gloria Sue's grandmother, but within a few months, she threw Zinnia Mae out for "sassin'" her. Zinnia Mae telephoned her older sister, who had become the virtual mother of the boy Zinnia Mae had when she was 14, asked for bus fare home, and was told there was no money to send. For nearly three years, no one in Trackton heard from Zinnia Mae, and those missing months remain a mystery. Her sister heard from her again in early 1985, when she telephoned to say she wanted to see her boy, she was living in Atlanta, had a little girl who was a year old, and she was expecting twins.

Although her sister had neither money nor inclination to send the boy to Zinnia Mae, she asked me to take pictures of the child to her if I was ever in Atlanta. A series of phone calls to Zinnia Mae opened the way for me to visit her in mid-1985 when her girl, Donna, was 16 months old, and her twin boys were only 2 months old. When I telephoned, she asked to meet me at a local fast-food restaurant and she took me to her apartment from there. Although a hundred pounds heavier than she had been as a teenager, Zinnia Mae still walked the skipping walk she had years earlier, and she smiled as timidly as she had in response to the neighborhood teases. We walked up the six flights of stairs ("the elevator don't work yet"), and in the living room of her apartment, we found a 12-year-old neighbor's child "mindin' the babies" who left when Zinnia Mae handed her a dollar bill. Zinnia Mae asked about my children, and we settled into talk of old acquaintances. When she asked about her son, I handed her the envelope of photographs. She held each one up to the light, looked at it silently, and gave them back, saying, "He's sure cute, ain't he?" She asked what I had been doing, and when I told her I was still trying to figure out how kids learned to talk, she said she wondered if her little girl would ever learn. While we had been talking, the child had been lying quietly sucking on a pacifier on the mattress on the floor where her child caregiver had left her. I assured Zinnia Mae that she would surely learn, she was young yet, and asked how Zinnia Mae spent her days with her children. She answered "Well, I ain't havin' no more, that's for sure. I have my tubes tied when the twins came. I've done all I'm doin' for menfolks who just pick up and leave when the music's gone." She paused, looked out the window, and then picked up my earlier question. "My days, you know, I just do what I can, can't get away much, watch some TV, try to keep 'em clean, get some groceries now and then." She volunteered that she had tried to get some work back before the twins came, but she could only find part-time dishwashing work at $4.25 an hour, and her welfare check gave her more than that. The babies' father sometimes used to bring formula and diapers and gave her cash for food and makeup.

Before I left that first visit, she mentioned again about wondering if her girl would learn to talk. Trying to reassure her, I bet her that the child had already begun to talk some, but Zinnia Mae just might not notice since there weren't any older children around for her little girl to play with. She laughed and said: "You bet there ain't. I can't haul her up and down those six flights of steps to get her out with them other kids, and the place in here is too cramped as it is; I sure can't have nobody else's babies in here, so me and Donna, we pretty much stay in here with the babies by ourselves 'cept when I get the neighbor girl to come in so I can go get some food for us to eat, 'n my girlfriends, they come by sometimes, but they don't like to climb them steps either." I suggested that she might hear Donna talk if she tape-recorded some of the hours during the day while she was bathing, dressing, and feeding her. Zinnia Mae agreed this might be a fun idea. I left and returned that afternoon with two tape recorders, several boxes of tapes, and a notebook and pencil. Zinnia Mae agreed to turn the tape recorder on for several hours on several days each week and to write down what she and Donna had been doing while the tape was being made. (For a discussion of this participatory data collection technique used with another dropout mother, see Heath & Branscombe, 1985; Heath & Branscombe, 1986.)

Between mid-1985 and mid-1987, Zinnia Mae taped over four hundred hours and wrote approximately 1,000 lines of notes about her activities. The two of us met together about every 6 months, listened to certain tapes together, and talked about what was happening on the tapes and in her notes. During these years, she remained on welfare, stayed in the same apartment, and remained unsuccessful in either obtaining work or getting Donna into a day-care center. She had two hospitalizations, both as a result of falls, and one of the twins had to be hospitalized once for a bronchial infection.

Analysis of Zinnia Mae's data through superimposing portions of the notes and tapes on those collected at similar ages for Trackton's children revealed four primary resources for organizing language socialization: spatial and time allotments, access to coparticipants and audience, availability of props (animate and inanimate), and the affective tone or mood of interactions.

The everyday life of Donna and her younger brothers was played out in the living room, bedroom, and bathroom of Zinnia Mae's apartment. Since the small kitchen opened off the living room, and a table sat at its entry, there was no available space for them in the kitchen. In the bedroom, Donna slept in her mother's bed and the twins on a pallet on the floor; in the living room, all three children played on both the floor – on a small mattress in the corner – and the sofa set before the television set. The six flights of stairs and the lack of either available outdoor space for sitting or easy transportation with three small children were the reasons Zinnia Mae gave for not taking the children out. After Donna could walk well and climb the steps on her own, Zinnia Mae took her to the grocery store with her once or twice a week. They walked the two-and-a-half blocks to the store, Donna sat in the cart, and they walked back – Donna carrying small packages and walking alone, while her mother usually held packages in both arms. The twins remained in the apartment with the teenage neighbor girl. Once every 2 or 3 weeks, she took sheets and towels to the nearby laundromat, and Donna went with her and waited, sitting on the high orange plastic chair in the waiting area.

As preschoolers, Zinnia Mae and her peers had lived primarily on the porches of Trackton's houses and in the dirt plaza out front. They rarely went into the homes of others, and unless the weather was exceptionally bad, they spent very few of their daylight hours inside their own family's house. Because there were few cars in Trackton, a trip to the supermarket occurred rarely, and the available shared space in any car making the trip went to adults. A small neighborhood grocery was within walking distance, and adults sent the community's neighborhood children there to buy what was needed. On any of these trips, older children would ask permission to carry toddlers astride their hips, often using some of the money they received for doing the errand to buy candy for the youngster. Infants and toddlers went to church with their families whenever car space was available. Those children whose fathers did not live within Trackton often went to spend weekends with their father's mother or other relatives.

Time allotments for preschool children in Trackton and Zinnia Mae's household seemed on the surface very similar. For the majority of time, the children's mothers did not work outside the home, and when Trackton mothers did, they depended on older children or made reciprocal arrangements with neighbor friends to take care of the youngest ones. Beneath the surface evidence, however, patterns of time usage differed greatly. Trackton mothers seemed "busy." Inside the house they cleaned and washed or got a big washing together to take to the nearby laundromat; each morning they prepared food that sat on the stove available for stand-up meals throughout the day. Once a day, at least, clocks in both the bedroom and the living room roused sleepers to get off to their shiftwork, and alerted family members who had moved out onto the front porch to their duty of making sure no one overslept. On the porch, women took whatever work they could bring outside: beans to string, mending to do, magazines to look through, newspapers to read, potatoes to peel, or the cigarette for relaxation. There, even without tasks to keep their hands busy, they always found neighbors who either joined them or walked by, and there were always children in the plaza to watch, tease, and scold. Gossip, quarrels, retold stories, chewed-over newspaper or mail items, and interactions with children on the plaza filled the air with sounds of busy-ness.

Zinnia Mae, in contrast, never described herself as "busy" but always as "overworked" or "tired." She woke with the children, changed diapers, fixed bottles for the twins and cereal for Donna, ate some toast and smoked a cigarette, closed the bedroom door, so the children would stay in the living room, and turned on the television before she sat down on the sofa. She had no clock in the house, but told time by matching television programs to *TV Guide* listings. When any of her girlfriends were not working, and when she had money to keep a telephone, she would call them and talk, often comparing notes on a particular television game show or soap opera. The pace of her life varied not at all for Saturdays or Sundays, except through the occasional extra availability of her girlfriends on the weekends for short visits. Zinnia Mae kept movie and television star magazines her girlfriends sometmes brought, and she would often thumb through these or the free advertisements for department and grocery stores that came to all the apartment mailboxes.

Each day, after she gave the children their morning meal, Zinnia Mae put the children down in the living room "to play." Donna centered her activities around the mattress, playing sometimes with utensils or plastic dishes from the kitchen, and as the twins got older, both she and they made a game of climbing on and off the sofa, hiding under the table at the kitchen entry or under the coffee table on which the television sat. They had no set meal of the day other than their breakfast, but the children called for food whenever they felt hungry or seemed bored.

Donna fed herself and the children to break the boredom of daylight hours. Zinnia Mae planned trips to the grocery or laundromat on the basis of need and the availability and mood of the neighbor's teenager who was not always anxious to sit with the twins. She made the bed, swept the floor, and cleaned the kitchen or bathroom if she knew a girlfriend was coming by, and often on the days when she came home from the laundromat. Thus her time seemed to flow endlessly with few interruptions, but engagement with or activities carried out directly with her children came rarely. The following episode illustrates the language and social interactional aspects of daily life. The episode took place when Donna was 2;4 and the twins were 1;2.

> [Donna picks up a movie magazine and begins tearing out its pages to place the separate pages around the living room floor. Zinnia Mae sits on the sofa watching a gameshow and hears the tearing pages.]
>
> Zinnia Mae: Hey, what do you think you're doing? [sounds of pages rustling and furniture movement]
> Donna: Makin' places, see, here?
> Zinnia Mae: You ain't tearin' up my books; get them playtoys over there. You hear? Shhh, I cain't hear.
> [sound of plastic banging on the floor]
> Zinnia Mae: Now, what you doin'? I told you I cain't hear. Put that thing down, I say.
> [Donna begins to cry.]

This episode characterizes the types of interactions that filled the tapes, that took place on my visits, and that Zinnia Mae wrote of in her notes:

> Monday: Watched TV, Donna eat cheers [Cheerios], babies cry and I catch Donna give cheers; she make a house under the chair.
> [Jan 9, 1986]

In a random selection of 20 hours of the tapes made over the 2 years, approximately 14% of recording sessions included talk between Zinnia Mae and any of her children. During these encounters, she asked direct questions about the children's immediate actions, offered comment on those actions (and her response to them), and gave directions or requested certain actions, usually in exchanges of talk that lasted less than 1 minute. During those sessions that contained more than four contingent exchanges between mother and child, 92% took place when someone else was in the room. A girlfriend or the neighbor girl as audience seemed to provoke talk as performance and invitations for others to comment on the children. Following the episode in which Donna had "set places," Zinnia Mae reported this to a visiting girlfriend (partly as explanation for the torn magazine). Seemingly speaking directly to Donna, she asked: 'You think you gonna be a waitress or something?" She then explained to her girlfriend that she and Donna had stopped at Burger King on the way home from the grocery last week, and Donna had liked the place mats. She then said "You ate them fries and drank that coke down." During these exchanges, Donna started several times to tell the girlfriend something that is unintelligible on the tape, but Zinnia Mae explained on hearing the tape several weeks later that Donna wanted to let the girlfriend know that she (Zinnia Mae) had spilled part of her coke, and it had run down off the table into Donna's lap. The intonational pattern and the length of sustained talk provide evidence that Donna was trying to offer some account of a past event – no doubt, the one her mother remembered as having made a considerable impression on Donna at the time.

The availability of coparticipants and audience, as well as access to props, was limited to girlfriends and neighbor girl, visits to the grocery and laundromat, and the usually traumatic visits to the doctor's office. In a large shoe box near the mattress, Donna had several plastic toys bought at the grocery store, pieces of a blanket, several plastic spoons and food cartoons, and a collection of fuzzy animals brought by Zinnia Mae's girlfriends. The twins inherited these toys and acquired in addition a small rubber ball, a roller skate abandoned in the apartment entryway downstairs, and several plastic cars. Zinnia Mae rarely brought anything into the living room, except diaper boxes, food items, or cigarettes. Occasionally, she left the open grocery bags on the living room floor for the children to crawl in and out of.

Zinnia Mae's most frequent words were "I'm so tired." She rarely laughed, except in response to something on television or to a jesting approach from one of her girlfriends. She met the needs her children made known for food, water, clean diapers, relief from pain, and occasional physical help (being lifted onto a sofa, into a chair, etc.). She held and hugged all the children when her mood was good and they approached her; she did not hit at them or push them away roughly. The tapes and her own talk about her notes and the tapes reveal that she waited for the children to address or approach her most of the time. In only 13 instances within the hours of taping did she initiate talk to one of the children that was not designed to give them a brief directive or query their actions or intentions. She once told Donna to come sit beside her to see the puppet on television, twice asked one of the twins to give her a bite of cookie and talked about why she liked that particular kind of cookie, and once she said to Donna that someone on television looked like one of her girlfriends. On 9 occasions, she talked to the children as a result of introducing some written artifact to them.

Often while watching television or sitting at the kitchen table smoking a cigarette, she read magazines and advertisements. She sometimes talked with her girlfriends about the magazine materials, commenting on the differences between two stories, changed events in the lives of certain television or movie stars, and certain hair styles or dress styles she liked or disliked. She read the advertisements to see pictures of hair and clothing styles and to learn about special sales at the only grocery store near enough for her to walk to. Her primary purposes for reading were thus instrumental and social interactional/recreational. She wrote as an aid to memory and occasionally to record financial records related to medicaid, food stamps, or her welfare payments. On three occasions, she brought Donna's attention to a magazine or paper by pointing to an object foreign to the child (swimming pool, horse, and large helium-filled balloon). She then asked her to look at the picture, named it, and commented on the item ("that's like a big bathtub," "you see one of them on TV," "that'll take you right up into the air"). Four times, she gave Donna a page of advertisements and a pencil and told her to draw; she circled one of the items to demonstrate what she meant. On two other occasions, she showed the children a cartoonlike figure in an advertisement that looked like one of the Saturday morning cartoon figures, saying "You know him, you seen him on TV." (For further treatment of the influence of literacy artifacts on prompting demonstration-type talk by mothers who do not otherwise point out environmental items and name them for their children, see Heath & Thomas, 1984; Heath & Branscombe, 1984.)

In summary, the language socialization resources of Trackton and Zinnia Mae's apartment contrast sharply along nearly every dimension of interaction. The spatial – and resultant social – isolation forced the great majority of interactions with her children to be dyadic rather than multiparty, as was the case in Trackton's open and shifting arena of speakers and listeners and play and work. In the absence of audience, almost no playful and teasing episodes, or requested routines or demonstration of physical feats by the children took place. The public dimensions of socialization in Trackton multiplied the number of interlocutors, events, genres, and goals of talking and listening for young and old. Without actors of her preceding generation to socialize her by direct and indirect teaching, and without the actors and props of her own socialization, Zinnia Mae did not assume a key role in enabling her children to learn to use language across a wide variety of genres, styles, and functions. Cut off from the family and community of her childhood, and walled in a transient community of people who remained strangers to her, Zinnia Mae's own language socialization had been brought to a halt. For most of her waking hours each day of the week, she was a passive spectator of television and movie or TV magazines, and a passive listener to the episodes of the worlds her girlfriends frequent. Her active engagement in spoken and written language resided primarily in instrumental exchanges. In her taped exchanges with her girlfriends, they talked nearly 80% of the time, and her contributions centered on queries about the events they told of, changes in welfare check rulings, or problems with medicaid, apartment tenants, and getting someone to stay with the twins while she shopped. Any talk of the future in her language was of the near future: how to get the papers to the welfare office, when Donna might start talking, whether day-care rulings might change, and what she would do if she could get her hands on the children's father who stopped sending money shortly after the twins were born. She did not talk of distant future events or accomplishments for the children or herself. The only group she talked of belonging to was "us women" – a term she used to signify females without male companions, mothers of young children without fathers, and competitors for welfare resources.

Rarely involved in manipulative activities (such as sewing) for any extended period of time, and engaging in these without talk of the activities while they were in process, Zinnia Mae could provide few occasions for guided or collaborative tasks with her children, few chances for mother and children to coconstruct tasks or talk for more than a fleeting minute or so. One exception to this relative absence of opportunities for guided interactions in task accomplishment was sweeping the floor. Once Donna was old enough to stand alone, she leaned on the broom as Zinnia Mae pushed it about, and later one of Donna's favorite activities was to try to sweep by herself. During these events, Zinnia Mae gave directives, sometimes laughed, and offered encouragement or admonishments after Donna initiated talk during the process. For Zinnia Mae, time did not flow between work – or accomplishful activities – and play or leisure. On the few occasions when she went out to interview for a job or tried a job for a few weeks (usually at the instigation of one of her girlfriends), she came back talking about those jobs (washing dishes in fast-food restaurants or waitressing) as "kids' jobs." She was convinced that employers wouldn't put anyone "as big and fat as me out there shoveling food in front of other people." Zinnia Mae expected the few people she met outside her apartment to hold the same opinions she held; their intentions, she judged by the immediate effect of their actions on her.

Staying home

The climate of despair about American inner cities that developed in the mid-1980s makes it easy to see Zinnia Mae's cultural membership as created (or obliterated) by her particular location and exacerbated by her own physical condition. Without contemporary accounts of the everyday life of other inner-city household units, the uniqueness of her situation is difficult to judge. It is, however, possible to compare the language socialization of her children with that of another young Trackton mother, Sissy, who did not leave home.

When Sissy had her first child at 16, she and her mother, Lillie Mae, and brothers and sisters had moved from Trackton to temporary housing to await placement in public housing. Located on a long street lined with shade trees, the house into which they moved had long been abandoned by the white families who used to live in this area of town. Without paint, running water, or heat, the single-family dwelling offered primarily a roof and four walls when Lillie Mae moved in. Now owned by a black man who lived "up North," the house rented on a short-term basis for $150 a month. Lillie Mae, Tony, and the older children set about clearing the weeds in the front yard, putting the bricks back into the sidewalk, patching holes in the floor, painting, and hounding the landlord to get a gasline run into the house. Sissy's baby, Denny, arrived within a few months of the move and slept in the bed with Lillie Mae and Sissy. From the outset, Lillie Mae and Tony took charge of the baby, carrying him about wherever they sat in the living room to visit or watch television. They knew no one in the neighborhood, made up primarily of transients waiting to go elsewhere, except Lillie Mae's cousin who lived several houses down and around the corner on a street of small well-kept houses owned by black families.

The competitive spirit of the families who came and went on Lillie Mae's street kept any long-term associations from building up. Most of the households consisted of women and children waiting to get into public housing and living on welfare. Those men who maintained close connections with their families usually lived with their mothers and aunts in another part of town, staying away from their own women and children to ensure continuation of AFDC payments. Some worked in other parts of the state on construction sites and came to town only occasionally. Few of the houses had front porches and those that did were ususaly filled with visiting family and friends who came by car on weekends. On these occasions, a mix across generations talked, teased, prepared to go to special church services, or planned coming weekend events.

Within Lillie Mae's house, Denny had Sissy's three brothers and younger sister to take him with them when they went to the nearby service station/grocery store or on errands to the cousin's house. When Denny was 8 months old, Lillie Mae agreed to tape-record half an hour or so several times each week when the baby was awake, and Sissy wrote several lines each week describing the baby's activities and the contexts of the tape recordings. These recordings began in December 1986 and continued through October 1987, when Denny was 18 months old. In addition, I visited about every 2 months. During most of the first 6 months of taping, Denny was a listener and spectator to multiparty interactions primarily in the living room and kitchen and at the cousin's house, where some of the taping was done. Denny's spatial world extended from this house to the corner store and three times to church services. His toys, contributed primarily by the cousin and Tony, stayed in a box in a corner of the living room and included a wooly puppy, large plastic ball, two cast-off hats from older boys, plastic eggs that came in two parts, and a toy gun holster found in the yard. He played with these or howled whenever he was not taken up as a toy himself by one or the other of the older children, who encouraged him to learn to crawl, sit up, walk, kick, and to resist their teasing. They let him play school with them from time to time when they did their homework, and from the time he was 16 months old, they kept him away from their books by giving him crayons and paper bags to draw on while they worked. Major responsibility for Denny rested with Lillie Mae, and, in days of tension over no word from the housing authority or threatened cuts in her check, she spoke harshly to Denny and chided Sissy for "doing nutn' to help us out." Sissy spent as much time as possible out of the house at the technical school, where she was taking a "modeling course." She and her girlfriends carpooled to nearby shopping centers, where they told Lillie Mae they had to do "homework." Unlike the days before the textile mills closed, Lillie Mae and her oldest children, Tony and Sissy, found few common work experiences outside the home to talk about. The stuff of shared stories, complaints, and jokes about working in the mill was no more, and a lot of talk at home focused on frustrations, disappointments, and anger over the failure to find work, to hear from the housing authority, or to keep the landlord from raising the rent.

Lillie Mae pored over the papers that came in the mail from various authorities and asked Tony to interpret them and write some kind of answer. Each day she read the local paper as well as the advertising brochures that came in the mail. While doing so, she often held Denny on her lap. She sometimes walked to her cousin's house with the paper, where they read and talked about local events. Her instrumental uses of reading and writing related primarily to keeping track of applications for housing, welfare, and medicaid, and occasionally writing a letter to relatives up North. She gave up going to church except on rare occasions when an out-of-town relative with a car came to take her. Tony went regularly, read church materials at home, and kept his college books around to read from time to time. Once he started computer training, he was rarely at home, and when he got a full-time job, he took his books and moved out on his own. On his visits, he sometimes helped the younger children with their homework, and Denny was always party to these occasions.

When they had tasks to do in the house or errands to run, he went along as well, and as soon as he could stand, he was sent on errands within the household and told to pick up things from the floor. By 13 months, he echoed end bits and pieces of the talk of those around him, usually with no acknowledgment that he was talking by the adults or older children present. When they initiated talk to him, they asked him to name family members or stop doing something they objected to. At 18 months, his vocabulary consisted of names of family members and two fixed phrases that he varied in two moods – happy and angry: "get it," and "open it." He called Lillie Mae "Ma" and all other family members by their given or nicknames. This pattern of language development matches that of Trackton's children, which moved through three stages: (1) a repetition stage, in which they picked up and repeated chunks of phrasal and clausal utterances of speakers around them; (2) a repetition with variation stage in which they manipulated pieces of the conversations they picked up from the discourse around them; (3) participation, usually reached around 2 years of age, during which they attempt to bring their own talk into that of adult conversation, making themselves part of the ongoing discourse (Heath, 1983: chap. 3).

Interaction time with Sissy differed little in flavor from time with all other members of the family (including the neighbor cousin) except Lillie Mae, who always kept watch over his whereabouts and inclusion in others' activities. On his monthly visits to the home of his father's parents (who called him their "gran"), he went with them to church, choir practices, shopping centers, and the grocery store. The 40 hours of tape and 10 pages of notes collected over 10 months indicate that during approximately 40% of the taped time at least three people were engaged in conversations that surrounded both work and leisure time (visiting, watching television, washing dishes, preparing to go somewhere). Talk consisting of more than a vocative or term of endearment directed specifically to Denny occurred on only 12 occasions, 10 of them bunched in the first few tapings and, no doubt, artificial performances for the benefit of the tape recorder. The two exceptions were teasing exchanges in the seventh and eighth months of taping. On both these occasions, Tony tried to get Denny to wear his hat and Denny kept throwing it on the floor. Tony repeatedly asked Denny who he thought he was, how he was going to the store without a hat, and where his hat was. Denny and Tony played this game on each occasion for more than five minutes, Denny interjecting "get it," each time he threw the hat on the floor.

Symbols in adaptation

Let's return to the question of the extent that Zinnia Mae and Sissy – as young mothers – now demonstrate that they sufficiently understood and retained the narratives, rituals, and everyday rhythm of their socialization as cultural members in Trackton, to adapt them in current circumstances. Although Trackton residents during the 1960s and 1970s saw their time there as temporary and hoped to "move on," they cohered as a group in their waiting. Although respectables separated themselves from the "real" transients and the "no-counts," the community's connections across residents of all ages met in their attempts to get and keep jobs, to enjoy weekends, to keep up on the news, and to keep from being "pulled down" by hard circumstances. The Black-Is-Beautiful spirit of the public media and the prominence given to black concerns through model city, CETA, head start, and human relations councils only added vocabulary and slogans for their performances and sometimes instrumental access to goods and services within their power. The intense publicity surrounding the first few years of desegregation, amidst frequent school shifts and openings and closings, gave them a sense of being players in a larger drama than that of their own small neighborhood. They read the local paper, shared news of events and people, and sustained a sense of connection as members to the outside world. Their young heard and felt much from these societal shifts in school, but only Tony, 8 years old when he moved to Trackton, could remember what came before in the slum dwellings across the tracks on the outskirts of town. He intensified his sense of otherness by going to a predominately white Southern college.

Those just behind him, such as Zinnia Mae and Sissy, remembered nothing before Trackton, and as children they listened to tales of cotton fields, dimestore counter sit-ins, and race riots with less involvement than to tales of last weekend's dance. Today, for Zinnia Mae and Sissy alike, the struggles are of the individual, not of the group, and the enemies are shifting, faceless, and largely unseeable – rulings, paperwork, neighbors downstairs or down the street who breed cockroaches or report to the welfare worker that Tony brought extra money home to Lillie Mae last week. In earlier days, the black church preached and sang of group struggles and the strength to be gained in comradeship, faith, and perseverance. Neither Zinnia Mae nor Sissy is connected to a black church or any other institution of voluntary membership.

These case studies suggest the power of groupings and allegiances beyond the immediate family to give a sustaining ideology of cultural membership. The sense of belonging was punctuated for Trackton's members by the black church (and its affiliated organizations, such as choirs), constant access to several generations and their tales of history, as well as the availability of commentators on the current scene (played by Trackton members who read their newspapers in porch groupings, listened to Trackton's self-appointed "mayor" talk about the human relations council, etc.). Moreover, recent sociological research underscores the importance of such contacts for the academic and mental health of young minorities – especially blacks. In a comparative study of black dropouts and high school graduates in Chicago, those who graduated found support in a system of school and community associations, as well as church attendance; 72% of the graduates reported regular church attendance, whereas only 14% of the dropouts did (Williams, 1987). In a Boston study, positive effects on the academic success of children came with the association of their mothers with organizational ties beyond the family (and with friends who had such ties also), nondenominational religious affiliations, and stability in the labor force over a number of years (Blau, 1981). Acceptance and assimilation within institutions beyond the home for both parent and child provide positive carryovers for mental health, academic retention, and job stability. Alienation from family and community – and subsequently school – appear to play a more critical role in determining whether or not a student finishes high school than the socioeconomic markers of family income, education level, and so on (Williams, 1987). For Sissy and Zinnia Mae, in the absence of such associations of sustenance and reinforcement of cultural membership, the intimate symbols of connectedness, pride, and perseverance have left them seemingly unable to adapt their own socialization for that of the next generation or to recreate new foundations of togetherness.

But what of the resources for adaptation that might lie within the symbols of the culture of their childhood? Were the porch tales, teasings, newspaper readings, church services, fussings, and other public performances sufficiently identified as theirs for their significance to be maintained? These texts of Trackton carried much of the same significance and ideological weight as similar performances detailed for other black communities (e.g., Baugh, 1983; Folb, 1980; Smitherman, 1977). Persistence, assertive problem solving, and adaptability – especially in human relations – emerge as primary individual and group survival characteristics from these texts. In addition, authoritative – firm but supportive – human bondings stand out as those most desirable (Spencer, Brookins, & Allen, 1985; Moses, 1985; Stack, 1974). However, in all studies reporting the celebration, performance, adaptation, and fitness of these characteristics, the contexts have been relatively free from external influences that cut at the heart of the extended and fictive kin family and the centrality of children to a group's sense of self-perpetuation. Currently, AFDC rulings that encourage fathers to remain outside the household of the mother and children, as well as public housing regulations limiting the number of occupants per unit of space, have cut away the traditional supportive contexts for key performances. Zinnia Mae's children have no entry into the contexts in which they might witness or participate in repetitive collaborative celebrations of persistence or assertive problem solving. Those available to Sissy's son are severely diminished from those of her own childhood, since Lillie Mae and she both find their struggles against individuals in the bureaucracies they encounter unsuitable for translation into verbal performance. Moreover, an absence of shared work and leisure experiences set mother and daughter apart in the shared background fundamental to leisure talk, and Sissy's continued socialization from womanhood and motherhod comes less and less from her own mother, but from other young women as adrift as she from either a past or a future.

Language socialization research currently gives primary attention to the role of social interactions in enabling children to become competent communicators in their sociocultural group. "Mutual tuning-in" (Schutz, 1951) and eventual linguistic and metalinguisitc awareness are said to rest in the fast-paced coconstructions of reality that adults and children create in everyday life (Rogoff & Wertsch, 1986; Vygotsky, 1978). In addition, however, linguists increasingly emphasize the subjective and alternative interpretations that children create as a result of their opportunities to constantly conform and inform through verbal and nonverbal means (Rice & Schiefelbusch, 1989a). Children call on numerous perceptual levels – seeing, hearing, touching, tasting – in their creation of representational systems for gaining, storing, and displaying information. The contexts of language socialization for the children of the children of Trackton in the cases offered here hold few opportunities for solidarity, social construction of reality, and guided learning through verbal direction, observation, or apprenticeship. The language socialization of these children holds little promise that they will enter school with the wide range of language uses, varieties of performances, types of genres, and perspectives on self-as-performer that Trackton's children had. Their association with written materials rests primarily in the instrumental and not in the confirmational, social interaction/ recreational, or news-related reading of their mother's childhood. (For discussions of the relevance of these ranges of uses of written language in academic achievement and school-defined "critical thinking," see Heath, 1983 and in press.) It is too early to predict the extent to which the pattern of language socialization for Sissy's son and her future children may come to match that of Zinnia Mae's. It is likely that Lillie Mae will be unable to secure public housing as long as Sissy and her son remain with her. If they have to leave Lillie Mae to strike out on their own, Sissy may be forced into the atomization and separation that small-apartment living of public housing imposes.[1]

Recent critiques within anthropology have suggested that those who have written ethnographies may well have made many mistakes of analysis and interpretation. They have been characterized as victims of alienated nostalgia (Clifford, 1983; Clifford & Marcus, 1986), prone to read too much into other people's ways of talking about their experiences and motives (Keesing, 1987), too willing to reveal the private ways of minority groups (Scheper-Hughes, 1987), too ready to focus on solidarity and sharedness (Fernandez, 1986), and unable to avoid championing the underdog (Foster, 1979). The current spirit of confessions and probings of methods of analysis and interpretation by ethnographers will contribute much to the sociology of knowledge and our understanding of the fact that just as those we describe have historically established contexts that define and sustain them, so do our descriptions. The reinterpretations and new considerations they bring can only improve our own understandings of what we do, have done, and can do (e.g., Keesing, 1982).

The task of describing American minorities, especially black Americans, is fraught not only with all the problems these critics have noted, but also with numerous others. It is essential that we see relationships of knowledge and power that both connect those within communities and disconnect them. In an era in which national and state policies strike at the core of intimate family relations – male to female, and grandparent to parent, and parent to child – tracing these con-nections depends on searching out some sense of covariance for role relations, everyday narratives and metaphors, problem-solving strate-gies, and a sense of future. We perhaps further our understanding of social change best when we can understand the relative extent of control that individuals both have and believe they have over the actual texts that enter their leisure and work time. We must be able to specify the nature of continuity between situations and the degree to which actors know they are making choices as they live under the rubric of change. Detailed studies will allow us to consider how collectively sustained are social structures, value systems, and other glosses "on the will to power" (Barth, 1981:83).

We must run the risk of demonstrating that fewer and fewer individuals in some minority groups define themselves in terms of webs of significance they themselves spin, and many may be caught without understanding, interpreting, or transmitting anything like the cultural patterns into which they themselves were socialized. In addition, interpreting in our own society, we cannot forget that what we have viewed as "normal" or stable contexts for children's socialization into a definable group may be ruled out for many under external policy impositions. The novelist George Eliot has warned that no fragment of a life can be "the sample of an even web." Today's social changes for American minority groups reinforce her message and remind us of both the fragility and the unevenness of the web.

Notes

1 In the spring of 1988, less than 6 months after this chapter was written, Sissy and Denny, as well as Lillie Mae and Sissy's younger brothers and sisters, moved together into a three-bedroom two-story public housing apartment. Tapes and notes made in the first 3 months following this move illustrate the power of mulitparty talk from extended family members on the language socialization of Denny. The full range of challenging language that surrounded toddlers on the plaza of Trackton in Sissy's childhood reappeared for Denny in a housing situation that kept the extended family together and provided numerous spaces for out-of-doors play under the watchful eye of family and neighbors. Language data and analysis that provide an update on the language socialization of Denny appear in Heath (1989b).

References

Barth, F. 1981. *Process and form in social life: Selected essays.* Vol. 1. London: Routledge & Kegan Paul.

Baugh, J. 1983. *Black street speech: Its history, structure, and survival.* Austin, TX: University of Texas Press.

Black Family Summit. 1984. Charge to task force on developing and mobilizing resources for supporting the black family. *The Crisis 91*(6):262–302.

Blau, Z. S. 1981. *Black children/white children: Competence, socialization, and social structure.* New York: Free Press.

Clifford, J. 1983. On ethnographic authority. *Representations 1*(2):118–46.

Clifford, J., & Marcus, G. (Eds.). 1986. *Writing culture: The poetics and politics of ethnography.* Berkeley: University of California Press.

Coleman, J. S., & Hoffer, T. 1987. *Public and private high schools: The impact of communities.* New York: Basic Books.

Edelman, M. W. 1987. *Families in peril.* Cambridge, MA: Harvard University Press.

Fernandez, J. W. 1986. The argument of images and the experience of returning to the whole. In V. W. Turner & E. M. Bruner (Eds.), *The anthropology of experience.* Urbana: University of Illinois Press.

Folb, E. A. 1980. *Runnin' down some lines: The language and culture of black teenagers.* Cambridge, MA: Harvard University Press.

Foster, G. W. et al. (Eds.). 1979. *Long-term field research in social anthropology.* New York: Academic Press.

Heath. S. B. 1983. *Ways with words: Language, life, and work in communities and classrooms.* Cambridge: Cambridge University Press.

1989a. The learner as cultural member. In M. L. Rice & R. L. Schiefelbusch (Ed.), *The teachability of language.* Baltimore, MD: Paul H. Brooks.

1989b. Oral and literate traditions among black Americans living in poverty. *American Psychologist 44*(2):45–56.

In press. The sense of being literate: Historical and cross-cultural features. In R. Barr (Ed.), *Handbook of Reading Research.* White Plains, NY: Longman.

Heath, S. B., & Branscombe, A. 1985. Intelligent writing in an audience community. In S. W. Freedom (Ed.), *The acquisition of written language: Revision and response.* Norwood, NJ: Ablex.

1986. The book as narrative prop in language acquisition. In B. B. Schieffelin & P. Gilmore (Eds.), *The acquisition of literacy: Ethnographic perspectives.* Norwood, NJ: Ablex.

Heath, S. B., & Thomas, C. 1984. The achievement of preschool literacy for mother and child. In H. Goelman, A. Obert, & F. Smith (Eds.), *Awakening to literacy.* Exeter, NH: Heinemann Educational Books.

Keesing, R. M. 1982. *Kwaio religion.* New York: Columbia University Press.

1987. Anthropology as interpretive quest. *Current Anthropology 28*(2):161–176.

Lefkowitz, B. 1987. *Tough change: Growing up on your own in America.* New York: Free Press.

Levine, L. W. 1977. *Black culture and black consciousness: Afro-American folk thought from slavery to freedom.* New York: Oxford University Press.

Moses, E. G. 1985. Advantages of being disadvantages: A paradox. *Journal of Negro Education 54*(3):333–343.

Moynihan, D. 1986. *Family and nation.* San Diego: Harcourt Brace Jovanovich.

Mulder, M. B. 1987. Adaptation and evolutionary approaches to anthropology. *Man 22*(1):25–41.

Ochs, E., & Schieffelin, B. B. 1984. Language acquisition and socialization: Three developmental stories and their implications. In R. Shweder & R. LeVine (Eds.), *Culture theory: Essays on mind, self, and emotion.* New York: Cambridge University Press.

Ogbu, J. 1981. School ethnography: A multilevel approach. *Anthroplogy and Education Quarterly 12*(1):3–29.

Rogoff, B., & Wertsch, J. V. (Eds.) 1984. *Children's learning in the "zone of proximal development."* San Francisco: Jossey-Bass.

Scheper-Hughes, N. 1987. The best of two worlds, the worst of two worlds: Reflections on culture and fieldwork among the rural Irish and Pueblo Indians. *Comparative Studies in Society and History 29*(1):56–75.

Schieffelin, B., & Ochs, E. 1986. Language socialization. *Annual Review of Anthropology 15*:163–191.

Schutz, A. 19851. Making music together: A sutdy in social relationship. *Social Research 18*(1):76–97.

Smitherman, G. 1977. *Talkin' and testifyin': The language of black America.* Boston: Houghton Mifflin.

Spencer, M., Brookins, G., & Allen. W (Eds.). 1985. *The social and affective development of black children.* Hillsdale, NJ: Lawrence Erlbaum.

Stack, C. B. 1974. *All our kin: strategies for survival in a black community.* New York: Harper & Row.

Vygotsky, L. S. 1978. *Mind in society: The development of higher psychological processes.* Cambridge, MA: Harvard University Press.

— 1985. *Culture, communication, and cognition: Vygotskian perspectives.* Cambridge: Cambridge University Press.

Whitten, Jr., N. E., & Szwed, J. F. (Eds.). 1970 *Afro-American anthropology: Contemporary perspectives.* New York: Free Press.

Williams, S. B. 1987. A comparative study of black dropouts and black high school graduates in an urban public school system. *Education and Urban Society 19*(3):311–319.

18
Cultural model, identity, and literacy

John U. Ogbu

The question that I address in this chapter is this: Why do some minority groups continue to experience difficulty in acquiring literacy? For the purpose of this essay, I define literacy as the ability to read, write, and compute in the form taught and expected in formal education. Put differently, I consider literacy to be synonymous with academic performance.

Theories of minority school failure

There are competing explanations of the lower school performance of some minority groups like Black Americans. One is the theory of inadequate genetic endowment. Jensen (1969), for instance, argues that because of genetic differences Black Americans not only perform lower than white Americans on IQ tests, but they also perform much lower than whites on those parts of the IQ tests requiring abstract reasoning and other cognitive skills associated with the higher academic performance of the whites. I have pointed out elsewhere (Ogbu, 1978, 1986) that the type of genetic differences that researchers have shown to exist between Blacks and whites do not warrant the type of generalizations made by Jensen. In addition, the so-called twin studies upon which much of Jensen's theory rests have now been called into question (Dorfman, 1978; Hearnshaw, 1979). Other theorists attribute the lower school performance to developmental deficiency. They argue that poor Black children grow up in home environments that do not provide them with the kind of early child experience that enhances the development of appropriate cognitive, linguistic, motivational, and social-emotional skills or competencies for school success (Hess & Shipman, 1967; Riessman, 1962; Hunt, 1969; Ramey & Suarez, 1985). The best criticism of the developmental deficiency theory is the failure of early childhood education programs to transmit to these children white-middle-class types of cognitive, linguistic, motivational, and social-emotional competencies on a relatively permanent basis and to inoculate them against later school failure (Goldberg, 1971; Ogbu, 1978, 1988; Ramey & Campbell, 1987). Institutional deficiency is another explanation. Proponents of this view believe that Black Americans and other involuntary castelike minorities do poorly in school because teachers do not expect them to succeed and because the educational system channels them into inferior schools and inferior classes and courses by means of biased testing and misclassification (U.S. Senate Select Committee, 1972). This account, too, fails to illuminate the problem because it does not explain why other minorities who attend the same inferior schools do relatively better than Blacks and similar minorities (Gibson, 1988; Suarez Orozco, 1987).

Many analysts prefer to attribute the low school performance to social class differences. They argue that Black students do less well in school than white students because more Blacks than whites come from lower-class backgrounds (Bond, 1981). Middle-class Blacks are said to be succeeding in school like their white middle-class counterparts, but lower-class blacks or underclass blacks do not succeed just like lower-class or underclass whites (van den Berghe, 1980; Wilson, 1980). Unfortunately, this argument is not supported by available research data. Generally, research evidence shows that at any given class level, Black students, on the average, do less well in school and on standardized tests than their white counterparts (see Haskins, 1980; Oliver, Rodriguez, & Mickelson 1985; Slade, 1982; Stern, 1986; Wigdor & Garner, 1982). Moreover, although there is a clear pattern for whites, so that children's academic performance level tends to rise as their parents' education (and therefore socioeconomic status) increases, there is no such clear pattern for Blacks. For example, in a recent study of the performance of eighth-grade students in California schools on the CAP test, it was found that (a) the gap between Black students whose parents are highly educated and those whose parents have little education is only about half as great as the gap between such groups among whites; (b) Black students whose parents have advanced degrees score, on the average, below Anglo students whose parents have completed only high school education; and (c) Black students whose parents completed only some college consistently outperformed Black students whose parents are college graduates (Haycock & Navarro, 1988). From this and other studies it is clear that class differences do not fully account for the lower school performance of Black students.

The last theory I wish to consider is that of cultural discontinuities, which posits that the lower school performance of Blacks and similar minorities is caused by cultural conflicts or cultural discontinuities in teaching and learning situations. It has indeed been well established through ethnographic studies that minority children come to school with distinct cognitive styles (Cohen, 1969; Ramirez & Castenada, 1974; Shade, 1982), communication styles (Gumperz, 1981; Kochman, 1982), interaction styles (Erickson & Mohatt, 1982), and learning styles (Philips, 1976, 1983). There is also evidence from research that these differences are associated with teaching and learning difficulties as well as with adjustment difficulties of minority children.

But there are some reasons to be skeptical about the cultural discontinuities explanation (see Ogbu, 1978, 1982, 1987a). One is that the studies on which the theory is based are not comparative in the sense that they do not include studies of other minorities who possess distinct cognitive styles, communication styles, interaction styles, and learning styles but still do relatively well in school. Why and how do such minorities cross cultural boundaries or overcome their cultural and language barriers to do well in school? It is instructive to note, too, that observations in Britain, Malaysia, New Zealand, and Spain suggest that in some instances the minorities who are more different in language and culture from the dominant group are the very ones who are more successful in school (Ogbu & Matute-Bianchi, 1986). Furthermore, cross-cultural studies also suggest that in some cases a minority group that does poorly in school in its country of origin, where its language and culture may be more or less similar to that of the dominant group and of the schools, tends to do quite well in school when its members emigrate to another society where its language and culture are now less similar to that of the dominant group and its schools. This is the case for Japan's Buraku outcastes in Japan and the United States (Ito, 1967).

On the whole, the theories I have reviewed fall short in three ways. One is that they ignore historical and wider societal forces that can encourage or discourage the acquisition of literacy by members of a population. For example, Cressey's study (1980) of literacy in 15th- and 16th-century England shows that the rates of literacy were high in those regions where it was socially and economically beneficial to be literate. The second problem is that the theories do not consider the collective basis of adoption of literacy and of subsequent orientation toward literacy. Instead, they assume that literacy acquisition is a matter of individual ability and effort coupled with family background. Third, just as theorists ignore the collective basis of adoption and orientation to literacy, they also fail to consider the people's own notions about literacy or schooling in the context of the people's interpretations of their social reality.

Rather than try to understand why minorities behave the way they do from the minorities' perceptions and interpretations of their social reality, researchers have been busy "evaluating" the minorities' behaviors in terms of white middle-class perceptions and interpretations of the social reality of white people and the social reality of the minorities as the former understand it. Thus, current theories have generally been constructed without the benefit of what the minorities think; and, from my point of view, they cannot adequately account for the variability in the school performance of Blacks and whites from similar social class backgrounds or the variability in the school performance of minority groups who experience cultural and language differences in school; nor can they explain the variability in the school performance of members of the same minority group from the same social class background, such as the variability in the school performance of Black students from the same social class. I suggest that to construct a more adequate explanation it is necessary to incorporate the perceptions and understandings that Blacks and similar minorities have of their social reality and schooling. To this end, I further suggest that the concept of *cultural model* is a useful tool.

What is a cultural model?

I define a cultural model as an understanding that a people have of their universe – social, physical, or both – as well as their understanding of their behavior in that universe. The cultural model of a population serves its members as a guide in their interpretation of events and elements within their universe; it also serves as a guide to their expectations and actions in that universe or environment. Furthermore, the cultural model underlies their folk theories or folk explanations of recurrent circumstances, events, and situations in various domains of life. It is used by members of the population to organize their knowledge about such recurrent events and situations. Members of a society or its segment develop their cultural model from collective historical experiences. The cultural model is sustained or modified by subsequent events or experiences in their universe. The cultural model has both instrumental and expressive dimensions (Figure 18.1).

Some students of cultural models focus on its cognitive organization – how cultural knowledge or the people's understanding of their universe is organized inside their head – and the relation of that organization to behaviors or actions (Holland & Quinn, 1987). Partly because this school of thought relies so much on "talk" for data, some find the relation of cognitive organization of knowledge or cultural model to behavior – the relation of thought to action – problematic.

My approach is different. I focus on the nature of cultural model as can be learned or constructed from what members of a population say (their "talk") as well as from what they actually do (their "behavior" or "action"), rather than on how their cultural model or cultural knowledge is organized inside their head. From this standpoint, cultural model is more or less similar to what Bohannan calls "the folk system," which he says is built up through perceived experiences and the interpretations of these experiences by the people themselves (Bohannan, 1957:4; Ogbu, 1974:16).

In a plural society like the United States, different segments of the society, such as the dominant whites and racial/ethnic minorities, tend to have their own cultural models – their own understanding of how U.S. society or any of its particular domains "work" and their respective places in that working order. The cultural model of the dominant group, like that of a given minority group, is neither right nor wrong; it is neither better nor worse than others. As Bohannan puts it in his study of the justice system of the Tiv in colonial Nigeria, "The folk systems (or cultural models) are *never* right nor wrong. They exist" (Bohannan, 1957:5), to guide behaviors and interpretations.

In the domain of education or schooling in the United States, the cultural model of the white middle class coexists with the models of Black Americans, American Indians, Mexican Americans, and other minorities. And the cultural model of each group provides its members with the framework for interpreting educational events, situations, and experiences and guides their behaviors in the schooling context. The cultural model of each group is thus implicated to some extent in the relative academic success or failure of the members of the group. Although the theories reviewed earlier may be self-consistent and satisfactory to their proponents, they do not necessarily reflect the realities they attempt to explain because they do not include the cultural models of the minorities and their consequences for the academic behaviors of the minorities (Ogbu, 1974).

In the remainder of this chapter I argue that what distinguishes minority groups that are doing relatively well in school from those that are not is not that the former possess a particular type of genetic endowment; not that they inhabit a cultural environment that enables them to develop the type of cognitive, linguistic, motivational, and socioemotional attributes characteristic of the white middle class; not that they attend schools that are without defects; not that they experience no economic, political, or other discriminatory treatment at the hands of white Americans; and not that they encounter no cultural barriers in the public schools. Rather, the more academically successful minorities differ from the less academically successful minorities in that the former possess a cultural model or understanding of the working of American society and their place in it that is more conducive to school success. And the difference in the cultural models arises from differences in the histories of the minorities.

Minority status and cultural models

The cultural models of minority groups that are relatively successful in school differ from the cultural models of the minorities that are relatively less successful for two reasons: (1) these two types of minorities differ with respect to their initial incorporation into U.S. society; and (2) they differ in the pattern of responses they make to subsequent treatment by white Americans. The relationship between terms of incorporation, white treatment, minority responses, and cultural model is represented in Figure 18.1. I now summarize the differences among the minorities.

Initial terms of incorporation into the United States society. By most accounts the minorities who do well in school are immigrants. *Immigrants* are people who have moved more or less *voluntarily* to the United States because they believed that this would lead to more economic well-being, better overall opportunities, or greater political freedom. These expectations continue to influence the way they perceive and respond to their treatment by white Americans and by the

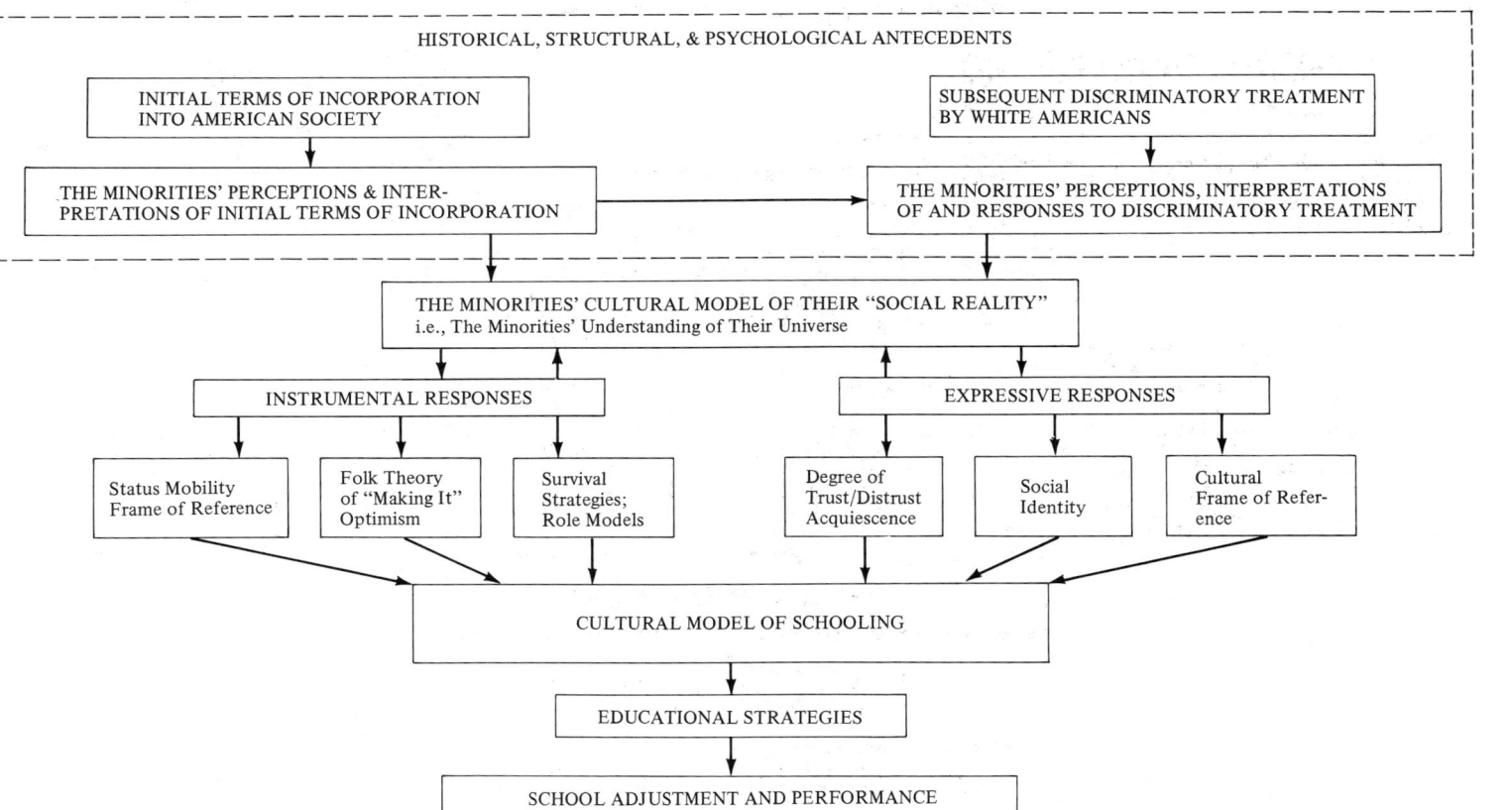

Figure 18.1. Cultural model sociocultural adaptation of minorities.

institutions controlled by the latter. The Chinese in Stockton, California, and the Punjabis in Valleyside, California, are representative examples (Gibson, 1988; Ogbu, 1974).

In contrast, nonimmigrant minorities whom I designate *involuntary minorities* are people who were initially brought into U.S. society through slavery, conquest, or colonization. They usually resent the loss of their former freedom and they perceive the social, political, and economic barriers against them as part of their undeserved oppression. American Indians, Black Americans, Mexican Americans in the Southwest, and Native Hawaiians are examples in the United States. Similar minorities exist in Japan (the Buraku outcastes and Japan's Koreans), as well as in New Zealand (the Maoris).

Response to subsequent treatment. Both the immigrants and the involuntary minorities experience prejudice and discrimination at the hands of white Americans. Both may, for example, be relegated to menial jobs, confronted with social and political barriers, given inferior education; and both may face intellectual and cultural derogation and exclusion from true assimilation into the mainstream of American life. The immigrants tend to interpret these *collective problems* one way and the involuntary minorities another. The immigrants tend to interpret the economic, political, and social barriers against them as more or less temporary problems, as problems they will overcome or can overcome with the passage of time and with hard work, especially by obtaining a good education. The immigrants often compare their situation in the United States with that of their former selves or of their peers "back home." When they make such comparisons they find much evidence to convince them that they have more and better opportunities in the United States for themselves or for their children. Owing to this positive dual frame of reference, the immigrants think that even if they are allowed only marginal jobs they are better off in the United States than they would be in their homeland. Furthermore, they may attribute their exclusion from better jobs to their status as "strangers" or "foreigners," or to the fact that they do not speak good English, or that they were not educated in the United States. As a result, the immigrants tend to share the folk theory of getting ahead with the white middle class (as the immigrants "understand it") and tend to behave accordingly, sometimes even in the face of barriers to opportunity. The immigrants do not necessarily bring such a theory from their homeland; they often accept the white middle-class theory when they arrive in the United States (Suarez-Orozco, 1987).

In contrast, involuntary minorities interpret the same barriers differently. Because they do not have a "homeland situation" to compare with the situation in the United States, they do not interpret their menial jobs and low wages as "better." Neither do they see their present situation as temporary. Quite the contrary, they tend to interpret the discrimination and prejudice against them as more or less permanent and institutionalized. Although they "wish" they could get ahead through education and ability like white Americans, they know they "can't." They have come to realize or believe that it requires more than education, and more than individual effort and hard work to overcome the barriers they encounter in economic, political, and social domains. Consequently, involuntary minorities tend to develop a folk theory of getting ahead that differs from that of white Americans in important respects. For instance, their folk theory tends to stress collective effort as providing the best chances for overcoming the barriers against their advancement.

Not only do the two types of minorities differ in their responses to instrumental barriers; they also differ in their cultural systems, which lead to differences in their responses to cultural and language differences. The cultural system of the immigrants is characterized by *primary cultural differences* in relation to the cultural system of white Americans (Ogbu, 1982). Primary cultural differences are those that existed *before* the immigrants came to the United States. Thus, Punjabi Indians in Valleyside, California, spoke Punjabi; practiced Sikh, Hindu, or Moslem religion; had arranged marriages; and males wore turbans before they came to the United States – where they continue these beliefs and practices to some extent. These cultural beliefs and practices sometimes cause difficulties for the Punjabis not only at school but in their relationship with mainstream society in general (Gibson, 1988). The Punjabis see some of the cultural differences and language differences as *barriers they have to overcome* to achieve the goals of their emigration. And they try to overcome the barriers by learning selectively the language and culture of mainstream Americans *without thinking* that they are giving up their own Punjabi culture and language.

The cultural system of involuntary minorities, on the other hand, tends to be characterized by *secondary cultural differences*, or differences that arose *after* such people became involuntary minorities. Involuntary minorities tend to develop certain beliefs and practices, including particular ways of communicating, as coping mechanisms under subordination. These beliefs and practices may be new creations of the minorities or their reinterpretation of old ones. On the whole, the beliefs and practices making up the secondary cultural differences constitute a new cultural frame of reference or ideal ways of believing and acting that identify one as a bona fide member of the group; and the minorities perceive their way to be not only different from that of their white "oppressors" but also oppositional to the latter. The cultural and language differences emerging under this condition thus serve as a boundary-maintaining mechanism. For this reason involuntary minorities do not interpret the cultural and language differences they encounter in school and society as barriers to be overcome; rather, they interpret them as *symbols of identity*. Their cultural frame of reference based on the secondary cultural differences gives them both a sense of collective social identity and a sense of self-worth.

With regard to social identity, the immigrants bring with them a sense of who they are, which they had before emigration. They perceive their social identity as primarily *different* rather than oppositional vis-à-vis the social identity of white Americans. And they seem to retain this social identity, at least during the first generation, even though they are learning the English language and other aspects of mainstream American culture.

Involuntary minorities, on the other hand, develop a new sense of peoplehood or social identity after their forced incorporation *and* because of subsequent discriminatory treatment *and* denial of true admission into mainstream society; or, in some cases, involuntary minorities develop a new identity because of forced integration into mainstream society (see Castile & Kushner, 1981; DeVos, 1967 1984; Spicer, 1966, 1971). Involuntary minorities do not see their new identity as merely being different from the social identity of their white "oppressors." They see their social identity as being more or less *oppositional* to that of white Americans. The oppositional nature of their interpretation is further reinforced because they perceive and experience treatment by whites as collective and enduring. They tend to believe that they could not expect to be treated like whites regardless of their individual differences in ability, training, or education; differences in place of residence or origin; or differences in economic status or physical appearance (Green, 1981). Furthermore, involuntary minorities know that they cannot easily escape from their birth-ascribed membership in a subordinate and disparaged group by "passing" or by returning to "a homeland" (DeVos, 1967; Ogbu, 1984). The oppositional social identity of involuntary minorities combines with their oppositional or ambivalent cultural frame of reference to make cross-cultural learning or "crossing cultural boundaries" difficult. For them to behave in a manner falling within the white American cultural frame of reference appears threatening to their own minority identity and security. Such behavior not only gives rise to peer pressure restraining them from doing so but also "affective disonnance" among the individuals concerned (DeVos, 1967, 1984).

One other element in the cultural model to be considered is the degree of trust that the minorities have for white Americans and the societal institutions the latter control. Although the two types of minorities may face similar problems in their relationship with white Americans and American institutions, they differ in interpretations of the problems and in the degree of trust in dealing with whites in trying to resolve the problems. It seems that the immigrants tend to acquiesce more and to rationalize the prejudice and discrimination against them by saying, for example, that they are "strangers in a foreign land (and) have no choice but to tolerate prejudice and discrimination" (Gibson, 1988). In their relationship with the schools the immigrants tend to rationalize their accommodation by saying that they came to the United States to give their children the opportunity to get an American education. Furthermore, the immigrants frequently find their relationship with the public schools to be "better" than their relationship with the schools of their homeland. They speak favorably of the fact that their children receive free textbooks and supplies in the U.S. public schools (Suarez-Orozco, 1987).

Involuntary minorities find no justification for the prejudice and discrimination against them in school and society other than the fact that they are minorities. A deep distrust runs through the relationship between involuntary minorities and white Americans as well as between the minorities and the public schools. In the case of Black Americans, for example, one finds many historical episodes that have left Blacks with the feeling that white Americans and their institutions cannot be trusted (Ogbu, 1987b). Public schools in the inner city are not particularly trusted to provide Black children with the "right education." This distrust arises partly from perceptions of past and current discrimination which, in the view of Black Americans, is more or less institutionalized and permanent. The discriminatory treatment has, of course, been documented throughout the history of Black Americans and their education (Bond, 1966, 1969; Kluger, 1977; Ogbu, 1978; Weinberg, 1977).

In sum, the cultural models of voluntary/ immigrant minorities and those of involuntary minorities differ in these key elements, namely, a frame of reference for comparing present status and future possibilities (i.e., a status mobility frame), a theory of getting ahead, a collective identity, a cultural frame of reference for judging appropriate behavior, and the degree of trust of white Americans and the institutions they control. I now explain how these elements might differentially influence the school orientations and performance of immigrant and involuntary minorities.

Cultural models and minority schooling

The contents of the cultural models of the minorities – status mobility frame, folk theory of getting ahead in the United States, survival strategies, trust, identity, and cultural frame of reference – enter into the schooling process by influencing the educational attitudes and strategies or behaviors of the minorities. The nature of the contents of the immigrants' cultural model (Figure 18.2) leads them to adopt attitudes and strategies more conducive to school success than is the case among the involuntary minorities (Figure 18.3). The immigrants have a dual status mobility frame and a folk theory of getting ahead that stresses the importance of school success by adopting appropriate academic attitudes and working hard. As already noted, the immigrants tend to believe that they have more and better opportunities to succeed in the United States than in their countries of origin and that, indeed, they may have come to the United States precisely to give their children an "American education" so that they can get ahead in the United States

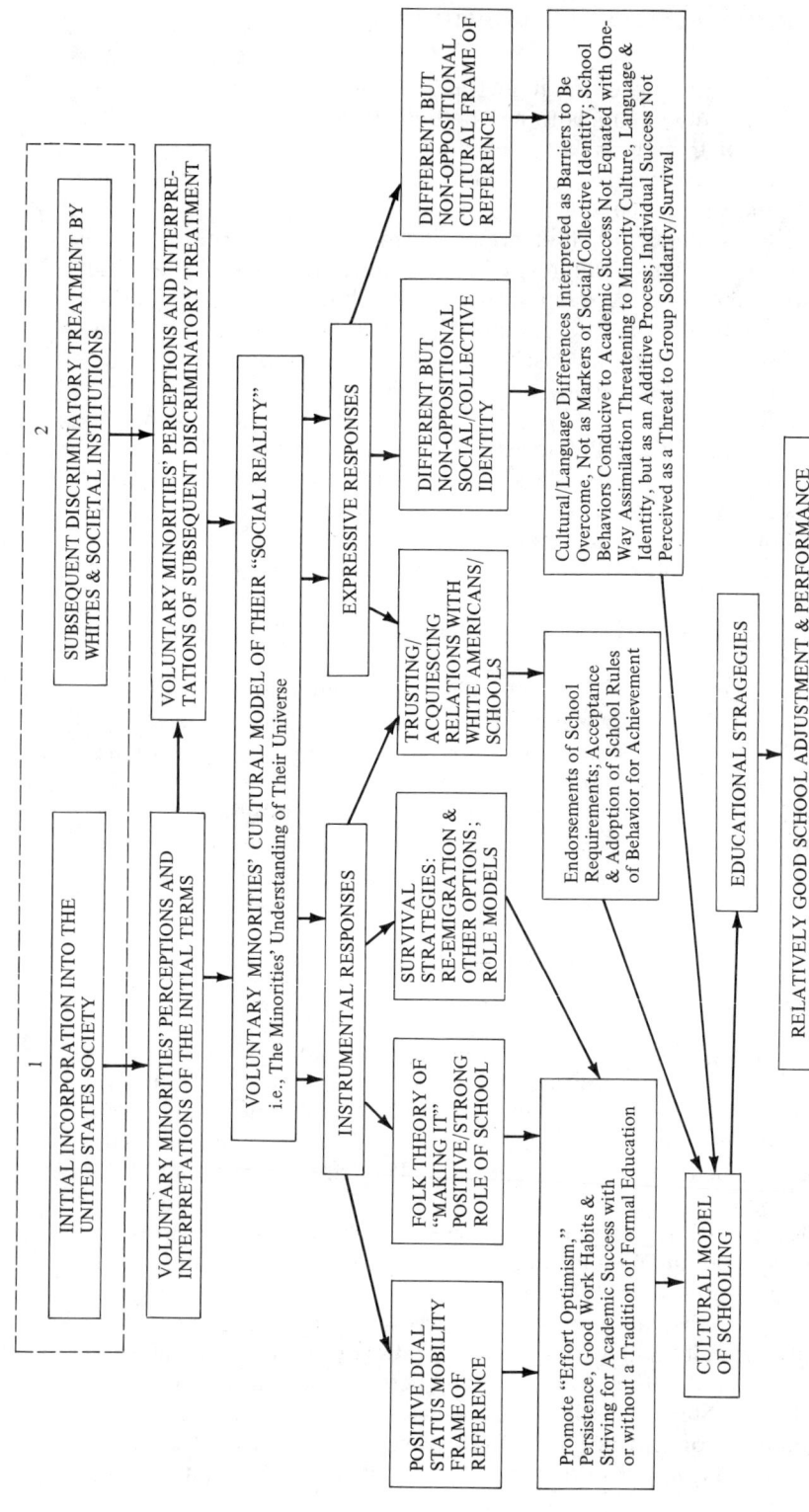

Figure 18.2. Cultural model and the school adjustment and performance of voluntary minorities.

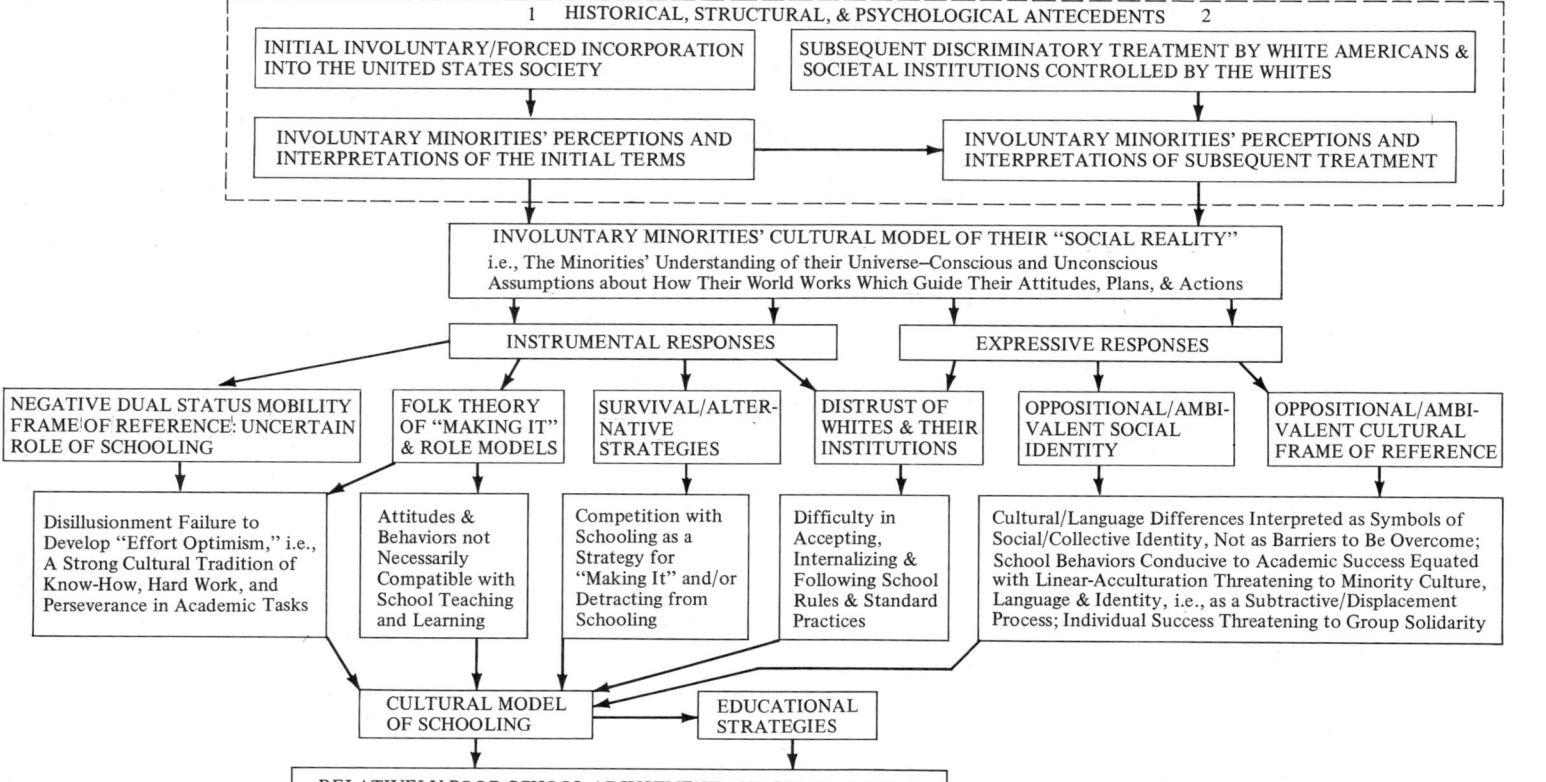

Figure 18.3. Cultural model and the school adjustment and performance of involuntary minorities.

or "back home," if they choose to return to their homeland. Thus, immigrant parents stress education and take steps to ensure that their children behave in a manner conducive to school success. For their part, the children – whether they are Chinese, Central and South Americans, Koreans, or Punjabis – appear to share their parents' attitudes toward an "American education," take their school work seriously, work hard, and persevere (Gibson, 1988; Kim-Eun-Young, 1987; Ogbu, 1983a; Suarez-Orozco, 1987; Ow, 1976).

The nonoppositional identity and nonoppositional cultural frame of reference of the immigrants permit them to cross cultural and language boundaries in the school context without peer pressure or "affective dissonance." They enable the immigrants to distinguish what they have to learn in order to achieve the goals of their emigration – such as the English language and the standard practices of the school and the workplace – *from* other aspects of mainstream American culture that may threaten their own minority language, culture, and identity. Another crucial point is that the immigrants interpret the language and cultural features necessary for school success – the language and cultural differences they encounter in school – as barriers that need to be overcome if they are to achieve school success and their long-range goals of future employment, economic well-being, and other benefits. Therefore, the immigrants do not go to school expecting the schools to teach them in their native language and culture, except as a temporary measure necessary for transition. Rather, they expect and are willing to learn the English language and the standard practices of the school. This does not mean that the immigrants do not experience problems in connection with cultural and language differences; the point is that immigrant children and their parents and communities perceive the language and cultural conflicts as temporary problems they have to overcome with appropriate help from the school.

Finally, the immigrants' acquiescing and somewhat trusting relationship with the teachers and other school personnel also promotes school success. Three factors account for this relative trust and acquiescence. One is that the immigrants consider the schools in the United States to be better than the schools of their homelands. Their comparative frame of reference is the school they left behind, not the school in the white suburb in the United States. Another reason is that the immigrants think that they are treated better by the U.S. public school personnel than the school personnel of their homeland (Suarez-Orozco, 1987). Finally, as noted previously, even where the immigrants experience prejudice and discrimination, which they certainly resent, they tend to rationalize such treatments in a way that does not discourage them from striving to succeed in school (Gibson, 1988). The overall impression one gains from ethnographic studies is that the immigrants teach their children to trust public school officials, accept, internalize and follow school rules and standard practices for academic success and that the children more or less do what their parents ask them to do.

In their dual status mobility frame, involuntary minorities, such as Black Americans, compare themselves unfavorably with Americans. And when they do they ususally conclude that they are worse off than they should be in spite of their education and ability. Thus, in their comparison the role of education is uncertain.

The folk theory of getting ahead developed by involuntary minorities emphasizes the importance of education, but this verbal endorsement is not usually accompanied by appropriate necessary effort. This is due, in part, to the fact that historically involuntary minorities have not received the same rewards for their educational effort as their white peers in terms of jobs and wages. Eventually, it seems, these minorities came to see their treatment in the job market as a part of institutionalized discrimination that they could not overcome merely by getting an education (Ogbu, 1981a). One result is that the minorities did not develop "effort optimism" toward academic work. That is, they did not develop a strong tradition of cultural know-how, hard work, and perseverance toward academic tasks. Another point to be elaborated later is that in the case of Black Americans, experience seemed to have taught them that collective action rather than individual perseverance offers the best chances for advancement (Ogbu, 1983b). Moreover, under this circumstance, involuntary minority parents appear to give their children contradictory messages about getting ahead through school success. The problem is that, on the one hand, the parents tell their children to get a good education and verbally encourage them to do well in school; those who can, help with homework; some reward their children with money for good report cards and beat them for poor report cards. On the other hand, the actual texture of the lives of these parents – in terms of low-level jobs, underemployment and unemployment – also comes through strongly, reproducing a second kind of message powerful enough to undo their exhortations. For, unavoidably, involuntary minority parents discuss their problems with the system as well as the problems of their relatives, friends, and neighbors in the presence of their children. The result is that involuntary minority children increasingly become disillusioned about their ability to succeed in adult life through the mainstream strategy of schooling.

The folk theory of getting ahead stresses other means than schooling, namely, survival strategies within and outside the mainstream economic system. The survival strategies affect the schooling of involuntary minority children in several ways. One is that some survival strategies generate attitudes and behaviors that are not conducive to good classroom teaching and learning. When survival strategies, such as collective struggle – in the case of Black Americans – succeed in increasing the pool of jobs and other resources for the minority community, they may encourage minority youths to work hard in school. But such success can also lead the youths to blame "the system" and to rationalize their lack of serious schoolwork effects. Furthermore, as indicated above, the effectiveness of collective struggle historically may have led some minorities like Black Americans to endorse collective action, instead of individual perseverance for education as offering the best chances for advancement. This pooling of efforts also probably weakens realistic perceptions and sidetracks the pursuit of schooling as a strategy for self-advancement. Clientship or Uncle Tomming (among Blacks) and Tio Tacoing (among Mexican Americans) is dysfunctional for minority youths because it does not create good role models for school success through hard work. Clientship teachers minority children manipulative knowledge, skills, and attitudes used by their parents in dealing with white Americans and their institutions. As the children become familiar with other survival strategies like hustling, pimping, and drug dealing, their attitudes toward schooling are adversely affected. For example, in the norms that support some of these strategies the work ethic is reversed by the insistence that one should make it without working, especially without "doing the white man's thing" (Ogbu, 1974, 1986). For students who are into hustling, social interactions in the classroom are seen as opportunities for exploitation, that is, opportunities to gain prestige by putting the other person or persons down. This may lead to class disruptions and suspensions (Ogbu, 1981a, 1987b).

Another problem is that the survival strategies can become serious competitors with schooling as ways of getting ahead, leading young people to channel their time and efforts into nonacademic activities. This is particularly true as involuntary minority children get older and become more aware of how some adult members of their communities "make it" without mainstream school credentials and employment (Bouie, 1981; Ogbu, 1974). For example, there is some evidence that among Black Americans, many young people view sports and entertainment, rather than education, as the way to get ahead; and their perceptions are reinforced by the realities they observe in the community and society at large and by the media. Black youths know that Blacks are overrepresented in the lucrative sports like baseball, basketball, and football. They may not know the exact earnings of Black players, but it is common knowledge that the average annual salary in teams of the National Basketball Association is over $300,000 and in those of the National Football Association it is over $90,000. It is also common knowledge that many of the superstars who earn between one and two million dollars a year are Black, people who probably were not particularly academically successful while they were in school. Furthermore, even though the number of such athletes may not be high, the media makes them and Black entertainers more visible to Black youths than they do Black lawyers, doctors, engineers, and scientists. There is some preliminary evidence, too, to suggest that Black parents encourage their children's athletic activities in the belief that such activities will lead to careers in professional sports (Wong, 1987).

Under this circumstance, involuntary minority children, like their parents, verbally express high interest in doing well in school and in obtaining good credentials for future employment in the mainstream economy. But they do not necessarily match their wishes and aspirations with effort, even though they know that to do well in school they would have to work hard. Black and Mexican American students in Stockton, California, whom I studied, for example, quite correctly explained that Chinese, Japanese, and white students in their schools were more academically successful than they themselves because the former expended more time and effort in their schoolwork, both at school and at home. The lack of serious academic attitudes and efforts seems to increase as involuntary minority students get older and apparently become aware of the reality that, as members of a subordinate minority group, they have a history of limited future opportunities for getting good jobs even with a good education. Simultaneously, they divert more and more of their time and effort into nonacademic activities.

The way voluntary minorities interpret the language and cultural differences they encounter in school adversely affects their ability to cross cultural and language boundaries in learning situations. As I pointed out previously, involuntary minorities interpret the cultural and language differences as markers of group or social identity to be maintained. This interpretation is due to their oppositional or ambivalent social identity and cultural frame of reference. In this context, the minorities do not appear to be able to make a clear distinction, as the immigrants do – as already mentioned – between what they have to learn to enhance their school success for future employment and other benefits (such as learning standard English, other aspects of school curriculum, and the standard practices of the school) *from* other aspects of white American culture and language or the cultural frame of reference of their white "oppressors," which may be detrimental to their own minority language, culture, and identity. Because they tend to equate standard English, the curriculum, and the standard school practices with white American culture and identity, the minorities more or less consciously and unconsciously resist learning these things. Youths who manifest attitudes and behaviors conducive to academic success are accused by their peers of "acting white" or, in the case of Black students, of being "Uncle Toms" (Fordham & Ogbu, 1986; Petroni, 1970) or of being "Tio Tacos," in the case of Mexican Americans (Matute-Bianchi, 1986). A case in point can be found in an ethnographic study of 33 Black high school students in Washington. DC (Fordham & Ogbu, 1986). The students regarded many behaviors associated with high academic achievement – speaking Standard English, studying long hours, striving to get good grades – as "acting white." Students who were known to engage in such behaviors were labeled "brainiacs," ridiculed, and ostracized as people who had abandoned the group. A number of bright students indicated in interviews that they had chosen to put "brakes" on their academic effort in order to avoid being labeled and harassed. Those who continued to try to succeed academically felt compelled to engage in behaviors that discredited studying or working hard. For example, they verbally belittled the value of schoolwork when among their peers; they did not speak up in class; they joined athletic teams or took part in other peer-approved extracurricular activities, and some behaved like class clowns. Some students got "bullies" to protect them against harassment by other students and in return they helped the "bullies" with their homework. These students were consciously aware of the choices they were making and they were careful not to brag about their academic success (see Fordham, 1985; Fordham & Ogbu, 1986; Ogbu, 1981b).

Furthermore, as DeVos (1976) has noted, even in the absence of such peer pressure, some involuntary minority students may not adopt serious academic attitudes or engage in behaviors conducive to academic success – that is, they may not persevere in academic tasks. The reason is that the students will have internalized their group's interpretations of such attitudes and behaviors as characteristic of and appropriate for their white "oppressors" and not safe for them. They also refrain from such attitudes and behaviors in part because they are uncertain that they would be received by White Americans if they succeed in learning to "act white" and thereby lost the support of members of their own group. This state of being, which DeVos calls "affective dissonance," keeps involuntary minority children from striving to succeed academically or in other mainstream activities. The dilemma of involuntary minority students, as Petroni (1970) rightly notes, is that they have to choose between striving for academic success and maintaining their minority identity and cultural frame of reference, a choice that does not seem to face the immigrants.

Involuntary minorities' distrust of white Americans and the schools that the latter control also adds to the lower academic success problem. Involuntary minorities distrust the public schools more than the immigrants do because the former do not have the advantage of a dual frame of reference that allows the immigrants to compare the public schools with the schools they knew "back home." Therefore, involuntary minorities evaluate their inferior and/or segregated schools more negatively. Since they do not trust the public schools and the white Americans controlling them, the minorities are usually skeptical that the schools can educate their children well. And this skepticism is communicated to children through family and community discussions as well as through public debate over the education of minority children in general or debates over particular issues in minority education, such as school desegregation. Another problem is that involuntary minorities – including parents, other adult members of the minority community, and students – tend to question school rules of behavior and standard practices rather than accept and follow them as the immigrants do. Indeed, involuntary minorities not infrequently interpret the school rules and practices as an imposition of a white cultural frame of reference that does not necessarily meet their "real educational needs."

My ethnographic research in Stockton provides several examples of instances in which Blacks and Mexican Americans expressed skepticism about what they were learning in school and related tasks. One occasion involved an incident at a public meeting after a riot in a predominantly minority high school. The question here was the "relevance" of a high school history textbook, *The Land of the Free*, to the experiences of various minority groups in the state of California. Another concerned the value of a preschool curriculum stressing social development rather than academic learning. Still another was the real purpose of job placement tests, especially in the civil service. The minorities in this case believed that such tests, whether given at school or elsewhere, whether given by white Americans or their minority representatives, are designed to keep them down.

The problems associated with the distrustful relationship become more complicated when one considers the tendency of the schools to approach the education of involuntary minorities defensively. I have suggested (Ogbu, 1988) that under this circumstance involuntary minority parents would have difficulty teaching their children to accept and follow school rules of behavior and standard practices that lead to academic success, and involuntary minority children, particularly the older ones, would have difficulty accepting and following the school rules of behavior and standard practices. In fact, during my ethnographic interviews, Black and Mexican American youths admitted that they do not always listen to their parents' advice concerning their school behaviors (Ogbu, 1974, 1984, 1987b, 1988).

Conclusion

I began this chapter by asking why some minority groups are more successful than others in acquiring literacy. Why are some minorities more academically successful than others? In the foregoing pages I have argued that the more successful minorities are immigrants and the less successful minorities are involuntary minorities. The immigrants are more successful in part because the initial terms of their incorporation into U.S. society enable them to form a cultural model conducive to academic striving and success. The initial terms of the incorporation of involuntary minorities, on the other hand, are different and compel them to interpret their subsequent experiences in U.S. society differently. Together, their interpretations of both the initial terms of their incorporation into U.S. society and their subsequent treatment by white Americans lead them to form a cultural model less conducive to academic striving and success. In other words, the contrasting historical experiences of the immigrants and the involuntary minorities result in contrasting cultural models and social identities that influence their school experiences or transmission and acquisition of literacy differently.[1]

Notes

1 My argument in this chapter should not be misinterpreted. I do not mean that minorities are solely or largely responsible for their own school success or

school failure. Rather, my point is that in addition to the role of the larger society and the school (Ogbu, 1974, 1978), minorities also contribute to their own school success or school failure because of the nature of their cultural model.

References

Bohannan, P. (1957). *Justice and Judgment among the Tiv*. London: Oxford University Press.

Bond, G. C. (1981). Social Economic Status and Educational Achievement: A Review Article. *Anthropology and Education Quarterly 12*(4):227–257.

Bond, H. M. (1966). *The Education of the Negro in the American Social Order*. New York: Octagon.

———(1969). *Negro Education in Alabama: A Study in Cotton and Steel*. New York: Atheneum.

Bouie, A. (1981). *Student Perceptions of Behavior and Misbehavior in the School Setting: An Exploratory Study and Discussion*. San Francisco: Far West Laboratory for Educational Research and Development.

Castile, G. P., & Kushner, G. (Eds.). (1981). *Persistent Peoples: Cultural Enclaves in Perspective*. Tuscon: University of Arizona Press.

Cohen, R. A. (1969). Conceptual Styles, Culture Conflict, and Non-Verbal Test of Intelligence. *American Anthropologist 71*:828–856.

Cressey, D. (1980). *Literacy and the Social Order: Reading and Writing in Tudor and Stuart England*. Cambridge, MA: Harvard University Press.

DeVos, G. A. (1967). Essential Elements of Caste: Psychological Determinants in Structural Theory. In G. A. DeVos & H. Wagatsuma (Eds.), *Japan's Invisible Race: Caste in Culture and Personality* (pp. 332–384). Berkeley: University of California Press.

———(1984). *Ethnic Persistence and Role Degradation: An Illustration from Japan*. Paper presented at the American-Soviet Symposium on Contemporary Ethnic Processes in the USA and the USSR, New Orleans, LA, April 14–16.

Dorfman, D. D. (1978). The Cyril Burt Question: New Findings. *Science 201*:1177–1186.

Erickson, F., & Mohatt, J. (1982). Cultural Organization of Participant Structure in Two Classrooms of Indian Students. In G. D. Spindler (Ed.), *Doing the Ethnography of Schooling: Educational Anthropology in Action* (pp. 132–175). New York: Holt.

Fordham, S. (1985). Black Student School Success as Related to Fictive Kinship. Final Report to the National Institute of Education, Washington, DC Unp. Ms.

Fordham, S., & Ogbu, J. U. (1986). Black Students' School Success: Coping with the Burden of "Acting White." *The Urban Review: Issues and Ideas in Public Education 18*(3):176–206.

Gibson, M. A. (1988). *Accommodation without Assimilation: Punjabi Sikh Immigrants in an American High School and Community*. Ithaca: Cornell University Press.

Goldberg, M. L. (1971). Socio-Psychological Issues in the Education of the Disadvantaged. In A. H. Passow (Ed.), *Urban Education in the 1970s* (pp. 61–93). New York: Teachers College Press.

Green, V. (1981). Blacks in the United States: The Creation of an Enduring

People? In G. P. Castile & G. Kushner (Eds.), *Persistent Peoples: Cultural Enclaves in Perspective* (pp. 69–77). Tucson: University of Arizona Press.

Gumperz, J. J. (1981). Conversational Inferences and Classroom Learning. In J. Green & C. Wallat (Eds.), *Ethnographic Approaches to Face-to-Face Interaction*. Norwood, NJ: Ablex.

Haskins, R. (1980). Race, Family Income, and School Achievement. Unp. Ms.

Haycock, K., & Navarro, S. (1988). Unfinished Business: A Report from the Achievement Council. Oakland, CA. Unp. Ms.

Hearnshaw, L. S. (1979). *Cyril Burt, Psychologist*. Ithaca: Cornell University Press.

Hess, R. D., & Shipman, V. C. (1967). Early Experience and the Socialization of Cognitive Modes in Children. In G. R. Medinnus, H. Keely, K. Mueller, & E. Rutherford (Eds.), *Problems of Children and Youth in Modern Society*. New York: Selected Academic Readings.

Holland, D., & Quinn, N. (Eds.). (1987). *Cultural Models in Language and Thought*. Cambridge: Cambridge University Press.

Hunt, J. McV. (1969). *The Challenge of Incompetence and Poverty: Papers on the Role of Early Education*. Urbana: University of Illinois Press.

Ito, H. (1967). Japan's Outcastes in the United States. In G. A. DeVos and H. Wagatsuma (Eds.), *Japan's Invisible Race: Caste in Culture and Personality* (pp. 200–221). Berkeley: University of California Press.

Jensen, A. R. (1969). How Much Can We Boost IQ and Scholastic Achievement? *Harvard Educational Review 39*:1–123.

Kim-Eun-Young (1987). *Folk Theory and Cultural Model among Korean Immigrants in the U.S.: Explanation for Immigrants' Economic Life and Children's Education/Schooling*. Special Project, Dept. of Anthropology, University of California, Berkeley. Unp. Ms.

Kluger, R. (1977). *Simple Justice*. New York: Vintage Books.

Kochman, T. (1982). *Black and White Styles in Conflict*. Chicago: University of Chicago Press.

Matute-Bianchi, M. E. (1986). Ethnic Identities and Patterns of School Success and Failure among Mexican-Descent and Japanese-American Students in a California High School: An Ethnographic Analysis. *American Journal of Education 95*(1):235–255.

Ogbu, J. U. (1974). *The Next Generation: An Ethnography of Education in an Urban Neighborhood*. New York: Academic Press.

—— (1978). Minority Education and Caste: The American System in Cross-Cultural Perspective. New York: Academic Press.

—— (1981a). *Schooling in the Ghetto: A Cultural-Ecological Perspective on Community and Home Influences*. ED 252 270. ERIC Clearinghouse.

—— (1981b). Origins of Human Competence: A Cultural-Ecological Perspective. *Child Development 52*:413–429.

—— (1982). Cultural Discontinuities and Schooling. *Anthropology and Education Quarterly 13*(4):290–307.

—— (1983a). Minority Status and Schooling in Plural Societies. *Comparative Education Review 27*(2):168–190.

—— (1983b). Schooling the Inner City. *Society 21*(1):75–79.

—— (1984). *Understanding Community Forces Affecting Minority Students' Academic Effort*. Paper prepared for the Achievement Council, Oakland, CA. Unp. Ms.

—— (1986). The Consequences of the American Caste System. In U. Neisser

(Ed.), *The School Achievement of Minority Children: New Perspectives* (pp. 19-56). Hillsdale, NJ: Lawrence Erlbaum.

(1987a). Variability in Minority School Performance: A Problem in Search of an Explanation. *Anthropology and Education Quarterly 18*(4):312-334.

(1987b). Opportunity Structure, Culture Boundaries, and Literacy. In J. A. Langer (Ed.), *Language, Literacy, and Culture: Issues of Society and Schooling* (pp. 149-177). Norwood, NJ: Ablex.

(1988). Diversity and Equity in Public Education: Community Forces and Minority School Adjustment and Performance. In R. Haskins & D. MaCrae (Eds.), *Policies for America's Public Schools: Teachers, Equity, and Indicators* (pp. 127-170). Norwood, NJ: Ablex.

Ogbu, J. U., & Matute-Bianchi, M. E. (1986). Understanding Sociocultural Factors: Knowledge, Identity and School Adjustment. In *Beyond Language: Social and Cultural Factors in Schooling Language Minority Students* (pp. 73-142). Bilingual Education Office, California State Department of Education, Sacramento.

Oliver, M. L., Rodriguez, C., & Mickelson, R. A. (1985). Black and Brown in White: The Social Adjustment and Academic Performance of Chicano and Black Students in a Predominantly White University. *Urban Review 17*(2):3-24.

Ow, P. (1976). *The Chinese and the American Educational System*. Special Project, Dept. of Anthropology, University of California, Berkeley. Unp. Ms.

Petroni, F. A. (1970). "Uncle Toms": White Stereotypes in the Black Movement. *Human Organization 29*(4):260-266.

Philips, S. U. (1976). Commentary: Access to Power and Maintenance of Ethnic Identity as Goals of Multicultural Education. In M. A. Gibson (Ed.). *Anthropology and Education Quarterly 7*(4):30-32.

(1983). *The Invisible Culture: Communication in Classroom and Community on the Warm Springs Indian Reservation*. New York: Longman.

Ramey, C. T., & Campbell, F. A. (1987). The Carolina Abecedarian Project: An Educational Experiment Concerning Human Malleability. In J. J. Gallagher & C. T. Ramey (Eds.), *The Malleability of Children* (pp. 115-125). Baltimore, MD: Paul H. Brookes.

Ramey, C. T., & Suarez, T. M. (1985). Early Intervention and the Early Experience Paradigm: Toward a Better Framework for Social Policy. *Journal of Children in Contemporary Society 7*(1):3-13.

Ramirez, M., & Castenada, A. (1974). *Cultural Democracy, Bicognitive Development and Education*. New York: Academic Press.

Riessman, F. (1962). *The Culturally Deprived Child*. New York: Harper and Row.

Shade, B. J. (1982). Afro-American Patterns of Cognition. Madison: Wisconsin Center for Educational Research. Unp. Ms.

Slade, M. (1982). Aptitude, Intelligence or What? *New York Times*, October 24, 1982.

Spicer, E. H. (1966). The Process of Cultural Enclavement in Middle America. *36th Congress of International de Americanistas, Seville 3*:267-279.

(1971). Persistent Cultural Systems: A Comparative Study of Identity Systems That Can Adapt to Contrasting Environments. *Science 174*:795-800.

Stern, S. P. (1986). School-Imposed Limits on Black Family "Participation": A View from Within and Below. Paper presented at the 85th annual meeting of the American Anthropological Association, Philadelphia, PA. December 4–7.

Suarez-Orozco, M. M. (1987). "Becoming Somebody": Central American Immigrants in U.S. Inner-City Schools. *Anthropology and Education Quarterly 18*(4):287–299.

U.S. Senate, Select Committee on Equal Educational Opportunity (1972). *Toward Equal Educational Opportunity: Report.* Washington, DC: U.S. Government Printing Office.

van den Berghe, P. (1980). A Review of Minority Education and Caste. *Comparative Education Review 24*(1):126–130.

Weinberg, M. (1977). *A Chance to Learn: A History of Race and Education in the United States.* New York: Cambridge University Press.

Wigdor, A. K., & Garner, W. R. (Eds.). (1982). *Ability Testing: Uses, Consequences, and Controversies.* Part 11: Documentation. Washington, DC: National Academy Press.

Wilson, W. J. (1980). Race, Class, and Public Policy in Education. A Lecture Given at the National Institute of Education Annual Vera Brown Memorial Seminar Series, Washington, DC, June 10.

Wong, M. L. (1987). Education Versus Sports. Special Project, University of California, Berkeley. Unp. Ms.

19

Mother love and child death in Northeast Brazil

Nancy Scheper-Hughes

I have seen death without weeping
the destiny of the Northeast is death
Cattle they kill
to the people they do something worse.

Tropical sadness

1965

I don't remember the blood, except that later on, much later I was trying to rub it off with spit and the palm of my hand. But my mouth was dry and it kept escaping me, sliding further up my arm until that night when the water boy came I could finally erase it....

And I don't remember saying, "Força, força, menina – push hard now, girl." Because she didn't have to, hardly, and suddenly the slippery blue-grey thing was in my hands, cold and wet as it slid over them. And they were dirty because it was lunchtime and the sticky bean stuff was still on them....

I knew I had to pull the tight, tense rope away from its scrawny neck, but it resisted and coiled in my hands like an angry telephone cord.

This chapter was written while the author was a Guggenheim Fellow and a Fellow at the Center for Advanced Study in the Behavioral Sciences, Stanford, California. The support of both and of the John D. and Catherine T. MacArthur Foundation is gratefully Acknowledged. It is based on a paper prepared for the 1987 Chicago Symposium on Culture and Human Development, University of Chicago, November 5–7, 1987. I am particularly grateful to the organizers of the symposium, especially Gilbert Herdt and Richard Shweder, for their incisive critiques and pertinent suggestions concerning the analysis and the presentation of difficult materials. In addition, Peter Homans (also a most creative discussant) opened up new areas of inquiry for me with his insistence that I sharpen my interpretations of grief, mourning, and disenchantment – most of which will, however, be treated in a forthcoming book. My husband, D. Micheal Hughes, and my daughter, Jennifer Scheper-Hughes, were field collaborators, responsible for much of the counting of child deaths in the cartório civil and who, together with my younger children, Sarah and Nathanael, gave the moral support necessary for the completion of the project.

"Scissors, scissors," I demanded, but the old women shook their heads, looking absently from one to the other, until Antonieta, Lourdes's sister, arrived sheepishly with a pair that had disappeared from my medical kit some weeks before. Lourdes wasn't crying, but the other one – the so little one – was. I couldn't look at it. It was me who had found Lourdes the job clearing the fields where she met Milton, who had just gotten out of Itamaraca, seven years on rape. Only this time it wasn't and he had gotten off scott-free while she came home with this belly. "Worms," she had told us, but of course we knew differently.

I laid it out on the lumpy straw mattress between her spread legs which had gone limp. It was dark and for this I was thankful. No windows, no door; just an opening at one side covered by Food for Peace bean sacks. Too dark to see the expression on her pinched-in little face with its matted, sweaty hair pasted against pale cheeks and forehead. But not too dark to see that her hurt mouth hung, like her thighs, loosely open, expectant.

I wanted to put out the smokey wood fire that burned in the corner and in the back of my throat. But there was no water in the jug. The smell of hot flesh and dried blood filled the single room. With Valdimar digging outside and hitting a stone, he stops to call out: "Is it here yet?" And the old women, clucking together in the corner by the fire and bent over a faintly squawking chicken, laugh and call back: "Oh-che, Valdimar, stop digging then. Do you think it is for a cow?" Inside I hear the wings flap madly one last time against the tin can, and then it is silent.

The cord stopped pulsating. It lay thin and cool between my fingers where I would cut. "Where's De-De with my first-aid kit?" I asked the old women irritably, but they were more interested in bleeding the chicken for the birthing meal. At least the smell of burning feathers, scorched off by the fire, was better than Lourdes's smell.

Lourdes squirmed on the bed and began to thrash her thin arms about. I wouldn't wait for De-De, but I needed string. There was my old key string, knotted and dirty in my pocket, but I would use it. My hand didn't want to cut, but even under the dull edge of the scissors it was less resistant than I had anticipated, but the sensation of hidden flesh giving way was at my fingers and up my spine, and I couldn't stop the screaming inside.

I called for help because the rest of it wouldn't come and her insides had gone slack, but the old women were gathered and nodding around the baby now, tied up in scraps of yellowed satin, torn ribbon, and lace. So little, I couldn't took. Outside I could hear Valdimar as his shovel again scraped against rock. My hands forced down into her soft belly while Antonieta pulled. Lourdes's mouth was open and crooked and no sound emerged until finally it slid out. With it in my hands, whole and yet in parts, folded in toward the center, I handed it to the women who wrapped it in a cloth and passed it through the opening to the waiting Valdimar. As if he were the father, so tender he was for her.

And it was blessedly cool and dark where I slid down. Cool and dark and wrapped up in the hollow, I am lifted high, high up into the Jesus tree behind our house. Hidden in green and brown. No one can see....

Valdimar – his black face twisted and lame is not really always laughing – is come to tell me softly what I already know. My head hurts, but the wet cloth feels cool against the afternoon air. Will I come and eat chicken with Lourdes? No, although I am hungry, I will wait, and will only come later when it is time to bury the baby. In its bits of faded silk and ribbon. So tiny and waxen, I will not look. In its cardboard box, covered with purple tissue and a silver paper cross (Valdimar will make it.) I am not deaf. I have heard the bells of Nossa Senhora das Dores, and they have touched the void. *De profundis clamavi ad te, Domine.*

I will not lose hold. There is much to be done. What time is it? My papers lay untouched where they had fallen and scattered on the mud floor. From my open window I can see Antonieta's wash caught up in a pretty white bundle, cradled in the tin basin outside her hut. And it's June and the tomatoes at home hang ripe and heavy on their vines.

So I slowly pick up the papers, watching Valdimar limp painfully up the hill. It is good to hear the milk goats knocking on the rocks outside my door. And it is even better to hear Antonieta sing and to see her swinging her full hips on the way down to the river, laundry poised gracefully on her head. And it very good, indeed, to think of Valdimar drinking and laughing and dancing to make Lourdes smile. But it is best of all to listen to the fat tomatoes split and fall, unpicked, from their vines.

1987

Lourdes who was 15 years old at the time of this story, had nine more pregnancies, seven of them by the rascal Milton, and two more by an older widower, Jaime, with whom she is now living. Only five of her children survived infancy and one of these, an initially rejected and severely neglected infant who nonetheless grew up to become, paradoxically, his mother's favorite child, was brutally murdered in the street by his lover's ex-husband.

Gentle Valdimar established a family not with Lourdes (obviously), but rather with her hapless older sister, Severina ("Biu") who is also a female worker in the cane. Biu had five children by Valdimar, two of whom died before Valdimar, unemployed, alcoholic, and depressed, finally hung himself, leaving Biu and their three remaining children to beg in the streets of the nearby capital city of Recife where no one she knew could witness her shame. One more child was dead before the year was out and another, the eldest, became a runaway and crazed: a *doida*. Later Biu returned home where she met another man, Oscar, by whom she had 10 more births and 6 surviving children. During the São João's day festivities in June of 1987 Oscar deserted Biu, taking the bed and the stove with him, for a younger woman who, he explained, still had her teeth. Eight months later (February 1988), during the pre-lenten carnival celebrations while Biu was trying to create a space of "forgetting" (see DaMatta, 1984), her rather "forgotten" 3-year-old daughter, Mercea, died at home of pneumonia.

Antonieta, the oldest sister of Lourdes and Biu, married well (which is defined on the Alto do Cruzeiro as a man who neither drinks nor runs around with other women and brings home the weekly market) and she eventually moved off the Alto and into a more respectable barro of Bom Jesus da mata. Antonieta's family of 10 children includes 3 *fihos de criacão* (foster children), one of whom was rescued from Biu during a particularly bleak period in her life when Biu was convinced she had no *jeito*, no "knack" for raising children that would survive infancy.

Lourdes, Antonieta, and Biu were my immediate neighbors when during 1964–1966 I first lived and worked on the Alto do Cruzeiro as a community health worker, a species of "barefoot doctor" called in those days a *visitadora*, a "house-caller" who, among other things, gave immunizations and glucose shots, distributed worm medicines, took blood and feces samples, dressed wounds, rubbed down bodies tormented by fevers of uncertain origin, and upon occasion delivered (or misdelivered) babies, like the "so little one" of Lourdes. Not infrequently *visitadores* were called upon to assist in preparing and burying the dead. In some localities (especially in urban areas) they also worked as community organizers. In Pernambuco the model for community organization, prior to the penetration of military repression in the nooks and crannies of social life, was that of Paulo Freire's (1970) *conscientizacão* through literacy (critical consciousness). And so my evenings were spent in small "cultural circles" where by the flickering light of kerosene lamps residents of the Alto organized around the founding of a popular grassroots organization, U.P.A.C., *União para o Progresso do Alto do Cruzeiro* (the Union for the Progress of Alto do Cruzeiro), and the collective building on the very top of the hill of a headquarters for local action, a "social center" that served as community school, day care cooperative, and meetinghouse for the often boisterous open "assemblies" held there each week. During this heady and exhilarating early phase of my work in Brazil I viewed the few anthropologists that I had met elsewhere in the state as remote intellectuals overly preoccupied with esoteric "exotica" and as largely out of touch with the practical realities of the people of the Northeast.

Nonetheless, by the time I finally returned to the Alto do Cruzeiro more than 15 years had elapsed and it was anthropology and not political activism that was the vehicle of my return. I came back not as *Dona* Nanci, *companheira*, but as *Doutora* Nanci, *antropolga*. As for Lourdes, Biu, and Antonieta, they joined my other former neighbors and coworkers in U.P.A.C. to become "key informants" and "research subjects" and "assistants." But the pressing research questions that emerged were ones that grew out of my original work with the people of the Alto, and these questions remain embedded in a political praxis that makes this work depart from "traditional" (if there can be said to be such a thing) ethnography in a number of ways that I shall make explicit.

The subject of my study is love and death on the Alto do Cruzeiro, but specifically *mother* love and *child* death. It concerns culture, economic and emotional scarcity, and their effects on maternal thinking and practice (see also Scheper-Hughes, 1984, 1985, 1987a). It is about the meanings and the effects of deprivation, loss, and abandonment on the ability to love, to nurture, to trust, and to have and keep faith in the broadest sense of those terms.

Because of the difficult subject of this research (mother love and child death) I am forced to create a different kind of dialogue with the reader, a pact that is perhaps best made explicit at the onset. These are not ordinary lives that I am describing. Rather, they are short, violent, and hungry lives. I am offering a small glimpse into Nordestino life through a glass darkly. Hence, reading entails a descent into a kind of Brazilian heart of darkness, and as it begins to touch upon and evoke, as Peter Homans noted (1987), some of our worst fears and unconscious dreads about "human nature," and about mothers and children, in particular, the reader may experience a kind of righteous indignation. Why am I being served this?

Death is never an easy topic, not for science, not for art. The ethnographer is engaged in a special kind of vision quest through which a specific interpretation of the human condition is forged and with it a kind of ethnographic poetics or ethnographic sensibility. In this case, the discourse, so to speak, demands an immediacy and a degree of raw and visceral emotion that interferes with the usual distance required in normative scientific writing and analysis. Given the topic, I found it impossible to conduct my work in a detached, distanced, and purely objective way. We are after all humans working with other humans and we can hardly help becoming involved (emotionally, and sometimes, as in this case, politically) in the lives of the sometimes desperate people with whom we have cast our lots, at least for the while. Hence, my particular sympathies are sometimes left painfully exposed, and I do, at times, enter into dialogue (sometimes into conflict) with my "subjects," challenging them on their interpretation of their situation, just as they challenge me on my interpretation of the world in which I live.

My theoretical and methodological approach is derived from critical or Marxist phenomenology. It has its intellectual roots in European critical theory, especially in the Frankfort School of Adorno, Fromm, and Horkheimer (see, e.g., Horkheimer & Adorno, 1972) and in the praxis of Antonio Gramsci (1971) and Franco Basaglia (see Scheper-Hughes & Lovell, 1987) in Italy. Taking my lead from Basaglia, I see my role as that of the "negative" intellectual, the one who tries to turn received wisdoms on their heads and inside out. Richard Shweder (personal communication) might see my role as that of the court jester, playing off the king (as representing authority, the normative) and against the "Loyal Opposition" (who I might cast in Gramscian terms as the "traditional" intellectual). The jester, the negative intellectual, works at the margins, "pulling at loose threads," deconstructing, looking at the world from a topsy-turvy position. Hence, the questions to be raised are the negative and oppositional ones, that point to contradictions, inconsistencies, and epistemic breaks in the logic of the established moral and social order.

Hence, I am taking a "negative" instance – the extraordinarily high "tax" of infant mortality in the shantytown of Alto do Cruzeiro in the Northeast of Brazil (approaching in some years almost 40% of all live births) – in order to ask with Gil Herdt (1987) why this predominantly Catholic social and moral order has "allowed" this situation to exist virtually without comment, censure, outrage, or organized response. Why is the carnage maintained as one of the "best kept, worst kept secrets" of an otherwise "good faith community" (Bourdieu (1977: 173)? This essay is a first step in a longer project on this subject (Scheper-Hughes, in press).

A second goal of this study is rather more abstract and theoretical. It represents the attempt to forge a dialogue between two competing views of maternity. On the one hand, I would situate the, perhaps, odd bedfellows of psychobiological attachment and "bonding" theorists (such as John Bowlby, Marshall Klauss and John Kennell, Alice Rossi, and Melvin Konner – for a review, see Sluckin, Herbert, & Sluckin, 1983) and the feminist "poetics of motherhood" authors (including Adrienne Rich, Nancy Chodorow, Carol Gilligan, and Sara Ruddick – see e.g., Rich, 1976; Chodorow, 1978; Gilligan, 1982), all of whom would posit the existence of a universal maternal script (whether biologically or social structurally derived). Sara Ruddick, for example, has defined the characteristic features of "maternal thinking" as an attentiveness to others, respect for difference, and a keen responsiveness to feeling. She suggests that it is "possible to identify interests that appear to govern maternal practice *throughout the species*" (1980:347). These *interests* concern attention to the *preservation*, *growth*, and *acceptability* of offspring. Similarly, bonding and attachment theorists suggest that owing to the precarious timing of human birth (i.e., the immaturity of the human neonate), mothering is "protected" by a strong, unlearned component – a maternal "instinct," as it were, that is genetically encoded in woman's evolutionary psychology. Klauss and Kennell and their associates (1983) have identified a "critical" or a "sensitive" period for maternal bonding believed to occur immediately postpartum. Maternal bonding is activated automatically in the mother's response to various innate infant behaviors such as crying, smiling, cooing, rooting, sucking, and clinging. The "milk-let-down" reflex in response to hungry infant cries is a case in point. Owing to the intensity of hormonally triggered maternal attachment to their newborn, Klaus suggests that grief, depression, and rage are more profound in mothers' responses to the death of a neonate than of a toddler or older child. Klaus equates the death of a neonate with a kind of "death-to-self" in the mother. I will return to this point with some contrary evidence from my own sample of mothers.

On the other side, I would situate the "history of childhood" theorists (including Lloyd deMause, Peter Laslett, William Langer, and Edward Shorter – see de Mause, 1974; Langer, 1974; Shorter, 1975), along with some of the child abuse and neglect writers, including Alice Miller (1983) and Maria Piers (1978), all of whom emphasize the existence of a universal "infanticidal impulse" in mothers (albeit one that is normally repressed). This impulse is elicited in mothers' responses and reactions to (especially) premature, sickly, deformed, or underweight neonates. A neonatalogist, practicing in a large urban children's hospital, reported that a great many mothers fear putting their hands into the incubator of their "preemie" because of an "irrational fear" that they might strike rather than stroke their tiny neonate. Maria Piers (1978) refers to maternal emotions of estrangement and disconnectedness ("basic strangeness") toward newborns that may actually precede emotions of attachment and "bonding." This primitive "basic strangeness" is, in fact, the opposite of empathy and love. It is an emotional state in which the mother "turns off" or "turns away" from the newborn, unable to recognize in the small creature a fellow human being. Such emotions of estrangement, suggests Piers, can account for the social history of infanticide that she schematically tries to develop later in her book. Langer (1974) attributes a great deal of unaccounted-for infant death in Europe from the Middle Ages through the 19th century to covert infanticide in the form of "accidental" maternal overlaying, for which women were not held accountable.

In other words, we have two rather extreme and stereotyped images of woman as mother – "earth mothers" versus "killer mothers" – surely inadequate and mythic models. But hardly surprising because of all the many factors that affect the lives and well-being of children, by far the most difficult to discuss with any degree of dispassionate "objectivity" is the quality of mothering. Social scientists, no less than the public at large, are prey to cultural stereotypes about "mother love" and "child-hood innocence," as well as their opposites. The terrible power and significance attributed to maternal behavior has caused mothers throughout history to appear in strange and distorted forms. They may appear as larger than life or, conversely, as invisible; as all powerful or as helpless; as malicious or angelic. And so, too, theories of a genetically encoded "maternal instinct" complete with theories of infanticidal, devouring women.

Both interpretive schools of thought – the bonding theorists and the infanticide/child abuse writers – *do* agree that external constraints affecting or threatening the mother's own well-being and survival can shape maternal sentiments, thinking, and practice. Poverty, scarcity, deprivation, and loss can turn some women into survival strategists in competition with their own offspring. The frequent experience of child death has always affected the ways in which women approach sexuality, reproduction, and parenting, for one producing a defensively high rate of fertility. A high expectancy of loss can produce a reproductive logic based on an assumption of the interchangeability and replaceability of offspring, and may lead to a decisive "underinvestment" in those infants seen as poor risks for survival, which may further contribute to the spiral of high fertility, high mortality in a kind of macabre lock-step dance of death.

Yet, we do not know and can scarce imagine what the death of individual children actually meant to those women living on the edge of the great demographic or epidemiologic transition of modern Europe when child mortality was still viewed as an unfortunate but altogether predictable natural occurrence and when a 30% to 40% mortality in the first year of life was not regarded as intolerable (Scheper-Hughes, 1987b). These women's histories are "minor" histories, left for the most part unrecorded, undocumented. In trying to fathom the meanings of lives very distant or very different from our own we are often tempted to attribute our own ways of feeling and thinking to them. Hence, any suggestion of patterns of passive infanticide or selective neglect based on the sex, health, or beauty of the infant – so abhorrent to our "modern" and class-based sensibilities – may be rejected out of hand as "impossible, unthinkable." Conversely, we may distance ourselves from the experiences of these women and suggest, as have several of the history of childhood writers on the basis of very little evidence, that until relatively recently in human history women so hardened their hearts against the threat of loss that they scarce knew how to love or to cherish their own children.

As a cultural anthropologist, I do not have the tools with which to probe the past, but I can closely examine the lives of women and children today living in parts of the world where economic and demographic conditions are similar to those that obtained throughout much of Western Europe prior to the demographic transition.

In order to understand the configuration of maternal sentiments and practices under conditions of high fertility/high mortality, I am drawing on the time-honored anthropological convention that Margaret Mead used to call the "anthropological veto" – that is, a single ethnographic instance, often the worst or most extreme case that might be found, in order to question a previously held and presumed to be universal theory of human behavior. In this case, then, I am going to explore the meanings of mothering within a larger world system, political-economic context that is utterly indifferent, indeed hostile to, child survival among certain classes of people.

My ethnographic instance, then, is a community of 35,000 (*Bom Jesus da Mata*) in the *zona da mata* of Northeast Brazil, a region dominated by a particularly crude form of agrarian capitalism: vast sugar plantations controlled by a class of semifeudal *senhorees de engenho* who keep their workers bound to them in a state of perpetual hunger, anxiety, and dependency. Sugarcane is self-devouring: It preempts more and more land, consumes humus in the soil, annihilates competing crops, and destroys the human capital on which its production is based. I have met many cane cutters and heads of families who go to work and go to bed hungry, and who mix half a cup of roughly refined sugar with a glass of contaminated river water to dull their pangs.

O Nordeste is a land of glaring contrasts and contradictions – cloying fields of sugarcane amidst hunger and disease; authoritarian landlords and libertarian social bandits; of an ancient penitential Catholicism coexisting with a new, politicized liberation theology. It is a land of many kinds of hungers and of a formidable thirst, so that infants who die from dehydration, their tongues, mothers say, blackened and hanging from their mouths, compete with equally vivid images of thirst-driven *sertaoejos* who have walked hundreds of kilometers to escape the drought of the *sertão* in order to sell themselves to plantation owners as *boas-frias*, temporary day laborers earning less in 1987 than $1.20/day.

Bom Jesus, centrally located and within easy commuting distance to several plantations and mills (*engenhos* and *usinas*) has become home to a new class of displaced and marginalized rural workers, many of whom have come to reside in the Alto do Cruzeiro, the largest, poorest, and most politically volatile of the three hillside shantytowns encircling the town. Over the past three decades many of the original rural migrants and squatters of O Cruzeiro have become permanent residents, and the original straw and mud huts have been largely replaced by small homes of adobe and brick. Pirated electricity and dangerous kerosene lamps have been replaced by electric bulbs, but most homes are without even dry, pit latrines, and no homes have running water. Sewage and poor sanitation remain precarious and life threatening to babies and young children who, from birth, are afflicted with parasites, skin infections, and gastroenteritis.

The infant and childhood mortality for the community is an absurdity – in some poor *barros* of Timbaúba 40% of all live births end in mortality before the end of the first year of life. In order to gauge the seriousness of the problem, natality and child mortality statistics were gathered from the original records kept in the huge ledger books at the Registro Civil for the years 1965, 1985, and 1987. We found that the official I.B.G.E. statistical summaries were not to be trusted, as, for example, annual "births" included *all* children who were registered for the first time, some of them as old as 4 or 5 years. Hence, the counting had to be done by hand. Although it is likely that most infant *deaths* after 1 month are registered (since no child may be buried in the municipal graveyard without an official certificate), *births* are underreported. Perhaps a better measure of the extent of the problem, then, is the proportion of childhood to adult deaths for each year surveyed.

In 1965, 526 childhood deaths (birth to 5 years) were recorded, of which the vast majority, 431, were of infants (birth to 1 year) from a total of 760 recorded live births; 47.1% of all deaths in Timbaúba for 1965 were of children under the age of 5.

Twenty years later, in 1985, there were 231 childhood deaths (174 of which were infant deaths) for 951 live births. The proportion of child to adult deaths remained fairly constant, at 42%. Finally, the statistics for 1987 gave 170 childhood deaths (141 of which were infant deaths) for 722 recorded live births. The proportion of child to adult deaths decreased in 1987 to 38.2%.

The geography of childhood mortality in Bom Jesus is virtually a map of social class stratification in the community: Over 90% of all childhood deaths originate in the poor and peripheral barros of Bom Jesus – the three Altos or morros, and at the rural margins and along the polluted river. A third of all childhood deaths reported to the *registro civil* in Timbaúba originated in the Alto do Cruzeiro which, with a population of 5,000 residents, represents only 15% of the population of the community. "Central" barro, the wealthy and middle-class neighborhood of the community, accounted for about 4% of all child and infant deaths in the three years surveyed.

Reproductive histories collected for 72 women of the Alto do Cruzeiro (ranging in age from 19 to 71) in 1982 (see Scheper-Hughes, 1985) likewise revealed the predictable pattern of high fertility/high childhood mortality. The women in the sample (the majority of whom had not yet completed their reproductive cycles) reported a total of 686 pregnancies (9.5/woman), and 251 child deaths among them (or 3.5/ woman). They reported an additional 101 abortions and stillbirths, which is lower than anticipated for this sample, representing perhaps some "selective" memory in this regard. Seventy percent of all child deaths had occurred in the first 6 months of life, and 82% by the end of the first year.

By any means of estimating child mortality for Bom Jesus and the Alto do Cruzeiro, the picture is one of what demographers like to refer to, cold-bloodedly, as a "great deal of reproductive waste." I want to turn these crude statistics into more embodied accounts of human suffering and human experience. The cluster of problems that I am addressing was one that began to crystallize for me during an intensely hot and dry summer in 1965 when I witnessed the wholesale die-out of Alto babies in the first months of their young lives. Some Alto mothers appeared to hasten the deaths caused by dehydration, malnutrition, and diarrhea with their own selective inattention to their babies' needs for water, food, and nurturance. Working then within the context of a community cooperative day-care center, a "creche," I found that while it was possible to rescue infants and toddlers from death by thirst and starvation, it was more difficult to encourage their mothers to participate in the rescue of a child they perceived as impossibly difficult (and costly) to raise. Reenter Lourdes.

In an earlier published piece (Scheper-Hughes, 1985) I told the story of Zezino, a severely neglected and malnourished 2-year-old whose young mother, Lourdes, had given up on him while she lavished a doting attentiveness on her second child, a newborn who she saw as a "better risk": a lively, robust, fair-headed little tyke. Unable to stand by while Zezino was gradually slipping away, I intervened and carried him to the "creche" and asked the activist women who participated in the cooperative to help me salvage what was left of the child. The Alto women, however, mocked my efforts to save "Ze," and cautioned that it was playing with death, that a child who "wanted" to die as much as this one did, should be left alone. Look, they said, you can already see his eyes sinking into the back of his head, a sign that he had already started on his journey into the next life. I managed (through force – for Ze refused to cooperate in eating) to save Ze, but I worried about the ethics of returning him to Lourdes in her scrap material lean-to, where she barely had the resources to care for herself and her new baby. Was this fair to her? To Zezino? Would he face a longer, more painful death from starvation at a later date?

Lourdes did agree to take Zezino back once he looked more human than spiritlike, and I left them to their own miserable resources. But I vowed never again to put so much effort into a situation where the odds were so poor. I was rapidly becoming socialized to Alto do Cruzeiro values. When I returned to the Alto in 1982, there among the women who formed my "sample" was my old neighbor, Lourdes, still battling to put together some semblance of a life for herself and her children, the oldest of whom was Zezino, now a young man of 19, and his mother's favorite, her *filho eleito*, elect son – her "arms and legs," as she called him. Zezino struck me as a slight, reserved young man, with a droll sense of humor. Much was made of our reunion and the story told again and again with much evident enjoyment of how I had force-fed "Ze" like a fiesta turkey, how he had been given up for dead, but managed to live and fool everyone. Ze would laugh at these survivor tales and of his near-miss with death, at the hands of his then-indifferent mother. Ze and his mother had an intensely intimate and affectionate relationship, one that took precedence over her relationship with the old and somewhat shadowy man with whom she was then living. When I asked Ze (in private) who was the one person he could count on in life, his very best friend in this world, he answered, "My mother, of course." A year later (after I again left the community) Zezino was dead – and on my return in 1987 I found his mother disconsolate and absorbed by a profound mourning that has all but disabled her. With tears coursing down her prematurely wrinkled cheeks, Lourdes said:

> Dona Nancí, if my Ze were alive today my life would not be the one that I have now, a life of suffering. None of my other children turned out like him. Even on the day he died he left my house filled with enough groceries for a month. It was almost as if he knew he would be leaving me. I couldn't eat for two weeks after the murder, but there was all this food from his hands: yams, pimentos, and beans. . . . The other children of mine, they only give me grief and worry, they only know how to ask for things. Ze never forgot who his mother was, even after he found himself a woman. How many mothers can say that about a son?

Her only joy is a young foster son adopted within months of Zezino's violent death.

My point is that *both* severe selective neglect *and* strong sentiments of maternal attachment coexist, dialectically, in this highly charged and physically threatening environment. Mother love is a richly elaborated theme in Brazilian Nordestino culture and society, celebrated in music, folk art, and in an intense devotion to the Virgin Mother and to San Antonio, patron saint of mothers and children. Nonetheless, the gradual selective neglect of certain ill-fated children is also common and is not criticized by other women or by popular healers in the community. Part of learning how to mother on the Alto do Cruzeiro includes learning when to "let go" of a child who shows that it "wants" to die. However, it is essential to look at the mother–child relationship *over time*, I found, and to follow the life history and the enfolding drama of attachment, separation, and loss that shapes the cultural expressions of maternal psychology and child-rearing practices.

Doença de Criança: mortal selective neglect

During the 1982 phase of fieldwork I had asked others to share with me their thoughts on the causes of childhood mortality. I posed this question in two ways. First, I asked a general question: "Why is it that so many babies die on the Alto do Cruzeiro?" Second, in the course of recording their reproductive histories, I asked each of the 72 women to explain the circumstances surrounding the death of each child, including their perceptions of key symptoms, the steps they took to remedy the illness, and their assessment of the primary cause of death.

It is important to note here that over 80% of all child deaths in Bom Jesus, according to the data recorded in the Registro Civil, occur *at home* and without the benefit of biomedical diagnosis (or, for that matter, without adequate treatment).[1] Hence, only the mothers themselves can give a clue as to the causes of death of their children, and, uneducated and illiterate, they quite naturally draw upon popular and "folk" diagnostic categories. Although Alto infants die without "medical testimony," as it is called on their death certificates, the majority were seen at the municipal or state health clinic, and treated with prescription drugs obtained from the mayor's personal dispensary or from one of a dozen pharmacies in Bom Jesus where clerks are all too willing to diagnose and sell restricted medications without prescription. In any event, no records are kept on nonpaying clients at any of the health posts or the municipal hospital, and clinic doctors prescribe drugs without the benefit of medical exams – normally without even laying a finger on a sick infant or child. Diagnosis is seen as a "luxury" in this community, and doctors merely treat key symptoms, so that I have witnessed a municipal doctor prescribe sleeping pills for a fussy, but clearly marasmic (starving) 2-year-old, whose mother complained that he was annoying her mother-in-law at night with his pathetic cries.

Women's responses to the two questions differed markedly and provide a clue with respect to the dynamics of mothering under extremely adverse conditions. When asked to reply to the *general* question, why do so many babies and young children of the Alto do Cruzeiro die, the women were quick to reply with a *general condemnation* of the *porcaria* [pig sty] in which they and their children were forced to live. They responded: "Our children die because we are poor, because we are hungry"; "they die because the water we drink is filthy with germs"; "they die because we cannot keep them in shoes or away from the human garbage dump we live in": "they die because the milk from our breasts is as contaminated and diseased as the water from the public faucets"; "they die because we get worthless medical care, 'street medicine'"; "they die because we have no safe place to leave them when we go off to work."

When asked what it is that infants need most in order to survive the first and precarious first year of life, Alto mothers invariably answered: "good food, strong milk, meat, vitamins." While they were quick to reject the value of their own breast milk, they were just as quick to denounce powdered milk as a "baby killer" in the Alto. As one mother commented, referring to the widespread practice of overdiluting powdered milk with contaminated water: "Babies fed on water, turn to water" [referring to the watery diarrheas that carry off so many Alto babies]. While these politically charged answers were given to my general questions, it was ironic that not a single Alto mother stated that hunger, dehydration, or malnutrition was a primary or even a contributing cause of death for any of her *own* children. Perhaps they must exercise a certain amount of denial because the alternative – the recognition that a child is slowly starving to death – is too painful. My more recent work – based on observations of mothers and malnourished babies on the Alto – enabled me to understand the moral dynamics of this denial at closer hand, as I shall describe in a few moments.

Turning to the mothers' explanations of the causes of death for each of her *own* children, most deaths were understood in naturalistic terms as bad things that just happen to people (fevers, parasites, measles, accidents, diarrheas), and, given the special vulnerabilities of babies, just carry them away. Although God and the saints were seen as the final arbiters of sickness and death, which are always attributed, in the final analysis, to God's will, 101 of the 251 deaths were attributed by the mothers to human agency and to their own actions in particular, including many instances of their "putting aside"[2] a baby seen as "better off dead" or as "having no *jeito*" (no "knack") for life, or as "wanting to die" or as having an "aversion" to the *luta* that is life. The majority of these individual diagnostic categories fell under the rubric of a flexible ethnomedical diagnostic syndrome: "*doença de criança.*" *Doença de criança* ("child sickness") subsumes at least 14 different "qualities" of sickness, each marked by ugly or horrible symptoms that are seen as harbingers of permanent disability/deformity in the child. Once labeled with "child sickness" by the mother *or* by a local *rezadeira* or a *parteira* (praying woman or midwife), the infant is virtually doomed. He or she will not receive the minimum care or attention necessary to sustain life. *Doença de criança* is – at least on the Alto do Cruziero – a death sentence.

Among the "qualities" (*qualidades*) or symptoms that result in a folk diagnosis of *doença do criança* are convulsions, eye rolling; explosive vomiting, diarrheas that leave the child *gasto*, spent, wasted; purple fingernails; infant yells and screams, grimaces, teeth gnashing; great laziness in the child – sleeps without waking even to eat; head-banging, out of control body movements; child's body is bruised, marked, discolored, battered or "crushed"; child foams at the mouth; child is hurt, damaged in the head; child is born with fraqueza, an innate weakness; child is "unnaturally" pale, deathly white, a "ghost child"; child is passive from a great *susto* – doesn't relate to anyone, anything; child looks like a spirit-child, wasted, old.

There are both *congenital* forms of *doença de criança* (also known as *attaque de memino*, child attack), and those that attack a child during its first year of life. A midwife offered me the following:

> When a baby is born *saudavel* (healthy), I always tell the mother to give the baby "cha de erva santa" to clean out the system and to strengthen the child. But if the infant is born "incomodo" (ill-fated) or *gasto* (puny, wasted), I tell them not to give the tea.
>
> Why? I asked.
>
> Because if she gives it, it may cure the baby.
>
> And why don't you want to cure it?
>
> It's better if it dies. If she cures it, it will be damaged. It happened like this with my own child. She was born little and weak and I decided not to "wash" her, and just to dust her with powder and wait for her to die. But it didn't happen that way. Her *madrinha* (godmother) gave her *cha*, and then *mingau* (baby gruel) so that she lived until she was 14 – *boba* (dumb); she just grunted; she never learned to talk or to walk. She lived pretty long, but then finally she died. She was born with *gasto*, and because of my *comadre I* suffered a lot in raising her until she died.

This pragmatic attitude toward sickness in childhood extends, as well, to the less stigmatized common childhood ailments, and another midwife replied to my question, "Do you 'pray' for sick babies?" (meaning do you "cure" them) as follows:

> I know how to "pray" all of the child illnesses – *mal olhado, susto, ventu caido*, but I don't have much faith in these prayers. Anyway, I don't want to take on the responsibility for all these sick babies. If I did my little house would be like this (knocks her knuckles together – meaning filled). I only pray for children to be born, not to cure them once they're here.

Once diagnosed with a *doença de criança*, the baby is said to be given up to Jesus to care for, or is *botou fora*, put aside to die quickly and quietly, especially when the illness entails convulsions or thrashing of arms and legs, the child beats its head against the wall or the floor. These particularly "ugly" symptoms are understood as the death throes itself or as death personified in the guise of a small child. As one mother said in response to my persistent question, "But what *is* doença de criança, *really*?": "Isn't it the *agonia* of death itself that appears in the child? No one can bear to look at it. So, we leave the baby alone."

Babies that are, conversely, passive, paralyzed, or wasted, are allowed to slip away more gradually. No heroic efforts are made to force food or water or healing herbal teas on them. They are not prayed over. Rather, they are fed "on demand." The problem is, however, that the demand is so weak, so underdeveloped. Mothers don't like deaths that take a long time; as one mother said of her premature twins, "It wasn't too bad. They just rolled their eyes to the back of their heads and were still."

No one blames a mother for turning away from such ill-fated infants and babies. Neither does the mother hold herself responsible or express any guilt for deaths that are hastened by severe neglect that entail starvation and extreme thirst. The true cause of the death is always seen as a deficiency *in the child*; not in the caretaker. Not only do conservative social scientists tend to "blame the victims" of misfortune. Here the infants are blamed for their foreshortened lives. Unfortunately, projection and denial are fairly universal defense strategies employed by individuals who dare not, who cannot face the consequences of behaviors over which they, in fact, have little control because they are, to a great extent, unconsciously motivated. One mother explained: "They die with this ugly disease because they have to die. If they were meant to live, then it would happen that way as well. I think that if a child was always weak, he wouldn't be able to defend himself." Another one offered: "These illnesses [*doença de criança*] we don't like to talk about. With these sicknesses it takes them a long time to die. It makes you sad. But if you treat the child he will never be right." What was sadly apparent, however, was that the symptoms of *doença de criança* or of a baby seen as difficult to raise, were often those produced by chronic hunger and dehydration interacting with high fevers and parasites. What mothers understood as an *innate* predisposition in the child toward chronic sickness, madness, and death were altogether treatable and transitory symptoms. Because the principal underlying maternal care and nurturance in the Alto is based on "demand," hungry and dehydrated babies are allowed to refuse food. Such babies shy away from human contact, are mournful and perpetually fussy. They are difficult to satisfy. Although slowly starving to death, they rarely cry for food, so that they appear to be *unnatural*, spiritlike beings. Because they are so passive, such babies are left alone for long periods of time, dangling in their hammocks while their mother is away or busy at some task, and sometimes not even a sibling or next-door neighbor (asked to look after the baby) may hear, amidst the loud, crashing din of Alto life, the feeble cries that signal a final crisis, so that many babies even manage to die alone and unattended, their faces set into a startled grimace that cannot be relaxed again before burial. A mother's single responsibility is to thrust a candle in the dying infant's hands – if she arrives too late to do this, she *will* be criticized as a "neglectful" mother, for the dead child may lose her way in her dark journey to the afterlife.

Afterward, the baby's body is washed and dressed in white and covered with tiny, sweet-smelling white flowers befitting a tiny angel. The plywood and cardboard coffin is gotten from the makeshift coffin factory behind the mayor's office, or a better one is purchased from one of the many shops where the coffins are arranged in order by size – many more of the tiny than of the larger ones. Children gather at the home to form the funeral procession, and the young girls take turns carrying the little box. From time to time the lid is lifted and ants are casually brushed away from the infant's face. The mother is not expected to attend the funeral, although *her* mother (the grandmother) may do so. Poor babies are buried in a common grave in the local cemetery and no headstone or even a simple wooden cross mark the spot where they are put to rest. No prayers are recited, and no priest attends the burial in this most Catholic of communities. The grave is never visited again.

Hungry mothers, hungry babies: the psychology of scarcity

What, finally, can be said, of these mothers? What are the emotions, affects, sentiments that motivate and drive them? How can they recover from one death after another only to carry yet another threatened life in their battered bodies? How do they make sense of their own lives? And of their babies' foreshortened lives? Their suffering and death? In short, what is the psychology of mothering under these conditions? How do mothers protect themselves from sorrow? From regret? From despair?

Women whose cumulative experiences lead them to expect that few of their offspring will survive infancy respond accordingly to the birth of a child. They arm themselves from the very start with a stance of what I have elsewhere called a guarded "watchful waiting." Although many Alto babies are still born at home, are put to the breast at least sporadically in the first few days or weeks of life, and generally sleep in the same bed or cot as the mother – in other words, there is at least some of that magical skin-on-skin contact that Klaus and Kennell see as the necessary foreplay of maternal "bonding" – women protect themselves from intense attachment through a form of nurturance and infant tending that is emotionally distanced and rather impersonal. Many Alto infants remain both unbaptized *and* unnamed until they begin to toddle. Although they might be given an amusing and affectionate nickname (for example, "Fiapo," a "little bit of nothing"), older siblings often wouldn't know if their little brother or sister has been given a name, or, if so, what it really is. I have myself walked to the cartorio civil with the father and aunt of a recently deceased year-old child in order to simultaneously register her birth and death only to have the father ask me the real name of his daughter, whom he only knew as "the skinny one."

Often a crisis and the fear of imminent death prompts an emergency baptism in which the mother or grandmother officiates. All too often, however, it is too late even for this, and so the dead infant must be baptized, conditionally, in her tiny coffin. Dona Amor tells the story of a young mother of the Alto who hastily buried her 4-month-old infant at a crossroad outside of Bom Jesus (a traditional rural practice) in order to avoid the cost of registering the death and birth (about $2.00 in 1987). Later that night she repented and told Amor, who suggested to the distraught woman that she ease her conscience by confessing her "sin" to the priest. The padre, however, told the woman that he could not give her absolution until she returned to the crossroads and dug up her baby and brought him to the church to be baptized. The woman left the confessional disconsolate for it seemed to her an "unholy" charge. The godfather chosen to officiate at the vampirish baptism refused to disturb the dead, and so performed a baptism over the approximate place of the burial (there was, of course, no marker) and left the rest to God.

Similarly, the affection shown the infant and young baby is diffuse – "Who doesn't enjoy a baby?" Alto people comment – but this attention and affection are not focused on any distinguishing traits of the infant as a separate little person. Alto infants are not held a great deal and are left alone for long periods of time. Recently delivered mothers are cautioned by older women not to *pegar* (grab or pick up) their infants until their 40-day *resguarda* is over. Hence, infants can generally be found lying on their backs or stomachs on the mother's bed or in a hammock. I have seen rather doting grandmothers get on their knees on a bed in order to engage a newborn in en face position *rather* than lift the infant and cuddle it in their arms. Breast-feeding is thought to be difficult, painful, and extremely draining on the mother (it can cause her to sicken with TB, for example), so it is not surprising that most Alto women desist after a few half-hearted attempts, saying that the infant doesn't know how to suck, or that their milk *naõ presta* (isn't worth anything), or that they are too weak and *acabada* to breast-feed. Hence, by the third day of life, *mingau* (powdered milk, manioc flour, sugar, and contaminated water) is offered the baby in a bottle. Young Alto mothers, however, often position the newborn on their laps, head at their knees – a very awkward and removed way of feeding a newborn.

What makes the distanced emotions possible is a different cultural construction of the infant and small baby. The infant is human, but decidedly less human than the older child or certainly than the adult. And, what may seem somewhat jarring to our own cultural sensibilities, the infant and small baby are understood as intrinsically *less valuable* than older children or than adults. When an infant dies, a neighbor woman will console the mother, drawing on the folk wisdom in a popular prayer to San Antonio (patron of mothers and children): "God knows what He is doing. He has the power. Better the baby should die than either you or I."

I recently questioned an old *beata* (a saintly, unmarried religious woman) of the Alto about the humaneness of this message, and she said:

> The worst thing that a mother can do is to be mad with grief for a child. I once heard a crazy woman weeping and say, "What good did it do for me to give birth and raise a child with so much sacrifice only to have God come look for him and eat him?"

> God – eat him? I asked, incredulously. Such "blasphemies" are extremely rare in this God-fearing community.

> Sim, senhora. Now wasn't that a lack of faith for her to curse God like that? Only a *doida* would do that.

Such outbursts are, however, extremely rare. Far more common is a tranquil resignation based on the belief that God "took" the baby so that the mother would suffer less in this life. The mandate not to express grief – and most especially not to shed tears – is strongly reinforced by a homely Catholic folk belief. Mothers of the Alto say that for the brief hours that the infant is in its coffin (children are buried on the day of their death) it is neither a human child nor yet a blessed angel, it is something Other, strange: a spirit struggling to leave this earth and find its way to the next world. It must climb. A mother's tears can impede the way.[3] "It is a grave sin for a mother to cry for the first 60 days after her baby's death," said Dona Marlene, "because their mother's tears will make the road from earth to heaven slippery and he will lose his footing and fall." Another woman told of a neighbor who was weeping for the death of her infant when she heard him call her from his little coffin: "Mae, don't cry for me, because *a mortalia* [the coffin] is very heavy." You see, she said, "The infant had to struggle even after death, and his mother was making it worse for him. He wasn't an angel yet, because angels never speak, they are *mudo* (mute)." What is being created here is an environment that teaches women from all sides to hold back, to hold off their affections during the precarious first year of life. It is, unfortunately, the voice of bitter experience.

Distance from the infant is also maintained by a failure to "anthropomorphize" the infant, to grant it an immediate and innate human status, as it were. By this I mean that no effort is made to attribute to the infant and small baby such human characteristics as consciousness, will, intentionality, self-awareness, and memory. Rosa said of her severely malnourished toddler with some pity for the creature, but little sense of personal responsibility: "Eh, eh, coitado, mas bichinos nao sentem nada" – "poor little thing, but little 'critters' don't have any feelings." The infant and baby is seen as incapable of real human suffering.

Similarly, mothers of the Alto are slow to personalize an infant by attributing specific meanings to their cries, facial expressions, their flailing of arms and legs, their kicks and screams – except when these are seen in the negative instance, as the harbingers of symptoms of *doença de criança*. Nor are they accustomed to scanning an infant's face to note his or her resemblance to mother, father, or other family members. At most, what is commented upon is the skin coloring – light, moreno, or preto – and hair type of the infant – and whether it is *bem forte* (strong) or *fraquino* (weak) or *xoxinho* (little, skinny). The infant, in short, does not have an individualized "self" that would make its death unbearably painful. Rather, the infant's humanness, its personhood, and its claims on the mother's attention and affections grow over time, slowly, tentatively, and anxiously.

In cases of severe malnutrition or dehydration there is, as well, a characteristic failure of mothers to recognize the symptoms of hunger and thirst, and therefore, an inability to respond adequately (see Scheper-Hugher 1988:451–453). Hungry babies are often described by their own healthy and relatively well-fed mothers as "sick" babies or as "fussy" or "difficult" babies, as hard to please. It *is* painful to see little famine victims sitting passively on the floor next to large, animated and nonchalant mothers. I must admit, but not without shame, that my own response was sometimes anger at the young mother, to which she would respond with great surprise. In visiting the hovel of an old friend, Dalina, age 77, I was taken aback to see in the same room a skeleton child in the arms of a somewhat older child of 12 or 13. "What is *wrong* with this baby?" I asked. Dalina, the great-grandmother, replied that he had been sick and "didn't like to eat." I asked to see the mother, a stocky and sullen 17-year-old girl who explained that Gil-Anderson was 11 months old and ate only a tablespoon of powdered milk in a bottle of water each day. The child weighed no more than 4 kilos. I challenged the young mother, "Your baby is *not* sick; your baby is hungry." Her reply was, however, that she had taken him to the municipal clinic and to the hospital and to the pharmacy and they had given her prescriptions to "treat" his sickness. I asked to see the medicines and was taken into her tiny lean-to behind Dalina's hovel, where over the child's hammock was a shelf with more than a dozen bottles of prescription drugs, all partly used and displayed like saints on an altar. There were antibiotics, painkillers, tranquilizers, sleeping pills ("Gil-Anderson cries all night and doesn't sleep regularly," she offered), and, most painful of all, there was an appetite stimulator. The child was being "fed" medicines and simultaneously denied food. Once again I decided to intervene and began to bring the child mashed vegetables, broths, soups, and fresh cow's milk. The boy ate greedily but very small amounts. The mother said she was surprised that he could eat such things. Each day, however, the foods I brought (meant to last for 2 or 3 days) would disappear. When questioned, the several women living in this extended, female-dominated household-cluster admitted to eating the foods that Gil-Anderson "didn't like, rather than to see them go to waste."

Similarly, when my field assistant, Cecilia, brought an antibiotic cream to the household to be used for a severe and infected heat rash bothering Gil's younger sibling, we discovered the women of the household passing it around among themselves, each one rubbing some of the cream onto her cheeks for her "blemishes." Meanwhile, the infant continued to be miserable.

My visits began to provoke arguments and jealousies in the household: Why was I giving so much to *this* baby and not to others in the family? The young mother of Gil-Anderson wanted me to take care of *her* – she had pains in her stomach. The aunt had a toothache. Worst of all, Dalina, the great-grandmother, began to cry pitifully. She said *she* had fallen from weakness on the way down the Alto, and now her bones were sore. When I walked across the tiny room to comfort her, she wailed saying: "*You* used to be a *mother* to me [referring to our close relationship 20 years earlier]. When I was hungry, you brought *me* good things to eat. When I was sick you took *me* to the hospital. Don't you care about *me* anymore?" I began to realize that no one in this household of adult single women was capable of nurturing Gil-Anderson, since all of them were still needing a "mother" and nurturing for themselves. Their needs and hungers were *real* enough and virtually insatiable. As one mother once told me with reference to why she could not breast-feed her infant: "Weak people can't give much milk – the babies suck an suck an all they will get is blood." Another Alto mother once told me, "We have nothing, nothing to give our children." These needy, virtually forgotten, and abandoned women are especially unable to respond when the baby shows symptoms of the hunger and thirst from which they themselves (at least emotionally) suffer. Hence, the child's hunger can even elicit rejection or denial. The sick or hungry child's incessant demands for a mother and mothering lead to role confusion, since it seems to remind impoverished women – even very old women like Dalina – of their own unsatisfied longings for a "good" mother, one that many of them never had. In the meantime, however, another sick or hungry child has died.

Nonetheless, I do not wish to leave you with the impression that Alto mothers, so concerned with their own basic needs, never suffer nor experience grief at the death of their children. In talking to women about their lives as women and mothers, amidst the generally controlled rendering of tragic events, the memory of a particularly painful and poignant loss would sometimes break through and shatter the stoicism and "conformity" to child death that is so valued. There would be cases of especially *older* toddlers who *had been* expected to live and whose death had taken their mother by surprise and unprepared. And there were cases of particularly loved or beautiful children in whom a mother's hopes for the future had been entrusted and she would weep in the telling of *this* particular death of all the many she had endured. This is particularly true of the death of the older baby or toddler. Dona Norinha had 11 children, 6 of whom she "gave to Jesus"; but it was only in telling me of the death of her 3-year-old *calçula*, the last born, that her composure disappeared:

> She was so beautiful, *que so vendo*. And *sabida* [smart] – she understood everything. The neighbors said, "Be careful – you'll never raise this one." And they were right. She was so beautiful and wise that Jesus took her for Himself. What could I do? You can't argue with Jesus. When she became ill I was almost crazy. I couldn't sleep, I couldn't eat. I could only think, God doesn't want me to have this child. He doesn't want me to have any comfort in this world. I had such friendship with this one child. I begged God to "forget" her, to leave this one for me. But my daughter said, "*Mamae*, let me go." I yelled at her: "Then die – go away, leave me, then." I was so *angry* at her. The poor little thing died like that, talking to me, telling me that she would be all right, asking me to forgive her, telling me not to cry.

But even in this touching story we can see the same evidence of role confusion and terrible neediness in the mother that makes her incapable of responding appropriately to her dying three-year-old. Whenever a woman of the Alto would break down in the telling of a death, other women present would calm the woman, and soon I, too, would fall into the ritualized words of consolation:

You are strong, D. Maria. Be grateful that *you* are still alive.
You will conform; it is useless to grieve. You have your own life.
You *will* endure.

And as the woman would gradually regain her composure I would wonder for how many generations women the world over had been telling each other the same words, shaping their experience of loss, controlling their reactions to that which could otherwise be unbearable, unmanageable. If there is, as feminists like to suggest, a universal sisterhood of women, no doubt it has its origins in this collective comforting of those weeping women, like the biblical Rachel, whose "children are no more."

And these women *are* survivors, just as many of their children, too, escape death and survive. And they have taught me a great lesson about human strength and resilience. After Biu finished telling me her life history, returning again and again to the themes of her child's death, husband's suicide, and abandonment both by her father and by her second husband, and all the other losses she has endured in her *long* 42 years, she roughly wiped the tears from the corners of her eyes with her charcoal-dirtied hands, making her look for all the world like a Welsh miner, and she concluded with great force:

> No, Dona Nancy, I *won't* cry: I *won't* worry myself, and I won't waste my time thinking about it from morning until night. I work all day,

what good would it do me to spend the night crying? Shall I fight with God for the state that I'm in? No! So I dance and I play, and yes, I laugh, and the people wonder at a *pobre* like me who can have such a good time. But if I don't enjoy myself, if I can't amuse myself a little...well, then, I would rather be dead.

In the end, what sustains and animates women like Biu and Lourdes and so many others whose own lives have been foreshortened by a brutal class-based selective neglect, is an altogether intact and persistent belief in the right to be alive, to take up space, to *gozar* – to take pleasure...in food, in sex, in *conversa*, and even in work. How that consistency of self is allowed to develop in this materially and psychologically hostile environment is a great puzzle, and the subject of ongoing research and writing (see Scheper-Hughes, in press). In the meantime, I will conclude here by pointing out that the experiences of these women and children suggest that both the maternal and bonding/poetics of motherhood and the infanticidal impulse views of motherhood are inadequate to describe the rich and complex psychologies, sentiments, and practices described here. That there must be a biological basis or foundation to maternal emotions and behavior is not disputed. In fact, one could read the *persistence* of so many mother–child attachments over time and through terrible adversity in this small threatened community in Northeast Brazil as demonstrating the tug of biology on ever so fragilely constituted human social relations. But that same biology is itself fragile and "nervous," shaped and transformed by specific social, economic, and historical circumstances.

Notes

1 The official indifference toward the reporting of child death among the poorer populations of Bom Jesus da Mata, and the failure of the civil government to inquire into the causes of so many hundreds of childhood deaths at home is, of course, symptomatic of the abandonment and "invisibility" and "no-accountability" of shanty-town residents. It contributes to the environment of "high expectancy" and routinization of daily childhood mortality that in turn contributes to the cycle.

2 The way that mothers express this is: *Eu boutei forar* or *tenho que boutar forar* – i.e., "I put him aside, or I had to put him out," meaning euphemistically, I let him die. Other women express the practice more critically: they say that a particular child was *jogado forar*, "thrown away" (by the mother). Other times, the cause of death is left ambiguous, as when the uncle of a child who died of untreated pneumonia at the age of 3 said as he baptized her in her little coffin: "I don't know if you were *chamada*, *tirada*, or *jogada* from this life [i.e., called, taken, or thrown away], but I pray that you find your way to heaven."

3 For a elaboration of this theme, see M. Nations and L.-A. Rebhun (1988). The Nations and Rebhun piece appeared while this manuscript was already in press. It will not escape the discerning reader that this article is also a critique of my "selective neglect" hypothesis first presented in my 1984, 1985 articles. The critique is based on Nations's research with a sample of women drawn

from a hospital clinic in the state of Ceára. Suffice it to say for now that the passive infanticide and mortal selective neglect that I am describing here is less often to be found in a clinically drawn sample than in the hammocks of miserable hovels in the shantytown. In these instances no treatment – biomedical or traditional – will be sought for "doomed" infants. The other questions raised by Nations and Rebhun concerning the cultural shaping of the experiences of attachment, loss, grief, and mourning will be treated at length in my forthcoming book.

References

Bourdieu, Pierre. 1977. *Outline of a Theory of Practice*. Cambridge: Cambridge University Press.

Chodorow, Nancy. 1978. *The Reproduction of Mothering*. Berkeley: University of California Press.

de Mause, Lloyd. 1974. *The History of Childhood*. New York: Psychohistory Press, 1974.

Freire, Paulo. 1970. *Pedagogy of the Oppressed*. New York: Seabury.

Gramsci, Antonio. 1971. *Selections from the Prison Notebooks*. London: Lawrence and Wishart.

Gilligan, Carol. 1982. *In a Different Voice*. Cambridge, MA: Harvard University Press.

Herdt, Gilbert. 1987. Commentary on Presentations by Robert LeVine and Nancy Scheper-Hughes. Chicago Symposium on Culture and Human Development, University of Chicago, November 5–7.

Homans, Peter. 1987. "Comments on Scheper-Hughes, 'Mother Love and Child Death.'" The Chicago Symposium on Culture and Human Development, November 6.

Horkheimer, Max, & Theodor W. Adorno. 1972. *Dialectic of Enlightenment* (John Cumming, Trans.). New York: Herder and Herder.

Klaus, Marshall, & John Kennell. 1983. *Parent–Infant Bonding*. St. Louis, MO: Mosby.

Langer, William. 1974. Infanticide: A Historical Survey. *History of Childhood Quarterly 1*:353–365.

Miller, Alice. *For Your Own Good: Hidden Cruelty in Child-Rearing and the Roots of Violence*. New York: Farrar, Straus, and Giroux.

Nations, M., & L.-A. Rebhun. 1988. Angels with Wet Wings Can't Fly: Maternal Sentiment in Brazil and the Image of Neglect. *Culture, Medicine and Psychiatry 12*:141–200.

Piers, Maria. 1978. *Infanticide*. New York: Norton.

Rich, Adrienne. 1976. *Of Woman Born*. New York: W. W. Norton.

Ruddick, Sara. 1980. Maternal Thinking. *Feminist Studies 6*:342–364.

Scheper-Hughes, Nancy. 1984. Infant Mortality and Infant Care: Cultural and Economic Constraints on Mothering in Northwest Brazil. *Social Science and Medicine 19*(5):535–546.

1985. Culture, Scarcity and Maternal Thinking: Maternal Detachment and Infant Survival in a Brazilian Shantytown. *Ethos. 13*(4):291–317.

1987a. "Basic Strangeness" – A Critique of Bonding Theory. In Charles Super (Ed.), *The Role of Culture in Developmental Disorder* (pp. 131–153). San Diego: Academic Press.

1987b. The Cultural Politics of Child Survival. In Scheper-Hughes (Ed.),

Child Survival (pp. 1–28). Dordrecht, Netherlands: D. Reidel.

1988. The Mothers of Hunger: Sickness, Delerium and Human Needs. *Culture, Medicine and Psychiatry 12*:429–458.

In press. *Mother Love and Child Death in Northeast Brazil.* Boston: Beacon.

Scheper-Hughes, Nancy, & Anne M. Lovel (Eds.). 1987. *Psychiatry Inside Out.* New York: Columbia University Press.

Shorter, Edward. 1975. *The Making of the Modern Family.* New York: Basic Books.

Sluckin, Wladyslaw, Martin Herbert, & Alice Sluckin. 1983. *Maternal Bonding.* Oxford: Basil Blackwell.

Part VII
A skeptical reflection

20
Social understanding and the inscription of self

Kenneth J. Gergen

The burning questions occupying self theorists of earlier decades now appear to be smoldering embers. No longer are we intrigued by the possibility that the theories of Freud, Erikson, Mead, or others might be applied across widely disparate cultural settings. We are less than excited by the possibility that there might be critical periods, rituals, or transition points whereby identity is achieved in various cultures. Even the possibility of cognitive bases of self-conception seems to capture little interest outside the cognitive and AI encampments. Rather, as we move through the period of what has variously been called post-structuralist, postmodern, symbolic, interpretive, hermeneutic, and constructionist, we have become acutely self-reflexive in our posture. Caution pervades the enterprise of description and explanation of other cultures, lest our etic preferences ride roughshod over the emic realities of the peoples we hope to understand. Within this context critical concern has shifted from the verification of peculiarly "Western" intelligibilities, already embraced, to the discovery of alien and/or exotic systems of understanding selves. What are the ontologies of personhood that serve to inform the treatment of individuals and to provide the forestructure from which selves emerge within the various cultures (see Carrithers, Collins, & Lukes, 1985; Gergen & Davis, 1985; Heelas & Lock, 1981; Marsella, DeVos, & Hsu, 1985; Shweder & Bourne, 1984)?

Within this latter work one finds increasing convergence around the assumption that the understandings of persons – the lay theories, systems of meaning, implicit beliefs, or ethnopsychologies – emerge out of particularized, sociohistorical circumstances. This is not an unfruitful intellectual space to occupy for a time – particularly as such analyses kindle an appreciation of alternative realities and undermine the confidence with which we imbue our own objectified system of understanding. At the same time, as agreement crystallizes, the task of social inquiry becomes substantially narrowed. For once we have agreed that cultural variation is primary, the paramount challenge is one of elucidating with greater clarity and sophistication the character of these variations. One is essentially challenged to furnish new enthographies, insights into the local conceptions of still other cultures, and so on. In this regard I cannot offer the benefit of newly garnered field notes from some exotic clime, nor a contrapuntal critique of some subtle malaise currently gripping Western culture. Perhaps this is just as well, as one might justifiably be fearful that I would be expanding further the ranks of those who are all too rapidly exhausting the remaining pool of exotic enclaves out of which are molded the dramas of cultural variation. However, it is possible to use this new wave of inquiry to pose further conceptual questions. And, as we elaborate these questions and consider possible answers, we can hopefully return to the topic of self with an expanded repertoire of concerns.

To be more specific, I wish to advance a series of interrelated arguments that begin with the problem of understanding other cultures. In spite of the attempt to treat method and theory independently, the methodological attempt to access the meaning systems of other peoples does not proceed in a theoretical vacuum. Rather, I propose that our methods of understanding others presuppose a conception of self that must invariably occlude the passage to exotic subjectivities. The search for understanding itself proceeds on assumptions that ultimately shape or delimit the conclusions that may be drawn about others' conceptions of the person. As I hope to demonstrate, there are major shortcomings inherent in the contemporary attempts to access the meaning systems of other cultures. As these shortcomings are revealed, we are confronted with the possibility of reconsidering the conceptions of self that form the conceptual foundations of these attempts at accessing meaning. It is at this point that I shall introduce the possibility of shifting from an individualist to a relational orientation to understanding selves. This relational account will not only enable us to see accounts of individual selves in a new, and possibly more fruitful light, but will offer an alternative orientation to ethnographic inscription.

Understanding as intersubjectivity

Most would agree that the behavioral movement within the social sciences is a failing enterprise. The behavioral movement, linked as it was to the positivist account of "truth through method," promised the development of objectively warranted theories of human conduct. With the deployment of controlled observation, sophisticated measurement, and associated statistical analysis, it was believed, the sciences could furnish objectively grounded propositions of no less consequence than those engendered within the natural sciences. Yet, within the philosophy of science most would agree that empiricist foundationalism is untenable. The prospects of positivist philosophers of the 1930s, along with empiricists and critical rationalists of later vintage, are no longer compelling. Within the human sciences, cultural anthropologists have been in the vanguard of those discerning the flaws in traditional empiricist assumptions. As it is variously argued, the mere observation and recording of human bodies moving through time and space does not furnish an adequate understanding of their actions. To say that a native moves his hands at a certain velocity in a certain direction at a certain time, regardless of the accuracy with which the event is recorded, does not furnish an adequate understanding of his actions. Rather, it is argued, understanding is achieved only when one has penetrated the *meaning* of the actions to the native him/herself. The researcher must be able to determine whether the observed action is, for example, a prayer, a status marker, a segment of an elaborate courting ritual, or something else. For it is the meaning assigned to actions that determines how they are related to other actions and to the reactions of others within the community. As it is said, people live in symbolic communities, and only as they share systems of meaning are their activities systematically patterned at all. These are now very familiar themes, virtually commonplace for many cultural anthropologists.

It is also worth reminding ourselves that this shift toward the symbolic is hardly a novel twist within the social sciences more generally. Contemporary arguments against behavioral reductionism echo many of the same themes developed by those contending within 19th-century Germany that the human sciences (*Geisteswissenschaften*) were of a different order than the natural sciences (*Naturwissenschaften*). One may thus locate a long, firm line of argumentation spanning virtually a century advocating the centrality of meaning in understanding others. Consider:

> In the human studies...[t]he nexus of psychic life constitutes originally a primitive and fundamental datum. We explain nature, we understand psychic life....Just as the system of culture – economy, law, religion, art and science – and the external organization of society in the ties of family, community, church and state, arise from the living nexus of the human mind (*Menschenseels*), so can they be understood only by reference to it. (Dilthey, 1894)

> Sociology...is a science that attempts the interpretive understanding of social action....In action is included all human behavior when and in so far as the acting individual attaches a subjective meaning to it. (Weber, 1904)

> When one is dealing with any kind of social (event), as opposed to physical, (its) character depends entirely on belonging in a certain way to a system of ideas or modes of living. It is only by reference to criteria governing that system of ideas or modes of life that they have an existence as...social events. (Winch, 1946)

> By culture we mean those historically created definitions of the situation which individuals acquire by virtue of participation in or contact with groups. (Kluckhohn, 1954)

> But whatever account or half-accurate sense one gets of what one's informants are "really like" comes from...the ability to construe their modes of expression. (Geertz, 1974)

This esteemed line of reasoning, now pervading the process of ethno-graphic inquiry, is wedded to further assumptions about the nature of human understanding. More broadly, it may be suggested that there is a deeply embedded conception of human understanding that furnishes the text of which the preceding excerpts are but manifestations. Several components of this sedimented conception of understanding are critical for our purposes. First, the process of understanding another is fun-damentally mental or psychological. As it is generally held, it is a major task of the mind to comprehend, ascertain, or essentially to understand the nature of the world – including others. Depending on the account, acts of thought, memory, feeling, intuition – all psychological in charac-ter – are variously required for understanding to occur. This view has early roots in both Plato and Aristotle, and it reappears in one form or another throughout the Western intellectual tradition. Virtually all clas-sic works on epistemology – including those of Locke, Kant, Berkeley, and Descartes – are concerned with the psychological process of under-standing as related to the world to be understood. As Derrida summa-rizes it, the Western tradition of letters is quintessentially *logocentric* – holding rational process as the primary basis of understanding and action.

Coupled with the long-standing assumption that understanding is essentially a mental process is a second and equally perduring commit-ment. As is held, understanding other persons is essentially a process of gaining access into their mental world. If one's own processes of understanding are mental, and it is understanding that largely governs one's activities, then to understand others must necessarily involve penetrating the exterior and grasping the character of their own under-standings. The mere recording of people's movements through time and space does not constitute understanding. Like the Jehovah of the New Testament, one does not understand until he or she "looketh upon the heart" of the other.

Given that the process of understanding is essentially a mental one, and that its object in the case of human action is essentially the mental world of the other, then we may properly speak of understanding as a form of intersubjective connection. When one's experience accurately maps the subjectivity of another, he or she is understood. As subjectivi-ties increasingly approximate each other, the possibility for mutual understanding is increased.

Space prevents the tracing of the various manifestations of this view across cultural history. To gain a sense of its pervasive hold, it will suffice to mention several of its more prominent instantiations. For example, as symbolic interactionists hold, social order depends on the capacity of actors to share in a common, psychological realm of sym-bols. Understanding within the psychoanalytic domain typically requires that the analyst grasp or gain access to the dynamics of the analysand's unconscious mind and the way in which they are represented in con-sciousness. For structuralists in a variety of domains (e.g., Lévi-

Strauss), understanding is achieved when one can decipher the overt signifiers in such a way as to grasp the internal structure of the signified. In Searle's (1970) theory of speech acts we have the pivotal *principle of expressibility*, which essentially says that "whatever can be meant can be said" – again distinguishing between inner meaning and outer manner of expression. Even Habermas's (1979) social theory of communication makes a strong claim to the ontological reality of intentionality and rational process as it forms the basis for communicative action.

Understanding and presumptions of selfhood

Informed by the view of human understanding as intersubjective connection, the process of ethnographic inquiry can proceed with direction. Whether through interview, dialogue, standardized categorization tasks, or analysis of folktales, the attempt is typically to gain access to the meanings, categories, concepts, or schemas of other peoples. And, for many investigators, such procedures have been employed to gain understanding of the others' conceptualization of selves. What is the concept of the person among the Balinese (Geertz, 1975), the Oriyas (Shweder & Bourne, 1984) or the Marquesans (Kirkpatrick, 1985); the conception of emotion among the Utka (Briggs, 1970), or the Ifaluk (Lutz, 1982); the understanding of knowledge and passion among the Ilongot (Rosaldo, 1980); or the concept of the self among the Chinese (Elvin, 1985) or the Brahmans of Kashmir (Sanderson, 1985)? As it is hoped, such inquiry can help us to look beneath the surface of the culture – to penetrate the exterior and to reveal the interior without which the exterior would indeed be unintelligible.

Within the context of such inquiry, the actual process of understanding itself recedes into the background. The investigator attempts to gain access into others' subjectivities, but the process itself seldom intrudes into the conclusions reached about others' conceptions of selves. Methods of accessing the meaning systems of others may be either sensitive or crude, but the method itself is held to be independent of the discoveries. In effect, the reader is informed, the method does not fashion the results. Yet, let us reconsider. Methods of understanding do not exist within an interpretive vacuum. In the broader sense, method, theory, and metatheory are all interdependent bodies of discourse, each deriving their validity from the other (Gergen, 1982). With specific regard to method, the very acceptance of a procedure as a relevant method depends on the way it is theoretically contextualized. A telescope fails to inform us about events within the stratosphere unless we possess preliminary theories concerning space, vision, the function of lenses, and so on. Within other ontological contexts the same instrument might furnish information on the future, the nature of God, or indeed, be of no utility at all in generating knowledge. In the same way, attempts at accessing implicit meaning systems of other peoples are themselves saturated with assumptions about the nature of human functioning – or to put it more directly – the nature of selves. To enter the field with a given view of the nature of human understanding is to circumscribe a priori the range of conclusions that may be drawn about the persons one wishes to understand. To elucidate such effects is to expand sensitivity to the typically unexplicated forestructure guiding ethnographic inscription (see also Clifford & Marcus, 1986; Fabian, 1983).

Let us consider a number of ways in which the view of understanding as intersubjectivity intrudes into the nature of ethnographic characterization – both into accounts of others as persons, and into the way others are held to characterize each other. At the outset, by virtue of the commitment to understanding as intersubjectivity, there is an abiding tendency in Western ethnography toward *individualization* of the other. That is, others tend to be characterized in terms of individual units, and to be understood as viewing each other in the same terms. Thus, whether treating the Trobriander's symbolizations of kinship (Blu, 1967), Navajo categorizations of objects at rest (Witherspoon, 1971), ideology in South India (Barnett, 1977) or social knowledge among the Kaluli (Ochs & Schieffelin, 1984), investigators treat the psychological processes of the individual as critical in understanding cultural patterns. This characterization of individuals as the fundamental units of culture is a logical cognate to the view of understanding as intersubjective connection. For, if understanding of persons is achieved through accessing their subjective worlds, then the individual is necessarily the focal unit of the culture. If understanding in general is achieved by treating persons as separate or individual entities, then other cultures must be constituted by such entities. (See also LaFontaine, 1985; MacFarlane, 1978; and Lukes, 1985, for further accounts of individualism and its place in anthropological inquiry.)

From this standpoint, social organization must necessarily be a derivative and fundamentally problematic achievement. It is the individual who represents the indefeasible unit; cultural organization is essentially contingent. Once in existence, the culture as a system may enter into the shaping of the young mind – thus duplicating itself. However, that which holds the cultural system together – the basis of its viability – is located within the minds of individuals. By way of contrast, consider the possibility of characterizing cultures without reference to individual actors, or treating individual actors as if they played the same function as pieces in a puzzle – essential particulars, but only as they fit within the overarching pattern of major interest. At present we have little in the way of anthropological theory treating cultures as information systems, spatial organizations, fields of power distribution, fulfillments of historical trajectories, or aesthetic configurations. This is not because such characterizations are less objective or "experientially grounded" than existing accounts, but, it would appear, because the prevailing construction of human understanding is unfavorable to them as cultural realities (or, at least, as realities of anything more than derivative interest). To a certain degree economic analyses of culture may stand as an exception to the general rule; however, in most such cases economic behavior is tied in the end to matters of rational process and motivation at the personal level.

It may be rebutted that many anthropologists have indeed expressed discontent with the ideology of individualism felt to be so basic to Western culture. However, as the present analysis suggests, this ethical posture is inconsistent with the prevailing conception of the process of understanding. A communitarian ethic is not a congenial companion to a logocentric conception of individual functioning. Thus, ethnographers such as Lee (1959), Geertz (1975), Shweder and Miller (1985), and Kirkpatrick (1985) all "find" less individualized and more communal conceptions of persons to prevail in other cultural settings. And in generating these ethnographies the individualistic conception of the person so dear to Western culture is relativized and problematicized. However, given the initial commitment to a logo-centered view of human understanding, such ethnographies fall short of a full invitation to communal forms of society. That is, the argument embedded within these analyses is essentially one that replaces communal forms, as cultural *realities,* with *conceptions* of community. Communal organization as an actuality is left at the periphery of the analysis – possibly existent, but possibly a conceptual construction alone. And, should such organization prove to be extant, its existence rests ultimately on the foundation of individual conceptualization. In effect, the theory of method impedes the kind of analysis that would give full expression to a more pluralistic or communal value system.

A second major aspect of ethnographic characterization tied to the assumption of understanding as intersubjective is its *dualistic presumption.* To the extent that an ethnographer believes that understanding necessitates the penetration of other minds, then it necessarily follows that those whom one sets out to understand are indeed mindful in nature. This presumption is essentially a priori; and it is difficult to imagine how any set of observations could serve to challenge it. It is essentially locked into Western metaphysics of persons. It is in this way that inquiry into the cognitive systems (Casson, 1981), emotions (Lutz, 1988), beliefs (Radcliffe-Brown, 1922), folk knowledge (LeVine, 1984), motives, and values of other peoples can proceed relatively unchallenged. We hold that such mental events can be opened to examination because our commitment to a conception of understanding guarantees the existence of such events. In addition to viewing the subjects of one's study as harboring minds within bodies, there is a pervasive tendency to hold that such subjects also hold such beliefs about each other. Thus, in characterizing the conception of self among the Wintu (Lee, 1959), emotions among the Pintupi (Myers, 1979), and conscious awareness among West Sumatrans (Errington, 1984), the presumption is that these conceptions are shared within the culture. The Bedoins understand each others' emotions when they hear the lyric *ghinnawas* (Abu-Lughod,

1987); the term *liget* reveals to the Ilongots the passion of their tribal mates (Rosaldo, 1980) and ancient Chinese poetry revealed to its audience information about people's decisions, emotions, and sense of obligation (Elvin, 1985). Such arguments may continue to strike us as true as long as we do not inquire into their grounds of validity. The question that will confront us shortly is, how could members of other cultures determine the underlying meaning of such symbols; and more directly, how can the ethnographer determine what states are implicated by the words, stories, gestures, and artifacts of other cultures?

Let us consider a third way in which the orienting belief in intersubjectivity insinuates itself into ethnographic characterization. Not only are there tendencies toward individualization and dualism, but particular *ascriptions of mental content* are also invited. In particular, there is a pervasive tendency to employ mental categories common to the Western cultural clime. Invited at the outset is the tendency to ascribe category systems to other persons. Within the Western tradition language is generally viewed as an expression of underlying categories or concepts (or in cognitivist terms, prototypes or schemas). Thus, when we use language of other peoples to access their subjectivities, it is essentially their category or conceptual systems that are at stake. Concepts are the bedrock of the archeology of the interior. Thus, research into cultural meaning systems (D'Andrade, 1984), folk knowledge (Holland, 1982), comparative cognition (Cole, 1981) along with ethnomedicine, ethnopsychology and the like, all borrow heavily from the conception of understanding as intersubjectivity. If we did not hold that language is an expression of underlying categories, but, for example, of doppelganger, demons, specific organs of the body, or God's will, traditional research vistas would lapse into unintelligibility. In effect, such research reifies the very assumptions that frame the undertaking.

Similarly, there is a deep tradition within Western culture of differentiating between rational processes (typically involving the deployment of categories or concepts) and those that are affective or emotional. Informed by this culturally sedimented distinction, one may set out to study whether all peoples share the same basic emotions, how emotional expressions differ across cultures, the socialization of emotions, the emotional vocabularies of other cultures, and the like (see Lutz and White's review, 1986). We can scarcely fail to undertake such explorations inasmuch as the emotions figure as essential to the makeup of the human person. A person without emotion simply fails, by common Western standards, to qualify as altogether human. To presume that members of other cultures had no emotions might be considered a pernicious form of ethnocentrism – not unlike the 19th-century consideration of whether black people possess souls. Does the contemporary study of emotion in other cultures rest on any stronger grounds than the earlier study of souls? We shall return to this problem shortly.

Finally, it should be added that the view of understanding as intersubjective connection invites the ethnographer to *stabilize* those cultures under study. If one sets out to discover systems of meaning, category structures, folk beliefs, symbol systems, and the like, the presumption must be made that the object of study is relatively perduring across time. If in continuous motion, then one could not hope for progressive approxima- tion. Individuals and the cultures that they constitute are thus characte- rized, by implication, as possessing an underlying structure, character, or essence. Should we choose not to view social understanding as a pro- gressive approximation to the underlying systems of others' thought, the presumption of stabilization would be less compelling. If social understanding were a matter of continuous unfolding, elaboration, and readjustment, without a fixed degree of success, then alternative views of other cultures would be invited. Processual, dynamic, and teleolo- gical characterizations of other persons might undergo a renaissance.

The impasse of inward access

We first considered the prevailing view of social understanding in contemporary ethnographic reporting. This view, stressing the inter- subjective connection among individuals, was found to rest on a set of interlocking assumptions concerning the nature of human functioning. Further, we found that these a priori assumptions concerning social understanding insinuate themselves into the ethnographic characteriza- tions of others. The tendencies toward individualization, dualism, a partitioning of the mental world and stabilization were all found compati- ble with the conception of understanding with which investigators enter the field. We are now prepared to take the next significant step. We must consider the possibility that the traditional conception of social under- standing is itself problematic. Although this conception seems eminently reasonable – both in academic and everyday circles – there is substantial reason for doubt. For, over the past few decades, a rhythm of adversarial counterpoint has become apparent. This critique is not limited to a single, tendentious minority, but emerges in a variety of differing contexts. As we explore the nature of this critique we must further be prepard to challenge the prevailing characterizations of other selves. Let us briefly consider three critical countercurrents.

WITTGENSTEIN AND THE DE-ONTOLOGIZING OF MENTAL TALK
One of the richest and most powerful bodies of scholarship countering the assumption of understanding as intersubjectivity can be traced to Wittgenstein. For Wittgenstein little merit could be found in the assumption that discourse about the mind was guided or corrected by the actuality of mental states. Rather, the limits placed upon such discourse derived from the conventional rules of language (or "language games") in which such terms were embedded. Consider such typical Wittgensteinian questions as "Does it sound queer to say 'He felt deep grief for one second.' because it so seldom happened?" or "Why is it

ridiculous to speak of a continuous feeling of familiar acquaintance? 'Well, because you don't feel one.' But is *that* the answer." Or again, "What does it mean to *believe* Goldback's theorem? What does this belief consist in? In a feeling of certainty as we state, hear, or think of the theorem?...And what are the characteristics of this feeling?" In attempting to answer such questions one rapidly realizes that mental observation (or introspection) furnishes no answers. At the same time, we become acutely aware of the powerful delimiting effects of conventional language use.

Inspired by such work, J. L. Austin (1962a) then went on to demonstrate the conceptual nightmare created by making ontological distinctions between the physical world or reality, on the one hand, and mental appearances on the other. How can appearance and reality be teased apart, when everything considered a reality from one standpoint is only an appearance from another? This attack on the assumption of perceptual inputs was coupled with an equally devastating critique by Gilbert Ryle (1949) on the concept of mind as an origin for action. As Ryle demonstrates, to presume that mental events, such as thinking, precede social actions leads one into an infinite regress of explanation. More recently, Rorty's *Philosophy and the Mirror of Nature* has provided an elegant and persuasive addition to the extension of the Wittgensteinian legacy. As Rorty argues, we have gone no further in our attempt to justify mental concepts than Descartes, who held them simply to be "incorrigibly known." As one breaks down the metaphoric view of minds as mirrors, the traditionally insoluable problems of epistemology vanish into a meaningless void.

As should be apparent, the general outcome of this line of argument is to leave the language of mind without reference. As Wittgenstein put it, "Try not to think of understanding as a mental process at all." And, if terms such as intention, thought, or emotion are merely components of linguistic practice, such that all that may be said about them is constrained by the rules of these practices, then it makes little sense to view understanding as a matter of discovering or penetrating other minds. If such terms as "perceive," "categorize," and "think" are bereft of an ontological base, then the assumption that understanding others requires mental representation – within either the knower or the person to be known – has little merit.

THE HERMENEUTIC CONUNDRUM

For over three centuries hermeneutic thinkers have labored over the problem of developing criteria for the valid interpretation of texts. Schleiermacher believed that to understand a text one needed to reexperience the mental processes of the text's author, This line of thought is later reiterated in Dilthey's concept of *Verstehen* and Collingwood's (1946) method of historical understanding. Because of the exotic character of the mental leap required to experience others' experiences, later theorists such as Betti (1980) and Hirsch (1976) attempted to establish more formal guidelines for interpretation. These guidelines emphasized logical inference and objective evidence. In many ways these later efforts ran parallel with logical empiricist thought, and have become subject to the many criticisms leveled against empiricist foundationalism.

With the deterioration of empiricism, and the renaissance of hermeneutic thought in recent years, it has become increasingly clear that the problem of validity in interpretation has not been satisfactorily solved. Consider for example, the confidence with which Charles Taylor wrote in 1964 about the possibility of verifying propositions about the purposive basis of behavior: "We must examine the phenomenon to see if the hypotheses of the kind proposed by rival theories hold of them, or whether, on the other hand, these theories, once in contact with the facts, begin to display the limitations mentioned in the last paragraph [e.g., unstable correlations, reliance on post hoc explanations]. In the latter case, we shall have good grounds for eliminating these rival theories, and the thesis of purposiveness will be correspondingly strengthened" (pp. 105–106). In contrast, consider Taylor, writing about the same problem in 1971, "making sense...[of another's actions] cannot but move in a hermeneutical circle. Our conviction that an account makes sense is contingent on our reading of action and situation. But these readings cannot be explained or justified except by reference to other such readings, and their relation to the whole. If an interlocutor does not understand this kind of reading, or will not accept it as valid, there is nowhere else the argument can go" (p. 127). Habermas (1979) has attempted to solve the problem of validity in interpretation by specifying ideal social conditions for communication. However, there is no rationale in Habermas's formulation as to why egalitarian social conditions should render the cognitive-intentional system transparent. Ricoeur (1981) has continued to wrestle with the problem of validity in interpretation – at times developing arguments favoring relativity and at others favoring valid understanding. However, as Wortham (1985) effectively demonstrates, Ricoeur cannot sustain the latter contention; problems surround him at every turn.

For many, the most continuously compelling refrain was originated by Gadamer (1960). As Gadamer proposed, the interpreter of texts always dwells within a unique historical context where particularized practices of interpretation prevail. These practices – or "foreconceptions" in Heidegger's terms – are employed in order to derive meaning from the text. They inevitably direct our attention and fashion our capacities to understand. Thus, understanding is primarily a product of the localized horizons of understanding and not the result of inner access to the author's true intent. Gadamer's view has yet to succumb to criticism.

For my own part, I believe there are principled difficulties underlying the hermeneutic attempt to establish validity in interpretation. The problem commences when one treats the text (or other social action) as opaque, and presumes a second level (an internal language) that must be located in order to render the overt transparent. Yet, all we have at our disposal in the process of understanding is a domain of public discourse (or action). We imagine there is a domain of private discourse to which this must be attached. Yet, we possess access neither to the private discourse itself nor to the rules by which it is tra￠ 'ated into the public domain. It follows that any attempt to translate (or understand) must be based on an analytic as opposed to a synthetic procedure. That is, readings or translations can only be rendered true by definition – by virtue of circularity rather than verification. We would face a similar problem if we assumed that all cloud formations were symbols of God's thoughts. Such thoughts could be read if we could but crack the code of how God's thoughts were transformed into nimbus as opposed to cirrus clouds, to thunderstorms and tornadoes. If such presumptions were made, what hope would we have of discovering through observation the impulses of God? All readings would inevitably be the result, first of an imaginary vernacular of the Holy One (e.g., God is a being who "wishes," "desires," wills," etc.), and a second set of imaginary translation rules (e.g., when God is angry the sky is dark). Once developed, such vehicles would indeed render God's thoughts transparent. However they would do so only by virtue of the imaginary system of definitions constructed to carry out the task. If there is no "inner voice" to which one can gain access, then all attempts to interpret the "inner" by virtue of the "outer" must be inherently circular.

At this point one may well wish to reconsider the initial presumption: that the level of overt language or action is itself opaque. Why have we allowed speech to be characterized as "mere sound," or writing to be defined as "mere markings"? A rose may be nothing more than "atomic particles," but this latter characterization seldom obstructs our immediate enjoyment of the flower. In daily life a rose is a rose; and so it should be as we confront the words and other actions of people.

THE DECONSTRUCTION OF THE AUTHOR

Within the literary domain, one of the most compelling but simultaneously controversial lines of thought to emerge within recent years has essentially questioned the capacity of the text to communicate an underlying meaning or intention. One of the foremost American proponents of this position, Stanley Fish (1980) has proposed that in literary interpretation the "interpreting entity (or agent), endowed with purposes and concerns is, by virtue of its very operating, determining what counts as the facts observed" (p. 8). As result of this reasoning, one is inclined to shift the focus of interpretation from the text to the "interpretive strategies," or "reading conventions" of the interpreter (see Davis, 1978). In many circles these operations carried out by the reader to incorporate the text into his/her preconceptions are termed "reader effects." How and to what extent the reader dominates the text has been a matter of vital and continuous concern (see Suleiman and Crosman's 1980 edited collection). In any case, to the extent that the reader appropriates the text, the author's intentions or meanings are essentially deconstructed.

It is in the writing of Derrida (1976) in particular that the deconstructionist thesis is most effectively launched against the dualistic assumption that overt actions, such as writing, are external expression of an inner reality. For Derrida, such an assumption is an expression of the misguided logocentrism of the Western tradition. His response is primarily a series of attempts to deconstruct the works of various contributors to the logocentric tradition – including Rousseau, Saussure, Lévi-Strauss, Husserl, and Searle. The force of such works is shown to depend not on the rational processes they celebrate, but on the use of literary figuration. The close analysis of these tropes reveals blind spots of paradox – or *aporia* – indicating that the works themselves fail to reveal any coherent system of underlying meaning. The works are essentially self-referring and deconstruct the very domain they attempt to represent.

As we see, each of these three bodies of argument raises serious questions concerning the traditional assumption that human understanding entails some form of psychological or intersubjective connection. From the Wittgensteinian perspective, critical conceptual problems are generated when one presumes that mental predicates possess ostensively definable referents. From this perspective, we are invited to abandon concern with the individual subjectivities that traditional arguments for human understanding have wished to conjoin. For many contemporary hermeneuticists, it is still fair play to posit a subjective realm. However, there is as yet no demonstrable way of accessing it. And, if there are principled arguments against validity in interpretation, then one wishes to know what is gained by positing such a world. If there are principled impediments to inner access, why should we presume its existence? For the deconstructionist, a similar conclusion seems warranted. As one reads, analyzes, characterizes, or criticizes the text, the author's intentions are deconstructed. Whether they exist or not is of little moment as the interpreter simply assimilates the text into his/her own preexisting frame.

It is not that these various lines of argument have failed utterly to enter anthropological dialogue. The Wittensteinian arguments have indeed been forcefully articulated in Rodney Needham's *Belief, Language and Experience*. As Needham's extensive analysis makes clear, anthropologists frequently produce extended accounts of belief systems in other cultures. Yet, when closely anlayzed, there are no indefeasible criteria for the existence of beliefs. "The [term *belief*] is often enough employed in ethnographical reports, and with an assurance which implies the assumption that we can directly and with confidence apply the concept of belief to others but it does not appear that the reportorial use of the word has in any instance provided a precise or verifiable description" (p. 189). In his more recent work, Needham (1981) has extended his analysis to the realm of psychological universals. Again on largely Wittgensteinian grounds, he concludes that the tendency to interpret exotic observations "as the varied expressions of universal inner states is in part a result of the uncritical employment of a traditional method of classification that conduces to this outcome. . . . It may be that European civilization. . . has afflicted much of the rest of the world with its perturbations about the self" (pp. 76–77). Although Needham does not follow through the implications of his argument, it follows that if the reading of other cultures in terms of universal states cannot be rendered valid, neither can the attempt to claim cultural differences. In his essay on emotion Solomon (1984) similarly demonstrates the paradoxical assumptions underlying the attempt to interpret emotional expression in other cultures. In more elaborate detail Wagner (1981) has described the means by which processes of discourse determine what we take to be the nature of self and society in anthropological study. Cultures are invented in discourse. As yet, however, such self-reflexive attempts as these have had but scant audiences.

The present chapter expands the basis of concern by raising doubts about the fundamental conception of social understanding as it undergirds ethnographic work. As is also apparent, as the traditional conception of understanding is eroded, so are the various associated characterizations of "the other" problematized. If the theory of understanding as intersubjective connection is found wanting, doubts must be raised concerning the propriety of individualizing others, assuming their dualistic existence, granting them stable and particularized mental states, and presuming that they view each other in these ways as well. A threat to the procedure of knowing simultaneously throws into jeopardy these ethnographic accounts that are its byproducts.

Toward a relational conception of social understanding

These various lines of argument are exceedingly valuable in generating doubt and provoking reflexive reconsideration of long-standing beliefs. Yet, we now reach a critical juncture. Although it is difficult in the face of such attacks to return to the traditions of comfort, we find ourselves at the end of this propaedeutic with neither a viable conception of what social understanding might be nor how it might proceed. Arguments in the Wittgensteinian mold make it difficult to ground psychological terminology; yet, how are we otherwise to account for processes of understanding and communication? The messages from both hermeneutic and deconstructionist analysis are also numbing in this regard. With increasing intensity one is informed that, indeed, human understanding may be impossible. We cannot probe the depths of others' intentional systems, as in the hermeneutic case. And, in the deconstructionist frame, we can never escape the prison of tropes that isolate us one from the other. This is indeed a bleak outcome. It is also an outcome difficult to reconcile with the very fact that we continue to read and write, and that Derrida himself would go to such great pains to deconstruct his own writings. It is just such attempts at negation that serve to undermine the deconstructionist conclusion. For, if it were true that our reading of texts were only a process of self-referring, there would be no need for such a self-immolating flourish. Deconstruction could proceed on its own without the author's assistance.

It is at just this point that one begins to consider the possibility for alternative accounts of understanding. If understanding as intersubjective connection ceases to compel, how are we to account for our continued engagement in a world of words? What is it we do when we share words with one another? And why, in many cases, would we go to such great efforts to do it? There are a number of fundamental conceptual issues that might be raised at this juncture. On what grounds do we demand a concept of understanding and communication; what valuational purposes are to be served by such an account? Are these terms themselves not so heavily encrusted by centuries of semantic chicanery as to be immobilizing? How is it possible to step outside the boundaries of our preconceptions to offer anything more than a recursive variant on existing conventions? I shall take the liberty of sidestepping such petulant questions for the moment, because I wish to take some preliminary steps toward an alternative account of understanding, expose them to possible shortcomings, and relate them both to ethnographic inscription and the cultural construction of self.

UNDERSTANDING AS ADJUDICATED COORDINATION

At the outset let us take seriously the outcomes of the above analysis, and abandon the presumption that mental entities or processes must serve as the critical constituents of the process of social understanding. If we are no longer committed to a conception of social knowledge as involving some form of mental representation, internal ordering, categorization, inference to other minds, and the like, then we are not compelled to recapitulate yet once again the foibles of empiricism as against rationalism or the failings of rationalism as exposed to long-standing empiricist critique. The attempt, then, is to extricate ourselves from the ingurgitating fray that has consumed most of Western epistemological thought for the past two thousand years (see also Gergen, 1985). This move enables us to treat actions, words, texts, and the like as what they are and not puzzling emanations from yet some other obscure, ontological realm. In abandoning the assumption that the locus of knowledge lies within the minds of single individuals, we also make an important move against the value of self-contained individualism that now appears so problematic for Western culture (Bellah, Madsen, Sullwin, Swindler, & Tipton, 1985; Sampson, 1977). No longer are we compelled to view insights, findings, theoretical breakthroughs, methodological discoveries, startling findings, and the like as the products of the single, heroic scientist arrogating to him/herself increments in power and prestige.

Once we have abandoned the assumption that understanding lies within the minds of single individuals, we are prepared to take a further step. The path has been cleared in this case by some of the theorists previously cited. It is essentially a path leading away from the single individual as the center of the social world to the relationship among persons. In moving away from the traditional hermeneutic structure, Taylor (1971) has contrasted "subjective meaning" (the possession of single individuals) with "intersubjective meanings," which are said to be "constitutive of the soical matrix in which individuals find themselves and act" (p. 48). In their analysis of communication Pearce and Cronen (1980) place a strong emphasis on the extent to which communication depends on the "coordinated management of meaning"; Mishler (1986) demonstrates this mutually interdependent character of meaning in the research interview. Within his analyses we find the meanings of utterances are not fixed but continue to shift over the course of a conversation as the participants manage their implications through recontextualization. Similarly, John Shotter (1980) has coined the concept of *joint-action* to refer to patterns of action for which the combined contribution is required of at least two persons. As he sees language, it is not essentially a vehicle for rendering accurate reports about the nature of the world. Rather, "the function of our communicative activities (is) to formulate the situations or states of affairs in which we are involved *as* situations, *as* states of affairs, to formulate them as topics or as common places in terms of which we can relate ourselves to one another" (1986, p. 71). In each case the theorist shifts attention away from the single individual; the central units of understanding become social collaborations or relational forms.

Against this backdrop let us press forward to consider an account of understanding as relational form. This account, termed *relational adjudication,* is lodged within three interdependent arguments.

Relational Nuclei. At the outset, it is clear that living beings are sustained only by virtue of their relationships with environments. On the biological level, we cannot sustain ourselves without relationships that engender oxygen, water, food, and so on. Relationships on the social level are essential in modern society for providing shelter, clothing, most of our foodstuffs, protection, health care, and so on. Yet, within the societal case, if each is dependent on others, then all personal outcomes are essentially contingent on interchange. The individual's well-being cannot be extricated from the web of relationships in which he/she is engaged. The character of the relationship depends, in turn, on the process of adjusting and readjusting actions. In effect, forms of relationship depend on the mutual coordination of actions. As this coordination is progressively realized, it may be said that a *relational nucleus* is formed. A relational nucleus may be viewed as a self-sustaining system of coordinated actions in which two or more persons are engaged. Thus, for example, as we encounter each other from day to day, our actions tend toward coordination. The movements of the eyes, hands, and feet, for example, or the number of words we speak, their volume and speed, and so on, are all in the process of becoming mutually coordinatd (we shall treat the exceptions shortly). As this coordination takes place – taking turns in conversation, adjusting the tone of voice so that the other may hear without discomfort, speaking in mutually acceptable patterns of words, walking together at similar speeds, and so on – we come to form a relational nucleus.

This line of reasoning furnishes an initial step toward an account of social understanding. As it may be proposed, such understanding first requires the cross-time coordination of action among persons. The extent to which this is so can be demonstrated in a variety of ways. For example, for me to extend my hand is itself a meaningless act, merely a spatiotemporal occurrence. However, should you smile and reach out to shake my extended hand, we have engendered meaning; it may properly be said that understanding has occurred. Yet, if I extend my hand and you, in turn, stop me with a stare, the coordinated achievement of a handshake rings hollow. I appear to have misunderstood; what have I forgotten, to what was I insensitive? Or, in a more extended conversation, either interlocutor may discredit the understanding of the other by treating his/her utterances as nonsense. For me to "make sense" in a conversation requires that you treat my discourse as sensible, and vice versa. Thus, virtually any arrangement of sounds, from Middle English to periodic grunts and groans, may generate a sense of understanding if the participants are willing to treat each other's utterances as integral to the existing pattern of relationship. A good example of the deterioration of the coordinated achievement of understanding has been furnished by Garfinkel (1967). As his students have demonstrated, relations are strained to the breaking point if one interlocutor treats another's utterances, however sensible by traditional standards, as mystifying. If I respond to everything you say with "I don't understand," "what do you mean?" or the equivalent, our relationship will soon be terminated.

The individual as intersection of relational nucleii. The mother and child form a prototype of a relational nucleus. Before birth, mutual accommodation is necessary for survival. However, as the child enters the culture he/she becomes embedded within a multiplicity of relational processes. Typically, with increasing age the range and intensity of these relationships continues to expand. In effect, the person becomes a constituent of multiple nuclei. On this view, what we have traditionally viewed as single individuals can more fruitfully be conceptualized as intersections of an array of relational units. Or, to put it another way, each of us carries with us an array of relational patterns of which we are a part. When any two of us come together, it is essentially the meeting point for the multiple systems of relatedness in which each of us is embedded. The trajectory of coordinated efforts of any two persons will thus be vitally influenced by these multiple enmeshments. As any two of us develop as a relational unit, we are the common interstice or point of confrontation for a multiplicity of relationships.

Adjudication and the generation of "understanding" as a social category. Within any relationship, isolated from context, the process of mutual adjustment or accommodation may proceed with relative ease. However, as one enters into multiple relationships the path to viable coordination becomes increasingly arduous. Because each individual is the common intersection of a variety of nuclei, the participants essentially confront the task of coordinating multiplicities. At times this convergence of individuals may be frustrated: For example, relationships with other members of the same gender may often favor patterns of mutual coordination that are inharmonious when imported into cross-gender relationships. The Amercian male who responds with jocularity to the female's account of her woes may be accused of failure in understanding, even though the same actions would be favored within the locker room. At other times the engagement in multiplicity may confront participants with mutually exclusive actions. Coordination within one relationship will be disastrous for another. By contemporary Western standards, one cannot easily be committed simultaneously to two "primary," intimate relationships. This is so because the requirement for bringing off such relationships is typically a commitment of exclusive proportion.

It is just such problems in coordination that set the stage for adjudication – for public judgments that particular actions are out of synchrony or do not fit within the emerging pattern. In particular, it is the language of "understanding," "knowledge," "insight," "savvy," "intuition," and the like that is deployed in both approbation and accrediting. In Austin's (1962b) terms, such language carries with it illocutionary implications. It serves to indicate in the relationship that a given action is prized (e.g., "You understand me very well"), or that it must be altered or abandoned. The announcement, "You just don't understand" is an invitation for the other to mend his/her ways. For one to respond to an action with "Oh, you just don't really know me" is not to say that the other has mentally failed to penetrate one's mental world; rather, it is to say that the preceding action fails to fit within the unfolding sequence of interrelated actions according to some criterion.

The origins for evaluative criteria against which coordination is judged may be several. In principle, the possibility for adjudication within a single, isolated relationship is minimal. Isolated relationships, within themselves, have no necessary trajectory, no essential goals to which they must aspire. Adjudication arises primarily within the context of multiple relationships – where comparisons among coordinated sequences are possible. In this case differences may be discerned and evaluations made. On this account, the master–slave relationship is not intrinsically undesirable for the slave; it becomes so primarily as advantageous alternatives become salient. Once various criteria have become articulated and buttressed by evaluative discourse, they may be deployed in wide-ranging relationships. Criteria of justice, peacefulness, or equality may be used to coordinate relations on some occasions, and criteria of competitiveness, sadomasochism, or aggressiveness may be employed in others. Patterns of love and cooperation require no less coordination of efforts among participants than do patterns of combat and slavery. Failures to meet the criteria of coordinated action in all cases may be judged in terms of a failed understanding.

On the present account, both judgments of success and failure are the result of joint or interdependent actions. Yet, even though the achievement is a product of relationships, one is neither obliged to credit nor to chastise all the participants in the case of success or failure. Rather, as scores of attribution and communication researchers have attempted to demonstrate, the locus of praise or blame can be shifted in a variety of ways. By obscuring portions of the relational sequence, any single individual may be rendered praiseworthy or culpable. It is this strategic deployment of the criteria that enables the individuals in the above illustrations to create ignorance or misunderstanding in the other. If I reach out to shake hands and you stop me with a stare, I may appear to have misunderstood. But this localization of misunderstanding need only be temporary. I may respond to your stare with a query into your visual capabilities, social skills, or the like – thus shifting the location of ignorance back to you. Or if an acquaintance treats my conversational utterances as nonsense, who has failed the task of human understanding? With an alternative shift in focus, one might equally discredit the one who has brought a halt to successful coordination through his/her questioning.

As this analysis should make clear, the concept of understanding as the possession of the single individual is abandoned as a misleading holdover from traditional and problematic assumptions of dualism. By and large we may view the common practice of holding single individuals responsible for achievements or deficits in human understanding as an exercise in practical rhetoric. In the same way that it is inappropriate to allocate depth of insight to single scientists, authors, philosophers, or statesmen, it is also problematic to discredit failing students, errant spouses, or Republican presidents for their failure in understanding. In each case such individuals are constituents of a complex array of relationships, and it is inappropriate from the present standpoint to disembed their actions from the relational sequences of which they are a part.

Relational understanding in the context of the ethnographic report

The position taken here can be clarified by returning to the process of ethnographic rendering. Let us first reconsider Geertz's views. Geertz

(1974) argues against Malinowski's proposal that some form of empathic leap is required to get inside the mind or experience of the native. One is not required, as in George Herbert Mead's case, to perform some exotic mental feat such as "taking the role of the other." In these arguments, Geertz's analysis is compatible with the position outlined thus far. However, in most of his writings, Geertz then goes on to adopt a form of soft dualism – respecting the interiority of the other while not elaborating on the inner ontology. As he points out in his essay on the evolution of mind (Geertz, 1973), "when we attribute mind to an organism, we are talking about neither the organism's actions nor its products per se, but about its capacities and proneness, its dispositions, to perform certain kinds of actions and produce certain kinds of products, a capacity and proneness we of course infer from the fact that he does sometimes perform such actions and produce such products" (p. 59). As one sees, this definition harbors a nettlesome circularity. Actions are those movements that are intended or mentally produced (as opposed to "behaviors," such as falling through the air); one must thus presume the mind in order to identify action and then use action to draw inferences to mind.

Nevertheless, the attempt of the anthropologist, Geertz contends, should be to capture the world "from the native's point of view." This capturing of "other peoples' subjectivities" is to be guided, for Geertz, by a form, not yet fully articulated, of hermeneutic analysis. One engages, says Geertz, in a "continuous dialectical tacking between the most local of detail and the most global of global structure in such a way as to bring both into view simultaneously" (1974:491). By this sort of "intellectual perpetual motion," the "penetration of other people's modes of thought" is made possible. As should be apparent, it is this line of argument that the earlier sections of the present chapter call into question. The hermeneutic circle that Geertz describes is, as we have seen, self-fulfilling; or in other terms, such an analysis will inevitably redeem the conceptual forestructure with which one commences. It is also in this sense that the present account is congenial with critics of cross-cultural (or paradigm) translation (see Fuller, 1986).

Geertz's analysis also suggests that it is possible for the ethnographer to return to his/her home culture with a form of description that can reveal a culture's system of thought. Such a possibility is also precluded by the present analysis. From the present standpoint, understanding is a relational achievement. Thus, understanding within the native setting results from the coordination of one's activities with theirs in such a way that success (as judged by their standards) is achieved. When the ethnographer returns to the home culture, the forms of coordination and the standards of relational success are typically of a different form. Relevant patterns of coordination in this case include the rendering of anthropological accounts. Institutionalized patterns of coordination (including the rhetorical rules for rendering objectivity) and evaluation will place powerful restrictions over putative acts of description.

These latter restrictions have gained considerable prominence in recent anthropological analyses. The work of Clifford (1983), Crapanzano (1986), Marcus (1982) and others has focused on the various rhetorical devices by which "the alien other" is rendered palpable, transparent, revealing, or informative. Additional attempts have been made to elucidate the value commitments informing or guiding contemporary inscriptions of the other (see Fabian, 1983; Marcus & Fischer, 1986; Said, 1979). Also emerging are a variety of innovative attempts to break through the forestructure of Western tradition, to share or diffuse ethnographic authorship. As Clifford (1983) has reviewed, varying investigators depict the web of discursive positionings from which their accounts emerge, furnish excerpts from ongoing dialogues with the natives, use polyphonic accounts in which native voices shape the reader's understanding of the culture, and produce collective ethnographies in which both natives and ethnographers participate.

Yet, in spite of the significance of these latter attempts in removing the mantel of authority from the words of the single ethnographer, and in expanding the means of ethnographic characterization, they do not fully solve the problems addressed in the present analysis. Each of these attempts suggests, at least implicitly, that the resulting ethnographies are somehow less biased – more accurate or fully rounded – than accounts produced by the single participant-observer of Western origin. Moreover, even if we suspend the question of who controls the final account in the home setting, such a conclusion is unwarranted – whether on empiricist, hermeneutic, or constructionist grounds. Most important for present purposes, the fact is that in all these cases the ethnographic account is finally transformed into the Western linguistic idiom. It must ultimately yield to the conventions of sense making within this cultural setting. Neither the words nor the putative actions of the native can appear within this idiom as nonsensical, else the ethnography must be considered a failed enterprise. Further, if the rendering does not speak to issues of common concern within the scholarly subculture it will also have failed to make an acceptable contribution to understanding. In effect, regardless of who participates in the writing of the ethnography, if it is to be considered intelligible communication, it must fit congenially into the conventional systems of coordinated action from which ascriptions of understanding emerge within the home culture.

In terms of the previous analysis, the ethnographer enters the field as an intersection of various relational nuclei within the home culture. Similarly, each denizen of the field culture is socially immersed – a "group carrier," as it were. When ethnographer and native interact, it is essentially the beginning of a new relational nucleus. Both will be engaged in adjusting actions over time to create a viable pattern of interchange according to some set of standards. In neither case will the participants be attempting to "read the minds" or "penetrate the subjectivities" of the other; nor will understanding of the other depend on translating their words or actions into one's home language. The new relationship is forged by the participants together as they adapt the resources and conventions supplied by the various relational trajectories of which they are a part.

When the ethnographer returns to the home culture – transformed in certain degree by the new relational forms in which he/she is now embedded – he/she essentially returns to the initial array of relational nuclei. The major task that must now be confronted is to contribute to the intelligibility system of the scholarly community (composed of intersecting relational nuclei). To do so requires a conformity to the kinds of conventions (relational forms) shared by that community concerning the kinds of inscriptions that may be appropriately included in an ethnographic report. Regardless of what transpires in the field, the ethnographer must return ultimately to the conventions of discourse within the professional culture. In this sense, ethnographic reports are not mimetic; they are pragmatic constituents of the relational nuclei making up the profession.

Two particularly nettlesome issues remain. First, does the present analysis suggest that ethnographic reporting must inevitably recapitulate the conventional? If the traditions of professional discourse guide and constrain the ontology of the other, is the discipline relegated to a continuous elaboration of the status quo? I think not. First, the preceding makes apparent that among the major constraints over contemporary ethnography is the conventional view of social understanding itself. As viable alternatives to this account are developed, then new forms of ethnographic representation are invited. It is to this end that much of the present discussion is directed. In addition, however, there is at least one major tradition in anthropological scholarship that is itself lodged against continuous replication of the norms. In particular, that scholarly offspring of the liberal tradition in anthropology – namely the attempt to elucidate cultural variation – can be a major antidote to ontological sedimentation. One may confront the field setting with either an eye toward universality or toward variation. If the latter route is selected, the ethnographer confronts the task of specifying an ontology that differs from that which is normative within the home culture. To be sure, this ontology cannot be wholly exotic, lest it resist intelligibility within the traditions of the home culture. However, it is at just this point that creative ethnographic writing may press against the boundaries of intelligibility. Much like the poet, the ethnographer can play at the margins of the acceptable – unsettling and reconstituting the language of representation so as to undermine the traditions and carve out a new domain of intelligibility. When the constructions of others attempt to submerge the individual within the communal, generate new gender categories, outline alternative forms of emotion, demonstrate exotic levels of self-consciousness, or help the reader understand the sense of seeing the spiritual as preeminent over the material, they are tampering with the discourse patterns of Western culture. In this context erosion and emancipation are close companions (see also Marcus & Fischer, 1986).

Numerous examples might be used to fortify and extend the argument. Lawrence Rosen's (1984) fascinating account of social relations in a Moroccan Muslim community is particularly apposite. As we have seen, ethnographic metatheory has undergone two major evolutions in recent decades: First, the symbolic-interpretive movement largely undermined the more empiricist-scientist account of behavioral study; however, in more recent times problems have been discerned within the symbolic-interpretive movement and vital interest has been generated in what might be termed postmodern ethnography. Within this vein investigators have begun to shift attention to the social construction of ethnographic reports. The present chapter is, of course, engaged in this latter project. What is most interesting in Rosen's case is that this movement in ethnographic metatheory essentially furnishes him with the conceptual implements for depicting Muslim social relations. That is, Rosen makes repeated visits to the field, spends 27 months immersed within the culture, and returns to portray the Muslims as people for whom Western ethnographic metatheory forms the "deep structures" of relationship. We are first informed that the culture is one in which intentional states are critical in judging persons, in determining their worth and their future trajectories. In effect, the denizens of the culture seek to identify the interiors of each other. Yet, as Rosen points out, this presents to the Moroccans "the problem of other minds." How is this hermeneutic problem solved but in a postmodern vein, by "bargaining with one another over the definition of the situation through which the others' intention is named and comprehended" (p. 56). In effect, Muslim community life reveals to the ethnographer the structure of metatheory within the Western community of scholars. Yet, this account of Rosen's work can be viewed as critical only if one is committed to the possibility of objective ethnography. From the present standpoint, Rosen's analysis is perfectly on target. In his elaboration of the process of social bargaining – the detailing of social typification, codes of entailment, and the logic of consequence – Rosen contributes to the dialogue currently absorbing the discipline. The account of Muslim culture succeeds in enriching the conceptual arena, stretching the boundaries of discourse in which the colloquy proceeds.

Finally, it must be asked, is all this to say that such accounts are fictitious, or without validity? Could they have been written without ever visiting the foreign culture (as in *Krippendorf's tribe*). Would a visitor to the alien culture, having read an ethnography, not be more suitably prepared for what was to follow than one who had not? At the outset, the present analysis does not conclude that the ethnographies are fictitious or invalid. Rather, questions of correspondence are simply irrelevant. Concepts of fact and fiction imply that, when properly used, scientific language can serve as a device with which one can mirror or map the world. Such metaphors of language use are simply irrelevant to the present account (see Gergen, 1986, for amplification). Good ethnographies can surely be written without relevant fieldwork, if by "good" is meant that the rhetorical conventions of the home culture (in this case of the anthropological community) are properly employed.

Yet, in spite of the bumptious character of these remarks, there nevertheless remains at least one important sense in which ethnographies may be said to vary in their validity, a sense in which a well-turned ethnography may give advantage to the newcomer to a given clime. The concept of validity in this case does not rest on standards of verisimilitude. Rather, it is a validity born of practical utility. That is, although words may not serve mimetic functions, they are embedded within ongoing relational practices, and they may be critical to the success of these practices. If a flash fire suddenly breaks out in your frying pan and you cry to your mate for the box of salt, much depends on whether the phrase "box of salt" has been used by the two of you to refer to a specific object. However, whether this object, ontologically speaking, is a box of salt – as opposed to sodium chloride, a molecular composition, a food additive, a taste of the sea, a granulated substance, or something else, is a matter of cultural convention. None of these labels possesses ontological significance; all have indexical utility within circumscribed, sociohistorical contexts. And so it is with ethnographic reports. To the extent that the forms of practice to which they are wedded have practical utility for the newly arriving visitor, they may be said to have validity – not because they are accurate, but because the practices that they invoke are advantageous in the impending process of mutual accommodation. It is only in this conventionalized sense that Holmes (1986) can be said to judge the relative accuracy of Mead's as opposed to Freeman's ethnography of the Samoans.

The relational understanding of mental discourse

Thus far we have explored important shortcomings in the traditional view of understanding as intersubjective connection, and have touched on the implications of this challenge for ethnographic characterization. As an alternative to the traditional conception, a preliminary sketch has been developed of understanding as adjudicated coordination. Various implications of this position for the process of ethnographic reporting have also been explored. However, we must at last return to a critical orienting theme within this chapter, namely the characterization of selves. As we previously saw, the conception of understanding as intersubjective connection is linked to particular views of the self; as long as ethnographic work remains committed to this conception of understanding other cultures, characterization of these cultures will bear the fingerprint of this view. It is clear from the earlier line of reasoning that there is no escape from discursive convention so long as one is striving toward intelligibility within the home culture. However, it is useful at this juncture to inquire into the characterization of other selves that would emerge from the relational account of understanding outlined earlier. If the reasoning behind this account is extended, how would other cultures be read? How would our current intelligibilities be altered?

This last turn is not to be taken lightly. That is, should the view of understanding as a relational process be extended, then we should no longer be able to replicate the traditional views of persons as individuals, possessing minds, thoughts, intentions, emotions, and so on. Alterations in our views of human selves would be required. Yet, it is also clear from the preceding analysis that such alterations cannot suddenly spring into existence. To be intelligible, language must be embedded in reliable ways within patterns of ongoing exchange. Novel conceptions cannot conveniently move past the shared patterns of interdependence that already exist. How then is transformation in discourse to take place? The attempt in the present case is to generate new meanings through reconstitution of existing practices. By assembling existing forms of discourse in alternative patterns, we may be able to borrow from the past while building into the future – to play at the edges of meaning, hoping that those edges may thus be extended without toppling into the void of opacity.

Let us first satisfy ourselves that there is a significant edge to be extended. First, consider the possibility that the very meaning of an individual's actions from moment to moment is derived from the manner in which such actions are embedded within ongoing relationships. We speak of persons as possessing motives, beliefs, understandings, plans, and so on, as if these are properties of individual selves. Yet, how is it that we formulate these expressions? If your arm is raised above your head there is little that may be said about your motives. Your action is merely a spatiotemporal configuration. In contrast, if another person is before you, crouching and grimacing, suddenly it becomes possible to speak of you as aggressive, oppressive, or ruthless. If the other is a child standing on tiptoes, arms outstretched, his ball lodged in a tree above your head, it becomes possible to characterize you as helpful or nurturant. Additional configurations of the other might yield the conclusion that you are playful, obedient, protective, proud, and so on. Note that your movement is similar in each case, yet, it is impossible to characterize you as an individual – until the relational context is articulated. Similarly, the other person's movements have little bearing on our description until they are seen within the context of your conduct. In effect, what we treat as individualized characteristics – aggressiveness, playfulness, altruism, and the like – are primarily products of joint configurations.

From this perspective, the discourse of relationship represents a vastly unarticulated subtext upon which rests the text of individual selves. The question to be addressed, then, is whether we can articulate this subtext. Can we bring into the foreground that which has remained obscure? It is as if we have at our disposal a rich language for characterizing rooks, pawns, and bishops but have yet to discover the game of chess. How can we redefine qualities of self in such a way that their derivation from the whole is made clear? Can we develop a language of understanding in which there are not powerful, helpful, intelligent, or depressed selves, for example, but in which these characterizations are derivative from more essential forms of relationship? Can we define the games in which the characteristics of self are rooted? Let us use the emotions as a test case.

EMOTIONS AS CONSTITUENTS OF RELATIONAL FORMS

Traditionally, the emotions are treated as private experiences or possessions of the individual. It is individuals who have emotions, who are struck or driven by their emotions, and who may or may not give expression to their emotions. It is this view that Lutz (1988) sees as a typical "Euroamerican construction" that "unconsciously serves as a normative device for judging the mental health of culturally different peoples" (p. 288). Further, it should also be clear from the preceding analysis of social understanding that the vocabulary of emotions could neither be derived from nor validated by accessing the minds of others. Yet, emotion terms are critical to our descriptions of persons; to abandon such terms would not only render ordinary actions unintelligible, but would jeopardize a great many relational patterns of significance. Patterns of relationship, indexed as love, friendship, motherhood, fatherhood, and so on would be substantially impoverished without an associated discourse of affect. Thus, the attempt is not to argue against the use of emotion terms, either in daily relations or ethnographic reporting, but to alter the way in which they figure within discourse. In particular, the move is toward refiguring emotional terms (along with the actions indexed by those terms) as components of more extended relational patterns – constitutents of relational nuclei (see also LeFevre's, 1987, analysis of creativity as a social act).

A convenient entry into relational space is furnished by various contributions to the view of emotion as social performance. Averill's work on hostility and on romantic love (Averill, 1982, 1985; see also Armon-Jones, 1985) is perhaps the best exemplar of this view. As Averill argues, emotions may be viewed as "transient social roles," or syndromes of action. Cognitive and physiological processes are not ruled out, but rather than determining emotional expression, they are recruited for effective execution. One uses one's capacities to present the performance more adequately. This position has a variety of advantages. It absorbs the many cross-cultural studies of variation in emotional patterning. It erases the problem of determining how many emotions there are, while recognizing the possibility that there may be different physiological patterns for various kinds of emotional performances (thus avoiding the naïveté of the "general arousal" assumption). Further, it does not reduce the human being to a one-dimensional cognizer.

For some, the metaphor of emotions as performance is not altogether a happy one, suggesting as it does that emotions are "playacted," or the result of superficial staging. However, such criticism depends on the extension of the metaphor beyond what Averill and others intend. Emotional performances can be dead serious.

Yet from the present standpoint the performance orientation possesses one significant shortcoming: In its present form it remains individualistic in form. That is, it adopts the traditional view that emotional syndromes are possessions of single individuals (or performers); from this perspective, one can understand emotions by focusing on the actions of single performers. Yet, following preceding arguments, spontaneous emotional performance, cut away from relational process, would be nonsensical. For example, if one's hostess at a dinner party suddenly bolted from her seat to express hostility, or buried her head in her lap and began loud sobbing, one would undoubtedly be unsettled or abashed. Further, if she could not make it clear how such outbursts were related to a series of preceding and/or anticipated events (essentially a narrative account) – if she announced that she merely felt like such outbursts for no particular reason – one might seriously consider her a candidate for psychiatric assistance. To be intelligible, the emotional action must be a constituent of a recognizable sequence. There is good reason, then, to view emotional performances as constituents of larger or more extended patterns of interaction. In Wittgenstein's terms, "Pain-behavior and the behavior of sorrow – these can only be described along with their external occasions. . . . Behavior and kind of occasion belong together. . . . Only surrounded by certain normal manifestations of life is there such a thing as an expression of pain. Only surrounded by an even more far-reaching particular manifestation of life, such a thing as the expression of sorrow or affection" (Wittgenstein, 1966). The present shift, then, is to these more extended "manifestations of life."

THE CASE OF ESCALATING HOSTILITY

Let us consider an initial line of research that presses these conceptions into practice. In this case we hope to elucidate at least one common interaction sequence in which emotional performance plays a critical role. An intriguing study by Richard Felson (1984) furnished a useful starting point for the analysis. Felson interviewed 380 male ex-criminal offenders and mental patients incarcerated for violent acts. Among other things, they were asked to describe an incident in which violence had occurred. In analyzing these accounts, Felson came to the conclusion that violent actions are not spontaneous, uncontrollable eruptions, but rather, are embedded in reliable patterns of interchange. In particular, the typical pattern of interaction is one in which person A violates a social rule or norm (e.g., playing the radio too loud, stepping in front of the line, interrupting others' privacy, etc.). A verbal exchange follows, in which person B typically reproaches A, blaming and ordering him/her to cease or correct the offensive behavior. Person A refuses to accept the blame or order, *B* threatens, *A* continues, and then *B* attacks *A*. In effect, Felson succeeded in revealing a common interaction scenario in which physical violence is an intelligible part.

By common standards, the relationship between violence and the emotions is an intimate one: Violence is typically viewed as an expression of hostile emotions. In this sense Felson's research provides a significant illustration of the fruitfulness of viewing emotions as relational components. Further study was thus undertaken to explore scenarios of hostility and violence in normal populations. This exploration was inspired, in part, by the work of Pearce and Cronen (1980) on the management of meaning. As they propose, many recurring patterns of interchange are unwanted by the participants, and yet are willingly repeated. Domestic violence may be a significant exemplar of such *unwanted repetitive patterns*. That is, neither husband nor wife may want physical violence, but once the pattern (or scenario) has begun, they may see little choice but to bear on toward its normative conclusion – physical abuse. This view also suggests that although the culture generally holds domestic violence in ill regard, for those embarked on the relational scenario the moves toward violence may all seem appropriate, if not desirable. To at least one of the participants violence may seem, at a given moment in a scenario, morally required.

With these concerns in mind research was designed to elucidate a relational scenario of *escalating hostility* (Harris, Gergen, & Lannamann, 1986). Often it appears both expected and desired in our culture that people will respond to acts of hostility with hostility; further, each escalation in hostility on the part of one member of a relationship will evoke increased hostility on the part of another. If such a scenario is carried out over time, participants should eventually come to see physical aggression as both normal and desirable.

To explore these issues research participants were exposed to unfolding stories involving two-person interaction. At the story's outset one protagonist mildly criticized the other. The story was interrupted at this point, and the participants asked to rate the probability, desirability, and advisability of each of a series of possible responses. The list of options ranged from highly conciliatory on the one extreme to physical violence at the other. Thus, for example, the participants read about a young married couple. In the first scene the husband mildly criticized his wife's cooking. The participants then rated a range of options (from embracing and kissing to physical striking) for the wife. After the evaluations were made, the participants turned the page to read that the reaction of the wife had been to escalate the hostility – she responded by criticizing her husband. Again, the story was halted and ratings made of the husband's probable reactions to his wife, along with their desirability and advisability. It is then found that he becomes harsher in his comments to his wife, and so on. Eight instances of escalation were thus furnished to participants with evaluations made after each.

Although a full review of the findings is beyond the scope of this discussion, the results depicted in Figure 20.1 are exemplary of the general pattern of findings for each of the stories. Specifically, the figure displays the ratings of probability for the most hostile options (combined) and the most conciliatory options (combined). As can be seen, the rated probability of hostile options increases over the eight intervals, while the probability of conciliation options decreases.

Most interestingly, however, this same pattern of mounting hostility and decreasing conciliation is generally revealed in both the ratings of desirability and advisability. That is, the research participants not only saw the increasing hostility as probable, but they also saw it as appropriate and praiseworthy. Although the participants would never recommend at the outset of the scenario that the husband or wife throw the dinner on the floor, by the end of four exchanges they are quite willing to endorse this option. The saw-tooth trajectory featured in Figure 20.1 is the result of the participants' ratings of the husband versus the wife in the story. The research participants generally endorsed more hostility for the female than the male. None of them advised that the husband should strike the female. Yet, in a second story, involving hostile interchanges between two male students, even physical violence was endorsed.

As such research suggests, when mild hostility is expressed, it seems both appropriate and desirable for the target to respond with hostility as well. And, although neither participant may wish an embittered antagonism, this early exchange invites the participants to engage in a widely shared cultural scenario. Each may righteously attack the other with slightly increasing intensity, and as the scenario unfolds there is little that

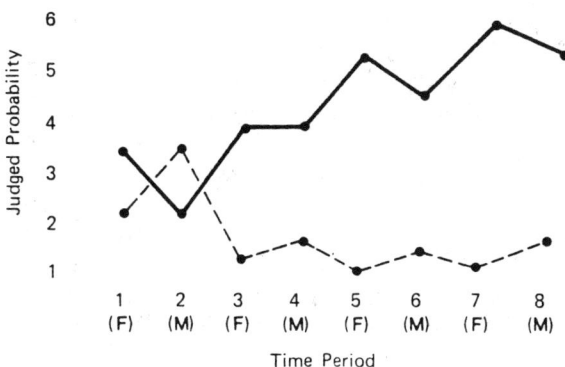

Figure 20.1. Aggressive (−) and conciliatory (− −) preferences over time.

either can do to change the direction of events. The parallel between such domestic incidents and relationships among nations is striking.

EMOTIONAL SCENARIOS: EXPANDING THE SPECTRUM

Encouraged by this line of inquiry, we broadened the perspective by exploring the way in which a variety of different emotional actions – including anger, depression, and happiness – fit within ongoing patterns of relationship. The research strategy in this case has been more open-ended than in the foregoing. Rather than trying to elucidate a single pattern, as in the case of escalating hostility, the attempt was to explore the possibility of multiple scenarios. That is, it seemed plausible that any given emotional expression might be embedded in a variety of common sequences or scenarios, just as a given move of the torso might figure in a variety of standard dances or the movement of the arm might be included in a variety of team maneuvers. This exploratory technique also seemed fruitful in pinpointing differences between effective or desirable scenarios as opposed to ineffectual or failing ones, that is, scenarios that might be judged as knowledge displays according to the terms of our earlier analysis.

In each of these cases research participants were presented with a vignette in which they were told of a friend who expressed to them one of the several emotions. Typically, for example, the friend was said to be a roommate who entered the room and expressed a given emotion – such as "I am really angry at you," "I'm feeling so depressed," or "I'm so happy." In each case the research participants were asked how they would respond to the expression. As a result of preliminary analysis it became apparent that such expressions would engender only a single form of reply, that of an *inquiry* into the cause. In effect, people are scarcely free to reply to a friend's expression of emotion in any way they wish. To remain intelligible by cultural standards, one must inquire into the source. Yet, this inquiry is far more than a cultural formality. In terms of our earlier discussion, the emotional expression is without sense or definition until it has been placed within an unfolding context of events. In this light the answer to the question "why are you feeling..." furnishes the recipient with an indication of what story is being played out. On a more metaphoric level, the answer has the perlocutionary effect of informing the listener what game is being played, or what dance is being performed. Without this information the recipient cannot generate further actions that will be sensible or appropriate. Indeed, in the present study, there was no participant who responded to the initial emotional expression with other than a query into cause.

The research participants were then furnished with a prepared reply to the query. The roommate was angry because the target (in this case the research participant) had revealed a failing grade to a mutual friend after pledging secrecy; depression was attributed to a general feeling that nothing was going right, classes were going badly, a recent breakup of a close relationship, no sleep, and so on; happiness was attributed to the general feeling that everything was going well – classes, a close relationship, and so on. The research participants were then asked to indicate how they would reply to this explanation. At this point in the research two rounds of turn taking (or interacts) had thus been achieved.

This array of partial scenarios was then used as the sample pool to explore a third round of turn taking. That is, sample protocols were selected at random from the initial pool of interchanges and were presented to a new group of research participants. This group was asked to take the part of the roommate who had initially engaged in the emotional expression, explained why he/she felt this way, and was then confronted by the roommate's response. Special note was made in this case, and later, of whether participants might feel the scenario was at an end. That is, if they indicated that there wasn't anything more to be said, or felt puzzled about what might be added, it was taken as a signal that the scenario was at an end. If such responses occurred, no further inquiries were made. If a response was made, the participants were then asked to supply what they felt would be the likely reaction of their roommate.

Responses at each phase of these scenario samples were then subjected to categorization. With such simplification it was hoped that it would be possible to generate an intelligible array of scenario forms. As this categorization proceeded, it became apparent that at *any* stage of interchange more than 90% of the responses could reliably be placed into one of three categories. In effect, it appears that at each choice point in the unfolding scenarios, participants typically faced at least three intelligible alternatives. The generality and limits of this pattern remain to be explored.

In order to appreciate the character of the fuller set of findings, consider the depiction of the anger scenarios in Figure 20.2. The case is particularly interesting in light of the results of the earlier study of escalating hostility. As this schematic makes clear, we first see that the initial interact is composed of the expression of anger, and the resultant questioning of the reason. In the second interact the explanation for the anger is given (as described above), and the research participants generated three major options. The most frequently selected option is *remorse* (e.g., "I'm very sorry I hurt your feelings"). The second most frequent reaction is that of *reframing*. The reframing response is one in which the interlocutor attempts to redefine the precipitating event in such a way that anger is no longer appropriate. In the present case, for example, participants tended to use two forms of reframing, the first a plea of ignorance over the wishes that the information remain secret, and the second, a claim of positive intent (e.g., "I only did it because I thought it would be helpful to you"). Ranking third in frequency of selection is the response of *anger* (e.g., "Don't you think you're overreacting a bit? It's not such a big deal"). This latter pattern points up an important limitation on the earlier study of escalating of hostility. As it appears, although escalation of hostility is a common scenario in our culture, it is neither essential nor necessary (e.g., required biologically). Rather, it is one possible option among several, and at least in the present case, not one that is typically preferred.

As Figure 20.2 demonstrates, with the third interact it becomes possible to bring the scenario to an end. Participants begin to find a natural break in the exchange. The most favored antecedent of the ending is the expression of remorse in the second interact. If remorse is expressed in this instance, two of the three replies (and the most favored two) lead to the end of the scenario. Remorse is likely to be followed by *compassion* ("That's OK, it really doesn't matter so much, I guess") or by *caution* ("Well, I hope you will never do that kind of thing again"). The reframing reply in the second interact is somewhat less successful in bringing the scenario to an end. Of the three options selected by participants, only the least preferred reaction (that of compassion) succeeds in bringing matters to a conclusion. The most frequent reaction to reframing, however, is an attempt on the part of the emotional person to reframe, typically so as to reinstate the validity of the initial claim to anger ("You knew very well it wouldn't help me"). However, a very common reaction to the reframing response is simply more anger. Reframing may be viewed as a form of insult as it challenges the person's capacities for understanding. In any case, if reframing engenders anger the story remains open.

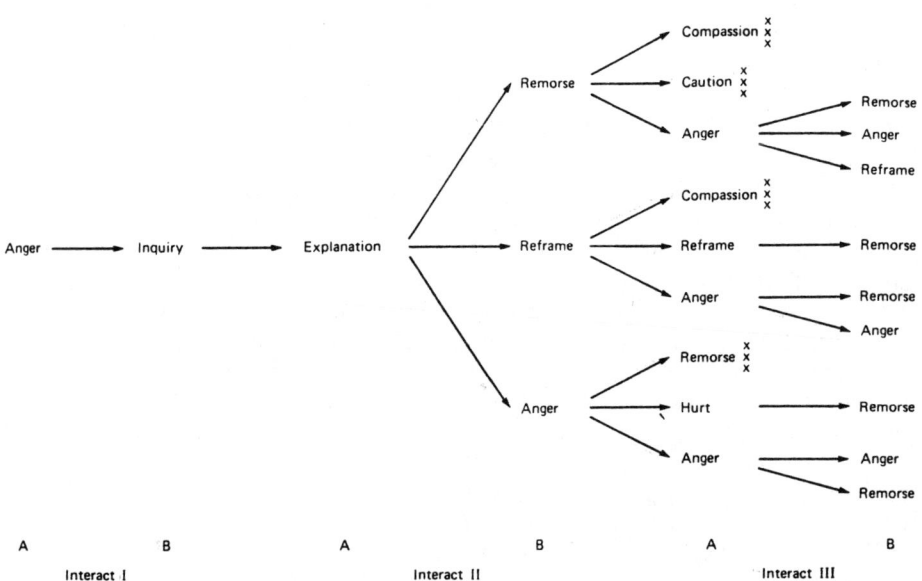

Figure 20.2. Anger scenarios.

Research exercises such as these are, of course, quite preliminary. They are artificially abstracted from the full-scale relational performances of everyday life; they employ only a nonrepresentative handful of research participants; and they speak only tangentially to the problems confronting the field researcher. Yet, they do prove useful in developing an alternative vocabulary of description and explanation, and most especially a vocabulary that does not reduce to the mental events of individuals. Through analysis of these various exercises, we begin to open a vocabulary of social scenarios – sequences of interrelated actions in which what we call "emotions" play a part, but in which a variety of other actions are also constituent parts. Through our research thus far we are led to the tentative conclusion that the prevailing function of scenarios in which emotional performance play a role is that of social regulation (including adjustment and solidification). The agonistic emotions (e.g., anger, depression, sadness) are most likely to occur when a given pattern of relationship has either begun to deteriorate or when an alteration is required in the existing pattern. Such a scenario is not complete until the participants have both signaled agreement (often through positive emotional performances) that the old pattern will be reinstated or that the new pattern is agreeable. When positive emotional performances (e.g., love, attraction, respect) are featured at the beginning of a scenario they often serve as invitations to the other to join in a particular form of relationship (e.g., a love affair, a friendship). Or during a particular scenario they may be used to solidify or acclaim the desirability of the existing relational form. In effect, it may be tentatively concluded that scenarios in which emotional performances play a significant role often act as metarelational devices: They operate to begin, end, or alter other relational forms.

If such an orientation were extended into the realm of ethnographic analysis, what would be the character of the resulting inscriptions? Initially, the putative object of analysis would no longer be the subjectivities of individual others, but the microsocial relationships making up the culture. Concerns with the structures of meaning, rational processes, the emotional bases of action, beliefs, and the like would slowly be replaced with accounts of relational patterns, the ways in which various actions fit within these patterns, the function of the patterns within the broader complexion of microsocial relationships, and so on. We would be less concerned with whether a given people experience the same emotions that we do, and more fascinated by the possibility that others solve problems of relational patterning in different and possibly more effective ways than we do. As relational forms are essentially diachronic, attention would shift toward cross-time process within the culture – the ways in which relational forms develop and deteriorate within a culture. The ethnographer would be less concerned with veridicality of reporting, as the concept of "descriptive truth" would itself be viewed as a misleading claim to authority. Understanding within the native culture would be essentially a process of participating successfully in its relational forms; understanding within the home culture would be achieved when the ethnographer could engender coherent dialogue within the relevant communities regarding relational configurations in other cultural settings.

Summary

I first proposed that the traditional conception of understanding as intersubjective connection not only informs the procedures of ethnographic inquiry, but also saturates the characterizations of other peoples. Reified by existing analyses are individuals (as opposed to relationships), synchronic or stable features (as opposed to diachronic process), a dualistic conception of persons, and distinctions between rational and irrational processes of mind. A critical examination of the conception of understanding as intersubjective connection was then undertaken and found to be seriously flawed. These shortcomings, in turn, raised questions concerning their cognate effects on ethnographic characterization of persons. The problematics of the traditional conception of understanding suggest a fundamental inadequacy in the prevailing characterizations of selves.

I then attempted to develop a set of grounding assumptions for an alternative theory of social understanding. In this case, the locus of understanding is removed from the heads of individual persons and placed within a relational space. More specifically, social understanding becomes characterized as a form of adjudicated coordination. Relational units are formed as individuals coordinate their actions with each other; however, the individual in this case is viewed as the intersection of a range of relational units. As these coordinations are judged according to some standard, "understanding" comes to be realized as a social fact and typically attributed to individual persons. This orientation was further elaborated in an inquiry into the emotions. As argued, emotions are not the possessions of individuals; rather, emotional performances are embedded within relational scenarios. What we term emotional understanding emerges as the result of judging the individual's adequacy within a recognized scenario.

References

Abu-Lughod, L. (1987). *Veiled sentiments*. Berkeley: University of California Press.

Armon-Jones, C. (1985). Presumption, explication and the social construction of emotion. *Journal for the Theory of Social Behavior 15*:1–22.

Austin, J. L. (1962a). *Sense and sensibilia*. London: Oxford University Press. (1962b). *How to do things with words*. Cambridge, MA: Harvard University Press.

Averill, J. R. (1982). *Anger and aggression: An essay on emotion*. New York: Springer-Verlag.

(1985). The social construction of emotion. In K. J. Gergen & K. E. Davis (Eds.), *The social construction of the person*. New York: Springer-Verlag.

Barnett, S. (1977). Identity, choice and caste ideology in contemporary South India. In K. David (Ed.), *The new wind: Identities in South Asia*. The Hague: Mouton.

Becker, H. S. (1963). *Outsiders*. New York: Free Press.

Bellah, R. N., Madsen, R., Sullivan, W. M., Swindler, A., & Tipton, S. M. (1985). *Habits of the heart*. Berkeley: University of California Press.

Betti, E. (1980). Hermeneutics as the general methodology of the *Weisteswissenschaften*. In J. Bleicher (Ed.), *Contemporary hermeneutics*. London: Routledge & Kegan Paul.

Blu, K. I. (1967). Kinship and culture: Affinity and the role of the father in the Trobriands. *Journal of Anthropological Research 23*(1):90–109.

Briggs, J. L. (1970). *Never in anger: Portrait of an Eskimo family*. Cambridge: Harvard University Press.

Carrithers, M., Collins, S., & Lukes, S. (1985). *The category of the person*. Cambridge: Cambridge University Press.

Casson, R. W. (1981). *Language, culture and cognition*. New York: Macmillan.

Clifford, J. (1983). On ethnographic authority. *Representations 1*:118–146.

Clifford, J., & Marcus, G. E. (1986). *Writing culture, the poetics and politics of ethnography*. Berkeley: University of California Press.

Cole, M. (1981). Intelligence as culture practice. In W. Kessen (Ed.), *Carmichael's handbook of child psychology*. New York: Wiley.

Collin, D. (1983). La discrète émancipation de Talasia: identité féminine et vision du monde d'une jeune Inuk. *Recherches Amerindiennes 13*:236–252.

Collingwood, R. (1946). *The idea of history*. Oxford: Clarendon Press.

Crapanzano, V. (1986). Hermes dilemma: The masking of subversion in ethnographic description. In J. Clifford & G. E. Marcus (Eds.), *Writing culture*. Berkeley: University of California Press.

D'Andrade, R. (1984). Cultural meaning systems. In R. A. Shweder & R. A. LeVine (Eds.), *Culture theory: Essays on mind, self and emotion*. Cambridge: Cambridge University Press.

Davis, K. E. (1978). *Advances in descriptive psychology* (Vol. 1), Greenwich. CT: JAI Press.

Derrida, J. (1976). *Of grammatology*. Baltimore, MD: Johns Hopkins University Press.

Dilthey, W. (1984). *Selected writings*. H. P. Rickman (Ed.). Cambridge: Cambridge University Press. (Originally published in 1914)

Elvin, M. (1985). Between the earth and heaven: Conceptions of the self in China. In M. Carrithers, S. Collins, & S. Lukes (Eds.), *The category of the person*. Cambridge: Cambridge University Press.

Errington, F. K. (1984). *Manners and meaning in West Sumatra: The social context of consciousness*. New Haven: Yale University Press.

Fabian, J. (1983). *Time and the other: How anthropology makes its object*. New York: Columbia University Press.

Felson, R. (1984). Patterns of aggressive social interaction. In A. Mummenday (Ed.), *Social psychology of aggression*. New York: Springer-Verlag.

Fish, S. (1980). *Is there a text in this class? The authority of interpretive communities*. Cambridge: Harvard University Press.

Fuller, S. (1986). The inscrutability of silence and the problem of knowledge in the human sciences. Unpublished paper: University of Colorado.

Gadamer, H. (1960). *Truth and method.* C. Barden & J. Cumming (Eds.). New York: Seabury.

Garfinkel, H. (1967). *Studies in ethnomethodology.* Englewood Cliffs, NJ: Prentice-Hall.

Geertz, C. (1973). *The interpretation of cultures.* New York: Basic Books.

(1974). From the native's point of view. *Bulletin of the Academy of Arts and Sciences.*

(1975). On the nature of anthropological understanding. *American Scientist* 63:47–53.

Gergen, K. J. (1982). *Toward transformation in social knowledge.* New York: Springer-Verlag.

Gergen, K. J. (1986). Correspondence vs. autonomy in the language of understanding human action. In D. Fiske & R. Shweder (Eds.), *Pluralism and subjectivity in social science.* Chicago: University of Chicago Press.

Gergen, K. J., & Davis, K. E. (1985). *The social construction of the person.* New York: Springer-Verlag.

Habermas, J. (1979). *Knowledge and human interest.* Boston: Beacon Press.

(1979). *Communication and the evolution of society.* Boston: Beacon Press.

Harris, L. M., Gergen, K. J., & Lannamann, J. W. (1986). Aggression rituals. *Communication Monographs* 53:252–265.

Heelas, P., & Lock, A. (1981). *Indigenous psychologies: The anthropology of the self.* Lancaster: Academic Press.

Hirsch, E., Jr. (1976). *The aims of interpretation.* Chicago: University of Chicago Press.

Holland, D. (1982). Samoan folk knowledge of mental disorders. In A. Marsella & G. White (Eds.), *Cultural conception of mental health & therapy.* Boston: Reidel.

Holmes, L. D. (1986). *Quest for the real Samoa.* South Hadley: Bergin & Garvey.

Kirkpatrick, J. (1985). How personal differences can make a difference. In K. J. Gergen & K. E. Davis (Eds.), *The social construction of the person.* New York: Springer- Verlag.

Kluckhohn, C. (1954). *Culture and behavior.* New York: Free Press.

La Fontaine, J. S. (1985). Person and individual: Some anthropological reflections. In M. Carrithers, S. Collins, & S. Lukes (Eds.), *The category of the person.* Cambridge: Cambridge University Press.

Latour, B., & Woolgar, S. (1979). *Laboratory life, the social construction of scientific facts.* Beverly Hills: Sage.

Le Fevre, K. B. (1987). *Invention as a social act.* Carbondale: Southern Illinois University Press.

Lee, D. (1959). *Freedom and culture.* Cambridge: Harvard University Press.

LeVine, R. (1984). Properties of culture: An ethnographic view. In R. A. Shweder & R. A. LeVine (Eds.), *Culture theory: Essays on mind, self & emotion.* Cambridge: Cambridge University Press.

Lukes, S. (1985). *Individualism.* Oxford: Basil Blackwell.

Lutz, C. (1982). The domain of emotion words on Ifaluk. *American Ethnology* 9:133–28.

(1985). Cultural patterns and individual differences in the child's emotional meaning system. *The socialization of emotions* (37–53). New York: Plenum.

(1988). *Unnatural emotions*. Chicago: University of Chicago Press.

Lutz, C., and White, G. (1986). The anthropology of emotions. *Annual Review of Anthropology 15*:405–436.

MacFarlane, A. (1978). *The origins of English individualism*. Oxford: Blackwell.

Marcus, G. (1980). Rhetoric and the ethnographic genre in anthropological research. *Current Anthropology 21*:507.

(1982). Ethnographies as text. *Annual Review of Anthropology 11*:25–69.

Marcus, G. E., & Fischer, M. J. (1986). *Anthropology as cultural critique*. Chicago: University of Chicago Press.

Marsella, A. J., DeVos, G., & Hsu, L. K. (1985). *Culture and self: Asian and Western perspectives*.New York: Tavistock.

Mink, L. D. (1968). Philosophical analysis and historical understanding. *Review of Metaphysics 21*:66–698.

Mischler, E. G. (1986). *Research interviewing: Context and narrative*. Cambridge: Harvard University Press.

Myers, F. R. (1979). Emotions and the self: A theory of personhood and political order among the Pintupi Aborigines. *Ethos 9*:343–370.

Needham, R. (1972). *Belief, language and experience*. Chicago: University of Chicago Press.

Needham, R. (1981). Inner states as universals: Skeptical reflections on human nature. In P. Heelas & A. Lock (Eds.), *Indigenous psychologies: The anthropology of self*. Berkeley: University of California Press.

Ochs, E., & Schieffelin, B. (1984). Language acquisition and socialization: Three developmental stories and their implications. In R. A. Shweder & R. A. Levine (Eds.), *Culture theory: Essays on mind, self and emotion*. Cambridge: Cambridge University Press.

Pearce, W. B., & Cronen, V. E. (1980). *Communication, action and meaning*. New York: Praeger.

Radcliffe-Brown, A. R. (1922). *The Andaman Islanders*. Cambridge: Cambridge University Press.

Ricoeur, P. (1981). *Hermeneutics and the human sciences* (J. Thompson, Trans.). New York: Cambridge University Press.

Rorty, R. (1979). *Philosophy and the mirror of nature*. Princeton: Princeton University Press.

Rosaldo, M. (1980). *Knowledge and passions: Ilongot notions of self and social life*. Cambridge: Cambridge University Press.

(1986). Ilongot hunting as story and experience. In V. W. Turner & E. D. Bruner (Eds.), *The anthropology of experience*. Chicago: University of Chicago Press.

Rosen, L. (1984). *Bargaining for reality. The construction of social relations in a Muslim community*. Chicago: University of Chicago Press.

Ryle, G. (1949). *The concept of mind*. London: Hutchinson.

Said, E. (1979). *Orientalism*. New York: Random House.

Sampson, E. E. (1977). Psychology and the American ideal. *Journal of Personality and Social Psychology 35*:767–782.

Sanderson, A. (1985). Purity and power among the Brahmans of Kashmin. In M. Carrithers, S. Collins, & S. Lukes (Eds.), *The category of the person*. Cambridge: Cambridge University Press.

Searle, J. R. (1970). *Speech acts*. London: Cambridge University Press.

Shotter, J. (1980). Action, joint action and intentionality. In M. Brenner (Ed.), *The structure of action*. Oxford: Blackwell.

606 KENNETH J. GERGEN

Shweder, R. A., & Bourne, E. (1984). Does the concept of the person vary cross-culturally? In R. Shweder & R. LeVine (Eds.), *Culture theory*. Cambridge: Cambridge University Press.

Shweder, R. A., & Miller, J. G. (1985). The social construction of the person: How is it possible? In K. J. Gergen & K. E. Davis (Eds.), *The social construction of the person*. New York: Springer-Verlag.

Solomon, R. C. (1984). Getting angry: The Jamesian theory of emotion in anthropology. In R. Schweder & R. LeVine (Eds.), *Culture theory*. Cambridge: Cambridge University Press.

Suleiman, S. R., & Crosman, I. (1980). *The reader in the text*. Princeton: Princeton University Press.

Taylor, C. (1964). *The explanation of behavior*. London: Routledge & Kegan Paul.

(1971). Interpretation and the sciences of man. *The Review of Metaphysics* 25(1).

Wagner, R. (1981). *The invention of culture*. Chicago: University of Chicago Press.

Weber, M. (1904). *Methodology of the social sciences*. Glencoe: Free Press.

White, H. (1978). *Tropics of discourse*. Baltimore, MD: Johns Hopkins University Press.

Winch, P. (1946). *The idea of a social science*. London: Routledge & Kegan paul.

Witherspoon, G. (1971). Navajo categories of objects at rest. *American Anthropologist* 73(1):110–117.

Wittgenstein, L. (1966). *Zettel*. (G. Anscombe, Trans.). London: Blackwell.

Wortham, S. (1985). *How justifiable are interpretive ladders? Possibilities for objective knowledge in the social sciences*. Senior Honors Thesis, Swarthmore College.

Conference participants

Wayne C. Booth, The University of Chicago
Norman M. Bradburn, Provost, The University of Chicago
Bertram J. Cohler, The University of Chicago
Vincent Crapanzano, Queens College, CUNY
Mihaly Csikszentmihalyi, The University of Chicago
Roy D'Andrade, University of California at San Diego
Takeo Doi, St. Luke's International Hospital, Tokyo, Japan
James W. Fernandez, The University of Chicago
Raymond D. Fogelson, The University of Chicago
Daniel G. Freedman, The University of Chicago
Clifford Geertz, Institute for Advanced Study, Princeton, New Jersey
Kenneth Gergen, Swarthmore College
Susan Goldin-Meadow, The University of Chicago
Jacqueline J. Goodnow, Macquarie University, Sidney, Australia
Thomas Gregor, Vanderbilt University
Gunhild Hagestad, Northwestern University
Shirley Brice Heath, Stanford University
Gilbert Herdt, The University of Chicago
Dennis P. Hogan, Pennsylvania State University
Peter Homans, The University of Chicago
Janellen Huttenlocher, The University of Chicago
Sudhir Kakar, The University of Chicago
Edward O. Laumann, Dean of Social Sciences, The University of
    Chicago
Jean Lave, University of California at Berkeley
Bennett Leventhal, The University of Chicago
Robert A. LeVine, Harvard University
Martha K. McClintock, The University of Chicago
Peggy J. Miller, The University of Chicago
Elinor Ochs, University of Southern California
John U. Ogbu, University of California at Berkeleey
Paul Rozin, University of Pennsylvania
Nancy Scheper-Hughes, University of California at Berkeley
Richard A. Shweder, The University of Chicago
Michael Silverstein, The University of Chicago
G. William Skinner, Stanford University

Dan I. Slobin, University of California at Berkeley
Melford E. Spiro, University of California at San Diego
Nancy L. Stein, The University of Chicago
James W. Stigler, The University of Chicago
Fred L. Strodtbeck, The University of Chicago
Tom Trabasso, The University of Chicago
Froma Walsh, The University of Chicago
John W. M. Whiting, Harvard University
Marvin Zonis, The University of Chicago

Name index

Subject index